HANDBOOK ON WELLBEING, HAPPINESS AND THE ENVIRONMENT

Handbook on Wellbeing, Happiness and the Environment

Edited by

David Maddison

Professor of Economics, University of Birmingham, UK

Katrin Rehdanz

Professor of Economics, Kiel University, Germany

Heinz Welsch

Professor Emeritus of Economics, University of Oldenburg, Germany

EE Edward Elgar PUBLISHING

Cheltenham, UK • Northampton, MA, USA

Published by
Edward Elgar Publishing Limited
The Lypiatts
15 Lansdown Road
Cheltenham
Glos GL50 2JA
UK

Edward Elgar Publishing, Inc.
William Pratt House
9 Dewey Court
Northampton
Massachusetts 01060
USA

A catalogue record for this book
is available from the British Library

Library of Congress Control Number: 2019956577

This book is available electronically in the **Elgar**online
Economics subject collection
DOI 10.4337/9781788119344

MIX
Paper from responsible sources
FSC® C013604

ISBN 978 1 78811 933 7 (cased)
ISBN 978 1 78811 934 4 (eBook)

Typeset by Servis Filmsetting Ltd, Stockport, Cheshire

Printed and bound by CPI Group (UK) Ltd, Croydon CR0 4YY

Contents

Contributors

Mona Ahmadiani, Wake Forest University, Eudaimonia Institute, NC, USA.

Michael Berlemann, Helmut-Schmidt-University Hamburg, Department of Economics and Social Sciences, Germany.

Finbarr Brereton, University College Dublin, School of Architecture, Planning and Environmental Policy, Ireland.

Luigino Bruni, University LUMSA (Rome), Department of Law, Economics, Politics and Modern Languages, Italy.

Xi Chen, Yale University, School of Public Health, CT, USA.

Carmen Amelia Coral-Guerrero, SEK International University, UISEK Business School, Ecuador.

Susana Ferreira, University of Georgia, Department of Agricultural and Applied Economics, USA.

Henk Folmer, University of Groningen, Department of Economic Geography, Faculty of Spatial Sciences, Netherlands.

Bruno S. Frey, University of Basel and CREMA – Center for Research in Economics, Management and the Arts, Zurich, Switzerland.

Daniel Fujiwara, London School of Economics, Centre for Economic Performance, UK and Simetrica, London, UK.

Fernando García-Quero, University of Granada, Faculty of Social Sciences and Law (Melilla Campus), Spain.

Iulian Gramatki, Simetrica, London, UK.

Jorge Guardiola, University of Granada, Institute of Peace and Conflicts and Department of Applied Economics, Spain.

Peter Howley, University of Leeds, Leeds University Business School, UK.

Benjamin A. Jones, University of New Mexico, Department of Economics, NM, USA.

Kazuki Kagohashi, Nanzan University, Department of Global Liberal Studies, Japan.

Shashi Kant, University of Toronto, Faculty of Forestry, Canada.

Kieran Keohane, Simetrica, London, UK.

Christian Krekel, London School of Economics, Department of Psychological and Behavioural Science and London School of Economics, Centre for Economic Performance (CEP), UK.

Kate Laffan, London School of Economics, Department of Psychological and Behavioural Science, UK.

Ricky N. Lawton, Simetrica, London, UK.

Arik Levinson, Georgetown University, Department of Economics, DC, USA.

George MacKerron, University of Sussex, Department of Economics, UK.

David Maddison, Birmingham University, Department of Economics, UK.

Shunsuke Managi, Kyushu University, Urban Institute, Japan.

Mirko Moro, University of Stirling, Stirling Management School, UK.

Susana Mourato, London School of Economics, Department of Geography and Environment, UK.

Judith Regner, Helmut-Schmidt-University Hamburg, Department of Economics and Social Sciences, Germany.

Katrin Rehdanz, Kiel University, Department of Economics, Germany.

Honghao Ren, Northwestern Polytechnical University (Xi'an, Shaanxi), School of Humanities, Economics and Law, China.

Teresa Ruckelshauß, Heidelberg University of Education, Research Group for Earth Observation, Germany.

Jianjun Tang, Renmin University of China, School of Agricultural Economics and Rural Development, China.

Tetsuya Tsurumi, Nanzan University, Faculty of Policy Studies, Japan.

Jascha Tutt, Helmut-Schmidt-University Hamburg, Department of Economics and Social Sciences, Germany.

Ruut Veenhoven, Erasmus University Rotterdam, Erasmus Happiness Economics Research Organization (EHERO), Netherlands and North-West University, Opentia Research Program, South Africa.

Ilan Vertinsky, University of British Columbia, Sauder School of Business, Canada.

Heinz Welsch, University of Oldenburg, Department of Business Administration, Economics and Law, Germany.

Xiaobo Zhang, Peking University, National School of Development, China.

Xin Zhang, Beijing Normal University, School of Statistics, China.

Bin Zheng, Nanjing Forestry University, College of Economics and Management, China.

Foreword

My reactions to this volume are principally of wonderment and of congratulation. This book is about what really matters to human life on the planet. Human wellbeing (and non-human wellbeing) should be our central concern as economists and social scientists. We are also starting to recognize what environmentalists have believed for a long time: the natural environment provides the foundation of people's lives and of civilization. As I write this, I have BBC radio on in the background. The BBC reporters are, at this moment in late summer in 2019 and literally as I type on my computer this afternoon, describing thousands of fires that are burning simultaneously across the Amazon rain forest in Brazil. This destruction of a vital environmental resource provides a salient example of the environmental changes that constitute the background for this volume and vividly illustrates that it is a timely contribution.

One of the contributions of the chapters in this volume is to provide a scientific way to prove – I believe I am using the word advisedly – the value of environmental influences for human wellbeing. Ultimately, the idea in the volume is that human happiness is a function of clean air, green space, lack of excessive noise, many other kinds of environmental influences, income, and standard social science variables. Crucially, the research literature blends this kind of conceptual approach with regression-equation techniques.

What then emerges, regardless of different approaches and alternative technical details, is estimates of the size of the effects of environmental factors upon the happiness and wellbeing of humans. In particular, by using data on reported happiness and life satisfaction, it is possible to calculate the 'happiness' marginal rate of substitution between factors such as clean air and income. For anyone interested in the history of social science, I recall looking at my first happiness equation in the year 1992 at the London School of Economics (in work with colleagues such as Andrew Clark and David Blanchflower) and, although I never dreamed then of entering environment variables as covariates, asking myself whether equations of this sort, and especially the notion of exploiting the estimated income coefficients, might ever be taken seriously by economists. It took a long and somewhat painful period to get referees at economics journals to be (if only partly) won over, and it will probably be half a century yet before that process is close to complete. But I would like particularly to salute certain colleagues for their seminal work: I recommend any young reader especially to read the five early papers listed below. I wish I had written them.

In my own view, these methods hand an intellectual tool not only to academia but also to committed environmentalists, and a potential lifeline to human beings.

Andrew Oswald
Professor of Economics and Behavioural Science
University of Warwick, UK
August 2019

REFERENCES

Brown, E.L. and W.R. Nelson (1971), 'Effects of a changing environment on human happiness and welfare', *Agricultural Science Review*, **9**, 27–30.
Frijters, P. and B. Van Praag (1998), 'The effects of climate on welfare and well-being in Russia', *Climate Change*, **39**, 61–81.
Rehdanz, K. and D. Maddison (2005), 'Climate and happiness', *Ecological Economics*, **52**, 111–125.
Van Praag, B. and B. Baarsma (2005), 'Using happiness surveys to value intangibles: the case of airport noise', *Economic Journal*, **115**, 224–246.
Welsch, H. (2002), 'Preferences over prosperity and pollution: environmental valuation based on happiness surveys', *Kyklos*, **55**, 473–494.

Introduction to the *Handbook on Wellbeing, Happiness and the Environment*

David Maddison, Katrin Rehdanz and Heinz Welsch

BACKGROUND

The past decades have seen a massive expansion of the field of wellbeing, happiness and the environment. The pertinent literature has used the term 'happiness' in a wider and a narrower sense. In the wider sense, happiness denotes what psychologists refer to as subjective wellbeing (SWB). As suggested by Diener (1984), SWB encompasses an affective and a cognitive component, that is, emotional states and evaluations of life, respectively. While happiness in the narrow sense refers to the affective component, the cognitive (evaluative) component is usually referred to as life satisfaction. However, since measures of affective and cognitive wellbeing are typically highly correlated with each other, it is nevertheless common to neglect the difference between them and to use the terms SWB, happiness and life satisfaction synonymously. We follow this practice unless stated otherwise.

Data on SWB are routinely elicited in large-scale social surveys at both the national and international levels. Important national data sources, among others, include the Keio Household Panel Survey (KHPS), the German Socio-Economic Panel (SOEP) and the UK Household Longitudinal Study (UKHLS). At the international level, SWB data are included, among others, in the Eurobarometer Surveys (covering the member countries of the European Union), the European Social Survey (covering 36 European countries), the World Values Survey (covering more than 80 countries worldwide) and the Gallup World Poll covering (156 countries). In these and similar surveys, people are asked questions about their happiness or life satisfaction. The European Social Survey, for instance, regularly asks representative samples of people. 'How happy are you?' (on a scale from 0 = extremely unhappy, to 10 = extremely happy) and 'All things considered, how satisfied are you with your life as a whole nowadays?' (from 0 = extremely dissatisfied, to 10 = extremely satisfied). While the samples used in international surveys typically change over time, national surveys like the KHPS, SOEP and UKHLS rely on fixed sets of people over several years, thus allowing longitudinal analyses of SWB and its correlates.

While SWB started to be studied by psychologists in the late 1940s (Diener et al., 1999), Easterlin (1974) was the first to focus explicitly on economic factors. His finding of a stationary level of self-rated happiness in the United States of America (USA), in spite of tremendous income growth, became known as the Easterlin paradox and is probably the best-known result in the economics of happiness. In addition to income, other economic correlates of happiness include unemployment, inflation and inequality. Survey articles on happiness and economics are Frey and Stutzer (2002), Kahneman and Krueger (2006), Di Tella and MacCulloch (2006), Dolan et al. (2008) and Graham (2017); a recent monograph is Frey (2018).

Happiness has received increasing attention not only in the academic but also in the political sphere. The kingdom of Bhutan adopted 'Gross National Happiness' as a policy target as far back as the 1970s. In 2008, French President Nicolas Sarkozy commissioned the development of a 'statistical system which goes beyond commercial activity to measure personal well-being' (Stiglitz et al., 2009). In 2014, the United Kingdom (UK) Office for Statistics launched its happiness and wellbeing statistics titled 'Measures of national well-being'. In 2019, the Treasury of New Zealand published its first Wellbeing Budget. At the international level, the United Nations started to release the annual World Happiness Report in 2011.

The connection between wellbeing, happiness and the environment started to be investigated about 20 years ago (Frijters and van Praag, 1998; Welsch, 2002; Rehdanz and Maddison, 2005; van Praag and Baarsma, 2005), focusing initially on climate, air pollution and noise nuisance. Since then, many more topics have been covered, as documented in this *Handbook*. Often the relevant studies have used happiness data as a novel tool for non-market valuation, in addition to the established stated and revealed preference approaches. Specifically, interpreting happiness or life satisfaction as measures of utility or individual welfare, and modelling utility as a function of income and environmental quality, allows researchers to estimate the amount of income individuals would be willing to trade off for a given change of environmental quality at constant utility levels; an implicit measure of willingness to pay for environmental quality (Welsch and Kühling, 2009).

EVOLUTION OF THE ECONOMIC LITERATURE

To track the evolution of the economic literature, we interrogate the EconLit database. We do this not only in order to illustrate the recent rapid growth of this approach but also to highlight the range of applications, and the geographical distribution of research activities. We also identify which journals have published this research. We further attempt to divine trends in the literature by describing the most recent contributions. By using the EconLit database, our literature survey focuses on the literature in the field of economics, acknowledging that literature published in interdisciplinary journals such as *Climatic Change* or *Global Environmental Change* are excluded. The literature is therefore likely to be larger than described below.

Our survey uses a Boolean search combining (happiness OR subjective wellbeing OR subjective well being OR subjective well-being OR life satisfaction OR life-satisfaction) anywhere in the text in conjunction with various *Journal of Economic Literature* (JEL) subject codes. Note that studies on subjective wellbeing tend to be identified by JEL code I31, but unfortunately this category also includes a large number of other issues: general welfare, basic needs, living standards, quality of life and (finally) happiness. Expanding our research to include publications with JEL subject code I31 would therefore incorporate a vast number of articles having nothing to do with subjective wellbeing.

Our interest lies in JEL subject codes Q relating to agricultural and natural resource economics, environmental and ecological economics. When we combine the aforementioned search string with the JEL code Q, the number of publications returned is 230 as of 14 April 2019. These 230 hits stretch back as far as 1999. While the number of items published in the ten-year period 1999–2008 was 31, over the following ten-year period of 2009–18 it was 197. Over the most recent five-year period, 2014–18, there were 118 research articles. It is thus possible to see that the number of items is growing very rapidly indeed. All but four of these articles were published in English. It might be helpful here to compare the number of items published in economics generally over the same period, 1999–2019, that contained these same terms: which was 4166. It is therefore apparent that the majority of research on subjective wellbeing, happiness and life satisfaction takes place in JEL subject areas other than the JEL subject category Q. We can also compare the total number of items recorded in EconLit over the same three time periods: 486 191, 606 620 and 286 560. On the basis of these figures it is therefore clear that research into subjective wellbeing and the environment is increasing faster than the number of economic research items recorded in EconLit. What happens if we do not insist on the word 'subjective' to precede the word 'wellbeing' or variants thereof? The number of hits increases markedly, to 3285, but it is apparent that the vast majority of these studies have nothing to do with the approach that concerns us. We cannot, however, exclude the possibility that some relevant items simply omit the word 'subjective' for brevity. What happens if we search for 'cantril', as in 'cantril scale' or 'cantril ladder'? Combining with the JEL code Q there are no hits whatsoever and only 19 hits in the entire EconLit database. We believe that the code I31 is outdated and that a new subject code that deals exclusively with approaches based on subjective wellbeing would be more useful.

In terms of where this research is located, 8 refer to Africa, 44 to Asia, 64 to Europe, 5 to Latin America and the Caribbean, 15 to North America and 9 to Oceania. Perhaps interesting is the fact that the number of publications from North America is relatively low, and the number from Asia is relatively high, in comparison to what one might have expected. This might reflect a certain scepticism regarding the approach in North America.

Of those items retrieved, 184 were published in academic journals, with the remainder published as edited volumes, books, dissertations and working papers. Notably, of the journal articles identified, no fewer than 43 were contained in one single journal: *Ecological Economics*. We also find 25 in *Social Indicators Research*, a journal publishing articles on diverse topics (not just the environment). The implication is that if one wishes to find an audience that is sympathetic to analyses of the field of subjective wellbeing and the environment, one should lean towards these two journals. *Environmental and Resource Economics*, *Journal of Economic Psychology*, *Journal of Public Economics* and *Kyklos* contained three articles each, with the remaining articles scattered through diverse journals. The *Journal of Environmental Economics and Management*, which was until recently the journal of the Association of Environmental and Resource Economists, contains two articles. It is notable that, together, the journals of the North American and European Associations of Environmental and Resource Economists included only five out of the 184 journal articles. We suspect that this means that the study of subjective wellbeing is still viewed as somewhat unorthodox.

Because the category Q also contains research on agriculture (which we believe holds little interest for researchers into subjective wellbeing), we also look at Q2 (renewable resources and conservation) and Q3 (non-renewable resources and conservation); these yielded 28 and 10 items, respectively, whereas Q4 (energy) resulted in 18 hits. Note that Q2 includes fisheries, land, water, forestry and the recreational aspects of natural resources.

It is surprising that these have not received greater attention from researchers, although there is a literature outside of economics.

Resulting in a somewhat larger number of hits (48) was Q51 (valuation), whilst Q53 (air pollution, water pollution, noise, hazardous waste, solid waste and recycling) resulted in 49 hits, and Q54 (climate, natural disasters and global warming) in 51. It is often the case that the same publication will have multiple JEL codes, and many items that deal with a particular environmental issue also value changes in environmental quality. The number of items using subjective wellbeing to value the environment is dwarfed by the number of items using, for example, contingent valuation (583) or hedonics (196) for the same purpose. Obviously if these search terms are included without the subject code Q51 these numbers increase to 2499 and 3618, respectively. Interestingly, the most popular subject area is found to be Q54, which includes studies that, for example, attempt to both explain differences in subjective wellbeing as a function of the climate and also attempt to value natural disasters such as earthquakes.

The rather nondescript category Q56 (environment and development, environment and trade, sustainability, environmental accounts and accounting, environmental equity and population growth) generated 34 hits, whilst Q57 (ecological economics, ecosystem services, biodiversity conservation, bio-economics and industrial ecology) resulted in 22 hits. Category Q57 includes those studies that see biodiversity and changes in biodiversity as an explanation for differences in subjective wellbeing.

We also investigate JEL subject codes I1 (health), R (urban, rural and regional economics) and R4 (transportation systems). These resulted in 456, 279 and 39 hits, respectively. There is, of course, a literature considering the impact of health status on the various measures of subjective wellbeing, which is considerably larger than the literature on the impact of the environment on subjective wellbeing. There is also a literature on regional differences in subjective wellbeing, some of which will naturally have their origins in differences in environmental quality. Other studies might focus exclusively on causes of differences in subjective wellbeing experienced by people living in urban areas on account of differences in environmental quality, for example differences in the abundance of green space. Finally, the literature of transportation systems seems to include the impact of commuting on subjective wellbeing rather than the environmental impacts of transportation.

Apart from counting the number of items on EconLit it is also of interest to count the number of items being presented at recent European Association of Environmental and Resource Economists (EAERE) conferences. In 2018 at the Gothenburg conference the number of presentations including the word 'happiness' was zero, whereas the number of presentations including the words 'life satisfaction' or variants thereof was one. The number of presentations including the phrase 'subjective wellbeing' or variants thereof was one. A further four presentations included the phrase 'wellbeing' or variants thereof, and of these, two papers very clearly dealt with subjective wellbeing, making six in total. In 2017 the same exercise was undertaken for Athens and the result was four; similarly for the 2016 conference in Zurich.

The Environmental Valuation Reference Inventory (EVRI) also offers the opportunity to search for studies using the subjective wellbeing approach, although without the Boolean search capabilities of EconLit. This inventory is for use by practitioners interested in project evaluation, and the site is maintained by Statistics Canada. Unlike

EconLit it also contains conference presentations and government reports, and although one may doubt how comprehensive the database is and whether it is up to date, its utility to practitioners is beyond question.

Searching for the term 'happiness' as a keyword generates 13 hits of which 4 were published in the last five years and 8 in the last ten years. Of these 6 were for Europe, 5 for Asia, 4 for North America and 2 for Oceania (some studies cover more than one region). The subject matter of these items (some of which were only conference presentations) was air (7), human (7), land (3), plants (2) and animals (1). The phrase 'life satisfaction' (whether hyphenated or not) generates 29 hits of which 7 were published in the last five years and 23 in the last ten years. The locations of the studies were Europe (16), Asia (10), North America (9) and Oceania (3). The subject matters were air (14), human (13), land (5), plants (4) and water (4). Subjective wellbeing brings up only 2 articles. These studies refer to Asia and to land and plants. The phrase 'subjective well being' (whether hyphenated or not) brings up 15 studies, of which 4 were published in the last five years and 9 in the last ten years: 11 in Europe, 5 in Asia, 5 in North America and 2 each in Africa and Oceania. These dealt with human (10), air (7) land (2), plants (2) and animals (1). These findings confirm that whilst the main geographical area of application is Europe, studies in Asia are more common than those in North America. Because the classification of studies is different it is not possible to compare the results directly with those in EconLit. Nevertheless, air pollution (including local, regional and global) and human health seem to be popular topics.

OVERVIEW OF THE *HANDBOOK*'S CONTENT

Part I of the book, dealing with social sciences, happiness and the environment, provides the basis for the thematic chapters included in Part II. Luigino Bruni (Chapter 1) opens this part of the *Handbook* by providing a historical perspective on economics, wellbeing and happiness. He highlights that the 'happiness transformation problem' – that is, how wealth becomes wellbeing – was a central point in some streams of the economic tradition. In particular, he shows that from Malthus to Pigou this economic tradition paid special attention to non-economic domains important for human happiness and that are affected by market choices.

As our description of the evolution of the literature reveals, social scientists are producing an ever-growing stream of research findings, while comparatively little attention has been paid to bringing available research findings together. In Chapter 2 Ruut Veenhoven describes the World Database of Happiness, a 'findings archive' that provides: (1) techniques for describing research findings in a comparable way; (2) a system for storing such descriptions in an easily accessible archive; and (3) a means to add research findings to this system on a continuous basis. The chapter describes how it works, and illustrates its use with an overview of research findings on two topics: (1) the relation between happiness and air pollution; and (2) the relation between happiness and economic growth.

Like environmental quality, subjective wellbeing varies widely across space. Chapter 3 by Mona Ahmadiani, Finbarr Brereton, Susana Ferreira and Mirko Moro presents evidence of the spatial variation in self-reported life satisfaction measured at the national, regional or local level, using a variety of datasets at different geographical scales. Noting that such variation is at odds with the notion of spatial equilibrium in hedonic markets, the chapter offers alternative explanations for the observed differences in life satisfaction across locations that remain after controlling for individual sociodemographic characteristics. To what extent regional differences in wellbeing can be explained by geocoded environmental data is identified as an important research question.

This issue is taken up in Chapter 4 by Heinz Welsch, who discusses the role of happiness in environmental economics. He shows that happiness research has established robust relationships between a variety of environmental indicators and subjective wellbeing, and explains how these relationships can be used to estimate the utility trade-off people are willing to make between income and the environment, thus providing a new tool for environmental valuation. He discusses the evidence that the happiness–consumption relationship involves consumption externalities that lead to market failures, in addition to those stemming from environmental externalities, and argues that consumption and environmental externalities combined suggest that optimal environmental regulation should be stricter than is suggested by traditional models of environmental policy.

Jianjun Tang, Honghao Ren and Henk Folmer (Chapter 5) argue that neoclassical economic valuation of environmental quality is subject to rigorous assumptions. They therefore present a framework in which subjective wellbeing is the basic concept in the valuation approach of environmental quality embedded in environmental social sciences. The framework combines economic concepts with psychological and sociological variables to account for the combined economic and socio-psychological roots of environmental behaviour. The notions of valuation, subjective wellbeing and happiness are multidimensional latent variables which can only be indirectly measured via observed indicators.

Part II of the book focuses on the relationship between the environment and happiness or subjective wellbeing by presenting individual case studies. David Maddison and Katrin Rehdanz (Chapter 6) start by addressing the role of the climate in explaining cross-country variations in subjective wellbeing. Their chapter highlights two key findings from the empirical analysis. First, it is important to distinguishing those climates where temperature varies across the annual cycle from those where it does not. Any analysis failing to distinguish between extreme 'continental' climates and mild 'maritime' ones risks erroneously finding that individuals do not care about the climate. Second, when appropriate representations of the climate are used, climate variables can be extremely important. Next to gross domestic product (GDP) per capita, it appears that climate is the most important variable in explaining cross-country variations in subjective wellbeing.

Michael Berlemann, Judith Regner and Jascha Tutt (Chapter 7) look at the relationship between natural disasters and subjective wellbeing. By combining data from the UK Household Longitudinal Study with precipitation data collected by the UK Centre for Ecology and Hydrology, the chapter studies whether extreme rainfall events have a significant impact on happiness and life satisfaction. While no significant impact of rainfall measures on happiness is found, a significantly negative effect on life satisfaction is detected, even when including numerous control variables which capture the direct impact of disaster events. The study provides evidence in favour of the hypothesis that the mere risk of being confronted with natural disasters decreases life satisfaction.

Chapter 8 by Benjamin A. Jones studies the hypothesis that by diminishing environmental quality, forest-attacking invasive species may affect happiness, and estimates the non-market costs. The study exploits a deforestation quasi-experiment caused by the invasive emerald ash borer (EAB) in the US to economically value changes in life satisfaction. A difference-in-differences approach is used, taking advantage of EAB detections across 14 US states. Results suggest that the detection of EAB in a county within the past five years is associated with a decline in life satisfaction that is equivalent to a US$176 loss in annual household income. This corresponds to US$5.8 billion in annual aggregate EAB-induced damages in those counties where this beetle was detected between 2006 and 2010. The causal interpretation of results is bolstered by finding that the happiness impacts of EAB are increasing over time as more trees die due to infestation.

Arik Levinson (Chapter 9) analyses the existing evidence on happiness and air pollution. He focuses on three questions: Does pollution make people unhappy? How much? And is the effect proportional to pollution's estimated effects on mortality and productivity? Answers to these three questions must overcome three obstacles: unobserved characteristics of locales correlated with both pollution and happiness; selection by pollution-averse individuals into less-polluted areas; and habituation by residents to local circumstances. The chapter discusses how the 30 pertinent studies published since 2010 tackle each of those three problems. In order to compare their findings, despite their different measures of both happiness and pollution, the happiness and income coefficients from each study are combined into a willingness-to-pay measure for a one-day, one-standard-deviation pollution reduction. The results reveal a surprising concordance between those calculated willingness-to-pay measures and new research assessing the effects of pollution on mortality and productivity.

Chapter 10 by Xin Zhang, Xi Chen and Xiaobo Zhang studies the impact of air pollution on subjective wellbeing in China, considering six main air pollutants, and three key dimensions of subjective wellbeing: life satisfaction, hedonic happiness and mental health. A nationally representative survey is matched with local air quality and a rich set of weather conditions according to the exact date and county of each interview. By making use of variations in exposures to air pollution across similar respondents living in the same county, particulate matter with a diameter smaller than 2.5 micrometers (PM2.5) is found to reduce hedonic happiness and to increase the rate of depressive symptoms, but not to affect life satisfaction. The results are taken to show that the benefits of reducing air pollution would be higher if the hidden costs of air pollution on SWB in China are taken into account.

Chapter 11 by Daniel Fujiwara and Ricky N. Lawton explores the state-of-the-art research on noise and subjective wellbeing, assessing the growing body of evidence that general noise pollution from road traffic, railways and airport operations is associated with lower levels of subjective wellbeing. The chapter presents a recent case study exploring the association between aviation noise and subjective wellbeing. Using two large UK datasets that involve different measurements of subjective wellbeing presents an opportunity to assess the association between aviation noise and wellbeing measures covering evaluative (life satisfaction), eudemonic (purpose) and hedonic measures (happiness and relaxation). Exploiting the panel nature of the data provides the strongest causal claims to date of a negative association between aviation noise and subjective wellbeing. In the final analysis, the chapter explores how such data may help to quantify the effects of aviation noise mitigation and compensation policies.

Chapter 12 by Daniel Fujiwara, Iulian Gramatki and Kieran Keohane measures the wellbeing and health impacts of sewage odour. It analyses the association between geographical proximity to sewage treatment works and subjective wellbeing. Controlling for a range of factors, including the size of the plant, the presence of odour reduction technologies, and relevant individual covariates such as age, employment status, marital status and others, the study finds that living in close proximity to an odour-emitting sewage treatment facility is negatively correlated with life satisfaction, implying that people would be willing to forgo part of their income in exchange for reductions in odour. The results are taken to be an indication of a negative impact of sewage odour on people's subjective wellbeing, although causality is not guaranteed.

Chapter 13 by Teresa Ruckelshauß studies the effect of green areas on life satisfaction using data from the 2012 European Quality of Life Survey and the Land Use and Coverage Area Frame Survey. Results indicate that, controlling for a wide range of individual and macro-level factors, there exists a significant relationship between subjectively perceived green space accessibility and life satisfaction in the 27 member states of the European Union as of 2012. An objective measure of the amount of green space, however, shows no significant relationship with life satisfaction.

George MacKerron and Susana Mourato (Chapter 14) investigate the relationship between momentary happiness and an individual's immediate environment within the UK, building on their earlier work in this area. Using a smartphone app, they collected millions of geolocated self-reports of happiness from tens of thousands of participants. Joining response locations with other spatial datasets, they estimate a fixed-effects model relating land cover types to happiness, using only within-individual variation, and controlling for daylight, weather, companionship, activity, type of location, time, day, and a response trend. Study participants are significantly happier outdoors in any green or natural habitat type than they are in urban environments. Of the natural habitats, coastal environments are ranked top.

Chapter 15 by Peter Howley addresses the relationship between health and wellbeing by focusing on two potentially important issues that have been inadequately explored by the health and wellbeing literature to date: legacy effects and individual heterogeneity. First, in terms of legacy effects, it is suggested that health conditions may have significant consequences for wellbeing, even after an individual feels that they have fully recovered. Second, while health clearly matters for wellbeing, there may be significant heterogeneity in this relationship. Focusing on cancer as a case study, the chapter provides preliminary evidence to suggest that individuals may not revert back to an initial set-point level of wellbeing even after they believe that they have fully recovered from cancer (legacy effects), and that the relationship between cancer and wellbeing differs sharply depending on personality traits (individual heterogeneity).

Chapter 16 by Christian Krekel discusses the use of wellbeing and hedonic price data for the valuation of infrastructure externalities, using the example of renewable energy plants. Focusing on wind turbines, the chapter lays out the data, methodological and conceptual issues surrounding the use of wellbeing data for valuation purposes, and discusses the relationship to results from hedonic pricing studies. The chapter offers practical recommendations and an outlook concerning future developments, including novel opportunities arising from big data and machine learning.

Heinz Welsch discusses, in Chapter 17, the recent wellbeing literature with respect to a set of issues relevant to contemporary energy policy. The chapter starts by discussing the channels through which various energy supply systems may affect wellbeing: air pollution, greenhouse gases, nuclear risk, visual and acoustic effects, and costs. Against this background, numerous issues are discussed. How do actual or perceived nuclear risks affect wellbeing? What are the wellbeing consequences of living close to energy facilities? How do energy-related natural hazards affect wellbeing? How does the affordability of energy affect wellbeing? What are citizens' preferences for alternative configurations of the energy system in terms of wellbeing?

Kate Laffan (Chapter 18) explores the relationship between pro-environmental behaviours and subjective wellbeing in the UK. Her chapter argues that conceptual clarity as to what wellbeing is can lead to a better understanding of how it relates to behaviour. In order to do so, the relationship between such behaviours and a range of measures of subjective wellbeing is examined. The results indicate that individuals who engage in pro-environmental behaviours have higher levels of life satisfaction and consider their activities to be more worthwhile, while at the same time reporting equivalent levels of happiness and anxiety as those who do not engage in them. Additionally, individuals who engage in relatively more common pro-environmental behaviours report higher wellbeing across all measures, which may relate to the relative social norms or costs associated with these behaviours. Together, the results contribute to both scholarly and policy discussions around how to promote both ecological and personal wellbeing.

Chapter 19 by Heinz Welsch on happiness and green lifestyle discusses the evidence that engaging in pro-environmental behaviours is associated with greater subjective wellbeing. Following a summary of relevant empirical studies, the chapter aims at contributing to a better understanding of how green lifestyle and wellbeing are related. To this end, it discusses possible motives underlying pro-environmental behaviours, and how they fit into explanatory models of the occurrence of such behaviours. The chapter proceeds by interpreting the available evidence in the light of those models, discussing in particular what the evidence implies with respect to the wellbeing benefits and costs of pro-environmental behaviours. In addition to these behaviours, the chapter discusses how green self-image relates to subjective wellbeing.

Tetsuya Tsurumi, Kazuki Kagohashi and Shunsuke Managi explore in Chapter 20 how environmental ethics affect the consumption–wellbeing relationship in Japan. The chapter argues that in order to engender the sustainable consumption advocated in the ongoing discourse on ecological footprints, planetary boundaries and the Sustainable Development Goals, current consumption levels in developed countries need to be re-examined. If there is acknowledgment that an increase in consumption is not related to an increase in the subjective wellbeing, at least by people with high environmental ethics, rampant consumption can be mitigated. Estimation results based on a large-scale survey show that although there is on average no satiation point concerning the consumption–wellbeing relationship for people in Japan, there are satiation points for people who have environmental ethics concerning 'intergenerational equity' or 'irreversibility'. Their results thus imply that environmental ethics is a key to achieving sustainable consumption.

Chapter 21 by Carmen Amelia Coral-Guerrero, Jorge Guardiola and Fernando García-Quero explores how the indigenous lifestyle of *Sumak Kawsay* relates to subjective wellbeing. The Andean indigenous way of life *Sumak Kawsay* ('living well' in Kichwa) is related to reciprocity, solidarity, collective participation, social justice, and harmony with nature and with the community. The chapter uses a representative national sample in Ecuador to assess how certain features of *Sumak Kawsay* relate to subjective wellbeing. It considers several variables associated with this particular way of life: collective participation activities (*mingas*), enjoying a portion of land (*chakra*), living in a rural area and indigenous identity. The results indicate that most *Sumak Kawsay* features are positively related to life and environmental satisfaction. It is suggested that *Sumak Kawsay* is important for subjective wellbeing in Ecuador, but indigenous people's subjective wellbeing would benefit if their needs are better taken into account in the political arena.

Chapter 22 by Shashi Kant, Ilan Vertinsky and Bin Zheng explores the relationship between traditional lifestyles and wellbeing of two Canadian First Nations communities. Key domains of wellbeing and respective contributing factors and linkages between contributing factors and domains are identified. Subjective wellbeing models and household welfare functions of income, traditional diet and trapping income are estimated. The social, cultural and land use domain is found to be the most important contributor to wellbeing, and factors from this domain contribute to all other domains' satisfactions. Estimates of the household welfare function indicate that as people's income increases, they need more income to be satisfied; however, an improvement of the quality of time spent on creating or strengthening social ties can reduce the amount of income for average income satisfaction. The phenomenon of preference drift is also observed in the household welfare function of traditional diet and trapping income.

In Part III, the final part of the book, Bruno S. Frey in Chapter 23 discusses happiness in retrospect and prospect. Subjective wellbeing research has produced many valuable insights concerning the determinants as well as the consequences of happiness. It is argued in this chapter that the causality issue should be dealt with in a more pragmatic way than is now the case. Various reasons are proposed for why happiness research has only partially been integrated into standard economics. The insights provided by happiness research should be introduced as one element in democratic political discourse. In future, care should be taken not to swamp the main messages of happiness research by ever more refined and detailed analyses. Various fruitful research topics are suggested; most importantly, the institutional and constitutional ones, the sociological determinants of happiness, as well as the impact of violent political conflict. Future research topics should come from issues in the real world rather than from problems mainly of interest within the research community.

REFERENCES

Diener, E. (1984), 'Subjective well-being', *Psychological Bulletin*, **95**, 542–575.

Diener, E., Suh, E.M., Lucas, R.E. and H.L. Smith (1999), 'Subjective well-being: three decades of progress', *Psychological Bulletin*, **125**, 276–302.

Di Tella, R. and R. MacCulloch (2006), 'Some uses of happiness data in economics', *Journal of Economic Perspectives*, **20**, 25–46.

Dolan, P., Peasgood, T. and M. White (2008), 'Do we really know what makes us happy? A review of the economic literature on the factors associated with subjective well-being', *Journal of Economic Psychology*, **29**, 94–122.

Easterlin, R. (1974), 'Does economic growth improve the human lot? Some empirical evidence', in P.A. David and M.W. Reder (eds), *Nations and Households in Economic Growth: Essays in Honour of Moses Abramovitz*, New York: Academic Press, pp. 89–125.

Frey, B.S. (2018), *Economics of Happiness*, Berlin: Springer.

Frey, B.S. and A. Stutzer (2002), 'What can economists learn from happiness research?', *Journal of Economic Literature*, **40**, 402–435.

Frijters, P. and B. Van Praag (1998), 'The effects of climate on welfare and well-being in Russia', *Climate Change*, **39**, 61–81.
Graham, C. (2017), 'Happiness and economics: insights for policy from the new "science" of well-being', *Journal of Behavioral Economics for Policy*, **1** (1), 69–72.
Kahneman, D. and A.B. Krueger (2006), 'Developments in the measurement of subjective well-being', *Journal of Economic Perspectives*, **20**, 3–24.
Rehdanz, K. and D. Maddison (2005), 'Climate and happiness', *Ecological Economics*, **52**, 111–125.
Stiglitz, J.E., Sen, A. and J.-P. Fitoussi (2009), 'Report by the Commission on the Measurement of Economic Performance and Social Progress (CMEPSP)', http://www.stiglitz-sen-fitoussi.fr/en/documents.htm.
Van Praag, B. and B. Baarsma (2005), 'Using happiness surveys to value intangibles: the case of airport noise', *Economic Journal*, **115**, 224–246.
Welsch, H. (2002), 'Preferences over prosperity and pollution: environmental valuation based on happiness surveys', *Kyklos*, **55**, 473–494.
Welsch, H. and J. Kühling (2009), 'Using happiness data for environmental valuation: issues and applications', *Journal of Economic Surveys*, **23**, 385–406.

PART I

SOCIAL SCIENCES, HAPPINESS AND THE ENVIRONMENT

1. Economics, wellbeing and happiness: a historical perspective*

Luigino Bruni

1.1 INTRODUCTION: OLD AND NEW HAPPINESS IN ECONOMICS

The *telos* of classical political economy was to reduce unhappiness by means of reducing material poverty, increasing the wealth of nations. This was the main operation that created its moral statute in the late modernity. The science of economics became known as the 'science of wealth', with the 'hope that poverty and ignorance may gradually be extinguished' and 'that all should start in the world with a fair chance of leading a cultured life, free from the pains of poverty and stagnating influences of excessive mechanical toil' (Marshall, 1890 [1945]: 3–4). This hope has inspired economists to study the 'nature and causes of the wealth' of persons and nations, with the hope and promise that an ever-increasing number of people can enjoy basic material needs, and therefore increase 'public happiness'.

In the last decades, however, something very subtle pertaining to human happiness has begun to creep into economic thought. Doubts about the moral value of economic growth and the ethical bases of progress have arisen, fostered by the recent (2008) financial and economic crisis, in Europe especially. A stream of inner critique of the values of modernity and market economy has characterized modernity since its very beginning.

J.J. Rousseau is the main representative of this anti-modernity tradition, pointing out that in the luxury, avarice and the search for wealth, lies the main vice of modern ages. Not only socialism and Marxism, but also utopian socialists and some branches of the co-operative movement, have continued Rousseau's radical critical attitude toward the market and modern economy, which has flowed in parallel to the capitalistic river. During deep and long economic and social crises this anti-market economy tradition has always emerged, gaining consensus in the public audience, the media and among intellectuals.

The literature on the 'paradoxes of happiness' offers material to the present-day critique of capitalism. In this chapter I will try to show that the messages that the issue of happiness has for economic life and theory are many, complex and old.

The expression 'paradox of happiness' or 'Easterlin paradox' refers to empirical data about two main different and controversial issues. In a nutshell, the 'happiness paradox' shows that per capita income has risen sharply in most countries in recent decades, whereas average happiness has stayed constant or has lower growth than traditional economics claims.[1]

The explanations of the paradox are many. There is, however, an idea present in all economic theories: economics, focused on its key variables (income, wealth, consumption), neglects something important which affects people's happiness. There are, in other words, some 'happiness externalities' that are not calculated in the standard economic analysis of income and wealth. In the 'transformation' of goods into wellbeing, something occurs to make the process more complex than standard economic theory supposes.

But apart from the technicalities of the debate on the economics of happiness today (where we find many nuances and interpretations), from it springs a very sharp cultural message: in contemporary market societies, wealth and income, at both the individual and social levels, are linked in a deep relation with wellbeing or happiness, both individually and socially. However, the most important words about our lot are those embodied in the 'transformation problem' of goods into wellbeing, of wealth into weal. But mainstream economics shows no interest in the transformation of commodities into happiness, stopping its discourse at the backyard of our wellbeing.

This chapter tries to show some of the 'whys' and 'hows' of the lack of attention for this kind of transformation problem in economics, following the mainstream of the history of the nexus of wealth and happiness but also some interrupted paths of economic traditions (the Italian civil economy and the Cambridge tradition), where the attention regarding the translation of goods into wellbeing was greater and in some cases central.

1.2 'WEALTH' OR 'HAPPINESS'?

Modern political economy is supposed to have been a by-product of the modern need to make the search for wealth and individual self-interest socially and morally legitimate. However, before Adam Smith published his *Wealth of Nations* in 1776 (Smith, 1776 [1976]), where he defined 'wealth' as the subject of the newborn discipline, a different approach had gained ground. In the mid-eighteenth century in French and Italian traditions the issue placed at the core of the modern economic reflection was 'public happiness'. The first author who used the expression '*pubblica felicità*' as the title of one of his books was the Italian philosopher Ludovico Antonio Muratori (*On Public Happiness*) in 1749, and after him the term 'happiness' appeared in the title of many books and pamphlets by Italian economists of that time: examples are Giuseppe Palmieri (*Reflections on the Public Happiness*, 1788), or Pietro Verri's (1781) *Discourse on Happiness*, among others. Happiness became a landmark of the Italian classical political (civil) economy: 'All our [Italian] economists, from whatever regional background, are dealing not so much, like Adam Smith, with the wealth of nations, but with public happiness' (Loria, 1893 [1904]: 85).

The eighteenth-century Italian tradition was in continuity with civic humanism, and with the idea in particular that comes from the Aristotlotelian–Tomistic tradition that happiness is 'social' by nature: man is a social animal, and therefore the happy man needs friends.

It should also be noted that in Italy the theme of public happiness was coupled with the idea of *ben vivere sociale* (the social weal),[2] an association that had been characteristic of the Italian civic humanist tradition from Francesco Petrarca to Leon Battista Alberti and Lodovico Antonio Muratori. A special Neapolitan echo of that tradition stayed alive in Naples, thanks to Giambattista Vico, Pietro Giannone and Paolo Mattia Doria (Bruni, 2006). Some years later, in France, philosopher-economists, such as Rousseau, Linguet, Maupertuis, Necker, Turgot, Condorcet and Sismondi, all gave a place to happiness in their analyses, and the *félicité publique* was one of the key ideas of the French

Enlightenment movement: 'The mass of the [English] nation seems to forget, as do philosophers, that the increase in riches is not the end of political economy, but the means by which to provide the happiness for all' (Sismondi, 1819 [1971]: 52).

Loria's and Sismondi's thesis has to be circumstantiated. In fact, if it is true that Smith or Ricardo did not give happiness a central place in their economic theories, nonetheless the issue of happiness was far from being absent in the British debate in their time; it suffices to remember that classical utilitarianism was an offspring of that intellectual climate. At the same time, we must however recognize that English classical political economy did not choose public happiness as a direct object of its enquiries, focusing instead on the wealth of nations, its distribution, creation and growth.

Smith's position is well known. In the *Theory of Moral Sentiments* (*TMS*) one can find the classical (Aristotelian) idea of happiness as the final goal of human life (Smith, 1759 [1976]: 166). Human happiness does not present a particular characteristic for human beings in respect of other creatures, and under the Stoic influence happiness is defined as 'tranquillity and enjoyment' (Smith, 1759 [1976]: 149). The idea that happiness is related to interpersonal relationships is not emphasized, although Smith's moral system is built on relational categories, such as 'fellow-feeling'; categories, however, absent in his economic theory of the *Wealth of Nations*.

The key idea in the relationship between wealth and happiness is that the former is instrumental to the latter; wealth is just a means for being happy (Smith, 1759 [1976]: 166), a thesis not far away from the classical one. However, Smith's vision of happiness in relation to the economic field is more complex than the simple equivalence 'more wealth equals more happiness'. The argument runs as follows. The emulation of the wealth and greatness of the rich is the engine of both social mobility and economic development. So the 'poor man's son' submits 'to more fatigue of body and more uneasiness of mind . . . he labours night and day to acquire talents superior to all his competitors' (Smith, 1759 [1976]: 181).

This dynamic, however, is based upon a deception, namely, the idea that the rich man is happier than the poor, or that he possesses 'more means for happiness' (Smith, 1759 [1976]: 182). In reality this is not true, but it is the engine of social and economic development (by means of the 'invisible hand' argument). It is this 'good deception' (for the common good) that is the core of Smith's theory of the 'invisible hand'.

Smith's illustration of the working of deceived human imagination is a piece of psychological analysis which finds its completion in the description of the real and actual condition of the rich, as people paradoxically sharing the same lot as the poor:

> It is to no purpose, that the proud and unfeeling landlord views his extensive fields, and without a thought for the wants of his brethren, in imagination consumes himself the whole harvest that grows upon them. The homely and vulgar proverb, that the eye is larger than the belly, never was more fully verified than with regard to him. The capacity of his stomach bears no proportion to the immensity of his desire, and will receive no more than that of the meanest peasant. (*TMS*: IV, 1, 10)

The fate of the rich, in fact, is merely that:

> they only select from the heap what is most precious and agreeable. They consume little more than the poor, and in spite of their natural selfishness and rapacity, though they mean only their

> own conveniency, though the sole end which they propose from the labours of all the thousands whom they employ, be the gratification of their own vain and insatiable desires, they divide with the poor the produce of all their improvements. They are led by an invisible hand to make nearly the same distribution of the necessaries of life, which would have been made, had the earth been divided into equal portions among all its inhabitants, and thus without intending it, without knowing it, advance the interest of the society, and afford means to the multiplication of the species. When Providence divided the earth among a few lordly masters, it neither forgot nor abandoned those who seemed to have been left out in the partition. These last too enjoy their share of all that it produces. In what constitutes the real happiness of human life, they are in no respect inferior to those who would seem so much above them. In ease of body and peace of mind, all the different ranks of life are nearly upon a level, and the beggar, who suns himself by the side of the highway, possesses that security which kings are fighting for. (*TMS*: IV, 1, 10)

Smith's use of the 'invisible hand' metaphor in the *TMS* parallels the logic of the 'happiness paradox' in the current literature. In Smith's moral theory, the rich and the ambitious are moved by frivolous and temporary illusions. 'Power and riches (IV, 1, 8) appear then to be, what they are, enormous and operose machines contrived to produce a few trifling conveniences to the body . . . which in spite of all our care are ready every moment to burst into pieces, and crush in their ruins their unfortunate possessor' (*TMS*: VI, 1, 9).

In the *Wealth of Nations* the issue of happiness is almost totally absent. The title of the book itself defines the object of the new-born political economy: it deals with wealth not with happiness, even if in Smith's choice of the word 'wealth' instead of 'riches' one can rightly see the idea that wealth (weal or wellbeing) is more and something different from simply possessing riches.[3]

Malthus, 'the first of the Cambridge economists', as J.M. Keynes (1933: 95) defined him, followed a different path. His *Essay on the Principle of Population* (Malthus, 1798 [1966]) reserves an important role for the issue of happiness, a word that appears even in the title of the second edition (1803) of the book.[4] In a very central passage he writes:

> The professed object of Dr Adam Smith's inquiry is the nature and causes of the wealth of nations. There is another inquiry however perhaps even more interesting, which he occasionally includes in his studies and that is the inquiry into the causes which affect the happiness of nations . . . I am sufficiently aware of the near connection of these two subjects and that the causes which tend to increase the wealth of a state tend also, generally speaking, to increase happiness . . . But perhaps Dr Adam Smith has considered these two inquiries as still more nearly connected than they really are. (Malthus, 1798 [1966]: 303–304)

From this sentence we have the main elements for us to be able to understand the key points of Malthus's idea of happiness and his evaluation of Smith's position. To Malthus happiness is not wealth, but in general he agrees with Smith that more wealth leads to more happiness. According to Malthus, however, Smith was not sufficiently aware that the relation between these two concepts is complex and worth investigating on its own: he was aware, then, of the 'happiness transformation problem'. In particular, Malthus belongs to a group of those economists (Sismondi, Genovesi and many Italians) who thought that the 'happiness of the nations' is 'another inquiry, however, perhaps still more interesting' (Malthus, 1798 [1966]: 304) than that of wealth, as the modern theorists of happiness also think (Bruni, 2017).

It is important to notice, however, that Malthus's wish to directly study happiness as the object of political economy did not last long. In his *Principles of Political Economy*

(Malthus, 1820 [1986]), there are no references to happiness, and the object of his enquiries becomes wealth, as in Smith and the classical mainstream tradition of economics (something similar will occur also to Marshall, as we will see later). In particular, although he was fully aware that political economy, in focusing on material and quantitative aspects of human interactions, was losing important elements of wellbeing, he left out all interpersonal dimensions of wealth:

> A man of fortune has the means of . . . collecting at his table persons from whom he is likely to hear the most agreeable and instructive conversation . . . It would not be denied, that these are some of the modes of employing wealth, which are always, and most justly, considered as much superior in respectability, to the purchase of fine clothes, spending on furniture, or costly jewels . . . But it is a wide step in advance of these concessions, at once to place in the category of wealth, leisure, agreeable conversation . . . The fact really is, that if we once desert matter in definition of wealth, there is no subsequent line of demarcation which has any tolerable degree of distinctness, or can be maintained with any tolerable consistency, till we have included such a mass of immaterial objects as utterly to confuse the meaning of the term, and render it impossible to speak with any approach towards precision, either of the wealth of different individuals, or different nations. (Malthus, 1820 [1986]: 31–32)

Here the main reason that brought political economy to avoid dealing with interpersonal qualitative aspects of economic transactions is clearly stated. Malthus was convinced not only that 'enjoying conversations' with friends is an important and 'superior' form of using wealth, but even that 'leisure and agreeable conversations' can rightly be considered as components of the wealth and welfare of a person. These components, however, he considered to be too ill-defined to be included within the economic domain that instead needs data and objective measurement, that is, needs 'matter'; a methodological position very close to the Austrian school of Menger at the end of the nineteenth century. Something had to be sacrificed on the altar of the new science of objective and scientific measurements, and one victim was the social and immaterial components of wealth. A science seeking to encompass the first 'scientific' reflections on economic relations chose to concentrate its analyses upon objective elements, such as labour value or redistribution of income. Such a science, however, does not have the tools to study the 'happiness of nations', as the young Malthus claimed.

1.3 THE CAMBRIDGE TRADITION

Alfred Marshall's analysis of happiness, an expression that he uses as synonymous with wellbeing, is strictly interrelated with his theory of sociality in economics. It is well known that Marshall made room for 'altruism' in his economics, denying, in contrast with economists such as Pantaleoni (Bruni and Sugden, 2007), that the individualistic self-interest is an essential requisite of economic science. He wanted to study the 'man in flesh and blood', and therefore any human dimension could find, theoretically, its place within his economics (Marshall, 1890 [1945]: 27 ff.). The only limitation of the economic domain is, for Marshall, the possibility of monetary measurement of economic variables: therefore, economic goods are those that 'can be measurable by a money price' (ibid.: 33).[5] It is a methodological operation very close to that performed by Malthus in Cambridge in shaping the boundaries of economic wealth.

The right of citizenship to altruism is not, however, an element of originality and breaking of Marshall's theory with regard to the economists who preceded him. The first name that comes into mind is Edgeworth, who allowed altruism to be present within the core of pure economics. The second is H.P. Wicksteed, who replaced egoism (and economic principle) with 'non-tuism', a concept open to a form of altruism (Bruni, 2006). Although Edgeworth preferred speaking of 'sympathy' or 'utilitarianism', and although he considered actions actuated or influenced by sympathy as not perfectly economic (consider his well-known definition: 'the first principle of Economics is that every agent is actuated only by self-interest'; Edgeworth, 1881: 16), he recognized that sympathetic or altruistic actions can perfectly well be present within economics (ibid.: 53; see Collard, 1978). Moreover, however, although self-interest as a dominant motive in economic matters was considered by classical and neoclassical economists (from Mill to Jevons) as one of the most basic and universal economic laws, this was more a commonsense thesis than an essential exigency of the theory.

Above I presented Malthus's position on happiness: apart from the reference to a direct study of happiness that one can find in the *Essay on the Principle of Population*, I have shown that he was sharp to spot the distinction between happiness and wealth, although in his economic analyses he chose to deal with wealth and only indirectly with happiness. This approach of the founder of the Cambridge tradition was continued by Marshall and his school (Pigou in particular). Marshall, opening his *Principles of Economics*, wrote the following:

> Political economy or economics is a study of mankind in the ordinary business of life; it examines that part of individual and social action which is most closely connected with the attainment and with the use of the material requisites of well-being. Thus it is on the one side a study of wealth; and on the other, and more important side, a part of the study of man. (Marshall, 1890 [1945]: 1)

In this Marshall was really a 'neo-'classical, his approach being fully in agreement with Malthus. Given his moral approach to economics, partially inherited from Ruskin and Carlyle (see Henderson, 2000), and his concern for poverty, he was very aware of the complexity of the happiness–wealth relationship. From the above passage, significantly placed at the beginning of his *Principles*, we get the basic elements of Marshall's vision of economic agency: economics does not deal directly with 'wellbeing' (that, to Marshall, is a substitute for happiness) but with the 'material requisites' of it. We do not find the word 'happiness' anymore (which in England was linked to the utilitarian and hedonistic philosophy, from which Marshall wanted to distance himself);[6] there is, however, the expression 'wellbeing' (not completely new among economists of his time), later translated by his follower, Pigou, into 'welfare', the key category of his *Economics of Welfare* (Pigou, 1912 [1920]).

The 'material requisites' of wellbeing essentially consist of 'wealth', in line with the Smithian classical tradition. In the 'Introduction' to the *Principles* we also find the theoretical key for understanding Marshall's idea of the relationship between happiness and wealth:

> It is true that in religion, in the family affections and in friendship, even the poor may find scope for many of those faculties which are the source of the highest happiness. But the conditions which surround extreme poverty, especially in densely crowded places, tend to deaden the higher

> faculties. Those who have been called the Residuum of our large towns have little opportunity for friendship; they know nothing of the decencies and the quiet, and very little even of the unity of family life; and religion often fails to reach them. (Marshall, 1890 [1945]: 2)

Happiness, to Marshall, depends largely on extra-economic factors that are not wealth in the usual economic sense, that do not pass through the market, such as religion; and, mainly, genuine interpersonal relationships, such as family affections and friendship. We still find in Marshall the classical (Aristotelian in particular) idea that happiness does not coincide with wealth, and also that happiness has a social nature. Nevertheless, poverty, even if in itself it does not necessarily mean unhappiness, determines those objective conditions that render it very difficult, if not impossible, to develop the dimensions of life and the interpersonal relationships on which happiness actually depends. Therefore, to Marshall the economists' role in society is very important: to study the ways of increasing wealth or reducing poverty, far from being in contrast with general wellbeing or happiness, is a means for directly increasing the 'standard of life' by fostering the interpersonal dimensions of life. Relevant to this is the fact that Marshall (following the German writers) was the first to use, in the English language, the word 'good' for 'commodity' in his *Principles*.

Anyone who knows Amartya Sen's (1987) theory of the 'the standard of living' will find a strong consonance between the two Cambridge economists:

> It is quite easy to be persuaded that being happy is an achievement that is valuable, and that in evaluating the standard of living, happiness is an object of value (or a collection of objects of value, if happiness is seen in a plural form). The interesting question regarding this approach is not the legitimacy of taking happiness to be valuable, which is convincing enough, but its exclusive legitimacy. Consider a very deprived person who is poor, exploited, overworked and ill, but who has been made satisfied with his lot by social conditioning (through, say, religion, political propaganda, or cultural pressure). Can we possibly believe that he is doing well just because he is happy and satisfied? Can the living standard of a person be high if the life that he or she leads is full of deprivation? The standard of life cannot be so detached from the nature of the life the person leads. (Sen, 1987: 7–8)

Marshall's line of thought was followed by his heir in Cambridge, Arthur Cecil Pigou, who moved the fulcrum of the issue at hand toward the other magic word in economics: 'welfare'. In his *Economics of Welfare*, Pigou (1912 [1920]: 16) states that he intends to deal only with the economic aspects of general welfare (what he calls 'economic welfare'), that part of total welfare that 'can be expressed, directly or indirectly, by a money measure'.

In this choice, which per se is legitimate, there was an important missing link: that consisting of analysing how and whether economic goods may become happiness, or wellbeing (without an adjective). In fact what we see today in the debate on economics and happiness is that the efforts to acquire material goods have systematic negative effects on the other components of wealth, in particular interpersonal relationships, and more income can lead (as the growing amount of literature on the paradox of happiness shows) to less wellbeing. Such a line of thought was also developed by Keynes (1930), in particular in his 'Economic possibilities for our grandchildren', where he distinguished between 'basic' and 'relative' (or relational) needs. To Keynes, economic or material growth can properly satisfy the basic needs, but the relative ones have only a tiny and indirect connection with income.

In Marshall's *Principles*, however, there is also an intuition of this possible inverse (and perverse) tendency that, instead, was completely ignored by the founders of contemporary economics. It is his theory of the 'standard of life', the last chapter of his *Principles*.

First of all Marshall, in this chapter, in a full Aristotelian flavour, states that 'the true key-note of economic progress is the development of new activities rather than new wants' (Marshall, 1890 [1945]: 688), specifying that the question that 'is of special urgency in our generation' is 'the connection between changes in the manner of living and the rate of earning' (ibid.).

In order to analyse this urgent question he distinguishes between two concepts: 'the standard of life' and 'the standard of comfort', where the 'standard of life is here taken to mean the standard of activity adjusted to wants' (ibid.: 689), and 'the standard of comfort [is] a term that may suggest a mere increase of artificial wants, among which perhaps the grosser wants may predominate' (ibid.: 690). Then he repeats his thesis that:

> It is true that every broad improvement in the standard of comfort is likely to bring with it a better manner of living, and to open the way to new and higher activities; while people who have hitherto had neither the necessaries nor the decencies of life, can hardly fail to get some increase in vitality and energy from an increase of comfort, however gross and material the view which they may take of it. Thus a rise in the standard of comfort will probably involve some rise in the standard of life. (ibid.)

But this is not always the case. The rest of the chapter, in fact, is an analysis, applied to the labour market and the 'burning question of the limitation of the hours of labour' (Edgeworth, 1891 [1970], III: 14), and to the related issues of minimum wage and redistribution of income, of the cases when rises of standard of comfort bring a fall in the standard of life. A first application of this analysis is Marshall's recommendation to reduce in general the hours of labour, which is likely to cause a little net material loss and much moral good, a case where a reduction of income can lead to a higher standard of life (happiness). At the end of the chapter Marshall explains why:

> Even if we took account only of the injury done to the young by living in a home in which the father and the mother lead joyless lives, it would be in the interest of society to afford some relief to them also. Able workers and good citizens are not likely to come from homes . . . from which the mother is absent during a great part of the day; nor from homes to which the father seldom returns till his children are asleep: and therefore society as a whole has a direct interest in the curtailment of extravagantly long hours of duty away from home. (Marshall, 1890 [1945]: 721)

1.4 THE NEW NAME OF HAPPINESS

Cambridge's approach to happiness did not become mainstream in England, or in neoclassical economics. The University College, where Bentham founded the Utilitarian tradition and Jevons studied economics, took the lead. In fact, it is impossible to reconstruct the evolution of the idea of happiness in economics without taking into account Utilitarianism, built around the golden rule of 'the greatest happiness for the greatest number'.

In Bentham's idea of happiness we immediately see that in his system happiness is equal to 'pleasure', as it comes straight from the very first lines of *An Introduction to the*

Principles of Morals and Legislation: 'Nature has placed mankind under the governance of two sovereign masters, pain and pleasure' (Bentham, 1789 [1996]: 11).

The Benthamite vision of happiness can therefore rightly be called psychological hedonism, having an individualistic nature; people are depicted as seekers of happiness/pleasure. This psychological feature is essential to the utilitarian programme in which social happiness is seen only as an aggregation, a sum of individual pleasures. J.S. Mill, who on happiness diverges deeply from Bentham and from his father James, in his *Utilitarianism* explicitly states that in early Utilitarianism there was an identification between pleasure and happiness: 'By happiness is intended pleasure' (Mill, 1861 [1963]: 210).

The other key word of Bentham is 'utility' (from which the term 'Utilitarianism' came), and the 'principle of utility' (inherited from Beccaria's '*Dei delitti e delle pene*') is stated appropriately, in the first page of his *Introduction*, as the 'foundation of the present work' (Bentham, 1789 [1996]: 11). In all his works the words 'happiness', 'pleasure' and 'utility' are used interchangeably as different ways of expressing the same basic concept of Utilitarianism. In Chapter 1 of *An Introduction to the Principles of Morals and Legislation* he wrote that by utility he meant 'that property in any object, whereby it tends to produce benefit, advantage, pleasure, good or happiness' (Bentham, 1789 [1996]: 12).

With Bentham the distinction between end (happiness) and means (wealth) disappeared; happiness/pleasure also became the direct end of economic actions. Bentham's approach to happiness, therefore, is far from both the classical vision of happiness (from Aristotle to Genovesi) and the Cambridge tradition that kept the distinction between happiness (the final end) and wealth.

Bentham's methodological project, as is well known, nurtured economics, thanks mainly to the works of Jevons and Edgeworth. Most of the leaders of the new economics based their subjectivist approach to economics on a hedonistic philosophy. In Edgeworth's early works up to *Mathematical Psychics* (Edgeworth, 1881), the Utilitarian and hedonist philosophy had a great impact. To him happiness means pleasure, and maximizing happiness means maximizing pleasure (Edgeworth, 1881: 7, 16). Jevons (1871 [1070]) defined economics as the science of utility, explicitly stating his acceptance of the Utilitarian philosophy of Bentham (Robbins, 1998: 262). Happiness entered neoclassical economics fully identified with utility, the new subject of the new economics. Jevons states not only the old Utilitarian thesis that happiness is related to utility, but also that economics is the 'calculus of pleasures and pain' (Jevons, 1871 [1970]: 'Introduction'). To Jevons, pleasures are different 'only in degree, not in kind' (Schabas, 1990: 39). Economics deals with the 'lowest' ones and he does not exclude the fact that men can renounce pleasures coming from the economic domain for the sake of ethical or superior pleasures; but, as Bentham's, his ethical rule is to maximize the sum of pleasures, both individually and socially. In the *Theory of Political Economy* he states: 'The theory which follows is entirely based on a calculus of pleasure and pain and the object of economics is to maximize happiness by purchasing pleasure as it were, at the lowest cost of pain' (Jevons, 1871 [1970]: 91). For British marginalist economists, economics became the science of the direct analysis of happiness/pleasure. The domain of economics was no longer 'wealth' but happiness/pleasure directly. Whilst the classical economists were dealing with objective, external aspects ('material prerequisites'), with Jevons or Edgeworth economics came back to a 'subjective' approach: the domain of economics is inside man's mind.

Contemporary rational choice theory (based on the preference satisfaction approach) is, from a methodological point of view, a continuation of the Benthamite approach: 'The analysis assumes that individuals maximize welfare as they conceive it' (Becker, 1996: 139). Contemporary rational choice theory is far from the classical or neoclassical economists and very close to Bentham or Jevons (more than they thought, if we consider Hicks's and Samuelson's battle against hedonism in economics in the 1930s). Why? First, like Jevons the domain of economics is 'maximizing' pleasure (preferences); second, the place of pleasure has been taken by preferences-satisfaction, but the core elements of the utilitarian approach are still there:

- the domain of economics is no more wealth or economic welfare (the material prerequisites), but to directly bring about happiness, which can be translated into concepts such as pleasure (old marginalists), ordinal utility or preferences (Hicks), or choices (Samuelson);
- the tools utilized for studying the 'means' (maximization, quantitative calculus, instrumental rationality) are now used for specifically studying 'happiness'.

After Bentham, happiness/pleasure became the object of economics: therefore, it is not true that happiness is not central in neoclassical economics. The reductionism of happiness/eudaimonia to utility/pleasure is the real breaking point in the history of happiness in economics: the distinction between material prerequisites and happiness, Cambridge's and classical political economy's cornerstone, has been lost.

1.5 CONCLUSION

Cambridge's epistemology was potentially open to making space for the analysis of some aspects of happiness within economics; the mainstream, however, has followed a completely different path, and the present resurgence of the 'paradox of happiness' is an eloquent sign that during the twentieth century mainstream economics has lost the methodological categories for even understanding the 'happiness transformation problem'.

The reasons for that are many. The most obvious is the cultural atmosphere of the 1930s, when modern microeconomics came to life, so much influenced by neo-positivism and behaviourism, which disregarded Marshall's social considerations and, at the same time, welcomed Paretian positive economics.

The word 'richness' is a distant derivative of *rex* in Latin (king), therefore it has to do with power and even with disposing of people through money and goods. To possess riches has always been and is still deeply connected with the possession of people; and the borderline where democracy turns into plutocracy (the rule of the rich) is always quite faint, fragile and little guarded by those sentinels who are not paid by the plutocrats.

But 'richness' also means 'wealth', and this English word comes from *weal*, meaning wellbeing, prosperity, individual and collective happiness. Adam Smith chose to use the word 'wealth' (and not 'riches') for his economic study (*The Wealth of Nations*) also to suggest that economic richness is something more than the mere sum of material goods or our gross national product.

In order to express this second type of richness, Italians and many economists from the Latin peoples chose the term '*felicità pubblica*' (public happiness) so as not to misvalue the complex passage from richness to happiness. From the second half of the nineteenth century the tradition of *pubblica felicità* became an underground river and the old idea of wellbeing understood by wealth gradually disappeared. And so in the whole of the West the semantic range of richness became much poorer; and so did we. We have created a financial type of capitalism that generated much of the wrong 'richness' that did not improve our lives or that of the planet. Then, maybe, the tradition of *pubblica felicità* can still have something important to say.

NOTES

* The chapter is based on Bruni (2016).

1. The index of 'very happy' responses in the United States National Surveys in the period 1946–90 has decreased (or has not increased), while the gross domestic product per capita has strongly increased.
2. The phrase was used in a well-known title by Ludovico Bianchini (1845), one of Italy's early historians, as a hallmark of Italian economic thought.
3. Also Smith's definition of wealth leaves room for interpersonal relationships as a form of wealth: 'Every man is rich or poor according to the degree in which he can afford to enjoy the necessaries, conveniences, and amusements of human life' (Smith, 1776 [1976], I: 32). In the expression 'amusements' one can find all kinds of social activities. Smith develops this idea further a few lines later: 'Wealth, as Mr. Hobbes says, is power' (ibid.: 33). In fact, Hobbes, in his *Leviathan* (Hobbes, 1651 [1954], I: x), says that riches is power 'because it procureth friends'.
4. In fact, the expression 'human happiness' was not present in the first edition.
5. The same thesis is present in Pigou (1912 [1920]: Ch. 1). For Marshall and his school, the domain of economics is determined by the strength of man's motives – 'not the motives themselves' – strength that 'can be approximately measured by the sum of money' (Marshall, 1890 [1945]: 15).
6. Fontaine's interpretation repeats the Humean theory of 'spheres of intimacy', also present in Smith. The key test for supporting their thesis is the following: 'the necessity or conveniency of mutual accommodation, very frequently produces a friendship not unlike that which takes place among those who are born to live in the same family. Colleagues in office, partners in trade, call one another brothers; and frequently feel towards one another as if they really were so . . . Even the trifling circumstance of living in the same neighbourhood, has some effect of the same kind. We respect the face of a man whom we see every day, provided he has never offended us. Neighbours can be very convenient, and they can be very troublesome, to one another' (Smith, 1759 [1976]: 223–224).

REFERENCES

Becker, Gary (ed.) (1996), *Accounting for Tastes*, Cambridge, MA, USA: Harvard University Press.

Bentham, Jeremy (1789 [1996]), *An Introduction to the Principles of Morals and Legislation*, reprinted in J.H. Burns and H.L.A. Hart (eds) (1996), *The Collected Works of Jeremy Bentham: An Introduction to the Principles of Morals and Legislation*, Oxford, UK: Clarendon Press.

Bianchini, Lodovico (ed.) (1845), *Della Scienza del ben Vivere Sociale e della Economia Degli Stati*, Palermo, Italy: Stamperia di Francesco Lao.

Bruni, Luigino (ed.) (2006), *Civil Happiness: Economics and Human Flourishing in Historical Perspective*, London, UK: Routledge.

Bruni, Luigino (2016), 'Economics, well-being and happiness: history and protagonists', in Luigino Bruni and Pier L. Porta (eds), *Handbook of Research Methods and Applications in Happiness and Quality of Life*, Cheltenham, UK and Northampton, MA, USA: Edward Elgar Publishing, pp. 334–348.

Bruni, Luigino (2017), 'On the concept of Economia Civile and Felicitas Publica: a comment on Federico D'Onofrio', *Journal of the History of Economic Thought*, **39** (2), 273–279.

Bruni, Luigino and Robert Sugden (2007), 'The road not taken: How psychology was removed from economics, and how it might be brought back', *Economic Journal*, **117** (516), 146–173.

Collard, David (ed.) (1978), *Altruism and Economy: A Study in Non-selfish Economics*, Oxford, UK: Oxford University Press.

Edgeworth, Francis Y. (ed.) (1881), *Mathematical Psychics*, London, UK: C. Kegan Paul.
Edgeworth, Francis Y. (1891 [1970]), *Papers Related to Political Economy*, reprinted in 1970, Vol. 3, New York, USA: Burt Franklin.
Henderson, William (ed.) (2000), *John Ruskin's Political Economy*, London, UK: Routledge.
Hobbes, Thomas (ed.) (1651 [1954]), *Leviathan*, reprinted in 1954, London, UK: Dent & Son.
Jevons, William S. (ed.) (1871 [1970]), *The Theory of Political Economy*, reprinted in 1970, New York, USA: Penguin Books.
Keynes, John Maynard (ed.) (1930), *Essays in Persuasion*, London, UK: Macmillan.
Keynes, John Maynard (ed.) (1933), *Essays in Biography*, London, UK: Macmillan.
Loria, Achille (ed.) (1893 [1904]), *Verso la Giustizia Sociale*, reprinted in 1904, Milan, Italy: Società Editrice Libraria.
Malthus, Thomas R. (ed.) (1798 [1966]), *An Essay on the Principle of Population*, reprinted in 1966, London, UK: Macmillan.
Malthus, Thomas R. (1820 [1986]), *Principles of Political Economy*, reprinted in E.A. Wrigley and D. Souden (eds) (1986), *The Works of Thomas Robert Malthus*, London, UK: Pickering.
Marshall, Alfred (ed.) (1890 [1945]), *Principles of Economics*, reprinted in 1945, London, UK: Macmillan.
Mill, John S. (1861 [1963]), *Utilitarianism*, reprinted in J.M. Robson and J. Stillinger (eds) (1963), *The Collected Works of John Stuart Mill*, Vol. X, Toronto, Canada: University of Toronto Press and London, UK: Routledge & Kegan Paul.
Muratori, Lodovico A. (ed.) (1749), *Della Pubblica Felicità*, Verona, Italy: Lucca.
Palmieri, Giuseppe (ed.) (1788), *Riflessioni sulla Pubblica Felicità Relativamente al Regno di Napoli*, Milan, Italy: Pirotta e Maspero.
Pigou, Arthur C. (ed.) (1912 [1920]), *Economics of Welfare*, reprinted in 1920, London, UK: Macmillan.
Robbins, Lionel (1998), *A History of Economic Thought: The LSE Lectures*, edited by Steven G. Medema and Warren J. Samuels, Princeton, NJ, USA and Oxford, UK: Princeton University Press.
Schabas, Margaret (ed.) (1990), *A World Ruled by Number: William Stanley Jevons and the Rise of Mathematical Economics*, Princeton, NJ, USA: Princeton University Press.
Sen, Amartya (ed.) (1987), *The Standard of Living*, Cambridge, UK: Cambridge University Press.
Sismondi, Jean-Charles-Léonhard Simonde de (1819 [1971]), *Nouveaux Principes d'Economie Politique: Ou de la Richesse dans ses Rapports avec la Population*, reprinted in 1971, Paris, France: Calmann-Lévy.
Smith, Adam (1759 [1976]), *The Theory of Moral Sentiments*, reprinted in A.L. Macfie and D.D. Raphael (eds) (1976), *The Glasgow Edition of the Works and Correspondence of Adam Smith*, Vol. I, Oxford: Oxford University Press.
Smith, Adam (1776 [1976]), *An Inquiry into the Nature and Causes of the Wealth of Nations*, reprinted in W.B. Todd (ed.) (1976), *Glasgow Edition of the Works and Correspondence of Adam Smith*, Vol. II, Oxford: Oxford University Press.
Verri, Pietro (ed.) (1781), *Sull'indole del Piacere e del Dolore*, Milan, Italy: Giuseppe Marelli.

2. World Database of Happiness: a 'findings archive'

Ruut Veenhoven

2.1 HAPPINESS RESEARCH

Over the ages the subject of happiness has absorbed a lot of thought. Happiness was a major theme in early Greek philosophy and gained renewed interest during the later Western European Enlightenment (Mauzi, 1960). The philosophic tradition has produced a lot of ideas, but little factual knowledge; philosophers have raised more questions about happiness than they have answered. Most of the controversies they have raised cannot be solved by the logic of reasoning, and settlement of arguments based on reality checks has long been handicapped by a lack of adequate research techniques.

In the 20th century, the social sciences brought about a breakthrough. New empirical research methods opened the possibility to identify conditions for happiness inductively and to test theories. This instigated a lot of research, most of which is embedded in the then newly established specializations of social indicators research, health-related quality of life research, and more recently in 'positive psychology' and 'happiness economics'.

2.1.1 Growing Number of Empirical Studies on Happiness

The stream of social scientific research is growing fast. The rising number of publications on happiness is depicted in Figure 2.1.[1] After take-off in the 1970s, the average annual growth rate has been approximately 5 per cent. The number of research reports published in 2019 on happiness defined as the subjective enjoyment of one's life as a whole (see section 2.2) is estimated to be some 800.[2]

Reviews of this research literature have been published by Veenhoven (1984), Argyle (1987), Diener (1999), Frey and Stutzer (2002), Dolan et al. (2006) and Diener and Biswas-Diener (2008). The growing interest in happiness is also reflected in the establishment of specialized scientific journals such as the *Journal of Happiness Studies*,[3] the first issue of which appeared in the year 2000.

2.1.2 Intriguing Findings on Happiness

The new line of research has produced several unexpected results, such as:

- The majority of humanity appears to enjoy life. Unhappiness is the exception rather than the rule. This is at odds with common misery counts in the social sciences (Diener and Diener, 1996).
- Average happiness is high in modern societies and the trend is for it to rise even higher. This finding contradicts longstanding pessimism about modernization (Cummins, 2000; Veenhoven, 2005; Veenhoven and Hagerty, 2005; Inglehart et al., 2008).

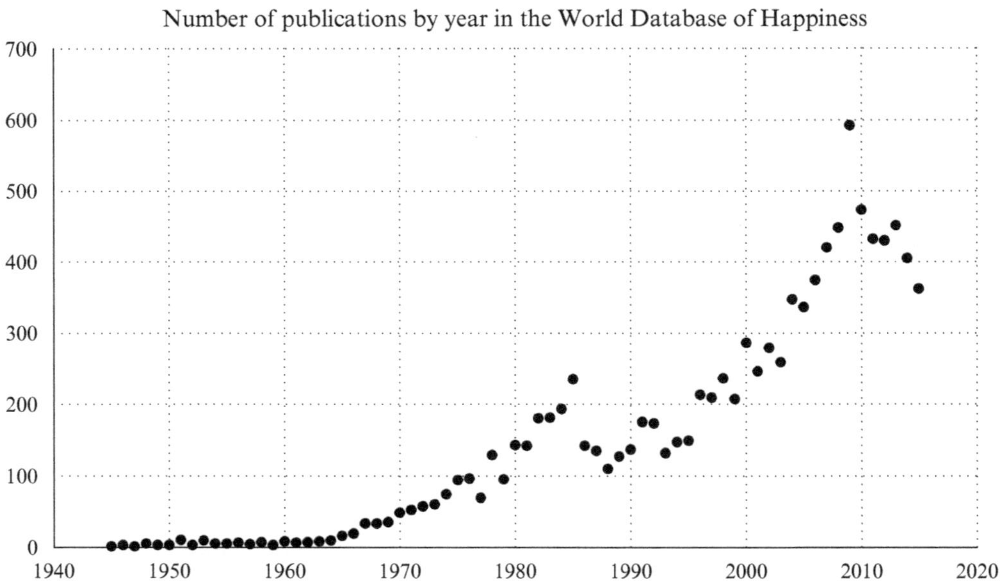

Source: Bibliography of Happiness, http://worlddatabaseofhappiness.eur.nl/hap_bib/bib_fp.php.

Figure 2.1 Yearly number of scientific publications on happiness since 1940

- In modern Western nations, happiness differs little across social categories, such as rich and poor, and males and females. The difference is rather in psychological competence (Headey and Wearing, 1992). This result is at odds with the common notion in sociology that happiness depends primarily on one's social position.
- Differences in happiness within nations (as measured by standard deviations) have tended to get smaller over time. This contradicts claims about growing inequality in modern society (Veenhoven, 2002).
- People live more happily in individualistic societies such as Denmark, than in collectivistic societies such as Japan (Veenhoven, 1999; Verne, 2009). This contradicts the view that modern society falls short in social cohesion, proclaimed in books such as *Bowling Alone* (Putman, 2000).
- People do not live more happily in welfare states than in equally rich nations where the 'father state' is less open-handed. Inequality of happiness does not appear to be smaller in welfare states either (Veenhoven, 2000). This finding conflicts with political left thinking.
- Happiness is not just a matter of being better off than others; though social comparison plays a role, it is not the whole story. This finding challenges cognitive theories of happiness, and supports affective explanations (Veenhoven, 1991, 1995, 2008).
- Happiness is not very trait-like; over a lifetime it appears to be quite variable. This finding does not fit the 'set-point' theory of happiness (Veenhoven, 1994; Ehrhardt et al., 2000; Headey, 2006).

2.1.3 Stagnating Progress in Understanding of Happiness

All this empirical research on happiness has not yet crystallized into a sound body of knowledge. Preliminary questions about conceptualization and measurement are now fairly well solved, but our understanding of the determinants and consequences of happiness is still tentative and very incomplete. There are several reasons why the growing stream of empirical research has not yet brought better understanding. In addition to complexities in the subject matter, such as contingencies, there are a number of practical problems.

Conceptual confusion

The first reason is 'confusion of tongues'. As there is no consensus on the use of words and terminology in the field, it is quite difficult to select the data that pertain to happiness in a particular sense, such as my usage here of satisfaction with one's life as a whole. I will discuss this in section 2.2.

Some researchers who state that their aim is to measure 'life satisfaction' end up measuring something else; for example, Neugarten et al. (1961), whose life satisfaction scale involves several items that measure social functioning rather than satisfaction with life. Conversely, some investigators focusing on mental health have used indicators that adequately reflect life satisfaction; for example, Gurin et al. (1960).

Lack of overview

The second reason for the stagnation in our field is lack of coordination. There is much redundancy in the research on happiness: the same issues are investigated over and over again, in the same way; for example, the correlation between happiness and income. As a result, the range of variables considered is still rather small and methodological progress is slow. A related problem is that the research findings are very scattered, and most of the observations cannot be traced in bibliographical systems. Consequently, many of the findings get 'lost'.

Scarce research on contingencies

A more basic reason for the stagnation in the study of happiness lies in the dominant research approach. The bulk of empirical happiness studies consist of cross-sectional surveys within particular countries. Typically, investigators try to identify universal conditions for happiness using local correlates. For instance, the observation found in American studies that the happy tend to have high incomes is seen to mean that money buys happiness in any country, and that the basic underlying mental process is social comparison.

Yet, conditions for happiness are probably not the same at all times and in all places. Neither are its consequences. Though there are obviously universal requirements for a happy life (Veenhoven, 2010b), some seem to be contingent on the characteristics of a person and situation. For instance, happiness correlates strongest to income in poor and socially unequal countries, and most so among materialistic persons. Usually, such contingencies cannot be detected in single studies in one country; they can only be identified if many studies are compared in a systematic meta-analysis, and this requires that the available findings be compiled in a suitable dataset.

Scarce research on causality

Correlations say little about cause and effect. If rich Americans tend to be happier, this does not prove that money buys happiness, because happiness can also boost earning chances. Separation of cause and effect requires studies that use techniques such as follow-up, experiment or instrumental variable analysis. Such studies are scarce as yet, and the results are difficult to retrieve. Progress in the field requires at least that these scattered findings be brought together.

2.1.4 Research Compilation on Happiness Required

Because of these problems, it is important to gather the available research findings on happiness and to present these in a comparable format. Without a complete and detailed view on the available findings, there will be little accumulation of knowledge. This need for a compilation of research findings on happiness becomes ever more pressing. The higher the pile of research reports, the greater the need for a good overview of the findings they contain.

Now that some 800 studies on happiness appear every year (see Figure 2.1), the heap of findings has grown too big to be handled using narrative research reviews; yet at the same time the stockpile is becoming ever more suitable for quantitative meta-analysis. Meta-analysis requires much investment in gathering of relevant research and in homogenizing the findings. This investment is particularly high if one wants to cover the entire world's research on a particular topic. Such investments are made in capital-intensive fields such as pharmacological research, but are uncommon in happiness research. The few meta-analyses of empirical happiness research to date have been based on small collections of research findings, for example Stock et al. (1983), Okun et al. (1984), Pinquart and Sörenson (2000, 2001) and Steel et al. (2008). As yet, all these meta-analyses have been one-time shots, leaving no common database to build on. Hence each new investigator has to make a new start. Not surprisingly, few do.

2.2 THE WORLD DATABASE OF HAPPINESS

The World Database of Happiness (Veenhoven, 2019a) is an archive of research findings on happiness defined as the subjective enjoyment of one's life as a whole. It is meant to facilitate research synthesis on this subject. Access to the archive is freely available on the Internet, at http://worlddatabaseofhappiness.eur.nl. The start page of this database is presented in Figure 2.2.

Below I describe this data system and present details of illustrative web pages. Technical terms used are summarized in Table 2.1.

2.2.1 Aims

The prime aim is to provide an empirical basis for policies that aim at greater happiness for a greater number of people[4] (Veenhoven, 2010c). The formation of such policies requires knowledge about the conditions for happiness and the consequences of happiness, and of possible variations in these across time, place and kinds of people. Empirical evidence on these matters is needed as an antidote to ideological presumption.

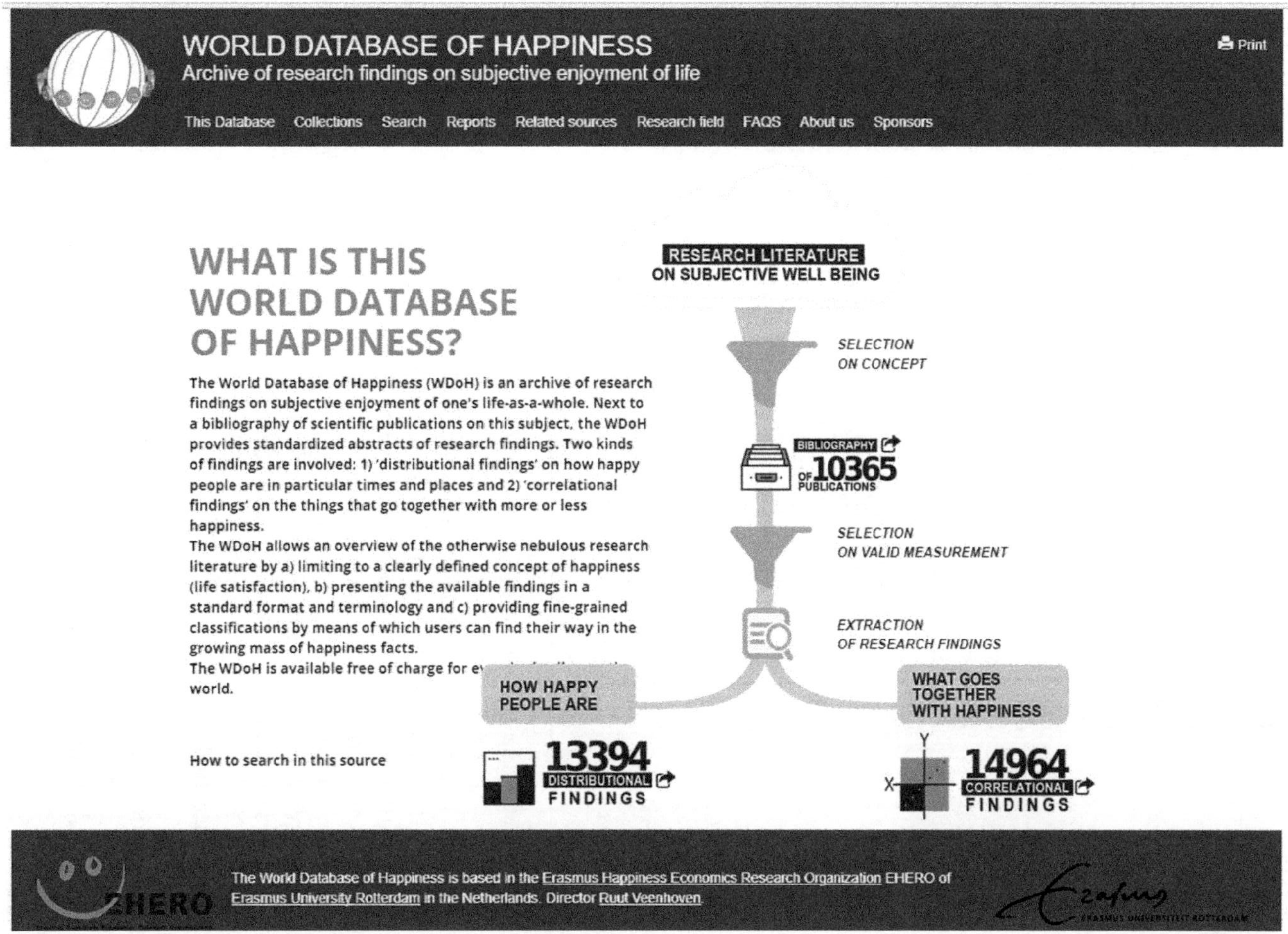

Figure 2.2 Start page of the World Database of Happiness

Table 2.1 Glossary of terms used

Terms	Definitions
Publication	A written report of scientific research on happiness, such as articles, books, dissertations and working papers. All publications that involve information about happiness in the sense of subjective enjoyment of life are gathered in the Bibliography of Happiness.* One publication can report more than one study.
Study	Investigation on happiness in a particular population.
Public	Kind of people investigated. Next to the general public in nations, this database distinguishes several 'special publics', such as the elderly and home makers.
Measure of happiness	Method for assessing how much people like the life they live.
Finding page	A structured presentation of a single research finding, which involves: (1) the publication in which this result was reported; (2) the population in which this result was observed; (3) the method used to obtain the result; (4) the observed distribution of happiness in the population; and (5) the observed covariates of happiness. Finding pages are 'dynamic', that is, they are made up instantly in response to a request from different collections in the data systems. Finding pages can be copied and saved as pdf files.
Findings report	Structured combination of multiple research findings. Examples are: (1) the ranking reports of happiness in nations; and (2) reports of correlational findings on particular topics such as on the relation between happiness and income.
Findings archive	Collection of results of empirical research, such as means and correlations.

Note: * https://worlddatabaseofhappiness.eur.nl/hap_bib/bib_fp.php.

A side aim of this project is to add to the technique of research synthesis. The method used here for the gathering of research findings on happiness can also be used for taking stock of research findings on other subjects, such as personal health and wealth. The method helps us to overcome several problems in research synthesis, such as poor visibility of data, non-comparable descriptions and lack of continuity. The method allows standard descriptions of research findings to be presented and stored in collections to which scholars can add their findings from all over the world.

2.2.2 Conceptual Focus

Happiness is defined as the subjective enjoyment of one's life as a whole. In other words, how much one likes the life one leads. Synonyms are 'life satisfaction' and 'subjective wellbeing'. This concept of happiness is currently the most used in the social sciences.

Within this concept of overall happiness, two components of happiness are discerned: an 'affective' component called 'hedonic level of affect' and a 'cognitive' component called 'contentment'. These components are seen to function as subtotals in the overall evaluation of life. This conceptualization of happiness is delineated in more detail in the book *Conditions of Happiness* (Veenhoven, 1984), and more recently in a paper entitled 'How do we assess how happy we are?' (Veenhoven, 2009a).

Selection of publications

All publications that use the word 'happiness' or related words in the title, abstract or contents are called in and inspected for fit with the above concept of happiness. This involves a lot of reading: since the start of this project in the 1980s some 20 000 publications have been inspected.

Publications that pass the test are entered in the Bibliography of Happiness, discussed below in section 2.2.5. As of 1 January 2019 (hereafter, 'to date'), this bibliography contains about 13 000 scientific publications on happiness. Happiness is not always the central issue of these publications, nor is it always called by the same name of 'happiness'. The same phenomenon is sometimes called 'life satisfaction' or 'subjective wellbeing', and in the 1950s the terms 'morale' and 'adjustment' have been used to denote what I call happiness.

Selection of empirical studies

If such a publication reports an empirical investigation, the next step is to check whether the measure of happiness used in the study fits the above definition of happiness adequately. This appears often not to be the case, since many questionnaires purportedly dealing with happiness measure broader phenomena, such as positive mental health, or satisfaction with particular domains of life rather than satisfaction with life as a whole. Studies that involve at least one acceptable indicator are described systematically on a study page, which will be discussed below in section 2.2.4.

2.2.3 Building Blocks

The basic elements of the database are pages, which are linked in various ways. Pages are organized in collections, from which reports are generated. Reports are bunches of pages on a particular subject. This make-up is presented graphically in Figure 2.3. These three elements are described in the next subsections: pages in section 2.2.4, collections in section 2.2.5 and reports in section 2.2.6.

2.2.4 Pages

Four kinds of pages are used: pages on: (1) a particular publication; (2) a particular study; (3) a particular measure of happiness; and (4) a particular research finding. All these pages use a standard format and a standard vocabulary.[5]

Pages on a particular publication

Pages of this kind are much like an old-fashioned catalogue card in a library. They enumerate author, title and bibliographical source. Unlike the traditional library card, pages also contain a link to the full text. As in a systematic library catalogue, publication pages also mention the subjects addressed in the publication, using a classification of topics in happiness research. In the case where a publication deals with an empirical study the results of which are entered in a findings collection, the page also gives a link

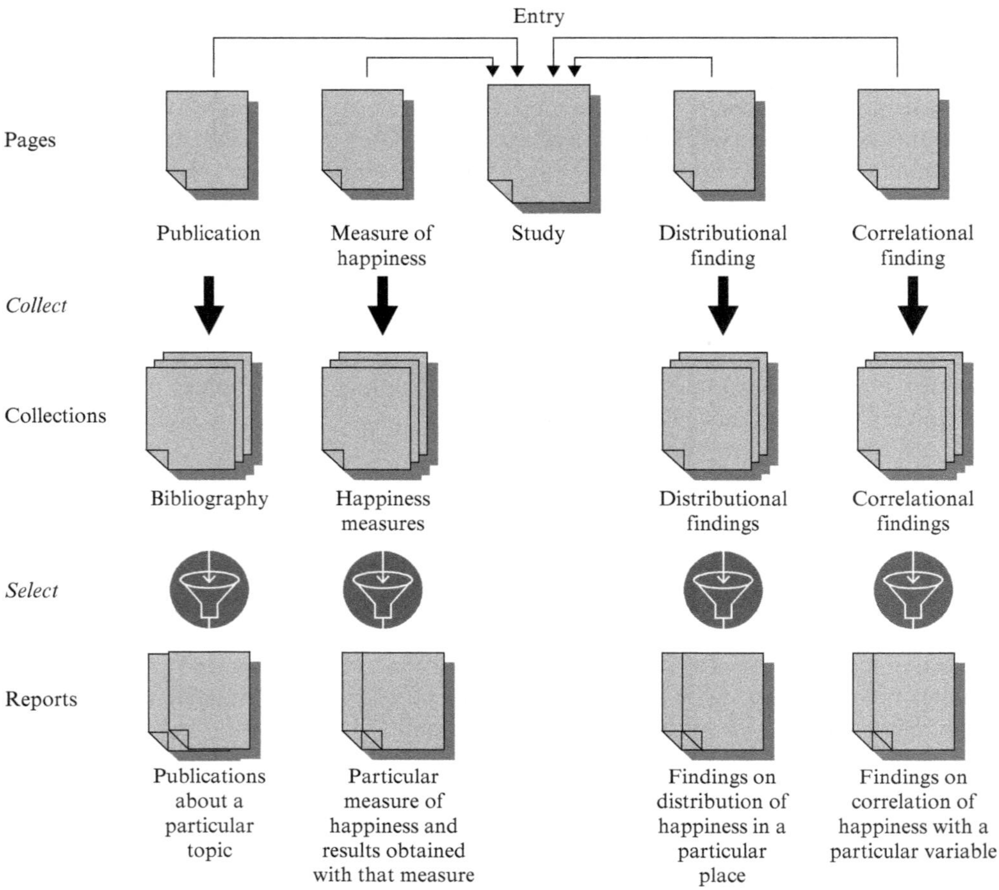

Figure 2.3 Building blocks of the findings archive

to the excerpt of that study. An example of a publication page can be found at http://worlddatabaseofhappiness.eur.nl/hap_bib/src_pubs.php?mode=2&author=8423.

Pages on a particular empirical study

If a publication reports results of an empirical investigation that used an acceptable measure of happiness, the investigation is described briefly on a study page. Standard descriptives are: the population under investigation (that is, public, place and time), sampling, response rate, number of participants (N), and method of observation, such as face-to-face interview or web questionnaire.

On each study page is a reference to the publication from which the information is drawn, when possible with a link to the full text. Study pages also have links to the pages discussed below regarding the measure of happiness used and the observed distributional and correlational findings. An example of a study page is found at http://worlddatabaseofhappiness.eur.nl/common/desc_study.php?studyid=15105. The full list of study pages is available at http://worlddatabaseofhappiness.eur.nl/hap_study/study_fp.htm.

Pages on a particular measure of happiness
Pages of this kind describe a particular way of measurement, mostly survey questions. Such pages present the full text of question and answer categories, and in the case of multiple questions, also how a sum-score is computed. If available, information in other languages is added. In the case of survey question using verbal response scales, the page also mentions weights for particular response options (for example, 8 for 'very happy'), with which scores can be transformed into a numerical 0–10 scale. These weights are obtained in the international Happiness Scale Interval Study (Veenhoven, 2009b).

These pages also have links to all the studies in which this particular measure is used, and to the findings obtained with that measure in each of these studies. An example of such a page can be found at http://worlddatabaseofhappiness.eur.nl/hap_cor/desc_hind.php?ind=401.

Pages on a particular research finding
At the heart of the archive are pages that summarize a particular research finding. Two kinds of findings are involved: (1) distributional findings, that is, observations on the spreading of happiness in a particular population; and (2) correlational findings about the degree to which other things than happiness go together with happiness.

Distributional finding A page of this kind describes how happy people are in a particular population, as observed using a particular measure of happiness. Next to the frequency distribution, the page reports two summary statistics (mean and standard deviation[6]) and the 95 per cent confidence interval around these. Information about the people under investigation is taken from the study page; information on the measure of happiness is taken from the happiness measure page; and information on the original research report from a publication page. An example of such a page on a distributional finding can be found at http://worlddatabaseofhappiness.eur.nl/common/desc_study.php?studyid=2195.

Correlational finding This kind of page contains the description of the observed statistical associations between happiness and something else (called a 'correlate') in a particular public and using a particular measure of happiness. The page is partly built from the above-mentioned pages on a particular publication, study and happiness measure. Additional elements are a description of the correlate and the observed statistical association.

The description of the correlate consists of three parts: the name by which the correlate is called in the original research report, detail about the measurement of the correlate, and a classification of the correlate by subject matter, using a taxonomy derived inductively from the available research findings.

Description of the observed statistical association of the correlate with happiness involves the following elements: the statistics used for quantifying the degree of association and for assessing statistical significance, the values obtained in the study, and particular elaborations or specifications. An example of a page with a correlational finding can be found at http://worlddatabaseofhappiness.eur.nl/hap_cor/desc_cor.php?sssid=24629.

2.2.5 Collections

The above-mentioned pages are gathered in collections. The World Database of Happiness has four such collections: (1) the Bibliography of Happiness; (2) the collection of Measures of Happiness; (3) the collection of Distributional Findings; and (4) the collection of Correlational Findings. The way in which these collections are linked is depicted in the flowchart on the start page of the website shown on Figure 2.2.

Bibliography of Happiness

All publications on happiness that passed a selection on conceptual fit (see section 2.2.2 above) are entered in the Bibliography of Happiness (Veenhoven, 2019b). This involves the making of a publication page as described above, the bibliography being a collection of such pages.

Most publications in the bibliography are books and journal articles; however, the collection is not limited to 'authorized' publications. Grey reports are also included. The main reason for this is that the publication process involves some systematic biases, one of which is under-reporting of non-correlations. By deliberately including 'unpublished' findings, this database allows a more realistic view on happiness. Synthesis of studies based on this source can therefore yield conclusions that differ from impressions based only on reviews of research published in journal articles.

The Bibliography of Happiness contains a detailed systematic subject index, which allows an easy overview of the field and helps us to trace literature on specific issues. An example of a selection on subject matter can be found at http://worlddatabaseofhappiness.eur.nl/hap_bib/src_pubs.php?mode=1&Subject=1911. Publications can also be searched by author, key words, place, time and medium of publication and by words used in the title.

To date the Bibliography contains some 13 000 scientific publications on happiness, sorted into some 450 subject categories. The coverage of the literature in English, German and Dutch is almost complete up to 2018. The Bibliography of Happiness can be found at http://worlddatabaseofhappiness.eur.nl/hap_bib/bib_fp.php.

Directory of Happiness Investigators

Authors of publications that are entered in the Bibliography of Happiness are automatically listed in the Directory of Happiness Investigators, which also lists names of scholars who are otherwise involved in the study of happiness. To date the directory contains some 20 000 names, for which about half have an email address. Addresses are limited to investigators who have published after 1975. The directory is fairly complete up to 2018.

Since the directory is linked to the bibliography, which is indexed by subject, one can easily select specialists on a particular topic within happiness research and because the bibliography is also indexed by year of publication, one can identify currently most active researchers, authors can also be selected on the country where they live. The directory is available on request to peer researchers, for scientific purposes only. In the last few years, it has been of great help in creating research networks on and around the themes of happiness.

Measures of Happiness collection

As noted in section 2.2, all measures of happiness used in empirical studies are checked for fit with the concept of happiness used here. The selection is quite stringent and about half of the indicators claimed to measure happiness are rejected. One of these is the much-used Satisfaction With Life Scale (Diener et al., 1985), because the last item in this scale reads: 'If I could live my life over, I would change nothing'. A positive answer to this question does not necessarily mean that the respondent dislikes the life they are actually living, and for that reason the entire scale is rejected. This restrictiveness has a price: the results of many otherwise good studies are not included in the findings collections. The gain is that we can be sure about what the selected findings mean. Accepted indicators of happiness are described on a page which enumerates the full text of questions or observation schedules and contains links to studies in which these measures have been applied. Together these pages constitute the Measures of Happiness collection.

The Measures of Happiness collection consists of a detailed classification of happiness measures, based on distinctions between happiness variants, time reference and methods of assessment. To date some 1000 variants have been distinguished. This seems to be a lot for the specific concept of happiness at hand. However, most of the differences concern minor variations in wording, such as whether the positive end of a response scale is labelled 'satisfied' or 'very satisfied'.

Though such variations may seem trivial at first sight, they can make a difference, for instance when responses to such nearly identical questions are used in trend analysis. Variations in wording or timeframe of questions should also be clear when it comes to explaining divergent outcomes. Research synthesis requires systematic and precise information about measurement, and this is what this fine-grained categorization provides.

The pages link to the studies that used this particular measure of happiness, and thereby the collection provides an easy overview of the scores yielded, using the same measures in different populations. The collection is therefore useful for selecting happiness measures that allow comparison with earlier research. It is also a valuable tool for identifying instrument effects. Users can search the collection by keywords or use the classification for selection by variant, time reference, method of observation or rating scale used. The Measures of Happiness collection can be found at http://worlddatabaseofhappiness.eur.nl/hap_quer/hqi_fp.htm.

Collections of distributional findings on happiness

Distributional findings are about how happy people are in a particular population. As indicated above, each such finding is noted on a separate page. These pages provide detail about sampling and interrogation and present the full frequency distribution of responses, together with mean and standard deviation. Comparison is facilitated by additional transformation of means and standard deviations to a common 0–10 scale and by presenting the 95 per cent confidence interval around these central tendency statistics. These pages are sorted in three collections, two of which focus in the first place on happiness in places, and one on happiness in particular publics.

Happiness in Nations Pages that report a finding on happiness in the general public of a country are gathered in the Happiness in Nations collection (Veenhoven, 2019c). Findings are ordered by country in nation reports. In these nation reports, findings are grouped by the kinds of happiness measure used, and within these categories by year. This sorting provides an easy view on trends over time.

The entire collection can be sorted by nation and by measure of happiness. From this collection, several further findings reports are generated, which will be discussed below in section 2.2.6. To date, this collection contains some 900 findings in 175 nations between 1945 and 2019. Though most of the data come from first world countries, the collection contains findings from almost all countries of the world and covers more than 95 per cent of the world's populations. Among these findings are time series of 25 years and longer for 15 developed nations. The collection is fairly complete up to 2018.

This collection provides a first set of international statistics on happiness. The data on average happiness serve to identify the macro-social factors that mark off more and less livable societies. These data are also used for monitoring social progress and decline; for example, by Veenhoven (2010a). The data on dispersion of happiness in nations can be used in comparative studies of inequality in life chances. The uses of these data are spelled out in more detail in Veenhoven (1993: Chapter 8) and Veenhoven (2002). The Happiness in Nations collection can be found at http://worlddatabaseofhappiness.eur.nl/hap_nat/nat_fp.php?mode=1.

Happiness in Regions Recently a similar collection of distributional findings has been added to the World Database of Happiness on happiness of the general public in geographical areas other than nations. Most of these areas are regions within nations, such as post-1990 Germany and the former East and West parts of the country. The collection also contains data on transnational regions, such as sub-Sahara Africa. A comparable collection of distributional findings on Happiness in Cities is in the making.

Most of the findings in this Happiness in Regions collection are extracted from national samples, often using pooled data from several surveys that use the same question on happiness and contain information about the place of residence of the respondent. Since such samples are designed to represent the population in the country rather than that in regions, the findings in this collection are less representative than the findings in the above-mentioned collection of distributional findings on Happiness in Nations.

To date, this collection contains some 4000 findings, in 2500 regions, mostly provinces, and cities. To view these findings, go once more to http://worlddatabaseofhappiness.eur.nl/hap_nat/nat_fp.php?mode=1 and click the ⊕ icon at the left of a nation. A list of regions will appear, each of which links to an overview of the available distributional findings on happiness in the general population of that area.

Happiness in Publics (particular kinds of people) Alongside the data on happiness of the general population in places, there is also a collection of findings on the degree of happiness among particular publics, that is, social categories within nations, such as aged people or psychiatric patients. Some 160 different categories have been discerned, among which are some rather unusual ones such as 'lottery winners' and 'prisoners'.

To date this collection contains about 2000 distributional findings, most of which concern particular kinds of people in first world nations. The collection is fairly complete up to 2015 and as such less complete than the Happiness in Nations collection. The collection can be searched in several ways: by public, by country, by year and by measure of happiness. The Happiness in Publics collection (Veenhoven, 2019c) can be found at http://worlddatabaseofhappiness.eur.nl/hap_pub/pub_fp.php.

Collection of Correlational Findings The World Database of Happiness also provides a large collection of 'correlational' findings (Veenhoven, 2019d). As noted above, research findings are condensed in standard abstracts, which are presented on pages. These finding pages provide details about: (1) the population investigated; (2) design of the study; (3) measures of happiness used; (4) measurement of the correlate; (5) the statistics used for quantifying the observed statistical association between happiness and that correlate; and (6) the observed effect size and statistical significance. Links lead to full detail about the publication in which the finding is reported, the measure of happiness used, and the statics applied for quantifying the statistical association between happiness and the correlate. To date there are about 15 500 such pages in the collection. Though this is rather a lot, the collection is far from complete; there is about twice as much waiting to be entered.

Pages on correlational findings are ordered by the kind of correlate involved. For instance, there are 204 pages about findings on the relation between happiness and age. The subject classification used is fine-grained and involves some 3000 categories. Though complicated at first sight, this detailed classification is quite helpful for tracing atypical findings that would otherwise fall out of sight in this expanding field. For instance, the few studies on happiness and social mobility can easily be found using this subject category and do not get lost in the pile of findings on happiness and social status. The collection can also be searched in several more ways, such as by happiness measure, public, nation and time. Something that is particular useful for identifying causality is that the search mechanism allows studies to be selected which used methods such as follow-up, experiments or instrumental variable analysis. The Correlational Findings collection on happiness can be found at http://worlddatabaseofhappiness.eur.nl/hap_cor/cor_fp.htm.

2.2.6 Reports

Selections of pages are assembled automatically from each of the above-mentioned collections, and presented in reports. Two kinds of reports are particularly useful in research synthesis: publication reports and findings reports.

Publication reports

Reports of this kind list the publications on a particular subject, using the subject classification of the Bibliography of Happiness. Unlike the findings reports mentioned below, these publication reports cover all that is written on the subject: not only research reports, but also literature studies and theoretical treatises. Among the research reports mentioned, the publication reports are not limited to publications on studies that used acceptable measures of happiness, but also contain publications on studies that are not included in the findings collections. As such, publication reports provide a complete overview of the literature, which is helpful in narrative research synthesis. An example of a publication report on happiness and urban green areas can be found at http://worlddatabaseofhappiness.eur.nl/hap_bib/src_pubs.php?mode=1&Subject=2262.

Findings reports

Reports of this kind are more focused and limited to empirical observations yielded using an accepted measure of happiness, that is, one of the indicators listed in the Measures of Happiness collection. Findings reports may list either distributional findings or correlational findings, and in the case of reports on happiness in specific publics they present both. An overview of all these reports can be found at http://worlddatabaseofhappiness.eur.nl/findingreportslinkpage.htm.

Reports on distributional findings As mentioned above, distributional findings are about how happy people are in a particular place and time. To date, the archive contains some 13 000 pages on this kind of findings, and the following kinds of reports can be gathered from that pool.

Nation reports present an overview of observed distributions of happiness in the general population in nation states. The reports are limited to findings in representative samples of the general population. These findings are ordered by the kinds of happiness measure used, and within these blocks by year. The list of nation reports can be found at http://worlddatabaseofhappiness.eur.nl/hap_nat/toc_secondary.php?mode=1.

Rank reports draw on the above nation reports and select findings yielded using the best comparable measure of happiness. Currently this is a single question on life satisfaction, responses to which are rated on a numerical scale ranging from 0 to 10 (measure types 122D+E). The current rank report is based on responses to this question in the last ten years. When the question has been used in several surveys during this ten-year period, the average is given in the rank report. The selected findings are marked in yellow in the nation reports.

Nation ranks are presented in four separate reports on, respectively: (1) average happiness in nations; (2) inequality of happiness in nations, as measured using the standard deviation; (3) inequality-adjusted happiness, which is an index combining mean and standard deviation; and (4) happy life years, which is a combination of average happiness and life-expectancy. Within these rank reports, the user can sort either alphabetically by name of the nations or by observed degree of happiness, by clicking in the head of the table. The rank report on average happiness can be found at http://worlddatabaseofhappiness.eur.nl/hap_nat/findingreports/RankReport_AverageHappiness.php.

Trend reports also draw on the above-mentioned nation reports and focus on those that involve repeated responses to the same question over the years. Trend reports are limited to countries for which at least 15 such data points are available over a period of at least 20 years. To date, there are 14 such cases.

As with the rank reports, there are four kinds of trend reports on happiness in nations, respectively on change over time in: (1) average happiness; (2) inequality of happiness; (3) inequality-adjusted happiness; and (4) happy life years. An example of the trend report on average happiness can be found at http://worlddatabaseofhappiness.eur.nl/hap_nat/findingreports/TrendReport2007-1.pdf.

Reports on correlational findings Findings reports can also be generated from the collection of Correlational Findings on happiness. These reports assemble finding pages on the same subject, using the main topics in the subject classification of that collection. To date, there are about 100 such reports in the database, some of which contain more than 100 finding pages, such as the findings report on income.

Reports on correlational findings start with a subclassification of the available findings in this subject category and enumerate the number of findings in each of these categories. This subclassification follows a standard categorization into: (1) over-time correlations, for instance the relation between earlier income and present happiness; this category is labelled 'career'; (2) same-time correlations, such as the association between present income and present happiness; this subcategory is labelled 'current'; and (3) attitudes to the subject matter, rather than the subject itself; for example, the observed correlation between income satisfaction and happiness.

Further distinctions are made within each of the subcategories; for instance, in the case of 'current income' between 'personal income' and 'household income'. These classifications of correlates of happiness are further tailored to the available findings on the particular topic involved and continuously refined. The richness of the available data is thus brought to the eye of the users. An example of such a classification of correlational findings on happiness and local environment can be found at http://worlddatabaseofhappiness.eur.nl/hap_cor/desc_topic.php?tid=2810.

The reports lay the foundation for research synthesis. They provide a set of research findings that is about a well-defined concept of happiness, and the findings are presented in a comparable way, using a standard format and a standard terminology. Conceptual and terminological ambiguities being cleared away, the real meta-analysis can start. The full list of reports on correlational findings is available at http://worlddatabaseofhappiness.eur.nl/hap_cor/CFmainsubj_reports.php.

Reports on happiness in special publics This kind of report gathers distributional findings and correlational findings observed in a specific public, rather than the general population. The findings are not presented as such, but the reports present links to the finding pages. To date, there are 160 such findings reports on happiness among particular kinds of people. The full list of public reports is available at http://worlddatabaseofhap piness.eur.nl/hap_pub/pub_fp.php.

2.3 USES OF THIS FINDINGS ARCHIVE FOR RESEARCH SYNTHESIS

Reviews of research typically summarize the main trends in research findings in verbal statements, followed by references to publications in which such findings have been reported. Though the source publications are listed at the end of the paper, they are not easily assembled by the reader and therefore the reviewer's interpretation cannot easily be controlled. This World Database of Happiness allows a new format that takes advantage of the online availability of detailed information. Review papers can now be directly linked to elements in the findings archive, such as to particular finding pages. Examples of such presentations are given in Table 2.2 and Figure 2.4 below.

This way of summarizing research findings has several advantages over traditional reviews that are limited to the possibilities of printed paper. Checking with the available data is easier, as the links provided in the text will lead the reader directly to standardized descriptions of research findings, all of which still contain a traditional reference to the original research report. Referencing is also more complete; traditional reviews must often cite selectively, since they cannot mention all the available data in the limited space available in a printed journal article. This method allows all research reports to be taken into account and should avoid the danger of 'cherry picking'. This new method also allows a more complete description of the findings. While traditional reviewers typically have to condense information into a few columns of a summary table, our new method allows easy access to much more detail in online finding pages. In short: this technique allows reviewers to make controllable statements about main trends in data without burdening the reader with detail, yet the reader can seek, and easily find, more detail if they wish.

2.3.1 Air Pollution Example

There is only a small amount of research literature on the relation between happiness and air pollution. An overview of that literature can be obtained as follows.

Overview of publications

Scientific publications in which the relationship between happiness and air pollution is a main topic are gathered in two subject sections of the Bibliography of Happiness section on 'pollution in the living environment'.[7] Both sections are linked and can be found in searches using the keywords 'pollution' and 'smog'. To date this section lists 31 publications, of which 25 contain information that is eligible for entering in the findings archive, 12 of which have been actually entered; that is, half the available research. In this example I focus on the results reported in these 13 publications.

Overview of correlational findings in table

Together, the 13 publications yield 13 separate finding pages, nine of which are classified in the collection of correlational findings under 'environmental quality in nations',[8] two under 'environment in region'[9] and two under 'local air pollution'.[10] Again, the subject sections are interlinked and can be found using the same keywords. Some of the pages report more than one finding, typically because the same data have been subjected for different analyses. Together the 11 pages yield 20 findings. All these research findings are presented as in Table 2.2. In this table, positive correlations are denoted '+', non-correlations '0', and negative correlations '−'. When statistically significant, plus and minus signs are printed in bold (**+ −**). In an online version (not supported here; see Notes to the table) each of the signs used contains a link to the finding page in the World Database of Happiness, where the reader will find full details of the research finding.

Comparing results of Table 2.2 one can see that air pollution relates negatively to happiness. The findings leave no doubt that air pollution tends to reduce happiness. Spurious correlation is unlikely to be involved, given the many partial correlations that are negative, though one study in Italy found a small positive correlation in an analysis that involved many control variables. Reverse correlation is not only unlikely in this case (that is, unhappiness causing air pollution) but also the longitudinal and experimental findings demonstrate that causality runs from air pollution to lower happiness.

Table 2.2 20 research findings on happiness and air pollution

Area	Method					
	Cross-sectional		Longitudinal		Experimental	
	Zero-order	Partial	Zero-order	Partial	Zero-order	Partial
National						
Actual	–	– – – – – – + – –				
Perceived						
Regional						
Actual						**–**
Perceived						
Local						
Actual		**+ – – – – –**				
Perceived		–				

Notes:
Signs denote the direction and significance of observed correlations:
+ = positive and significant; + = positive not significant; 0 = no correlation, – = negative and not significant; **–** = negative and significant.
Embedded links (not supported here) are available in an online version of this table at https://personal.eur.nl/veenhoven/Pub2020s/2020a-supplement.pdf. In that table, place the cursor on a sign and use Control+Click. A 'finding page' with full detail will pop up on your screen.

2.3.2 Overview of Research Findings on Economic Growth and Average Happiness in Nations

There is a considerable research literature on the relation between happiness and economic growth in nations, most of which has been inspired by the 'Easterlin paradox' (Easterlin, 1974), which holds that individual income does add to happiness, but that a rise in the national income per head does not.

Overview of publications

To date, 127 publications on this subject have been listed in the Bibliography of Happiness in the subject category 'economic growth/decline',[11] which links to the related subject category of 'personal income'.[12]

Overview of correlational findings

To date, 25 finding pages on this subject are available in the collection of Correlational Findings, in the subject category 'economic growth/decline',[13] which links to the related subjects of 'personal income'[14] and 'relative income'.[15]

Presentation of correlational findings in a stem–leaf diagram

Most of the 25 finding pages contain information about strengths of the statistical relationship observed between economic growth and change of average happiness in nations. These pages together provide 23 standardized effect sizes.[16] This allows presentation in

Stem	Leaves
+1.0	
+0.9	
+0.8	
+0.7	
+0.6	3
+0.5	1 8
+0.4	1 1
+0.3	1 4
+0.2	0 1 3 4
+0.1	7
+0.0	01 01 01 01 02 02 03 05 06 08 1 7 8
–0.1	
–0.2	
–0.3	
–0.4	
–0.5	
–0.6	
–0.7	
–0.8	
–0.9	
–1.0	

Notes:
Numbers represent the size of an observed correlation.
Embedded links (not supported here) to detail for these findings in the World Database of Happiness are available in an online version of this figure at https://personal.eur.nl/veenhoven/Pub2020s/2020a-supplement.pdf. In that table, place the cursor on a sign and use Control+Click. A 'finding page' with full detail will pop up on your screen.

Source: Slag (2017).

Figure 2.4 25 research findings on economic growth on change in average happiness in nations, presented in a stem–leaf diagram

a stem–leaf diagram, as shown in Figure 2.4. In this diagram, the observed effect sizes are presented vertically (stem) on the possible range from +1 to −1, while the specific correlations at each level are presented horizontally (leaves). The number 3 next to +0.6 means that a correlation of +0.63 has been observed.

At a glance one can see that there is considerable difference in the observed relationships between economic growth and change of average happiness in nations, correlations varying between +0.01 and +0.63. These differences are due to variations in the countries and periods considered, as well as to differences in measurement and statistical analysis. In an online version (not supported here; see Notes to the figure), by following the links the reader can see the particularities behind each correlation coefficient. Most of the correlations are positive, and this means that the Easterlin paradox describes exceptions rather than the rule.

2.4 CONCLUSION

The findings archive technique described in this chapter allows us to keep an eye on the growing stream of research findings on happiness, and contributes as such to the accumulation of knowledge on this subject. The technique can also be applied to other subjects.

NOTES

1. This count is based on publications about happiness in the sense of 'subjective enjoyment of one's life as a whole', and that passed the test for conceptual fit described in section 2.2.2.
2. To date (1 January 2018), we have not yet screened and entered everything published after 2010, so the declining numbers at the right of Figure 2.1 do not denote that less has been published on the subject since then.
3. https://www.springer.com/social+sciences/wellbeing+&+quality-of-life/journal/10902.
4. In moral philosophy, this pursuit of greater happiness for a greater number is known as (political) utilitarianism. The aim is to achieve that a greater part of the population enjoys life (not to increase the number of people), and this concerns not only the present generation but also future generations. A recent account of this creed is given in Layard (2000).
5. Rules for standard notation of research findings are described at http://worlddatabaseofhappiness.eur.nl/hap_cor/introtexts/introcor3.pdf.
6. Computing means and standard deviations would require a cardinal level of measurement, while happiness is measured at the ordinal level. Though problematic in theory, treating these ordinal data as cardinal does not involve substantial problems in practice (e.g., Kristoffersen, 2017).
7. https://worlddatabaseofhappiness.eur.nl/hap_bib/src_pubs.php?mode=1&Subject=1592.
8. https://worlddatabaseofhappiness.eur.nl/hap_cor/desc_sub.php?sid=5935.
9. https://worlddatabaseofhappiness.eur.nl/hap_bib/src_pubs.php?mode=1&Subject=2278.
10. https://worlddatabaseofhappiness.eur.nl/hap_cor/desc_sub.php?sid=5935.
11. https://worlddatabaseofhappiness.eur.nl/hap_bib/src_pubs.php?mode=1&Subject=122.
12. https://worlddatabaseofhappiness.eur.nl/hap_bib/src_pubs.php?mode=1&Subject=122.
13. https://worlddatabaseofhappiness.eur.nl/hap_cor/desc_sub.php?sid=3431.
14. https://worlddatabaseofhappiness.eur.nl/hap_cor/desc_sub.php?sid=1742.
15. https://worlddatabaseofhappiness.eur.nl/hap_cor/desc_sub.php?sid=1757.
16. Many of the findings are reported in unstandardized regressions coefficients or in ordered probits which do not allow comparison of strength of correlations across studies. Such findings can be included in overviews using = or – signs (as in Table 2.2), but not in stem–leaf diagrams as in Figure 2.4.

REFERENCES

Argyle, Michael (ed.) (1987), *The Psychology of Happiness*, London, UK and New York, USA: Methuen.

Cummins, R.A. (2000), 'Happiness and progress' (Editorial introduction), *Journal of Happiness Studies*, **1** (3), 3–6.

Diener, E. (1999), 'Subjective wellbeing, three decades of progress', *Psychological Bulletin*, **125** (2), 276–301.

Diener, E. and R. Biswas-Diener (eds) (2008), *Happiness: Unlocking the Mysteries of Psychological Wealth*, Malden, MA, USA: Blackwell Publishing.

Diener, E. and C. Diener (1996), 'Most people are happy', *Psychological Science*, **7** (3), 181–185.

Diener, E., Emmons, R., Griffin, S. and R. Larsen (1985), 'The satisfaction with life scale', *Journal of Personality Assessment*, **49** (1), 71–75.

Dolan, P., Peasgood, T. and M. White (2006), 'Review of research on the influences on personal wellbeing and application to policy making', Defra report, London, UK.

Easterlin, Richard A. (1974), 'Does economic growth improve the human lot? Some empirical evidence', in Paul A. David and Melvin W. Reder (eds), *Nations and Households in Economic Growth*, New York, USA: Academic Press, pp. 89–125.

Ehrhardt, J., Saris, W. and R. Veenhoven (2000), 'Stability of life-satisfaction over time in a national panel', *Journal of Happiness Studies*, **1** (2), 177–205.

Frey, Bruno S. and Alois Stutzer (eds) (2002), *Happiness and Economics*, Princeton, NJ, USA: Princeton University Press.
Gurin, G., Feld, S. and J. Veroff (eds) (1960), *Americans View their Mental Health: A Nationwide Interview Survey*, New York, USA: Basic Books.
Headey, B. (2006), 'Happiness: revising set point theory and dynamic equilibrium theory to account for long term change', Discussion Paper 607, DIW Berlin, Germany.
Headey, B. and A. Wearing (eds) (1992), *Understanding Happiness, a Theory of Subjective Wellbeing*, Melbourne, Australia: Longman Cheshire.
Inglehart, R., Foa, R., Peterson, C. and C. Welzel (2008), 'Development, freedom, and rising happiness: a global perspective (1981–2007)', *Perspectives on Psychological Science*, **3** (4), 264–285.
Kristoffersen, I. (2017), 'The metrics of subjective wellbeing data: an empirical evaluation of the ordinal and cardinal comparability of life satisfaction scores', *Social Indicators Research*, **130** (2), 845–865.
Mauzi, Robert (ed.) (1960), *L'Idée du Bonheur dans la Littérature et la Pensée Française au 18e Siècle* (*The Idea of Happiness in French Thought and Literature in the 18th Century*), Paris, France: Librairie Armand Colin.
Neugarten, B.L., Havighurst, R.J. and S.S. Tobin (1961), 'The measurement of life satisfaction', *Journal of Gerontology*, **16** (2), 134–143.
Okun, M.A., Haring-Hidore, M.J., Stock, W.A. and R.A. Witter (1984), 'Health and subjective well-being: a meta-analysis', *International Journal of Aging and Human Development*, **19** (2), 111–132.
Pinquart, M. and S. Sörensen (2000), 'Influence of socioeconomic status, social network, and competence and subjective well-being in later life: a meta-analysis', *Psychology and Aging*, **15** (2), 187–224.
Pinquart, M. and S. Sörensen (2001), 'Gender differences in self-concept and psychological well-being in old age: a meta-analysis', *Journal of Gerontology: Series B*, **56** (4), 195–213.
Putman, R.D. (ed.) (2000), *Bowling Alone: The Collapse and Revival of American Community*, New York, USA: Simon & Schuster Paperbacks.
Slag, M. (2017), 'Tests of the Easterlin Paradox: a meta-analysis', Master's thesis, Erasmus University Rotterdam, School of Economics.
Steel, P., Schmidt, J. and J. Shultz (2008), 'Refining the relationship between personality and subjective well-being', *Psychological Bulletin*, **134** (1), 138–161.
Stock, W.A., Haring-Hidore, M.J., Okun, M.A. and R.A. Witter (1983), 'Age differences in subjective wellbeing: a meta-analysis', *Evaluation Studies Review Annual*, **8**, 279–302.
Veenhoven, R. (ed.) (1984), *Conditions of Happiness*, Dordrecht, Netherlands: Kluwer Academic Publishers.
Veenhoven, R. (1991), 'Is happiness relative?', *Social Indicators Research*, **24**, 1–34.
Veenhoven, R. (ed.) (1993), *Happiness in Nations: Subjective Appreciation of Life in 56 Nations, 1946–1992*, Rotterdam, Netherlands: Erasmus University Rotterdam, RISBO.
Veenhoven, R. (1994), 'Is happiness a trait? Tests of the theory that a better society does not make people any happier', *Social Indicators Research*, **32**, 101–160.
Veenhoven, R. (1995), 'Developments in satisfaction research', *Social Indicators Research*, **37**, 1–46.
Veenhoven, R. (1999), 'Quality of life in individualistic society', *Social Indicators Research*, **48** (2), 159–188.
Veenhoven, R. (2000), 'Wellbeing in the welfare state: level not higher, distribution not more equitable', *Journal of Comparative Policy Analysis*, **2** (1), 91–125.
Veenhoven, R. (2002), 'Return of inequality in modern society? Trends in dispersion of life-satisfaction in EU-nations 1973–1996', published in German in Wolfgang Glatzer, Roland Habich and Karl Ulrich Maier (eds), *Sozialer Wandel und Gesellschaftliche Dauerbeobachtung*, Opladen, Germany: Leske + Bundrich, pp. 273–294.
Veenhoven, R. (2005), 'Is life getting better? How long and happily do people live in modern society?', *European Psychologist*, **10**, 330–343.
Veenhoven, R. (2008), 'Sociological theories of subjective well-being', in Michael Eid and Randy Larsen (eds), *The Science of Subjective Well-being*, New York, USA: Guilford Press, pp. 44–61.
Veenhoven, R. (2009a), 'How do we assess how happy we are?', in Amitava K. Dutt and Benjamin Radcliff (eds), *Happiness, Economics and Politics: Towards a Multi-Disciplinary Approach*, Cheltenham, UK and Northampton, MA, USA: Edward Elgar Publishing, pp. 45–69.
Veenhoven, R. (2009b), 'International scale interval study: improving the comparability of responses to survey questions about happiness', in Valerie Møller and Dennis Huschka (eds), *Quality of Life and the Millennium Challenge: Advances in Quality-of-Life Studies, Theory and Research*, Social Indicators Research Series, Vol. 35, Dordrecht, Netherlands: Springer, pp. 45–58.
Veenhoven, R. (2010a), 'Life is getting better: societal evolution and fit with human nature', *Social Indicators Research*, **97** (1), 105–122.
Veenhoven, R. (2010b), 'How universal is happiness?', in Ed Diener, John F. Helliwell and Daniel Kahneman (eds), *International Differences in Well-Being*, New York, USA: Oxford University Press, pp. 328–350.
Veenhoven, R. (2010c), 'Greater happiness for a greater number: is that possible and desirable?', *Journal of Happiness Studies*, **11** (5), 605–629.
Veenhoven, R. (2019a), 'World Database of Happiness: continuous register of scientific research on subjective

enjoyment of life', Erasmus University Rotterdam, the Netherlands. Available at: http://worlddatabaseofhappiness.eur.nl.

Veenhoven, R. (2019b), 'Bibliography of Happiness', World Database of Happiness, Erasmus University Rotterdam, the Netherlands. Available at: http://worlddatabaseofhappiness.eur.nl/hap_bib/bib_fp.php.

Veenhoven, R. (2019c), 'Happiness in Nations', World Database of Happiness, Erasmus University Rotterdam, the Netherlands. Available at: http://worlddatabaseofhappiness.eur.nl/hap_nat/nat_fp.php?mode=1.

Veenhoven, R. (2019d), 'Correlates of Happiness', World Database of Happiness, Erasmus University Rotterdam, the Netherlands. Available at: http://worlddatabaseofhappiness.eur.nl/hap_cor/cor_fp.htm.

Veenhoven, R. and M. Hagerty (2005), 'Rising happiness in nations 1946–2004: a reply to Easterlin', *Social Indicators Research*, **79** (3), 421–436.

Verne, P. (2009), 'Happiness, freedom and control', *Journal of Economic Behavior and Organization*, **71** (2), 146–161.

3. Spatial variation in life satisfaction: a happiness puzzle

Mona Ahmadiani, Finbarr Brereton, Susana Ferreira and Mirko Moro

3.1 INTRODUCTION

With a renewed awareness of the limitations of conventional economic indicators (for example, gross domestic product and gross national product) to measure economic and social progress, there has been a growing interest by economists and policy makers in using a broader set of indicators, including self-reported measures of subjective wellbeing (SWB) (Stiglitz, 2009; Stiglitz et al., 2009; Fleurbaey, 2009; Deaton and Stone, 2013a). A more widespread use of SWB data to measure quality of life has inevitably been accompanied by an increased scrutiny of the measures themselves and attempts to explain 'happiness puzzles' or findings in the literature that do not accord to intuition (Deaton and Stone, 2013a).

A vast literature examines the most famous puzzle, the 'Easterlin paradox', that while income has a positive impact on SWB at a point in time, there is little effect of economic growth after a certain level of gross domestic product per capita has been attained (Easterlin, 1974; Stevenson and Wolfers, 2008; Clark et al., 2008; Deaton, 2008; Inglehart et al., 2008; Easterlin et al., 2010).[1] Another puzzle that has received considerably less attention concerns the existence of large spatial differences in SWB across nations, regions and communities. The analysis of this puzzle is the focus of this chapter.

Income dominates the explanation of spatial differences in SWB; its variation explains a sizeable proportion of the variation in SWB both within and between countries (Deaton, 2008; Stevenson and Wolfers, 2008; Inglehart et al., 2008; Helliwell and Barrington-Leigh, 2010). However, income is not everything. Countries such as Ireland, Denmark and the Netherlands consistently rank highly in comparison with countries such as Italy, France, Germany and Portugal despite similar levels of affluence. As reported in Kahneman et al. (2004), 64 per cent of Danish respondents described themselves as 'very satisfied' with their lives in a Eurobarometer survey, against only 16 per cent of French respondents (see also Senik, 2014). More generally, analyses of all available international datasets – the World Values Survey (WVS), the World Gallup Poll, the European Social Survey (ESS), the Eurobarometer survey – lead to the same conclusion: observable socio-economic and demographic characteristics are not sufficient to explain international differences in SWB; in all the cross-national models estimating life satisfaction or happiness, country dummies always remain highly significant, even after controlling for macroeconomic and institutional characteristics. International differences in wellbeing, moreover, are stable over time (Inglehart et al., 2008; Senik, 2014).

In this chapter, we present evidence of the international heterogeneity in self-reported life satisfaction (LS) using data from two widely used international surveys, the WVS and the Eurobarometer, and explore possible reasons for these differences. One straightforward explanation is that people cannot freely move across borders. Although in the standard interurban equilibrium model (Rosen, 1979; Roback, 1982) an individual chooses to live in a location with the basket of wages, rents and locational characteristics that maximizes their utility, equalization of utility in equilibrium requires a very restrictive set of conditions including perfect information, and zero mobility and transaction costs to be met, that clearly do not hold internationally.

Mobility within a nation should be less costly, but we show that for the United States (US), LS also varies widely spatially even after controlling for individual observable characteristics. Oswald and Wu (2010, 2011), Goetzke and Islam (2017) and Ahmadiani and Ferreira (2019) document the spatial heterogeneity in LS in the US. Similar results have been reported in other, smaller countries (for example, Canada in Helliwell and Barrington-Leigh, 2010; Germany in Maddison and Rehdanz, 2007). Even in a country as small as Ireland, Ferreira and Moro (2010) report a difference of more than two standard deviations in LS between the local authorities with the largest and lowest LS (Galway county and Dublin South, respectively).

Like in an international setting, statistically significant differences in spatial fixed effects within a country could reflect obstacles to free mobility or the existence of different labour and housing markets, especially in large and diverse countries such as the US. These spatial fixed effects thus might capture differences in objective local living conditions that are not capitalized in labour and housing markets. Brereton et al. (2008) and Ahmadiani and Ferreira (2019) show that objective differences in environmental amenities do explain a non-negligible fraction of the variation in LS in Ireland and the US, respectively, and that – although to a lesser extent – this is also the case in specifications that control for wages and rents.

In addition to considering the possibility that LS can vary due to differences in extrinsic, objective living conditions that are not or cannot be arbitraged away, in this chapter we also review a large literature that considers people's intrinsic cultural dispositions, mental attitudes and representations as important factors driving differences in self-reported LS, which go beyond language differences and translation effects (Senik, 2014). Respondents living in different regions or countries might use different thresholds when collapsing their wellbeing into the ordinal scale provided in the LS questionnaires, even if they experienced the same level of latent true wellbeing (King et al., 2004). It could also be that people in different cultures facing similar objective characteristics have different 'happiness functions' which transform circumstances into wellbeing at different rates. That is, although there are universal causes of wellbeing across cultures and nations, there are also specific ways in which wellbeing is experienced (and reported) in various cultures (Diener and Tov, 2007).

Disentangling the relative importance of objective conditions and cultural dispositions to explain away the spatial fixed effects remains difficult. Although an increasing availability of high resolution, geospatial data at the subnational level reduces the number of variables that remain 'unobservable' to the researcher, the concern remains that it is not feasible to measure and control for absolutely every possible influence in LS. By definition, spatial fixed effects control for all region-specific, time-invariant unobservable factors. Some authors have proposed the use of anchoring vignettes as a tool to correct for self-assessment biases (King et al., 2004; King and Wand, 2006). However, as noted by Senik (2014), it is not clear that these 'biases' are purely nominal differences that should be treated as misleading measurement errors; they convey important information on the cultural differences that we may be interested in explaining or that are correlated with other factors of interest. An interesting new approach compares the LS of natives to that of immigrants to disentangle cultural from circumstantial influences. There is also the argument that LS may not be a suitable proxy for utility (Glaeser et al., 2016), and we explore this point of view as well.

The chapter proceeds as follows: in section 3.2 we present evidence of the spatial heterogeneity in self-reported LS using data from several international and national surveys; in section 3.3 we present the conventional economic explanation (the violation of the spatial equilibrium condition) for these differences, while in section 3.4 we review a large literature that considers the influence of cultural dispositions, mental attitudes and representations in driving differences in self-reported LS. In section 3.5 we discuss some of the challenges, and promising approaches to explain and control for the influence of spatial fixed effects; in section 3.6, we explore the implications of the assumption that LS is a proxy for utility. Section 3.7 concludes.

3.2 MAPPING HAPPINESS ACROSS SPACE

The advent of large cross-national surveys such as the WVS, the Eurobarometer and the ESS, over the last four decades, has allowed social scientists to compare and track the changes in SWB of people at different geographical levels. The WVS has documented individual LS in almost 100 countries since it was launched in 1981. In each round the following LS question has been asked, 'All things considered, how satisfied are you with your life as a whole these days?', and respondents have chosen their responses from a ten-point scale from 'completely dissatisfied' to 'completely satisfied'. Since 1973, the Eurobarometer has also tracked individual LS in European countries: 'On the whole, are you very satisfied, fairly satisfied, not very satisfied, or not at all satisfied with the life you lead?' Respondents choose their response from a 1–4 scale, where 1 is 'not satisfied at all' and 4 stands for 'very satisfied'.

We use data from the five most recent waves (1989–93, 1994–98, 1999–2004, 2005–09, 2010–14) of the WVS for a total of 98 world countries (see Appendix 3A.1, Table 3A.1 for the list of countries in each wave), and yearly data from the Eurobarometer for the period 2004–14 for 38 European countries, to show the spatial variation in LS across the world and in Europe in Figures 3.1 and 3.2, respectively. Both figures depict the regression-adjusted mean LS for each country. That is, they depict the country fixed effect (FE) plus the estimated constant obtained in a regression of individual LS on a set of year dummies and country FEs. In panel B, in addition, the regressions control for individual-level characteristics including marital status, general health, age, sex, education, employment status and income.[2]

Consistent with what we observe in the maps, the null hypothesis of equal mean LS across world nations is rejected in both specifications. The F-statistics of the joint test for both specifications illustrate the significance of country FEs.[3] The country with the minimum LS over the last 25 years is Tanzania and the most satisfied (that is, the country with the highest LS) is the territory of Puerto Rico (Appendix 3A.2, Table 3A.2). Interestingly, after controlling for individual characteristics and income, some rich countries such as the

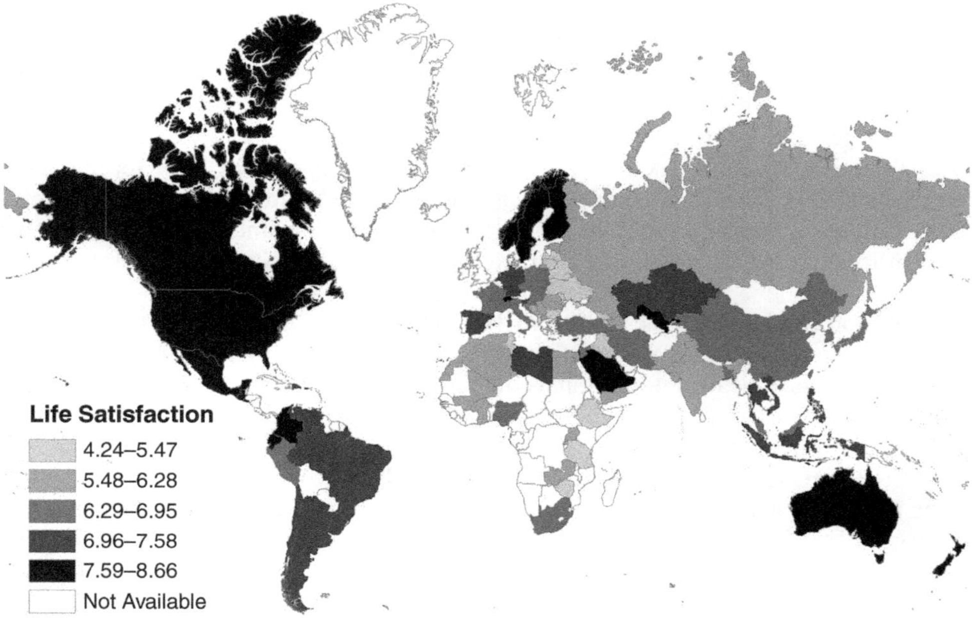

Panel A: Excludes individual-level controls

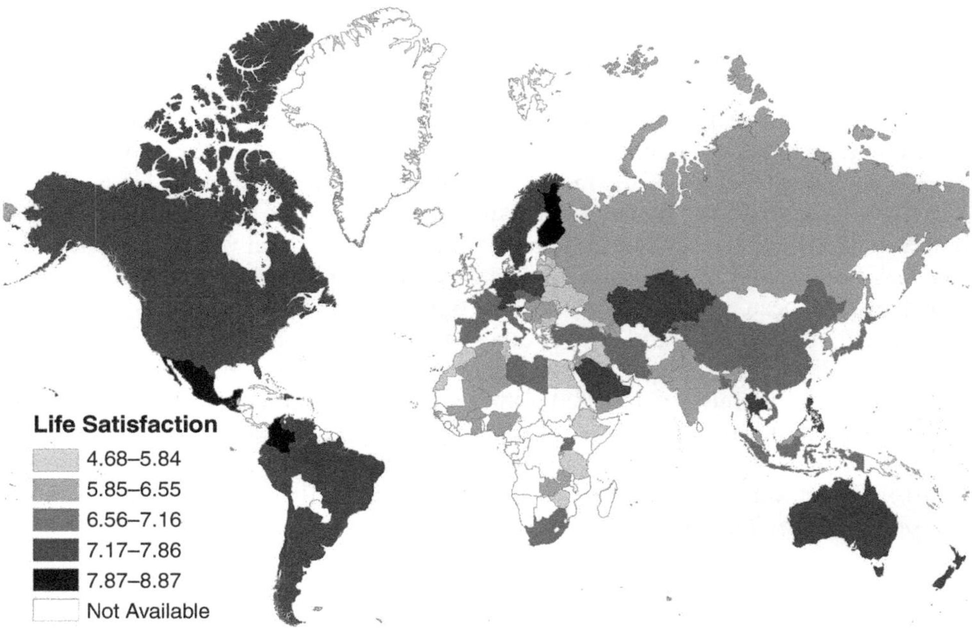

Panel B: Includes individual-level controls

Source: Authors from WVS data.

Figure 3.1 Regression-adjusted mean life satisfaction from 1989 to 2014, World

US, Canada, Norway, Sweden and Saudi Arabia; but also other middle- and low-income countries such as Uzbekistan, Ecuador, Nigeria, Libya and Indonesia exhibit lower LS.

Zooming into Europe, and using Eurobarometer data, we also observe a sizeable spatial variation in LS from similar regressions. Results from tests of equality of LS across countries reject the null hypothesis that LS is identical for both specifications.[4] Appendix 3A.2, Table 3A.3 presents the list and the ranking of countries for both specifications. The most satisfied European country during the period is Denmark while the least satisfied is Bulgaria. Comparison of Panels A and B in the table and in Figure 3.2 reveals that controlling for individual-level characteristics does not make a big difference in the rankings.

A common finding in studies analysing the 'geography of happiness' is that LS varies widely across space. As it is evident from Figures 3.1 and 3.2, and reported in previous studies, this is the case for international comparisons (Inglehart et al., 2008), but also for regional comparison of SWB within the same country (Moro et al., 2008; Ahmadiani and Ferreira, 2019). To explore regional variation in LS, we map the LS scores for the US using data from the Behavioral Risk Surveillance System (BRFSS).

The BRFSS is a US, state-based system of health surveys conducted annually under the auspices of the Centers for Disease Control and Prevention (CDC) in all 50 states. Between 2005 and 2010, its questionnaire contained a standard four-point scale LS question: 'In general, how satisfied you are with your life?', where 1 denotes 'very dissatisfied' and 4 denotes 'very satisfied'. Because the BRFSS reports the county of residence of the respondent, in Figure 3.3, regression-adjusted LS scores can be plotted at the county level.[5]

Panels A and B in Figure 3.3, illustrate statistically significant differences in LS across US counties.[6] Controlling for individual characteristics (education, sex, age, marital status, race, employment status and income) slightly mitigates the differences in LS across counties, but does not change the results of the tests. Table 3A.4 in Appendix 3A.2 presents an abbreviated list of the most and least satisfied counties in the US.

The graphical analysis poses an interesting question: how do people make residential choices and why would they live in 'unhappy' places? The spatial variation in individual SWB has been linked to the physical, social and economic environment in which the individuals are located. Oswald and Wu (2010) demonstrate that the variation in SWB (that is, the subjective quality of life) across location conforms with the variation in objective quality of life in conventional interurban equilibrium models (Rosen, 1979; Roback, 1982; Blomquist et al., 1988). Other studies have shown that LS depends on a wide range of location characteristics including the level of urbanization, and endowed natural amenities and disamenities (Brereton et al., 2008; Glaeser et al., 2016; Albouy et al., 2016; Winters and Li, 2017; Ahmadiani and Ferreira, 2019). In the following sections we explore these and other explanations.

3.3 RESIDENTIAL CHOICE: SPATIAL/INTERURBAN EQUILIBRIUM AND LIFE SATISFACTION

The way economists think about individuals making residential decisions can be traced back to Tiebout (1956). Interestingly, Tiebout's seminal work was about provision of

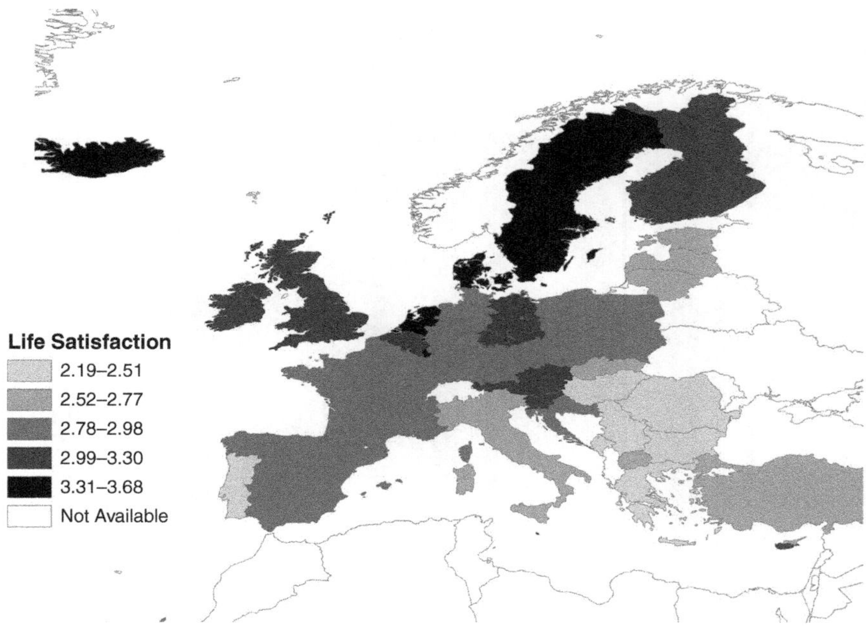

Panel A: Excludes individual-level controls

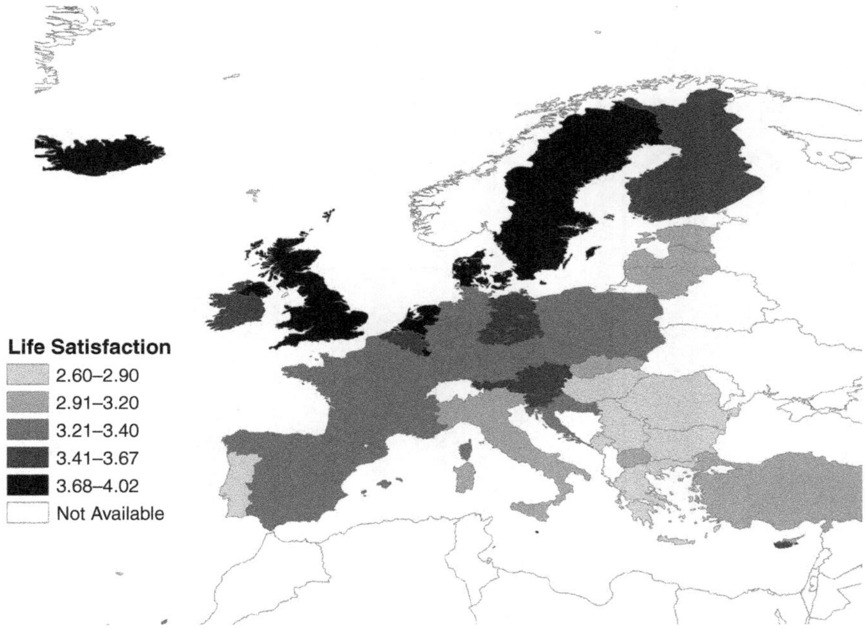

Panel B: Includes individual-level controls

Source: Authors from Eurobarometer data.

Figure 3.2 Regression-adjusted mean life satisfaction from 2004 to 2014, Europe

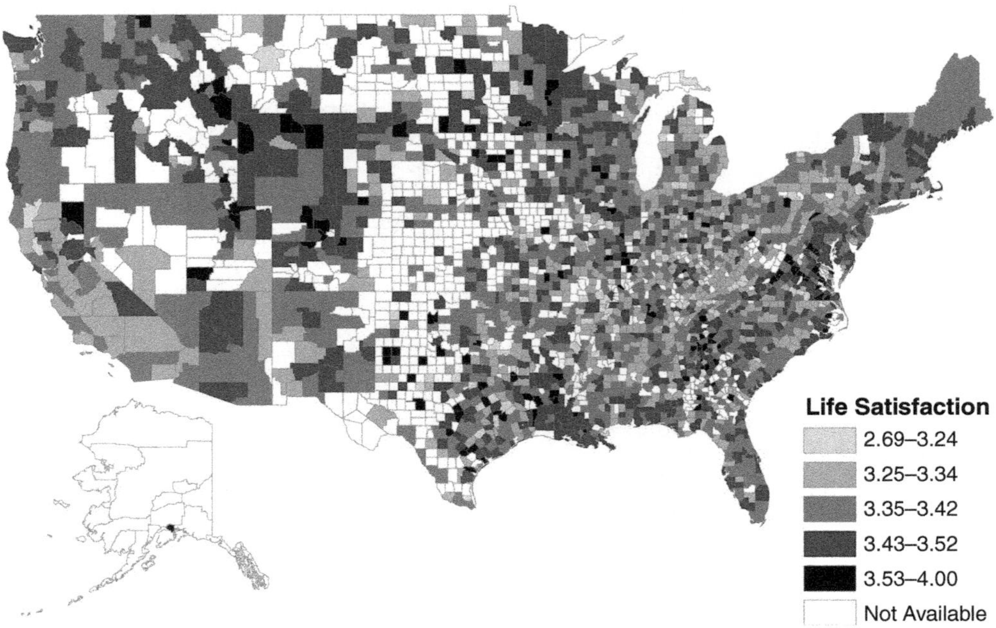

Panel A: Excludes individual-level controls

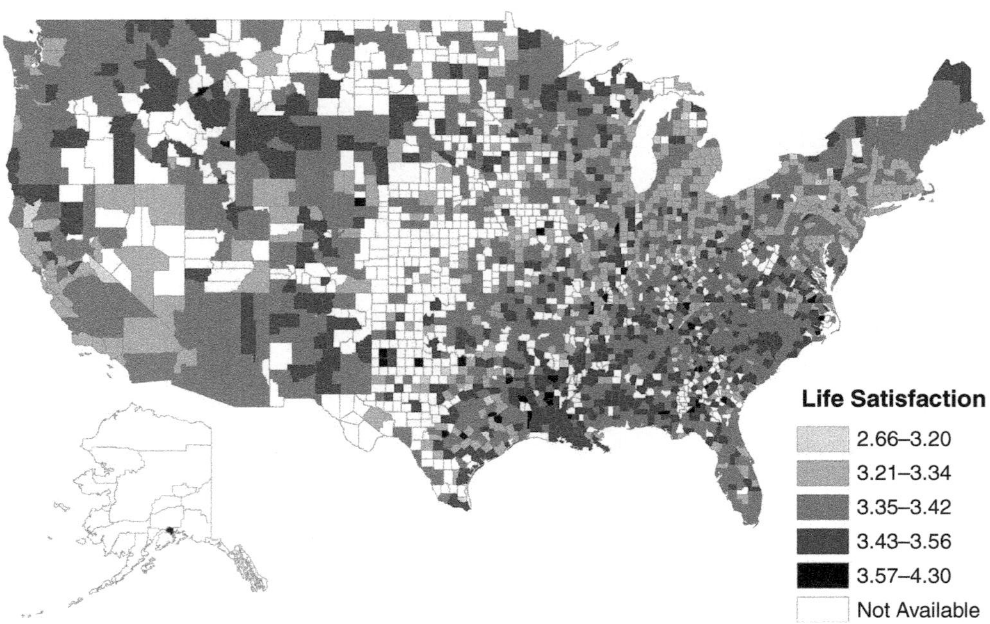

Panel B: Includes individual-level controls

Source: Authors from BRFSS data.

Figure 3.3 Regression-adjusted life satisfaction from 2005 to 2010, US

public goods, but it spurred a literature that focused on urban and spatial economics. Individuals have preferences towards local public goods and sort themselves across space according to these preferences. The model showed that markets for public, non-market goods, such as the climate, air quality, scenic beauty and better schools, could be 'revealed' by residential choices. Individuals with a taste for high-quality local amenities would be 'voting with their feet' by leaving behind undesired (low-quality) locations and moving to more desired ones.

The same building blocks based on the residential choice framework can be found in later works on hedonic models aimed at measuring quality of life across urban areas. Rosen (1979) showed that places can be seen as bundles of wages, rents and local amenities and that residential choices are affected by, and affect, these factors. Roback (1982) expanded Rosen's work to include the behaviour of firms and the housing market in a general equilibrium setting.

The conclusion of these interurban hedonic models is that workers will be willing to live in cities with lower levels of amenities if compensated by higher wages and lower rents. As in Tiebout's model, when choosing between different locations, individuals make trade-offs that reveal something about the value they place on surrounding local amenities. This choice affects the levels of rents and wages. Thus, rental price and wage differentials among locations can be used to compute the implicit price of amenities. A further useful feature is that these estimated implicit prices can be used as weights to construct quality of life indices that are theoretically sound and do not suffer – or suffer to a lesser extent – from the arbitrariness behind the weighting schemes used to construct this type of indices in the popular press.

3.3.1 A Simple Interurban Equilibrium Model

More formally, following Roback (1982) we can write down a utility maximization problem in which workers derive utility from consuming a composite good x (which we can describe as a numeraire paid with wage w), land (l^c) (which can be paid with unit rent r) and an exogenous amenity a. The model assumes that every worker is identical and free to move (with negligible costs) across locations endowed by different levels of amenities. 'Location' here is a general term that can refer to neighbourhoods, cities, regions or even countries. Workers are optimizers and have information and preferences over sets of amenities in different locations. Workers maximize their utility subject to their budget constraint that depends on total rent (rl^c) and total income; wages (w) plus non-labour income I (assumed to be non-location specific for simplicity):

$$max\ U(x, l^c, a)\ s.t.\ x + r\, l^c = w + I. \tag{3.1}$$

Solving (3.1) yields the indirect utility function $v(w, r, a)$, which depends on the level of wage, rents and amenities in each location. The workhorse of this framework is the spatial equilibrium condition; this model is in equilibrium only when workers do not have any incentive to move across locations; that is, conditional on amenities a, wages and rents must adjust so as to equalize utility across every location:

$$v(w, r, a) = k. \tag{3.2}$$

Differentiating this equation yields:

$$(dv/da) = (\partial v/\partial w \; dw/da) + (\partial v/\partial r \; dr/da) + (\partial v/\partial a) = 0. \tag{3.3}$$

Rearranging equation (3.3) gives the implicit marginal price of the amenity, p^a, that is, the marginal rate of substitution between w and a:

$$p^a = (\partial v/\partial a)/(\partial v/\partial w) = -(dw/da) - (\partial v/\partial r \; dr/da) \, / \, (\partial v/\partial w). \tag{3.4}$$

In the revealed preference world, equation (3.4) is not useful because it cannot be estimated directly, but after applying Roy's identity, and some algebra, it can be rewritten as

$$p^a = (\partial v/\partial a)/(\partial v/\partial w) = l^c dr/da - dw/da, \tag{3.5}$$

which shows that the implicit price of a (p^a) depends on the land consumed times the impact of the amenity on rents minus the impact on wages. These can be estimated from rent and wage regressions across different locations with different amounts of amenities. The (hedonic) index of quality of life is obtained by multiplying these prices, p^a, by the quantity of different amenities in different locations.

3.3.2 How Does this Model Speak to the Life Satisfaction Literature?

The typical way is to think of LS as a proxy for indirect utility (v). More formally, one way to interpret the indirect utility function and equation (3.2) is to give a latent variable interpretation to the LS scores observed. Given M ordered categories (from, say, 'completely dissatisfied' to 'completely satisfied'), there exist an underlying continuous indirect utility function v and $M+1$ ordered threshold parameters μ ($-\infty < \mu_0, \ldots, \mu_M < +\infty$) such that:

$$LS = m \text{ if } \mu_{m-1} < v \leq \mu_m \text{ for } m = 1 \text{ to } M. \tag{3.6}$$

In equation (3.6), LS is the reported LS score and v is the latent variable corresponding to the true indirect utility. Given a rich set of geocoded data this relationship can now be modelled as a linear combination of the variables of interest and estimated using ordered response models. In most applications, however, researchers report estimates from OLS instead, as the results do not vary much and OLS estimates are easier to interpret (Ferrer-i-Carbonell and Frijters, 2004).

The assumption that LS is a proxy for v has profound consequences. In theory, equation (3.2) can now be tested using geocoded LS data. If the null hypothesis that LS is equal across locations is rejected, then the ensuing question is: why does LS not equalize across locations? There are different reasons.

An explanation that has received considerable attention in the literature is the violation of the equilibrium condition, which is based on strong assumptions of rationality, perfect information and no obstacles to the free mobility of individuals across space. A vast literature in behavioural economics documents the limits of the rational choice model and that people do make systematic, predictable 'mistakes'.[7] Transaction costs may include informational, searching costs (for a new house, new schools, and so on), moving costs, as well as psychological costs (the psychic burden – disutility – of leaving a known place, friends and family) and idiosyncratic preferences towards one's own birth place or family traditional residence. They can be compounded by language, cultural and other migratory barriers in the case of international mobility.

While the set of assumptions behind the spatial equilibrium models is restrictive, the idea that systematic differences in LS across locations reflect spatial disequilibrium resulting from the violation of those assumptions requires the additional assumptions that LS is a good proxy for utility, and that it is comparable across individuals and across cultures.[8] In the next section we show that differences in LS could still be consistent with the spatial equilibrium framework to the extent to which they are explained by differences in reporting styles, cultural or social norms.

3.4 CULTURE AND REPORTING BIASES: ARE PEOPLE REPORTING THEIR 'TRUE' LIFE SATISFACTION?

When reporting their LS, individuals provide an evaluative measure of SWB (that is, their global satisfaction with life) which is a function of their individual characteristics and circumstances, forming their *true ex post* utility (that is, experienced utility) plus an error term:

$$LS_{ij} = f(true\ LS_{ij}) + e_{ij} \tag{3.7}$$

It is possible that people answer differently to LS questions for several reasons. Firstly, they may interpret the question identically, but have differing levels of SWB due to differences in socio-economic and demographic characteristics and circumstances; that is, their true LS is different. This is the standard starting point in the economics of happiness literature; that is, that the answers to the SWB question are interpersonally comparable, and that differences are due to circumstantial (individual and contextual) factors (for a review, see Dolan et al., 2008).

Secondly, they may interpret the LS question being asked of them differently, for example due to language barriers, or differences in translation (see, e.g., Jowel et al., 2007). For example, research criticizing the cross-country comparability of ESS questions on values (Davidov, 2010) and education (Schneider, 2010) has been published, despite the rigorous translation protocols employed in that survey (Jowel et al., 2007).

Thirdly, respondents may interpret the question identically *and* experience identical circumstances but answer differently due to differences in scale interpretation. Differential item functioning (DIF) is the interpersonal, intercultural variation that exists in people's interpretation and uses of specific response categories for the same question (Angelini et al., 2014: 664). It may be the case that the DIF is exacerbated in cross-cultural and cross-lingual research. That is, respondents living in different regions or countries may use different scales when converting their wellbeing into a number on the ordinal scale provided in the LS questionnaires, even if they experienced the same level of latent true wellbeing.

In practice, issues two and three can manifest in respondents providing answers that reflect context effects (Oishi et al., 2003; Deaton and Stone, 2013b; OECD, 2013), social desirability bias (Diener et al., 1991), reference scale bias (OECD, 2013), or certain response styles such as extreme responding and acquiescence.[9] To the extent that these differences are randomly distributed among populations of interest, they will contribute to random 'noise' in the data without necessarily posing a fundamental challenge for analysis. However, they have been linked, more generally, to cultural differences (Kroeber and Kluckhohn, 1952; Tov and Diener, 2007; Powdthavee, 2007), whereby they affect certain groups, nationalities or cultures differently, making the interpretation of group, sample and spatial differences in LS problematic. For instance, the tendency toward showing modesty among groups of respondents – namely, moderate-responding bias (Lau et al., 2005; Cummins and Lau, 2010) – or toward extreme responding to maintain social desirability, are examples of cultural expressions (as in a study by Van Herk et al., 2004 showing that extreme response style is more prevalent among Spanish and Italian respondents compared to the French). Lau et al. (2005) found that the average value of the personal wellbeing index (PWI) for the Australian population falls within the Western average of 70–80 (on a 0–100 scale), while the average PWI for the Hong Kong Chinese is lower as they reflect a 'bliss-like mental state about accepting and being grateful'.

Fourthly, respondents may interpret the question *and* scale identically, *and* experience identical circumstances, but culturally they interpret their lives differently (for example, collectivist versus individualist societies) (e.g., Tov and Diener, 2007). This issue is more complex and relates to cultural interpretation of values in society, with Suh et al. (1998: 484) stating that the 'influence of culture on life satisfaction judgments . . . may be chronic'.

In their seminal paper, Kroeber and Kluckhohn (1952) critically review the definitions and theoretical significance of the concept of 'culture'. Culture is 'understood as the set of long-run persistent attitudes, beliefs and values that characterize groups of people' (Senik, 2014: 381). It is important in the study of SWB, as 'conceptions of happiness may vary across different societies' (Tov and Diener, 2007), with Suh et al. (1998: 491) going so far as to state that 'the "good life" cannot be defined universally but has a different locus, depending on one's culture'. However, 'culture' is not stable over time, and 'should be conceived as an open system that consistently absorbs and reflects the dynamic changes of its social setting (e.g. modernization)' (Suh et al., 1998: 491). Diener and Tov (2007) state that 'although there are universal causes of wellbeing across cultures and nations [such as temperament and positive relationships], as the experience of wellbeing has certain pancultural aspects, there are also unique influences', and that 'cultures should differ in SWB to the extent that they provide people with different levels of autonomy, meaning, and relationships'.

Empirically, it is evident that the literature equates 'culture' with 'country' or 'nation'; that is, they are used interchangeably (Near and Rechner, 1993; Diener et al., 1995; Senik, 2014), with cross-country analysis taken to equate cross-cultural analysis. For example, in their study of cross-cultural predictors of LS, Near and Rechner (1993) discuss the difference between Japanese and US levels of work satisfaction, using the nation as their spatial unit of analysis. While the former could be seen as somewhat culturally homogeneous, it would be difficult to attribute this to the latter. Interestingly, Tov and Diener (2007), report that the Amish enjoy somewhat comparable levels of SWB with the richest Americans. It is also evident that even where the theoretical focus of an article is not nation-dependent (see, for example, Suh et al., 1998: 485, where discussions are focused on cultural rather than geographical or national levels), the analysis reverts to the national borders. This empirical strategy is prone to miss intra-national cultural differences which might be important. Even in a 'relatively homogenous country like Ireland' (as reported by Brereton et al., 2008: 390), there is still a high degree of diversity.[10]

While predictors of SWB may differ across cultures (Tov and Diener, 2007), and Diener et al. (1995) use cultural characteristics as a determinant of national wellbeing, using countries as the unit of analysis may be problematic because, as Tov and Diener (2007) point out, 'cultural influences often permeate national boundaries, cultures are not completely independent of one another'. For a review of the literature concerning the influence of cultures on SWB and the methodological challenges to assessing SWB in different cultures, see Tov and Diener (2007).

3.5 DEALING WITH SPATIAL HETEROGENEITY EMPIRICALLY

In a standard LS regression of the kind estimated in the 'economics of happiness' literature, LS is a function of individual traits, objective life circumstances, location and time FEs. What are the implications of the aspects discussed in the previous sections for this model?

$$LS_{ijt} = \alpha_i + \boldsymbol{x}_{ijt}'\boldsymbol{\beta} + \gamma_j + \delta_t + e_{ijt} \tag{3.8}$$

Whenever possible, researchers tend to favour specifications that, like (3.8), include individual FE, α_i. They account for a significant proportion of variance across individuals.[11] By definition, however, they embed any life circumstance that does not change over the sample period, including any location-specific, time-invariant factor (for example, residing close to the beach) if individuals do not change locations.

The impact of measurable, objective life circumstances is captured in the term $\boldsymbol{x}_{ijt}'\boldsymbol{\beta}$. These can refer to socio-economic and demographic characteristics at the individual level (such as education attainment, race, income, marital status), and when available, location-specific macroeconomic, institutional, cultural and environmental factors, as long as they vary over time (otherwise they would be embedded into the individual or spatial FE). Although consistent data for cross-national comparisons are typically only available at the national level, at a subnational level there is an increasing availability of geocoded socio-economic and environmental data. While the advent of 'big data' can mitigate potential omitted variable bias, particularly at a subnational level, it is difficult to control for every potential regional influence on SWB. When location-specific factors do not vary over time, their influence on LS is captured in the spatial FE, γ_j. In fact, although cultural and geographical boundaries do not necessarily overlap, spatial FEs are taken to measure the contribution of national or cultural factors over and above objective life circumstances.[12]

In equation (3.8) the contribution of objective life circumstances to LS, $\boldsymbol{\beta}$, is assumed to be constant, but it is possible that individual, cultural and national factors mediate how people subjectively feel about their wellbeing. For example, Helliwell et al. (2009) estimate country-by-country LS regressions where the cross-cultural differences between countries show up as differences in the constant terms but also as differences in the estimated coefficients of the covariates of interest. This would be equivalent to introducing interaction terms of country FEs with the individual life circumstances. Whether the betas are constant can then be statistically tested. If they are indeed found to be constant, then the researcher interested in studying the impact of life circumstances on LS can safely run equation (3.8).

However, things are complicated if the objective of the researcher is to study the drivers of spatial differences. In practice, it is not easy to disentangle the different components (environmental, macroeconomic, institutional and cultural) embedded in the FEs. Moreover, the FEs also include systematic differences in translation (e.g., Veenhoven, 2008; Oishi, 2010), differences in susceptibility to certain response styles (Hamamura et al., 2008; Minkov, 2009; Van Herk et al., 2004), or the cultural relevance and sensitivity of certain subjective wellbeing questions (Oishi, 2006; Vittersø et al., 2005).

Careful survey design seeks to minimize self-reporting biases, for example placing SWB questions near the start of the survey or randomizing where they appear; using introductory text and transition questions can eliminate the context effect to some extent (Deaton and Stone, 2013b). Differences in response styles and cultural biases can also be alleviated by comparing changes in the pattern of LS over time, rather than focusing on its absolute level (Cummins and Lau, 2010). Another approach is the anchoring vignettes technique, presented by King et al. (2004) as a method to address comparability issues in survey research; that is, what to do when respondents interpret identical questions in different ways. King et al. (2004) propose an ordered probit model that aims at anchoring subjective scores against vignettes incorporating the heterogeneity observed via the vignettes into the threshold parameters. However, Senik (2014: 384) questions whether this method is sufficient (or even necessary) to control for the effects of culture on SWB, and states that 'anchoring biases can be viewed as a cultural but nonetheless integral part of happiness'.

An innovative approach to disentangle cultural from circumstantial influences is to study the LS of immigrants to a country, as in Senik (2014), where mentality (the set of specific intrinsic attitudes, beliefs, ideals and ways of apprehending reality) is influenced by the culture of the originating country (at least in the short term) and circumstances (institutions, regulations and general living conditions) in the country of residence.

In their study of Switzerland, Frey et al. (2000) found that foreigners exhibit a significantly lower probability of reaching high happiness scores compared to the Swiss. However, they control for 'foreigners' using one aggregate dummy variable. It could be hypothesized that part of the reason is cultural, or the absence of cultural familiarity. Fulmer et al. (2010) find a cultural congruence effect in that people are happier if their characteristics match the cultural norms.

Hence, there may also be a need to control for the length of time an immigrant or foreigner has been in a country. Senik (2014) does this and finds that 'the longer immigrants have sojourned in a given country, the closer their level of happiness gets to that of natives'. Interestingly, she finds that 'the happiness level declared by European expatriates (of the second generation) is correlated to the average happiness of their home-fellows' (Senik, 2014: 381). The cultural congruence effect may help to explain these findings in relation to the length of time immigrants have resided in a host nation; that is, cultural convergence with the host nation.

Additionally, whether someone is escaping a 'repressive culture' (for example, suffering repression because they are homosexual, or female; or due to corruption) may be important. Senik (2014: 381) states that 'in a given country, say France, natives and immigrants share the same contextual circumstances', a view echoed by Frey and Stutzer (2000). However, individuals, including immigrants, can be excluded from certain services (for example, housing, education, employment opportunities) depending on cultural similarity.[13]

Further research is needed to inform the best approach to international comparisons. For example, additional research could study the LS of the same ethnic or cultural group across different national boundaries. Also, because cultural influences permeate national borders, spatial econometric methods and gravity models might be used to model the spatial dependence of this unobserved component. Additionally, more and better use could be made of the cultural and sociological variables in the WVS and the ESS (individualism, traditionalism, religiosity), especially by economists (for example, to control for culture, rather than nation). Having said this there is evidence to suggest that these issues do not extensively bias the analysis of determinants in micro-data (Helliwell, 2008; Fleche et al., 2011). At the national level, there remain clear and consistent relationships between objective life circumstances and subjective wellbeing (Helliwell, 2008), and these differences are reflected in mean scores.

3.6 LIFE SATISFACTION AND UTILITY

So far we have discussed potential reasons for the empirical finding that LS is different across space, whether across or within countries. Differences in LS can still be consistent with the spatial equilibrium framework if they can be explained by different reporting styles, cultural or social norms. In other words, one cannot invoke the breakdown of the spatial equilibrium model because LS does not equalize across space without further assumptions on how true utility converts into reported utility.

In this section, we discuss a more general view which concludes that geographical differences in LS do not necessarily challenge the notion of a spatial equilibrium. According to this view, rather than a proxy for utility, LS is an argument of the utility function among many others: private goods, environmental services, leisure, and so on. This idea is compatible with an interpretation of utility which is neither happiness, nor pleasure, but a mere representation of choice that can be disjointed to any link to emotions, pleasure and pain (Fisher, 1892 [2007]). In this view, LS data do not necessarily represent revealed-preference utility 'in the sense of what individuals would choose if their prediction of the [life satisfaction] consequences of their choices were not biased' (Benjamin et al., 2012: 2107).

In specific settings and periods of their lives, individuals may decide to trade off their happiness or LS for other goals (sense of achievement, self-esteem, bequest motives, religious fervour). Perhaps these motivations are more noticeable in sports. Most Olympic athletes sacrifice their youth to compete in a single event every four years for very little money, fame or reward (most of them will not win a medal). Serious mountaineers endure climbs that 'tend to be one unrelenting misery from beginning to end' (Loewenstein, 1999: 317).

It is conceivable that people make some of these trade-offs in the ordinary business of life too. The question is then an empirical one. To what extent LS is a good proxy for utility is very difficult to establish empirically with secondary data. Recent studies using ad hoc surveys show that LS is indeed a good predictor for hypothetical choices (Benjamin et al., 2012). Most respondents choose alternatives that maximize predicted LS in most settings. This is comforting for applied researchers who use LS as a proxy for utility. However, hypothetical choices and predicted LS seem to diverge systematically in settings where one alternative involves higher income or more money. From an environmental economics perspective, this suggests that individuals may be willing to trade off higher incomes for lower satisfaction. Although based on hypothetical scenarios, this research can serve as a cautionary tale for happiness researchers regarding the practice of using LS regressions to compute compensating variation and welfare measures similar to willingness to pay in stated-preference models (Benjamin et al., 2012, 2014).

Back to our original question: how to interpret differences in LS across space within this alternative framework? If LS is an argument in the utility function, differences across space are to be expected: 'individuals in less happy areas are foregoing wellbeing in order to gain some other advantage' (Glaeser et al., 2016: 23). Note that this alternative view is not incompatible with the idea that self-reported SWB is an important and meaningful outcome that should be investigated by social scientists, but does not invoke a parallel with utility; SWB is a uniquely important argument of the utility function, but people do not seek to maximize SWB exclusively.

3.7 CONCLUDING REMARKS

Subjective wellbeing varies widely across space. We use data from the WVS, the Eurobarometer and the BRFSS to compare self-reported life satisfaction in countries around the world, European countries and counties in the US. We find statistically significant differences in LS scores both between and within countries, and explore alternative explanations to this apparent puzzle. The spatial variation in subjective wellbeing has been linked to differences in physical, social and economic environment across locations, but even conditioning on (some of) those factors, the literature shows that country and regional dummies remain stubbornly significant.

Why would people choose to live in miserable places? What explains this puzzle? The conventional explanation in economics is that there are obstacles to free mobility: individuals have imperfect information (they may not know what they are missing), moving is costly (particularly internationally); or that another assumption (for example, perfect rationality) underlying a spatial equilibrium of equal satisfaction across locations does not hold.

It is also possible, however, that differences in reporting styles, cultural and social norms result in systematic differences on how LS is reported and/or experienced across administrative borders. Econometrically, spatial fixed effects have been used to capture and control for these differences and other time-invariant omitted variables. However, this strategy is of little use when the question being asked is, precisely: what are the factors driving regional differences in wellbeing; that is, what is inside the FE 'black box'? From a public policy perspective, a better understanding of the relative contribution of cultural factors versus other environmental and economic factors (which are more amenable to policy interventions and more easily measurable) can help to design more effective policy to close the LS gap across locations.

To what extent regional differences in wellbeing can be explained by better socio-economic and environmental geocoded data is an important research question; one that can be tackled with fully saturated models (with interactions between each variable and each location) and, in the age of big data, with the collection of representative samples at smaller geographical units. The remaining differences will then reflect culture. If the objective of the researcher is to further disentangle these differences then a truly interdisciplinary approach that attempts to measure different psychological and cultural aspects discussed in section 3.4 is required.

It is probably fair to state that if differences are still persistent either because they reflect culture or because people may trade happiness off in some circumstances, then one needs to be cautious in interpreting indexes of quality of life based on subjective wellbeing even within countries.

NOTES

1. Figures between \$10 000 (Frey and Stutzer, 2002: 146) and \$15 000 (Layard, 2005: 149) have been reported in the literature (Stevenson and Wolfers, 2008: 22).
2. For the WVS, the individual-level controls are marital status, general health, employment status, income, education, age and sex. For the Eurobarometer, they are marital status, employment status, education, sex and age. In both sets of regressions, we cluster the standard errors at the country level.
3. Excluding individual-level controls: $F(4, 97) = 307.58$ and p-value < 0.0000; including individual-level controls: $F(38, 97) = 1.6e{+}05$ and p-value < 0.0000; and the test of pairwise comparison of estimated country FEs after the regressions confirm that 4156 out of 4636 pairs of means (90 per cent in the regressions without individual controls, and 4221 of the 4752 pairs of means (89 per cent) in the regressions with individual controls are significantly different at the 1 per cent significance level, respectively.
4. Without individual-level controls: $F(10, 35) = 9.1e{+}08$ and p-value < 0.0000; and with individual level controls: $F(23, 35) = 1.8e{+}08$ and p-value < 0.0000. The test of pairwise comparison of FEs concludes that 99.6 per cent and 99.2 per cent of the means for specifications without and with individual-level controls, respectively, are different.
5. Our analysis includes a total number of 2367 and 1669 counties across the US for the specifications without and with individual-level controls, respectively. In addition to clustering standard errors at the county level to control for the intra-county correlation of residuals, we exclude counties with fewer than 50 observations per year to estimate an accurate county-level mean life satisfaction. This is consistent with the BRFSS guidelines of not reporting or interpreting FIPS county codes for any county with less than 50 respondents ('2010 SMART: BRFSS City and County data and documentation, comparability of data', retrieved from http://www.cdc.gov/brfss/smart/2010/compare_10.pdf).
6. $F(5, 2366) = 22398.92$ and p-value < 0.0000 excluding individual-level controls; $F(34, 1668) = 51708.60$ and p-value < 0.0000 including individual-level controls.
7. The valuation of local amenities elicited from individual choices in private markets might be biased in cases of imperfections, bounded rationality, and in general when transaction costs are non-negligible (Freeman, 2003; Frey and Stutzer, 2004, 2005; Kahneman and Sudgen, 2005). For example, Bayer et al. (2009) show that in the presence of moving costs, the variation in housing prices and wages across locations may no longer reflect the value of differences in local amenities.
8. Kahneman et al. (1997) distinguish between experienced utility, defined as a subjective hedonic experience, and decision utility, which is the weight of an outcome in a decision. In their terminology, the requirement would be that LS is a good proxy for experienced utility and that decision utility and experienced utility do not diverge, for example due to failures in affective forecasting, that is, in anticipating the utility consequences of one's choice (see Loewenstein et al., 2003 and references therein).
9. For a comprehensive list of biases that distort the reported LS from the true LS see the Organisation for Economic Co-operation and Development (OECD) guidelines for measuring SWB (OECD, 2013: 64).
10. For example, the Central Statistics Office (CSO) of Ireland reports that 13 per cent of the population spoke a foreign language at home in 2016; see http://www.cso.ie/en/media/csoie/newsevents/documents/pressreleases/2017/prCensussummarypart1.pdf.

11. For example, in two national panel studies, Lucas and Donnellan (2011) found that 34–38 per cent of variance in LS was due to stable trait differences, and a further 29–34 per cent to an autoregressive component which was stable in the short term but could fluctuate over longer time periods. However, this study did not include measures of the objective life circumstances that might affect both stable traits and autoregressive components.
12. The time invariance of spatial FE can be relaxed in specifications where location dummies are interacted with time dummies, or time trends, potentially in a flexible way.
13. Levitt and Dubner's (2005) famous *Freakonomics* demonstrates examples of discrimination based solely on race.

REFERENCES

Ahmadiani, M. and S. Ferreira (2019), 'Environmental amenities and quality of life across the United States', *Ecological Economics*, **164**, 106341.

Albouy, D., Graf, W., Kellogg, R. and H. Wolff (2016), 'Climate amenities, climate change, and American quality of life', *Journal of the Association of Environmental and Resource Economists*, **3** (1), 205–246.

Angelini, V., Cavapozzi, D., Corazzini, L. and O. Paccagnella (2014), 'Do Danes and Italians rate life satisfaction in the same way? Using vignettes to correct for individual-specific scale biases', *Oxford Bulletin of Economics and Statistics*, **76** (5), 643–666.

Bayer, P., Keohane, N. and C. Timmins (2009), 'Migration and hedonic valuation: the case of air quality', *Journal of Environmental Economics and Management*, **58** (1), 1–14.

Benjamin, D.J., Heffetz, O., Kimball, M.S. and A. Rees-Jones (2012), 'What do you think would make you happier? What do you think you would choose?', *American Economic Review*, **102** (5), 2083–2110.

Benjamin, D.J., Heffetz, O., Kimball, M.S. and A. Rees-Jones (2014), 'Can marginal rates of substitution be inferred from happiness data? Evidence from residency choices', *American Economic Review*, **104** (11), 3498–3528.

Blomquist, G.C., Berger, M.C. and J.P. Hoehn (1988), 'New estimates of quality of life in urban areas', *American Economic Review*, **78** (1), 89–107.

Brereton, F., Clinch, J.P. and S. Ferreira (2008), 'Happiness, geography and the environment', *Ecological Economics*, **65** (2), 386–396.

Clark, A.E., Frijters, P. and M. Shields (2008), 'Relative income, happiness and utility: an explanation for the easterlin paradox and other puzzles', *Journal of Economic Literature*, **46** (1), 95–144.

Cummins, R.A. and A.L.D. Lau (2010), 'Well-being across cultures: issues of measurement and the interpretation of data', in K.D. Keith (ed.), *Cross-Cultural Psychology: A Contemporary Reader*, New York, USA: Wiley/Blackwell, pp. 365–379.

Davidov, E. (2010), 'Testing for comparability of human values across countries and time with the third round of the European Social Survey', *International Journal of Comparative Sociology*, **51** (3), 171–191.

Deaton, A. (2008), 'Income, health, and well-being around the world: evidence from the Gallup World Poll', *Journal of Economic Perspectives*, **22** (2), 53–72.

Deaton, A. and A.S. Stone (2013a), 'Two happiness puzzles', *American Economic Review*, **103** (3), 591–597.

Deaton, A. and A.S. Stone (2013b), 'Do context effects limit the usefulness of self-reported well-being measures?', Research Program in Development Studies Working Paper No. 288.

Diener, E. and W. Tov (2007), 'Culture and subjective well-being', in Shinobu Kitayama and Dov Cohen (eds), *Handbook of Cultural Psychology*, New York, USA: Guilford Press, pp. 691–713.

Diener, E., Diener, M. and C. Diener (1995), 'Factors predicting the subjective well-being of nations', *Journal of Personality and Social Psychology*, **69** (5), 851–864.

Diener, E., Sandvik, E., Pavot, W. and D. Gallagher (1991), 'Response artifacts in the measurement of subjective well-being', *Social Indicators Research*, **24** (1), 35–56.

Dolan, P., Peasgood, T. and M. White (2008), 'Do we really know what makes us happy? A review of the economic literature on the factors associated with subjective well-being', *Journal of Economic Psychology*, **29** (1), 94–122.

Easterlin, R.A. (1974), 'Does economic growth improve the human lot?', in Paul A. David and Melvin W. Reder (eds), *Nations and Households in Economic Growth: Essays in Honor of Moses Abramovitz*, New York, USA: Academic Press, pp. 89–125.

Easterlin, R.A., McVey, L.A., Switek, M., Sawangfa, O. and J.S. Zweig (2010), 'The happiness–income paradox revisited', *PNAS*, **107** (52), 22463–22468.

Ferreira, S. and M. Moro (2010), 'On the use of subjective well-being data for environmental valuation', *Environmental and Resource Economics*, **46** (3), 249–273.

Ferrer-i-Carbonell, A. and P. Frijters (2004), 'How important is methodology for the estimates of the determinants of happiness?', *Economic Journal*, **114** (497), 641–659.

Fisher, Irving (ed.) (1892 [2007]), *Mathematical Investigations in the Theory of Value and Prices*, 2007 reprint, New York, USA: Cosimo.

Fleche, S., Smith, C. and P. Sorsa (2011), 'Exploring determinants of subjective wellbeing in OECD countries'. Paper published at https://www.oecd-ilibrary.org/.

Fleurbaey, M. (2009), 'Beyond GDP: the quest for a measure of social welfare', *Journal of Economic Literature*, **47** (4), 1029–1075.

Freeman, A. Myrick (ed.) (2003), *The Measurement of Environmental and Resources Values: Theory and Methods*, Washington, DC, USA: Resources for the Future.

Frey, B.S., Luechinger, S. and A. Stutzer (2004), 'Valuing public goods: the life satisfaction approach', IEW Working Paper No. 184.

Frey, B.S. and A. Stutzer (2000), 'Happiness, economy and institutions', *Economic Journal*, **110** (466), 918–938.

Frey, B.S. and A. Stutzer (2002), 'What can economists learn from happiness research?', *Journal of Economic Literature*, **40** (2), 402–435.

Frey, B.S. and A. Stutzer (2005), 'Happiness research: state and prospects', *Review of Social Economy*, **63** (2), 207–228.

Fulmer, C.A., Gelfand, M.J., Kruglanski, A.W., Kim-Prieto, C., Diener, E., et al. (2010), 'On "feeling right" in cultural context: how person–culture match affects self-esteem and subjective well-being', *Psychological Science*, **21** (11), 1563–1569.

Glaeser, E.L., Gottlieb, J.D. and O. Ziv (2016), 'Unhappy cities', *Journal of Labor Economics*, **34** (S2), S129–S182.

Goetzke, F. and S. Islam (2017), 'Testing for spatial equilibrium using happiness data', *Journal of Regional Science*, **57** (2), 199–217.

Hamamura, T., Heine, S.J. and D.L. Paulhus (2008), 'Cultural differences in response styles: the role of dialectical thinking', *Personality and Individual Differences*, **44** (4), 932–942.

Helliwell, J.F. (2008), 'Life satisfaction and the quality of development', NBER Working Paper, No. 14507.

Helliwell, J.F. and C.P. Barrington-Leigh (2010), 'Measuring and understanding subjective well-being', *Canadian Journal of Economics / Revue canadienne d'économique*, **43** (3), 729–753.

Helliwell, J.F., Barrington-Leigh, C.P., Harris, A. and H. Huang (2009), 'International evidence on the social context of well-being', NBER Working Paper, No. 14720.

Inglehart, R., Foa, R., Peterson, C. and C. Welzel (2008), 'Development, freedom, and rising happiness: a global perspective (1981–2007)', *Perspectives on Psychological Science*, **3** (4), 264–285.

Jowell, R., Roberts, C., Fitzgerald, R. and G. Eva (eds) (2007), *Measuring Attitudes Cross-Nationally: Lessons from the European Social Survey*, London, UK: SAGE Publications.

Kahneman, D. and R. Sugden (2005), 'Experienced utility as a standard of policy evaluation', *Environmental and Resource Economics*, **32** (1), 161–181.

Kahneman, D., Wakker, P.P. and R. Sarin (1997), 'Back to Bentham? Explorations of experienced utility', *Quarterly Journal of Economics*, **112** (2), 375–406.

Kahneman, D., Krueger, A.B., Schkade, D., Schwarz, N. and A. Stone (2004), 'Toward national well-being accounts', *American Economic Review*, **94** (2), 429–434.

King, G. and J. Wand (2006), 'Comparing incomparable survey responses: evaluating and selecting anchoring vignettes', *Political Analysis*, **15** (1), 46–66.

King, G., Murray, C.J., Salomon, J.A. and A. Tandon (2004), 'Enhancing the validity and cross-cultural comparability of measurement in survey research', *American Political Science Review*, **98** (1), 191–207.

Kroeber, A.L. and C. Kluckhohn (1952), 'Culture: a critical review of concepts and definitions', *Papers of the Peabody Museum of Archaeology and Ethnology, Harvard University*, **47** (1), viii, 22.

Lau, A.L.D., Cummins, R.A. and W. McPherson (2005), 'An investigation into the cross-cultural equivalence of the Personal Wellbeing Index', *Social Indicators Research*, **72** (3), 403–430.

Layard, R. (2005), 'Rethinking public economics: the implications of rivalry and habit', in P.L. Porta and L. Bruni (eds), *Economics and Happiness: Framing the Analysis*, Oxford, UK: Oxford University Press, pp. 147–169.

Levitt, S.D. and S.J. Dubner (eds) (2005), *Freakonomics: A Rogue Economist Explores the Hidden Side of Everything*, New York, USA: HarperCollins Publishers.

Loewenstein, G. (1999), 'Because it is there: the challenge of mountaineering for utility theory', *Kyklos*, **52** (3), 315–343.

Loewenstein, G., O'Donohue, T. and M. Rabin (2003), 'Projection bias in predicting future utility', *Quarterly Journal of Economics*, **118** (4), 1209–1248.

Lucas, R.E. and M.B. Donnellan (2011), 'Personality development across the life span: longitudinal analyses with a national sample from Germany', *Journal of Personality and Social Psychology*, **101** (4), 847–861.

Maddison, D.J. and K. Rehdanz (2007), 'Are regional differences in utility eliminated over time? Evidence from Germany', SOEP Papers on Multidisciplinary Panel Data Research 16, DIW Berlin, German Socio-Economic Panel (SOEP).

Minkov, M. (2009), 'Predictors of differences in subjective well-being across 97 nations', *Cross-Cultural Research*, **43** (2), 152–179.

Moro, M., Brereton, F., Ferreira, S. and J.P. Clinch (2008), 'Ranking quality of life using subjective well-being data', *Ecological Economics*, **65** (3), 448–460.

Near, J.P. and P.L. Rechner (1993), 'Cross-cultural variations in predictors of life satisfaction: an historical view of differences among West European countries', *Social Indicators Research*, **29** (1), 109–121.

OECD (2013), *OECD Guidelines on Measuring Subjective Well-being*, Paris: OECD Publishing. https://doi.org/10.1787/9789264191655-en.

Oishi, S. (2006), 'The concept of life satisfaction across cultures: an IRT analysis', *Journal of Research in Personality*, **40** (4), 411–423.

Oishi, S. (2010), 'Culture and well-being: conceptual and methodological issues', in E. Diener, D. Kahneman and J. Helliwell (eds), *International Differences in Well-Being*, Oxford, UK: Oxford University Press, pp. 34–69.

Oishi, S., Schimmack, U. and S.J. Colcombe (2003), 'The contextual and systematic nature of life satisfaction judgments', *Journal of Experimental Social Psychology*, **39** (3), 232–247.

Oswald, A.J. and S. Wu (2010), 'Objective confirmation of subjective measures of human well-being: evidence from the USA', *Science*, **327** (5965), 576–579.

Oswald, A.J. and S. Wu (2011), 'Well-being across America', *Review of Economics and Statistics*, **93** (4), 1118–1134.

Powdthavee, N. (2007), 'Economics of happiness: a review of literature and applications', *Chulalongkorn Journal of Economics*, **19** (1), 51–73.

Roback, J. (1982), 'Wages, rents, and the quality of life', *Journal of Political Economy*, **90** (6), 1257–1278.

Rosen, S. (1979), 'Wage-based indexes of urban quality of life', in P. Mieszkowski and M. Straszheim (eds), *Current Issues in Urban Economics*, Baltimore, MD, USA: Johns Hopkins University Press, pp. 74–104.

Schneider, S.L. (2010), 'Nominal comparability is not enough: (in-)equivalence of construct validity of cross-national measures of educational attainment in the European Social Survey', *Research in Social Stratification and Mobility*, **28** (3), 343–357.

Senik, C. (2014), 'The French unhappiness puzzle: the cultural dimension of happiness', *Journal of Economic Behavior and Organization*, **106**, 379–401.

Stevenson, B. and J. Wolfers (2008), 'Economic growth and subjective well-being: reassessing the Easterlin Paradox', NBER Working Paper No. 14292.

Stiglitz, J.E. (2009), 'GDP fetishism', *Economists' Voice*, **6** (8), 1–3.

Stiglitz, J.E., Sen, A. and J.-P. Fitoussi (2009), 'Report by the Commission on the Measurement of Economic Performance and Social Progress', Paris, France.

Suh, E., Diener, E., Oishi, S. and H.C. Triandis (1998), 'The shifting basis of life satisfaction judgments across cultures: emotions versus norms', *Journal of Personality and Social Psychology*, **74** (2), 482–493.

Tiebout, C.M. (1956), 'A pure theory of local expenditures', *Journal of Political Economy*, **64** (5), 416–424.

Tov, W. and E. Diener (2007), 'Culture and subjective well-being', in S. Kitayama and D. Cohen (eds), *Handbook of Cultural Psychology*, New York, USA: Guilford Press, pp. 691–713.

Van Herk, H., Poortinga, Y.H. and T.M.M. Verhallen (2004), 'Response styles in rating scales: evidence of method bias in data from six EU countries', *Journal of Cross-Cultural Psychology*, **35** (3), 346–360.

Veenhoven, R. (2008), 'The international scale interval study: improving the comparability of responses to survey questions about happiness', in V. Moller and D. Huschka (eds), *Quality of Life and the Millennium Challenge: Advances in Quality-of-Life Studies, Theory and Research*, Social Indicators Research Series, Vol. 35, Dordrecht, Netherlands: Springer, pp. 45–58.

Vitterso, J., Biswas-Diener, R., Vittersø, J. and E. Diener (2005), 'Most people are pretty happy, but there is cultural variation: the Inughuit, the Amish, and the Maasai', *Journal of Happiness Studies*, **6** (3), 205–226.

Winters, J.V. and Y. Li (2017), 'Urbanisation, natural amenities and subjective well-being: evidence from US counties', *Urban Studies*, **54** (8), 1956–1973.

APPENDIX 3A.1

Table 3A.1 Summary of used datasets, period and list of countries/regions

	Names of countries/regions	#	Period
WVS	Albania, Algeria, Andorra, Azerbaijan, Argentina, Australia, Bahrain, Bangladesh, Armenia, Bosnia, Brazil, Bulgaria, Belarus, Canada, Chile, China, Taiwan, Colombia, Cyprus, Czech Rep., Dominican Rep., Ecuador, El Salvador, Ethiopia, Estonia, Finland, France, Georgia, Palestine, Germany, Ghana, Guatemala, Hong Kong, Hungary, India, Indonesia, Iran, Iraq, Italy, Japan, Kazakhstan, Jordan, South Korea, Kuwait, Kyrgyzstan, Lebanon, Latvia, Libya, Lithuania, Malaysia, Mali, Mexico, Moldova, Montenegro, Morocco, Netherlands, New Zealand, Nigeria, Norway, Pakistan, Peru, Philippines, Poland, Puerto Rico, Qatar, Romania, Russia, Rwanda, Saudi Arabia, Serbia, Singapore, Slovakia, Viet Nam, Slovenia, South Africa, Zimbabwe, Spain, Sweden, Switzerland, Thailand, Trinidad and Tobago, Tunisia, Turkey, Uganda, Ukraine, Macedonia, Egypt, Great Britain, Tanzania, United States, Burkina Faso, Uruguay, Uzbekistan, Venezuela, Yemen, Serbia and Montenegro, Zambia, Bosnia	98	1989–2014 Repeated cross-section of world countries for five waves of 1989–93, 1994–98, 1999–2004, 2005–09, 2010–14
Eurobarometer	Austria, Belgium, Bulgaria, Croatia, Cyprus (Northern), Cyprus (Rep.), Czech Republic, Denmark, Estonia, Finland, France, Germany-East, Germany-West, Great Britain, Greece, Hungary, Iceland, Ireland, Italy, Latvia, Lithuania, Luxembourg, Macedonia (FYROM), Malta, Montenegro, Netherlands, Northern Ireland, Poland, Portugal, Romania, Serbia, Slovakia, Slovenia, Spain, Sweden, Turkey	38	2004–14
BRFSS	US counties	2366	2005–10

APPENDIX 3A.2

Table 3A.2 Regression-adjusted mean life satisfaction from 1989 to 2014, World

Panel A: Excludes individual-level controls		Panel B: Includes individual-level controls	
Country/region name	Life satisfaction	Country/region name	Life satisfaction
Puerto Rico	8.814	Puerto Rico	8.869
Colombia	8.641	Colombia	8.667
Mexico	8.342	Guatemala	8.554
Switzerland	8.308	Mexico	8.462
Norway	8.184	Finland	8.178
Finland	8.143	Switzerland	7.864
Guatemala	8.096	El Salvador	7.832
Canada	8.069	Ecuador	7.791
El Salvador	8.041	Norway	7.791
New Zealand	7.981	Dominican Rep.	7.745
Qatar	7.918	Canada	7.735
Sweden	7.912	Brazil	7.730
Dominican Rep.	7.866	Netherlands	7.636
Saudi Arabia	7.853	Argentina	7.603
Ecuador	7.836	Sweden	7.565
Uzbekistan	7.797	Uzbekistan	7.532
United States	7.747	Uruguay	7.490
Australia	7.727	New Zealand	7.477
Great Britain	7.691	Chile	7.435
Argentina	7.670	Australia	7.408
Brazil	7.610	Venezuela	7.408
Uruguay	7.603	United States	7.397
Netherlands	7.563	Peru	7.388
Chile	7.424	Philippines	7.375
Trinidad and Tobago	7.404	Saudi Arabia	7.339
Thailand	7.399	Slovenia	7.337
Slovenia	7.339	Great Britain	7.314
Venezuela	7.316	Trinidad and Tobago	7.298
Germany	7.312	Germany	7.254
Andorra	7.285	Qatar	7.249
Philippines	7.210	Poland	7.239
Spain	7.195	Thailand	7.213
Cyprus	7.187	Kazakhstan	7.193
Viet Nam	7.187	Spain	7.157
Kazakhstan	7.166	Japan	7.130
Indonesia	7.160	Viet Nam	7.118
Kuwait	7.150	Czech Rep.	7.079
Libya	7.127	France	7.070
Poland	7.079	Italy	7.005
China	7.072	China	6.975
Italy	7.027	Indonesia	6.963
Malaysia	7.023	Andorra	6.917
Peru	7.009	Cyprus	6.882

Table 3A.2 (continued)

Panel A: Excludes individual-level controls		Panel B: Includes individual-level controls	
Country/region name	Life satisfaction	Country/region name	Life satisfaction
Czech Rep.	6.993	Kyrgyzstan	6.881
Japan	6.987	Turkey	6.876
France	6.974	Slovakia	6.832
Taiwan	6.926	Bangladesh	6.805
Kyrgyzstan	6.925	Libya	6.762
Nigeria	6.900	Taiwan	6.739
Singapore	6.867	Kuwait	6.735
South Africa	6.833	Hong Kong	6.706
Bahrain	6.798	South Africa	6.685
Turkey	6.786	Bahrain	6.639
Bangladesh	6.755	Bosnia	6.598
Iran	6.699	Iran	6.590
Slovakia	6.661	Uganda	6.574
Hong Kong	6.631	Malaysia	6.545
South Korea	6.590	Algeria	6.515
Mali	6.568	Singapore	6.496
Bosnia	6.551	Nigeria	6.494
Pakistan	6.492	South Korea	6.405
Lebanon	6.453	Zambia	6.359
Zambia	6.443	Azerbaijan	6.353
Ghana	6.384	Mali	6.350
Jordan	6.336	India	6.309
Uganda	6.280	Serbia and Montenegro	6.278
India	6.278	Estonia	6.274
Bosnia	6.263	Bosnia	6.267
Montenegro	6.261	Serbia	6.229
Azerbaijan	6.220	Pakistan	6.222
Algeria	6.208	Ghana	6.198
Serbia	6.175	Jordan	6.186
Serbia and Montenegro	6.142	Hungary	6.183
Yemen	6.062	Lebanon	6.182
Morocco	6.034	Romania	6.168
Rwanda	6.020	Yemen	6.144
Romania	5.999	Rwanda	6.142
Hungary	5.985	Montenegro	6.094
Estonia	5.932	Russia	6.083
Burkina Faso	5.886	Burkina Faso	5.882
Macedonia	5.856	Morocco	5.844
Russia	5.768	Macedonia	5.819
Egypt	5.722	Georgia	5.772
Tunisia	5.637	Ukraine	5.757
Palestine	5.586	Latvia	5.713
Lithuania	5.532	Egypt	5.639
Albania	5.530	Belarus	5.595
Latvia	5.466	Tunisia	5.574

Table 3A.2 (continued)

Panel A: Excludes individual-level controls		Panel B: Includes individual-level controls	
Country/region name	Life satisfaction	Country/region name	Life satisfaction
Zimbabwe	5.437	Palestine	5.484
Bulgaria	5.301	Zimbabwe	5.475
Iraq	5.299	Moldova	5.469
Belarus	5.294	Lithuania	5.429
Ukraine	5.294	Armenia	5.423
Georgia	5.195	Bulgaria	5.388
Ethiopia	5.118	Albania	5.306
Moldova	4.995	Iraq	5.271
Armenia	4.977	Ethiopia	5.135
Tanzania	4.337	Tanzania	4.683

Table 3A.3 Regression-adjusted mean life satisfaction from 2004 to 2014, Europe

Panel A: Excludes individual-level controls		Panel B: Includes individual-level controls	
Country/region name	Life satisfaction	Country/region name	Life satisfaction
Denmark	3.675	Denmark	4.020
Iceland	3.595	Iceland	3.881
Sweden	3.469	Sweden	3.824
Netherlands	3.458	Netherlands	3.823
Luxembourg	3.379	Northern Ireland	3.764
Northern Ireland	3.321	Luxembourg	3.749
Finland	3.300	Great Britain	3.701
Great Britain	3.274	Finland	3.671
Ireland	3.238	Ireland	3.648
Belgium	3.201	Belgium	3.588
Germany-West	3.135	Germany-West	3.536
Malta	3.091	Malta	3.529
Cyprus (Rep.)	3.084	Cyprus (Rep.)	3.495
Austria	3.078	Austria	3.492
Slovenia	3.072	Slovenia	3.451
France	2.981	Spain	3.400
Spain	2.936	France	3.384
Czech Republic	2.908	Germany-East	3.338
Germany-East	2.891	Czech Republic	3.300
Poland	2.852	Poland	3.245
Croatia	2.802	Croatia	3.232
Turkey	2.772	Turkey	3.203
Estonia	2.772	Estonia	3.155
Slovakia	2.749	Slovakia	3.146
Cyprus (Northern)	2.710	Italy	3.107
Italy	2.707	Cyprus (Northern)	3.083
Latvia	2.645	Macedonia (fyrom)	3.051
Lithuania	2.634	Lithuania	3.046
Macedonia (fyrom)	2.578	Latvia	3.035
Montenegro	2.508	Montenegro	2.900
Hungary	2.426	Hungary	2.893
Greece	2.384	Portugal	2.877
Romania	2.378	Greece	2.809
Portugal	2.378	Romania	2.777
Serbia	2.313	Serbia	2.695
Bulgaria	2.186	Bulgaria	2.601

Table 3A.4 Regression-adjusted mean life satisfaction from 2005 to 2010, US

Panel A: Excludes individual-level controls			Panel B: Includes individual-level controls		
State name	County name	Life satisfaction	State name	County name	Life satisfaction
Most satisfied			*Most satisfied*		
Alaska	Anchorage	4.004	Virginia	Covington City	4.303
Texas	King	4.001	Virginia	Galax City	4.231
Virginia	Covington City	4.001	Alaska	Anchorage	4.094
Virginia	Galax City	4.001	Texas	King	3.870
Texas	Camp	3.758	North Carolina	Pamlico	3.762
Texas	Madison	3.710	Texas	Lamb	3.734
Virginia	Williamsburg City	3.702	Georgia	Butts	3.688
Texas	Lampasas	3.689	Virginia	Harrisonburg City	3.669
North Carolina	Washington	3.676	Texas	Newton	3.661
North Carolina	Pamlico	3.675	Louisiana	West Feliciana	3.659
Texas	Kendall	3.671	Illinois	Piatt	3.659
Virginia	Harrisonburg City	3.661	Missouri	Linn	3.654
Texas	Hockley	3.653	Texas	Upshur	3.637
Georgia	Hart	3.642	Georgia	Worth	3.634
Georgia	Bleckley	3.635	North Carolina	Washington	3.626
Texas	Upshur	3.633	Illinois	White	3.621
Georgia	Harris	3.631	Georgia	Mitchell	3.621
Pennsylvania	Juniata	3.627	Louisiana	Grant	3.617
Virginia	Southampton	3.627	Texas	Madison	3.617
Least satisfied			*Least satisfied*		
Virginia	Buchanan	3.124	Iowa	Mills	3.142
Texas	Trinity	3.117	Michigan	Branch	3.140
Texas	Morris	3.116	Georgia	Haralson	3.125
Pennsylvania	Greene	3.116	Texas	Jones	3.120
Illinois	Mason	3.111	Michigan	Mason	3.117
Illinois	Bond	3.102	Texas	Morris	3.089
Tennessee	Campbell	3.061	Arkansas	Drew	3.087
Virginia	Charlotte	3.029	Texas	Freestone	3.078
Texas	Jones	3.028	Virginia	Charlotte	3.065
Texas	Freestone	3.019	Kentucky	Bourbon	3.038
Illinois	Union	3.019	Illinois	Mason	3.033
Pennsylvania	Fulton	3.016	Pennsylvania	Fulton	3.022
Texas	Willacy	3.014	Virginia	Madison	3.009
Virginia	Emporia City	3.001	Illinois	Union	2.995
Virginia	Lexington City	3.001	Virginia	Waynesboro City	2.971
Virginia	Staunton City	2.998	Virginia	Emporia City	2.922
Virginia	Waynesboro City	2.994	Virginia	Manassas City	2.784
Virginia	Madison	2.983	Virginia	Lexington City	2.756
Virginia	Manassas City	2.909	Virginia	Staunton City	2.753

4. Happiness and environmental economics

Heinz Welsch

4.1 INTRODUCTION

Textbooks in general economics maintain that human wellbeing, or utility u, rises with consumption c: $u = u(c)$. Many, accordingly, view growth of consumption (or income) as the overarching goal of economic policy. Textbooks in environmental economics, however, assert that the utility function is more complex, including environmental quality Q as an additional argument: $u = u(c, Q)$.

The literature on the economics of happiness has contributed to the understanding and measurement of the utility function in several ways. First, starting with Easterlin (1974), the role of economic growth for human wellbeing has been scrutinized. Second, the role of environmental quality for wellbeing has been empirically established. Third, the trade-off people are willing to make between consumption and protection of the environment has been measured in a more direct manner.

The methodology used in addressing these issues involves using data on subjective wellbeing (SWB) – often referred to as happiness or satisfaction – as a proxy for utility.[1] While economists rejected the idea of direct measurement of utility throughout much of the twentieth century, using such data has recently become widely accepted in the economics profession due to an increased awareness of their scientific quality (Frey and Stutzer, 2002) and the advantages this offers.

One advantage of using happiness data lies in avoiding reliance on non-testable assumptions that need to be made when applying some methods of standard non-market valuation techniques. Indeed, happiness data not only permit avoidance of such assumptions, but also permit the testing of assumptions previously considered untestable, for example, the assumption of spatial equilibrium in hedonic approaches to non-market valuation (Ferreira and Moro, 2010) or the assumption of utility maximization in environmentally relevant consumer choice (Welsch and Kühling, 2011).

While happiness data offer one useful way of measuring the utility function and assessing its role for the analysis of economic behavior, happiness economics often benefits from complementary evidence from other approaches, in particular experimental economics. Experimental economics involves the study of choice behavior, whereas happiness economics is concerned with the utility consequences of economic choices. The two approaches often lead to similar conclusions, which sometimes are at odds with assumptions of standard economics. Due to their complementarity, they are sometimes considered to be branches of a common discipline, called behavioral economics (BE).

The next section provides some background on happiness economics, behavioral economics and their relationship to the standard economic model. Section 4.3 discusses the nature of the relationship between consumption, growth and happiness, and the implications for environmental policy analysis. Section 4.4 addresses the relationship between environmental quality and happiness, and the happiness trade-off between consumption and environmental quality. Section 4.5 concludes.

4.2 BACKGROUND: BEHAVIORAL ECONOMICS AND THE STANDARD ECONOMIC MODEL

4.2.1 The Standard Economic Model

Like other fields of economics, environmental economics builds on a simple but powerful model of behavior. The core assumption of this model is rational choice (RC): individuals make choices such as to maximize a utility function that represents a complete and consistent (transitive) preference ordering over a given set of options. In addition to the RC assumption, the utility function is usually assumed to possess a set of typical properties. Arguably the most important of these is that preferences are affected only by the levels of one's own pay-offs, not by changes of pay-offs relative to some reference point or by the pay-offs of other individuals. In choices involving uncertainty, individuals are assumed to maximize expected utility, and in intertemporal choices, preferences are assumed to be time-consistent, involving a constant discount factor (DellaVigna, 2009).

These assumptions constitute what can be called the standard economic model (SEM). Laboratory and field evidence on decision making, however, raises serious questions about the validity of the SEM and has inspired the development of the field of behavioral economics.

4.2.2 Alternative Models of Decision Making

BE involves the incorporation of insights from psychology into economic analysis. As suggested by Sent (2004), BE can be differentiated into an "old" BE and a "new" BE. Whereas new BE retains utility maximization as a goal of decision makers but asserts that they frequently fail to achieve that goal, old BE, dating back at least to Simon (1955), questions whether individuals even attempt to maximize utility. Instead of striving to maximize utility, proponents of old BE suggest that, given cognitive limitations, individuals engage in "satisficing," that is, applying heuristics and routines that yield outcomes which individuals consider satisfactory, without being optimal.

New BE has accumulated a set of typical deviations from the SEM, so-called anomalies, some of which can be rationalized by a behavioral model that is more general than the SEM. The first and most fundamental anomaly is framing: rather than choosing from a given set of unambiguous options, individuals need to interpret and "edit" the choice situation, and editing systematically influences the choices being made. In particular, a fundamental difference arises depending on whether outcomes are interpreted as gains or as losses relative to some reference point, and this interpretation depends on the semantic framing of the situation. A famous example involves a medical treatment program (vaccination against a dangerous disease, say) whose outcome is stochastic and described to decision makers in terms of either the expected number of lives saved or the expected number of lives lost, relative to a no-treatment option (Tversky and Kahneman, 1981). Robust experimental evidence found the rate of approval to the program to be significantly higher when the framing highlights lives saved rather than lives lost. This is a typical example of the phenomenon of loss aversion, and of how it affects choices depending on the framing of the choice situation.

In addition to the issue of framing, the medical treatment example involves two aspects that constitute a deviation from the SEM. The first is that preferences involve differences from a reference point (lives lost or saved relative to no treatment) rather than level variables (number of people alive after treatment/no-treatment). The other is probability weighting: in their decision making individuals typically do not use statistical probabilities (even if known), but attach disproportionally high weights to outcomes with low probability and disproportionately low weights to outcomes with high probability. In other words, they do not behave as expected-utility maximizers.

Many deviations of decision-making behavior from the SEM can be rationalized by prospect theory (Kahneman and Tversky, 1979). Prospect theory (PT) generalizes expected-utility theory in the following ways. First, the choice situation is edited, that is, the outcomes of the various options are interpreted as differences from a reference point (for example, the status quo). Second, the utility function is defined over those differences rather than the levels of the outcome variable. Third, the utility function incorporates loss aversion, that is, it is more sensitive to deteriorations (with respect to the reference point) than to improvements. Fourth, uncertain outcomes are valued according to probability weights that are higher than the statistical probability for low-probability outcomes and lower than the statistical probability for high-probability outcomes.

PT is an extension of the SEM that applies to choice situations without social interaction or social interdependence. The SEM has also been challenged, however, with respect to strategic choices; that is, situations in which several people's outcomes are mutually dependent on those people's choices. With respect to strategic choices (games), the SEM predicts that players are guided only by their own outcomes, not by those of other players. In other words, the SEM assumes preferences to be entirely self-regarding. In contrast to this assumption, experimental evidence abounds which is inconsistent with this assumption. In particular, individuals typically reject options that entail pay-offs that are poor relative to those of others. Specifically, people are willing to forego certain amounts of absolute pay-off if they perceive their pay-off to be unfair in relation to the pay-offs that others receive. While the SEM cannot account for such behaviors, models involving other-regarding preferences (e.g., Fehr and Schmidt, 1999; Bolton and Ockenfels, 2000) yield predictions largely in agreement with such evidence.

As this discussion suggests, a common theme of BE applications to both strategic and non-strategic choices is the relevance of reference points for decision making. In non-strategic choices, a reference point may be the status quo, whereas in strategic choices it may be the outcome for others. As will be seen later, reference points are important not only for our understanding of the making of decisions, but also for their consequences in terms of utility and welfare.

4.2.3 Experienced Utility and Subjective Wellbeing

BE involves the incorporation of insights from psychology into economic analysis. As sketched in the preceding subsection, such insights have led to significant revisions of the SEM of decision making. Specifically, alternatives to the utility function underlying economic decisions have been proposed. Psychological considerations, however, have shaped our understanding not only of the objectives people pursue in making decisions, but also of the utility consequences of individual and collective choices.

Highlighting the distinction between utility as an objective and utility as a consequence of economic behavior, Kahneman et al. (1997) have introduced the notions of decision utility and experienced utility. Experienced utility is the *ex post* hedonic quality associated with an (economic) outcome. Decision utility describes the *ex ante* expectation of experienced utility. Experienced utility thus entails a retrospective (or contemporaneous) assessment of outcomes, whereas decision utility involves a prospective assessment. Ideally, decision utility and experienced utility would coincide, but evidence from BE casts doubt on their equivalence. Specifically, deviations between decision utility and experienced utility (and the associated decision errors) may arise because of failures in affective forecasting; that is, in figuring out the utility consequences of one's choices (Loewenstein and Adler, 1995; Loewenstein and Schkade, 1999; Loewenstein et al., 2003; Wilson and Gilbert, 2003).

The title of the paper in which Kahneman et al. (1997) introduced the notion of experienced utility is "Back to Bentham?" This title perfectly conveys the neo-utilitarian flavor of the concept. Since experienced utility can be measured by means of reported SWB (for example, happiness or life satisfaction), its policy relevance was soon noticed. For instance, a group of renowned economists have advocated using SWB as a standard of reference of economic and social performance (Stiglitz et al., 2009).

In addition to their greater policy relevance, an advantage of SWB measures relates to economic methodology: the availability of SWB data provides researchers with generic data on the utility consequences of behaviors. To assess utility we thus do not have to rely on inferences from behaviors (Frey and Stutzer, 2002). Moreover, by using SWB as a measure of utility, we are able to test the assumptions typically made to derive such inferences, in particular the assumptions of the SEM. In this sense, experimental economics and happiness economics are complementary to each other as they permit a cross-validation of their respective results.

One issue where such cross-validation has found highly consistent results is the importance of relative concerns for both behaviors and utility outcomes. Relative concerns and their implications for environmental economics and policy will be discussed in the next section.

4.3 HAPPINESS AND THE PROVISION OF ENVIRONMENTAL GOODS

4.3.1 Happiness, Growth and Relative Concerns

With respect to the key environmental economics issues to which happiness economics contributes (see the introduction to this chapter), important insights come from the study of the wellbeing effects of consumption, income and growth. The role of economic growth for human wellbeing was first studied by Easterlin (1974). He found average happiness in the United States (US) after World War II to be stationary in spite of a tremendous increase in per capita income. This initial finding has since been corroborated using data for many developed economies (Easterlin et al., 2010).

These findings on the macro level – involving per capita income – can be contrasted with micro-level evidence according to which: (1) within countries, individuals with higher incomes are happier than individuals with lower incomes; and (2) over time, increases in individuals' real income are associated with increases in their happiness, even if transitory (Clark et al., 2008).

A reconciliation of the macro and micro evidence relies on the idea that the income–happiness relationship involves relative concerns: individuals evaluate their income not in absolute terms but in comparison with some benchmark. Benchmarks can be the income of relevant others and one's own income in the past (Easterlin, 1995, 2001).

With respect to the income of others, a distinction is usually made between relative deprivation and relative satisfaction. Relative deprivation is said to prevail if the income of the individual in question is lower than the relevant comparison income, whereas relative satisfaction prevails if the individual's income is higher than comparison income. A standard finding in the income comparison literature is that higher comparison income reduces the individual's wellbeing (Clark and D'Ambrosio, 2015) through either greater deprivation or lower satisfaction. Comparison income – the income of others – thus yields a negative externality. Due to such mutual income externalities, the social marginal utility of income is smaller than the private marginal utility of income.

In addition to the income of others, a benchmark for evaluating one's income is the income earned in the past. Income earned in the past creates an aspiration level for the income which the individual deems satisfactory, such that only increases relative to that prior level lead to additional wellbeing. The reason for this effect is hedonic adaptation. With hedonic adaptation, increases in income have only (or mainly) transient effects because individuals become accustomed to their new circumstances. In economics terms, the tendency of satisfaction of returning to some baseline level implies that the long-term marginal utility of income (or consumption) is smaller than the short-term marginal utility. Taking into account both social comparison and hedonic adaptation can explain Easterlin's finding that increases in per capita income of developed economies tend to have no long-term consequences for wellbeing (Clark et al., 2008).

4.3.2 Consumption Externalities

Though the above discussion was in terms of income, social comparison and hedonic adaptation in effect refer to consumption. In particular, social comparison is likely to refer to consumption (of cars and status goods more generally) rather than income, because the former is observable whereas the latter is less so. In this sense, findings from happiness economics have contributed to a more realistic understanding of the structure of the utility function $u(c)$.

Comparison and adaptation effects have long been discussed in the economics literature on consumption behavior (Veblen, 1899; Duesenberry, 1949), but their implications for welfare analysis and public policy have been elaborated only recently. In a welfare economic perspective, the circumstance that one individual's consumption negatively affects other individuals' utility means that consumption yields negative externalities.[2] Standard microeconomic analysis suggests that in the presence of negative externalities individuals choose inefficiently high levels of the action that causes the externality, because people's choices do not take into account the negative effect they inflict on others. Individuals' choices are hence not socially optimal.

Similarly, the circumstance that an individual's past consumption level negatively affects their current utility can be referred to as an "internality" (Frank, 1985). In the case of consumption internalities (intra-personal externalities), fully rational (forward-looking) decision making would internalize the intra-personal externality; that is, individuals would anticipate the adaptation-related negative effect of higher consumption today on utility in the future. However, an important finding from BE is that adaptation to consumption levels is largely unforeseen in the individual's decision making, due to a failure in affective forecasting (Loewenstein et al., 2003; Wilson and Gilbert, 2003). Individuals, in other words, tend to behave in a myopic rather than a forward-looking way, disregarding the internality in their consumption choices. Similar to classical (interpersonal) externalities, negative intra-personal externalities then imply that the chosen level of consumption is higher than the optimal level. More specifically, consumption choices not only fail to be socially optimal (due to social comparison), but also fail to be individually optimal (due to unanticipated adaptation).

Such reasoning has been formalized by Layard (2006) in a model of income–leisure choice, which he showed to be biased to the disadvantage of leisure due to social comparison and unforeseen adaptation.[3] This result suggests that an income or consumption tax is not necessarily distortionary, as suggested by standard public economics, but may to some extent be warranted to correct for distorted decision making.

4.3.3 Implications for Environmental Regulation

In addition to such implications for public economics and taxation, consumption externalities and "internalities" have been shown to affect optimal environmental policy and regulation (Brekke and Howarth, 2002; Howarth, 1996; Ng and Wang, 1993; Welsch, 2009). These studies typically assume income to be exogenous (taking the income–leisure choice as given) and focus on the allocation of income to a (private) consumption good and a contribution to a public environmental good, invoking "standard" and "revised" versions of the environmental economics utility function $u(c, Q)$, with Q being the sum of individual contributions.

In such a framework, the standard model of environmental policy analysis (which disregards relative consumption) implies market failure in the following sense. While individually optimal choice implies that the marginal rate of substitution (MRS) between consumption and the environmental contribution be equal to the price ratio, the social optimum requires equality of the sum (across all individuals) of marginal rates of substitution and the price ratio (Samuelson rule). The intuition is that every individual's environmental contribution yields utility not only for themself, but for all individuals. The familiar overall result is that the socially optimal level of environmental quality is greater than the level of environmental quality in an unregulated market.

If one extends the textbook model of environmental policy to include consumption externalities due to social comparison, the condition for individually optimal behavior is unchanged, but the condition for a social optimum changes, accounting not only for the public-good character of the environment, but in addition for the consumption externality. In comparison with the standard condition for a social optimum, the negative consumption externality creates an additional gap between the individually rational market outcome and the social optimum. Specifically, not only is the social marginal utility of the environmental contribution greater than the associated private marginal utility, but in addition the social marginal utility of consumption is smaller than its private counterpart. The discrepancy between the private and the social marginal utility of consumption implies that from a societal point of view the choice between consumption and the environmental contribution involves an additional distortion to the disadvantage of the latter. Due to this additional distortion, the gap between the socially optimal level of environmental quality and the market outcome is greater than implied by the standard model of environmental economics (Welsch, 2009).[4]

Similar to the case of social comparison, the phenomenon of adaptation to consumption levels may affect the optimal level of environmental quality (Welsch, 2009). Anticipation of the adaptation effect (forward-looking choice) implies that the MRS (or, respectively, the sum of the marginal rates of substitution) should be smaller than the price ratio. Intuitively, choice under correct affective forecasting would recognize that more consumption today raises the benchmark for the evaluation of consumption tomorrow. Myopic choice neglects this mechanism and the associated negative internality. As a consequence, if the market outcome is based on myopic behavior, whereas the social optimum accounts for adaptation, then the gap between the unregulated market outcome and the socially optimal outcome is greater than in the standard model. In addition, failure to anticipate adaptation implies that the individually chosen environmental contribution is not only smaller than the socially optimal value, but also smaller than the individually rational choice.[5]

In sum, negative consumption externalities and unanticipated adaptation to consumption levels suggested by recent happiness research may imply distortions away from optimal environmental quality in addition to the distortions stemming from environmental public goods. Optimal environmental regulation may thus be stricter than suggested by standard models of environmental policy analysis.

4.4 HAPPINESS AND ENVIRONMENTAL VALUATION

4.4.1 Environment, Utility and Non-Market Valuation

By adopting the $u(c, Q)$ framework, the discussion in the preceding section (and the pertinent literature) has assumed that environmental quality in fact has an influence on utility or wellbeing. In addition to traditional approaches to eliciting preferences for environmental quality, happiness economics has established a new way of measuring the relationship between utility and the environment. Indeed, as demonstrated in Part II of this *Handbook*, there is by now an impressive body of evidence demonstrating the wellbeing relevance of environmental quality.

A more specific question with respect to the effects of environmental quality on wellbeing is how individuals value these effects. This issue basically involves determining, in a $u(c, Q)$ framework, what amount of the market good c the individual is willing to give up in exchange for a specified increase in Q. Environmental valuation, in this sense, is an important element of the benefit–cost analysis of environmental policy.

Using happiness data constitutes a novel approach to measuring the wellbeing trade-off between consumption and environmental amenities. While traditional stated and revealed preference approaches to non-market valuation (Freeman, 2003) rely on decision utility, involving choices in hypothetical or actual markets, the happiness approach relies on experienced utility.[6] As argued by Welsch and Ferreira (2013), the value of a good, environmental or other, is its contribution to experienced utility.[7] To differentiate the happiness approach from both stated and revealed preference approaches, they refer to it as the experienced preference method (EPM) of preference elicitation.

The EPM consists of correlating people's reported SWB with local environmental amenities. It thus relies on a purely statistical association between wellbeing and environmental conditions. In this way, it avoids strategic responses and other biases characteristic of stated preference methods, and assumptions concerning the functioning of markets necessary for revealed preference methods (e.g., Welsch and Ferreira, 2013). In particular, it avoids assuming spatial equilibrium in the housing market, a necessary assumption for the hedonic pricing method to fully capture the value of environmental conditions (Roback, 1982).

More fundamentally, by focusing on experienced utility directly, the EPM avoids reliance on people's guesswork as to the utility consequences of (hypothetical and actual) choices.[8] Figuring out such consequences *ex ante* requires, as a minimum, that people are aware of causal relationships between environmental conditions and wellbeing. Such awareness is unnecessary for establishing a statistically valid and substantively meaningful relationship. All that is necessary for valid inference is soundness of empirical methodology and consistency with theoretically plausible mechanisms of influence. For instance, air pollution may affect wellbeing through cardiovascular problems, and wellbeing research may uncover the pollution–wellbeing relationship even if affected individuals are unaware of it.

However, it is possible that the EPM fails to capture effects on future wellbeing, whereas stated and revealed preference have the potential to do so. For instance, SWB was found to be unrelated to the spatial pattern of radioactive radiation after the Fukushima nuclear meltdown (Rehdanz et al., 2015), whereas property prices displayed a significant decrease in areas with higher radiation levels, presumably capitalizing expected future wellbeing effects (Welsch, 2016). Similar considerations may apply to long-term effects of climate change, but the issue does not seem to have been explored systematically as yet.

4.4.2 The Experienced Preference Method of Environmental Valuation

To be concise, the basic idea of the EPM is to use survey data on self-rated happiness, and to model an individual's happiness as a function of their income and the prevailing environmental conditions, controlling for other relevant circumstances. The estimated relationship is used to calculate the trade-off people would be willing to make between income and environmental conditions; that is, the increase in income necessary to compensate individuals for the loss in utility from a given deterioration of environmental quality.

The general form of the happiness function can be stated as follows:

$$H_{ist} = f(y_{ist}, Q_{st}, controls_{ist}, error_{ist}), \tag{4.1}$$

where H_{ist} is the stated SWB (happiness) of individual i in location s at time t, y_{ist} is the individual's income, and Q_{st} describes environmental quality in place s at time t.[9] The function $f(.)$ is usually specified as being linear in (transformations of) the independent variables. Depending on whether the happiness measure is taken as a cardinal or ordinal variable, estimation of $f(.)$ uses least squares or ordered probit or logit estimators. Whichever method is used, the ratio of the coefficients on y and Q is typically found to be very similar. For example, a study on happiness and electricity supply by Welsch and Biermann (2014) found that the coefficients on income and the supply shares of various types of electricity generation yielded very similar monetary values of substituting solar and wind power for nuclear power.

To obtain unbiased estimates, the vector of controls should include those utility-relevant variables that are correlated with Q. Given the possibility that the benefits of particular environmental goods become capitalized into differences in property prices, one such variable is the cost of housing: in spatial equilibrium, housing should be less expensive in more environmentally degraded places, inducing a positive correlation between housing prices and environmental quality. Indeed, if environmental quality is completely capitalized in housing prices and wages (income), the coefficient on Q in equation (4.1) should be non-significant. If significant despite the inclusion of housing costs, this suggests that the data do not represent a spatial equilibrium (Ferreira and Moro, 2010; Welsch and Ferreira, 2013). The EPM may thus provide a test of the hedonic pricing model.[10]

Notwithstanding the above issues, once estimated, the happiness function can be used to derive a monetary valuation of changes in environmental quality. The value of a marginal change in environmental quality is the MRS of income for environmental quality. In the case of an environmental improvement, it is the amount by which income can be reduced when environmental quality rises marginally, such that the level of utility (happiness) remains unchanged. Likewise, it is the amount by which income needs to rise when environmental quality decreases marginally and utility is to be kept constant. Diagrammatically, it is the slope of the indifference curve in the y–Q plain.

Computationally, as basic microeconomics suggests, the MRS is obtained by dividing the derivative of $f(.)$ with respect to Q (the coefficient on Q) by the derivative of $f(.)$ with respect to y (the coefficient on y). Since the ratio of those coefficients is fairly invariant with respect to the estimation method (see above), so is the MRS obtained.

The MRS is the utility-constant valuation of marginal changes in environmental quality. If non-marginal changes are to be evaluated, the Hicksian welfare measures are appropriate (Johansson, 1987), that is, the compensating surplus (CS) and the equivalent surplus (ES). The CS is the amount by which – after an environmental change – income would need to be raised or reduced to fix wellbeing at the original level. The ES is the amount by which income would need to be adjusted to attain the same level of wellbeing as that which arises after the environmental change, assuming that the latter did not take place.

4.4.3 Discussion and Open Questions[11]

In applications of the EPM it has often been observed that the valuations obtained – that is, the MRS of income for the environmental good under study – are "too high" (e.g., MacKerron and Mourato, 2009; Ferreira and Moro, 2010), in particular in comparison with results from hedonic pricing studies.[12] As discussed in the preceding subsection, however, hedonic pricing need not capture the full value of environmental quality because the condition of spatial equilibrium may not be satisfied. Another reason why hedonic pricing studies may be an inappropriate standard against which to assess the plausibility of EPM results is the disjunction between decision and experienced utility: in making purchase decisions, people may underrate the utility effects of the environmental variables.

Though expectations as to "reasonable" magnitudes for the value of environmental quality may be misleading, a bias can nevertheless arise from a biased estimate of the marginal utility of income, the denominator of the MRS. One source of bias can be endogeneity of income due to reverse causality, omitted variable bias and measurement error. Reverse causality means that happier people may earn higher incomes, for example, because they are more committed to their work. With respect to omitted variable bias, one important point is that specifications of wellbeing regressions often fail to control for the disutility from income generation (working hours, commuting and stress) and thus tend to deliver the net rather than the "full" marginal utility of income (Luechinger, 2009). Finally, measurement of income is a tricky task. For example, the income of homeowners should include an element representing the rental value of their home. Another frequently encountered issue is the use of income categories and the top-coding problem.

In addressing the endogeneity issue, Powdthavee (2010) found that the income coefficient in an instrumental-variables specification of the wellbeing regression is larger than in a least-squares specification, suggesting that the latter would otherwise overstate the MRS of income for the environmental good. Ambrey and Fleming (2014) also provide evidence of an overstatement of the MRS due to endogeneity of income.

Another point relates to the relative income effects discussed in section 4.3. The findings on relative income effects might suggest to include in the wellbeing regression not only current own income but also lagged own income and the income of others. Because lagged own income and the income of others affect wellbeing negatively but both are likely to be positively correlated with current own income, omission of those controls is expected to lead to a smaller coefficient on current own income than their inclusion.

It is however open to debate whether this constitutes a bias or whether both specifications yield meaningful, though different insights. When lagged own income and the income of others are controlled for, the coefficient on current own income captures utility gains from short-term improvements in relative socio-economic status, that is, the short-term private marginal utility of income. When lagged own income and the income of others are omitted, the coefficient on current own income incorporates the negative "internality" of past income and the negative externality of others' income. The coefficient can thus be interpreted as capturing the long-term social marginal utility of income, which is less than the short-term private marginal utility of income (Layard, 2006).

Following this reasoning, standard EPM studies, which include only current own income, should be taken as delivering the value of environmental quality in terms of the long-term social value of income. The value of environmental quality so obtained may be larger than its counterpart in terms of the short-term private value of income.[13] To the extent that individuals fail to account for negative consumption (income) "internalities" and externalities in making (actual or hypothetical) choices (as argued, for example, by Frank, 1985), conventional revealed and stated valuation approaches may be thought of as relying on the short-term private value of income. It is arguably the long-term social value of income rather than its short-term private value that should be the basis for environmental benefit–cost analysis.

4.5 CONCLUSION

While psychologists started exploring happiness in the late 1940s, the economics of happiness is a more recent phenomenon. Studying happiness or, more broadly, SWB from an economics perspective has the potential to clarify important issues in welfare economics, since SWB can serve as a proxy for the fundamental economic notion of utility previously deemed unobservable.

Starting in the 1970s, happiness economics has accumulated a considerable body of insights on how economic, institutional and environmental factors contribute to human wellbeing. Put more formally, happiness economics (and BE more generally) has changed our understanding of the structure of the utility function. While traditional microeconomics has been concerned with consumption as the sole source of utility, happiness economics has established that a whole array of factors contribute to utility. Specifically, using happiness data it has been shown empirically that environmental quality affects utility. What is more, happiness data have enabled researchers to estimate the trade-off people are willing to make between consumption and the environment, thus providing a new tool for environmental valuation and environmental benefit–cost analysis.

An important aspect of the utility trade-off between consumption and the environment concerns how exactly consumption affects wellbeing. While standard microeconomics assumed that higher levels of consumption lead to greater wellbeing without regard to contextual factors, happiness economics has found evidence for the view held by some that people evaluate consumption not in absolute terms, but in relation to the consumption of others and to their own consumption in the past. This creates consumption externalities that lead to market failures in addition to those stemming from environmental externalities. Consumption and environmental externalities combined suggest that the gap between optimal environmental quality and that delivered by unregulated markets may be larger than suggested by traditional models of environmental policy. Though certain aspects of the valuation of the environment using happiness data are subject to debate, the use of such data has established itself as a fruitful contribution to the environmental economics toolbox.

NOTES

1. Unless stated otherwise, the terms (subjective) wellbeing, happiness, (life) satisfaction, and (experienced) utility are used interchangeably in this chapter.
2. Externalities are defined as unpriced, unintended and uncompensated side effects of one agent's actions that directly affect the welfare of another agent (Baumol and Oates, 1988).
3. This analysis presumes that relative concerns do not apply to leisure. This assumption reflects common findings that social life, time spent with family, and other intrinsically motivated activities are much less affected by relative concerns than is consumption (Gui and Sugden, 2005). According to Solnick and Hemenway (1998, 2005), leisure time has the lowest status effect of all goods considered in the respective studies.
4. Howarth (2006) found in a calibrated model of optimal carbon dioxide abatement that the optimal level of abatement is significantly larger when relative consumption effects are accounted for.

5. As will be discussed in Chapter 19 in this *Handbook*, studies of happiness and pro-environmental behavior have found evidence consistent with the idea that individuals' choice between consumption and contributions to environmental quality may in fact be distorted to the disadvantage of the latter.
6. Stated preference methods (for example, contingent valuation) involve asking people directly how they value hypothetical changes of the environmental good in question. Revealed preference methods rely on complementarity relationships between market goods (for example, houses) and local environmental quality to infer the value attributed to the latter from choices (and resulting prices) concerning the former.
7. While this assumption may be questionable in some cases of pure existence value, experienced utility can be considered a source of value for most environmental goods.
8. Ideally, decision utility (which guides people's choices) and experienced utility would coincide, but evidence from behavioral economics casts doubt on the general validity of their equivalence. As discussed in subsection 4.2.3, deviations between decision utility and experienced utility (and the associated decision errors) may arise because of failures in affective forecasting; that is, in figuring out the utility consequences of one's choices.
9. In practice, Q is often measured in an inverse fashion, using data on pollution. This is not a substantive but an empirical matter.
10. For a comparison of studies that do and do not control for property prices, see Chapter 6 by Maddison and Rehdanz in this *Handbook*.
11. This subsection draws on Welsch and Ferreira (2013).
12. For example, MacKerron and Mourato (2009) estimated that a 1 percent increase in nitrogen dioxide (NO_2) levels is equivalent, in SWB terms, to a 5.3 percent drop in income, and they note that: "Notwithstanding that the NO_2 variable here may indicate more general pollution levels, this figure is unrealistically high, both intuitively and in comparison with results from revealed and stated preference studies. Although this result may be due in part to the high incomes of the survey sample, surprisingly high values seem to be a fairly common finding in LS [life satisfaction] research to date."
13. Regarding habituation, Menz and Welsch (2010) experiment with including lagged income and find it to enter negatively and to considerably raise the coefficient on current income. In contrast to income, Menz (2011) found no habituation with respect to environmental quality.

REFERENCES

Ambrey, C. and C. Fleming (2014), 'The causal effect of income on life satisfaction and the implications for valuing non-market goods', *Economics Letters*, **123** (2), 131–134.

Baumol, W.J. and W.E. Oates (eds) (1988), *The Theory of Environmental Policy*, 2nd edition, Cambridge, UK: Cambridge University Press.

Bolton, G.E. and R. Ockenfels (2000), 'ERC: a theory of equity, reciprocity, and competition', *American Economic Review*, **90** (1), 166–193.

Brekke, K.A. and R.B. Howarth (eds) (2002), *Status, Growth and the Environment: Goods as Symbols in Applied Welfare Economics*, Cheltenham, UK and Northampton, MA, USA: Edward Elgar Publishing.

Clark, A.E. and C. D'Ambrosio (2015), 'Attitudes to income inequality: experimental and survey evidence', in Anthony B. Atkinson and François Bourguignon (eds), *Handbook of Income Distribution*, Amsterdam, Netherlands: Elsevier, pp. 1147–1208.

Clark, A.E., Frijters, P. and M.A. Shields (2008), 'Relative income, happiness and utility: an explanation for the easterlin paradox and other puzzles', *Journal of Economic Literature*, **46** (1), 95–144.

DellaVigna, S. (2009), 'Psychology and economics: evidence from the field', *Journal of Economic Literature*, **47** (2), 315–372.

Duesenberry, J.S. (1949), *Income, Saving, and the Theory of Consumer Behavior*, Cambridge, MA, USA and London, UK: Harvard University Press.

Easterlin, R.A. (1974), 'Does economic growth improve the human lot? Some empirical evidence', in Paul R. David and Melvin W. Reder (eds), *Nations and Households in Economic Growth: Essays in Honor of Moses Abramowitz*, New York, USA: Academic Press, pp. 89–125.

Easterlin, R.A. (1995), 'Will raising the incomes of all increase the happiness of all?', *Journal of Economic Behavior and Organization*, **27** (1), 35–47.

Easterlin, R.A. (2001), 'Income and happiness: towards a unified theory', *Economic Journal*, **111** (473), 465–484.

Easterlin, R.A., Angelescu-McVey, L., Switek, M., Sawangfa O. and J. Zweig (2010), 'The happiness–income paradox revisited', *PNAS*, **107**, 22463–22468.

Fehr, E. and K.M. Schmidt (1999), 'A theory of fairness, competition and co-operation', *Quarterly Journal of Economics*, **114** (3), 817–868.

Ferreira, S. and M. Moro (2010), 'On the use of subjective well-being data for environmental valuation', *Environmental and Resource Economics*, **46** (3), 249–273.

Frank, Robert H. (ed.) (1985), *Choosing the Right Pond: Human Behavior and the Quest for Status*, New York, USA: Oxford University Press.

Freeman, A. Myrrick (ed.) (2003), *The Measurement of Environmental and Resource Values: Theory and Methods*, 2nd edition, Washington, DC, USA: Resources for the Future.

Frey, B.S. and A. Stutzer (2002), 'What can economists learn from happiness research?', *Journal of Economic Literature*, **40** (2), 402–435.

Gui, B. and R. Sugden (eds) (2005), *Economics and Social Interaction*, Cambridge, UK: Cambridge University Press.

Howarth, R.B. (1996), 'Status effects and environmental externalities', *Ecological Economics*, **16** (1), 25–34.

Howarth, R.B. (2006), 'Optimal environmental taxes under relative consumption effects', *Ecological Economics*, **58**, 209–219.

Johansson, P-O. (ed.) (1987), *The Economic Theory and Measurement of Environmental Benefits*, Cambridge, UK: Cambridge University Press.

Kahneman, D. and A. Tversky (1979), 'Prospect theory: an analysis of decision under risk', *Econometrica*, **47**, 263–291.

Kahneman, D., Wakker, P.P. and R. Sarin (1997), 'Back to Bentham? Explorations of experienced utility', *Quarterly Journal of Economics*, **112** (2), 375–405.

Layard, R. (2006), 'Happiness and public policy: a challenge to the profession', *Economic Journal*, **116** (510), C24–C33.

Loewenstein, G. and D. Adler (1995), 'A bias in the prediction of tastes', *Economic Journal*, **105** (431), 929–937.

Loewenstein, G. and D.A. Schkade (1999), 'Wouldn't it be nice? Predicting future feelings', in Daniel Kahneman, Ed Diener and Norbert Schwarz (eds), *Well Being: The Foundations of Hedonic Psychology*, New York, USA: Russell Sage Foundation.

Loewenstein, G., O'Donohue, T. and M. Rabin (2003), 'Projection bias in predicting future utility', *Quarterly Journal of Economics*, **118** (4), 1209–1248.

Luechinger, S. (2009), 'Valuing air quality using the life satisfaction approach', *Economic Journal*, **119** (536), 482–515.

MacKerron, G. and S. Mourato (2009), 'Life satisfaction and air quality in London', *Ecological Economics*, **68** (5), 1441–1453.

Menz, T. (2011), 'Do people habituate to air pollution? Evidence from international life satisfaction data', *Ecological Economics*, **71**, 211–219.

Menz, T. and H. Welsch (2010), 'Population aging and environmental preferences in OECD countries: The case of air pollution', *Ecological Economics*, **69** (12), 2582–2589.

Ng, Y.K. and J. Wang (1993), 'Relative income, aspirations, environmental quality, individual and political myopia: why may the rat-race for material growth be welfare reducing?', *Mathematical Social Sciences*, **23** (1), 3–23.

Powdthavee, N. (2010), 'How much does money really matter? Estimating the causal effect of income on happiness', *Empirical Economics*, **39** (1), 77–92.

Rehdanz, K., Welsch, H., Narita, D. and T. Okubo (2015), 'Well-being effects of a major natural disaster: the case of Fukushima', *Journal of Economic Behavior and Organization*, **116**, 500–517.

Roback, J. (1982), 'Wages, rents, and the quality of life', *Journal of Political Economy*, **90** (6), 1257–1278.

Sent, E.M. (2004), 'Behavioral economics: how psychology made its (limited) way back into economics', *History of Political Economy*, **36** (4), 735–760.

Simon, H.A. (1955), 'A behavioral model of rational choice', *Quarterly Journal of Economics*, **69** (1), 99–118.

Solnick, S.J. and D. Hemenway (1998), 'Is more always better? A survey on positional concerns', *Journal of Economic Behavior and Organization*, **37** (3), 373–383.

Solnick, S.J. and D. Hemenway (2005), 'Are positional concerns stronger in some domains than in others?', *American Economic Review*, **95** (2), 147–151.

Stiglitz, J.E., Sen, A. and J.P. Fitoussi (2009), 'Report by the Commission on the Measurement of Economic Performance and Social Progress (CMEPSP)', accessed 16 November 2017 at http://www.stiglitz-sen-fitoussi.fr/en/documents.htm.

Tversky, A. and D. Kahneman (1981), 'The framing of decisions and the psychology of choice', *Science*, **211** (4481), 453–458.

Veblen, T. (ed.) (1899), *The Theory of the Leisure Class*, London, UK: Macmillan, George Allen & Unwin.

Welsch, H. (2009), 'Implications of happiness research for environmental economics', *Ecological Economics*, **68** (11), 2735–2742

Welsch, H. (2016), 'Electricity externalities, siting, and the energy mix: a survey', *International Review of Environmental and Resource Economics*, **10** (1), 57–94.

Welsch, H. and P. Biermann (2014), 'Electricity supply preferences in Europe, evidence from subjective well-being data', *Resource and Energy Economics*, **38**, 38–60.

Welsch, H. and J. Kühling (2011), 'Are pro-environmental consumption choices utility maximizing? Evidence from subjective well-being data', *Ecological Economics*, **72**, 75–87.
Welsch, H. and S. Ferreira (2013), 'Environment, well-being, and experienced preference', *International Review of Environmental and Resource Economics*, **7**, 205–239.
Wilson, T.D. and D.T. Gilbert (2003), 'Affective forecasting', in Mark P. Zanna (ed.), *Advances in Experimental Social Psychology*, Vol. 35, New York, USA: Elsevier, pp. 345–411.

5. Subjective wellbeing as valuation system of environmental quality: an environmental social sciences approach

Jianjun Tang, Honghao Ren and Henk Folmer

5.1 INTRODUCTION

A key objective of environmental economics is to develop a thorough understanding of the interaction between the environment and the economy, and of the development of policy handles to promote sustainable use of the environment. For the latter purpose, the balancing of the marginal benefits and marginal costs of the environmental goods to be preserved or to be sacrificed is needed. For goods that carry prices, balancing of marginal benefits and costs of a good is based on its price, so as to determine the marginal rate of substitution of income for the good. However, the use of most environmental goods does not involve market transactions. Consequently, they do not carry market-determined prices, thus hampering the trade-off between their marginal costs and marginal benefits.

As an alternative, a variety of methods has been developed to assess the value of environmental assets. The methods are based on the notions of compensating (equivalent) variation, which refer to the amount of money that needs to be changed to an individual's income after (before) a change in condition, for example, a price change of a good or change in environmental quality, so that the individual's utility is the same as without (with) the change in economic conditions (Hicks, 1941; van Kooten and Folmer, 2004; Kollmuss and Agyeman, 2002). In environmental economics, the concepts of compensating and equivalent variation are used to elicit an individual's maximum willingness to pay (WTP) in monetary terms for improved environmental quality, or the minimum willingness to accept (WTA) for compensation for foregoing the environmental good or for incurring environmental degradation. The information collected is used as input into the development of policy handles aimed at promoting environmentally friendly behaviors.

As in other subfields of neoclassical economics, valuation in environmental economics relies upon utility maximization, which is assumed to sufficiently and accurately capture an individual's decision-making framework. In this setting, consumers are assumed to be rational agents who have stable preferences, possess perfect information, and make utility-maximizing choices (van Kooten and Folmer, 2004). However, the theoretical framework of utility maximization disregards the complexity of human decision making and does not necessarily represent actual individual behavior (Folmer, 2009; Lindenberg, 2001a). Consequently, it suffers from several drawbacks. First, it was shown in a variety of contexts that economic preferences may manifest systematic deviations from the predictions of utility maximization (Simon, 1957; Thaler, 2016). That is, in addition to, or combined with, maximizing utility, humans often act based on regret minimization (Chorus et al., 2011), risk and uncertainty aversion (Tversky and Kahneman, 1991; Wakker, 2010), or loss aversion (Abdellaoui et al., 2016). Stationarity in preferences is also challenged in that preferences are not a priori well formed, but rather are formed through a process of repetition and experience (Ariely et al., 2003; List, 2003; Bateman et al., 2008; Lindenberg, 2001a, 2001b). Furthermore, individuals usually do not possess perfect information, nor do they have the cognitive capability to fully process the information they carry, limiting their abilities to make perfectly rational decisions. Finally, decisions are usually concluded in the context of norms, values, manners and customs, and social interaction, rather than by individual agents in isolation (Lindenberg, 2001a, 2001b). Although some of the assumptions are sometimes relaxed (for example, Stiglitz, 2000 on asymmetric information), modifications of the standard model are merely incidental "on-top" modifications rather than basic alterations of the utility maximization model, leaving the fundamental utilitarian framework untouched (Keen, 2001).

When it comes to modeling an individual's demand for environmental amenities, neoclassical environmental economics typically utilizes capitalized environmental outcomes. That is, an individual's valuation of environmental quality is given by the willingness to pay or accept in monetary terms (Welsch and Ferreira, 2014). However, based on the argument that an individual's preferences may deviate systematically from utility maximization, it is questionable whether capitalized environmental outcome adequately and fully captures one's valuation of environmental quality. Furthermore, utility arising from money alone is unlikely to catch all aspects of environmental quality, because in the neoclassical setting valuation rests on decision utility, that is, the prospective assessment of future outcomes. Kahneman et al. (1997) showed that decision utility is less measurable than experienced utility, which refers to an individual's assessment of their retrospective hedonic experience. The reason is that individuals have a clearer sense of the hedonic consequences of their past actions than of the influence of their attitudes on future acts (Kahneman and Sugden, 2005). Thus, respondents in contingent valuation studies as well as in other preference surveys, which measure respondents' willingness to pay for environmental goods, are often uncertain or unfamiliar with the interview context, particularly the assessment of hypothetical situations. This may lead to systematic errors because their choices are reflections of their attitudes which cannot be well translated into preferences in monetary terms (Kahneman and Sugden, 2005).

The shortcomings of the utility maximization framework listed above are key topics of the social science sister disciplines of economics, notably psychology, sociology, law, anthropology and political sciences. A natural approach to overcome the weaknesses of the neoclassical environmental economics framework is then to integrate it with the sister social sciences, leading to what we would call environmental social sciences (ESS).[1] It offers a more comprehensive and more adequate framework for the understanding of complex human–environment interactions by uniting complementary disciplinary theoretical frameworks and research methods.[2] Adequate understanding of environmental valuation and behavior requires the integration of economic factors as well as psychological and sociological factors, such as perception, knowledge, social networks and norms, which goes beyond the partial and incidental status of economic factors in neoclassical environmental economics models (Folmer, 2009). The above claims are supported by evidence from psychological and behavioral economics theories and experiments as well as neuro-economics, which have challenged the assumption of self-interested and utility-maximizing individuals with stable preferences. Research in these areas has shown that humans have limited and imperfect knowledge, distorted memory and limited processing capability, which lead to context-specific choices made without careful deliberation, and are affected by physiological and emotional states as well as perceptions and social norms (Samson, 2014).

Several of the shortcomings of the traditional methods premised on the decision utility framework used to value environmental functions can be overcome by using the notion of happiness or subjective wellbeing. This is because people make more accurate hedonic assessments based on past experiences than in forecasting hedonic outcomes of future choices (Welsch and Ferreira, 2014; Kahneman and Thaler, 2006). From this it follows that the value of an environmental good is its contribution to subjective wellbeing. Subjective wellbeing is thus an appropriate substitute to decision utility theory in environmental valuations. By regressing subjective wellbeing on environmental quality and income, it is possible to calculate the marginal rate of substitution of income for environmental quality (Welsch, 2009). In addition, psychologists have provided validated and reliable (survey) instruments to measure subjective wellbeing (Diener et al., 2017), as opposed to stated preference methods (for example, discrete-choice experiments) which often require respondents to answer a battery of cognitively more demanding questions (Day et al., 2012). Finally, as a reliable empirical substitute of decision-based utility, subjective wellbeing is a fundamental tool in welfare analysis and cost–benefit studies.

The objective of this chapter is to present a framework in which subjective wellbeing is the basic concept in the valuation approach of environmental quality embedded in environmental social sciences. The remainder of the chapter is organized as follows. Section 5.2 summarizes the basic features of neoclassical environmental valuation, describes the notions of experienced utility and subjective wellbeing, and outlines the basic features of an environmental social science. In section 5.3, we present the econometric approach LISREL and PLS which are suitable to measure subjective wellbeing from an environmental social sciences perspective. Section 5.4 discusses an environmental social sciences case study with subjective wellbeing as the outcome, and section 5.5 concludes.

5.2 NEOCLASSICAL ECONOMIC VALUATION, EXPERIENCED UTILITY, SUBJECTIVE WELLBEING AND ENVIRONMENTAL SOCIAL SCIENCES

The first subsection presents a brief summary of the key neoclassical economic concepts to value environmental quality – that is, the willingness to pay (WTP), the willingness to accept (WTA), equivalent variation (EV) and compensating variation (CV) – and their properties and shortcomings.

5.2.1 Neoclassical Economic Valuation of Environmental Quality

The starting point of the neoclassical economic valuation framework is a "rational" utility-maximizing agent with utility function (van Kooten and Folmer, 2004):

$$U = F(I, G, X, e) \tag{5.1}$$

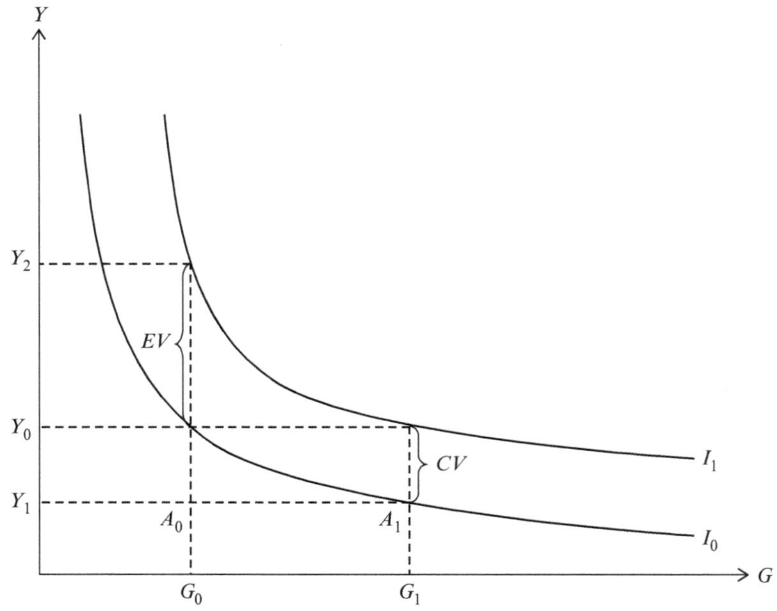

Source: Adapted from van Kooten and Folmer (2004).

Figure 5.1 Compensating surplus and equivalent surplus

where U denotes utility, I income, G environmental quality, $\boldsymbol{X}$ a vector of control variables, for example socio-demographic characteristics, and e the error term. F represents the (often linear) relationship between U and $I, G, \boldsymbol{X}$ and e.

From (5.1) the key neoclassical economic concepts to measure environmental quality are derived, as illustrated in Figure 5.1. An agent has income Y_0 and consumes the current quantity of environmental good G_0 which gives utility U_0 on the indifference curve I_0. An improvement of the consumption from G_0 to G_1 increases utility to U_1 on indifference curve I_1. Two types of measures can be applied to measure the welfare change: the compensating variation (CV) and the equivalent variation (EV). The CV is defined as follows. In the case of an improvement in environmental quality, it is the income change, that is, payment, that makes the agent indifferent between consuming the original level G_0 and the higher level G_1. In the case of a deterioration the income change is a compensation. Hence, the CV is a payment/compensation such that the individual remains at their initial level of utility. It can be represented as: $U(G_0, Y_0) \sim U(G_1, Y_0 - CV)$ where $CV = Y_0 - Y_1$. The EV is a compensation/payment such that the individual attains the same level of welfare as if the environmental quality were improved/deteriorated. Hence, it is a compensation for an improvement in environmental quality that fails to occur and it is a willingness to pay for preventing deterioration of environmental quality. It can be represented as: $U(G_0, Y_0 + EV) \sim U(G_1, Y_0)$ where $EV = Y_2 - Y_0$. The CV is typically used to measure an agent's willingness to pay for an environmental improvement. By contrast, EV quantifies the agent's willingness to accept (income gain) for forgoing an environmental improvement. In practice, various methods have been developed to measure people's evaluation of environmental quality based on the above concepts, notably the WTP, that is, the maximum amount of money an individual is willing to sacrifice to obtain a good. For an introductory overview, see Shechter (2000).

Despite the fact that the estimation of WTA/WTP has received broad applications, it suffers from several drawbacks. First, people may find they are uneasy about making trade-offs between environmental amenities and money, so that the CV or EV is likely to be measured with substantial error (Kahneman and Thaler, 2006). In addition, stated preference methods such as contingent valuation typically assess respondents' attitudes towards the environmental good, rather than their preferences for the good (Kahneman and Sugden, 2005). Preferences, in the strict sense of the term, are absolute values and are extensional so that \$3 are preferred to \$2 if \$2 are preferred to \$1. However, attitudes are non-extensional, limiting respondents' ability to transform their attitudes into absolute WTP monetary values. Suppose an individual holds a positive attitude towards wildlife conservation. When asked whether they are willing to pay to the fund of an endangered species conservation program, they may express their positive attitude, but may find it difficult to express this attitude in monetary terms. When presented with an open-ended question where respondents can state their WTP in monetary units, their WTP for saving one endangered species is often similar to the WTP for saving two endangered species (known as scope insensitivity; Veisten et al., 2004). Furthermore, stated preference questions are often unfamiliar to respondents, especially with regard to discrete-choice experiments which have a specification of multiple attributes and levels. This means that respondents do not have a clear idea of the monetary values of the scenarios questioned. Meanwhile, it might also be questionable to allocate a predetermined reference price where respondents could indicate whether they are willing to pay the price or not. This is because the closed-ended design is often susceptible to anchoring, which refers to the phenomenon through which the presentation of a predetermined price creates an illusion to respondents that the price is the "correct" price. Hence, respondents might anchor their prior unknown WTP to the given price (Chien et al., 2005; Carlsson et al., 2007).

Another weakness of monetary WTP and WTA measures is that money only captures the materialistic aspect of the environmental good while other aspects of wellbeing, for example social connectedness and inequality, are not taken into consideration. Laboratory experiments have suggested that people in a social context are often motivated by other objectives beyond their self-interests, such as praise and approbation, known as pro-social preferences (Charness and Rabin, 2002). In addition, WTP and WTA studies often suffer from social desirability biases as a result of altruism or "warm-glow" effects where respondents often give false positive views to please interviewers to create a positive social image (Andreoni, 1990).

5.2.2 Experienced Utility and Subjective Wellbeing Approach

In this subsection, we show that several of the above-mentioned drawbacks can be overcome by the notion of subjective wellbeing (SWB) in the valuation of environmental assets. According to Diener (2000), SWB refers to the affective and cognitive evaluation of a good and related emotional experience. Although SWB is typically used interchangeably with the notion of happiness or life satisfaction,[3] it is a much broader concept than happiness. Specifically, it is an umbrella term that includes several separable components: (1) global life satisfaction; (2) satisfaction with important domains; (3) indicates positive effects; and (4) low levels of negative effects (Diener et al., 2017).

The notion of SWB is rooted in experienced utility and replaces the utility-based notion (Welsch, 2009; Welsch and Kuhling, 2009). A general framework can be formulated as follows:

$$SWB = F(I, G, \boldsymbol{X}, e) \tag{5.2}$$

where I, G, $\boldsymbol{X}$, and e are the same as in (5.1) and SWB represents subjective-wellbeing. If F represents a linear relationship we have:

$$SWB = \beta_1 I + \beta_2 G + \beta_3 \boldsymbol{X} + e \tag{5.3}$$

Estimating (5.3) provides a marginal subjective wellbeing derived from income $(\frac{\partial SWB}{\partial I} = \beta_1)$ and from environmental quality $(\frac{\partial SWB}{\partial G} = \beta_2)$. Consequently, the marginal value of improved environmental quality equals the constant marginal rate of substitution (MRS) between income and the need for environmental goods:

$$MRS = \frac{\dfrac{\partial SWB}{\partial G}}{\dfrac{\partial SWB}{\partial I}} = \frac{\beta_2}{\beta_1} \tag{5.4}$$

The above experienced utility approach is a more appropriate approach to evaluate environmental assets for the following reasons. First, it is a measure of experienced utility (hedonic experience) which is a better measure of utility than the decision utility measure (that is, WTP). This is because economic agents often make systematic errors by basing their forecasts of future choices on intuition rather than on carefully considered judgments (Kahneman and Thaler, 2006). Subjective wellbeing, on the other hand, is a measure of experienced utility – that is, an *ex post* assessment of past outcomes – which allows agents to make forecasts based on past memories and thus provides more accurate hedonic forecasts (Kahneman and Thaler, 2006). Second, SWB and environmental conditions can be elicited independently so that respondents need not take into account that the two concepts are related (von Möllendorff and Welsch, 2017). For instance, a higher level of air pollution is in theory likely to be associated with a lower level of subjective wellbeing. However, the questions relating to SWB need not be directly related to air pollution. This is in principle preferable to conventional valuation techniques, which are based on the direct relationship between WTP and air quality and require respondents to answer unfamiliar and cognitively complicated questions, such as making trade-offs between environmental improvements and income (Carlsson et al., 2012).

5.2.3 Environmental Social Sciences

In this section, we show that estimation of equation (5.3) can benefit from insights from environmental social sciences (ESS). In the ESS framework, the general (or substantive) goal of a social agent has three hierarchically ordered layers, the highest of which is the improvement of subjective wellbeing, followed by two general goals, namely physical and social wellbeing. In addition, there are instrumental goals for realizing the higher-level goals (Lindenberg, 2001c). To achieve these goals, Lindenberg (2001b) proposed a general model of human behavior with six features (known as RREEMM):

- the agent has the rationality to develop ways to achieve the goals (denoted as "Resourceful");
- under restrictions (denoted as "Restricted");
- has the ability to learn from experience (denoted as "Expectations");
- to make valuations of different alternatives (denoted as "Evaluating");
- has the motivation to improve the conditions to achieve the goals (denoted as "Motivated");
- and to identify the elements useful to define choice-situations (denoted as "Meaningful").

Lindenberg (2001b) and Folmer (2009) showed that neoclassical economics is a submodel of RREEMM. Particularly, neoclassical economics assumes that an agent is subject to a budget constraint (Restricted), has the desire (Motivation) to achieve a goal (that is, utility maximization), has the ability to think of ways to achieve the goal (Resourceful) and to attach values to different products (Evaluating). Meaningful and Expectations are irrelevant in the neoclassical framework because of complete information on price and products. Therefore, under the umbrella of environmental social sciences, neoclassical environmental economics should go beyond its boundaries (Folmer and Johansson-Stenman, 2011; Lindenberg, 2001a, 2001b).

Environmental models in the areas of the sister social sciences fit into the EES framework as well. Environmental psychology and sociology study the interactions between humans and the environment by modeling the psycho-social roots of pro-environmental behaviors (Steg et al., 2014). Typical psycho-social factors related to environmental behaviors include awareness, knowledge, attitudes and social norms. Some well-known theories of the foundations synthesizing these factors in the environmental domain are the theory of planned behavior (Ajzen, 1991, 1985, 2015), the norm-activation model (Schwartz and Howard, 1981; Onwezen et al., 2013), and the value–belief–norm theory (Stern, 2000; Fornara et al., 2016).

The theory of planned behavior assumes that pro-environmental behavior is influenced by three core psychological constructs: the attitude towards pro-environmental behavior, that is, the positive feelings about the behavior in question and the desirability of its outcome; the subjective norm, that is, the belief about the social environment surrounding the behavior and the social pressure to perform the behavior; and perceived behavioral control which refers to the easiness and the perceived self-efficacy to perform the behavior. The attitude, subjective norm and perceived behavioral control are intercorrelated and complement each other in the process of strengthening intention.

The norm activation model was originally developed to explain altruism and pro-social behaviors but was adopted to study environmental behavior at a later stage. The core of the model is that the formation of personal norms is an antecedent to pro-environmental (or social) behaviors (Onwezen et al., 2013; Schwartz, 1977). Two other concepts that are relevant to environmental behaviors are: responsibility, that is, a person's feelings of responsibility for their behaviors; and awareness of consequences, that is, the understanding of the positive (negative) consequences for others when the behavior is (is not) performed. De Groot and Steg (2009) empirically demonstrated that personal norms are induced by responsibility, which in turn is activated by the awareness of consequences. The value–belief–norm theory, which is an extension of the norm activation model, considers the role of personal values – that is, egoistic, altruistic and biospheric values – as the ultimate roots for environmentalism (Stern, 2000). It postulates that behavior is directly induced by personal norms and assumes a causal chain of five psychological factors (namely: personal values, general environmental attitudes, awareness of consequences, the ascription of responsibility, and personal norms) such that each factor in the chain is an antecedent of the next factor. Supplementary to the individual-focused models described above, Axsen and Kurani (2012) drew attention to the interpersonal interactions among multiple individuals in the context of a social network through which pro-environmental behaviors may spread from one individual to another.

These theoretical frameworks have received empirical support when it comes to the prediction of pro-environmental behaviors. For instance, the theory of planned behavior was found to be empirically appropriate to predict consumers' purchase intentions of energy-efficient household appliances (Tan et al., 2017), and employees' engagement in environmental behaviors in a workplace setting (Greaves et al., 2013). The norm activation model was applied to analyze the psychological roots of employees' electricity-saving behavior (Zhang et al., 2013). The value–belief–norm theory was used to model the intention among households to use renewable energy sources (Fornara et al., 2016), and the intent of a group of young travelers to behave in an environmentally friendly way while traveling (Kiatkawsin and Han, 2017).

The above-mentioned models entail psychological factors, such as intention, awareness and perception, which are not directly observable; that is, are latent. To measure and analyze latent variables, structural equation models can be applied. They are discussed in the next section.

5.3 METHODS TO ESTIMATE SUBJECTIVE WELLBEING (AND OTHER LATENT VARIABLES): STRUCTURAL EQUATION MODELS

5.3.1 Latent Variables

Measurement of subjective wellbeing or happiness is typically measured on an 11-point scale by the single question (Welsch, 2009; Diener, 2000; Kahneman and Krueger, 2006): "All things considered, how satisfied are you with your life as a whole these days?" The single question, however, may be subject to measurement error due, for example, to misinterpretation of the question or incorrect recording of the answers. In addition, it does not capture the multidimensional nature of subjective wellbeing (Folmer and Oud, 2008; Little et al., 2002). Both problems can be overcome by taking subjective wellbeing as a latent variable or a theoretical construct.

Latent variables refer to the phenomena that are supposed to exist but cannot be directly observed (Bollen and Lennox, 1991; Fornell and Larcker, 1981). Well-known examples of latent variables are intelligence, propensity to consume, social inequality, socio-economic status, economic expectation and permanent income. Since latent variables cannot be directly observed, they are given empirical meanings by directly observable variables derived from experience (correspondence statements). For instance, intelligence is measured by intelligence tests; socio-economic status by income, education and profession. Note that observable indicators of a latent variable are contaminated with measurement error, except when there is a one-to-one correspondence between a latent variable and its indicator (Cheung and Rensvold, 2002; Steenkamp and Baumgartner, 2000).

Based on their causal relationship, latent variables or theoretical constructs can be divided into two categories: (1) reflective latent variables which "cause" the corresponding indicators; for example, the scores on intelligence tests are caused by the latent variable intelligence; and (2) formative latent variables where the latent variables are "formed" (caused) by their indicators. For instance, income and education make up socio-economic status (Bollen and Lennox, 1991; Haenlein and Kaplan, 2004). The measurement models of latent variables differ for these two categories.

Reflective indicators depend on their associated latent variables. In the example shown in Figure 5.2(a), the observable indicators y_1, y_2 and y_3 are caused by the latent variable η. Specifically, the relationships between the three reflective indicators and the corresponding latent variable η read as follows:

$$y_1 = \lambda_1\eta + \varepsilon_1 \tag{5.5}$$

$$y_2 = \lambda_2\eta + \varepsilon_2 \tag{5.6}$$

$$y_3 = \lambda_3\eta + \varepsilon_3 \tag{5.7}$$

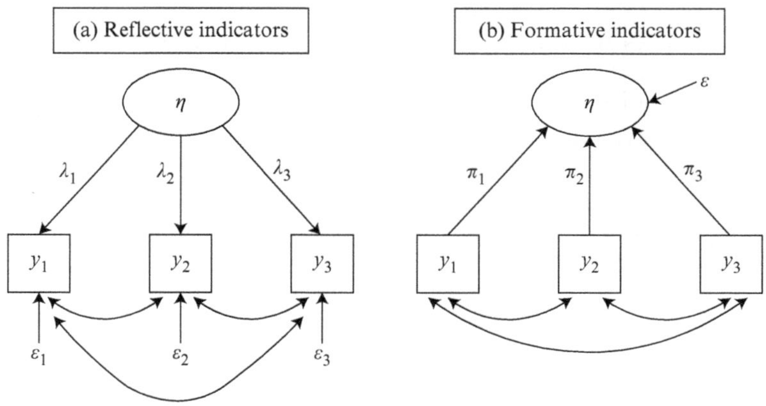

Note: Latent variables are presented in ellipses and observable indicators in boxes.

Source: Modified from Monecke and Leisch (2012).

Figure 5.2 Path diagrams of (a) reflective and (b) formative indicators

where λ_1, λ_2 and λ_3 are factor loadings indicating the impacts of η on the indicators, and ε_1, ε_2 and ε_3 are *i.i.d.* error terms. Equations (5.5), (5.6) and (5.7) indicate that changes in the latent variable η bring about changes in all three indicators. This means that (positive) reflective indicators of the same latent variable are highly positively correlated because they measure the same underlying latent variable (Bollen and Lennox, 1991). For instance, a high score on one intelligence test is likely to go together with a high score on other tests.

By contrast, in the case of formative indicators, the influences are from the indicators to the latent variable. For instance, the latent variable "environment quality" is a combination of formative indicators such as lack of clean water, presence of sulfur dioxide (SO_2), dissolved oxygen in rivers, fecal coliforms in rivers, municipal waste per capita and carbon emission per capita (Shafik, 1994). An increase of carbon emission per capita results in a decrease of environment quality. But a decrease of environment quality does not necessarily imply an increase of carbon emission per capita. Figure 5.2(b) depicts the relationships between the latent variable η and its formative indicators y_1, y_2 and y_3. The relationship reads:

$$\eta = \pi_1 y_1 + \pi_2 y_2 + \pi_3 y_3 + \varepsilon \tag{5.8}$$

where π_1, π_2 and π_3 are coefficients and ε is an *i.i.d.* error term. Formative indicators can have positive, negative or zero relationships with one another (Hulland, 1999). A change in one indicator need not go together with a change in other indicators; and if it does, not in the same direction (Chin and Newsted, 1999). For instance, an increase of carbon emission per capita does not necessarily imply an increase of sulphur dioxide (SO_2).

5.3.2 LISREL-SEM

LISREL-SEM (LISREL for short), which owes its prominence to the well-known software package LISREL (Jöreskog and Sörbom, 2006), is the best-known model to handle latent variables and their indicators within one framework (Haenlein and Kaplan, 2004). A general LISREL consists of two parts: a measurement model (equation 5.9 for the endogenous latent variables and equation 5.10 for the exogenous latent variables, respectively) and a structural model (equation 5.11). The measurement model specifies how the latent variables affect their reflective indicators, and the structural model specifies the causal relationships among the latent endogenous and latent exogenous variables as well as the relationships among the latent endogenous variables mutually. A LISREL can be represented as follows:

$$\boldsymbol{y} = \boldsymbol{\Lambda}_y \boldsymbol{\eta} + \boldsymbol{\varepsilon} \tag{5.9}$$

$$\boldsymbol{x} = \boldsymbol{\Lambda}_x \boldsymbol{\xi} + \boldsymbol{\delta} \tag{5.10}$$

$$\boldsymbol{\eta} = \boldsymbol{B}\boldsymbol{\eta} + \boldsymbol{\Gamma}\boldsymbol{\xi} + \boldsymbol{\zeta} \tag{5.11}$$

where $\boldsymbol{\eta}$ is an $m \times 1$ vector of endogenous latent variables, $\boldsymbol{y}$ a $p \times 1$ vector of observed variables to measure the endogenous latent variables, $\boldsymbol{\xi}$ an $n \times 1$ vector of exogeneous latent variables, $\boldsymbol{x}$ a $q \times 1$ vector of observed variables to measure the exogenous latent variables ξ, $\boldsymbol{\Lambda}_y$ and $\boldsymbol{\Lambda}_x$ are $p \times m$ and $q \times n$ matrices which specify the relationships between $\boldsymbol{\eta}$ and ξ and their indicators $\boldsymbol{y}$ and $\boldsymbol{x}$, respectively, and $\boldsymbol{\varepsilon}$ $(p \times 1)$ and $\boldsymbol{\delta}$ $(q \times 1)$ are *i.i.d.* error terms. In the structural equation (5.11), $\boldsymbol{B}$ $(m \times m)$ represents the relationship among the endogenous variables, $\boldsymbol{\Gamma}$ $(q \times n)$ the relationship between the exogenous latent variables and endogenous latent variables, and ζ $(m \times 1)$ is an *i.i.d.* error term. The covariance matrices of $\boldsymbol{\varepsilon}$, $\boldsymbol{\delta}$, ζ, and ξ are:

$$\mathrm{cov}(\boldsymbol{\varepsilon}) = \boldsymbol{\Theta}_{\varepsilon}\,\mathrm{cov}(\boldsymbol{\delta}) = \boldsymbol{\Theta}_{\delta}$$

$$\mathrm{cov}(\zeta) = \boldsymbol{\Psi}\,\mathrm{cov}(\xi) = \boldsymbol{\Phi}$$

where $\boldsymbol{\Theta}_{\varepsilon}$ is a $p \times p$ matrix, $\boldsymbol{\Theta}_{\delta}$ a $q \times q$ matrix, $\boldsymbol{\Psi}$ a $m \times m$ matrix, and $\boldsymbol{\Phi}$ a $n \times n$ matrix. For details we refer to Jöreskog and Sörbom (1996), Kline (2015), Muthén (1984) and Schumacker and Lomax (2004).

Estimation of LISREL focuses on estimating the unknown model parameters in such a way that the distance (in some metric) between the theoretical covariance matrix (in terms of the unknown parameters in 5.9–5.11) and the observed covariance matrix is minimized (Hair et al., 2011; Rigdon, 1998). The most common estimator is maximum likelihood, although various alternatives are available. For an overview of model identification, estimation, testing and model modification, we refer to Reinartz et al. (2009), Haenlein and Kaplan (2004), Jöreskog and Sörbom (1996), Kline (2015), MacCallum et al. (1996) and Olsson et al. (2000).

5.3.3 PLS-SEM

PLS-SEM (PLS for short) was introduced by Wold (1975) under the name NIPALS (non-linear iterative partial least squares). Like LISREL, PLS is made up of two components: a measurement model and a structural model (Chin and Newsted, 1999; Haenlein and Kaplan, 2004). The measurement models, referred to as outer models in the PLS literature, represent the relationships between the latent variables and their associated observable indicators (Joe et al., 2014; Monecke and Leisch, 2012). Observable indicators may correlate with each other, but each observable indicator is related to only one latent variable. The structural model, also referred to as the inner model in the PLS literature, depicts the relationship among the latent variables (Chin, 2010).

PLS can deal with models which have formative or reflective indicators, or both. For models with reflective indicators, the measurement models and the structural model in PLS have the same equations as in LISREL. For models with formative indicators, the measurement models in PLS are:

$$\boldsymbol{\eta} = \boldsymbol{\pi}_{\eta}\mathbf{y} + \boldsymbol{\varepsilon} \tag{5.12}$$

$$\xi = \boldsymbol{\pi}_{\xi}\mathbf{x} + \mathbf{v} \tag{5.13}$$

$$\boldsymbol{\eta} = \boldsymbol{B}\boldsymbol{\eta} + \boldsymbol{\Gamma}\xi + \zeta \tag{5.14}$$

where $\boldsymbol{\eta}$, ξ, $\boldsymbol{y}$, $\boldsymbol{x}$, $\boldsymbol{B}$, $\boldsymbol{\Gamma}$, and ζ are defined as in (5.9)–(5.11). $\boldsymbol{\pi}_\eta$ and $\boldsymbol{\pi}_\xi$ are $m \times p$ and $n \times q$ matrices of the linear relationships between the endogenous and exogenous latent variables with their indicators, respectively. $\boldsymbol{\eta}$ and ξ do not necessarily have the same number of indicators. $\boldsymbol{\varepsilon}$ and $\boldsymbol{v}$ are *i.i.d.* error terms. The covariance matrices of $\boldsymbol{\varepsilon}$ and $\boldsymbol{v}$ are:

$$\text{cov}(\varepsilon) = \boldsymbol{\Theta}_\varepsilon \text{cov}(v) = \boldsymbol{\Theta}_v$$

where $\boldsymbol{\Theta}_\varepsilon$ is a $p \times p$ matrix and $\boldsymbol{\Theta}_v$ a $q \times q$ matrix.

Unlike LISREL, the PLS algorithm is based on maximization of the variance of the dependent variables as explained by the independent ones (Haenlein and Kaplan, 2004; Shmueli et al., 2016). The PLS algorithm is an iterative procedure that generates estimates of the latent variables which fit into the structural and measurement models. The algorithm follows a five-step approach (Hair et al., 2011). In step 1, proxies of the latent variables are computed as the weighted sum of the indicators. For reflective indicators, the computation follows equations (5.9) and (5.10), while for formative indicators it follows equations (5.12) and (5.13) (Fornell and Bookstein, 1982). A weighted sum of indicators can serve as a proxy for a given latent variable. For instance, in SmartPLS, a uniform value of 1 is taken as a weight. In step 2, proxies for the structural model coefficients ($\boldsymbol{B}$ and $\boldsymbol{\Gamma}$) are computed. There are three common weighting schemes to do the computation, namely path weighting, centroid weighting and factor weighting. The centroid weighting scheme only takes into account the sign of the correlations between the latent variable and its neighboring latent variables; the factor weighting scheme uses the strength of correlation between the focal latent variable and its neighbors; and the path weighting scheme considers the standing of the latent variables in the structural model. Antecedents and consequences of the focal latent variables play different roles in the relationships such that the path weighting scheme endows different weights to them. See Chin (1998) for a detailed discussion about the three weighting schemes.

When recursive relationships appear in the structural model, all three weighting schemes can be applied (Hair et al., 2011; Monecke and Leisch, 2012). When recursive relationships do not exist, a centroid weighting scheme or a factor weighting scheme should be applied (Henseler and Sarstedt, 2013). In step 3, estimates of $\boldsymbol{B}$ and $\boldsymbol{\Gamma}$, obtained in step 2, are used to calculate proxies of $\boldsymbol{\eta}$ and ξ. Step 4 calculates the weights between the latent variables and their correlated indicators. The above four steps are repeated until the relative changes of the weights in the outer models between two iterations are smaller than a predefined tolerance (Monecke and Leisch, 2012). Once the weights estimated in step 4 converge to those in step 1, the weights are used to calculate the final values of the latent variables. Then, ordinary least squares (OLS) can be applied to estimate the relationships between latent variables, that is, the coefficients in $\boldsymbol{B}$ and $\boldsymbol{\Gamma}$ (see Hair et al., 2011; Monecke and Leisch, 2012).

Compared to LISREL, the PLS has some advantages. Firstly, it can handle models with formative indicators. Secondly, in contrast to LISREL which was designed for normally distributed variables, particularly observed endogenous variables, PLS works efficiently with variables which do not follow a normal distribution, for instance nominal, ordinal and interval scaled variables. Thirdly, it also works well when each latent variable within a model has a large number of indicators (for example, 200 indicators per latent variable; Haenlein and Kaplan, 2004). Finally, it works well for small samples.

For instance, Sarstedt et al. (2014) showed that PLS provides consistent estimates with 125 observations.

5.4 A CASE STUDY

The focus of this section is on PLS since, as argued above, subjective wellbeing is a formative latent variable. Before going into detail, however, we refer to Li et al. (2014), who applied LISREL to measure subjective wellbeing as a reflective latent variable and to analyze its relationship with other environmental social sciences concepts, particularly risk perception and environmental knowledge.

Using PLS, Musa et al. (2018) developed a community happiness index for Putrajaya, Malaysia. Community happiness was defined as the subjective wellbeing among the residents within a community arising from interaction with fellow residents and the state of the natural environment in the community. It was taken as a formative latent variable which was decomposed hierarchically, as shown in Figure 5.3. First, it was split into two domains, namely eco-environmental wellbeing and human wellbeing, with the former further decomposed into two subdomains (that is, environmental wellbeing and urban governance), and the latter into another two subdomains, namely social wellbeing and economic wellbeing.[4] To take into account the multidimensional nature of environment quality, a Delphi survey was applied among experts from different disciplines. To validate

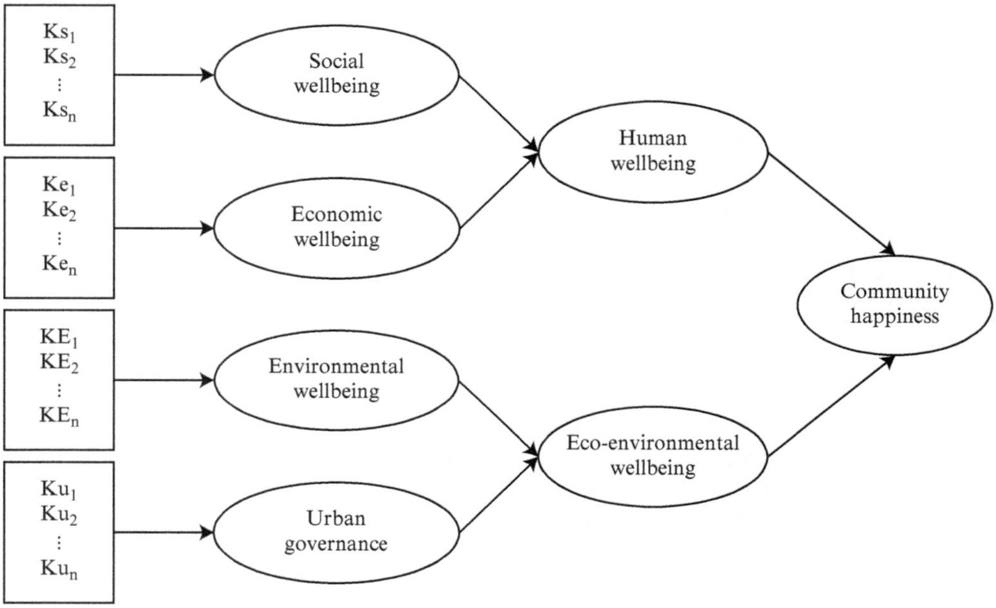

Note: Latent variables are presented in ellipses and observable indicators in boxes.

Source: Musa et al. (2018). Modified by the authors.

Figure 5.3 Hierarchical structural model of CH

the efficacy of the 11 environmental indicators, an empirical analysis was conducted based on a survey of 400 residents. The decision to use PLS as the estimator was appropriate because the environmental elements "caused" environmental wellbeing, and not the other way around. The empirical results showed that an increase of subjective assessment of each of the 11 environment indicators resulted in higher environmental wellbeing. It was also shown that environmental wellbeing contributed most to the formation of community happiness, followed by economic wellbeing, social wellbeing and, finally, urban governance.

5.5 CONCLUSIONS AND DISCUSSIONS

Neoclassical economics and its subdisciplines, including environmental economics, rest on utility-maximizing and stationary economic preferences of agents who possess perfect information and perform perfectly rational decisions. Based on this fundamental assumption, neoclassical environmental economics applies the concepts of compensating and equivalent variation to model an individual's demand for environmental amenities in terms of the maximum willingness to pay or, to a lesser extent, the minimum willingness to accept compensation, for environmental goods. However, the assumptions of neoclassical economics are far too extreme to adequately model behavior. Individuals typically have limited cognitive capability and imperfect information, leading to economic behavior based on "bounded rationality." And preferences are not stationary but are formed through a process of repetition and experience in a social setting. The ultimate outcome is satisficing behavior rather than utility maximization (Simon, 1957). Another shortcoming of neoclassical environmental economics is that it often utilizes capitalized environmental quality which only captures the materialistic aspect of subjective wellbeing and disregards the social aspect of subjective wellbeing. Consequently, a monetary WTP or WTA measure that represents an individual's valuing of the environment is materially unobservable and measured with error.

To overcome several of the above-mentioned drawbacks, we have suggested the environmental social sciences (ESS) approach, with subjective wellbeing as the key measurement concept of environmental quality. We have summarized three main features of the alternative approach. Firstly, subjective wellbeing is based on the assumption that individuals are expected to make valuations based on their past actions (experienced utility) rather than on future actions (decision utility). It differs from conventional WTP and WTA methods (for example, discrete-choice experiments) which often require respondents to answer cognitively demanding questions, for example, making trade-offs between environmental assets and monies. The alternative system allows SWB and environmental conditions to be elicited independently which makes it possible to quantify the willingness to pay under constant utility (Rehdanz et al., 2015; von Möllendorff and Welsch, 2017; Welsch and Biermann, 2016). Note, however, that the association between income and subjective wellbeing may be difficult to identify and subject to biases (Welsch, 2009) which limit the application of the approach.

Secondly, psychological and sociological control variables play important roles in analyzing and predicting environmental behaviors. Ignoring these variables leads to model underspecification and biased and inconsistent estimators of the other (conventional) determinants of environmental behaviors (known as omitted-variable bias). Several typical latent psychological and sociological theories are reviewed in section 5.2. The causality between subjective wellbeing and these psychological variables can be handled by structural equation modelling as well.

Thirdly, subjective wellbeing is usually measured by a single question (see subsection 5.3.1). However, this measurement approach is subject to measurement error and ignorance of the multidimensionality of subjective wellbeing. These problems can be overcome by taking subjective wellbeing as a latent variable, notably as a formative latent variable which allows a closer correspondence between theory and empirics. We discussed the LISREL and PLS frameworks to handle latent variables and their indicators simultaneously, with the latter tailored to handle subjective wellbeing as a formative latent variable. What is more, PLS is robust to non-normally distributed variables and small sample sizes.

As an illustration of PLS, we discussed the case study by Musa et al. (2018) that analyzed community happiness as a formative latent variable with subjective assessment of environment quality as one of its components. It demonstrated the advantage of utilizing PLS in environmental studies. However, it did not take into account psychological variables such as risk perception and environmental knowledge, as in, for example, Li et al. (2014). Psychological variables, such as environmental knowledge and personal norms, influence subjective assessment of environment quality. Particularly, individuals with different environmental knowledge and personal norms are likely to rate environment quality differently. Consequently, the impact of environment quality on subjective wellbeing varies.

To sum up, subjective wellbeing embedded in an environmental social sciences framework allows estimation by structural equation methods that can handle latent and observable variables simultaneously, as an alternative to valuation methods based on neoclassical premises. Detailed (comparative) empirical studies are needed to shed further light on this.

NOTES

1. Similar remarks apply to other subdisciplines of economics, and economics in general. Lindenberg's (2001b, 2001c) social rationality model is a general social science model. Folmer (2009) argues that the utility maximization model is a submodel of Lindenberg's social rationality model.
2. One of the few definitions of environmental social sciences (EES) is given by Moran (2010). He also includes the natural sciences, notably ecology, in his definition. In this chapter, we apply a limited definition of EES restricted to the social sciences only.
3. Welsch and Ferreira (2014) argued that the concept of happiness pertains to the affective aspect of subjective wellbeing, whereas life satisfaction refers to the evaluative aspect.
4. Below we focus on environmental wellbeing and its indicators. See Musa et al. (2018) for detailed discussion about social wellbeing, economic wellbeing and urban governance.

REFERENCES

Abdellaoui, M., Bleichrodt, H., L'Haridon, O. and D. van Dolder (2016), 'Measuring loss aversion under ambiguity: a method to make prospect theory completely observable', *Journal of Risk and Uncertainty*, **52** (1), 1–20.

Ajzen, I. (1985), 'From intentions to actions: a theory of planned behavior', in Julius Kuhl and Jürgen Beckmann (eds), *Action Control: From Cognition to Behavior*, New York, USA: Springer, pp. 11–39.
Ajzen, I. (1991), 'The theory of planned behavior', *Organizational Behavior and Human Decision Processes*, **50** (2), 179–211.
Ajzen, I. (2015), 'The theory of planned behaviour is alive and well, and not ready to retire: a commentary on Sniehotta, Presseau, and Araújo-Soares', *Health Psychology Review*, **9** (2), 131–137.
Andreoni, J. (1990), 'Impure altruism and donations to public goods: a theory of warm-glow giving', *Economic Journal*, **100** (401), 464–477.
Ariely, D., Loewenstein, G. and D. Prelec (2003), '"Coherent arbitrariness": stable demand curves without stable preferences', *Quarterly Journal of Economics*, **118** (1), 73–106.
Axsen, J. and K.S. Kurani (2012), 'Social influence, consumer behavior, and low-carbon energy transitions', *Annual Review of Environment and Resources*, **37** (1), 311–340.
Bateman, I.J., Burgess, D., Hutchinson, W.G. and D.I. Matthews (2008), 'Learning design contingent valuation (LDCV): NOAA guidelines, preference learning and coherent arbitrariness', *Journal of Environmental Economics and Management*, **55** (2), 127–141.
Bollen, K. and R. Lennox (1991), 'Conventional wisdom on measurement: a structural equation perspective', *Psychological Bulletin*, **110** (2), 305–314.
Carlsson, F., Frykblom, P. and C.J. Lagerkvist (2007), 'Preferences with and without prices – does the price attribute affect behavior in stated preference surveys?', *Environmental and Resource Economics*, **38** (2), 155–164.
Carlsson, F., Mørkbak, M.R. and S.B. Olsen (2012), 'The first time is the hardest: a test of ordering effects in choice experiments', *Journal of Choice Modelling*, **5** (2), 19–37.
Charness, G. and M. Rabin (2002), 'Understanding social preferences with simple tests', *Quarterly Journal of Economics*, **117** (3), 817–869.
Cheung, G.W. and R.B. Rensvold (2002), 'Evaluating goodness-of-fit indexes for testing measurement invariance', *Structural Equation Modeling: A Multidisciplinary Journal*, **9** (2), 233–255.
Chien, Y.L., Huang, C.J. and D. Shaw (2005), 'A general model of starting point bias in double-bounded dichotomous contingent valuation surveys', *Journal of Environmental Economics and Management*, **50** (2), 362–377.
Chin, W.W. (1998), 'The partial least squares approach for structural equation modeling', in George A. Marcoulides (ed.), *Modern Methods for Business Research*, Mahwah, NJ, USA: Lawrence Erlbaum Associates Publishers, pp. 295–336.
Chin, W.W. (2010), 'How to write up and report PLS analyses', in Vincenzo Esposito Vinzi, Wynne W. Chin, Jörg Henseler and Huiwen Wang (eds), *Handbook of Partial Least Squares: Concepts, Methods and Applications*, Berlin and Heidelberg, Germany: Springer Berlin Heidelberg, pp. 655–690.
Chin, W.W. and P.R. Newsted (1999), 'Structural equation modeling analysis with small samples using partial least squares', *Statistical Strategies for Small Sample Research*, **1** (1), 307–341.
Chorus, C.G., Annema, J.A., Mouter, N. and B. van Wee (2011), 'Modeling politicians' preferences for road pricing policies: a regret-based and utilitarian perspective', *Transport Policy*, **18** (6), 856–861.
Day, B., Bateman, I.J., Carson, R.T., Dupont, D., Louviere, J.J., et al. (2012), 'Ordering effects and choice set awareness in repeat-response stated preference studies', *Journal of Environmental Economics and Management*, **63** (1), 73–91.
De Groot, J.I.M. and L. Steg (2009), 'Morality and prosocial behavior: the role of awareness, responsibility, and norms in the norm activation model', *Journal of Social Psychology*, **149** (4), 425–449.
Diener, E. (2000), 'Subjective well-being: the science of happiness and a proposal for a national index', *American Psychologist*, **55** (1), 34–43.
Diener, E., Heintzelman, S.J., Kushlev, K., Tay, L., Wirtz, D., et al. (2017), 'Findings all psychologists should know from the new science on subjective well-being', *Canadian Psychology/Psychologie canadienne*, **58** (2), 87–104.
Folmer, H. (2009), 'Why sociology is better conditioned to explain economic behaviour than economics', *Kyklos*, **62** (2), 258–274.
Folmer, H. and O. Johansson-Stenman (2011), 'Does environmental economics produce aeroplanes without engines? On the need for an environmental social science', *Environmental and Resource Economics*, **48** (3), 337–361.
Folmer, H. and J. Oud (2008), 'How to get rid of W: a latent variables approach to modelling spatially lagged variables', *Environment and Planning A: Economy and Space*, **40** (10), 2526–2538.
Fornara, F., Pattitoni, P., Mura, M. and E. Strazzera (2016), 'Predicting intention to improve household energy efficiency: the role of value–belief–norm theory, normative and informational influence, and specific attitude', *Journal of Environmental Psychology*, **45**, 1–10.
Fornell, C. and F.L. Bookstein (1982), 'Two structural equation models: LISREL and PLS applied to consumer exit-voice theory', *Journal of Marketing Research*, **19** (4), 440–452.

Fornell, C. and D.F. Larcker (1981), 'Evaluating structural equation models with unobservable variables and measurement error', *Journal of Marketing Research*, **18** (1), 39–50.

Greaves, M., Zibarras, L.D. and C. Stride (2013), 'Using the theory of planned behavior to explore environmental behavioral intentions in the workplace', *Journal of Environmental Psychology*, **34**, 109–120.

Haenlein, M. and Kaplan, A.M. (2004), 'A beginner's guide to partial least squares analysis', *Understanding Statistics*, **3** (4), 283–297.

Hair, J.F., Ringle, C.M. and M. Sarstedt (2011), 'PLS-SEM: indeed a silver bullet', *Journal of Marketing Theory and Practice*, **19** (2), 139–152.

Henseler, J. and M. Sarstedt (2013), 'Goodness-of-fit indices for partial least squares path modeling', *Computational Statistics*, **28** (2), 565–580.

Hicks, J.R. (1941), 'The rehabilitation of consumers' surplus', *Review of Economic Studies*, **8** (2), 108–116.

Hulland, J. (1999), 'Use of partial least squares (PLS) in strategic management research: a review of four recent studies', *Strategic Management Journal*, **20** (2), 195–204.

Joe, F.H.J., Marko, S., Lucas, H. and G.K. Volker (2014), 'Partial least squares structural equation modeling (PLS-SEM): an emerging tool in business research', *European Business Review*, **26** (2), 106–121.

Jöreskog, Karl G. and D. Sörbom (eds) (1996), *LISREL 8: User's Reference Guide*, Lincolnwood, IL, USA: Scientific Software International.

Jöreskog, K.G. and D. Sörbom (2006), *LISREL 8.80 for Windows*, Skokie, IL, USA: Scientific Software International.

Kahneman, D. and A.B. Krueger (2006), 'Developments in the measurement of subjective well-being', *Journal of Economic Perspectives*, **20** (1), 3–24.

Kahneman, D. and R. Sugden (2005), 'Experienced utility as a standard of policy evaluation', *Environmental and Resource Economics*, **32** (1), 161–181.

Kahneman, D. and R.H. Thaler (2006), 'Anomalies: utility maximization and experienced utility', *Journal of Economic Perspectives*, **20** (1), 221–234.

Kahneman, D., Wakker, P.P. and R. Sarin (1997), 'Back to Bentham? Explorations of experienced utility', *Quarterly Journal of Economics*, **112** (2), 375–406.

Keen, S. (ed.) (2001), *Debunking Economics: The Naked Emperor of the Social Sciences*, Annandale, Australia: Pluto Press Australia.

Kiatkawsin, K. and H. Han (2017), 'Young travelers' intention to behave pro-environmentally: merging the value–belief–norm theory and the expectancy theory', *Tourism Management*, **59**, 76–88.

Kline, Rex B. (ed.) (2015), *Principles and Practice of Structural Equation Modeling*, New York, USA: Guilford Press.

Kollmuss, A. and J. Agyeman (2002), 'Mind the gap: why do people act environmentally and what are the barriers to pro-environmental behavior?', *Environmental Education Research*, **8** (3), 239–260.

Li, Z., Folmer, H. and J. Xue (2014), 'To what extent does air pollution affect happiness? The case of the Jinchuan mining area, China', *Ecological Economics*, **99**, 88–99.

Lindenberg, S. (2001a), 'Intrinsic motivation in a new light', *Kyklos*, **54** (2–3), 317–342.

Lindenberg, S. (2001b), 'Social rationality as a unified model of man (including bounded rationality)', *Journal of Management and Governance*, **5** (3), 239–251.

Lindenberg, S. (2001c), 'Social rationality versus rational egoism', in Jonathan H. Turner (ed.), *Handbook of Sociological Theory*, Boston, MA, USA: Springer US, pp. 635–668.

List, J.A. (2003), 'Does market experience eliminate market anomalies?', *Quarterly Journal of Economics*, **118** (1), 41–71.

Little, T.D., Cunningham, W.A., Shahar, G. and K.F. Widaman (2002), 'To parcel or not to parcel: exploring the question, weighing the merits', *Structural Equation Modeling*, **9** (2), 151–173.

MacCallum, R.C., Browne, M.W. and H.M. Sugawara (1996), 'Power analysis and determination of sample size for covariance structure modeling', *Psychological Methods*, **1** (2), 130–149.

Monecke, A. and F. Leisch (2012), 'semPLS: structural equation modeling using partial least squares', *Journal of Statistical Software*, **48** (3), 1–32.

Moran, E.F. (2010), 'The challenge of human–environment interactions research', in Emilio F. Moran (ed.), *Environmental Social Science: Human–Environment Interactions and Sustainability*, Chichester, UK: Wiley-Blackwell, pp. 1–24.

Musa, H.D., Yacob, M.R., Abdullah, A.M. and M.Y. Ishak (2018), 'Enhancing subjective well-being through strategic urban planning: development and application of community happiness index', *Sustainable Cities and Society*, **38**, 184–194.

Muthén, B. (1984), 'A general structural equation model with dichotomous, ordered categorical, and continuous latent variable indicators', *Psychometrika*, **49** (1), 115–132.

Olsson, U.H., Foss, T., Troye, S.V. and R.D. Howell (2000), 'The performance of ML, GLS, and WLS estimation in structural equation modeling under conditions of misspecification and nonnormality', *Structural Equation Modeling: A Multidisciplinary Journal*, **7** (4), 557–595.

Onwezen, M.C., Antonides, G. and J. Bartels (2013), 'The norm activation model: an exploration of the functions of anticipated pride and guilt in pro-environmental behaviour', *Journal of Economic Psychology*, **39**, 141–153.

Rehdanz, K., Welsch, H., Narita, D. and T. Okubo (2015), 'Well-being effects of a major natural disaster: the case of Fukushima', *Journal of Economic Behavior and Organization*, **116**, 500–517.

Reinartz, W., Haenlein, M. and J. Henseler (2009), 'An empirical comparison of the efficacy of covariance-based and variance-based SEM', *International Journal of Research in Marketing*, **26** (4), 332–344.

Rigdon, E.E. (1998), 'Structural equation modeling', in George A. Marcoulides (ed.), *Modern Methods for Business Research*, Mahwah, NJ, USA: Lawrence Erlbaum Associates Publishers, pp. 251–294.

Samson, A. (2014), 'An introduction to behavioral economics', in Alain Samson (ed.), *The Behavioral Economics Guide 2014*, pp. 1–12. https://www.behavioraleconomics.com/resources/introduction-behavioral-economics/.

Sarstedt, M., Ringle, C.M., Smith, D., Reams, R. and J.F. Hair (2014), 'Partial least squares structural equation modeling (PLS-SEM): a useful tool for family business researchers', *Journal of Family Business Strategy*, **5** (1), 105–115.

Schumacker, R.E. and R.G. Lomax (eds) (2004), *A Beginner's Guide to Structural Equation Modeling*, New York, USA and London, UK: Routledge.

Schwartz, S.H. (1977), 'Normative influences on altruism', in Leonard Berkowitz (ed.), *Advances in Experimental Social Psychology*, New York, USA: Academic Press, pp. 221–279.

Schwartz, S.H. and J.A. Howard (1981), 'A normative decision-making model of altruism', in J. Philippe Rushton and Richard M. Sorrentino (eds), *Altruism and Helping Behaviour: Social, Personality and Developmental Perspectives*, Hillsdale, NJ, USA: L. Erlbaum Associates, pp. 189–211.

Shafik, N. (1994), 'Economic development and environmental quality: an econometric analysis', *Oxford Economic Papers*, **46**, 757–773.

Shechter, M. (2000), 'Valuing the environment', in Henk Folmer and H. Landis Gabel (eds), *Principles of Environmental and Resource Economics*, Cheltenham, UK and Northampton, MA, USA: Edward Elgar Publishing, pp. 72–103.

Shmueli, G., Ray, S., Velasquez Estrada, J.M. and S.B. Chatla (2016), 'The elephant in the room: predictive performance of PLS models', *Journal of Business Research*, **69** (10), 4552–4564.

Simon, H.A. (ed.) (1957), *Models of Man: Social and Rational*, New York, USA: John Wiley & Sons.

Steenkamp, J.-B.E.M. and H. Baumgartner (2000), 'On the use of structural equation models for marketing modeling', *International Journal of Research in Marketing*, **17** (2), 195–202.

Steg, L., Bolderdijk, J.W., Keizer, K. and G. Perlaviciute (2014), 'An integrated framework for encouraging pro-environmental behaviour: the role of values, situational factors and goals', *Journal of Environmental Psychology*, **38**, 104–115.

Stern, P.C. (2000), 'New environmental theories: toward a coherent theory of environmentally significant behavior', *Journal of Social Issues*, **56** (3), 407–424.

Stiglitz, J.E. (2000), 'The contributions of the economics of information to twentieth century economics', *Quarterly Journal of Economics*, **115** (4), 1441–1478.

Tan, C.S., Ooi, H.Y. and Y.N. Goh (2017), 'A moral extension of the theory of planned behavior to predict consumers' purchase intention for energy-efficient household appliances in Malaysia', *Energy Policy*, **107**, 459–471.

Thaler, R.H. (2016), 'Behavioral economics: past, present, and future', *American Economic Review*, **106** (7), 1577–1600.

Tversky, A. and D. Kahneman (1991), 'Loss aversion in riskless choice: a reference-dependent model', *Quarterly Journal of Economics*, **106** (4), 1039–1061.

Van Kooten, G.C. and H. Folmer (eds) (2004), *Land and Forest Economics*, Cheltenham, UK and Northhampton, MA, USA: Edward Elgar Publishing.

Veisten, K., Fredrik Hoen, H., Navrud, S. and J. Strand (2004), 'Scope insensitivity in contingent valuation of complex environmental amenities', *Journal of Environmental Management*, **73** (4), 317–331.

Von Möllendorff, C. and H. Welsch (2017), 'Measuring renewable energy externalities: evidence from subjective well-being data', *Land Economics*, **93** (1), 109–126.

Wakker, Peter P. (ed.) (2010), *Prospect Theory for Risk and Ambiguity*, Cambridge, UK: Cambridge University Press.

Welsch, H. (2009), 'Implications of happiness research for environmental economics', *Ecological Economics*, **68** (11), 2735–2742.

Welsch, H. and P. Biermann (2016), 'Measuring nuclear power plant externalities using life satisfaction data: a spatial analysis for Switzerland', *Ecological Economics*, **126**, 98–111.

Welsch, H. and S. Ferreira (2014), 'Environment, well-being, and experienced preference', *International Review of Environmental and Resource Economics*, **7** (3–4), 205–239.

Welsch, H. and J. Kuhling (2009), 'Using happiness data for environmental valuation: issues and applications', *Journal of Economic Surveys*, **23** (2), 385–406.

Wold, H. (1975), 'Path models with latent variables: the NIPALS approach', in Hubert M. Blalock, Abel G. Aganbegian, F.M. Borodkin, Raymond Boudon and Vittorio Capecchi (eds), *Quantitative Sociology*, Cambridge, MA, USA: Academic Press, pp. 307–357.

Zhang, Y., Wang, Z. and G. Zhou (2013), 'Antecedents of employee electricity saving behavior in organizations: an empirical study based on norm activation model', *Energy Policy*, **62**, 1120–1127.

PART II

CASE STUDIES ON HAPPINESS AND THE ENVIRONMENT

6. Cross-country variations in subjective wellbeing explained by the climate

David Maddison and Katrin Rehdanz

6.1 INTRODUCTION

Although significant research has been directed towards predicting the wider impacts of climate change, noticeably less research has attempted to value the direct impacts of climate change on households. The value of climate to households can best be motivated using Becker's household production function (HPF) theory (Becker, 1965). According to this theory, households do not consume marketed commodities directly, but instead combine them with non-market environmental goods – for example, the climate – to produce service flows. It is the resulting service flows that are of direct value to the household.

HPF theory explains why households living in locations characterised by different climates purchase different patterns of commodities, even when confronted by the same vector of market prices and identical incomes. This is often referred to as adaptation (see, e.g., Ebert and Welsch, 2012). The same theoretical framework also explains why such households achieve very different levels of welfare. Essentially, because particular climates are conducive to the production of certain service flows, households are able to produce such flows at lower cost.

But although HPF theory explains why climate might be of value to households, few researchers have actually attempted to use the HPF theory for the purposes of valuing changes in the climate (Maddison, 2003). The first problem is that service flows are themselves unobservable. The value to households of changes in the climate can only be deduced through examining the expenditure patterns of households confronted by different climates, incomes and prices, but in order to do so additional restrictions are necessary. Essentially, these restrictions require the existence of a price vector at which marginal changes in the climate have no value to the household (Bradford and Hildebrandt, 1977). Whether there is indeed some price vector at which changes in the climate would cease to matter seems doubtful. Where only one market good is involved, the situation is usually framed in terms of averting or defensive expenditures; for example, Bartik (1988) or Lanz and Provins (2017). If there is no price vector at which marginal changes in the value of the climate cease to matter – for example, if climate variables enter the utility in an additive fashion – then the value of any changes in the climate cannot be valued using this technique.

Although it serves to motivate the inclusion of climate variables into the utility function, due to the difficulty of conducting a convincing analysis into the value of the climate using HPF theory there has been a search for 'alternative' means of valuing climate amenities. One possibility is that the value of particular sorts of climate become capitalised into house prices and wage rates (e.g., Rehdanz and Maddison, 2009). If households optimally position themselves on the hedonic price schedule – that is, make a locational choice – it is possible to infer the implicit price of climate amenities to the household. Note that we say 'alternative' because the hedonic technique is itself an application of the HPF method. More specifically, if there is a price vector such that marginal changes in the non-market environmental good cease to matter, then it is possible to value changes in the provision of the good. The important price here is the price of housing: if the price of housing in a particular location is so high that one chooses not to live there, then the climate of that location does not matter. For a discussion of the relationship between HPF and revealed preference valuation techniques, see Ebert (2007). One difficulty with applying the hedonic technique to valuing climate amenities, however, is the assumption that households are willing and without cost able to move a significant distance in order to enjoy particular sorts of climate. Considering the distances over which climate amenities vary significantly, this seems not entirely plausible.

An alternative valuation methodology, and one which this chapter focuses on, is provided by analyses of subjective wellbeing (SWB). The methodology underlying such studies is described elsewhere in this *Handbook*, but basically, SWB studies analyse the trade-off between climate and income, holding SWB constant. The key assumption here is that different individuals nonetheless use a common function to convert utility into SWB, measured for example on a 1–10 scale.

One important advantage of the SWB technique is the fact that the estimates of SWB are provided by individuals already inhabiting particular climates. The individual has thus already experienced and presumably adapted themselves to the local climate. By contrast, stated preference valuation techniques simply probe individuals about their willingness to pay (or accept compensation) for a climate that they themselves have never experienced other than for brief periods, if at all. With the SWB approach it is moreover not necessary to place any restrictions on household preferences in order to estimate the value of the climate. Neither is it necessary to assume the absence of significant barriers to relocation that would prevent elimination of the net benefits of particular locations; a proposition that the SWB itself can be used to test.

Previous research reviewed below establishes that particular sorts of climate do indeed appear to influence levels of SWB in a manner consistent with common sense. This research makes use of data from single countries as well as cross-country data on SWB. Evidence on the value of the climate uncovered by these studies has even been used by some to produce monetary estimates of the impact of climate change (Tol, 2018). More specifically, information on the substitutability between climate variables and income has been combined with predictions of future climate change associated with particular greenhouse gas emissions scenarios. Care must be taken, since analyses of the impact of climate on SWB studies attempt to value only a subset of the impacts of climate change: the direct impact of climate change on households. Other sorts of impacts, such as those relating to changes in incomes or the prices of marketed goods, are omitted using this technique. Other non-market environmental goods valued by households whose abundance is affected by the climate might be inadvertently included.

Although promising, research into SWB and the climate is in some respects still in an exploratory phase. There is no single definitive study of SWB and the climate, rather a series of studies each of which has its own (sometimes significant) shortcomings. One reason for this is constraints on the use of the SWB data, which although generally unimportant have significant consequences for valuing changes in the climate. Foremost among these are restrictions on providing researchers with information on the precise location of the respondent for confidentiality purposes (although this may be less important than for other environmental goods, for example noise, where noise levels vary at even shorter distances). The SWB technique also has numerous known weaknesses that are not specific to valuing changes in climate. The justification for concerning ourselves with this technique, therefore, is not that the values provided by analyses of SWB are necessarily better than those provided by other methodologies, but rather that all available techniques depend upon assumptions which may be more or less palatable.

The goal of this chapter is to survey the literature on SWB and the climate and to provide further empirical evidence on this relationship. Compared to our earlier study explaining cross-country variations in SWB (Rehdanz and Maddison, 2005; Maddison and Rehdanz, 2011), this study uses a far larger number of countries offering a greater degree of climatic diversity. We also investigate the robustness of the relationship between climate and SWB by examining whether alternative representations of the climate provide an equivalent account of the role of the climate. In addition we examine whether the observed relationships are stable across different subsamples of data and unaffected by changes in the econometric procedures we adopt. Although we stop short of attempting to combine these data to project the impact of climate change, our results could nevertheless be used to estimate the impact of climate change on welfare.

The remainder of the chapter is organised as follows. Section 6.2 critically surveys the literature linking SWB and the climate. Section 6.3 briefly describes the methodology underlying such studies. Section 6.4 describes the data underlying the empirical analysis that is presented in section 6.5. These results are subject to additional analyses in section 6.6, and the section 6.7 concludes.

6.2 LITERATURE SURVEY

The ECONLIT database was accessed on 3 December 2018 to locate articles containing the phrase 'subjective well-being' OR 'subjective wellbeing' OR 'happiness' OR 'life satisfaction' AND 'climate', resulting in 81 hits, with publication dates ranging from 1998 to 2018. Of these, 60 were in academic journals whereas ten were working papers and seven were books. Of the remainder, three were theses and there was one article in a collective volume. A significant number of these hits referred to articles in the publications *Social Indicators Research* (11) and *Ecological Economics* (8).

Only a minority of the publications discovered by ECONLIT actually involved any research into SWB and the climate. Many articles use the word 'climate' in a broader sense, for example the 'business climate'; whereas in other articles the word 'climate' is used incorrectly to refer to the weather. Studies delving purely into the effects of weather on SWB, although not uninteresting, are excluded from what follows. Also excluded are a number of literature reviews discussing publications concerning climate and SWB. Along with studies in which the climate is the main focus we do, however, include in our review studies that include climate variables, even if they are not the main focus.

Chronologically, Frijters and Van Praag (1998) appear to be the first to use the SWB technique to value climate. They analyse surveys undertaken 1993–94 in which Russians rate their satisfaction with their life on a 0–10 Cantril scale. This is in addition to their utilisation of an alternative valuation technique referred to as the income evaluation question, in which individuals are asked about the minimum household income required in order to be able to describe it as, for example, 'good' or even 'very good'.

Although this is an extremely early implementation of the SWB technique to value non-market environmental goods it is interesting to see the authors anticipate some of the possible problems of the technique; for example, the variability of responses in response to transient events such as the weather, and whether it is safe to assume a common response from people belonging to different cultures.

The chief limitation of the study is that, despite the unparallelled climatic diversity of Russia, the authors were able to identify only 35 different climatic regions. Those climate variables appearing to be significant in the ordered probit regressions are January wind speed, the interaction between January temperature and January wind speed, and average annual temperature interacted with average annual humidity. Wind speed in January has a depressing effect on SWB, especially in areas with lower temperatures. The combination of high humidity and high temperature also reduces SWB.

Rehdanz and Maddison (2005) appears to be the first cross-country analysis of happiness and climate and is undertaken with the primary intention of valuing the impacts of climate change. The paper further explains the relative advantages of using SWB to value climate amenities relative to other methodologies. For example, in order to value climate using the hedonic technique the authors note that it is necessary to assume equilibrium in the housing and labour markets. The approach of demand dependency – that is, inferring the value of the climate by analysing patterns of household expenditure – by contrast is argued to require the imposition of untestable restrictions on preferences.

Data are drawn from the World Database of Happiness and range from 1972 to 2000. There are 187 observations on 67 countries. These data use four categories of response and refer to the concept of happiness. The authors include a large number of economic variables, including for example gross domestic product (GDP) per capita in 1995 USD, inflation and GDP growth rates. An index of freedom and information on demographic characteristics of the population is also included along with geographical variables.

A number of different ways of representing the climate are considered. These include maximum and minimum monthly values for temperature and precipitation, as well as annual averages and counts of hot and cold and wet and dry months. The climate records for each country represent the weighted averages of different climate records for major cities within each country. For example, the climate of Italy is the population-weighted average of the climate records for Milan, Rome and Naples. Absolute latitude is included to control for the variation in the hours of daylight across the annual cycle.

The regression is population-weighted and standard errors are clustered at the level of the country. The best specification in terms of maximising the R-squared statistic involves using the hottest and coldest and wettest and driest months. The authors then combine their estimates with country-specific predictions of future climate change, and it transpires that the impacts of climate change uniformly benefit high-latitude countries.

Bjørnskov et al. (2008) also present a cross-country analysis of variations in SWB. Unlike the preceding effort, however, climate is not the main focus of the analysis and the only climate variable included is the average temperature of each country's capital. Such a concept frankly does not seem capable of testing the stated hypothesis that a moderate climate is conducive to life satisfaction.

The analysis incorporates individual data from 90 000 different individuals inhabiting 70 different countries. Responses are analysed using an ordered probit model in view of the ordinal nature of the dependent variable. Data are taken from the World Value Survey and refer to the years 1997–2000. The authors analyse 'life satisfaction these days' on a 1–10 scale, rather than happiness, even though the World Value Survey includes both. They note the surprisingly low correlation between life satisfaction and happiness. Unsurprisingly, in none of the regressions is the mean temperature of the capital city of the country statistically significant.

Brereton et al. (2008) examine SWB and climate for Ireland. The key contribution of this paper is that climate is measured at the highest level of resolution consistent with maintaining respondent anonymity. The exercise is based upon 1467 surveys conducted in Ireland, using a seven-point scale referring to the balance of good things and bad things in a person's life. Apart from climate variables their dataset includes a range of other variables; for example, the homicide rate, distance to the coastline and presence of waste facilities.

The authors take professional advice with regards to which climate variables they include in their empirical analysis. This advice leads them to include the minimum temperature in January and maximum temperature in July as well as mean annual precipitation, annually averaged wind speed and the duration of sunshine measured in hours. They find that wind speed exerts a statistically significant negative impact on SWB. By contrast, warmer temperatures for both January and July increase SWB, with January temperatures having a particularly large effect. Mean annual precipitation and hours of sunshine are not statistically significant in either an ordered probit or an ordinary least squares (OLS) regression.

Using the same data as Brereton et al. (2008), Ferreira and Moro (2010) use the SWB approach to calculate the compensating surplus for small changes in climate variables. They find that one of the underlying assumptions of the hedonic technique – namely that the net benefits of particular locations have been eliminated – is soundly rejected for Ireland. On this basis, the authors conclude that hedonic analysis cannot deliver the correct valuation of non-market environmental goods.

The authors estimate a regression which controls for variations in housing rental prices and wage rates to control for the extent that these capitalise differences in environmental variables, and then proceed to calculate the value of changes in the climate. The results seem to be implausibly large: several thousand euros for a relatively minor change in temperature. For example, the compensating surplus corresponding to the difference between the average values for all Ireland and the average value for the Dublin regions is €4200 per person per annum for a 0.3°C increase in minimum January temperatures. This is a not uncommon finding in the SWB literature, and the authors consider a number of possible explanations including the mismeasurement of the marginal utility of income caused by the use of income categories.

Maddison and Rehdanz (2011) present an analysis updating their earlier paper. They use evidence from 87 countries taken from the World Values Survey and introduce monthly temperature deviations as a way of representing the climate. There are 178 observations from 1981 to 2008 and these use a 1–10-point scale for satisfaction with life as a whole. 'Deviations' here refers to the number of positive and negative deviations from a monthly mean temperature of 18.3°C summed over 12 months (see later for more details). Consideration is given to the nature of the welfare impacts that can be captured and those that are not, using the SWB technique. Excluded are the impacts of climate change on prices and on incomes, and the only impacts included are the direct impacts of climate change on household utility.

The paper calculates willingness to accept compensation for changes in the climate of different countries. Maddison and Rehdanz (2011) criticise their earlier use of maximum and minimum values because such a specification fails to distinguish between those locations where the temperature in the coldest month is already high, and those locations where the temperature in the hottest month is still quite low. As in their previous work, the climate variables are the population-weighted averages for the largest cities. The number of records per country depends on the geographical area of the country concerned.

It appears that the effects of negative deviations and positive deviations are equal, permitting the authors to propose a simple representation of the climate: cumulated absolute monthly deviations from 18.3°C. Furthermore, although the authors assume a base of 18.3°C (65°F), they also demonstrate that such a temperature base is optimal when compared to other temperature bases. More specifically, they note a decline in the T-statistic on the coefficient of 'degree-months' using temperature bases either side of 65°F.

Ferreira et al. (2013) has as its primary objective determining the effects of air quality on SWB in Europe. The paper uses regional data from the first three waves of the European Social Survey 2002–07 at the Nomenclature of Territorial Units for Statistics (NUTS) level. These data refer to 23 different countries and include approximately 75 000 respondents. The usual controls are present along with sulphur dioxide (SO_2) concentrations as the main focus of the analysis. Most important for our purposes is the inclusion of the maximum July temperatures and minimum January temperatures along with mean annual precipitation. There is evidence that higher maximum July temperatures reduce SWB, whereas higher mean annual precipitation increases SWB. The coefficient on minimum January temperatures is positive, as expected, but insignificant.

Cuñado and de Gracia (2013) use data drawn from the European Social Survey for Spain for the year 2008. The objective is to analyse the impacts of air pollution and climate. These data are combined with socio-demographic information on the Spanish regions, along with information on air pollution and climate from the Spanish Meteorological Agency. Climate data are 30-year averages, and average January and July temperatures are included along with January and July averages for precipitation. Data from regions having more than one weather station were averaged. The dependent variable is happiness on a 1–10 scale. The SWB equation is estimated using OLS. The climate variables perform poorly, although this might be because there are actually only 17 regions, and curiously the authors include both minimum and maximum and January and July temperatures in the same specification. Only July precipitation appears to have a significant impact, and the value of July precipitation ranges from €500–€1000 per millimetre per annum depending on the specification.

Murray et al. (2013) is perhaps the most compelling study into SWB and the climate to date. What makes it so persuasive is the fact that the authors use information from the 1999–2000 third wave of the European Values Survey covering 17 500 respondents and NUTS regions of 24 countries. There is thus a great deal of climatic variation present in the data, whilst the climate is measured much more accurately than, for example, Maddison and Rehdanz (2011). The SWB question refers to satisfaction with life as a whole these days on a 1–10-point scale. The authors use the usual set of controls for analysing individual data along with NUTS-2 and NUTS-3 level regional information.

The climate data include: temperature, precipitation, frost-days, sunshine, relative humidity, rain-days and wind speed. These are all available as monthly averages for the 209 NUTS regions identified. The specification of the climate variables includes linear and quadratic terms as well as the standard deviation of all the climate variables across the 12 months. Interestingly, it is only when the standard deviation of climate variables is included that any climate variables appear to be significant. But when these variables are included, the climate variables become significant even at the 0.1 per cent level. This indicates a correlation between the level of some climate variables and their standard deviations. The most important variables are humidity, which lowers satisfaction, and sunshine, which increases SWB. A high standard deviation in both temperature and the number of rain-days both decrease SWB.

The description of the climate is much more detailed than in any other study, and a variety of ways of representing the climate are compared. Furthermore, the study goes on to calculate the marginal rate of substitution between household income and the different climate variables. The final part of the paper calculates a climatic quality of life index using the estimated coefficients from the SWB regression. Interestingly, the climatic quality of life index points towards the most pleasant climate being found in those countries bordering the Mediterranean, whilst the least pleasant climate is found in those countries bordering the Baltic. Unfortunately, the fact remains that the implied values for climate are implausibly large.

A radically different sort of study is presented by Goetz et al. (2015), who seek to explain the number of days of mental ill-health across 2905 United States (US) counties averaged over the period 2002–08. The authors include dummies representing US states with similar climates. However, the authors also include the average number of days of sunshine in January in an attempt to control for seasonal affective disorder. An increase in this variable is found to decrease significantly the number of days of mental ill-health. However, it is unfortunate that the authors did not also include latitude in their analysis (although the state dummies might to some extent serve the same purpose), since this would have enabled them to distinguish the length of winter days from the amount of sunshine. Tantalisingly, some of the regional dummies were also highly significant, although precisely what other feature(s) of the climate causes the number of days of mental ill-health to vary, if any, is unclear.

Federsen et al. (2016) present an interesting piece of research evaluating the relative contributions of weather and climate to explaining the variation in SWB responses. Although we are mainly interested in the latter, there is obviously a concern about whether the preferences for particular sorts of climate continue to be present after controlling for weather at the time of the respondent interview. The title of the article gives away the main finding: weather matters, but climate does not. That weather should matter is unsurprising, since SWB responses appear to be affected by other occurrences, such as finding a dime on a photocopier (Schwarz and Strack, 1991) resulting in increases in SWB that cannot be explained by reference to any change in income.

The authors use a large, representative sample from Australia where information is available on the weather at the time of the interview. There are 96472 interviewees in the survey, which is conducted in multiple years beginning in 2001. The question refers to overall life satisfaction, which is measured on a 0–10 scale. The analysis includes numerous controls all commonly encountered in surveys of SWB. The location, time and date of the survey are recorded, making it possible to match the respondents not only to their climate but also to the prevailing weather conditions at the time of the interview. The authors moreover report that over 90 per cent of the respondents live within 20 km of a weather station, and they take a distance-weighted average of the nearest three weather stations' records as a representation of the climate of the individual respondents.

Including annual averages of temperature, precipitation, sunshine and wind speed results in statistically significant results for some of these climate variables even when state dummies are included. However, when respondent controls are included the statistical significance of the climate variables vanishes, whereas that of the weather variables lingers. The explanation provided for the insignificance of climate in this exercise is that in the long run individuals are able to adapt to all sorts of climate. The authors' perhaps somewhat speculative explanation for the significant effects encountered in other studies is that more-satisfied people tend to inhabit particular sorts of climate.

Whilst this is undoubtedly an interesting paper, it is however somewhat difficult to reconcile its findings with the existence of a large number of other studies pointing to the importance of climate. These include not only studies into SWB but also hedonic studies, studies that examine climate as a determinant of migration, studies that find climate to be an important determinant of household expenditure patterns, and studies in which individuals living in different locations report different incomes necessary to achieve the same verbal description of well-being. The most likely explanation for the insignificance of climate is therefore either that the specification of the climate is inadequate and/or the presence of compensating hedonic house-price rentals and wage rates not controlled for in the regression.

Kelley (2016) squarely addresses the issue of climate change and preferences for particular sorts of climates with a national Internet-based survey of 2295 respondents in the US. The author remarks that, unlike other surveys on climate change, this survey did not prompt respondents by mentioning the issue of climate change.

The survey is somewhat unusual because it measures directly satisfaction with the summer and with the winter weather, using a 100-point scale ranging from 'terrible' to 'delighted'. There are significant differences between the responses, as those in the north of the country are, on average, more pleased with the summer weather than residents in the south of the country. These findings are reversed for satisfaction with winter weather, whereby southerners are now more delighted by the winter weather than northerners. Satisfaction with the climate will therefore not necessarily be jeopardised by climate change, but rather it depends on the nature of the change.

The justification for interest in the weather variables is that if they are important, better controlling for them in surveys should lead to more accurate results. This is particularly critical if whatever is of interest is actually correlated with weather variables; for example, air pollution and wind speed. It might also matter if a survey is undertaken at a particular time of the year; for example, when the weather is typically clement. The significance of weather variables could also be indicative of the cognitive complexity of questions concerning life satisfaction.

Barrington-Leigh and Behzadnejad (2017) demonstrate that, after controlling for individual characteristics and the weather, there is no role for climate variables as a determinant of SWB. Their study uses two large-scale Canadian surveys probing life satisfaction: the Canadian Community Health Survey and the National Population Health Survey. The latter consists of four waves from 2004–10, whereas the former consists of six waves from 2005–11. The question in both studies refers to satisfaction with life in general, and this was measured on either a five-point or an eleven-point scale. Respondents are linked to contemporaneous weather and climate data from the nearest weather station. The analysis is conducted using both fixed individual effects but also as a pooled cross-section in which individual characteristics are included.

For the analysis of climate the authors retain dummy variables for each province but include average values for a variety of climate variables. The specification includes temperature, temperature range, rain, snow and hours of sunshine. There is no strong evidence that any of these are important, except perhaps for temperature range. Once more, however, just like the Federsen et al. (2016) study, the specification of the climate is extremely simple and there are no controls for compensating wage and house price differentials.

What is to be concluded from these published papers? There seems to be a clear consensus that extreme climates not only impact upon but typically reduce SWB. The evidence for this is the success in explaining cross-country variations in SWB using monthly deviations from a baseline temperature of 18.3°C, and the fact that in some specifications adding the standard deviation of climate variables across the 12 months results in a vast improvement in fit. Furthermore, although the majority of papers use temperature and precipitation, there is evidence that when information on hours of sunshine, humidity and rain-days are included these too are often highly significant. There have been noticeably fewer attempts to investigate whether climate variables interact with one another; and no attempts whatsoever to use synthetic indices such as the wind chill factor, combining temperature and wind speed to produce a 'feels like' temperature.

The results from studies that analyse differences in SWB from within a single country do not seem to point to such an important role for climate as do the studies that consider multiple countries. This is hardly surprising since there is likely to be greater variation in climate in cross-country analyses. But there is another explanation: in a developed country with an itinerant population it is likely that differences in climate amenities are capitalised into differences in house prices and wage rates. Unless variations in house prices and wage rates are controlled for, the contribution of climate is therefore incorrectly measured. It is noteworthy that the only single-country study that controlled for differences in house prices and wage rates (Ferreira and Moro, 2010) found a substantial role for climate.

There seem to be several significant challenges for future analyses of the effect of climate change on SWB. The first of these is to resolve problems relating to the measurement of the marginal utility of income currently causing the implied marginal willingness to pay for climate to be implausibly large. This problem, however, is not unique to the measurement of the value of climate variables.

Another challenge lies in understanding whether the manner in which SWB is elicited actually matters. Put differently, does enquiring about overall life satisfaction result in a similar set of results concerning the role of climate as a question referring to happiness 'these days'? Furthermore, does it matter for the purposes of valuing climate variables whether the survey of SWB is undertaken at a particular time of the year, and does the value of climate variables change according to the weather at the time when the interview takes place?

The final challenge relates to the measurement of the climate variables themselves. Clearly there is an advantage in cross-country studies, since these ensure greater variation in the climate. But whereas single-country studies tend to possess information on the (approximate) location of respondents, cross-country studies often use aggregate data and average across the climate of different cities. Such a procedure is obviously problematical in countries with diverse climates such as, for example, the US. The ideal is to use cross-country data, thereby guaranteeing significant variation in the climate variables, whilst at the same time being able to place respondents into climatically homogeneous regions within these countries.

6.3 METHODOLOGY

In analyses of SWB, survey respondents are typically confronted by a question such as: 'On a scale of 1–10 how satisfied are you with your life, where 1 is the least satisfied and 10 is the most satisfied?' In some surveys the question might alternatively refer to some other concept such as happiness, and there may be a reference to a particular time period, for example, 'these days'. If we interpret the response as a measure of utility u, this requires that individuals are able to map their true utility onto an ordinal scale using a function where s_i is the reported satisfaction of individual i, and g_i describes the monotonic function used to map u_i on to s_i:

$$s_i = g_i(u_i)$$

If, however, we intend to go further and compare individuals it is in addition necessary to assume that all individuals share a common function g for converting utility into satisfaction. Moreover, given that the function g is unknown it is safest to assume only an ordinal relationship between satisfaction and utility. That is to say, the only thing that may be inferred when someone responds, for example, with an 8 rather than a 7 on the 1–10 scale is that they enjoy higher utility. Many researchers, however, analyse the data as if the relationship between utility and life satisfaction were cardinal rather than ordinal in nature. This choice is on the basis of the finding that analysing the responses using an ordinal probit rather than OLS often makes very little difference, at least if one is interested in the ratios of coefficients.

If we specify the indirect utility function v as:

$$u = v(p, y, x, z)$$

where p is prices, y is (after-tax) income, x is the characteristics of the individual and z is the level of some non-market environmental good, then the marginal willingness to pay (MWTP) for changes in the level of the non-market environmental good is given by:

$$MWTP = \frac{\partial g(u)/\partial u \times \partial u/\partial z}{\partial g(u)/\partial u \times \partial u/\partial y} = \frac{\partial u/\partial z}{\partial u/\partial y}$$

In empirical work it is also common to assume that each individual faces the same set of prices such that these become incorporated into the constant term. This would not be a good assumption, however, if it were felt that the prices of some commodities – for example, the rental price of housing – were affected by the level of the non-market environmental good. It is also common to include the equivalised income of the household rather than total income, to account for households of differing demographic composition.

6.4 DATA

The data underlying the empirical analysis are from a variety of sources. Data on SWB are sourced from the online data appendix of Chapter 2 of Helliwell et al. (2016). These data contain information from surveys undertaken 2005–15 and include information from 165 countries. The dependent variable in our analysis is the nationally averaged response to the question:

> Please imagine a ladder, with steps numbered from 0 at the bottom to 10 at the top. The top of the ladder represents the best possible life for you and the bottom of the ladder represents the worst possible life for you. On which step of the ladder would you say you personally feel you stand at this time?

Also included in these data is a measure of personal freedom. This is the response to the question: 'Are you satisfied or dissatisfied with your freedom to choose what you do with your life?' The response is recorded as a binary variable.

Based on the findings of earlier studies, these data are then supplemented by a range of socio-economic data. For example, following Easterlin (1974), income has been identified as significantly affecting SWB. Further economic variables alleged to be important are inflation (Di Tella et al., 2001) and unemployment (Clark and Oswald, 1994). Data on these variables are taken from the World Bank Databank. We include GDP per capita in terms of purchasing power parity constant 2011 international dollars, the rate of consumer price inflation and the modelled rate of unemployment. We also control for basic demographic features of the countries; namely, the proportion of individuals who are under 15 years of age and the proportion of individuals who are 65 years or older. We use the geographical area of the country to calculate population density. These data are also taken from the World Bank Databank.

We include the absolute latitude of the country in order to control for the variation in the length of daylight across the annual cycle. Absolute latitude is measured in decimalised degrees and refers to country centroids. This information is taken from the Central Intelligence Agency. We include this variable because absolute latitude and climate are clearly correlated. We also identify to which continent a country belongs. For each country we calculate the mean temperature of every month in °C. These monthly data are in almost all cases the weighted averages of individual climate records. The weights correspond to the populations of the largest cities within each country. The number of cities selected varies according to the geographical area of the country.

As noted in the earlier section a major concern is that the climate can be represented in a variety of ways. Careful consideration must therefore be given as to what is the best representation of the climate. Following in the footsteps of Cushing (1987), we represent the climate in a variety of ways. The simplest way of controlling for the climate is to include the temperature of the hottest and coldest month. Although simple, this is not an entirely satisfactory way of representing the climate since it suggests that the impact of a uniform 1°C centigrade increase in temperature is independent of the annual average temperature. Using the average temperature and the average temperature squared, by contrast, does not distinguish between countries having a 'continental' climate and those possessing a more 'maritime' one. Another way of representing the climate is in terms of deviations from a base temperature. Our preferred way of doing this is to measure deviations across the 12 months from a base of 18.3°C, where *POS* stands for positive deviations:

$$HDM = POS(18.3 - T_{Jan}) + POS(18.3 - T_{Feb}) + \ldots + POS(18.3 - T_{Dec})$$

$$CDM = POS(T_{Jan} - 18.3) + POS(T_{Feb} - 18.3) + \ldots + POS(T_{Dec} - 18.3)$$

This parodies the more familiar concept of heating and cooling degree-days, but instead uses monthly data to obtain heating degree-months (*HDM*) and cooling degree-months (*CDM*). The weakness of such a measure is the need to assume an appropriate temperature base. We choose 18.3°C simply because this is the temperature most often used to calculate degree-days and our previous research also suggests that this is the best temperature base. Note that we nonetheless treat positive and negative deviations differently. Table 6.1 summarises the statistics.

6.5 RESULTS

Before running any regressions we consider the weighting of the observations, each of which represents the average SWB for every country. These countries, however, are of different sizes in terms of population. In order to better represent the population of interest for each year we weight these observations according to the population of the country relative to the population of all the countries included in the same survey year. This procedure means that within each survey year the weights are proportional to population, and each survey year has the same weight in the regression.

In addition to weighting the data we also include dummy variables for each of the survey years contained in the analysis, which run from 2005 to 2015. Following the advice in Stock and Watson (2008), we further use the 'cluster' option at the level of the country in order to allow for the possibility that the disturbances are not identically distributed or there is serial correlation.

A number of observations have missing values. In what follows these are imputed by taking the average non-missing values for each of the 11 years. Below, we show that this makes little if any difference to the results, but it does prevent the number of countries included in the analysis falling from 165 to 150. With these preliminaries out of the way, we now present a variety of models.

We begin our analysis by comparing the different ways of parsimoniously representing the climate. In Model 1 in Table 6.2 we observe that the climate variables are individually statistically insignificant, even at 10 per cent. It should further be noted that these

Table 6.1 Summary statistics (N = 1274)

Variable	Description	Mean	Std Dev.	Min.	Max.
SWB	Overall life satisfaction, measured on a scale from 0 ('worst possible life') to 10 ('best possible life')	5.4372	1.1191	2.6876	8.0189
Meantemp	Mean monthly temperature (°C)	18.1312	7.1576	−0.553	29.7917
Mintemp	Lowest monthly temperature (°C)	11.2637	10.86121	−20.02	27
Maxtemp	Highest monthly temperature (°C)	24.55938	4.731508	11	36
HDM	Number of heating degree months (°C)	44.8192	51.84963	0	226.2458
CDM	Number of cooling degree months (°C)	42.79903	40.89886	0	137.9
Log(GDPPC)	Log of GDP per capita (2001 USD, PPP)	9.2112	1.1667	6.4572	11.7703
Inflation	Rate of consumer price inflation (%)	5.5281	6.7822	−8.975	121.7381
Unemployment	Rate of unemployment (%)	7.7888	5.5865	0.1600	34.9300
Young	Proportion of population under 15 years of age	0.2779	0.1082	0.1106	0.5022
Old	Proportion of population 65 years or older	0.0853	0.0569	0.0075	0.2602
Population density	Population density (persons per km^2)	226.4174	788.2143	1.6682	7806.7730
Latitude	Absolute latitude at the centroid of a country (in absolute decimalised degrees)	28.7922	16.9157	0	65
Freedom	Freedom to make life choices; 0 (lowest level) to 1 (highest level)	0.7200	0.1457	0.2575	0.9799
Northamerica	Continent dummy, 1 if country belongs to North America, 0 otherwise	0.0156986	0.1243555	0	1
Southamerica	Continent dummy, 1 if country belongs to South America, 0 otherwise	0.0800628	0.271497	0	1

Table 6.1 (continued)

Variable	Description	Mean	Std Dev.	Min.	Max.
Asia	Continent dummy, 1 if country belongs to Asia, 0 otherwise	0.3265306	0.469128	0	1
Africa	Continent dummy, 1 if country belongs to Africa, 0 otherwise	0.233124	0.4229866	0	1
Oceania	Continent dummy, 1 if country belongs to Oceania, 0 otherwise	0.0141287	0.118068	0	1
Year2005	Year dummy, 1 if 2005, 0 otherwise	0.0212	0.1441	0	1
Year2006	Year dummy, 1 if 2006, 0 otherwise	0.0706	0.2563	0	1
Year2007	Year dummy, 1 if 2007, 0 otherwise	0.0801	0.2715	0	1
Year2008	Year dummy, 1 if 2008, 0 otherwise	0.0863	0.2810	0	1
Year2009	Year dummy, 1 if 2009, 0 otherwise	0.0895	0.2856	0	1
Year2010	Year dummy, 1 if 2010, 0 otherwise	0.0973	0.2965	0	1
Year2011	Year dummy, 1 if 2011, 0 otherwise	0.1146	0.3187	0	1
Year2012	Year dummy, 1 if 2012, 0 otherwise	0.1115	0.3148	0	1
Year2013	Year dummy, 1 if 2013, 0 otherwise	0.1075	0.3099	0	1
Year2014	Year dummy, 1 if 2014, 0 otherwise	0.1146	0.3187	0	1

Sources: See text.

variables are also jointly insignificant even at 10 per cent. The implication is clear enough: representing the climate only in terms of annual averages essentially captures nothing.

Despite the insignificance of the climate variables, some of the other variables nevertheless have the expected signs and provide a statistically significant explanation of the cross-country variation in SWB. Leaving aside discussion of the year dummies, as expected, the single most important variable is log GDP per capita, which is positively signed and significant at 1 per cent. Inflation and unemployment, however, are both statistically insignificant at 10 per cent. The fraction of people under 15 is highly significant and positively related to SWB. The number of old people is also positively related to SWB, although this coefficient is not statistically significant at 10 per cent. This pattern is suggestive of the familiar result whereby there is a U-shaped relationship between SWB and age. Neither population density nor the absolute latitude of the country is

Table 6.2 Results

	Model 1	Model 2	Model 3
Meantemp	0.0482		
	(0.98)		
Meantemp (squared)	−0.00119		
	(−0.99)		
Mintemp		0.0328***	
		(3.72)	
Maxtemp		−0.0554***	
		(−3.64)	
HDM			−0.0115***
			(−4.43)
CDM			−0.00782***
			(−4.29)
Log (GDPPC)	0.940***	0.840***	0.852***
	(9.70)	(10.08)	(11.53)
Inflation	0.003	−0.00257	0.0043
	(0.49)	(−0.55)	(0.77)
Unemployment	−0.0186	−0.0276*	−0.0338*
	(−1.24)	(−2.00)	(−2.48)
Young	4.275***	1.76	2.688*
	(3.37)	(1.35)	(2.41)
Old	4.342	0.986	3.12
	(1.55)	(0.54)	(1.21)
Population density	−8.7E-05	−0.0001	−0.00013
	(−0.61)	(−0.96)	(−1.06)
Latitude	−0.00632	0.00634	0.0105
	(−0.57)	(0.67)	(1.23)
Freedom	1.499**	1.006	1.407**
	(2.84)	(1.70)	(3.10)
Year2005	0.464**	0.479**	0.371*
	(3.34)	(2.97)	(2.57)
Year2006	0.34	0.31	0.356
	(1.40)	(1.18)	(1.44)
Year2007	0.460***	0.416**	0.447**
	(3.58)	(2.83)	(3.27)
Year2008	0.342	0.34	0.329
	(1.82)	(1.77)	(1.68)
Year2009	0.21	0.174	0.21
	(1.41)	(1.06)	(1.35)
Year2010	0.25	0.233	0.243
	(1.49)	(1.29)	(1.38)
Year2011	0.191*	0.202*	0.180*
	(2.52)	(2.43)	(2.20)
Year2012	0.251*	0.227	0.241*
	(2.11)	(1.94)	(2.01)

Table 6.2 (continued)

	Model 1	Model 2	Model 3
Year2013	0.116*	0.108	0.110*
	(2.19)	(1.97)	(2.03)
Year2014	0.123**	0.118**	0.117**
	(2.87)	(2.66)	(2.74)
Constant	−6.194***	−2.697*	−3.876***
	(−5.24)	(−2.16)	(−3.94)
N	1274	1274	1274
R^2	0.7183	0.7484	0.7609

Note: Estimation based on OLS with clustered standard errors; * significant at the 5 per cent level; ** significant at the 1 per cent level; *** significant at the 0.1 per cent level; t-statistics in parentheses.

statistically significant at 10 per cent, but the freedom variable is significant at 1 per cent. The R-squared is 0.7183.

Turning now to Model 2, the R-squared rises to 0.7484 when representing the climate by mean temperature in the coldest and hottest months. Both of these are individually significant at 1 per cent. The results point to a strong preference for less extreme climates. More specifically, SWB increases with higher temperatures in the coldest month and declines with higher temperatures in the hottest month. Several of the other explanatory variables that were statistically significant in Model 1 are now statistically insignificant, and it is clear that apart from log GDP per capita, temperature extremes are now statistically speaking the most important determinants of SWB. Indeed, such is the dominance of log GDP per capita and minimum and maximum temperatures that, as a group, the other control variables contained in the regression are significant only at 5 per cent.

In Model 3, the R-squared rises further to 0.7609. The increase in the R-squared is attributable to the use of *HDM* and *CDM* as a means of representing the climate. Because each of the models discussed so far contains the same number of explanatory variables, it is possible to select the best model on the basis of the R-squared. The coefficients on both *HDM* and *CDM* are negative, indicating that climates where monthly temperatures are often below 18.3°C strongly reduce SWB, as do those where monthly temperatures are often above 18.3°C. The further that monthly temperatures are either above or below this base temperature, the greater the reduction in SWB. It is interesting to enquire whether positive and negative deviations have a similar impact on SWB. In fact it is impossible to reject the hypothesis that, rather than *HDM*and *CDM*, individuals are actually concerned about *DM*: deviations from 18.3°C in whatever direction (results not shown).

6.6 ROBUSTNESS CHECKS

Having investigated models differing in terms of the manner in which the climate variables are specified, we now investigate how robust these findings are (Table 6.3). Hitherto we have used data in which missing values have been imputed. Model 4 considers whether the analysis is affected by this procedure. If observations with missing values are instead

Table 6.3 Further results

	Model 4	Model 5	Model 6	Model 7	Model 8	Model 9	Model 10
	Excluding interpolated values	No use of probability weights	Colder countries (mean temp ≤ 18.1667°C)	Warmer countries (mean temp > 18.1667°C)	Richer countries (GDPPC > 11 225 USD)	Poorer countries (GDPPC ≤ 11 225 USD)	Controlling for continents
HDM	−0.0118***	−0.00423*	−0.00930***	−0.0438*	−0.00959**	−0.00740*	−0.00760***
	(−4.37)	(−2.40)	(−3.46)	(−2.53)	(−2.95)	(−2.37)	(−3.88)
CDM	−0.00800***	−0.00570***	−0.0234***	−0.00940***	−0.00381*	−0.0107***	−0.00366**
	(−4.12)	(−3.60)	(−4.67)	(−4.04)	(−2.10)	(−4.48)	(−2.92)
Log(GDPPC)	0.870***	0.683***	0.872***	0.691***	0.463***	0.960***	0.666***
	(10.98)	(8.69)	(10.85)	(6.71)	(3.59)	(8.66)	(10.35)
Inflation	0.00923	−0.00105	−0.008	−0.00574	−0.00195	0.00382	−0.00399
	(1.05)	(−0.18)	(−1.93)	(−0.77)	(−0.28)	(0.59)	(−0.96)
Unemployment	−0.0361*	−0.0283**	−0.0381*	−0.0277	−0.012	−0.0373*	−0.0279**
	(−2.54)	(−3.23)	(−2.51)	(−1.32)	(−0.68)	(−2.44)	(−3.27)
Young	2.700*	1.074	2.871*	0.786	0.886	0.629	2.625**
	(2.15)	(1.05)	(2.30)	(0.50)	(0.55)	(0.37)	(2.65)
Old	2.888	1.776	0.824	12.27*	3.75	−0.771	2.031*
	(1.08)	(1.20)	(0.44)	(2.13)	(0.75)	(−0.24)	(2.09)
Population density	−0.00014	−0.00011	−0.00062	−0.00018	3.37E-05	−0.000249**	−4.4E-05
	(−1.09)	(−1.51)	(−1.50)	(−1.61)	(0.16)	(−2.97)	(−0.51)
Latitude	0.012	0.00362	0.0138	0.00358	0.00741	−0.00602	0.00795
	(1.33)	(0.53)	(1.39)	(0.45)	(0.71)	(−0.50)	(1.30)
Freedom	1.371**	1.861***	1.926***	−0.126	0.411	2.748***	1.068**
	(2.93)	(5.73)	(3.85)	(0.27)	(0.82)	(6.33)	(2.87)
North America							0.285*
							(2.24)

Table 6.3 (continued)

	Model 4	Model 5	Model 6	Model 7	Model 8	Model 9	Model 10
	Excluding interpolated values	No use of probability weights	Colder countries (mean temp ≤ 18.1667°C)	Warmer countries (mean temp > 18.1667°C)	Richer countries (GDPPC > 11 225 USD)	Poorer countries (GDPPC ≤ 11 225 USD)	Controlling for continents
South America							0.264
							(1.61)
Asia							−0.557***
							(−6.29)
Africa							−0.828***
							(−7.29)
Oceania							0.678***
							(6.62)
Year2005	0.403**	0.324**	0.0585	0.861***	0.619***	0.196*	0.344*
	(2.80)	(3.09)	(0.41)	(4.58)	(3.72)	(2.04)	(2.41)
Year2006	0.492	0.0855	−0.00011	0.632	0.484	0.108	0.248
	(1.66)	(1.56)	(−0.00)	(1.78)	(1.70)	(1.00)	(0.96)
Year2007	0.524***	0.288***	0.248***	0.586**	0.582***	0.262***	0.357*
	(3.54)	(4.49)	(3.54)	(3.13)	(3.72)	(3.90)	(2.55)
Year2008	0.393	0.277***	0.102	0.514	0.492*	0.287***	0.289
	(1.97)	(3.96)	(0.84)	(1.87)	(2.19)	(5.02)	(1.51)
Year2009	0.273*	0.276***	−0.0656	0.366***	0.270*	0.317**	0.13
	(2.54)	(5.11)	(−0.30)	(4.80)	(2.51)	(3.39)	(0.80)
Year2010	0.303*	0.209***	−0.0452	0.490**	0.394*	0.290***	0.202
	(2.05)	(4.23)	(0.25)	(2.76)	(2.14)	(4.54)	(1.11)

Year2011	0.244***	0.164***	0.0521	0.353***	0.364***	0.195**	0.173*
	(3.42)	(3.48)	(0.55)	(3.85)	(3.65)	(3.39)	(2.10)
Year2012	0.310**	0.132**	0.0599	0.302**	0.402***	0.204**	0.219
	(2.81)	(2.97)	(0.63)	(2.87)	(3.43)	(3.36)	(1.92)
Year2013	0.175*	0.0609	0.0847	0.107	0.0712	0.0956	0.0971
	(2.55)	(1.43)	(0.94)	(1.44)	(0.99)	(0.95)	(1.78)
Year2014	0.143**	0.0652	0.0648	0.142*	0.102	0.101	0.104*
	(3.06)	(1.73)	(1.37)	(2.58)	(1.68)	(1.86)	(2.39)
Constant	−4.087***	−2.218*	−3.990***	−0.984	0.134	−4.564***	−1.681*
	(−3.45)	(−2.16)	(−4.44)	(−0.61)	(0.08)	(−4.07)	(−1.98)
N	1150	1274	631	643	607	667	1274
R^2	0.7731	0.7151	0.8822	0.6823	0.3385	0.7559	0.8197

Note: Estimation based on OLS with clustered standard errors; * significant at the 5 per cent level; ** significant at the 1 per cent level; *** significant at the 0.1 per cent level; t-statistics in parentheses.

dropped, the number of countries included in the sample falls from 165 to 150 and the number of observations drops from 1274 to 1150. The statistical significance of *HDM* and *CDM* is unaffected: both remain statistically significant at 1 per cent and the coefficients themselves change little. Unemployment and the fraction of individuals under 15 are both significant at 5 per cent. Freedom is statistically significant at 1 per cent.

Reverting to the data with imputed values, Model 5 continues to assume clustered errors and use dummy variables for the different years. However, in this model the observations are no longer population-weighted: small countries and large countries have the same weight, and survey years including more countries have more weight. Despite these changes there is, however, only a minor impact on the *HDM* and *CDM* coefficients. The statistical significance of the *HDM* variable slips from 1 per cent to 5 per cent. The statistical significance of the *CDM* variable stays at 1 per cent.

The next analysis distinguishes between countries whose mean temperature is above or below the median temperature (which happens to be 18.1667°C, curiously close to the temperature threshold of 18.3°C used to calculate the temperature deviations). The results are displayed in Models 6 and 7, where it is observed that in cold countries both *HDM* and *CDM* remain statistically significant at the 1 per cent level of confidence. For countries whose mean temperature is $>$ 18.1667°C, *HDM* is now significant at 5 per cent whereas *CDM* remains statistically significant at 1 per cent. This suggests that the base temperature for calculating temperature deviations does not depend on mean annual temperature.

We now investigate whether preferences for *HDM* and *CDM* differ with respect to income. In order to accomplish this we divide the data according to the median level of GDP per capita of US$11 225 (Models 8 and 9). The results suggest that the preference for climate is indeed independent of income. More specifically, the coefficients from the two regressions do not appear to be different. We also investigated this point by interacting both *HDM* and *CDM* with the log of income per capita. Neither of the newly created variables was statistically significant at 5 per cent. This is important because climate policy needs to know whether future (hopefully richer) generations will value climate differently.

Finally, we add additional variables denoting the different continents (Model 10). We identify with a dummy variable countries in North America, South America, Asia, Africa and Oceania, with European countries as the comparator group. Note that there are insufficient observations to run separate regressions for any one continent. The dummy variables denoting Asian and African countries are negative and statistically significant. implying that compared to Europe, SWB is lower in these continents for reasons not captured in the regression model. But although including these dummy variables might be expected to diminish the statistical significance of the climate variables, both *HDM* and *CDM* continue to be statistically significant at 1 per cent. We conclude that the climate variables are not in some way compensating for otherwise ignored differences across the different continents.

6.7 CONCLUSIONS

In this chapter we review the literature on the role of the climate in explaining geographical variations in SWB. We also use more recent and more extensive data to update our earlier research on the importance of the climate in explaining cross-country variations in SWB.

According to the results of the literature review (and also those of our empirical analysis) two key findings emerge. The first relates to the importance of distinguishing those climates where temperature varies across the annual cycle from those where it does not. Any analysis failing to distinguish between extreme 'continental' climates and mild 'maritime' ones is in danger of erroneously finding that individuals do not care about the climate. The second finding is that when appropriate representations of the climate are used, then climate variables are incredibly important. Next to GDP per capita, it appears that climate is the most important variable in explaining cross-country variations in SWB. This finding underlines the magnitude of the potential threat to wellbeing in some locations posed by climate change. Equally, we should not discount the possibility of substantial gains in other locations. These gains and losses of course refer only to the direct impacts.

We also identify a large number of research issues which future researchers ought to address. One challenge is that in order to analyse the impacts of climate change it is necessary to use data in which the location of the respondents is known with a far greater degree of precision. This requires the use of subnational data. A further unresolved issue is whether only temperature matters, or whether some other climate variables matter too. There appears to be some evidence that hours of sunshine and the number of rain-days impact upon SWB, along with humidity. There is also a concern as to whether systematically conducting surveys at particular times of the year might somehow be responsible for the result that climate is a highly significant determinant of SWB. We think that it is necessary to conduct all-year-round surveys, or else avoid the use of SWB questions that invite a response which depends on experiences, for example, over the last 30 days. There is also concern that analyses using data from regions across which households can easily migrate might exhibit compensating wage and house price differentials. These should be controlled for as part of the analysis. It also seems important to confirm that different sorts of approaches – for example, the hedonic and HPF approaches – yield similar results notwithstanding their limitations.

Finally, we encourage future researchers not merely to conduct analyses into SWB and the climate, but then to use the results of such analyses to make predictions about the impacts of climate change. This implies using the results of SWB analyses to calculate the implicit values of climate variables across different times of the year, and then combining them with actual projections of climate change obtained under different emissions scenarios. Although we have not done so in this chapter, in our opinion such estimates could help to improve the valuation of climate impacts, permitting (perhaps) a more informed discussion of the costs and benefits of measures to slow the rate of climate change.

REFERENCES

Barrington-Leigh, C. and F. Behzadnejad (2017), 'The impact of daily weather conditions on life satisfaction: evidence from cross-sectional and panel data', *Journal of Economic Psychology*, **59**, 145–163.

Bartik, T. (1988), 'Evaluating the benefits of non-marginal reductions in pollution using information on defensive expenditures', *Journal of Environmental Economics and Management*, **15** (1), 111–127.

Becker, G. (1965), 'A theory of the allocation of time', *Economic Journal*, **75** (299), 493–517.

Bjørnskov, C., Dreher, A. and J.A.V. Fischer (2008), 'Cross-country determinants of life satisfaction: exploring different determinants across groups in society', *Social Choice Welfare*, **30** (1), 119–173.
Bradford, D. and G.G. Hildebrandt (1977), 'Observable public good preferences', *Journal of Public Economics*, **8** (2), 111–131.
Brereton, F., Clinch, J.P. and S. Ferreira (2008),'Happiness, geography and the environment', *Ecological Economics*, **65** (2), 386–396.
Clark, A.E. and A.J. Oswald (1994), 'Unhappiness and unemployment', *Economic Journal*, **104** (424), 648–659.
Cuñado, J. and F.P. De Gracia (2013), 'Environment and happiness: new evidence for Spain', *Social Indicators Research*, **112** (3), 549–567.
Cushing, B.J. (1987), 'A note on the specification of climate variables in models of population migration', *Journal of Regional Science*, **27** (4), 641–649.
Di Tella, R., MacCulloch, R.J. and S.J. Oswald (2001), 'Preferences over inflation and unemployment: evidence from surveys of happiness', *American Economic Review*, **91** (1), 335–341.
Easterlin, R.A. (1974), 'Does economic growth improve the human lot? Some empirical evidence', in Paul A. David and Melvin W. Reder (eds), *Nations and Households in Economic Growth: Essays in Honor of Moses Abramovitz*, New York, USA: Academic Press, pp. 89–125.
Ebert, U. (2007), 'Revealed preference and household production', *Journal of Environmental Economics and Management*, **53** (2), 276–289.
Ebert, U. and H. Welsch (2012), 'Adaptation and mitigation in global pollution problems: economic impacts of productivity, sensitivity, and adaptive capacity', *Environment and Resource Economics*, **52** (1), 49–64.
Federsen, J., Metcalfe, R. and M. Wooden (2016), 'Subjective wellbeing: why weather matters', *Journal of the Royal Statistical Society: Series A (Statistics in Society)*, **179** (1), 203–228.
Ferreira, S., Akay, A., Brereton, F., Cuñado, J., Martinsson, P., et al. (2013), 'Life satisfaction and air quality in Europe', *Ecological Economics*, **88**, 1–10.
Ferreira, S. and M. Moro (2010), 'On the use of subjective well-being data for environmental valuation', *Environmental and Resource Economics*, **46** (3), 249–273.
Frijters, P. and B. Van Praag (1998), 'The effects of climate on welfare and well-being in Russia', *Climatic Change*, **39** (1), 61–81.
Goetz, S.J., Davlasheridze, M. and Y. Han (2015), 'County-level determinants of mental health, 2002–2008', *Social Indicators Research*, **124** (2), 657–670.
Helliwell, J., Layard, R. and J. Sachs (2016), *World Happiness Report, Update (Vol. I)*, New York, USA: Sustainable Development Solutions Network.
Kelley, J. (2016), 'Human gains and losses from global warming: satisfaction with the climate in the USA, winter and summer, north and south', *Social Indicators Research*, **131** (1), 345–366.
Lanz, B. and A. Provins (2017), 'Using averting expenditures to estimate the demand for public goods: combining objective and perceived quality', *Resource and Energy Economics*, **47**, 20–35.
Maddison, D. (2003), 'The amenity value of the climate: the household production function approach', *Energy and Resource Economics*, **25** (2), 155–175.
Maddison, D. and K. Rehdanz (2011), 'The impact of climate on life satisfaction', *Ecological Economics*, **70** (12), 2437–2445.
Murray, T., Maddison, D. and K. Rehdanz (2013), 'Do geographical variations in climate influence life satisfaction?', *Climate Change Economics*, **4** (1), 2–23.
Rehdanz, K. and D. Maddison (2005), 'Climate and happiness', *Ecological Economics*, **52** (1), 111–125.
Rehdanz, K. and D. Maddison (2009), 'The amenity value of climate to German households', *Oxford Economic Papers*, **61** (1), 150–167.
Schwarz, N. and F. Strack (1991), 'Evaluating one's life: a judgment model of subjective well-being', in Fritz Strack, Michael Argyle and Norbert Schwarz (eds), *Subjective Well-Being: An Interdisciplinary Perspective*, Oxford, UK: Pergamon Press.
Stock, J.H. and M.W. Watson (2008), 'Heteroskedasticity-robust standard errors for fixed effects panel data regression', *Econometrica*, **76** (1), 155–174.
Tol, R.S.J. (2018), 'The economic impacts of climate change', *Review of Environmental Economics and Policy*, **12** (1), 4–25.

7. Natural disasters and self-reported wellbeing: empirical evidence for rainfall extremes in the United Kingdom

Michael Berlemann, Judith Regner and Jascha Tutt

7.1 INTRODUCTION

Natural disasters have always affected life on planet Earth. However, only recently have economists started analysing the effects of natural disasters on economic development. The rising interest in the effects of natural disasters was largely triggered by the expectation that the ongoing process of global warming increases the frequency or at least the severity of certain types of natural hazards and extreme weather events. Under a warming climate, extreme temperatures and precipitation events are expected to occur more often (Banholzer et al., 2014). The same holds true for the length, frequency and/or intensity of heatwaves (IPCC, 2013). For other natural hazards such as tropical storms the picture is less clear (see, e.g., Callaghan and Power, 2011; Grinsted et al., 2012; Thomas, 2014; Wang and Lee, 2008), as tropical storms become natural disasters typically only when making landfall, and global warming tends to affect tropical cyclone tracks (Murakami and Wang, 2010).

Economists mostly measure material living standards in terms of the level and growth of the gross domestic product (GDP). It is thus not surprising that most of the existing (economic) literature on the effects of natural disasters is concerned with their growth effects. In their comprehensive analysis of the short-term effects of different sorts of natural disasters, Felbermayr and Gröschl (2014) conclude that the effect of natural disasters on short-term economic growth is 'naturally negative'. While up to now little attention has been devoted to the question whether natural disasters have medium- and long-term growth effects, some recent papers indicate that natural disasters affect economic growth patterns even over longer periods of time (Hsiang and Jina, 2014; Berlemann and Wenzel, 2016, 2018).

Recently, considerable effort has been devoted to studying the effects of natural disasters on the microeconomic level. An important strand of this literature analyses the effect of natural disasters on measures of self-reported individual wellbeing. Both dimensions of self-reported wellbeing have been considered: happiness and life satisfaction. Although the terms 'happiness' and 'life satisfaction' are often used interchangeably, the two concepts do not coincide. Happiness refers to the comparatively short-term, affective and thus more volatile component of individual wellbeing; while life satisfaction can thus be thought of as the cognitive and less volatile long-term component of individual wellbeing (Berlemann, 2016).

When natural disasters occur they might affect individuals in various different ways. In the most extreme case, a natural disaster may exact a death toll. But even if an individual survives a natural disaster, a disaster might affect their health status negatively, for example by causing more or less severe injuries. Besides, natural disasters often destroy individual property, thereby causing negative wealth effects for the affected individuals (at least, when they are not fully insured). Disasters might also affect an individual's employment status, for example because affected firms have to dismiss employees. And even if their job status remains unchanged, the individual's income might change, for example as a consequence of a changing demand for goods and services. Thus, whenever natural disasters occur and affect health status, cause wealth or income effects, or change employment status, we should expect this to translate into wellbeing effects as all these variables have shown to be important determinants of happiness and life satisfaction (see e.g. Frey and Stutzer, 2002; van Praag and Ferrer-i-Carbonell, 2004; Frey, 2008; Diener and Biswas-Diener, 2008).

However, natural disasters might also affect individual wellbeing through a psychological channel. The mere possibility that natural disasters might occur and affect individual living conditions might be an additional source of individual disutility. If this holds true, higher disaster risk should go along with lower self-reported wellbeing. However, this issue has rarely been studied. In this chapter, we contribute to closing this gap in the literature by delivering an analysis of extreme rainfall events on both measures of self-reported wellbeing: happiness and life satisfaction. In our empirical analysis we regress both wellbeing measures on a number of control variables and a measure of regionally occurring extreme rainfall events. The effects of actual events are captured by the control variables, among them income, employment and health status. Thus, whenever we find a systematic effect for the extreme rainfall indicator, we might interpret this finding as evidence in favour of the earlier described psychological channel.

In order to do so, we employ data from the United Kingdom (UK) Household Longitudinal Study and combine it with precipitation data, collected by the UK Meteorological Office (Met Office). The case of the United Kingdom is interesting and relevant as several studies for the United Kingdom found an increase in rainfall totals in winter and fewer but more intense rainfall events and a slight decrease in summer. Moreover, the last decade in the United Kingdom was meteorologically characterised by some of the wettest events since the beginning of weather recording (Jones et al., 2013; Fowler and Kilsby, 2003). We opted for the year 2012 as the winter of 2011 and the whole year 2012 was characterised by several intense weather anomalies. Early winter storms in December 2011 with record-breaking wind speeds caused power cuts and school closures in Scotland and resulted in heavy rainfall over the coast of Wales and southern England (Met Office, 2012). The year 2012 started with heavy storms in January, continued with exceptionally wet weather in the summer, and witnessed broken records in precipitation in the autumn. Several heavy precipitation events occurring close after one another in late November 2012 led to the wettest weeks in England in the last five decades (Met Office, 2016). Again, the resulting floods that lasted until Christmas that year disrupted public transport because of damage to railways and infrastructure. Hundreds of people were evacuated and several fatalities were reported (Met Office, 2013).

In our empirical analysis we find no systematic effect of the deviation of rainfall from its long-run mean on both measures of self-reported wellbeing. Thus, rainfall in general seems to be unrelated to happiness and life satisfaction. Turning to extreme rainfall events, we find a different picture. While extreme rainfall events that occurred in the region in the year before being surveyed turn out to have no effect on self-reported happiness, we find a systematically negative and significant effect of these events for life satisfaction. Thus, when evaluating their general satisfaction with life, individuals seem to take the risk of being confronted with extreme rainfall events into account.

The chapter is structured as follows. Section 7.2 delivers a brief review of the related literature. Section 7.3 explains the estimation approach and introduces the employed data. It also delivers some summary statistics of the employed dataset. In section 7.4, we report and discuss the results. Section 7.5 concludes.

7.2 REVIEW OF THE RELATED LITERATURE

The empirical literature on the influence of natural disasters on measures of subjective wellbeing is comparatively young and has developed since early this century. The existing literature can broadly be subdivided into two groups.

The first group of papers evolved within the literature on environmental evaluation. As an alternative to conventional methods (such as contingent valuation, travel cost models and hedonic approaches) the value of environmental goods (or 'bads') can be assessed using subjective wellbeing data. The idea behind this approach is to regress a measure of subjective wellbeing on a number of likely determinants – including household or Organisation for Economic Co-operation and Development (OECD) equivalence income – and a measure of the environmental good to be evaluated. The value of the environmental good can then be assessed on the basis of the marginal rate of substitution between income and the level of the environmental good. This approach has been used to assess the value of environmental quality (Welsch, 2002; van Praag and Baarsma, 2005; Welsch, 2006; Rehdanz and Maddison, 2008; MacKerron and Mourato, 2009; Luechinger, 2009; Ferreira and Moro, 2010), urban regeneration schemes (Dolan and Metcalfe, 2008) and climate (Van der Vliert et al., 2004; Rehdanz and Maddison, 2005; Maddison and Rehdanz, 2011).

A few papers applied the approach to the evaluation of natural disasters. Carroll et al. (2008) attempted to quantify the costs of droughts in Australia throughout the period of 2001 to 2004. They find that, at least in rural areas, life satisfaction significantly decreases during droughts. Luechinger and Raschky (2009) apply the valuation method to flood disasters in a sample of 15 European countries and find a significantly negative and robust effect on life satisfaction. The effect starts to decay one year after the disasters occurred, and completely vanishes after two years. Kountouris and Remoundou (2011) are concerned with quantifying the welfare costs of wildfires in the Mediterranean region, and find life satisfaction of the rural population to be negatively affected. Rehdanz et al. (2015) study the effects of the Fukushima catastrophe, and find a significantly negative effect on subjective wellbeing that turns out to be the larger, the closer individuals live to Fukushima.

The second group of papers makes no attempt of monetising the effect of disasters, but directly focuses on the effects of disasters on economic wellbeing. Kimball et al. (2006) use happiness data from the University of Michigan Consumer Survey to study the effects of two natural disasters: Hurricane Katrina in August 2005, and a large earthquake in Pakistan in October 2005. The authors report a decrease in happiness in early September 2005 which lasted for 2–3 weeks and which was most pronounced in the south central region of the United States, which was closest to the devastation of Katrina. The authors also found happiness in the United States to decrease after the Pakistan earthquake, thereby indicating that the respondents did not only care about disasters in their own country but also in places far away. Berger (2010) uses the 1986 wave of the German Socio-Economic Panel (SOEP) to study the reaction of the panel members (from households in Germany) to the Chernobyl disaster, which occurred in late April 1986. She finds no significant effect on self-reported life satisfaction when controlling for a bunch of sociodemographic control variables. Yamamura (2012) studies the long-term effects of the large earthquake in Kobe which occurred in 1995. After controlling for various sociodemographic control variables, Yamamura (2012) finds the survivors of the Kobe earthquake to be significantly happier than the respondents from other Japanese regions. The author concludes that surviving a large natural disaster has a long-lasting positive effect on subjective wellbeing. Von Möllendorff and Hirschfeld (2016) study the effect of floods, storms and hail events on life satisfaction based on 11 waves of the German Socio-Economic Panel (SOEP). They find that storms and hail events have a rather short-term negative effect on life satisfaction, while the effect of floods is more long-lived. They attribute this finding to the fact that the insurance coverage for storms and hail events is much larger than for floods. Sekulova and van den Bergh (2016) study the impact of a number of floods on life satisfaction in Bulgaria, based on a survey conducted among 600 affected individuals. Besides finding a negative short-term impact on life satisfaction, the authors also detect that self-reported worries about future disaster depress life satisfaction. Finally, Berlemann (2016) studies the effect of hurricane risk on a sample of 80 countries, based on data from the Integrated European and World Value Survey and the Best Track Dataset of tropical cyclones. Hurricane risk turned out to affect happiness only in the subsample of less developed countries, whereas the risk of tropical cyclones affects life satisfaction in the sample of both developed and underdeveloped countries.

7.3 DATA AND ESTIMATION APPROACH

7.3.1 General Estimation Approach

Our estimation approach consists of regressing a measure of self-reported wellbeing on a number of control variables and an indicator of (extreme) precipitation risk. Self-reported wellbeing is typically measured on ordinal scales with only a few discrete outcomes. Thus, estimating a linear model using ordinary least squares (OLS) is inappropriate, here. In our estimation approach, we make use of generalised linear model (GLM) estimation methods. More precisely, we opt for the ordered logit approach and estimate the model:

$$Prob(W_{i,j} = k) = Prob(\pi_{k-1} < \alpha + \beta X_i + \gamma R_j + \varepsilon_{i,j} \leq \pi_k) \qquad (7.1)$$

where $W_{i,j}$ is a measure of wellbeing (either happiness or life satisfaction) of individual i, living in region j (we explain below which regional level we use in our analysis, as this choice had to be based on the available data). The vector X includes the control variables on the individual level. R is a rainfall indicator, which is available on the regional level. We estimate the model using the maximum likelihood technique. As the rainfall indicator has the same value for all individuals living in the same region, we cluster the error term on the regional level (see Chamberlain, 1980; Ferrer-i-Carbonell and Frijters, 2004).

7.3.2 Data

For our study, we employ two different datasets. The data on self-reported wellbeing as well as numerous control variables come from the UK Household Longitudinal Study. As this study does not contain information on rainfall events, we extract this information from a precipitation dataset collected by the UK Meteorological Office, and combine it with the survey data. In the following, we describe both data sources and the extracted variables. The reported summary statistics refer to the 34988 respondents for which all variables that we use in the subsequent empirical analysis are available.

Survey data

The survey data that we use in our empirical study comes from the UK Household Longitudinal Study (UKHLS), which is also known as 'Understanding Society'. The UKHLS is an annual longitudinal household panel survey, managed by the Institute for Social and Economic Research (ISER) at the University of Essex. The multi-focus, multi-topic social survey started in 2009 with a nationally representative stratified, clustered sample of 27000 households living in the United Kingdom. In addition to the face-to-face interviews, the household members fill out questionnaires. The survey is organised into several modules and covers topics such as health, work, education, income, family and social life. The resulting data also come with data on the place of living of the surveyed (local authority unit level, upper level) and are used extensively in the social sciences. For our empirical analysis, we need measures of general individual wellbeing. The survey contains two such measures: *Life Satisfaction Overall* and *General Happiness*. In our empirical analysis, we use both variables.

In the UKHLS, respondents are asked, as part of the self-completion questionnaire, to rate on a seven-point scale how satisfied they are with their 'life overall'. All scale points are labelled and range from 'completely dissatisfied' to 'completely satisfied'. Figure 7.1 gives an overview of the distribution of the answers. The mean of 5.08 reveals a comparatively high level of life satisfaction of the survey participants, and the median of 6.0 shows that over 50 per cent of the respondents are 'mostly' or 'completely satisfied' with their lives.

The second wellbeing variable, *General Happiness*, is measured by the answers to the question: 'Have you recently been feeling reasonably happy, all things considered?'. Four answering categories are available: 'more so than usual' (1), 'about the same as usual' (2), 'less so than usual' (3) and 'much less than usual' (4). As the happiness variable is coded in a way that higher values go along with less happiness, we recoded it inversely. Figure 7.2 gives an overview on the frequencies of occurrence of the four answers. The mean of 2.95 and the median of 3.0 indicate that the majority of the survey participants do not feel any change in their usual level of happiness.

The employed set of control variables also comes from the UKHLS. We oriented our choice of the control variables on those variables which have often been found to have a significant impact on subjective measures of wellbeing, and which are available in the survey. First, we control for the age of the survey participants. In line with most of the

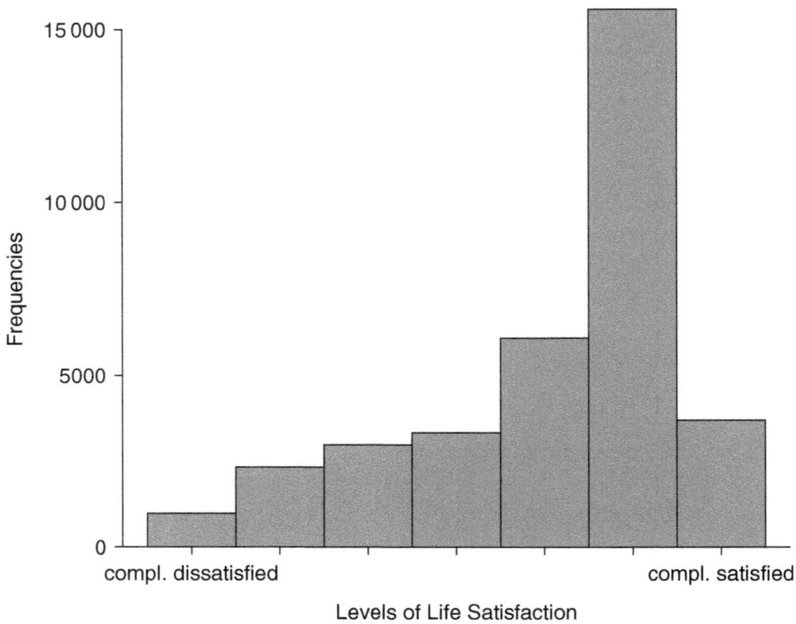

Source: Own calculations based on UK Household Longitudinal Study, Wave 2012.

Figure 7.1 Distribution of survey respondents' levels of life satisfaction (N = 34 988)

literature, we allow for a linear-quadratic impact of age. Second, we have information on a respondent's gender. In the empirical analysis, we use a dummy variable for female respondents. Third, we control for education by adding a dummy variable for highly educated individuals. We construct this dummy on the basis of the answers to the question on the highest qualification ever reached. We classify all individuals with a degree or a higher degree as highly educated. Fourth, we control for the self-reported individual health status, which is measured on a five-point ordinal scale: 'excellent' (1), 'very good' (2), 'good' (3), 'fair' (4), 'poor' (5). Thus, low indicator values go along with good health. Fifth, we take the marital status into account. In order to do so, we code a number of control variables for single, married, separated, divorced and widowed individuals as well as for individuals living as a couple without being married. All other sorts of marital status form a final subgroup. Sixth, we control for the job status and create a dummy variable for employed individuals. Seventh, we add self-reported total net personal monthly income to the set of control variables. Besides these control variables, we also have information on the local authority units (LAUs), upper level, that the respondents live in.

Table 7.1 reports on the summary statistics of the described control variables. On average, the survey respondents in our sample are 47 years old. The share of female respondents (55.7 per cent) is considerably larger than that for males. The median health status turns out to be 'very good'. Slightly more than one-third of the sample are highly educated. Roughly half of the respondents in our sample are married (51.2 per cent); another 12.4 per cent are living as unmarried couples; 21.8 per cent in our sample are

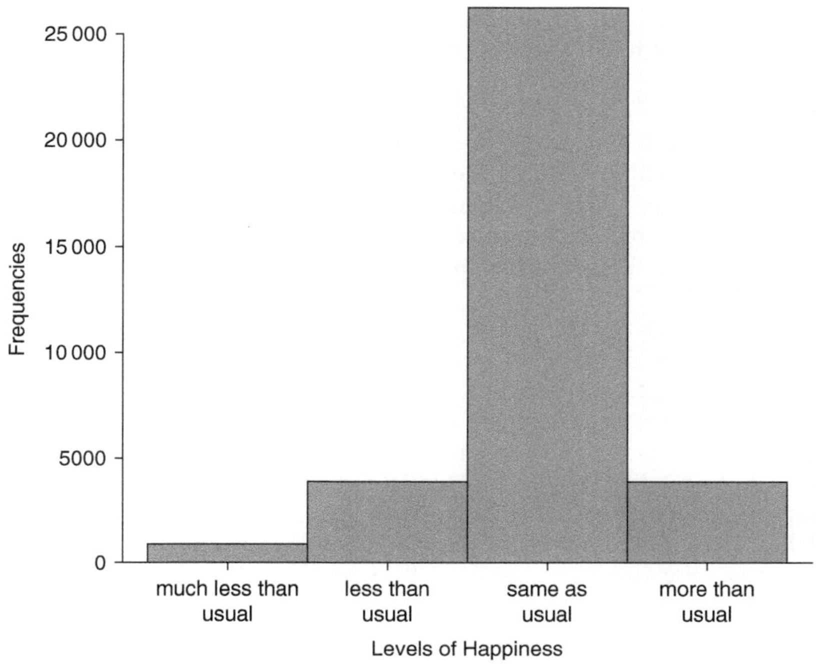

Source: Own calculations based on UK Household Longitudinal Study, Wave 2012.

Figure 7.2 Distribution of survey respondents' recent level of happiness (N = 34 988)

Table 7.1 Summary statistics for control variables (N = 34 988)

	Min.	Max.	Mean	Median	Std dev.
Age	16	99	47.148	46	18.1
Female	0	1	0.557	1	0.497
Single	0	1	0.218	0	0.413
Health status	1	5	2.58	2	1.096
Highly educated	0	1	0.357	0	0.479
Single	0	1	0.218	0	0.413
Married	0	1	0.512	1	0.500
Couple	0	1	0.124	0	0.329
Separated	0	1	0.018	0	0.134
Divorced	0	1	0.068	0	0.253
Widowed	0	1	0.056	0	0.231
Other marital status	0	1	0.003	0	0.054
Employed	0	1	0.569	1	0.495
Net income (£)	0	15000	1382.143	1182.67	1263.869

Source: Own calculations based on UK Household Longitudinal Study, Wave 2012.

singles. Almost 57 per cent of the respondents are employed. The average monthly net personal income amounts to slightly less than £1400.

Rainfall data

The precipitation data that we use in our empirical analysis were provided by the UK Centre for Ecology and Hydrology (we used the CEH-GEAR-NetCDF4 files provided by Tanguy et al., 2016). The CEH-GEAR datasets contain a 1 km x 1 km grid of monthly rainfall amounts for Great Britain since 1890. Originally, the rainfall grids were designed for hydrological modelling, which requires a tight grid with a high spatial resolution (Keller et al., 2015).

Rainfall in the CEH-GEAR datasets is defined as the sum of liquid precipitation and the corresponding liquid amount of any solid precipitation. The rainfall data are based on records by the UK Meteorological Office (Met Office). The Met Office started recording precipitation in the nineteenth century and established a network of standardised storage rain gauges (Keller et al., 2015). The grid has grown rapidly over the last century (Tanguy et al., 2016), but it is still irregular in its spatial distribution. At some locations, the coverage is denser than at others (Keller et al., 2015). Hence, creating a uniform grid required interpolation (Keller et al., 2015), a geospatial method to estimate values for locations where no actual observations are available (Stoyan et al., 1997).

To be able to combine the rainfall data with the earlier described survey data, each grid cell and the associated rainfall amount in the CEH-GEAR datasets had to be assigned to a specific district. For this purpose, a layer containing the spatial extents of the local authority units (LAUs), taken from the Office of National Statistics, was added and intersected with the CEH-GEAR grid (see Figure 7.3). The districts usually contain several grid points. Whenever this was the case, we used overall average values for our calculations.

Based on the rainfall data, we calculated several indicators (see Table 7.2). First, we calculated the average rainfall over the last 30 years (1986–2015) for each district. We then computed the mean rainfall anomaly in the survey year in a region as the deviation of rainfall from the long-term average. Second, we calculated dummy variables for each survey participant, which capture whether they live in a district which experienced at least one extreme precipitation event over the last (half) year before they were surveyed. These dummy variables take the value of 1 whenever precipitation exceeded at least once the value of the 90 per cent quantile of the rainfall distribution of all rainfall events (alternatively the 75 per cent quantile). In Figure 7.3 we show how many surveyed individuals lived in a district which experienced at least one extreme precipitation event throughout the year before being surveyed.

7.4 ESTIMATION RESULTS

7.4.1 Baseline Estimation

In the first step of our empirical analysis, we regress our two measures of self-reported wellbeing, happiness and life satisfaction only on the earlier-described set of control variables. The estimation results are shown in Table 7.3.

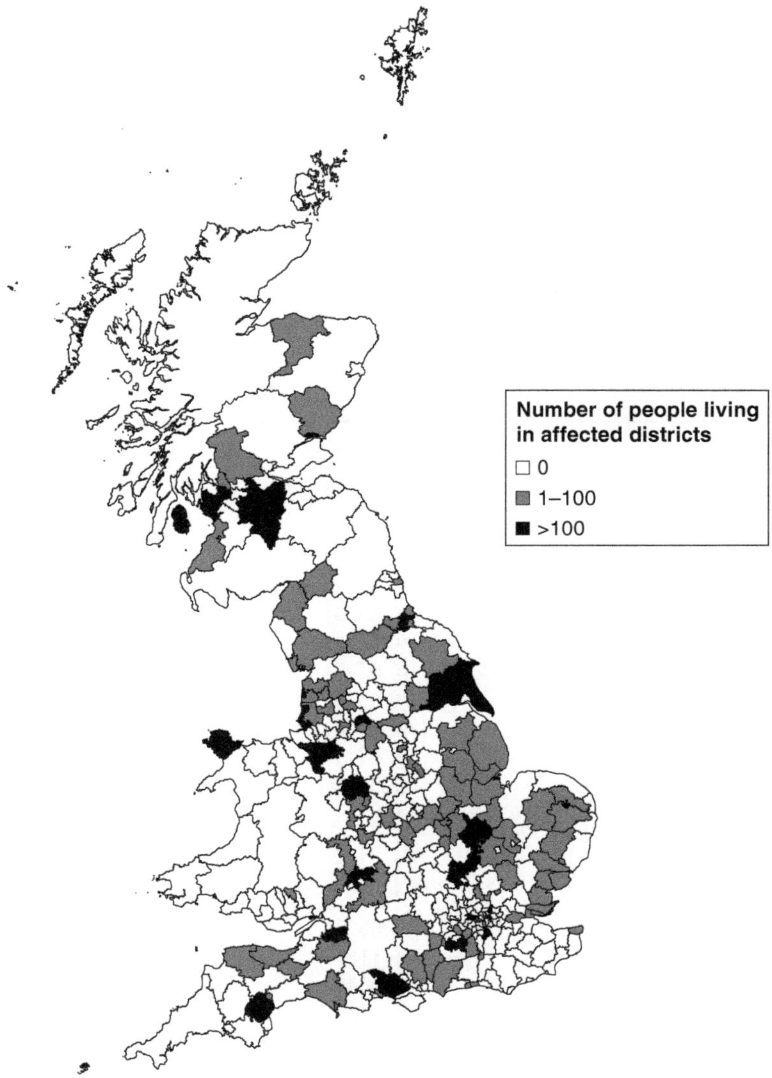

Figure 7.3 *Respondents living in districts of Great Britain in 2012, affected by at least one extreme rainfall event in the year before being surveyed (30-year 90% quantile)*

The explanatory power of the happiness regressions measured by Nagelkerke's pseudo R squared, is satisfactory as compared to similar studies. Age turns out to affect happiness in the well-known U-shaped manner. Female respondents exhibit a significantly lower degree of happiness than men. Better health goes along with higher levels of happiness,[1] while education remains without a happiness effect. Married people report (on average) higher degrees of happiness than the comparison group of singles. All other marital statuses do not differ significantly from singles in terms of reported happiness. While

Table 7.2 Definition of precipitation variables

Variable	Description
PA	Precipitation anomaly: difference between rainfall in last 12 months before survey was conducted and 30-year average
PE_90_LY	Precipitation extreme: at least one precipitation event exceeding the 90% quantile of all rainfall events throughout the year before survey was conducted
PE_75_LY	Precipitation extreme: at least one precipitation event exceeding the 75% quantile of all rainfall events throughout the year before survey was conducted

Table 7.3 Determinants of self-reported wellbeing (ordered logit estimations)

Variable	Happiness	Life satisfaction
	coefficient (std err.)	coefficient (std err.)
Age	−0.0656***	−0.0760***
	(0.0047)	(0.0041)
Age squared	0.0007***	0.0009***
	(0.0000)	(0.0000)
Female	−0.1898***	0.0890***
	(0.0227)	(0.0190)
Highly educated	0.0333	0.0526**
	(0.0274)	(0.0216)
Health status	−0.4744***	−0.5871***
	(0.0131)	(0.0103)
Married	0.0903*	0.4797***
	(0.0480)	(0.0345)
Couple	0.0523	0.3118***
	(0.0562)	(0.0399)
Separated	−0.0551	−0.1609**
	(0.1187)	(0.0712)
Divorced	−0.0049	−0.0674
	(0.0649)	(0.0453)
Widowed	−0.0189	0.0751
	(0.0654)	(0.0582)
Other marital status	0.2189	0.5643**
	(0.3382)	(0.2417)
Employed	0.2268***	0.0056
	(0.0315)	(0.0284)
Net income (in £1000)	0.0023	0.0405***
	(0.0105)	(0.0091)
Observations	34988	34988
Nagelkerke R squared	0.077	0.140
Likelihood ratio test (Chi squared)	2218.86***	5050.82***

Note: The regression results refer to an unemployed, low-educated, single male. We report standard errors clustered on region level. ***: $p < 0.01$, **: $p < 0.05$, *: $p < 0.10$.

employed individuals turn out to be significantly happier than the unemployed, no systematic effect of net income could be detected.

The explanatory power of the life satisfaction regression, again measured by Nagelkerke's pseudo R squared, is considerably higher than in the happiness regression. Again, we find evidence in favour of a U-shaped age effect. Female individuals turn out to be significantly more satisfied with their life than men. Highly educated and more healthy individuals also report significantly higher life satisfaction. Married individuals and respondents living in unmarried couples exhibit higher levels of life satisfaction as singles, whereas separated individuals are significantly less satisfied. We find no effect of the employment status; however, there is a positive effect of net income.

7.4.2 Wellbeing and Precipitation

In the next step of our analysis, we add the earlier-described rainfall indicator to the regression equations. The results are displayed in Table 7.4. The estimated coefficients for the control variables remain almost unchanged. We find no significant effect of the rainfall variable on happiness, nor on life satisfaction. Thus, the actual rainfall anomaly when being interviewed – that is, the difference between actual rainfall from the long-run mean – seems to remain without any systematic influence on self-reported measures of wellbeing.

7.4.3 Wellbeing and Precipitation Extremes

In the second step of our analysis, we turn to an analysis of precipitation extremes. In order to do so, we now add the earlier-described measures of the occurrence of rainfall extremes in the home districts throughout the last year before being surveyed to the regression equation.

The results for happiness are shown in Table 7.5. While the coefficients for both indicators of precipitation extremes turn out to be negative, they are both insignificant. Thus, actual happiness seems to be unaffected by having experienced extreme precipitation in the home district over the last year before being surveyed.

When turning to life satisfaction (see Table 7.6), and thus the long-run component of wellbeing, the occurrence of extreme precipitation events turns out to be relevant. For both measures, based on either the 90 per cent or the 75 per cent quantile of the long-run precipitation distribution, we find a negative and significant effect on life satisfaction. Thus, when evaluating their general satisfaction with life, the respondents seem to take into account their experiences with extreme precipitation over a one-year period. This result is the more interesting as extreme precipitation is not usually a threat to life in a highly developed country such as the United Kingdom.

One might be interested in obtaining an impression of the magnitude of the effects. As the marginal effects in ordered logit estimations depend on the levels of the variables, we report the effects for an average individual, who is a female, married, non-highly educated and employed respondent of 47.1 years old, earning a net monthly income of £1382. In Table 7.7 we report the probabilities with which this individual will report life satisfaction on the seven different levels without having experienced an extreme precipitation event (column 2). Column 3 reports the values which apply for the same individual, provided

Table 7.4 Effect of precipitation deviation from long-run mean on subjective wellbeing (ordered logit estimations)

Variable	Happiness	Life satisfaction
	coefficient (std err.)	coefficient (std err.)
Age	−0.0656***	−0.0760***
	(0.0047)	(0.0041)
Age squared	0.0007***	0.0009***
	(0.0000)	(0.0000)
Female	−0.1898***	0.0887***
	(0.0227)	(0.0190)
Highly educated	0.0333	0.0526**
	(0.0274)	(0.0216)
Health status	−0.4744***	−0.5870***
	(0.0131)	(0.0102)
Married	0.0903*	0.4801***
	(0.0480)	(0.0344)
Couple	0.0522	0.3122***
	(0.0562)	(0.0398)
Separated	−0.0552	−0.1605**
	(0.1187)	(0.0711)
Divorced	−0.0049	−0.0674
	(0.0648)	(0.0453)
Widowed	−0.0188	0.0747
	(0.0654)	(0.0582)
Other marital status	0.2189	0.5635**
	(0.3382)	(0.2420)
Employed	0.2268***	0.0051
	(0.0315)	(0.0283)
Net income	0.0023	0.0407***
	(0.0105)	(0.0091)
Precipitation deviation from long-run mean	0.0001	−0.0008
	(0.006)	(0.0006)
Observations	34988	34988
Nagelkerke R squared	0.077	0.140
Likelihood ratio test (Chi squared)	2218.88***	5053.48***

Note: The regression results refer to an unemployed, low-educated, single male. We report standard errors clustered on region level. ***: $p < 0.01$, **: $p < 0.05$, *: $p < 0.10$.

it has experienced at least one precipitation event over the last 12 months before being surveyed (we report the 90 per cent quantile version).

As Table 7.7 shows, experiencing an extreme precipitation event decreases the probability to report the highest life satisfaction levels, 6 and 7. The probability to report the highest level of 7 decreases by some 0.5 percentage points, whereas the likelihood to report a life satisfaction level of 6 decreases by almost 0.8 percentage points. The likelihood to report the other levels of life satisfaction decrease. Altogether, the expected mean of reported life satisfaction decreases by 0.04 units. Thus, the total effect is not too large,

Table 7.5 Effect of extreme precipitation on happiness (ordered logit estimations)

Variable	90% quantile	75% quantile
	coefficient (std err.)	coefficient (std err.)
Age	−0.0656***	−0.0656***
	(0.0047)	(0.0047)
Age squared	0.0007***	0.0007***
	(0.0000)	(0.0000)
Female	−0.1899***	−0.1897***
	(0.0227)	(0.0227)
Highly educated	0.0333	0.0332
	(0.0274)	(0.0274)
Health status	−0.4743***	−0.4745***
	(0.0131)	(0.0131)
Married	0.0904*	0.0905*
	(0.0480)	(0.0480)
Couple	0.0523	0.0525
	(0.0562)	(0.0562)
Separated	−0.0550	−0.0551
	(0.1187)	(0.1187)
Divorced	−0.0048	−0.0048
	(0.0648)	(0.0648)
Widowed	−0.0190	−0.0184
	(0.0654)	(0.0655)
Other marital status	0.2190	0.2194
	(0.3384)	(0.3380)
Employed	0.2267***	0.2271***
	(0.0315)	(0.0315)
Net income	0.0022	0.0023
	(0.0105)	(0.0105)
Living in district with extreme precipitation event (90% quantile of long-run distribution)	−0.0062 (0.0288)	0.0248 (0.0419)
Observations	34988	34988
Nagelkerke R squared	0.077	0.077
Likelihood ratio test (Chi squared)	2218.90***	2219.22***

Note: The regression results refer to an unemployed, low-educated, single male. We report standard errors clustered on region level. ***: $p < 0.01$, **: $p < 0.05$, *: $p < 0.10$.

which seems to be reasonable given that it is the largely psychological effect of being exposed to extreme precipitation risk.

Table 7.6 Effect of extreme precipitation on life satisfaction (ordered logit estimations)

Variable	90% quantile coefficient (std err.)	75% quantile coefficient (std err.)
Age	−0.0761***	−0.0761***
	(0.0041)	(0.0041)
Age squared	0.0009***	0.0009***
	(0.0000)	(0.0000)
Female	0.0885***	0.0886***
	(0.0190)	(0.0190)
Highly educated	0.0531**	0.0529**
	(0.0216)	(0.0216)
Health status	−0.5869***	−0.5868***
	(0.0103)	(0.0103)
Married	0.4800***	0.4794***
	(0.0345)	(0.0345)
Couple	0.3125***	0.3113***
	(0.0399)	(0.0399)
Separated	−0.1601**	−0.1611**
	(0.0712)	(0.0711)
Divorced	−0.0661	−0.0667
	(0.0453)	(0.0454)
Widowed	0.0745	0.0732
	(0.0582)	(0.0582)
Other marital status	0.5657**	0.5632**
	(0.2418)	(0.2415)
Employed	0.0045	0.0043
	(0.0283)	(0.0283)
Net income	0.0408***	0.0406***
	(0.0091)	(0.0091)
Living in district with extreme precipitation event (90% quantile of long-run distribution)	−0.0542*	−0.0916**
	(0.0293)	(0.0362)
Observations	34988	34988
Nagelkerke R squared	0.140	0.140
Likelihood ratio test (Chi squared)	5055.39***	5058.37***

Note: The regression results refer to an unemployed, low-educated, single male. We report standard errors clustered on region level. ***: $p < 0.01$, **: $p < 0.05$, *: $p < 0.10$.

Table 7.7 Marginal effects for having experienced an extreme precipitation event (90% quantile)

Life satisfaction level	Reporting probability without extreme precipitation event	Change in reporting probability when precipitation event occurred
1	0.01685577	0.000921233
2	0.04370726	0.002233954
3	0.06364531	0.002856153
4	0.08238815	0.003005700
5	0.17567076	0.003848792
6	0.50656759	−0.007626983
7	0.11116516	−0.005238848
Mean	5.320674	5.283465

Note: We report the effects for a female, married, non-highly educated and employed respondent of 47.1 years old, earning a net monthly income of £1382.

7.5 SUMMARY AND CONCLUSIONS

In this chapter, we study the effect of (extreme) rainfall on happiness and life satisfaction. Based on survey data from the UK Household Longitudinal Study for a cross-section of 2012, we found that actual rainfall patterns do not play a significant role in determining self-reported measures of individual wellbeing. We also fail to find any significant effect of precipitation extremes occurring in the region of residence over the year before being surveyed on reported happiness. Thus, when reporting on actual happiness, extreme precipitation risk turns out to be unimportant. However, we find that respondents in districts which experienced at least one extreme rainfall event over the last year systematically report lower life satisfaction than the respondents from other districts. When this effect is driven by the direct harm caused by such an event, we should expect to find the same effect for the more short-run-oriented happiness measure. The absence of this effect suggests that individuals update their disaster expectations (here: extreme precipitation, and closely related issues such as floods) by recently occurring events. We thus might interpret our results as an indication that disaster risk has a systematically negative impact on life satisfaction. Our findings are in line with the results reported in Berlemann (2016), who finds a much more pronounced effect of hurricanes on life satisfaction than on happiness.

Altogether, we might conclude that a further increase in disaster risk, which is the likely consequence of the ongoing process of climate change, is thus not only associated with higher expected costs, which have a direct negative effect on both happiness and life satisfaction of the affected individuals: in addition, the mere risk of being hit by more or more severe natural disasters tends to decrease life satisfaction.

NOTE

1. Note that higher values of the health variable are indicating lower levels of health.

REFERENCES

Banholzer, S., Kossin, J. and S. Donner (2014), 'The impact of climate change on natural disasters', in Ashbindu Singh and Zinta Zommers (eds), *Reducing Disaster: Early Warning Systems for Climate Change*, Dordrecht, Netherlands: Springer Science+Business Media, pp. 21–49.

Berger, E.M. (2010), 'The Chernobyl disaster, concern about the environment, and life satisfaction', *Kyklos*, **63** (1), 1–8.

Berlemann, M. (2016), 'Does hurricane risk affect individual well-being? Empirical evidence on the indirect effects of natural disasters', *Ecological Economics*, **124** (C), 99–113.

Berlemann, M. and D. Wenzel (2016), 'Long-term growth effects of natural disasters: empirical evidence for droughts', *Economics Bulletin*, **36** (1), 464–476.

Berlemann, M. and D. Wenzel (2018), 'Hurricanes, economic growth and transmission channels: empirical evidence for countries on differing levels of development', *World Development*, **105** (C), 231–247.

Callaghan, J. and S. Power (2011), 'Variability and decline in the number of severe tropical cyclones making land-fall over eastern Australia since the late nineteenth century', *Climate Dynamics*, **37** (3), 647–662.

Carroll, N., Frijters, P. and M.A. Shields (2008), 'Quantifying the costs of drought: new evidence from life satisfaction data', *Journal of Population Economics*, **22** (2), 445–461.

Chamberlain, G. (1980), 'Analysis of covariance with qualitative data', *Review of Economic Studies*, **47** (1), 225–238.

Diener, E. and R. Biswas-Diener (eds) (2008), *Happiness: Unlocking the Mysteries of Psychological Wealth*, Boston, MA, USA: Blackwell Publishing.

Dolan, P. and R. Metcalfe (2008), 'Comparing willingness-to-pay and subjective well-being in the context of non-market goods', CEP Discussion Paper No. 890.

Felbermayr, G. and J. Gröschl (2014), 'Naturally negative: the growth effects of natural disasters', *Journal of Development Economics*, **111** (C), 92–106.

Ferreira, S. and M. Moro (2010), 'On the use of subjective well-being data for environmental valuation', *Environmental and Resource Economics*, **46** (3), 249–273.

Ferrer-i-Carbonell, A. and P. Frijters (2004), 'How important is the methodology for the estimates of the determinants of happiness?', *Economic Journal*, **114**, 641–659.

Fowler, H.J. and C.G. Kilsby (2003), 'A regional frequency analysis of United Kingdom extreme rainfall from 1961 to 2000', *International Journal of Climatology*, **23**, 1313–1334.

Frey, Bruno S. (ed.) (2008), *Happiness: A Revolution in Economics*, Cambridge, MA, USA: MIT Press.

Frey, Bruno S. and A. Stutzer (eds) (2002), *Happiness Economics: How the Economy and Institutions Affect Human Well-being*, Princeton, NJ, USA: Princeton University Press.

Grinsted, A., Moore, J.C. and S. Jevrejeva (2012), 'Homogeneous record of Atlantic hurricane surge threat since 1923', *PNAS*, **109** (48), 19601–19605.

Hsiang, S.M. and A.S. Jina (2014), 'The causal effect of environmental catastrophe on long-run economic growth: evidence from 6700 cyclones', NBER Working Paper No. 20352.

IPCC (2013), *Climate Change 2013: The Physical Science Basis. Contribution of Working Group I to the Fifth Assessment Report of the Intergovernmental Panel on Climate Change*, T.F. Stocker, D. Qin, G.-K. Plattner, M. Tignor, S.K. Allen, et al. (eds), Cambridge, UK and New York, USA: Cambridge University Press.

Jones, M.R., Fowler, H.J., Kilsby, C.G. and S. Blenkinsop (2013), 'An assessment of changes in seasonal and annual extreme rainfall in the UK between 1961 and 2009', *International Journal of Climatology*, **33** (5), 1178–1194.

Keller, V.D.J., Tanguy, M., Prosdocimi, I., Terry, J.A., Hitt, O., et al. (2015), 'CEH-GEAR: 1 km resolution daily and monthly areal rainfall estimates for the UK for hydrological and other applications', *Earth System Science Data*, **7**, 143–155.

Kimball, M., Levy, H., Ohtake, F. and Y. Tsutsui (2006), 'Unhappiness after Hurricane Katrina', NBER Working Paper No. 12062.

Kountouris, Y. and K. Remoundou (2011), 'Valuing the welfare cost of forest fires: a life satisfaction approach', *Kyklos*, **64** (4), 556–578.

Luechinger, S. (2009), 'Valuing air quality using the life satisfcation approach', *Economic Journal*, **119** (536), 482–515.

Luechinger, S. and P.A. Raschky (2009), 'Valuing flood disaster using the life satisfaction approach', *Journal of Public Economics*, **93** (3–4), 620–633.

MacKerron, G. and S. Mourato (2009), 'Life satisfaction and air quality in London', *Ecological Economics*, **68** (5), 1441–1453.

Maddison, D. and K. Rehdanz (2011), 'The impact of climate on life satisfaction', *Ecological Economics*, **70** (12), 2437–2449.

MetOffice (2012), 'Early winter storms, late 2011'. Accessed 24 April 2018 at https://www.metoffice.gov.uk/climate/uk/interesting/2011_decwind.

MetOffice (2013), 'Exceptionally wet weather – November 2012'. Accessed 18 April 2018 at https://www.metoffice.gov.uk/climate/uk/interesting/november-2012.

MetOffice (2016), 'Past weather events'. Accessed 18 April 2018 at https://www.metoffice.gov.uk/climate/uk/interesting.

Murakami, H. and B. Wang (2010), 'Future change of North Atlantic tropical cyclone tracks: projection by a 20-km-mesh global atmospheric model', *Journal of Climate*, **23** (10), 2699–2721.

Rehdanz, K. and D. Maddison (2005), 'Climate and happiness', *Ecological Economics*, **52** (1), 111–125.

Rehdanz, K. and D. Maddison (2008), 'Local environmental quality and life satisfaction in Germany', *Ecological Economics*, **64** (4), 787–797.

Rehdanz, K., Welsch, H., Narita, D. and T. Okuba (2015), 'Well-being effect of a major natural disaster: the case of Fukushima', *Journal of Economic Behavior and Organization*, **160**, 500–517.

Sekulova, F. and J.C.J.M. van den Bergh (2016), 'Floods and happiness: empirical evidence from Bulgaria', *Ecological Economics*, **126**, 51–57.

Stoyan, D., Stoyan H. and U. Jansen (eds) (1997), *Umweltstatistik – Statistische Verarbeitung und Analyse von Umweltdaten*, Teubner-Reihe Umwelt, Leipzig, Germany: Vieweg+Teubner Verlag.

Tanguy, M., Dixon, H., Prosdocimi, I., Morris, D.G. and V.D.J. Keller (2016), 'Gridded estimates of daily and monthly areal rainfall for the United Kingdom (1890–2015) [CEH-GEAR]', NERC Environmental Information Data Centre.

Thomas, V. (2014), 'Confronting climate-related disasters in Asia and the Pacific', *Review of Economics*, **65** (2), 163–207.

Van der Vliert, E., Huang, X. and P. Parker (2004), 'Do hotter and colder climates make richer societies more, but poorer societies less, happy and altruistic?', *Journal of Environmental Psychology*, **24** (1), 17–30.

Van Praag, B.M.S and B.E. Baarsma (2005), 'Using happiness surveys to value intangibles: the case of airport noise', *Ecological Economics*, **115** (500), 224–246.

Van Praag, B.M.S. and A. Ferrer-i-Carbonell (eds) (2004), *Happiness Quantified: A Satisfaction Calculus Approach*, Oxford, UK: Oxford University Press.

Von Möllendorff, C. and J. Hirschfeld (2016), 'Measuring impacts of extreme weather events using the life satisfaction approach', *Ecological Economics*, **121**, 108–116.

Wang, C. and S.-K. Lee (2008), 'Global warming and United States landfalling hurricanes', *Geophysical Research Letters*, **35**, L02708.

Welsch, H. (2002), 'Preferences over prosperity and pollution: environmental valuation based on happiness surveys', *Kyklos*, **55** (4), 473–494.

Welsch, H. (2006), 'Environment and happiness: valuation of air pollution using life satisfaction data', *Ecological Economics*, **58** (4), 801–813.

Yamamura, E. (2012), 'Experience of technological and natural disasters and their impact on the perceived risk of nuclear accidents after the Fukushima nuclear disaster in Japan 2011: a cross-country analysis', *Journal of Socio-Economics*, **41** (4), 360–363.

8. Happiness and forest-attacking invasive alien species

Benjamin A. Jones

8.1 INTRODUCTION

For better or for worse, invasive alien species are disrupting environmental quality across the globe. A nascent branch of research and institutional attention on the broader, multidimensional impacts of invasive species has taken shape over the last decade that moves beyond defining "impact" as limited to direct, first-order effects on ecosystems and biological systems. This shift in attention has been buttressed by calls in prominent research outlets (for example, *Science*, *Proceedings of the National Academy of Sciences*) and governmental and quasi-governmental organizations (for example, the World Health Organization, European Environment Agency) for new approaches for capturing the broad-based impacts of invasive alien pests on human health, behavior and overall wellbeing (Civitello et al., 2015; WHO, 2015; Boyd et al., 2013; European Environment Agency, 2012).

There is growing concern that tree-attacking pests, in particular, are leading to consequential changes in human wellbeing through changes in environmental quality and the provision of ecosystem services (Jones, 2016; Boyd et al., 2013). For example, the invasive Asian longhorned beetle and the emerald ash borer have destroyed tens of millions of trees across North America over the past decade, reducing beneficial ecosystem services provided by forests such as pollutant deposition, shade and opportunities for recreation (McPherson et al., 2005). There is mounting empirical evidence that invasive-induced changes in forest ecology and forest health are associated with human mortality and morbidity outcomes (Donovan et al., 2015; Donovan et al., 2013),[1] changes in the labor–leisure trade-off (Jones, 2016) and happiness decrements (Jones, 2017).

However, aside from Jones (2017), not enough is known about the values that individuals place on the broader, multidimensional impacts of tree pests, such as those values derived from invasive-induced perturbations to utility. For example, destruction of ash trees in an urban park by an invasive species may lead to individual welfare loss due to lost aesthetic value or lost recreational opportunities, creating non-market economic damages. Hence, utility-theoretic costs associated with invasive species introductions may be substantial. Holmes et al. (2009) argue that the damages to non-market economic values created by tree-attacking invasives are at "least as important" as market damages such as timber output, and lack of inclusion of non-market values is a "potentially enormous source of bias" in cost estimates of forest pests. Limiting discussions of invasive species economic costs to market effects or first-order direct impacts (for example, cost of replacing an infested tree) ignores the growing body of research on how environmental disruptions in coupled human and natural systems create cascades of effects (Liu et al., 2007), imposing costs on society. More to the point, however, is that understanding the totality of societal damages imposed by invasive species has the potential to improve pest management policy by leading to more accurate risk assessments.

I am not the first to argue for inclusion of more broad-based costs of forest pests in invasive species risk assessments (e.g., Boyd et al., 2013). There are more than a few non-market value estimates of invasive species impacts, primarily using stated preference methods (e.g., Moore, 2008; MacDonald et al., 1997; Jakus, 1992) or the hedonic pricing method (Holmes et al., 2006); see Holmes et al. (2009) for a review of this literature. However, a major shortcoming of the extant literature is that it does not value the totality of invasive impacts on individuals. Rather, prior work has focused on non-market values associated with invasive species control, forest management and residential landscapes, which only represent a subset of the possible ways in which invasive species may affect individual wellbeing (e.g., Pejchar and Mooney, 2009). By contrast, this chapter takes a different approach from the extant literature by estimating the utility-theoretic damages produced by invasive species using the life satisfaction or "happiness" valuation approach. Unlike other non-market valuation techniques, the life satisfaction approach will fully capture the costs associated with all invasive-induced changes to welfare, including changes from multidimensional sources or indirect effects through changes in the provision of ecosystem services.[2] Additionally, these estimates can be interpreted as causally consistent (but not causal) because they exploit a natural experimental setting provided by quasi-random detections of a tree-attacking pest, which is an improvement over purely cross-sectional estimates where issues of residential sorting and environmental confounding are concerns (Graff Zivin and Neidell, 2013). Thus, this work answers calls for new approaches to capturing broad-based impacts of forest pests and human welfare.

The life satisfaction approach provides arguably more credible evidence of the true damages associated with invasive species, because costs are identified through observed changes in "experienced utility" (Kahneman et al., 1997). Unlike stated preference approaches to non-market valuation (for example, contingent valuation, choice experiments), the life satisfaction approach does not suffer from problems of hypothetical bias, strategic biases or framing problems (Levinson, 2012). Furthermore, unlike revealed preference approaches (for example, hedonics, damage function approach), assumptions on the rationality of agents and well-functioning markets are not required (Welsch, 2006). Perhaps the most important advantage of the life satisfaction approach is that it can capture those aspects and effects of environmental conditions that individuals may or may not be consciously aware of (Welsch and Kühling, 2009; Welsch, 2006). In the present context, this allows measurement of invasive species costs that may arise through indirect or second-order effects such as costly changes in behavior patterns, health outcomes or mental wellbeing.

The main contribution of this chapter is to provide causally consistent, utility-theoretic estimates of forest-attacking invasive species costs using an exemplar invasion that has destroyed wide swaths of forests across the United States (US) within a relatively short period of time.[3] It applies the life satisfaction approach to the natural experiment provided by the emerald ash borer (EAB hereafter), which is a virulent tree-attacking invasive beetle that has destroyed tens of millions of ash trees in the US since first being detected in 2002. Using nationally representative data over 2006–10 and a repeated cross-sectional state fixed effects design, it is found that detection of EAB in an infested county within the past five years is associated with a decline in life satisfaction that is equivalent to a \$176 loss in annual household income. This corresponds to \$5.8 billion in annual aggregate EAB-induced damages in the counties where the beetle was detected between 2006 and 2010. Individuals in the third and fourth highest in-sample household income quartiles experience annual damages of \$280 and \$621, respectively, suggesting that EAB eradication is a normal good. Lastly, results suggest that the welfare damages of EAB are larger among individuals in poor health, larger in urban areas, and disproportionally affect communities predominantly composed of racial and ethnic minorities. Several robustness checks and alternative specifications are completed throughout the analysis.

8.2 LIFE SATISFACTION APPROACH IN ECONOMICS

Known by various terms in the economics literature, happiness, subjective wellbeing or life satisfaction is a prominent strand of research that uses approximations of experienced utility, often from surveys, to investigate important economic relationships (MacKerron, 2012; Clark et al., 2008; Kahneman and Krueger, 2006; Kahneman et al., 1997). Life satisfaction is most commonly measured by asking people a question, such as, "Taken all together, would you say that you are very happy, pretty happy, or not too happy?" This question is used to provide an evaluative overview of a person's welfare. There is a vast empirical literature on life satisfaction (see review in Kahneman et al., 1999), encompassing topics such as income and wellbeing, trade-offs between inflation and unemployment, the effect of cigarette taxes on welfare, and air pollution and welfare (Levinson, 2012; Krueger and Schkade, 2008). In their assessment of the reliability of life satisfaction for economic analyses, Krueger and Schkade (2008) conclude that it is "probably sufficiently high to support much of the research that is currently being undertaken," though the method is not without controversy: see Smith (2008).

Environmental applications of life satisfaction began in earnest with Welsch (2002) and with follow-up work in Welsch (2006, 2007). A strong case for using happiness data in environmental contexts was also made in Kahneman and Sugden (2005). These works brought about the life satisfaction approach to environmental valuation where regression estimated compensating differentials of the marginal utility of income and the marginal utility (or disutility) of environmental quality were used to calculate willingness to pay for environmental goods. The approach has been used, among other applications, to value climate (Rehdanz and Maddison, 2005), air pollution (Luechinger, 2009; Welsch, 2006), airport noise (van Praag and Baarsma, 2005) and drought (Carroll et al., 2009).

To understand how these values are estimated, I begin with a conceptual model of life satisfaction:

$$LS_{it} = F(Q_{it}, I_{it}, X_{it}, \varepsilon_{it}) \tag{8.1}$$

where LS_{it} is the subjective life satisfaction of individual i at time t, which is said to be a function of environmental quality (Q_{it}), income (I_{it}), individual-level and macro-level determinants of life satisfaction (X_{it}), and an idiosyncratic error term containing unobserved determinants (ε_{it}). Welsch and Kühling (2009) refer to equation (8.1) as an operationalization of the indirect utility function.

To calculate the amount of money income necessary to compensate an individual for a marginal change in environmental quality while holding life satisfaction constant, I totally differentiate (8.1), set $dLS = 0$, and solve for the compensating differential between environmental quality and income:

$$\frac{dI}{dQ} = -\frac{\partial F/\partial Q}{\partial F/\partial I} \tag{8.2}$$

Equation (8.2) is the amount of income necessary to offset a unit change (either an increment or decrement) in environmental quality. Alternatively, it is the trade-off between income and environmental quality that will leave the average person equally happy. Technically, equation (8.2) is a marginal rate of substitution, though following Levinson (2012) and the conventional terminology in this literature I will refer to it as "marginal willingness to pay."

For non-marginal changes in environmental quality (ΔQ), Welsch and Kühling (2009) relate equation (8.2) to the more familiar Hicksian welfare measures of compensating variation (CV) and equivalent variation (EV):

$$CV{:}\ F(Q, I, X, \varepsilon) = F(Q + \Delta Q, I - CV, X, \varepsilon)$$

$$EV{:}\ F(Q + \Delta Q, I, X, \varepsilon) = F(Q, I + EV, X, \varepsilon)$$

Thus, the life satisfaction approach is tractable with the general theory on non-market valuation, and willingness to pay is estimated in a similar spirit as in stated and revealed preference approaches.

To produce more defensible estimates of environmental values using the life satisfaction approach, several caveats should be addressed. The first caveat is based on the well-known Easterlin paradox (Easterlin, 1974) that happiness increases with income across individuals within a country at a given point in time, but does not increase with income across countries or within a given country over time. Some work has challenged this paradox (e.g., Deaton, 2008), while others have upheld it (e.g., Layard, 2006; Oswald, 1997). If this paradox is true, then it implies that in order to identify the impact of invasive species on life satisfaction we must compare similar individuals living in the same location who responded to a happiness question on or around the same date. Use of location and time fixed effects in addition to controls for observable individual-level characteristics will allow for the relevant comparisons to be made.

Another caveat of this approach raised by Levinson (2012) is that measures of environmental quality are often aggregated at state or national levels, which not only masks quality heterogeneity, but can introduce noise into the data in cases where individual-level experiences significantly differ from aggregated outcomes. Authors have dealt with this concern by obtaining environmental quality data at higher spatial resolutions. For example, Ferreira and Moro (2010) linked location-specific attributes to an individual's residence using geographic information system (GIS) modeling. Jones (2017) takes a similar approach and links quasi-random county-level invasive species detections to individual life satisfaction outcomes within a given county of residence.

To increase the credibility of these results, I will address each of these caveats in my empirical design. Furthermore, I argue that these results, while falling short of causation, are still stronger than cross-sectional estimates because I exploit a unique natural experiment where treatment assignment is quasi-randomly determined by invasive species spread. In the next section, I apply the life satisfaction approach to an exemplar forest-attacking invasive species, EAB.

8.3 EAB, ENVIRONMENTAL QUALITY AND LIFE SATISFACTION

EAB is a small phloem-feeding invasive beetle first detected in the US state of Michigan in 2002. It is believed to have traveled over from Asia through infested ash and ash by-products. Adult EAB lay eggs in the conductive tissue of ash trees and their larvae feed on this tissue, disrupting the transfer of nutrients and water. This process, repeated over several EAB lifecycles, eventually results in tree mortality. Adult ash typically die within 5–7 years after initial infestation (Herms et al., 2014; Poland and McCullough, 2006).

Adult EAB and their larvae are extremely resistant to the North American climate and face few existential threats from natural predators in the areas they have infested (Herms and McCullough, 2014). EAB attack all North American species of ash (*Fraxinus* spp.), including both stressed and relatively healthy trees. In light of the sheer abundance of ash across the US, coupled with few natural constraints on growth, EAB have spread quickly since initial detection in 2002, and as of June 2016 were present in 27 US states and the District of Columbia. It is unknown exactly how many ash trees have been killed by EAB, but the estimates are in the tens of millions, if not more (Herms and McCullough, 2014).

There have been massive and largely unprecedented federal, state and local responses to EAB; see Herms and McCullough (2014) for a history. Unfortunately, eradication and containment efforts (including insecticide use, releases of natural predators, and quarantines) have proven largely ineffective at stopping spread, through research is ongoing (McCullough and Mercader, 2012). In the meantime, newly detected areas are discovered weekly, on average, and experts believe that the entire stock of some 8 billion North American ash may be threatened (Sydnor et al., 2011).

By destroying ash trees, which often comprise 10–40 percent of urban forest canopies (Wise, 2015), EAB bring about significant changes in environmental quality. This is because trees are an important and recognized source of ecosystem services. Trees provide shade, reduce storm water runoff, intercept rainfall and capture air pollution (McPherson et al., 2005). There is a vast literature on the association between trees, public health and wellbeing; see Nilsson et al. (2011) for a comprehensive survey. For example, Hansmann et al. (2007) found that individuals visiting an urban forest were significantly less likely to suffer from headaches and stress and were more likely to feel well balanced. Tree cover is also known to impact community identity and pride, and is associated with community capacity and trust (Elmendorf, 2008). In a series of papers, Nowak and colleagues have modeled the significant magnitudes of urban air pollutants removed by trees and their subsequent health impacts (Nowak et al., 2013; Nowak et al., 2006; Nowak et al., 2000).

The sudden loss of ash in a community might thus affect welfare across multiple direct and indirect channels. Green spaces and structures that were once shaded may no longer be so; ash-forested parks, urban green spaces and areas of recreation may now lack or have severely reduced forest coverage; or the trees that once lined the streets in one's neighborhood or that were in the front or backyard may now be gone. If ash were uncommon or located far from where people lived and worked, then we might not expect their loss to have significant impacts on wellbeing. However, it is the fact that ash trees are common in urban areas, particularly in the eastern US where millions of people are congregated, that underscores the nature of the potential threat to life satisfaction posed by EAB.

Several high-profile studies have captured EAB's impacts on individual outcomes. Donovan et al. (2015) and Donovan et al. (2013) produced causally consistent estimates of the association between EAB detection and decrements to cardio-respiratory mortality and morbidity health outcomes. Jones (2016) found the labor–leisure trade-off had been altered in EAB-infested counties. In particular, individuals spent less time recreating outdoors and more time inside working. The work that comes closest to this one is Jones (2017), where it was found that EAB detection was associated with significantly lower life satisfaction after a five-year lag. However, that work did not proceed to value changes in life satisfaction, as is done here.

Two other studies have calculated the costs of EAB damage, which may be as high as \$10.7–\$12.5 billion over a ten-year period (Kovacs et al., 2011; Kovacs et al., 2010). However, neither study includes the harder-to-measure non-market values associated with EAB and ash loss, meaning that these estimates are likely extreme lower bounds on actual EAB economic costs. At present, the utility-theoretic costs of EAB, one of the worst ecological catastrophes ever experienced in the US (McCullough, 2013), are unknown. In the following sections, I describe the data and methods used to estimate these costs for the first time.

8.4 DATA

The study area consists of all US counties where initial EAB detection occurred between 2006 and 2010. Dates and location of detections were provided by the United States Department of Agriculture Animal Plant Health Inspection Service (USDA APHIS). Detections are made at the county level, and once a county is infested it is considered to be infested indefinitely. Over the study period, EAB was detected in 173 counties across 14 US states and the District of Columbia (Figure 8.1).

Figure 8.1 illustrates the quasi-random nature of EAB spread, a key feature of my identification strategy. EAB spread is characterized by degrees of randomness due to idiosyncratic, stochastic flight patterns ("insect flight") and long-range dispersal through ash transport ("insect ride") (Prasad et al., 2010). This leads to cases of outlier detected counties and situations where some counties (containing ash) are completely surrounded by EAB, yet no EAB have been detected in them. As recognized elsewhere (e.g., Jones, 2017; Donovan et al., 2015), this feature of EAB establishes a natural experiment where treatment assignment (that is, EAB detection) is determined by a quasi-random process. Exploiting natural experiments in environmental valuation contexts can strengthen the causal interpretation of results, as discussed in Graff Zivin and Neidell (2013).

Subjective life satisfaction data come from the US Centers for Disease Control and Prevention (CDC) Behavioral Risk Factor Surveillance System (BRFSS) annual products. The BRFSS is a nationally representative repeated cross-sectional survey of

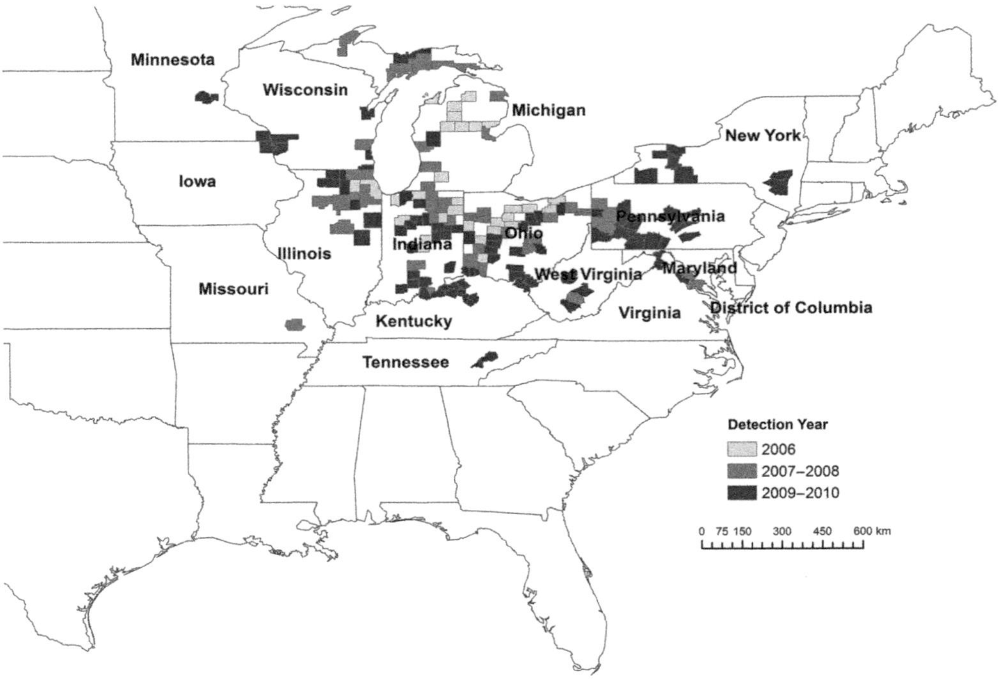

Source: USDA APHIS.

Figure 8.1 EAB detections, 2006–10

behavioral outcomes and risk factors among adult Americans (≥ 18 years). During the years 2006–10, the following question on life satisfaction was asked as part of the core questionnaire: "In general, how satisfied are you with your life? – (1) Very Satisfied, (2) Satisfied, (3) Dissatisfied, (4) Very Dissatisfied." This is the outcome variable of interest in what follows. The BRFSS also contains data on respondent demographics and socio-economics, which I additionally use.

Income is a categorical variable in the BRFSS, which is a potential source of measurement error (Ligon, 1989). Following the recommendations in Hout (2004) and Ligon (1989) for mitigating this concern, income categories were converted into real values by taking the midpoints of the closed intervals, solving the top coding problem, and were adjusted for inflation.[4] The resulting income values are log adjusted to account for the declining marginal effect of income on wellbeing.

One previously mentioned caveat of the life satisfaction approach concerned the spatial resolution at which individual-level life satisfaction measures were mapped to environmental conditions. In this regard, the BRFSS is advantageous because it identifies a respondent's county of residence in all instances where the total county adult population is greater than 10000 residents and there are more than 50 respondents in the county.[5] Therefore, county-level EAB detections can be mapped to a BRFSS respondent's county of residence. This yields a fairly high spatial resolution (the average county size is 532.0 square miles or 1377.9 square kilometers) at which the impacts of detection on life satisfaction are being assessed, especially compared to the extant literature where environmental quality is sometimes measured at the state, region or even national level (e.g., Di Tella and MacCulloch, 2008; Welsch, 2006).

I have one further note concerning my identification strategy. In any given study year, a subset of US counties contain EAB while another subset are EAB-free. One strategy would be to compare life satisfaction among individuals in EAB-detected counties to similar individuals in counties without EAB. However, a potential problem with this strategy is that if there existed some unobserved non-random driver of EAB spread, then observed differences in life satisfaction might be due to the non-random driver and not to EAB. A similar point was raised in Jones (2017); however, Donovan et al. (2013) note that they have been unable to identify any such driver of EAB spread that is also correlated with individual-level outcomes. Regardless, since non-random drivers of spread cannot be completely ruled out, a more convincing counterfactual might consist of counties that are EAB free concurrent-to-treatment, but where EAB is eventually detected. In other words, I make the reasonable assumption that EAB-detected counties are more comparable to EAB "ever detected" counties as opposed to a pure cross-section of US counties. In practice, this means that I compare individuals living in the 173 counties where detection occurred over 2006–10 to individuals in counties where detection ever occurs from 2002 (the first year EAB was detected) onward.[6]

Descriptive statistics for the final dataset are presented in Table 8.1. After dropping missing and no-response observations, 414737 individual observations remain. Mean life satisfaction is 3.38 on a four-point scale, between "satisfied" and "very satisfied." Year of average EAB detection is 2012, and the mean length of time since initial detection is only a few months. Mean household income is \$78778, which is similar to the 2014 US Census Bureau estimate of \$72641.

8.5 EMPIRICAL MODEL

Versions of the following function are estimated:

$$LS_{ict} = \beta_0 + \beta_1 EAB_{ct} + \beta_2 \ln Y_{it} + \beta_3 X_{ict} + \gamma_{state} + \delta_{year} + \varepsilon_{ict} \tag{8.3}$$

where LS_{ict} is the life satisfaction of individual i in county c in month and year t, EAB_{ct} is an indicator of EAB detection in county c and year t, $\ln Y_{it}$ is log household income, X_{ict} is a vector of respondent demographic and socio-economic characteristics, γ_{state} is a state fixed effect, δ_{year} is a year fixed effect, and ε_{ict} is the idiosyncratic error term. The use of the fixed effects means that unobservable time-invariant state-level heterogeneity in life satisfaction will not bias the coefficient estimates (for example, time-invariant labor market conditions, local institutional and political arrangements, culture, economic opportunities, environmental exposures). Additionally, using time and location fixed effects allows us to address the main implications of the Easterlin paradox.

Covariates included in X are: sex, age, age (squared), household size, married, employed, retired, college graduate, general health status, health insurance status, and controls for survey day of week and whether the survey day was a major holiday.

Table 8.1 Descriptive statistics

Variable	Coding	Mean	Std dev.
Life Satisfaction	1 = very dissatisfied, 2 = dissatisfied, 3 = satisfied, 4 = very satisfied	3.38	0.63
EAB Detection Year	continuous	2012.12	2.87
Years since Initial EAB Detection	continuous	0.26	0.82
Household Income	continuous	78 777.51	61 016.26
Sex	1 = male, 2 = female	1.61	0.49
Age	continuous	53.84	16.17
Household Size*	continuous	2.41	1.37
Married	0 = no, 1 = yes	0.55	0.50
Employed	0 = no, 1 = yes	0.49	0.50
Retired	0 = no, 1 = yes	0.24	0.43
College Graduate	0 = no, 1 = yes	0.39	0.49
General Health Status			
Excellent	0 = no, 1 = yes	0.19	0.39
Very Good	0 = no, 1 = yes	0.34	0.47
Good	0 = no, 1 = yes	0.29	0.46
Fair	0 = no, 1 = yes	0.12	0.33
Poor	0 = no, 1 = yes	0.05	0.22
Has Health Insurance	0 = no, 1 = yes	0.92	0.28
Urban	0 = no, 1 = yes	0.82	0.39
No. of obs. = 414 737			

Note: * Sum of adults and children living in the primary residence.

Sources: US CDC BRFSS and USDA APHIS.

Following equation (8.2), the average compensating differential between income and EAB detection is calculated as:

$$\frac{\partial Y}{\partial EAB} = -Y\frac{\hat{\beta}_1}{\hat{\beta}_2} \tag{8.4}$$

where $\hat{\beta}_1$ and $\hat{\beta}_2$ are the estimated coefficients on EAB detection and income, respectively. In words, equation (8.4) is the amount of income compensation required to exactly offset changes in experienced utility due to EAB, which I refer to as an estimate of marginal willingness to pay (WTP). That is, it represents average WTP for eradication of EAB from an infested county.

There is a well-established latency period between initial EAB detection and ash tree mortality, and hence changes in environmental quality (Herms and McCullough, 2014). Previous work on life satisfaction and EAB by Jones (2017) found significant effects only after a five-year lag, concurrent with the average timing of infested ash mortality (Herms et al., 2014). Others have found a stronger magnitude of effects in year 5 after detection than in earlier years (Donovan et al., 2013). Consistent with these findings and in order to provide a more conservative lower bound on results, the EAB detection variable is lagged by five years. In the robustness checks, additional lag lengths are explored.

Equation (8.3) is estimated as a generalized linear regression model, following the conventional econometric approach for estimating life satisfaction models (e.g., von Möllendorff and Hirschfeld, 2016; Levinson, 2012; Welsch, 2006). Furthermore, there is no consensus on how to appropriately apply fixed effects in ordered regression models, though research is ongoing (Baetschmann et al., 2015). However, as a robustness check, a discrete choice fixed effects logit model is also estimated to show that the main result holds across specifications.

In the results that follow, standard errors are clustered by county-year since observations are likely non-independent for individuals living in the same county during the same year. Additionally, survey weights are used to account for the complex BRFSS sampling design.

8.6 RESULTS

The first set of results are the regression estimates of the impact of lagged EAB detection on life satisfaction (Table 8.2). Results from three models are presented, differing in their inclusion of control covariates and fixed effects. In column 1, which only includes EAB detection and income, we see a negative but insignificant relationship between EAB detection within the past five years and life satisfaction. Detection of EAB is associated with a small 0.00006 decrease in life satisfaction on a four-point scale. Conversely, there is a positive and highly significant association between income and life satisfaction. A 10 percent increase in household income is associated with a 0.018 increase in life satisfaction. No WTP is estimated for the model in column 1 since the coefficient on EAB is insignificant.

In column 2, state and year fixed effects are added to the regression. Here, a larger and marginally significant effect of EAB on life satisfaction is observed. Detection of EAB within the past five years lowers wellbeing by 0.00015. The sign and significance on income are similar to before. WTP is calculated by substituting the coefficient estimates for EAB detection (-0.000149) and income (0.185) into equation (8.4) and then multiplying by the negative of mean respondent income ($78 778). This produces an estimate on the value of EAB eradication at $63 per year. This represents an estimate of the amount of annual household income that increases happiness by the same amount as eradication of EAB, given that the county has contained EAB for at least five years. Using the delta method, the standard error on this estimate is produced in parentheses.

The baseline specification (column 3, Table 8.2) includes all demographic and socioeconomic covariates and all fixed effects. Adding these controls again increases the magnitude and significance of the coefficient on EAB detection. Now, individuals living in EAB-infested counties have a 0.00020 lower life satisfaction on a four-point scale. The signs and magnitudes on the other covariates are as expected. Wellbeing is higher among females, non-linearly decreasing in age, and increasing in household size. Employed, married and retired people have significantly higher life satisfaction, as do college graduates and those in better general health. These results are consistent with past research on EAB

Table 8.2 Regression estimates of the impact of EAB detection on life satisfaction

Variables	(1)	(2)	(3)
	Detection and income only	Add time and location FE's	Baseline specification
EAB Detection (≥ 5 years ago)	−0.0000575	−0.000149*	−0.000204**
	(0.000106)	(0.000088)	(0.00010)
Household Income (log)	0.184***	0.185***	0.090***
	(0.002)	(0.003)	(0.003)
Sex			0.026***
			(0.003)
Age			−0.013***
			(0.0006)
Age (squared)			0.0002***
			(0.000005)
Household Size			0.003**
			(0.002)
Married			0.170***
			(0.004)
Employed			0.032***
			(0.004)
Retired			0.103***
			(0.005)
College Graduate			0.031***
			(0.003)
General Health Status			
Excellent			0.719***
			(0.011)
Very Good			0.574***
			(0.011)
Good			0.401***
			(0.011)
Fair			0.253***
			(0.011)
Has Health Insurance			0.068***
			(0.007)
Constant	1.37***	1.49***	1.99***
	(0.03)	(0.07)	(0.07)
Year Fixed Effects	No	Yes	Yes
State Fixed Effects	No	Yes	Yes
Day-of-Week and Holiday Fixed Effects	No	No	Yes
R-squared	0.073	0.080	0.176
Observations	414737	414737	414737
WTP for eradication of EAB in an infested county	–	$63*	$176**
		(38)	(89)

Notes:
The dependent variable is life satisfaction (0 = very dissatisfied, 1 = dissatisfied, 2 = satisfied, 3 = very satisfied). Fixed effects linear regressions used. WTP calculated based on mean income for the sample. Omitted health status category is "Poor". Standard errors presented in parenthesis and adjusted for clustering by county-year and are survey weighted. Standard errors for WTP calculated using the delta method.
* $p < 0.1$; ** $p < 0.05$; *** $p < 0.01$.

and life satisfaction (e.g., Jones, 2017), and life satisfaction and environmental quality more generally (e.g., Levinson, 2012).

In the baseline specification, the effect of EAB detection on individual welfare is equivalent to a \$176 drop in annual household income, which is significantly different from zero at the 1 percent level. This is the penultimate result of the chapter. Put differently, it was found that the average US adult is willing to trade off \$176 per year in household income for eradication of EAB in an infested county, after controlling for many known individual-level and unobservable time- and location-specific predictors of life satisfaction. In other words, a person would be willing to forgo \$176 per year of household income to compensate them for EAB infestation in their county.

8.6.1 Demographic Nonlinearities and Location Heterogeneity

One way to test whether the previous results are truly measuring the impact of EAB detection is to check whether they reasonably correlate with individual characteristics. To investigate nonlinearities in the impact of EAB according to demographic characteristics, I separately interacted the detection variable with an indicator for self-reported health being fair or poor, and a continuous variable for the percentage of the county population composed of racial and ethnic minorities. Data on county racial characteristics were obtained from the US Census Bureau Profile of General Demographic Characteristics. These demographic variables were selected for interaction based on past research suggesting that minorities and individuals in poor health are disproportionally affected by changes in environmental quality (Nilsson et al., 2011; Pastor et al., 2001).

Results of including these interactions in the baseline specification are presented in Table 8.3. In column 1, we observe a negative and significant coefficient on the interaction between EAB detection and health being fair or poor, suggesting that the welfare impact of EAB is greater among people with lower health status. The coefficient on EAB detection is no longer significant, though it is still negative as before. WTP is now calculated differently due to the presence of the interaction:

$$\frac{\partial Y}{\partial EAB} = -Y\left(\frac{\hat{\beta}_1 + \hat{\pi}I}{\hat{\beta}_2}\right) \tag{8.5}$$

where $\hat{\pi}$ is the estimated interaction coefficient and I is the interacted variable, which is health status being fair or poor in this case. Using equation (8.5), WTP for EAB eradication among individuals in fair or poor health is calculated as \$150, compared to \$95 for individuals in good or better health (column 1, Table 8.3), suggesting that the value of eliminating EAB is a decreasing function of overall health status. However, neither WTP value is significantly different from zero.

Next, I interacted EAB detection with the percentage minority population (column 2, Table 8.3). It was found that individuals in counties with higher proportions of racial and ethnic minorities face greater life satisfaction decrements during the five years since initial detection. This is evidenced by the negative and significant coefficient on the interaction term. We can also observe that the coefficient on EAB detection is still negative and significant, as was the case in the baseline specification. As shown in the bottom of Table 8.3, people in the 25th percentile of county minority population are willing to pay \$256

Table 8.3 Non-linearities and location heterogeneity in impacts of EAB detection

Variables	(1)[a]	(2)[b]	(3)[c]	(4)[d]
	Health fair or poor interaction	% Minority interaction	Urban	Rural
EAB Detection (≥ 5 years ago)	−0.000110 (0.00013)	−0.00520*** (0.0016)	−0.000201** (0.00010)	−0.000200 (0.00020)
Household Income (log)	0.090*** (0.003)	0.090*** (0.003)	0.087*** (0.003)	0.108*** (0.005)
Interaction Coefficient	−0.00046** (0.0002)	−0.00005*** (0.00002)		
Interacted Variable Coefficient	−0.400*** (0.011)	−0.0004 (0.003)		
Includes same covariates and fixed effects as in Table 8.2, model (3)	Yes	Yes	Yes	Yes
R-squared	0.176	0.176	0.175	0.200
Observations	414737	414737	339169	75163
WTP for eradication of EAB from infested county			\$180** (91)	\$144 (142)
WTP for eradication of EAB from infested county when interaction = 0	\$95 (111)			
WTP for eradication of EAB from infested county when interaction = 1	\$150 (101)			
WTP for eradication of EAB from infested county when interaction = 25th percentile		\$256*** (85)		
WTP for eradication of EAB from infested county when interaction =75th percentile		\$1353*** (414)		

Notes:
[a] Model (1) interacts income with an indicator for respondent health being fair or poor.
[b] Model (2) interacts income with a continuous variable for the percentage of the county population that is racial and ethnic minorities.
[c] Model (3) restricts the sample to residents of an urban area.
[d] Model (4) restricts the sample to residents of rural areas.
The dependent variable is life satisfaction (0 = very dissatisfied, 1 = dissatisfied, 2 = satisfied, 3 = very satisfied). WTP calculated based on mean income for the sample. For interacted models, WTP calculated based on varying outcomes of the interacted variable as noted. The interacted variable coefficient is the coefficient on the non-interacted variable by itself (for example, on health fair or poor in Model 1, on urban in Model 3, etc.). Standard errors presented in parenthesis and adjusted for clustering by county-year and are survey weighted. Standard errors for WTP calculated using the delta method.
* $p < 0.1$; ** $p < 0.05$; *** $p < 0.01$.

of household income to eradicate EAB, and people in the 75th percentile are willing to pay $1353 of household income. Both values are highly significant, suggestive of an environmental justice story with regards to welfare changes associated with EAB (that is, communities of color appear to be disproportionally affected by EAB).

Another potential source of heterogeneity in EAB impacts may exist based on location. As previously mentioned, the ash is a popular and relatively common urban tree, often making up 10–40 percent of the total urban forest canopy. Much of the research on the connections between trees and wellbeing is based on people having regular or semi-regular interactions and experiences with trees, which is more likely in a forested urban or suburban setting (Nilsson et al., 2011). Hence, and for multiple reasons, we might expect the impact of EAB to be greater in urban areas.

To explore this hypothesis, separate regressions were performed of the baseline model for individuals living in urban and rural areas. The results of these regressions are presented in columns 3 and 4, respectively, of Table 8.3. Results are consistent with expectations. While the life satisfaction impact of EAB detection is negative in both urban and rural areas, only the coefficient on the urban model is statistically significant. Willingness to pay, calculated in the same way as in the baseline model, is $180 for urban areas and $144 for rural areas, though only the former is significantly different from zero. This suggests, consistent with my earlier hypothesis, that the utility-theoretic value associated with EAB is being primarily driven by urban residents, who appear to face the greatest welfare decrements.

8.6.2 Impacts by Income Quartiles

Past literature on EAB (e.g., Donovan et al., 2013) and changes to environmental quality more generally (e.g., Levinson, 2012) has found that environmental decrements are increasing in income; that is, that environmental quality is a normal good. To explore whether this is the case here, separate versions of the baseline model were regressed by respondent income quartiles (Table 8.4). There are two important findings. First, we can in fact observe that WTP is an increasing function of income, consistent with EAB eradication being a normal good. More importantly, the magnitude of the difference is quite striking. In the top two income quartiles, people are willing to pay $280 and $621, respectively, to eliminate EAB in an infested county. This compares to $176 in the baseline specification. Second, EAB detection has no significant association with life satisfaction for individuals in either of the bottom two income quartiles. It is only people at or above median income in the sample ($48 583) who appear to be negatively impacted. This could be because ash trees are more common in wealthier areas and hence these areas experience greater loss, as hypothesized elsewhere (Jones and McDermott, 2015).

8.6.3 Alternative Specifications and Robustness Checks

Several alternative specifications and robustness checks were performed on the baseline specification in order to address some of the modeling choices made throughout the analysis (Table 8.5). First, as an alternative specification, median income was used instead of mean income in the calculation of WTP (column 1). Since median income ($48 583) is lower than mean ($78 778) this has the effect of lowering WTP to $110 from $176 in

Table 8.4 Impacts of EAB detection by income quartiles

Variables	(1)	(2)	(3)	(4)
	0–25th quartile	25–50th quartile	50–75th quartile	75–100th quartile
EAB Detection (≥ 5 years ago)	−0.000262	−0.000200	−0.000255**	−0.000286**
	(0.00024)	(0.0013)	(0.00012)	(0.00013)
Household Income (log)	0.056***	0.073***	0.087***	0.077*
	(0.009)	(0.019)	(0.012)	(0.461)
Includes same covariates and fixed effects as in Table 8.2, model (3)	Yes	Yes	Yes	Yes
R-squared	0.154	0.135	0.122	0.110
Observations	106783	110438	95773	101743
WTP for eradication of EAB in an infested county	\$83	\$115	\$280**	\$621**
	(79)	(83)	(133)	(315)

Notes:
Models are estimated on a subset of respondents within the given income quartile. The dependent variable is life satisfaction (0 = very dissatisfied, 1 = dissatisfied, 2 = satisfied, 3 = very satisfied).
WTP calculated based on mean income within the quartile. Standard errors presented in parenthesis and adjusted for clustering by county-year and are survey weighted. Standard errors for WTP calculated using the delta method.
* $p < 0.1$; ** $p < 0.05$; *** $p < 0.01$.

the baseline model. Second, in column 2 I have performed a lead-lag analysis, meaning that I have added additional indicator variables to the baseline specification for three years prior to initial EAB detection (the leads) and five years after initial detection (the lags). Remember that the baseline model did not consider EAB impacts prior to the five-year lag. Here I consider those lags. In order for these results to be consistent with an EAB-induced life satisfaction story, we should expect to observe significant lag effects, but insignificant lead effects; that is, if EAB is to have an impact on life satisfaction it should be in the years after detection, but not in the years before detection. This finding, if observed, would be consistent with a causal story as described in Angrist and Pischke (2009). Indeed, this is what we observe. In fact, the only lag effect that is significant is the five-year lag, suggesting that the baseline results would be essentially unchanged if we did not include the ash mortality latency period. These results demonstrate not only that the results are causally consistent due to the insignificance of the lead coefficients, but also that the impacts of EAB are largely concurrent with actual ash tree mortality, which peaks 5+ years after initial detection. Finally, I estimated a discrete choice logit model comparing life satisfaction level "very satisfied" (= 1) to all other categories (= 0) (column 3, Table 8.5). This is a check on using a generalized linear model in the main results. Logit results are consistent with earlier findings in that EAB detection is significantly associated with lower life satisfaction.

Table 8.5 Alternative specifications of baseline model

Variables	(1)	(2)	(3)
	Median income	Lead-lag analysis	Logit model
EAB Detection (≥ 5 years ago)	−0.000204** (0.00010)		−0.00043** (0.00021)
Detection −3 Years		−0.000010 (0.000022)	
Detection −2 Years		−0.000004 (0.000028)	
Detection −1 Year		−0.000010 (0.000019)	
Detection +1 Year		0.00002 (0.00002)	
Detection +2 Years		−0.000006 (0.000027)	
Detection +3 Years		0.000012 (0.00002)	
Detection +4 Years		−0.000001 (0.00002)	
Detection +5 Years		−0.000203** (0.00010)	
Household Income (log)	0.090*** (0.003)	0.090*** (0.003)	0.300*** (0.010)
Includes same covariates and fixed effects as in Table 8.2, model (3)	Yes	Yes	Yes
R-squared	0.176	0.176	0.107
Observations	414737	414737	414737
WTP for eradication of EAB in an infested county	$110** (55)	$175** (89)	–

Notes:
Model (1) uses the median income of the sample ($48 583) to estimate WTP.
Model (2) estimates the impacts of EAB for three years prior to initial detection (lead) and for five years after initial detection (lag).
Model (3) is a logit regression on a binary dependent variable that = 1 if life satisfaction is "very satisfied" and = 0 otherwise.
Except in model (3), the dependent variable is life satisfaction (0 = very dissatisfied, 1 = dissatisfied, 2 = satisfied, 3 = very satisfied).
WTP calculated based on mean income for the sample unless otherwise noted. Standard errors presented in parenthesis and adjusted for clustering by county-year and are survey weighted. Standard errors for WTP calculated using the delta method.
* $p < 0.1$; ** $p < 0.05$; *** $p < 0.01$.

8.7 CONCLUSIONS

This chapter provides the first utility-theoretic cost estimates associated with a non-indigenous forest-invading pest using the life satisfaction approach. The main advantage of this approach over other non-market valuation techniques is that it is able to fully capture all costs actually borne by an individual, whether from direct or indirect sources, even if individuals were not consciously aware that their wellbeing was being affected.

Exploiting a natural experiment caused by the destruction of millions of ash trees in the US due to EAB, it was found that life satisfaction is significantly lower five years after initial EAB detection and that impacts vary predictably by individual characteristics. In the baseline specification, detection of EAB is associated with a decline in life satisfaction that is equal to a $176 drop in annual household income. Several important validity checks on these results suggest that this is indeed capturing the true costs of EAB, though causation remains elusive.

Since the data are nationally representative, a national value of EAB-induced costs by aggregating estimated average WTP across all individuals in EAB-detected counties over 2006–10 may be produced.[7] Doing so produces an estimate of $5.8 billion in lost welfare due to EAB over 2006–10, or about $965 million in annual EAB-induced costs. This is an estimate of the national non-market costs created by individual-level changes in wellbeing. This estimate is only slightly lower than the estimated market costs of EAB, which Kovacs et al. (2010) report as $1.07 billion per year. Combining the market and non-market point estimates suggests that EAB is associated with approximately $2 billion in annual impacts, which is nearly double the current estimates in Kovacs et al. (2010) that are often cited as the costs of EAB.

There are several limitations of this work. First, county-level detections of EAB are a less-than-ideal measure of changes in environmental quality. Some people in EAB-detected counties may have few if any ash trees around their place of residence or in areas that they frequently visit. This may introduce noise into the effect estimates. Second, unobserved individual-level characteristics were not controlled for due to the cross-sectional nature of the data. Future work would benefit from using life satisfaction panel data. Finally, BRFSS data limitations prevent the investigation of impacts after 2010; that is, BRFSS stopped asking the life satisfaction question after 2010. A longer time series data set might be useful for revealing longer-term impacts.

In closing, I see this work as contributing to invasive species policy by demonstrating not only the significant utility-theoretic costs associated with forest-attacking pests, but also the rich heterogeneity in costs across observable characteristics. As our understanding of human–nature connections continue to grow, it is my hope and desire that economic analyses of invasive species also grow to include the costs of induced welfare decrements to society brought about through changing environmental quality. Especially important, but not well understood, are the multiple channels by which changes in the natural environment affect welfare, including air pollution, recreation habits, scenic amenities and behavior, among other mechanisms. Given the explosive growth of invasive species spread and the substantial resources employed to contain them, future research has the potential to be highly impactful in this regard. Lastly, this chapter demonstrates how the life satisfaction approach can be applied to value wellbeing impacts of invasive species. In light of continued global spread of invasives, and predictions that climate change may exacerbate the anthropogenic impacts of invasive species (Hellmann et al., 2008), there is a strong need for further applications of happiness data to other invasive species contexts (for example, aquatic, vegetative, mammalian). I hope that this work spurs additional research in this topic area.

NOTES

1. For example, quasi-experimental evidence has shown that deforestation in the US due to the invasive emerald ash borer has led to increased cardio-respiratory deaths (Donovan et al., 2015), possibly due to increased air pollution, as trees act as pollutant sinks (Jones and McDermott, 2018).
2. By contrast, stated preference methods will only capture non-market values associated with the scenario described in a survey, which may or may not be exhaustive of the total impacts experienced by individuals. Likewise, hedonic price methods or revealed preference methods more generally will only capture values associated with actual responses to changes in environmental quality. The life satisfaction approach does not rely on descriptions of environmental impacts or behavioral changes to estimate values.
3. Recent work by Jones (2017) has similarly examined the life satisfaction consequences of the same forest-attacking pest considered here; however, that paper did not proceed to valuation as is done here. Moreover, the present chapter examines several additional complexities and extensions.
4. The top coding problem refers to the issue (found in many surveys) where respondents are asked their income category (for example, \$55 000–\$65 000) with the exception of the highest income category, which has an open-ended top (for example, \$150 000+). Following Hout (2004), we solve the top coding problem by extrapolating from the next-to-last category's midpoint using the frequencies of both the next-to-last and last (open-ended) categories. The following formula is used: $M_{top}=\frac{1}{2}L_{top}(1+\frac{v}{v-1})$ where $V=\frac{\ln(f_{top-1}+f_{top})-\ln(f_{top})}{\ln(L_{top})-\ln(L_{top-1})}$, where L_{top} is the lower limit of the top income category, L_{top-1} is the lower. limit of the category before the top one, f_{top} is the frequency in the top category, f_{top-1} is the frequency in the category before the top one, and M_{top} is the midpoint of the top income category. In our regressions, we use M_{top} as the top income category.
5. This censoring protects respondent identity from being compromised and results in a loss of five counties out of 173 where EAB was detected in 2006–10.
6. We also collected data on macro-level variables (for example, unemployment, poverty, size of the college educated population, and so on), but found them to be insignificant predictors of life satisfaction, and hence they were left out of the final models. Unfortunately, no national data are available on county-level ash tree canopy extents that includes both urban and rural areas. This is not much of a limitation because we know that EAB are only detected in counties containing ash, and that EAB-induced ash mortality exceeds 99 percent in infested areas (Herms and McCullough, 2014). Thus, it follows that detection of EAB will almost certainly lead to changes in environmental quality.
7. The 173 counties where EAB was detected between 2006 and 2010 have a combined population of 32 903 430 in the 2010 US Census. The national value is found as: (32 903 430) x (\$176) = \$5 791 003 680.

REFERENCES

Angrist, J.D. and J-S. Pischke (eds) (2009), *Mostly Harmless Econometrics*, Princeton, NJ, USA: Princeton University Press.

Baetschmann, G., Staub, K.E. and R. Winkelmann (2015), 'Consistent estimation of the fixed effects ordered logit model', *Journal of the Royal Statistical Society, Series A*, **178** (3), 685–703.

Boyd, I.L., Freer-Smith, P.H., Gilligan, C.A. and H.C.J. Godfray (2013), 'The consequence of tree pests and diseases for ecosystem services', *Science*, **342** (6160), 1235773.

Carroll, N., Frijters, P. and M.A. Shields (2009), 'Quantifying the costs of drought: new evidence from life satisfaction data', *Journal of Population Economics*, **22** (2), 445–461.

Civitello, D.J., Cohen, J., Fatima, H., Halstead, N.T., Liriano, J., et al. (2015), 'Biodiversity inhibits parasites: broad evidence for the dilution effect', *PNAS*, **112** (28), 8667–8671.

Clark, A.E., Frijters, P. and M.A. Shields (2008), 'Relative income, happiness, and utility: an explanation for the Easterlin paradox and other puzzles', *Journal of Economic Literature*, **46** (1), 95–144.

Deaton, A. (2008), 'Income, aging, health and wellbeing around the world: evidence from the Gallup World Poll', *Journal of Economic Perspectives*, **22** (2), 53–72.

Di Tella, R. and R. MacCulloch (2008), 'Gross national happiness as an answer to the Easterlin Paradox?', *Journal of Development Economics*, **86** (1), 22–42.

Donovan, G.H., Butry, D.T., Michael, Y.L., Prestemon, J.P., Liebhold, A.M., et al. (2013), 'The relationship between trees and human health: evidence from the spread of the emerald ash borer', *American Journal of Preventive Medicine*, **44** (2), 139–145.

Donovan, G.H., Michael, Y.L., Gatziolis, D., Prestemon, J.P. and E.A. Whitsel (2015), 'Is tree loss associated with cardiovascular-disease risk in the Women's Health Initiative? A natural experiment', *Health and Place*, **36**, 1–7.

Easterlin, R.A. (1974), 'Does economic growth improve the human lot? Some empirical evidence', *Nations and Households in Economic Growth*, **89**, 89–125.
Elmendorf, W. (2008), 'The importance of trees and nature in community: a review of the relative literature', *Arboriculture and Urban Forestry*, **34** (3), 152–156.
European Environment Agency (2012), 'The impacts of invasive alien species in Europe', Copenhagen, Denmark.
Ferreira, S. and M. Moro (2010), 'On the use of subjective well-being data for environmental valuation', *Environmental and Resource Economics*, **46** (3), 249–273.
Graff Zivin, J. and M. Neidell (2013), 'Environment, health, and human capital', *Journal of Economic Literature*, **51** (3), 689–730.
Hansmann, R., Hug, S.M. and K. Seeland (2007), 'Restoration and stress relief through physical activities in forests and parks', *Urban Forestry and Urban Greening*, **6** (4), 213–225.
Hellmann, J.J., Byers, J.E., Bierwagen, B.G. and J.S. Dukes (2008), 'Five potential consequences of climate change for invasive species', *Conservation Biology*, **22** (3), 534–543.
Herms, D.A. and D.G. McCullough (2014), 'Emerald ash borer invasion of North America: history, biology, ecology, impacts, and management', *Annual Review of Entomology*, **59**, 13–30.
Herms, D.A., McCullough, D.G., Smitley, D.R., Sadof, C.S. and W. Cranshaw (2014), 'Insecticide options for protecting ash trees from emerald ash borer', 2nd edition (North Central IPM Center). Accessed April 4, 2019 at http://www.emeraldashborer.info/documents/Multistate_EAB_Insecticide_Fact_Sheet.pdf.
Holmes, T.P., Murphy, E.A. and K.P. Bell (2006), 'Exotic forest insects and residential property values', *Agricultural and Resource Economics Review*, **35**, 155–166.
Holmes, T.P., Aukema, J.E., Von Holle, B., Liebhold, A. and E. Sills (2009), 'Economic impacts of invasive species in forests', *Annals of the New York Academy of Sciences*, **1162** (1), 18–38.
Hout, M. (2004), 'Getting the most out of the GSS income measures', GSS Methodological Report No. 101, University of California, Berkeley, Survey Research Center.
Jakus, P.M. (1992), 'Valuing the private and public dimensions of a mixed good: an application to pest control', PhD thesis, North Carolina State University, Raleigh.
Jones, B.A. (2016), 'Work more and play less? Time use impacts of changing ecosystem services: the case of the invasive emerald ash borer', *Ecological Economics*, **124**, 49–58.
Jones, B.A. (2017), 'Invasive species impacts on human well-being using the life satisfaction index', *Ecological Economics*, **134**, 250–257.
Jones, B.A. and S.M. McDermott (2015), 'Linking environmental management to health outcomes: a case study of the emerald ash borer', *Applied Economics Letters*, **22** (17), 1409–1414.
Jones, B.A. and S.M. McDermott (2018), 'Health impacts of invasive species through an altered natural environment: assessing air pollution sinks as a causal pathway', *Environmental and Resource Economics*, **71** (1), 23–43.
Kahneman, D. and A.B. Krueger (2006), 'Developments in the measurement of subjective well-being', *Journal of Economic Perspectives*, **20** (1), 3–24.
Kahneman, D. and R. Sugden (2005), 'Experienced utility as a standard of policy evaluation', *Environmental and Resource Economics*, **32** (1), 161–181.
Kahneman, D., Diener, E. and N. Schwarz (eds) (1999), *Well-being: Foundations of Hedonic Psychology*, New York, USA: Russell Sage Foundation.
Kahneman, D., Wakker, P.P. and R. Sarin (1997),'Back to Bentham? Explorations of experienced utility', *Quarterly Journal of Economics*, **112** (2), 375–405.
Kovacs, K.F., Haight, R.G., McCullough, D.G., Mercader, R.J., Siegert, N.W. and A.M. Liebhold (2010), 'Cost of potential emerald ash borer damage in US communities, 2009–2019', *Ecological Economics*, **69** (3), 569–578.
Kovacs, K.F., Mercader, R.J., Haight, R.G., Siegert, N.W., McCullough, D.G. and A.M. Liebhold (2011), 'The influence of satellite populations of emerald ash borer on projected economic costs in US communities, 2010–2020', *Journal of Environmental Management*, **92** (9), 2170–2181.
Krueger, A.B. and D.A. Schkade (2008), 'The reliability of subjective well-being measures', *Journal of Public Economics*, **92** (8), 1833–1845.
Layard, R. (2006), 'Happiness and public policy: a challenge to the profession', *Economic Journal*, **116** (510), C24–C33.
Levinson, A. (2012), 'Valuing public goods using happiness data: the case of air quality', *Journal of Public Economics*, **96** (9), 869–880.
Ligon, E. (1989), 'The development and use of a consistent income measure for the General Social Survey', GSS Methodological Report No. 64, University of Chicago, NORC.
Liu, J., Dietz, T., Carpenter, S.R., Folke, C., Alberti, M., et al. (2007), 'Coupled human and natural systems', *AMBIO*, **36** (8), 639–649.
Luechinger, S. (2009), 'Valuing air quality using the life satisfaction approach', *Economic Journal*, **119** (536), 482–515.
MacDonald, H., McKenney, D.W. and V. Nealis (1997), 'A bug is a bug is a bug: symbolic responses to contin-

gent valuation questions about forest pest control programs?', *Canadian Journal of Agricultural Economics*, **45** (2), 145–163.
MacKerron, G. (2012), 'Happiness economics from 35000 feet', *Journal of Economic Surveys*, **26** (4), 705–735.
McCullough, D.G. (2013), 'Will we kiss our ash goodbye?, *American Forests*, Winter 2013.
McCullough, D.G. and R.J. Mercader (2012), 'Evaluation of potential strategies to SLow Ash Mortality (SLAM) caused by emerald ash borer (Agrilus planipennis): SLAM in an urban forest', *International Journal of Pest Management*, **58** (1), 9–23.
McPherson, G., Simpson, J.R., Peper, P.J., Maco, S.E. and Q. Xiao (2005), 'Municipal forest benefits and costs in five US cities', *Journal of Forestry*, **103** (8), 411–416.
Moore, C.C. (2008), 'Using empirical benefit estimates in a bioeconomic model of invasive species control', PhD thesis, North Carolina State University, Raleigh.
Nilsson, K., Sangster, M. and C.C. Konijnendijk (2011), 'Forests, trees and human health and well-being: introduction', in Kjell Nilsson, Marcus Sangster, Christos Gallis, Terry Hartig, Sjerp de Vries, et al. (eds), *Forests, Trees and Human Health*, Dordrecht, Netherlands: Springer Science and Business Media, pp. 1–19.
Nowak, D.J., Crane, D.E. and J.C. Stevens (2006), 'Air pollution removal by urban trees and shrubs in the United States', *Urban Forestry and Urban Greening*, **4** (3), 115–123.
Nowak, D.J., Hirabayashi, S., Bodine, A. and R. Hoehn (2013), 'Modeled PM 2.5 removal by trees in ten US cities and associated health effects', *Environmental Pollution*, **178**, 395–402.
Nowak, D.J., Civerolo, K.L., Rao, S.T., Sistla, G., Luley, C.J. and D.E. Crane (2000), 'A modeling study of the impact of urban trees on ozone', *Atmospheric Environment*, **34** (10), 1601–1613.
Oswald, A.J. (1997), 'Happiness and economic performance', *Economic Journal*, **107** (445), 1815–1831.
Pastor, M., Sadd, J. and J. Hipp (2001), 'Which came first? Toxic facilities, minority move-in, and environmental justice', *Journal of Urban Affairs*, **23** (1), 1–21.
Pejchar, L. and H.A. Mooney (2009), 'Invasive species, ecosystem services and human well-being', *Trends in Ecology and Evolution*, **24** (9), 497–504.
Poland, T.M. and D.G. McCullough (2006), 'Emerald ash borer: invasion of the urban forest and the threat to North America's ash resource', *Journal of Forestry*, **104** (3), 118–124.
Prasad, A.M., Iverson, L.R., Peters, M.P., Bossenbroek, J.M., Matthews, S.N., et al. (2010), 'Modeling the invasive emerald ash borer risk of spread using a spatially explicit cellular model', *Landscape Ecology*, **25** (3), 353–369.
Rehdanz, K. and D. Maddison (2005), 'Climate and happiness', *Ecological Economics*, **52** (1), 111–125.
Smith, V.K. (2008), 'Reflections on the literature', *Review of Environmental Economics and Policy*, **2** (2), 292–308.
Sydnor, T.D., Bumgardner, M. and S. Subburayalu (2011), 'Community ash densities and economic impact potential of emerald ash borer (Agrilus planipennis) in four Midwestern states', *Arboriculture and Urban Forestry*, **37** (2), 84–89.
Van Praag, B. and B.E. Baarsma (2005), 'Using happiness surveys to value intangibles: the case of airport noise', *Economic Journal*, **115** (500), 224–246.
Von Möllendorff, C. and J. Hirschfeld (2016), 'Measuring impacts of extreme weather events using the life satisfaction approach', *Ecological Economics*, **121**, 108–116.
Welsch, H. (2002), 'Preferences over prosperity and pollution: environmental valuation based on happiness surveys', *Kyklos*, **55** (4), 473–494.
Welsch, H. (2006), 'Environment and happiness: valuation of air pollution using life satisfaction data', *Ecological Economics*, **58** (4), 801–813.
Welsch, H. (2007), 'Environmental welfare analysis: a life satisfaction approach', *Ecological Economics*, **62** (3), 544–551.
Welsch, H. and J. Kühling (2009), 'Using happiness data for environmental valuation: issues and applications', *Journal of Economic Surveys*, **23** (2), 385–406.
Wise, M. (2015), 'Emerald ash borer and urban trees'. Accessed April 4, 2019 at https://www.fpl.fs.fed.us/labnotes/?p=5480.
World Health Organization (WHO) (2015), 'Connecting global priorities: biodiversity and human health: a state of knowledge review', World Health Organization and Secretariat of the Convention on Biological Diversity, Geneva, Switzerland.

9. Happiness and air pollution*

Arik Levinson

9.1 INTRODUCTION

Air pollution makes people sick and sometimes kills them. It reduces workers' productivity, decreases students' test scores, damages buildings and reduces property values.[1] Given all these consequences, it may be obvious that air pollution also makes people less happy. And yet demonstrating the direct, cause-and-effect relationship between pollution and happiness is difficult. Researchers cannot merely ask a standard survey question about wellbeing or life satisfaction in polluted and clean places and then interpret the results as the effect of pollution on happiness. That will not work, for three reasons: omitted variables, selection, and habituation.

The first reason, omitted variable bias, involves a simple and ubiquitous statistical problem. Lots of things affect people's happiness, many of which are correlated with pollution. One example is income. Researchers and activists concerned about "environmental justice" have long observed that lower-income people live in more-polluted places. And happiness researchers have long debated the degree to which income makes people happy. If poor people live in polluted places and income makes people happy, then people living with pollution may be less happy because they are poor rather than because of the local pollution. In this narrow example, the solution is simple: any estimate of the effect of pollution on people's happiness must control statistically for their incomes. But that leaves open the concern that other characteristics of people or the places they live may also be correlated with both pollution and happiness. Automobile traffic causes pollution and makes people unhappy. Homes near the ocean have cleaner air but may have happier occupants because of the beach access. Any successful estimate of the effect of pollution on happiness must control statistically for all of those possibilities: the ones we can see and measure, and the ones we cannot.

The second problem, selection, involves a slightly more complex but still standard statistical problem. People choose where to live, and those who care the most about pollution presumably choose cleaner places. Survey respondents who have chosen polluted places might express no less happiness than respondents who chose less-polluted places. They chose the polluted places because they care less about pollution. But that does not mean that increasing pollution in the clean places would not make their residents less happy. The selection by people into polluted and unpolluted places may mask any true direct effect of pollution on happiness for a representative person.

The third problem, habituation, pertains especially to this topic. Graham (2009) summarizes evidence that people become inured to, or habituated to, things such as poor health, crime, corruption and democracy. That is, unhealthy people living in dangerous, corrupt, undemocratic places are not any less happy as a consequence, at least not in the long run. They become habituated to those problems. It makes sense that people might also become habituated to pollution. People living in Los Angeles, California may be no less happy than comparable people living in Portland, Oregon, even though the air pollution is worse in Los Angeles. Similarly, Los Angeles residents may be no happier today than their counterparts 40 years ago when the city's air was dirtier. They are habituated to better air quality than past Los Angeles residents, and to worse air quality than current Portland residents.

There is a solution to all three problems – omitted variables, selection, and habituation – but it is not an easy one. We need to examine differences in people's happiness in response to differences in pollution that are not correlated with other unobserved differences, are not the result of selection by the survey respondents, and are not long-lasting enough for the respondents to become habituated. As I show in what follows, few if any of the growing list of papers on this topic accomplish that ideal.

A few asides before proceeding. First, those three obstacles are one reason this chapter is about local air pollution in particular and not about other environmental problems such as groundwater contamination or climate change. Air pollution varies from location to location on a daily or even hourly basis, leaving open lots of statistical options for identifying the causal effect of the pollution, across locations and across time periods, in a short enough time so that people do not become habituated.

As a second aside, researchers use various terms of art in this context: happiness, subjective wellbeing, life satisfaction. Here I use "happiness" as a catch-all, though I recognize important differences. Partly, my imprecision arises because many of the surveys ask imprecise questions. The General Social Survey in the United States (US) asks how "things are these days." That could be interpreted as a wellbeing question about this week, or a life satisfaction question about recent years. Some, such as the World Values Survey (WVS), just ask how "happy" people are without specifying a time period. Others use language that conflates the two. The German Socio-Economic Panel (SOEP) asks, "How satisfied are you with your life, at present?" And the European Social Survey (ESS) asks, "How satisfied are you with your life as a whole nowadays?"

But another reason I use happiness to mean both temporary wellbeing and life satisfaction is because psychologists find that even if the survey questions do not conflate those ideas, survey respondents do. Schwarz and Clore (1983) provide a stark example. They telephoned people randomly on rainy and sunny days and asked them two questions: a question about their current state of mind, "How happy do you feel at this moment?" and an overall life satisfaction question, "How happy do you feel about your life as a whole?" Those called on sunny days reported higher wellbeing in response to both questions. That is a puzzle. If people make true assessments about their satisfaction with their entire lives, sunshine on the survey date should be immaterial.

A final reason to conflate life satisfaction and happiness is that pollution studies differ in whether they use daily fluctuations in pollution, which should affect momentary wellbeing but not life satisfaction, or local long-term pollution averages, which should affect life satisfaction and not momentary wellbeing, but might affect neither if people become habituated. Table 9.1 catalogs some of the happiness questions used in the studies surveyed in this chapter.

In sum, life satisfaction might be the right question to ask in theory about long-term differences in pollution, but if people become habituated then the effect may only be discernable in short-term local variations, which should not affect overall life satisfaction. So I use "happiness," blurring all of those distinctions.

Table 9.1 Happiness survey questions

Data source	Acronym	Question
European Social Survey	ESS	"All things considered, how satisfied are you with your life as a whole nowadays?" From 0 (extremely dissatisfied) to 10 (extremely satisfied)
World Values Survey	WVS	"Would you say you are happy or not?" From 1 (very happy) to 4 (not at all happy)
German Socio-Economic Panel	SOEP	"How satisfied are you with your life, at present, all things considered?" Ten-point scale
Eurobarometer		"On the whole, are you very satisfied, fairly satisfied, not very satisfied, or not at all satisfied with the life you lead?"
Spanish Quality of Working Life Survey (Encuesta de Calidad de Vida en el Trabajo)	ECVT	"Please, rate between 0 (not satisfied at all), and 10 (very satisfied), your degree of satisfaction with your personal life."
Chinese General Social Survey	CGSS	"Are you happy with your life?" From 1 (very unhappy) to 5 (completely happy)
Taiwan Social Change Survey	TSCS	Life satisfaction, five-point scale
UK Annual Population Survey	UK APS	Satisfaction: "Overall, how satisfied are you with your life nowadays?" 11–point scale Happiness: "Overall, how happy did you feel yesterday?"
Swiss Household Panel Survey	SHPS	"In general, how satisfied are you with your life if 0 means 'not at all satisfied' and 10 means 'completely satisfied'?"
Behavioral Risk Factor Surveillance System	BRFSS	"In general, how satisfied are you with your life?" From 1 (very satisfied) to 4 (very dissatisfied)
China Family Panel Studies	CFPS	"Overall, how satisfied are you with your life?" On a scale from 1 (not satisfied at all) to 5 (very satisfied)
Canadian Community Health Survey	CCHS	"How satisfied are you with your life in general" 5 or 11 levels, depending on year

In this chapter I address three questions. First, can the direct, causal effect of pollution on happiness be measured directly? Answering that question requires dealing with the three main problems identified: omitted variables, selection, and habituation. I survey recent work, and discuss the degree to which it surmounts those problems.

Second, how much does pollution decrease happiness? That is not easy to answer either, because many of the more than 30 recent published papers on this topic study different countries and time periods, use different measures of pollution and income, and ask different happiness questions. What does it mean that in one study, a one-day increase in the number of days particulate matter <10 microns (PM10) exceeds 50 micrograms per cubic meter ($\mu g/m^3$) reduces life satisfaction by 0.0005 on an 11-point scale (García-Mainar et al., 2015), while another study finds that a 1 $\mu g/m^3$ increase in sulfur dioxide (SO_2) decreases happiness by 0.07 units on a four-point scale (Menz and Welsch, 2012)? Which is larger?

To compare magnitudes across studies, I translate each into a willingness to pay for a one-standard-deviation improvement in air quality, for one day, in 2016 USD. Every one of the papers includes income as a covariate, and the ratio of the pollution and income coefficients indicates the amount of extra money (typically, annual income) an average respondent needs to compensate for a one-unit increase in pollution. Multiply that by the standard deviation in the pollutant, divide by 365 days per year, convert to US dollars and adjust for inflation to 2016, and we have an apples-to-apples comparison.

The third question I address is whether the measured willingness to pay derived from happiness studies comports with other negative effects of pollution. An enormous and growing body of research studies the effect of pollution on outcomes more tangible than happiness: health, mortality, productivity, test scores, and so on. It turns out, perhaps surprisingly, that these disparate methods of valuing air quality match up well. The dollar value of willingness to pay for air quality derived from happiness studies looks remarkably similar to the dollar value typically assigned to decreased mortality or to the increased productivity from that air quality.

9.2 LITERATURE REVIEW: THE EVIDENCE AS OF 2010

A recent review (Frey et al., 2010) cited seven noteworthy studies estimating the effect of pollution on happiness, controlling for other covariates. Two used single surveys from one point in time – cross-sections – comparing happiness of people in more- and less-polluted places (Welsch, 2002; MacKerron and Mourato, 2009). They estimate models such as:

$$H_{ij} = f(P_{ij}, Y_{ij}, \boldsymbol{X}_{ij}, \varepsilon_{ij}) \tag{9.1}$$

where H_{ij} is some measure of happiness or stated wellbeing for person i in location j, P is some measure of pollution, Y is income, $\boldsymbol{X}$ is a vector of other control variables, and ε is an error term. Some estimate linear regression versions of (9.1); some estimate discrete choice models such as ordered probits, acknowledging that happiness measures usually come in discrete categories; and some present robustness checks with multiple approaches. But most papers note that their qualitative findings do not depend on the choice of specification.

In the cross-section estimates of (9.1), pollution differs across observations because the survey respondents live in different places. As Frey et al. (2010) note, comparing pollution and happiness in different places is "prone to omitted variable bias," the first of the three statistical obstacles highlighted above. In short, there are likely unobserved characteristics of locations correlated with both pollution and happiness. The error term ε is correlated with P and H, imparting a bias on the estimate of $\partial H/\partial P$.

To address omitted variable bias, four of the studies cited by Frey et al. use surveys collected at multiple times: repeated cross-sections (Welsch, 2006; Di Tella and MacCulloch, 2006; Levinson, 2012; Luechinger, 2010). Repeated cross-sections help, making it feasible to control statistically for characteristics of places that are correlated with pollution and happiness but do not change over time. Consider proximity to the ocean. A single cross-section has to compare the happiness of respondents in ocean-side unpolluted neighborhoods to inland polluted neighborhoods, conflating the effect of beach access on happiness with that of pollution on happiness. Repeated cross-sections can compare respondents in either ocean-side or inland neighborhoods when the air quality changes and beach access has not. They estimate models such as:

$$H_{ijt} = f(P_{jt}, Y_{it}, \boldsymbol{X}_{ijt}, \boldsymbol{\delta}_j, \boldsymbol{\delta}_t, \varepsilon_{ijt}) \tag{9.2}$$

where observations are individuals i surveyed in location j at time t. The vector $\boldsymbol{\delta}_t$ is a set of time dummy variables, and $\boldsymbol{\delta}_j$ is a set of location-specific dummy variables that capture unobserved fixed characteristics of locations, such as proximity to the ocean. In (9.2) the estimate of $\partial H/\partial P$ is identified thanks to relative changes in pollution within locations over time. It asks: if a particular community becomes more polluted, do its inhabitants become less happy? By not comparing pollution and happiness across different communities, (9.2) avoids omitted variable bias due to unobserved community characteristics that are fixed over time and correlated with both happiness and pollution.

But that still leaves open the two harder problems: selection and habituation. Two of the papers surveyed by Frey et al. tackle those. My paper (Levinson, 2012) uses repeated annual cross-sections and daily variations in pollution. The idea is to compare similar individuals, in the same place during the same year, who happen to be surveyed on different days with more or less pollution. Respondents surveyed on polluted days are less happy. But respondents in polluted places with relatively high annual average pollution are not less happy. Short-term changes in pollution make people less happy, as expected. However, long-term differences do not, either because people become habituated or because people who care most about pollution choose the least-polluted places.

The one other paper surveyed by Frey et al. that addresses selection and habituation is Luechinger (2009). His is also the only to use panel data, repeated observations of the same individuals at different times. Panel data enables estimation of:

$$H_{ijt} = f(P_{jt}, Y_{it}, \boldsymbol{X}_{ijt}, \boldsymbol{\delta}_j, \boldsymbol{\delta}_t, \boldsymbol{\delta}_i, \varepsilon_{ijt}) \tag{9.3}$$

where the novel addition is the vector $\boldsymbol{\delta}_i$: individual-specific dummy variables. The estimate of $\partial H/\partial P$ in (9.3) is identified for a particular individual (who has presumably chosen to live in a clean or dirty place), when the air quality in that place changes over time. Luechinger measures annual sulfur dioxide (SO_2) levels at 533 monitoring stations in Germany for 19 years. To control for sorting by individuals into different locales, he compares responses by people who live downwind of large power plants that installed SO_2 emissions control equipment, before and after the equipment was installed. And he compares the responses of downwind people whose air quality improved to those of similar people living upwind of the same power plants, before and after the equipment installation. Luechinger finds that the downwind people got happier after the installation, relative to their upwind neighbors who experienced less of an air quality improvement.

As of 2010, Luechinger's approach was state-of-the-art. His paper addresses omitted variable bias by comparing pollution in the same places before and after changes in air quality. It solves the selection problem by comparing responses by the same individuals before and after the change. And it addresses habituation, so long as we believe that it takes longer than a year or so to occur.

Since 2010 then there have been over 30 new published papers on this topic. They are summarized in Table 9.2. Below I describe how well these new papers overcome the three

Table 9.2 New published papers on pollution and happiness

Study	Pollutant	Data	Number of observations	Main result	Willingness to pay for a 1 std deviation improvement (2016 $US per day)*
	(1)	(2)	(3)	(4)	(5)
Perceived air pollution					
Rehdanz and Maddison (2008)	Perceived air pollution	SOEP in 1994, 1999 and 2004	23014		
Beja (2012)	Perceived air pollution	2005 WVS	43408	Pollution and happiness negatively correlated in Latin America, not elsewhere	
Goetzke and Rave (2015)	Perceived air pollution and air pollution factor (comprised of SO_2, NO_x, PM10)	SOEP, perceived and actual pollution	7802	Perceived pollution endogenous	
Ozdamar (2016)	Self-reported exposure to air pollution	Turkish health survey 2010, 2012	14400		
Xu and Li (2016)	"Seriousness" of pollution, four-point scale	2007 WVS for China	1991	Perceived seriousness of pollution negatively associated with happiness.	
MacKerron and Mourato (2009)	NO_x	Original survey of London	400	Both perceived and actual air quality affect happiness	
Cross-sections					
Welsch (2007)	NO_2	Cross-section of average national happiness and income in 1995	54		
Smyth et al. (2008)	SO_2 emissions per capita	Chinese cross-section, 30 cities in 2003	8890		
Ferreira and Moro (2010)	PM10 (annual local mean)	Cross-section of Irish locations	1184	€945 per $\mu g/m^3$	$9.56

Table 9.2 (continued)

Study	Pollutant	Data	Number of observations	Main result	Willingness to pay for a 1 std deviation improvement (2016 $US per day)*
	(1)	(2)	(3)	(4)	(5)
Ferreira and Moro (2013)	PM10 (annual local mean)	Cross-section of Irish locations	1063	€2496 per μg/m^3	$31.57
Cuñado and De Gracia (2013)	CO_2, NO_2, PM10	European Social Survey 2008 for 17 regions of Spain	2565	€325–€609 for one day reduction in days >50 μg/m^3	No std dev. reported
Ambrey et al. (2014)	PM10 (local days per year exceeding guidelines)	HILDA Survey Australia 2001	919	AU$5164 for one day reduction	$30.12
Jidong and Yiran (2015)	NO_2 (annual local means)	Chinese cities (CGSS)	6626	RMB 1144 per μg/m^3	$6.48
León and Araña (2015)	NO_2, SO_2 (projected local levels at time of survey)	UK, Norway, Sweden, 2010	3830	NO_2: €402 in UK €918 in Norway SO_2: €763 in UK €1439 in Sweden	NO_2: $1.61 (UK) $3.38 (Norway) SO_2: $3.05 (UK) $5.76 (Sweden)
Tsurumi et al. (2015)	SPM at time of survey	Japan 2013 BLI Survey	2921	$0.18 per μg/m^3	$0.01
Tsurumi and Managi (2017)	SPM at time of survey	Japan 2013 BLI.	2921	Insignificant	--
Liao et al. (2015)	% days in June 2010 when local pollution index below "good"	Taiwan 2010 (TSCS)	1055	Negative (pollution increases happiness)	--
Dolan and Laffan (2016)	PM2.5 (annual local mean)	UK APS	≈130 000	£261.25 per μg/m^3	$170.65
Glaeser et al. (2016)	PM10	US cities in 2000 (BRFSS)	1 182 563	Insignificant	--
Zhang et al. (2017b)	PM2.5	China cities 2014	21 589		$8.11

Repeated cross-sections					
Menz and Welsch (2010)	PM10	25 OECD countries, 1990–2004, World Values Survey	136	\$98–\$185 per μg/m³	\$2.55–\$3.29
Menz (2011)	PM10 (annual mean, urban population weighted)	48 countries 1990–2006	253	\$136 per μg/m³	\$11.23
Menz and Welsch (2012)	SO_2, NO_2 (annual national mean)	Eurobarometer, 10 EU countries 1990–97	59437	€210 per μg/m³ SO_2 €139 per μg/m³ NO_2	\$10.23 (SO_2) \$7.25 (NO_2)
Ferreira et al. (2013)	SO_2 (annual regional means)	ESS, 23 EU countries, 248 regions, 2002–07	≈70000	€2925 per μg/m³ SO_2	\$44.81
García-Mainar et al. (2015)	PM10 (days >50 μg/m³)	ECVT, Spain, 17 regions, 2006–10	32317	€17–€20 per one day reduction	\$3.69–\$4.35
Orru et al. (2016)	PM10	Europe (ESS 2010, 2012)	3770	Omits absolute income covariate.	–
Barrington-Leigh and Behzadnejad (2017)	SO_2 (daily local mean)	CCHS 2005–11	322233	\$890 per μg/m³	\$19.99
Panel data					
Giovanis and Ozdamar (2016)	O_3, SO_2, NO_2, CO, PM10 (annual means)	Switzerland (SHPS) 2000–2013	71804	O_3: \$8900 per μg/m³ SO_2: \$11985 NO_2: \$6580 CO: \$1940 PM10: \$2320	O_3: \$25.12 SO_2: \$33.83 NO_2: \$18.57 CO: \$5.48 PM10: \$6.55
Ozdamar and Giovanis (2017)	NO_x, O_3, CO (weekly local average)	British Household Panel Survey, 1991–2009	5000	O_3: £1550 per std dev. NO_x: £1070 CO: insignificant	O_3: \$7.22 NO_x: \$4.99 CO: –
Zhang et al. (2017a)	API	China Family Panel Studies 2010, 2012, 2014	49333		\$4.29

Notes:
Pollutants: nitrous oxides (NO_x), nitrogen dioxide (NO_2), sulfur dioxide (SO_2), carbon monoxide (CO), ozone (O_3), particulates smaller than 10 microns (PM10), smaller than 2.5 microns (PM2.5) suspended particulate matter (SPM), Air Pollution Index (API).
* Monetary values converted to 2016 USD by first using average exchange rates, and then inflating by the CPI-U.

obstacles – omitted variables, selection, and habituation – and the answers they provide to the three questions: does pollution make people less happy? How much? And is the effect proportional to the estimates of pollution's effects on health and productivity?

9.3 DOES POLLUTION MAKE PEOPLE LESS HAPPY, AND HOW MUCH? QUESTIONS 1 AND 2

One of the very first papers to examine the relationship between environmental quality and happiness (Welsch, 2002) recognized the importance of controlling for income, and in doing so, the possibility of examining the trade-off between income and environmental quality as determinants of happiness. In short, the estimate of $\partial H/\partial P$ in equation (9.1) intends to capture the happiness reduction from a one-unit change in pollution; and the estimate $\partial H/\partial Y$ intends to capture the happiness increase from a one-unit change in income. Combined, the ratio:

$$\frac{\partial H/\partial P}{\partial H/\partial Y} = \left.\frac{-dY}{dP}\right|_{dH=0} = MWTP \tag{9.4}$$

then captures the amount of money necessary to compensate for a one-unit change in pollution. It is the marginal willingness to pay (MWTP) for a one-unit improvement in air quality. In a linear regression version of equation (9.1), that amounts simply to the ratio of the coefficient on pollution divided by the coefficient on income. Welsch calls this the "life satisfaction" approach to measuring willingness to pay for air quality. His 2002 paper estimates equation (9.4) in a simple way, using a cross-section of 54 countries, national average reported wellbeing, national average pollution levels and national per capita incomes. Though simple, the approach illustrated the methodology for subsequent research: the papers surveyed in Frey et al. (2010) and the 30-plus published since.

9.3.1 Perceived Pollution

Among the 30 new papers, five use survey respondents' perceptions of local air quality rather than actual measured local pollution. Using self-reported perceived pollution has the convenience that all of the data are contained in one survey. But relying on perceived air pollution comes with obvious difficulties. Most critically, perceived pollution seems likely to be endogenous even if actual pollution is not. People most sensitive to poor air quality may both describe pollution as worse and be less happy. Some papers that estimate versions of equation (9.1) or (9.2) using perceived P ignore the endogeneity issue, while others acknowledge the problem and demonstrate its significance empirically.

Beja (2012) finds that perceived poor local air quality reduces respondents' happiness in Latin America, but is unable to show statistically significant results for other analyzed regions (Europe and US, sub-Saharan Africa, Asia and Pacific). MacKerron and Mourato (2009) use their own survey of Londoners to show that both perceived and actual pollution is correlated with happiness. Of course, both could be endogenous for different reasons.

Only one paper, Goetzke and Rave (2015), deals directly with the endogeneity of perceived P, controlling for both perceived and actual air pollution. The authors find that perceived air pollution is associated with lower happiness, but actual measured air pollution is associated with greater happiness. They instrument for perceived pollution using actual pollution, and the result is an insignificant but positive coefficient. Their explanation makes sense: both perceived and actual air pollution are endogenous for different reasons. Perceived pollution because people who care most about air pollution are least happy when they perceive it to be bad; and actual pollution, presumably, because of omitted variable bias and selection.

Beyond endogeneity concerns, using perceived air pollution from the same survey that asks about happiness raises concerns about standard survey biases: framing, question order, and so on. By asking about air quality, the survey might make pollution more salient, or suggest to respondents that they should care about it or be less happy if it is bad, or happier if it is good. One of the advantages of the life satisfaction approach to valuing air quality is that measures of pollution taken from monitor readings independent of the happiness survey are unquestionably exogenous. For all of these reasons, most of the studies surveyed in Table 9.2 use actual air quality rather than perceived pollution.

9.3.2 Cross-Sections

Almost half of the new happiness-and-pollution studies published since the Frey et al. (2010) survey use cross-section estimates of equation (9.1). They show that people who live in more-polluted places are less happy, usually but not always, and infer that pollution decreases happiness. That approach cannot account for any of the three obstacles: omitted variables, selection, or habituation. I list them in Table 9.2 for inclusiveness, but the time has probably come to stop publishing estimates from models that use only single cross-sections.

9.3.3 Repeated Cross-Sections

Table 9.2 lists seven papers that estimate equation (9.2) using repeated cross-sections, enabling the inclusion of location fixed effects ($\boldsymbol{\delta}_j$) to control for unobserved location characteristics that may be correlated with happiness and pollution (for example, beach access). Then $\partial H/\partial P$ can be identified by examining how happiness changes when pollution changes within a location.

Two of the repeated cross-sections use country average measures of pollution and income (Menz and Welsch, 2010; Menz, 2011). That is, P is measured as the country-wide average level of pollution, and Y is some national average measure of per capita income. That is not necessarily problematic, but it does aggregate away much of the variation. Both income and pollution vary less across countries than within countries. In the US, for example, the standard deviation of PM10 within locations across days is twice as large as it is across states or across years (Levinson, 2013).

Orru et al. (2016) examine 3770 observations from Estonia and two years of the ESS. They find local PM10 pollution to be negatively correlated with life satisfaction. But they do not seem to include local regional dummy variables ($\boldsymbol{\delta}_j$ in equation (9.2)), so it is hard to tell whether or not the study capitalizes on the repeated cross-sections to address omitted variable bias. And the income variables included are feelings about the households' incomes, rather than actual incomes, making trade-offs difficult to interpret.

Menz and Welsch (2012) take an important step in the right direction, using five repeated cross-sections of more than 59 000 individuals in ten countries. The income and other covariates are at the individual level. But the pollution measures are still country average concentrations of SO_2 and nitrogen dioxide (NO_2). The authors address this shortcoming, noting that "there is some variation of ambient SO_2 concentrations" within France and within Italy, but that "all of Great Britain, Belgium, the Netherlands, Luxembourg, and Germany are more polluted than the other countries [*sic*] in our sample." And they argue that using country averages for SO_2 and NO_2 is less problematic than for PM10. Regardless of how much pollution varies within countries, their use of annual averages means that despite having 59 000 observations, they only have 50 different pollution readings: one for each of ten countries in five different years.

Ferreira et al. (2013) take a bigger step closer to the ideal, examining more than 70 000 survey responses from the European Social Survey over six years. They regress happiness on annual average concentrations of SO_2 and find a negative and significant relationship. An increase of one $\mu g/m^3$ is associated with a decline of from 0.016 to 0.030 points on an 11-point life satisfaction scale. Most of the regressions control for 23 country fixed effects but not the 248 regions used to characterize annual mean SO_2 concentrations. So it is impossible to say how much of the 0.016 to 0.030 happiness effect is identified by cross-region differences and how much is attributable to changes in SO_2 within regions over time. The cross-region differences will be affected by selection and habituation. The within-region differences perhaps less so. The largest negative relationship between SO_2 and wellbeing is estimated in the one regression with regional fixed effects.

Ferreira et al. do not translate their findings into MWTP, but their paper provides all the results necessary to do so. If we divide their pollution coefficient (0.0302) by their log income coefficient (0.361) and multiply by the average income in the sample (34 975), that yields the MWTP for a one-unit change in annual mean SO_2 concentrations. Multiplying by the standard deviation in SO_2 and dividing by 365 gives willingness to pay for a one-standard-deviation change in pollution, for one day. That number is reported in Table 9.2: US$44.81 in 2016 USD. It is among the highest such valuations.

García-Mainar et al. (2015) conduct a similar exercise, focusing on PM10 pollution in Spain. Their measure of pollution is the number of days per year that the average PM10 concentration in the respondent's region exceeds 50 $\mu g/m^3$. They find that an increase in the number of days PM10 exceeds that threshold reduces happiness by the same amount as a €17 decrease in annual income. Multiplying by the standard deviation of pollution, dividing by 365, and converting to 2016 USD yields a willingness to pay of $3.69 to $4.35 to avoid each day of high pollution. This estimate is among the lowest such valuations.

Barrington-Leigh and Behzadnejad (2017) is the only new paper listed in Table 9.2 that uses pollution which varies on a short time frame, daily in their case. They use repeated cross-sections of a non-public version of the Canadian Community Health Survey (CCHS) during 2005–11, which identifies the interview date and postal code for each respondent. They then match each response to the pollution at nearby pollution monitors on the date of the interview. This approach is closest in spirit to my own paper (Levinson, 2012). Barrington-Leigh and Behzadnejad find MWTP of around US$2000 for an annual, one-part-per-billion improvement in SO_2, or about US$20 for a one-standard-deviation change for a day. That is nearly exactly the amount I found, though curiously they find the effect for SO_2 and not for other pollutants such as particulates, while I found the effect for particulates and not for other pollutants such as SO_2. They explain the lack of effect for particulates as a result of the fact that levels are stable, mostly captured by geographic fixed effects. I explain the lack of effect for SO_2 in my paper as the result of the fact that most areas in my study do not have significant SO_2 pollution. SO_2 being less ubiquitous, it poses a problem mostly downwind of coal-fired power plants. Neither explanation seems implausible on its own, but combined they start to sound like *ex post* rationalizations of potentially spurious results.

9.3.4 Panels

Ideally, to solve the three problems of omitted variables, selection, and habituation, we would have panel data on the same individuals surveyed at different times and experiencing different air pollution. Three recent papers use panel data. Giovanis and Ozdamar (2016) use the Swiss Household Panel Survey (SHPS) from 2000 to 2013 to estimate a version of equation (9.3) that includes individual respondent fixed effects ($\boldsymbol{\delta}_i$). They include local daily air pollution at the location of the survey on the date of the survey. They find large and statistically significant MWTP for ozone (O_3), SO_2 and NO_2, and smaller and less significant MWTP for carbon monoxide (CO) and PM10. The results, summarized in Table 9.2, are not dissimilar from prior work using less sophisticated data.

Those same two authors, Ozdamar and Giovanis (2017), conduct a similar exercise for the United Kingdom. They use the British Household Panel Survey (BHPS) for 18 years, from 1991 to 2009. Instead of a standard happiness or life satisfaction question, the BHPS asks 12 questions about "mental wellbeing." Ozdamar and Giovanis combine those 12 answers into one scalar. They focus on non-movers because those are less likely to have made choices based on the local conditions such as pollution. The main results use only households eligible for public assistance, so the findings cannot necessarily be interpreted generally. All three of the pollutants studied – O_3, nitrous oxides (NO_x) and CO – are associated with more reported mental stress, though not statistically significantly so for CO. That makes sense, given that ambient CO mostly passes unnoticed. Income is negatively associated with mental stress. And the trade-off between income and pollution is smaller than in the authors' Swiss study: the numbers for O_3 and NO_x are about one-third as large.

Zhang et al. (2017a) conduct a third such exercise, this time for China. They use three waves of the China Family Panel Studies (CFPS) from 2010, 2012 and 2014. The authors track individuals over time, and know the place and date of each interview so that it can be matched to local pollution data. All three waves of the CFPS ask the life satisfaction question, "Overall, how satisfied are you with your life?" Respondents were also asked questions closer to momentary hedonic happiness: one about current depressive symptoms, and another about whether they were "hard to cheer up in the past month." Controlling for other things, including individual respondent fixed effects, Zhang et al. find current local air pollution to be uncorrelated with the life satisfaction question, but significantly correlated with the two measures of current happiness.

Notably, despite all its strengths, Zhang et al. generate a result that is remarkably consistent with papers that lack those advantages. A one-standard-deviation improvement in air quality raises the average person's happiness by an amount equivalent to income of US$4 per day. That similarity deserves caution, however. Most of the other studies in Table 9.2 focus on developed countries, Europe or the US. It stands to reason that MWTP might be different in China, where pollution levels are higher and incomes are lower. But more importantly, most of the other studies use a life satisfaction question, ignoring the fact that daily variations in pollution should not affect overall life satisfaction. Zhang et al. find no effect of pollution on life satisfaction, which contrasts with prior published studies but is to be expected, and do find an effect on hedonic happiness, which they use to generate their US$4 MWTP.

9.4 COMPARISONS OF EFFECTS OF POLLUTION ON HEALTH AND PRODUCTIVITY: QUESTION 3

As noted at the top of this chapter, pollution makes people sick and less productive. For researchers who might be skeptical of "happiness" survey questions or willingness to pay estimates derived from the life satisfaction approach, a natural question to ask is how the happiness results in Table 9.2 compare with the results of the health and productivity research.

Luechinger (2014) provides an excellent such comparison. He uses the exact same empirical strategy as in his 2009 happiness paper: examining respondents upwind and downwind of power plants before and after they install technology to reduce SO_2 emissions. Except, instead of happiness, his 2014 paper examines infant mortality. He finds that a 1 μg/m^3 increase in SO_2 results in 0.026 to 0.045 extra infant deaths per 1000 live births. His 2009 paper finds a willingness to pay for clean air of €183 to €313, or $230 to $349 in 2016 USD. Putting these two estimates together yields a value of statistical life (VSL) of $5.1 to $15.2 million. This estimate is remarkably consistent with VSL estimates used in policy analysis. For example, the US Environmental Protection Agency (EPA) uses a central VSL estimate of US$8.8 million.

To my knowledge there are no other papers like the pair by Luechinger, estimating effects of pollution on happiness and some less subjective measure of welfare. But there are many health and productivity papers that could be compared to the happiness papers in Table 9.2. Here is an example. Heutel and Ruhm (2016) estimate that a one-standard-deviation increase in CO increases mortality rates by 1.6 percent. Underlying mortality rates average 8.2 per 1000, so that is 0.13 additional deaths per 1000 per year. Giovanis and Ozdamar (2016) calculate a happiness-based willingness to pay for a one-standard-deviation reduction in CO of US$5.48. Putting those two together yields a VSL of US$15.6 million.

Other examples come from work comparing pollution and productivity. Graff Zivin and Neidell (2012) show that a 10 ppb decrease in ozone concentrations increases agricultural worker productivity in California by 5.5 percent. That is approximately a one-standard-deviation change. If workers earn the minimum wage of US$10.10 per hour, or $80.80 per eight-hour day, a 5.5 percent change is worth about $4.50, not out of line with the estimates on the rightmost column of Table 9.2.

Here is another productivity example. He et al. (2017) show that a 10 μg/m^3 increase in particulate matter smaller than 2.5 microns (PM2.5) reduces factory worker productivity in China by 1 percent.[2] The standard deviation of PM2.5 in their sample is 35.3, and the average output per worker per shift is US$20. So a one-standard-deviation change in PM2.5 costs about $0.75. That is considerably smaller than the US$6.55 Giovanis and

Ozdamar estimated for PM10 in Switzerland. But Chinese income per capita is less than one-fourth that of Switzerland.

Many papers similar in spirit to these four examples estimate the effect of pollution on health, mortality and productivity. Graff Zivin and Neidell (2013) and Currie et al. (2014) provide comprehensive reviews. The sampling here suggests that the papers estimating the effect of pollution on happiness generate comparable results.

9.5 DISCUSSION

9.5.1 Few Studies Address Omitted Variables, Selection, or Habituation

I raised three concerns at the start of this review. Many of the published papers to date do mention concerns about omitted variables, though few address the issue directly. Most papers ignore selection, and almost none mention habituation. Most papers rely on cross-sections of data, comparing annual average national pollution in different countries. Only two papers measure happiness as a function of daily fluctuations in air quality, on the date and in the place the survey question was asked. Only four use panels, following the same individual as pollution changes in the same place over time. And only one of the panel studies uses daily fluctuations: Zhang et al. (2017a) for China. That seems to be the current state-of-the-art methodology, and a strategy worth replicating. How do the same individuals respond to changing daily air pollution?

For the cross-section studies listed in Table 9.2, which ignore all three concerns, it may not be surprising that the results vary widely, from negative (pollution makes people happier) to a willingness to pay of US$170 per day for a one-standard-deviation reduction in pollution. But the range of magnitudes is much smaller and more sensible among repeated cross-sections, which at least address omitted fixed location characteristics. Those estimates range from a few dollars to US$44. That is not a wide range, given the variety of pollutants, countries and happiness questions involved. As for the few studies using panels or daily fluctuations, it is too early to say whether there is a consensus. The estimates of willingness to pay range from about US$4 (for an index of air pollution in China) to US$34 ($SO_2$ in Switzerland), a range similar to that for repeated cross-sections that do not account for selection or habituation as well.

To be clear, just because the estimates from papers that account for selection and habituation fall in the same general range does not excuse ignoring those issues. And just because the few studies that do use panel data or daily fluctuations have estimates within a relatively narrow bound does not mean they are correct. There remain large concerns that almost none of the papers in Table 9.2 address. One of those is that income itself may be endogenous.

9.5.2 Endogenous Income

Using happiness to value air quality requires estimating both the numerator and the denominator of equation (9.4). For the denominator, $\partial H/\partial Y$, we need to know the effect of income on happiness, but income may be endogenous. Inherently happier people may earn higher incomes. Luttmer (2005) estimates the effect of income on happiness where he instruments for household income using interactions between the respondents' and spouses' industry, occupation and location. He finds income coefficients in instrumental variables specifications that are larger than in ordinary least squares (OLS) specifications, suggesting that equation (9.4) overstates the MWTP for clean air.[3] Almost none of the papers in Table 9.2 even remark upon this concern, let alone try to address it. Luechinger (2009) and Levinson (2012) instrument for income using instruments such as Luttmer's, lowering the MWTP. But since then, most papers have ignored the issue.

9.5.3 Selection, Migration and Contagious Unhappiness

Another possible concern with these analyses is that the type of people who choose to live in polluted areas, or even areas likely to have occasional polluted days, may be different from people who live in reliably clean areas. Only a few of the papers in Table 9.2 address this. In their two papers, Giovanis and Ozdamar distinguish between people who have moved recently and those who have not, on the grounds that pollution may have played a role in movers' choice of where to move. And the studies that use daily fluctuations, such as Zhang et al. (2017a) and Barrington-Leigh and Behzadnejad (2017), control for selection by identifying the effect of pollution on happiness in a time frame that is shorter than those during which people typically would have time to move. But even those studies ignore the fact that areas known to have occasional highly polluted days may attract residents who are less sensitive to pollution.

More subtly, once we open the door to selection of location by residents, maybe we should be concerned about why, in equilibrium, there are any differences in happiness across jurisdictions. After controlling for everything on the right-hand-side, shouldn't happiness be equal everywhere? If not, people should move to the happier places. But Glaeser et al. (2016) show that people continue to move to cities in the US with lower-than-average levels of stated wellbeing, or happiness, and that individuals who migrate to cities with lower happiness become less happy themselves.

Glaeser et al.'s results have multiple possible interpretations for this happiness–pollution line of research. The fact that people migrate to low-happiness places could mean that people less concerned about the particular features of those target cities that make their residents unhappy are more likely to move there. Pollution-sensitive people do not move to polluted cities. That is concerning, because it means that regressions of happiness on pollution will understate how much pollution reduces happiness for a typical person.

Another interpretation is that happiness itself may be contagious. Glaeser et al. show that people who move to unhappy cities become less happy themselves. If the decline in happiness is the result of the underlying characteristics of those cities, such as pollution, then it would seem to be related to the causal effect of pollution on happiness, even though the migrants have selected the cities. But if the decline in happiness results from being surrounded by other unhappy people, then that spurious correlation plagues all of the pollution–happiness results in Table 9.2. If pollution makes you and everyone around you unhappy, then you are unhappy for two reasons: the direct effect of the pollution, and the indirect effect of pollution through everybody else. That poses a daunting empirical challenge, because your and everybody else's happiness will be correlated with all the same observable and unobservable local conditions.

9.5.4 Habituation, Short-Termism Bias and Using Happiness to Value Air Quality

People get habituated, which means that long-lasting circumstances have curiously small effects on life satisfaction. But a similar problem happens in reverse. Earlier I described how people report greater overall life satisfaction if they happen to be surveyed on a sunny day. Schwarz and Strack (1991) describe an even more trivial effect. They randomly placed 10 cents where some survey respondents could find it, and then interviewed those people about their life satisfaction. Those who found the coin were significantly more satisfied with their lives. A life satisfaction methodology would suggest that people are willing to give up a significant amount of annual income in exchange for finding 10 cents. Call it "short-termism." So habituation means that long-lasting circumstances affect life satisfaction too little, and short-termism means that even inconsequential temporary circumstances affect life satisfaction too much. That seems problematic for using reported wellbeing to value air quality – either long-lasting differences in pollution or temporary daily fluctuations.

In brief, the happiness approach to evaluating policy has shortcomings. Using daily fluctuations is problematic if public policy is aimed at long-term changes in air quality. But if people become habituated to long-term average levels, the happiness approach may be useless except as identified by short-term fluctuations.

Can we use happiness to value air quality anyway? An optimistic, or maybe even "Pollyanna-ish," view would be that we are fortunate that people exhibit both behaviors. Habituation without short-termism would mean that there would be no way of using happiness to value air quality. People would be habituated to long-term changes and would not mistake short-term changes for permanence. There would be no effect on life satisfaction of either local annual average air pollution levels across regions, thanks to habituation, or to daily fluctuations within regions, thanks to the lack of short-termism bias. Fortunately, responses to life satisfaction questions do vary with temporary circumstances, such as today's sunshine or pollution. Short-termism may partly save this methodology from habituation. On the other hand, there is no guarantee that the valuations of public goods with habituation and short-termism would be the same as the valuations with neither, or that the magnitudes would be comparable.

The pessimistic view was stated by Schwarz and Strack (1999) even before the recent growth of policy applications began: "What is being assessed, and how, seems too context dependent to provide reliable information about a population's well-being, let alone information that can guide public policy." If that seems too negative, recall that other methods of valuing environmental quality – hedonic property values regressions, travel cost models, contingent valuation – have their own biases and unaddressed issues. The past 15 years have seen the introduction of happiness economics as a new methodology for valuing air quality, a tool with its own new set of hurdles and biases that must be confronted.

9.6 CONCLUSIONS

I promised answers to three questions: Does pollution make people unhappy? How much? And is the effect proportional to estimates of pollution's effects on health and productivity? The answer to the first is unequivocal: "yes." There are now dozens of studies measuring negative correlations between happiness and pollution, in a variety of countries, using different wellbeing questions, pollution measures and empirical strategies.

The second question, "How much?," is tougher to answer. Because all the studies use different units, the coefficients on pollution cannot be compared directly. One way of comparing the pollution coefficients across different studies is to examine how they each relate to the income coefficient within the same studies, as in equation (9.4). Even if we do not consider this a valid approach to valuing air quality, it is a means of comparing results across studies that use different units of pollution and wellbeing. Here there is a division. Papers using only single cross-sections have results that vary from negative (pollution increases happiness), to people being willing to pay hundreds of dollars for a single day of cleaner air. Neither is credible. But if we focus only on the studies that use repeated cross-sections, or better yet use panels of data or daily fluctuations in air quality, the results fall into a reasonable range, from US$4 to US$40 for a day of cleaner air.

Third, how do these results compare to estimates of pollution's effect on more tangible outcomes, such as health and productivity? If we take the MWTP estimate from the happiness papers, and apply them to recent studies of the effect of pollution on mortality, we get an estimate of the VSL. These VSL numbers are similar to those used by policy makers, and that come directly from hedonic wage regressions or contingent valuation questions. In the same way, if we take the MWTP from happiness papers and apply them to recent studies of the effect of pollution on productivity, we find that the monetary value of people's lost happiness from pollution is comparable to their lost productivity.

Taken all together, the answers provide the grounds for cautious optimism about this line of inquiry. Caution, because most of the studies to date suffer from problems associated with omitted variables, selection, and habituation, as well as endogenous income and contagious happiness. But optimism, because a small handful of studies now use panel data and short-term fluctuations in pollution to address some of these problems. And those newer studies provide estimates of willingness to pay for air quality that are consistent with outcomes that economists have more experience and comfort in measuring, such as health and productivity.

NOTES

* Kevin Ankney and Lina Yu provided especially helpful insights and research assistance. Chris Barrington-Leigh, Simon Luechinger, Mirko Moro, Katrin Rehdanz and Heinz Welsch helped with thoughtful feedback on early drafts. Some of the material used here appeared in draft form as NBER Working Paper 19329 (Levinson, 2013).

1. See, for example, OECD (2016), Neidell (2017) and Ebenstein et al. (2016).
2. PM10 refers to particulate matter smaller than 10 microns, and PM2.5 to particulate matter smaller than 2.5 microns.
3. But see Pischke and Schwant (2012) for a note of caution about Luttmer's approach to instrumenting for income.

REFERENCES

Ambrey, C., Fleming, C. and A. Yiu-Chung Chan (2014), 'Estimating the cost of air pollution in South East Queensland: an application of the life satisfaction non-market valuation approach', *Ecological Economics*, **97**, 172–181.

Barrington-Leigh, C. and F. Behzadnejad (2017), 'Evaluating the short-term cost of low-level local air pollution: a life satisfaction approach', *Environmental Economics and Policy Studies*, **19** (2), 269–298.

Beja, E.L. (2012), 'Subjective well-being approach to environmental valuation: evidence for greenhouse gas emissions', *Social Indicators Research*, **109** (2), 243–266.

Cuñado, J. and F. Perez de Gracia (2013), 'Environment and happiness: new evidence for Spain', *Social Indicators Research*, **112** (3), 549–567.

Currie, J., Graff Zivin, J., Mullins, J. and M. Neidell (2014), 'What do we know about short- and long-term effects of early-life exposure to pollution?', *Annual Review of Resource Economics*, **6**, 217–247.

Di Tella, R. and R.J. MacCulloch (2007), 'Gross national happiness as an answer to the Easterlin paradox?', *Journal of Development Economics*, **86** (1), 22–42.

Dolan, P. and K. Laffan (2016), 'Bad air days: the effects of air quality on different measures of subjective well-being', *Journal of Benefit–Cost Analysis*, **7** (1), 147–195.

Ebenstein, A., Lavy, V. and S. Roth (2016), 'The long-run economic consequences of high-stakes examinations: evidence from transitory variation in pollution', *American Economic Journal: Applied Economics*, **8** (4), 36–65.

Ferreira, S. and M. Moro (2010), 'On the use of subjective well-being data for environmental valuation', *Environmental and Resource Economics*, **46** (3), 249–273.

Ferreira, S. and M. Moro (2013), 'Income and preferences for the environment: evidence from subjective well-being data', *Environment and Planning A*, **45** (3), 650–667.

Ferreira, S., Akay, A., Brereton, F., Cuñado, J., Martinsson, P., et al. (2013), 'Life satisfaction and air quality in Europe', *Ecological Economics*, **88**, 1–10.

Frey, B.S., Luechinger, S. and A. Stutzer (2010), 'Life satisfaction approach to environmental valuation', *Annual Review of Resource Economics*, **2**, 139–160.

García-Mainar, I., Montuenga, V.M. and M. Navarro-Paniagua (2015), 'Workplace environmental conditions and life satisfaction in Spain', *Ecological Economics*, **119**, 136–146.

Giovanis, E. and O. Ozdamar (2016), 'Structural equation modelling and the causal effect of permanent income on life satisfaction: the case of air pollution valuation in Switzerland', *Journal of Economic Surveys*, **30** (3), 430–459.

Glaeser, E.L., Gottlieb, J.D. and O. Ziv (2016), 'Unhappy cities', *Journal of Labor Economics*, **34** (S2), S129–S182.

Goetzke, F. and T. Rave (2015), 'Regional air quality and happiness in Germany', *International Regional Science Review*, **38** (4), 437–451.

Graff Zivin, J. and M. Neidell (2012), 'The impact of pollution on worker productivity', *American Economic Review*, **102** (7), 3652–3673.

Graff Zivin, J. and M. Neidell (2013), 'Environment, health, and human capital', *Journal of Economic Literature*, **51** (3), 689–730.

Graham, C. (2009), 'Why societies stay stuck in bad equilibrium: insights from happiness studies amidst prosperity and adversity', paper presented to the IZA Conference on Frontiers in Labor Economics: The Economics of Well-Being and Happiness, Washington, DC.

He, J., Liu, H. and A. Salvo (2019), 'Severe air pollution and labor productivity: evidence from industrial towns in China', *American Economic Journal: Applied Economics*, **11** (1), 173–201.

Heutel, G. and C. Ruhm (2016), 'Air pollution and procyclical mortality', *Journal of the Association of Environmental and Resource Economists*, **3** (3), 667–706.

Jidong, Y. and Z. Yiran (2015), 'Happiness and air pollution', *China Economist*, **10** (5), 62–77.

León, C.J. and J.E. Araña (2015), 'A Bayesian model averaging approach to the transfer of subjective well-being values of air quality', in Robert J. Johnston, John Rolfe, Randall S. Rosenberger and Roy Brouwer (eds), *Benefit Transfer of Environmental and Resource Values*, The Economics of Non-Market Goods and Resources series, Vol. 14, Dordrecht, Netherlands: Springer, pp. 489–505.

Levinson, A. (2012), 'Valuing public goods using happiness data: the case of air quality', *Journal of Public Economics*, **96** (9–10), 869–880.

Levinson, A. (2013), 'Happiness, behavioral economics, and public policy', NBER Working Paper No. 19329.

Liao, P.S., Shaw, D. and Y.M. Lin (2015), 'Environmental quality and life satisfaction: subjective versus objective measures of air quality', *Social Indicators Research*, **124** (2), 599–616.

Luechinger, S. (2009), 'Valuing air quality using the life satisfaction approach', *Economic Journal*, **119** (536), 482–515.

Luechinger, S. (2010), 'Life satisfaction and transboundary air pollution', *Economics Letters*, **107** (1), 4–6.

Luechinger, S. (2014), 'Air pollution and infant mortality: a natural experiment from power plant desulfurization', *Journal of Health Economics*, **37**, 219–231.

Luttmer, E.F.P. (2005), 'Neighbors as negatives: relative earnings and well-being', *Quarterly Journal of Economics*, **120** (3), 963–1002.

MacKerron, G. and S. Mourato (2009), 'Life satisfaction and air quality in London', *Ecological Economics*, **68** (5), 1441–1453.

Menz, T. (2011), 'Do people habituate to air pollution? Evidence from international life satisfaction data', *Ecological Economics*, **71**, 211–219.
Menz, T. and H. Welsch (2010), 'Population aging and environmental preferences in OECD countries: the case of air pollution', *Ecological Economics*, **69** (12), 2582–2589.
Menz, T. and H. Welsch (2012), 'Life-cycle and cohort effects in the valuation of air quality: evidence from subjective well-being data', *Land Economics*, **88** (2), 300–325.
Neidell, M. (2017), 'Air pollution and worker productivity', IZA World of Labor 2017 No. 363. Accessed April 4, 2019 at https://wol.iza.org/articles/air-pollution-and-worker-productivity/long.
OECD (2016), *The Economic Consequences of Outdoor Air Pollution*, Paris, France: OECD Publishing.
Orru, K., Orru, H., Maasikmets, M., Hendrikson, R. and M. Ainsaar (2016), 'Well-being and environmental quality: does pollution affect life satisfaction?', *Quality of Life Research*, **25** (3), 699–705.
Ozdamar, O. (2016), 'Exposure to air pollution and crime in the neighbourhood: evidence from life satisfaction data in Turkey', *International Journal of Social Economics*, **43** (12), 1233–1253.
Ozdamar, O. and E. Giovanis (2017), 'The causal effects of income support and housing benefits on mental well-being: an application of a Bayesian network', *Metroeconomica*, **68** (3), 398–424.
Pischke, J-S. and H. Schwandt (2012), 'A cautionary note on using industry affiliation to predict income', NBER Working Paper No. 18384.
Rehdanz, K. and D. Maddison (2008), 'Local environmental quality and life-satisfaction in Germany', *Ecological Economics*, **64** (4), 787–797.
Schwarz, N. and G.L. Clore (1983), 'Mood, misattribution, and judgments of well-being: informative and directive functions of affective states', *Journal of Personality and Social Psychology*, **45** (3), 513–523.
Schwarz, N. and F. Strack (1991), 'Evaluating one's life: a judgment model of subjective well-being', in Fritz Strack, Michael Argyle and Norbert Schwarz (eds), *Subjective Well-Being: An Interdisciplinary Perspective*, Oxford, UK: Pergamon Press, pp. 27–47.
Schwarz, N. and F. Strack (1999), 'Reports of subjective well-being: judgmental processes and their methodological implications', in Daniel Kahneman, Ed Diener and Norbert Schwarz (eds), *Well Being: The Foundation of Hedonic Psychology*, New York, USA: Russell Sage Foundation, pp. 61–84.
Smyth, R., Mishra, V. and X. Qian (2008), 'The environment and well-being in urban China', *Ecological Economics*, **68** (1–2), 547–555.
Tsurumi, T. and S. Managi (2017), 'Monetary valuations of life conditions in a consistent framework: the life satisfaction approach', *Journal of Happiness Studies*, **18** (5), 1275–1303.
Tsurumi, T., Mizobuchi, H. and S. Managi (2015), 'A monetary evaluation of life: life satisfaction approach', in Shunsuke Managi (ed.), *The Economics of Green Growth: New Indicators for Sustainable Societies*, Abingdon, UK and New York, USA: Routledge, pp. 157–195.
Welsch, H. (2002), 'Preferences over prosperity and pollution: environmental valuation based on happiness surveys', *Kyklos*, **55** (4), 473–494.
Welsch, H. (2006), 'Environment and happiness: valuation of air pollution using life satisfaction data', *Ecological Economics*, **58** (4), 801–813.
Welsch, H. (2007), 'Environmental welfare analysis: a life satisfaction approach', *Ecological Economics*, **62** (3–4), 544–551.
Xu, J. and J. Li (2016), 'Tax payment, social contribution for pollution prevention and happiness', *Problemy Ekorozwoju – Problems of Sustainable Development*, **11** (1), 59–64.
Zhang, X., Zhang, X. and X. Chen (2017a), 'Happiness in the air: how does a dirty sky affect mental health and subjective well-being?', *Journal of Environmental Economics and Management*, **85**, 81–94.
Zhang, X., Zhang, X. and X. Chen (2017b), 'Valuing air quality using happiness data: the case of China', *Ecological Economics*, **137**, 29–36.

10. The effects of exposure to air pollution on subjective wellbeing in China

Xin Zhang, Xi Chen and Xiaobo Zhang

10.1 INTRODUCTION

There has been a burgeoning body of studies examining the impact of exposure to air pollution on a wide range of health measures in China, especially diseases and mortality (e.g., Alberini and Krupnick, 1998; Chen et al., 2013; Tanaka, 2015; He et al., 2016). Health includes not only physical health and the absence of diseases, but also mental health.[1] Subjective wellbeing (SWB) plays an important role in maintaining physical health (National Research Council and Institute of Medicine, 2009). SWB has been listed as an important component in policy making in more and more countries (Levinson, 2013). However, the link between air pollution and SWB, such as happiness and mental health, has not been well studied in China compared to the link with physical health, until recently.

In responding to severe air pollution in some developing countries, a few studies have directly tested the link between air pollution and key psychological outcomes, including mental health and happiness. For instance, Li et al. (2014) show that both intensity of exposure to polluted air and hazard of pollutants affect people's happiness in mining areas in China. Using a nationally representative sample, Zhang et al. (2017a) find salient negative effect of fine particulates on hedonic happiness.

However, these studies focus only on hedonic happiness, but ignore evaluative measures of happiness. Both measures have been used in the SWB literature (Kahneman and Deaton, 2010; Deaton and Stone, 2013). Hedonic happiness refers to moment-to-moment experienced utility and directly links to immediate emotions and affection. Evaluative happiness, such as life satisfaction, reflecting an overall assessment of the entire life, is less likely subject to short-term changes in the external environment, such as daily air pollution. The time window of measuring mental health sits between evaluative and hedonic happiness. Therefore, the effect of air pollution on mental health tends to be smaller than the effect on hedonic happiness but larger than that on life satisfaction. Zhang et al. (2017b) for the first time compare the effect of air pollution on various SWB measures by using Chinese longitudinal data to remove individual heterogeneity in the reporting of SWB. Following Zhang et al. (2017b), this chapter simultaneously estimates the effects of specific air pollutants on three key measures of SWB.

However, due to the lack of air pollutant data, Zhang et al. (2017b) use only an air pollution index (API), a comprehensive index for air pollution. The API has a shortcoming in that it does not reveal specific air pollutant concentrations,[2] although different pollutants may affect SWB through different channels. Investigating differential effects of air pollutants on SWB may help us to understand which channels work and which do not. This improved knowledge could in turn guide evidence-based policy making to mitigate specific sources of pollutants.

Studies have shown that finer particulate matter, such as that with a diameter smaller than 2.5 micrometers (PM2.5), tends to be more detrimental to health than larger particulates, such as PM10 (Cao et al., 2014; Pal et al., 2016). PM10 is usually trapped in the upper airways and can be cleared by mucociliary mechanisms. However, due to its miniature size, PM2.5 can penetrate lungs at the alveolar level, translocate directly through the alveolar capillaries into the circulatory system, and leave toxic substances in the blood, causing cumulative damage to the body (Stanek et al., 2011). Ozone (O_3) can react with body molecules to create toxins, causing asthma and respiratory problems (Sanders, 2012). High levels of O_3 and sulfur dioxide (SO_2) are found to cause psychiatric distress (Rotton and Frey, 1984). Carbon monoxide (CO) prevents the body from releasing adequate oxygen to vital organs, in particular to the brain, which consume a large fraction of total oxygen intake. High concentrations of CO and nitrogen dioxide (NO_2) are significantly associated with headache, eye irritation and respiratory problems (Nattero and Enrico, 1996). In this chapter, we examine the impact of these six main pollutants: PM2.5, PM10, NO_2, SO_2, CO and ozone.

We merge a nationally representative survey – the China Family Panel Studies (CFPS) – with newly released daily air quality data that contain rich information on six main pollutants and weather conditions at the time and county of each interview. A key assumption for our identification strategy is that day-to-day fluctuations of air quality in a given county have little to do with the characteristics of individual respondents. More generally, under the assumption that locational sorting in response to air pollution occurs more slowly than changes in SWB caused by transitory air pollution, pollution is literally random to survey subjects.[3]

We find that PM2.5 significantly reduces hedonic happiness and raises the rate of depressive symptoms, while PM10 only marginally lowers hedonic happiness. Both PM2.5 and PM10 have little effect on life satisfaction. Other pollutants impose negligible effects on SWB measures. Given that air pollution is ubiquitous in many developing countries such as Bangladesh, India and Nepal, our study on China can shed some light on other developing countries as well.[4]

The rest of the chapter is organized as follows. Section 10.2 describes the data. Section 10.3 lays out the empirical strategy. Section 10.4 presents our main findings, including robustness checks and heterogeneous tests. Finally, section 10.5 concludes.

10.2 DATA

10.2.1 Subjective Wellbeing Measures

Our SWB measures come from the China Family Panel Studies (CFPS), a nationally representative survey of Chinese communities, families and individuals. The CFPS is carried out by the Institute of Social Science Survey of Peking University. There are three advantages of the CFPS for our purposes. First, rich measures ranging from long-term life satisfaction to moment-to-moment hedonic happiness allow us to compare the effects of air pollution in various time frames. Second, information about geographic locations and dates of interviews for all respondents enables us to precisely match individual SWB measures in the survey with external air quality data. Third, the survey collected rich information at multiple levels, allowing us to control for a wide range of covariates.

We make use of three types of SWB measures in the third wave of the CFPS survey, conducted in 2014. The first is life satisfaction. The CFPS asked each respondent to answer the question, "Overall, how satisfied are you with your life?" on a scale from 1 (not satisfied at all) to 5 (very satisfied). With no specified time frame, life satisfaction, an evaluative measure of SWB, reflects the extent to which people's own experiences match their long-term aspirations and expectations about their lives as a whole (Stone and Mackie, 2014). Life circumstances, such as income, education and social status, are among the main determinants of life satisfaction.

The second SWB measure comes from the six-item Kessler Psychological Distress Scale (K6) developed by Kessler et al. (2003), a self-reported scale designed to measure the current level of depressive symptomatology in the general population (see Appendix 10A.2). Each item in the K6 scores from 0 (never) to 4 (almost every day), with a total score ranging from 0 to 24. We create a binary indicator to define depressive symptoms as those with total K6 scores no less than 4. Compared to life satisfaction, the K6 highlights multidimensional emotional experiences that affect people in a shorter period.

The third SWB measure gauges short-term hedonic happiness. The first item in the K6 asks respondents to what extent they felt hard to cheer up in the past month, ranging from 0 (almost every day) to 4 (never). The higher the number, the happier the respondents are. Compared to evaluative wellbeing, depression symptoms and hedonic happiness belong to hedonic wellbeing and are more directly related to the environment as well as to people's affective state in day-to-day and moment-to-moment life (Stone and Mackie, 2014).[5]

10.2.2 Interpolation of Air Pollution and Weather Measures

We obtain air pollution measures from the daily air quality report published by the Ministry of Ecology and Environment of China (MEE). The report started to publish daily concentrations of six pollutants – PM2.5, PM10, carbon monoxide (CO), nitrogen dioxide (NO_2), ozone (O_3) and sulfur dioxide (SO_2) – in 2014. The dataset we use in our analysis covers 947 monitoring stations along with longitude and altitude information for each station. Figure 10A.1 and Figure 10A.2 in Appendix 10A.1 indicate that particulate matters (PM2.5 and PM10) are highly concentrated and are dominant sources of air pollution on most days in China.

We also include rich weather data in our analysis to help isolate the impact of air pollution from other weather patterns. The weather data come from the National Climatic Data Center under the United States (US) National Oceanic and Atmospheric Administration. The dataset contains daily records of temperature, precipitation, wind speed and an indicator for bad weather[6] from 402 monitoring stations in China. Sunshine duration is obtained from the 194 monitoring stations of the China National Meteorological Information Center. Sunshine may affect individuals' moods, social behavior and health (Cunningham, 1979; Wolfson, 2013).

To merge the CFPS sample with the air pollution readings, we calculate the weighted average values of all the monitoring stations within 60 km of the centroids of each CFPS county, where the weights are equal to the inverse of distance between stations and the county centroids. In the absence of stations within this radius, we obtain air quality from the nearest station within 100 kilometers. Weather controls are matched in the same way.[7] The binary indicators for bad weather and the sunshine duration are obtained from the nearest monitoring station regardless of the distance.

The 2014 wave of CFPS has 31 832 individuals, of which 22 896 could be matched to air quality and weather data within 100 kilometers.[8] Due to 21 missing values for life satisfaction, 51 missing values for hedonic happiness, 105 missing values for depressive symptoms, and 1256 missing values for household demographics, the final dataset for analyses includes 21 619 observations for life satisfaction, 21 589 observations for hedonic happiness, and 21 535 observations for depressive symptoms.[9]

10.3 EMPIRICAL STRATEGY

Our baseline econometric specification is as follows:

$$H_{ijt} = \alpha P_{jt} + \beta \ln Y_{ijt} + X'_{ijt} r + W'_{jt} \phi + \delta_j + \eta_t + \varepsilon_{ijt} \quad (10.1)$$

The dependent variable H_{ijt} is the SWB measure of respondent i in county j at date t. The key variable P_{jt} is the concentrations of air pollutants in county j at date t, the day of the interview. $\ln Y_{ijt}$ is the log form of household per capita income. We control for a set of demographic covariates X_{ijt}, including age and its squared term, gender, marital status, years of education, unemployment status, party membership and health status. W_{jt} indicates a vector of rich weather conditions on the day of the interview, to mitigate the concern that they are correlated with both SWB and air quality and therefore might bias our estimations. δ_j represents county fixed effect; η_t indicates month and day-of-week fixed effects. ε_{ijt} is the error term. Standard errors are clustered at the county level. Table 10.1 describes key variables and their summary statistics.

Figure 10A.3 in Appendix 10A.1 shows the distribution of interview months in our final sample, ranging between July and December 2014. Most surveys were conducted in July and August, during which college students on their summer break were recruited as numerators for the surveys. Our identification makes use of variations in exposure to air pollution across similar respondents living in the same county in the same year. There is substantial within-county variation in air quality during the more than four months survey in most counties.[10]

10.4 RESULTS

10.4.1 Baseline Results

We report the baseline results of air pollution on various SWB measures in Table 10.2 through Table 10.4. In each table, columns (1) through (6) estimate equation (10.1) respectively using PM2.5, PM10, CO, NO_2, O_3 and SO_2 as the air pollution measures.

Table 10.2 presents the baseline results on life satisfaction. Column (1) begins with PM2.5. We do not find any significant relationship between PM2.5 and life satisfaction. Household per capita income is positively correlated with life satisfaction. Consistent with

Table 10.1 Summary statistics of key variables

Variable	Definition	Mean	Std Dev.
Life satisfaction	life satisfaction, ranging from 1 to 5, the higher the better	3.572	1.156
Hedonic happiness	ranging from 0 to 4, higher numbers represent greater happiness	3.233	0.938
Depressive symptoms	indicator for depressive symptoms (= 1 if K6 total scores ≤ 4)	0.328	0.470
PM2.5	particulate matter with a diameter smaller than 2.5 micrometers (μg/m^3)	47.858	33.260
PM10	particulate matter with a diameter smaller than 10 micrometers (μg/m^3)	81.046	46.721
CO	carbon monoxide (μg/m^3)	1.004×10^3	0.615×10^3
NO_2	nitrogen dioxide (μg/m^3)	28.940	14.878
O_3	ozone (μg/m^3)	119.899	59.102
SO_2	sulfur dioxide (μg/m^3)	22.062	20.619
Household per capita income (log)	household per capita income (Chinese *yuan*)	9.031	1.214
Male	indicator for being male	0.486	0.500
Age (÷10)	age (÷10)	4.660	1.678
Married	indicator for being married	0.797	0.402
Education years	education years	7.480	4.983
Unemployed	indicator for being unemployed	0.012	0.109
Party	indicator for being a Communist Party member	0.077	0.267
Chronic disease	indicator for suffering from chronic diseases	0.170	0.376

Source: China Family Panel Studies 2014.

Table 10.2 Effects of air pollution on life satisfaction

Dependent variable	Pollutant					
Life satisfaction	PM2.5 (μg/m^3)	PM10 (μg/m^3)	CO (μg/m^3)	NO_2 (μg/m^3)	O_3 (μg/m^3)	SO_2 (μg/m^3)
	(1)	(2)	(3)	(4)	(5)	(6)
Pollutant (÷1000)	−0.105	−0.047	8.723×10^{-3}	1.250	0.120	0.421
	(0.409)	(0.313)	(0.016)	(0.768)	(0.178)	(0.784)
Household per capita income (log)	0.037***	0.037***	0.037***	0.037***	0.037***	0.037***
	(0.008)	(0.008)	(0.008)	(0.008)	(0.008)	(0.008)
Male	−0.013	−0.013	−0.013	−0.013	−0.013	−0.013
	(0.013)	(0.013)	(0.013)	(0.013)	(0.013)	(0.013)
Age (÷10)	−0.290***	−0.289***	−0.289***	−0.290***	−0.289***	−0.290***
	(0.033)	(0.033)	(0.033)	(0.033)	(0.033)	(0.033)
Age (÷10) squared	0.032***	0.032***	0.032***	0.032***	0.032***	0.032***
	(0.003)	(0.003)	(0.003)	(0.003)	(0.003)	(0.003)
Married	0.183***	0.183***	0.183***	0.183***	0.183***	0.183***
	(0.023)	(0.023)	(0.023)	(0.023)	(0.023)	(0.023)
Years of Education	0.004	0.004	0.004	0.004	0.004	0.004
	(0.003)	(0.003)	(0.003)	(0.003)	(0.003)	(0.003)
Unemployed	−0.348***	−0.348***	−0.347***	−0.347***	−0.348***	−0.348***
	(0.073)	(0.073)	(0.073)	(0.073)	(0.073)	(0.073)
Party	0.126***	0.126***	0.126***	0.126***	0.126***	0.126***
	(0.025)	(0.025)	(0.025)	(0.025)	(0.025)	(0.025)
Chronic disease	−0.135***	−0.135***	−0.135***	−0.135***	−0.135***	−0.135***
	(0.024)	(0.024)	(0.024)	(0.024)	(0.024)	(0.024)
County fixed effects	Yes	Yes	Yes	Yes	Yes	Yes
Month, day-of-week fixed effects	Yes	Yes	Yes	Yes	Yes	Yes
Weather controls	Yes	Yes	Yes	Yes	Yes	Yes
Observations	21 619	21 619	21 619	21 619	21 619	21 619
Adjusted R-squared	0.185	0.185	0.185	0.185	0.185	0.185

Note: The weather controls include sunshine duration, mean temperature and its square, total precipitation, mean wind speed, and a dummy for bad weather. Robust standard errors, clustered at the county level, are presented in parentheses. *10% significance level. **5% significance level. ***1% significance level.

Source: China Family Panel Studies 2014.

the happiness literature, there is a U-shaped relationship between age and life satisfaction with the lowest level being around age 45. Unemployed people who are in poor health or divorced report lower life satisfaction. Party membership is associated with a higher degree of life satisfaction. Similar to the results on PM2.5, there are not strong correlations between other air pollutants and life satisfaction.

Table 10.3 reports the estimates for hedonic happiness. Column (1) shows that hedonic happiness decreases with PM2.5 on the day of interview. The effects are significant at the 5 percent level. A 1 μg/m^3 increase in PM2.5 leads to a decline in happiness by 0.565‰. Household income is positively associated with hedonic happiness. A 1 percent increase in household per capita income raises happiness by 0.15‰. Therefore, in order to keep their happiness constant, people are on average willing to pay 3.8 percent of their annual income for a 1 μg/m^3 reduction in PM2.5 on the day of the interview. To put this into context, note that one standard deviation (SD) of PM2.5 is 33.260 μg/m^3. A one SD increase in PM2.5 results in a decline in happiness by 1.879 percent (= 33.260 × 0.565‰). Married, more-educated and healthier men tend to be happier.

Column (2) of Table 10.3 identifies the impact of PM10 on hedonic happiness. A one SD increase in PM10 is statistically significantly associated with a decline in happiness by 1.635 percent (= 46.721 × 0.350‰), a little smaller than PM2.5. The different estimates between PM2.5 and PM10 suggest that people are more sensitive to finer particulates (PM2.5) than coarse particulates (PM10). Considering that the related literature in China has largely focused on coarse particulates, this finding highlights the importance of giving more attention to finer particulates.

Column (3) presents results for CO. The coefficient on CO is statistically insignificant and much smaller than PM2.5 in magnitude. The difference may stem from the fact that CO is only a dominant source of air pollution for 2 percent of days (Figure 10A.2). Besides, CO is odorless, colorless and thus less noticeable.

Column (5) estimates the effects of NO_2 on hedonic happiness. The marginal effect of NO_2 is about half of the size of PM2.5, with no significance. The National Ambient Air Quality Standards (NAAQS) of the US Environmental Protection Agency (EPA) stipulates that the cut-off value for NO_2 is 53 ppb (100 μg/m^3). The mean and SD in our sample are both within this safety range, thus NO_2 is a minor pollutant in China.

Similarly, the coefficient on ozone presented in column (5) is statistically insignificant and the size is basically the same as NO_2. Ozone is a dominant pollutant in more than 10 percent of days a year (Figure 10A.2), but its concentration in our sample may only trigger discomfort among vulnerable people, such as those with lung diseases.[11]

The last column reports results for SO_2. Several papers examine the effects of annual average SO_2 on life satisfaction (Luechinger, 2009, 2010; Ferreira et al., 2013). In our case, the coefficient on SO_2 is still statistically insignificant.

Table 10.4 reports the effects of air pollution on depressive symptoms. Column (1) shows that depressive symptoms are positively correlated with PM2.5. A one SD increase in PM2.5 corresponds to an increase in the probability of having depressive symptoms by 7.450 (= 33.260 × 0.224) percentage points. However, as presented in column (2), PM10 does not appear to be related to depressive symptoms. By comparison, PM2.5 is a much stronger risk factor for depressive symptoms than PM10. Consistent with hedonic happiness, we do not find any significant effects of other air pollutants, including CO, NO_2, ozone and SO_2, on depressive symptoms.

Table 10.3 Effects of air pollution on hedonic happiness

Dependent variable	Pollutant					
Hedonic happiness	PM2.5 (μg/m³)	PM10 (μg/m³)	CO (μg/m³)	NO_2 (μg/m³)	O_3 (μg/m³)	SO_2 (μg/m³)
	(1)	(2)	(3)	(4)	(5)	(6)
Pollutant (÷1000)	−0.565**	−0.350*	-2.836×10^{-3}	−0.256	−0.252	−0.696
	(0.242)	(0.211)	(0.014)	(0.991)	(0.155)	(0.617)
Household per capita income (log)	0.015**	0.015**	0.015**	0.015**	0.014**	0.015**
	(0.006)	(0.006)	(0.006)	(0.006)	(0.006)	(0.006)
Male	0.097***	0.097***	0.097***	0.097***	0.097***	0.097***
	(0.014)	(0.014)	(0.014)	(0.014)	(0.014)	(0.014)
Age (÷10)	−0.011	−0.011	−0.011	−0.011	−0.012	−0.011
	(0.023)	(0.023)	(0.023)	(0.023)	(0.023)	(0.023)
Age (÷10) squared	0.005**	0.005**	0.005**	0.005**	0.005**	0.005**
	(0.002)	(0.002)	(0.002)	(0.002)	(0.002)	(0.002)
Married	0.059***	0.059***	0.059***	0.059***	0.059***	0.059***
	(0.019)	(0.019)	(0.019)	(0.019)	(0.019)	(0.019)
Years of Education	0.006***	0.006***	0.006***	0.006***	0.006***	0.006***
	(0.002)	(0.002)	(0.002)	(0.002)	(0.002)	(0.002)
Unemployed	−0.187***	−0.186***	−0.186***	−0.186***	−0.185***	−0.186***
	(0.062)	(0.062)	(0.063)	(0.063)	(0.063)	(0.062)
Party	0.033	0.033	0.033	0.033	0.033	0.033
	(0.024)	(0.024)	(0.024)	(0.024)	(0.024)	(0.024)
Chronic disease	−0.371***	−0.371***	−0.371***	−0.371***	−0.371***	−0.371***
	(0.022)	(0.022)	(0.022)	(0.022)	(0.022)	(0.022)
County fixed effects	Yes	Yes	Yes	Yes	Yes	Yes
Month, day-of-week fixed effects	Yes	Yes	Yes	Yes	Yes	Yes
Weather controls	Yes	Yes	Yes	Yes	Yes	Yes
Observations	21 589	21 589	21 589	21 589	21 589	21 589
Adjusted R-squared	0.076	0.076	0.076	0.076	0.076	0.076

Note: The weather controls include sunshine duration, mean temperature and its square, total precipitation, mean wind speed, and a dummy for bad weather. Robust standard errors, clustered at the county level, are presented in parentheses. *10% significance level. **5% significance level. ***1% significance level.

Source: China Family Panel Studies 2014.

Table 10.4 Effects of air pollution on depressive symptoms

Dependent variable	Pollutant					
Depressive symptoms	PM2.5 ($\mu g/m^3$)	PM10 ($\mu g/m^3$)	CO ($\mu g/m^3$)	NO_2 ($\mu g/m^3$)	O_3 ($\mu g/m^3$)	SO_2 ($\mu g/m^3$)
	(1)	(2)	(3)	(4)	(5)	(6)
Pollutant (÷1000)	0.242**	0.146	-0.288×10^{-3}	0.286	0.104	0.262
	(0.121)	(0.103)	(0.007)	(0.397)	(0.087)	(0.286)
Household per capita income (log)	−0.013***	−0.013***	−0.013***	−0.013***	−0.013***	−0.013***
	(0.003)	(0.003)	(0.003)	(0.003)	(0.003)	(0.003)
Male	−0.061***	−0.061***	−0.061***	−0.061***	−0.061***	−0.061***
	(0.006)	(0.006)	(0.006)	(0.006)	(0.006)	(0.006)
Age (÷10)	0.001	0.001	0.001	0.001	0.002	0.001
	(0.012)	(0.012)	(0.012)	(0.012)	(0.012)	(0.012)
Age (÷10) squared	−0.001	−0.001	−0.001	−0.001	−0.001	−0.001
	(0.001)	(0.001)	(0.001)	(0.001)	(0.001)	(0.001)
Married	−0.061***	−0.061***	−0.061***	−0.061***	−0.061***	−0.061***
	(0.009)	(0.009)	(0.009)	(0.009)	(0.009)	(0.009)
Years of Education	−0.006***	−0.006***	−0.006***	−0.006***	−0.006***	−0.006***
	(0.001)	(0.001)	(0.001)	(0.001)	(0.001)	(0.001)
Unemployed	0.090***	0.089***	0.089***	0.089***	0.089***	0.089***
	(0.032)	(0.032)	(0.032)	(0.032)	(0.032)	(0.032)
Party	−0.022*	−0.022*	−0.022*	−0.022*	−0.022*	−0.022*
	(0.012)	(0.012)	(0.012)	(0.012)	(0.012)	(0.012)
Chronic disease	0.171***	0.171***	0.171***	0.171***	0.171***	0.171***
	(0.011)	(0.011)	(0.011)	(0.011)	(0.011)	(0.011)
County fixed effects	Yes	Yes	Yes	Yes	Yes	Yes
Month, day-of-week fixed effects	Yes	Yes	Yes	Yes	Yes	Yes
Weather controls	Yes	Yes	Yes	Yes	Yes	Yes
Observations	21 535	21 535	21 535	21 535	21 535	21 535
Adjusted R-squared	0.089	0.089	0.089	0.089	0.089	0.089

Note: The weather controls include sunshine duration, mean temperature and its square, total precipitation, mean wind speed, and a dummy for bad weather. Robust standard errors, clustered at the county level, are presented in parentheses. *10% significance level. **5% significance level. ***1% significance level.

Source: China Family Panel Studies 2014.

10.4.2 Robustness Checks

In Table 10.5, we perform a set of alternative specifications to check the robustness of our main results. We focus on PM2.5 because it is associated with more detrimental health effects as shown in the baseline. Panels A, B and C present results for life satisfaction, hedonic happiness and depressive symptoms, respectively.

Column (1) replicates the baseline results in columns (1) of Table 10.2 through Table 10.4 for ease comparison. Column (2) adds a control variable, the PM2.5 level on the day prior to the interview date, to account for the lagged effect of pollution. After its inclusion, the negative effect of contemporaneous PM2.5 on hedonic happiness and mental wellbeing amplifies. However, the effect on life satisfaction remains insignificant.

Since the K6 scale asks for people's feelings in the past month, we use average local PM2.5 in the past 30 days instead of contemporaneous PM2.5 level to examine the long-term effects of air pollution on SWB. As reported in column (3), there is no significant relationship between longer-term air pollution and SWB, suggesting that people care more about their current exposure. There is another possibility, that daily PM2.5 on the date of the interview reflects average pollution in a county over a longer period, such as one month. To mitigate this concern, column (4) adds monthly mean PM2.5. The coefficient for monthly PM2.5 level is insignificant, while daily PM2.5 remains significant and essentially the same magnitude, confirming that day-to-day fluctuations in air quality drive our results.

Column (5) estimates equation (10.1) using an ordered probit model.[12] In panel A, the coefficient on PM2.5 remains insignificant for life satisfaction. As shown in panel B and panel C, PM2.5 is negatively correlated with hedonic happiness and depressive symptoms with statistical significance level at 5 percent or higher. Overall, our baseline results are robust to several alternative specifications.

10.4.3 Heterogeneous Effects

This subsection examines the heterogeneous effects of air pollution on hedonic wellbeing. First, we check whether the effect varies by age or not. Columns (1) through (5) in panel A and panel B of Table 10.6 present the impact of air pollution by gender and age cohort, respectively. Results suggest that men respond more strongly to air pollution than women. Interestingly, age differences vary with the choice of outcome variables. Specifically, young people are more sensitive to air pollution in hedonic happiness, while mental health among the elderly is more saliently affected.

Second, we examine the heterogeneity by education level. It has been shown in some literature that more education may enable one to acquire and digest information about air quality and become more concerned (Levinson, 2012; Greenstone and Hanna, 2014; Li et al., 2014). As revealed in columns (1) through (2) of Panel C and Panel D, people who finished at least six years of education are indeed more affected in terms of hedonic happiness than those who are less educated.

Third, we check whether the effect differs by pollution level. People living in more-polluted areas could be more (or less) sensitive to pollution than those in less-polluted areas. The net effect may rely on which force dominates, dose–response relationship or habituation. Columns (3) and (4) of panels C and D report the regression results for two

Table 10.5 Robustness checks

	Baseline	Add lagged PM2.5	Average PM2.5 in the past month		Ordered probit
	(1)	(2)	(3)	(4)	(5)
A. Life satisfaction					
PM2.5 (÷1000)	−0.105	−0.314		−0.179	−0.125
	(0.409)	(0.415)		(0.383)	(0.415)
lagged PM2.5 (÷1000)		0.406			
		(0.376)			
Average PM2.5 in the past month (÷1000)			0.777	0.943	
			(1.514)	(1.456)	
Observations	21 619	21 619	21 619	21 619	21 619
Adjusted R-squared	0.185	0.185	0.185	0.185	0.068#
B. Hedonic happiness					
PM2.5 (÷1000)	−0.565**	−0.695***		−0.550**	−0.887***
	(0.242)	(0.251)		(0.230)	(0.317)
lagged PM2.5 (÷1000)		0.254			
		(0.313)			
Average PM2.5 in the past month (÷1000)			−0.691	−0.182	
			(1.104)	(1.084)	
Observations	21 589	21 589	21 589	21 589	21 589
Adjusted R-squared	0.076	0.076	0.076	0.076	0.044#
C. Depressive symptoms					
PM2.5 (÷1000)	0.242**	0.298**		0.237**	0.729**
	(0.121)	(0.124)		(0.113)	(0.357)
lagged PM2.5 (÷1000)		−0.109			
		(0.139)			
Average PM2.5 in the past month (÷1000)			0.281	0.062	
			(0.613)	(0.610)	
Observations	21 535	21 535	21 535	21 535	21 535
Adjusted R-squared	0.089	0.089	0.089	0.089	0.080#

Note: Other covariates and fixed effects are the same as those in Column (1) of Table 10.2. Robust standard errors, clustered at the county level, are presented in parentheses. *10% significance level. **5% significance level. ***1% significance level. # indicates the Pseudo R2.

Source: China Family Panel Studies 2014.

Table 10.6 Heterogeneous effects of PM2.5

	Age			Gender	
	Young	Middle	Old	Male	Female
	(1)	(2)	(3)	(4)	(5)
A. Hedonic happiness					
PM2.5 (÷1000)	−0.914**	−0.621	−0.404	−0.824***	−0.295
	(0.400)	(0.408)	(0.373)	(0.307)	(0.321)
Observations	6247	8274	7068	10496	11093
Adjusted R-squared	0.062	0.083	0.093	0.068	0.078
B. Depressive symptoms					
PM2.5 (mg/m^3)	0.083	0.178	0.371*	0.360**	0.122
	(0.232)	(0.199)	(0.192)	(0.160)	(0.152)
Observations	6246	8264	7025	10476	11059
Adjusted R-squared	0.057	0.102	0.131	0.078	0.087

	Education		Pollution level		Children younger than six	
	≤ 6 years	> 6 years	Low	High	Yes	No
	(1)	(2)	(3)	(4)	(5)	(6)
C. Hedonic happiness						
PM2.5 (÷1000)	−0.293	−0.712**	−0.616	−0.604**	−1.182*	−0.553**
	(0.366)	(0.301)	(0.482)	(0.276)	(0.674)	(0.244)
Observations	9577	12012	10791	10798	2548	18519
Adjusted R-squared	0.091	0.068	0.071	0.081	0.069	0.080
D. Depressive symptoms						
PM2.5 (÷1000)	0.248	0.208	0.329	0.255*	0.606*	0.182
	(0.195)	(0.152)	(0.256)	(0.133)	(0.352)	(0.119)
Observations	9536	11999	10751	10784	2548	18466
Adjusted R-squared	0.122	0.062	0.099	0.075	0.061	0.097

Note: Other covariates and fixed effects are the same as those in Column (1) of Table 10.2. Robust standard errors, clustered at the county level, are presented in parentheses. *10% significance level. **5% significance level. ***1% significance level.

Source: China Family Panel Studies 2014.

subsamples according to the median level of yearly mean PM2.5. Apparently, the effects of air pollution are more salient in highly polluted areas, indicating that the dose–response relationship may dominate.

Finally, families with small children may be more concerned about bad air quality. We divide the sample according to whether or not a family has a child younger than age six. As revealed in columns (5) and (6) of Panels C and D, families with young children are marginally more vulnerable to air pollution in terms of both hedonic happiness and depressive symptoms.

10.5 CONCLUSION

This chapter estimates the impact of six air pollutants on long-term life satisfaction, short-term hedonic happiness and depressive symptoms by matching various self-reported SWB measures in the CFPS, a nationally representative survey, with daily air quality data according to the exact date and county of each interview. PM2.5 and PM10 are found to be negatively associated with hedonic happiness. For depressive symptoms, only PM2.5 matters. Other pollutants are not correlated with any of the three SWB measures. We also find some heterogenous effects. People who receive more education, reside in more-polluted areas or have young children are more sensitive to air pollution in terms of hedonic happiness.

Our results have important policy implications. China has been making real progress in striving for cleaner air according to its national plan 2016–20.[13] The optimal environmental regulations depend on the cost–benefit trade-offs. Our findings indicate that the currently estimated costs of pollution may understate some important social costs. By counting them in, the benefits of reducing pollution would be higher. Many other developing countries also face serious air pollution problems; the lessons learned from China can shed light on these countries as well.

NOTES

1. http://www.who.int/about/mission/.
2. API is generated by a piecewise linear transformation from the concentrations of air pollutants, including sulfur dioxide (SO_2), nitrogen dioxide (NO_2) and fine particulate matter smaller than 10 micrometers (PM10).
3. Several studies have made such assumption in their analyses; for example, Levinson (2012) and Currie et al. (2014) provide an excellent review of this approach.
4. According to the 2016 Environmental Performance Index published by Yale University, the world's top five most air polluted countries are Bangladesh, China, India, Nepal and Laos.
5. Hedonic wellbeing is closely related to the often-used terms "experienced well being" and "emotional wellbeing." They are often used interchangeably in the literature.
6. Bad weather includes fog, rain/drizzle, snow/ice pellets, hail, thunder and tornadoes/funnel clouds.
7. We use the same interpolation approach as Zhang et al. (2017a). The median matching distance is 33 km. PM2.5 particles are light and can stay in the atmosphere for 3–4 days. They can be transported by wind for more than 100 km (Barwick et al., 2017). Our baseline results are robust to matching using narrower radiuses, but the current set of results is reported to retain more observations in the analysis. Meanwhile, these baseline results are robust to alternative weights, including inverse of the square root distance or squared distance between the monitoring stations and the county centroids.
8. Counties unmatched to any air quality or weather monitoring station within 100 kilometers are dropped. The matching rate, 71.9 percent (= 22 896/31 832), is within a reasonable range. For example, a highly

comparable study Levinson (2012) retained 52.3 percent of the observations when matching the US General Social Survey with PM10 readings from the EPA's Air Quality System.
9. We use different sets of individuals for the three SWB measures to retain more observations in the analysis. Our results are robust to restricting the sample to the same set of individuals across regressions.
10. Although most interviews were conducted in the summer, the interview period often lasted for more than four months in each county, sometimes extended to November and December, when air quality is generally worse.
11. Source: https://www3.epa.gov/airnow/aqi-technical-assistance-document-dec2013.pdf.
12. For depressive symptoms, we simply run a probit model.
13. The national plan stipulates that air quality of cities at and above the prefectural level must be good or excellent for 80 percent of days each year. Please refer to http://language.chinadaily.com.cn/2016-03/18/content_23944369_2.htm.

REFERENCES

Alberini, A. and A. Krupnick (1998), 'Air quality and episodes of acute respiratory illness in Taiwan cities: evidence from survey data', *Journal of Urban Economics*, **44** (1), 68–92.

Barwick, P.J., Li, S., Rao, D. and N.B. Zahur (2017), 'Air pollution, health spending and willingness to pay for clean air in China', working paper.

Cao, C., Jiang, W., Wang, B., Fang, J., Lang, J., et al. (2014), 'Inhalable microorganisms in Beijing's PM2.5 and PM10 pollutants during a severe smog event', *Environmental Science and Technology*, **48** (3), 1499–1507.

Chen, Y., Ebenstein, A., Greenstone, M. and H. Li (2013), 'Evidence on the impact of sustained exposure to air pollution on life expectancy from China's Huai River policy', *PNAS*, **110** (32), 12936–12941.

Cunningham, M.R. (1979), 'Weather, mood, and helping behavior: quasi-experiments with the sunshine Samaritan', *Journal of Personality and Social Psychology*, **37** (11), 1947–1956.

Currie, J., Graff Zivin, J., Mullins, J. and M. Neidell (2014), 'What do we know about short- and long-term effects of early-life exposure to pollution?', *Annual Review of Resource Economics*, **6** (1), 217–247.

Deaton, A. and A.A. Stone (2013), 'Two happiness puzzles', *American Economic Review*, **103** (3), 591–597.

Ferreira, S., Akay, A., Brereton, F., Cuñado, J., Martinsson, P., et al. (2013), 'Life satisfaction and air quality in Europe', *Ecological Economics*, **88**, 1–10.

Greenstone, M. and R. Hanna (2014), 'Environmental regulations, air and water pollution, and infant mortality in India', *American Economic Review*, **104** (10), 3038–3072.

He, G., Fan, M. and M. Zhou (2016), 'The effect of air pollution on mortality in China: evidence from the 2008 Beijing Olympic Games', *Journal of Environmental Economics and Management*, **79**, 18–39.

Kahneman, D. and A. Deaton (2010), 'High income improves evaluation of life but not emotional well-being', *PNAS*, **107** (38), 16489–16493.

Kessler, R.C., Barker, P.R., Colpe, L.J., Epstein, J.F., Gfroerer, J.C., et al. (2003), 'Screening for serious mental illness in the general population', *Archives of General Psychiatry*, **60** (2), 184–189.

Levinson, A. (2012), 'Valuing public goods using happiness data: the case of air quality', *Journal of Public Economics*, **96** (9–10), 869–880.

Levinson, A. (2013), 'Happiness, behavioral economics, and public policy', NBER Working Papers No. 19329.

Li, Z., Folmer, H. and J. Xue (2014), 'To what extent does air pollution affect happiness? The case of the Jinchuan mining area, China', *Ecological Economics*, **99**, 88–99.

Luechinger, S. (2009), 'Valuing air quality using the life satisfaction approach', *Economic Journal*, **119** (536), 482–515.

Luechinger, S. (2010), 'Life satisfaction and transboundary air pollution', *Economics Letters*, **107** (1), 4–6.

National Research Council and Institute of Medicine (2009), *Preventing Mental, Emotional, and Behavioral Disorders Among Young People: Progress and Possibilities*, Washington, DC, USA: National Academies Press.

Nattero, G. and A. Enrico (1996), 'Outdoor pollution and headache', *Headache*, **36** (4), 243–245.

Pal, C., Bengtsson-Palme, J., Kristiansson, E. and D.G. Joakim Larsson (2016), 'The structure and diversity of human, animal and environmental resistomes', *Microbiome*, **4** (1), 4–54.

Rotton, J. and J. Frey (1984), 'Psychological costs of air pollution: atmospheric conditions, seasonal trends, and psychiatric emergencies', *Population and Environment*, **7** (1), 3–16.

Sanders, N.J. (2012), 'What doesn't kill you makes you weaker: prenatal pollution exposure and educational outcomes', *Journal of Human Resources*, **47** (3), 826–850.

Stanek, L.W., Brown, J.S., Stanek, J., Gift, J. and D.L. Costa (2011), 'Air pollution toxicology: a brief review of the role of the science in shaping the current understanding of air pollution health risks', *Toxicological Sciences*, **120** (S1), S8–S27.

Stone, A.A. and C. Mackie (eds) (2014), *Subjective Well-Being: Measuring Happiness, Suffering, and Other Dimensions of Experience*, Washington, DC, USA: National Research Council, National Academies Press.
Tanaka, S. (2015), 'Environmental regulations on air pollution in China and their impact on infant mortality', *Journal of Health Economics*, **42**, 90–103.
Wolfson, E. (2013), 'Your zodiac sign, your health', *Atlantic*, November 15.
Zhang, X., Zhang, X. and X. Chen (2017a), 'Valuing air quality using happiness data: the case of China', *Ecological Economics*, **137**, 29–36.
Zhang, X., Zhang, X. and X. Chen (2017b), 'Happiness in the air: how does a dirty sky affect mental health and subjective well-being', *Journal of Environmental Economics and Management*, **85**, 81–94.

APPENDIX 10A.1 SUPPLEMENTARY FIGURES

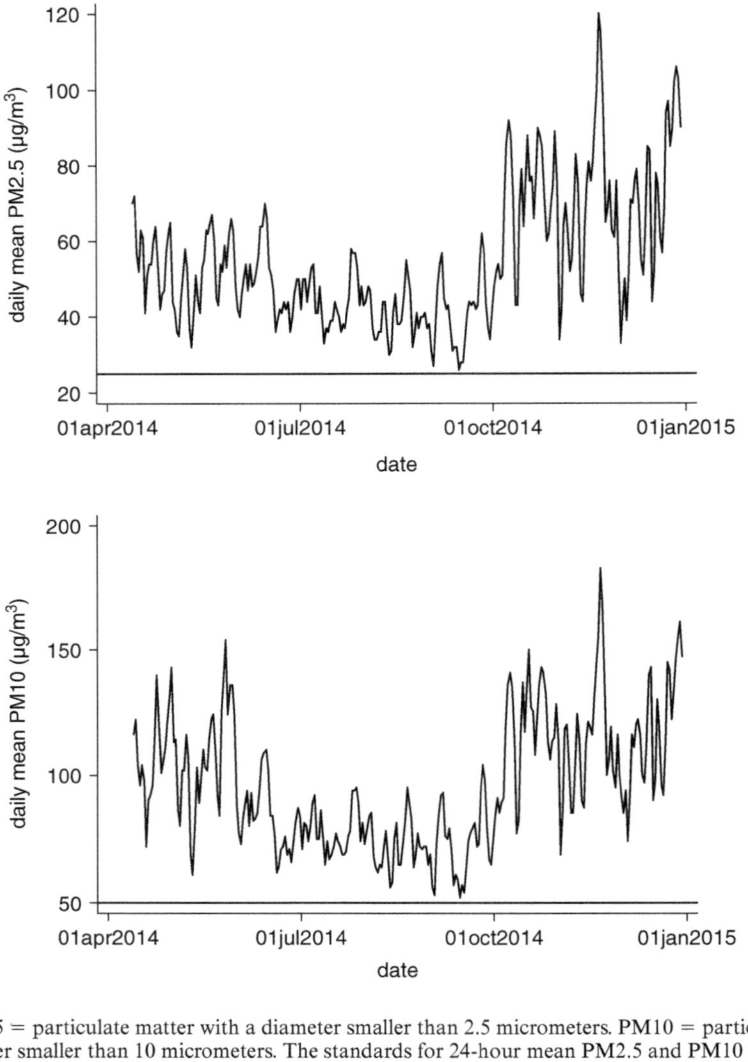

Note: PM2.5 = particulate matter with a diameter smaller than 2.5 micrometers. PM10 = particulate matter with a diameter smaller than 10 micrometers. The standards for 24-hour mean PM2.5 and PM10 published by WHO, plotted as horizontal lines, are 25 µg/m³ and 50 µg/m³, respectively.

Source: Ministry of Ecology and Environment of the People's Republic of China.

Figure 10A.1 Daily mean PM2.5 and PM10 (µg/m³) in China

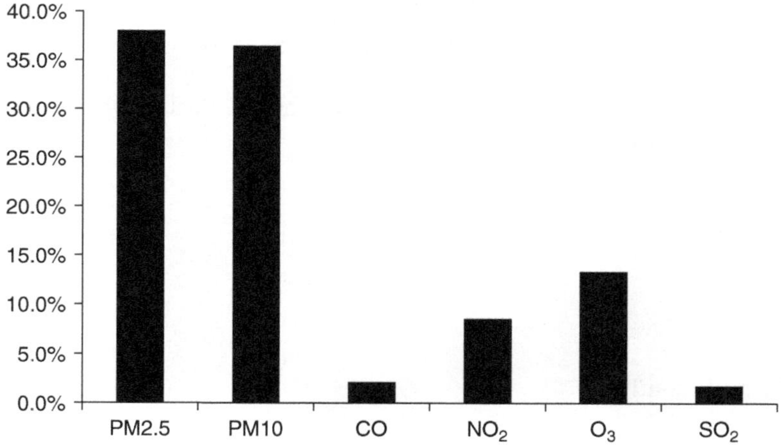

Note: CO = carbon monoxide. NO_2 = nitrogen dioxide. O_3 = ozone. PM2.5 = particulate matter with a diameter smaller than 2.5 micrometers. PM10 = particulate matter with a diameter smaller than 10 micrometers. SO_2 = sulfur dioxide.

Source: Ministry of Ecology and Environment of the People's Republic of China.

Figure 10A.2 Proportion of days each pollutant dominates the air quality index

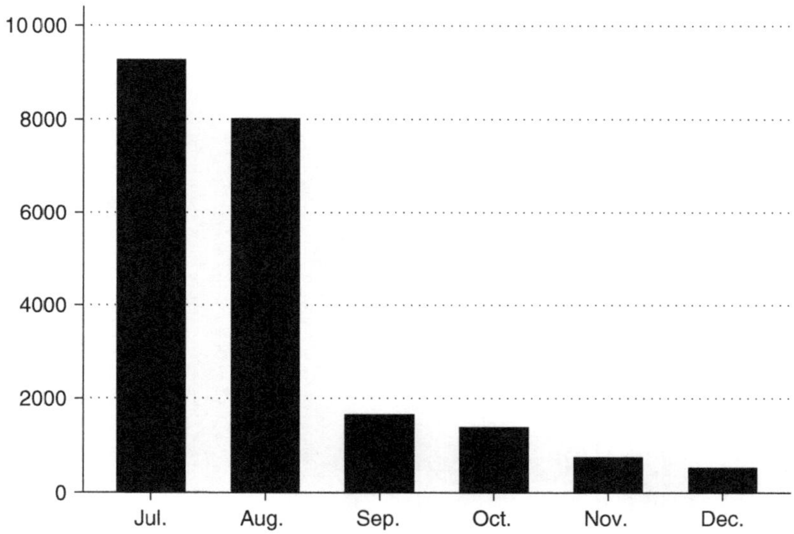

Source: China Family Panel Studies 2014.

Figure 10A.3 Distribution of interviews by month in 2014

APPENDIX 10A.2 KESSLER PSYCHOLOGICAL DISTRESS SCALE (K6) IN CFPS 2014

Below is a list of the ways you might have felt or behaved. Please tell me how often you have felt this way during the past month.

0. Never
1. Sometimes
2. Half the Time
3. Often
4. Almost Every Day

During the past month:

1. I felt so depressed that nothing could cheer me up.
2. I felt nervous.
3. I felt restless or fidgety.
4. I felt hopeless.
5. I felt that everything was an effort.
6. I felt that life was meaningless.

11. Noise and subjective wellbeing

Daniel Fujiwara and Ricky N. Lawton

11.1 INTRODUCTION

Environmental noise is a leading public complaint in the European Union (EU) (EU Directive 2002/49/EC). Transportation noise arising from road, rail and air traffic can cause adverse effects on human welfare (WHO, 2011) through four impact pathways: health and wellbeing; amenity; productivity; and ecosystems (Defra, 2014). A large amount of research has been devoted to understanding the health impacts of noise, with strong evidence of the links between exposure to noise and a comprehensive list of health outcomes, including annoyance, mental health, physiological impacts (particularly cardiovascular problems), poor general health status, tiredness, stress, anxiety and hypertension (Berry and Flindell, 2009; Defra, 2014; Navrud, 2002; WHO, 2011). Other areas of research have identified heterogeneous impacts of noise on school children (Berry and Flindell, 2009 provide a comprehensive review of the literature in this field). Less attention is given to the impacts on psychological wellbeing, despite the broad World Health Organization definition of health as 'a state of complete physical, mental and social wellbeing and not merely the absence of disease or infirmity'.

In this chapter we focus on one of the most politically contentious sources of noise intrusion. Aviation noise is a leading environmental complaint in the EU (European Parliament, 2002), and an issue of intense public debate for residents in affected areas around airports (Howarth and Griggs, 2013). Aviation noise and pollution are associated with negative health and wellbeing effects (Black et al., 2007; Clark and Stansfeld, 2011; Franssen et al., 2004), and environmental damages (Wolfe et al., 2014). However, with air traffic in Europe expected to increase between 1.4 and 2.2 times between 2012 and 2030 (EuroControl, 2013), demand for airport expansion continues to grow. As a consequence, airport expansion is an issue of intense public debate for environmental groups and local residents in affected areas around airports (Howarth and Griggs, 2013), due to their anticipated impacts on global climate change (Chapman, 2007) and the quality of life of affected local communities (Yim et al., 2013). Noise is regulated to some extent at all European airports through a combination of noise limits, flight path variations and restrictions on night flights. To mitigate the impact of aviation noise, aircraft paths are generally designed to fly over the least populated areas, while compensation measures are commonly proposed by airport operators, such as grant schemes to install sound insulation in affected homes.

Analysing how living with noise explains variation in people's responses to subjective wellbeing (SWB) in large-scale national datasets provides an innovative way of appraising societal impacts. With increasing consensus around the metrics for measuring wellbeing in evaluations and decision making (Helliwell et al., 2013; O'Donnell et al., 2014), SWB data are taking an increasingly prominent role in policy decisions and academic research, evidenced by the growing number of academic publications and recent government-level guidance on using wellbeing metrics in policy evaluation (Fujiwara and Campbell, 2011; OECD, 2013).

To date, few studies have addressed the impacts of noise on SWB, or they have been confined to one measure of SWB and subjective measures of noise 'nuisance' rather than objectively measured noise levels (Navrud, 2002; Van Praag and Baarsma, 2005), or to modelled changes in wellbeing associated with infrastructure interventions (Braubach et al., 2015). The SWB approach, which measures how SWB is associated with environmental quality, is particularly attractive because it excludes the possibility of framing effects and response bias that arise when asking people directly about their experience of living with noise (Kahneman and Tversky, 1984). This provides a more direct account of the effects on people's welfare of a non-market good such as environmental noise.

In this chapter we first review the growing body of evidence that general noise pollution, including from traffic and airport operations, is associated with lower levels of SWB. Our review considers methodological best practice for measuring the impacts of noise on health – where the gold standard of evidence is a dose–response relationship between health outcomes and increasing levels of noise – and explores the current state of knowledge in analysis of noise and SWB. We present two recent case studies which explore the association between aviation noise and SWB on large population datasets. This provides an opportunity to assess noise against a full range of wellbeing measures covering evaluative measures (life satisfaction), eudemonic measures (sense of purpose) and hedonic measures captured in the experience (happiness and relaxation).[1] This means that we can assess the association with wellbeing both in the moment and at a more global evaluative level. In the final analysis, we explore how such data may be used to quantify the effects of aviation noise mitigation and compensation policies.

11.2 LITERATURE REVIEW

Population-based studies have found strong evidence that people living in noisier locations suffer higher rates of clinical morbidity or mortality as a consequence of exposure to noise (Berry and Flindell, 2009; Defra, 2014; Navrud, 2002; Stansfeld et al., 1993; WHO, 2011). Evidence has also been identified of the links between noise and mental health (Hardoy et al., 2005; Morrell et al., 1997). Some groups, such as children and the elderly, are thought to be especially vulnerable to the effects of noise (Haines et al., 2001). Berry and Flindell (2009) found meta-analytical evidence of a dose–response relationship between increased risk of cardiovascular health problems with rising noise levels, and provided a methodology to monetize this risk (IGCB(N), 2010: Appendix A).[2] Evidence of a dose–response relationship was also found for hypertension and sleep disturbance, but the evidence was not sufficient to monetize these impacts.

Based on the available evidence of the links between noise and a number of health problems, the World Health Organization (WHO) (2009) developed a set of guidelines for maximum noise exposure at the residential level. The WHO concluded that daytime noise levels above 55 decibels (dB) are sufficiently associated with cardiovascular effects to be classed a major public health concern. Adverse health effects are also observed at the level above 40 dB, such as self-reported sleep disturbance, environmental insomnia, and increased use of somnifacient drugs and sedatives.

In the field of SWB, while there is evidence that general noise pollution reduces SWB (Dolan et al., 2008), as well as evidence in other domains of wellbeing such as housing (neighbour noise; see Fujiwara, 2013)[3] and energy production (Pedersen and Waye, 2007), we focus on transport noise in this chapter, as this is where the most consistent efforts to assess SWB have been undertaken (He et al., 2014).

In terms of road traffic noise, Lercher and Kofler (1996) measured the impact of noise level from traffic on the wellbeing of a cross-sectional dataset of 1989 individuals aged 25–65 from five rural alpine communities in Austria. They found significant associations between noise exposure >55 dB and loss of life satisfaction. These results are supported by Rehdanz and Maddison (2008), who utilized a larger sample of 23000 individuals in Germany to measure the impact of local noise nuisance on life satisfaction. The authors find that for each step reduction in feeling adversely affected by noise (on a five-point scale from 'not all affected' to 'very strongly affected'), a person is less likely to score average life satisfaction levels and more likely to report the highest levels of life satisfaction.

Braubach et al. (2015) predict wellbeing impacts before and after transport interventions modelled to affect noise exposure (subjective noise measures) for three cities: Basel (Swiss Household Panel Survey 2012), Rotterdam and Thessaloniki (European Quality of Life Survey 2012 (EQLS2012)). Future predicted levels of noise (up to 2020) are categorized into different noise perception categories, and relative differences in the probability of high/low wellbeing between current populations within these thresholds are compared.[4] Lowest wellbeing probability is found for the population group reporting high levels of noise. In only one case study (Rotterdam) is there a straight dose–response relationship indicating that less noise is associated with a higher wellbeing probability. The evidence suggests that baseline noise levels are important: a stronger wellbeing improvement is found for residents reporting high noise levels (increase of 0.8 per cent in their predicted wellbeing probability). Less-affluent populations report high noise perception more frequently, but there is no indication of a generally stronger wellbeing benefit for the less-affluent population in all three cities.

Turning to aircraft noise, Van Praag and Baarsma (2005) surveyed 1400 respondents living within a radius of 50 km around the Amsterdam Airport Schiphol. Questions on noise pollution were embedded within a broader question area of health and wellbeing to avoid bias. The survey asked a 'quality of life' (QoL) ladder question (Cantril, 1966). The authors found no significant effect on wellbeing from objective noise (measured in Kosten units). Where the survey asked about respondents' subjective noise perception, it found a significant and negative association with wellbeing. The impact on life satisfaction was lower if households had noise insulation. The limitations to this study lie in its failure to find association between objective levels of aviation noise and SWB. This may be accounted for by the choice of wellbeing variable used (the single metric of the Cantril ladder).

Kroesen et al. (2010) assessed the effects of aircraft noise on residential satisfaction, using a survey of the population living within a 25 km radius of Amsterdam Airport Schiphol. In comparison to other environment effects (road traffic noise annoyance and neighbour noise annoyance), aircraft noise was not a strong predictor of residential satisfaction. In contrast, the total effect of aircraft noise exposure ranks higher than the effect of aircraft noise annoyance, suggesting that the objective level of aircraft noise exposure was found to be a better predictor of residential satisfaction.

Overall, there is a lack of consensus around a physiological explanation of how noise causes health impacts. One of the key considerations in analysis of noise and SWB is the choice of objective measures of noise (reported or modelled noise levels measured in decibels) or subjective measures of noise 'annoyance' reported by the individual. Previous noise studies have demonstrated an incongruity between objective and subjective indicators of residential traffic noise exposure. Riedel et al. (2014) model the interplay of objective noise exposure and serious noise annoyance, by comparing objective noise levels (L_{den}) with noise annoyance (Likert scale) in one 'exposure' variable, and self-rated health in two German population-based studies, the Dortmund Health Study (DHS) and the Spatial Analysis of Households' Vulnerability to their Local Environment (SAVE) survey. A moderate association between objective and subjective indicators of resident exposure to road traffic noise was found in both samples. More than two-thirds of participants exposed to road traffic noise levels >55 dB did not report being seriously annoyed. The authors conclude that annoyance of road traffic noise is dependent to some extent on objective exposure, but the association between the two indicators is merely moderate.

We note that the link between objective and subjective noise measures may not operate in a linear way. As Braubach et al. (2015) note, although quantitative noise changes may occur for the largest part of the population, they only cause a change of noise perception category for a very small part of the population. The authors argue that a range of noise studies provide dose–response relations between transport noise levels and noise annoyance, but that noise annoyance may not adequately reflect the multifaceted concept of general SWB. To date, dose–response relationships have not been found between SWB and objective noise measures.

11.3 DATA

The two case studies that we report in this section assess SWB associated with presence within aircraft noise contours through surveys at two levels: household-level data on evaluative, hedonic and eudemonic SWB measures – life satisfaction, happiness yesterday, anxiety yesterday, and sense of purpose – within the Annual Population Survey (APS), a cross-sectional United Kingdom (UK) survey; and the Mappiness experience sampling method (ESM) survey which collected frequent affective wellbeing measures concerned with a person's feelings 'in the moment', both positive and negative (Kahneman et al., 2003; Pavot and Diener, 1993; Schwarz and Clore, 1983). Positive feelings are often measured in terms of happiness, and negative feelings as stress and anxiety. Affective wellbeing is typically measured on a more frequent basis than evaluative measures, and within Mappiness can be geolinked to the time and place in which the survey takes place. The ESM approach, due to its panel nature, provides the closest estimate to causal effects that can be achieved with wellbeing data (Csikszentmihalyi and Hunter, 2003; Hektner et al., 2007). This means that the level of causal inference that can be made of the results in the case study are stronger than in existing studies using cross-sectional data (Lawton and Fujiwara, 2016; Navrud, 2002; Van Praag and Baarsma, 2005).

Noise measurement maps are compiled by the UK Department for Environment, Food and Rural Affairs (Defra) from airport operators in England using geographical location data (including postcodes; lower-layer super output area, LSOA; and census output area,

OA).[5] This captures aviation impacts through the presence of aircraft noise contours for those English airports covered by the Environmental Noise Directive (consisting of the 17 main airports in England[6]). Noise contour data were derived from annual average noise levels from 2012 airport operator strategic noise maps at the geographical level of residential dwelling OA. Airport noise data were comprised of daytime (0700–2300 hours local time) noise (L_{Aeq16h}) and night-time (2300–0700 hours) noise (L_{night}) calculated over the 92-day summer period from 16 June to 15 September.[7] This is the most common international measure of aircraft noise (WHO, 2009). Averaging out means that the day's high and low levels of noise are levelled out to give a single figure. In each case, a maximum value is given across the OA derived from annual average noise levels from the 2012 airport operator strategic noise map results, as well as an arithmetic dwelling-weighted average derived from the 2011 annual average noise levels. The choice of maximum noise levels follows from the literature which indicates that peak noise levels are associated with greater health effects (Clark and Stansfeld, 2011; WHO, 2009).

We take the presence of aircraft noise to begin at 55 dB (L_{Aeq16h}) for daytime noise and 50 dB (L_{night}) for night-time noise. These are the lowest bands of aircraft noise provided in the noise map dataset. Standard reporting for airport noise data begins at 57 dB (L_{eq}). There is, however, a strong argument to begin at the 55/50 dB(A) levels from the literature on health and stress effects (WHO, 2009).

11.4 ANALYSIS

We apply multivariate regression analysis to estimate the association between aviation aircraft noise and wellbeing, allowing us to control for the main determinants of SWB, including ethnicity, household income, health status, marital status, employment status, housing status, gender, age, geographic region, religion and education (Fujiwara and Campbell, 2011). This allows us to make better-informed claims about the effects of aviation noise on SWB.

We used the following regression model as the base for all of the analyses:

$$SWB_i = \alpha + \beta_1 AN_i + \beta_2 AP_i + \beta_3 X_i + \varepsilon_i \tag{11.1}$$

where SWB_i is a wellbeing measure for individual i; X_i is a vector of other determinants of life satisfaction; and ε_i is the error term. AN_i is airport noise measured in dB. AP_i is a dummy variable for airport proximity within 5 km of the centre point of the airport.

Two methodological challenges in particular emerge in estimating the impacts of noise on health and wellbeing. First, contamination, whereby other variables related to noise, such as air pollution, severance, pedestrian risk and safety, vibration, visual intrusion, and dust and dirt may also have an impact on wellbeing. For instance, there is evidence that concentrations of air pollutants in areas reduce residents' SWB (Bjørner, 2004; Frey and Stutzer, 2010; Welsch, 2006; Wolfe et al., 2014).

Second, selection, where populations living within noisy areas are subject to non-random 'selection'. For instance, an individual's socio-economic or ethnic background may make them more likely to live in a noisy area, but these sociodemographic characteristics are also known to be significant factors associated with lower wellbeing at the population level. This leads to the question of whether individuals have lower wellbeing because they are subject to noise, or because they are economically marginalized and can only afford to live in these areas. At the same time, individuals who are able to adapt to higher levels of noise may also select into noisier areas, on the basis that the increased utility they gain from lower house costs more than offsets any potential loss of welfare through exposure to noise. Wherever possible it is recommended to design models to control for these potential confounding factors, and to caveat claims of causality related to any dose–response results.

The channels by which noise impacts on wellbeing may be related to health, sleep, air pollution, unpredictability, and so on. There may also be positive effects bundled in among negative effects. For instance, the positive aspects of living close to airports (for example, improved transport infrastructure, access to jobs and cheaper property) may offset the negative effects (for example, noise, pollution and visual disamenity). This adds to the challenges of assessing the impacts of airport developments: for example, small changes in factors such as the level of social interaction may have significant effects on the wellbeing of individuals since their characteristics and psychological health are known to affect SWB (Dolan et al., 2008).

To respond to these issues, in case study 1 we test for possible selection effects by regressing airport proximity on a set of socio-economic variables, using a logistic regression:

$$AP_i = \alpha + \beta_1 X_i + \varepsilon_i \tag{11.2}$$

where AP_i is a dummy for household proximity within 5 km of an English airport for individual i; X_i is a vector of sociodemographic variables from model (11.1); and ε_i is the error term.

11.4.1 Case Study 1: Association between Noise and SWB: Retrospective SWB Data

In case study 1, presence within airport noise contours was provided by geolinking postcodes positioned within aircraft noise contours with survey data on 190000 households (APS 2011–13), over 20 times that of previous studies on the effects of aviation noise on SWB.[8] These results were first published in Lawton and Fujiwara (2016), and are expanded upon within this chapter.

We run ordinary least squares (OLS) regressions for equation (11.1) where SWB_i is tested through a separate regression for each wellbeing measure – life satisfaction, happiness yesterday, anxiety yesterday, and sense of purpose, and positive affect balance – for individual i. All SWB variables in case study 1 are measured on a scale of 0–10, where 0 is ‘not at all’, and 10 is ‘completely’. Table 11.1 provides full variable descriptions for case study 1.

AN_i is presence within an airport noise contour. Separate regressions are run for: daytime noise for presence within noise contours of 55dB and above (Table 11.2); night-time noise within noise contours of 50 dB and above (results not reported here); continuous daytime noise contours of 55dB and above (Table 11.3). As well as standard sociodemographic controls, we also control for those living within 5 km of an airport, to account for potential positive and negative effects at the local level.

This allowed us to test for associations between aviation noise and SWB at a finer level

Table 11.1 Variable descriptions

Variable	Description	Mean	n (= 1)	N
Gender	1 = female; 0 = male (reference)	0.56	134675	240808
Age	Age of respondent as continuous variable	51.30		240808
Age Squared	Non-linear function of age	2935.62		240808
BME	Black or minority ethnic	0.10	23091	240651
Religion – Yes	1 = Religious; 0 = no religion (reference)	0.75	179291	240479
Single	Marital status: 1 = Single; 0 = Married (reference)	0.26	62934	240808
Separated	Marital status: 1 = Separated; 0 = Married (reference)	0.50	120787	240808
Divorced	Marital status: 1 = Divorced; 0 = Married (reference)	0.03	8428	240808
Widowed	Marital status: 1 = Widowed; 0 = Married (reference)	0.12	27868	240808
Civil_Partner	Marital status: 1 = Civil partner; 0 = Married (reference)	0.09	20791	240808
No child	1 = No dependent children; 0 = Dependent children (reference)	0.70	169684	240786
LimitingHealth	Health: 1 = Individual reports health to be limiting on their day to day life; 0 = No limiting health conditions (reference)	0.23	54504	240808
Smoker – Ex	Smoking: 1 = Ex-smoker; 0 = No smoking (reference)	0.38	91033	239147
Smoker – Yes	Smoking: 1 = Current smoker; 0 = No smoking (reference)	0.20	47625	239147
OwnHouse	Accommodation status: 1 = Owns house; 0 = Mortgage (reference)	0.67	161481	240606
RentPrivate	Accommodation status: 1 = Private renter; 0 = Mortgage (reference)	0.15	36899	240606
RentSocial	Accommodation status: 1 = Social housing; 0 = Mortgage (reference)	0.17	40363	240808
No rent/ squatters	Accommodation status: 1 = Not paying rent/squatting; 0 = Mortgage (reference)	0.01	1897	240606
Higher_Ed	Education: 1 = Higher education; 0 = Degree (reference)	0.34	68388	200365
Alevel	Education: 1 = A-level; 0 = Degree (reference)	0.22	44329	200365
GCSE	Education: 1 = GCSE; 0 = Degree (reference)	0.22	43917	200365
Ed_Other	Education: 1 = Other educational training; 0 = Degree (reference)	0.10	20514	200365
Ed_None	Education: 1 = No education; 0 = Degree (reference)	0.12	23217	200365
Inactive – seeking	Employment: 1 = Inactive seeking work; 0 = Full-time employed 1st pay quintile (reference)	0.00	1144	231780

Table 11.1 (continued)

Variable	Description	Mean	n (= 1)	N
Inactive – not seeking but wants to work	Employment: 1 = Inactive not seeking work but wants work; 0 = Full-time employed 1st pay quintile (reference)	0.04	9555	231 780
Inactive – not seeking not want to work	Employment: 1 = Inactive not seeking work doesn't want work; 0 = Full-time employed 1st pay quintile (reference)	0.09	21 518	231 780
Inactive – retired	Employment: 1 = Retired; 0 = Full-time employed 1st pay quintile (reference)	0.27	63 353	231 780
Unemployed	Employment: 1 = Unemployed; 0 = Full-time employed 1st pay quintile (reference)	0.05	10 870	231 780
Student	Employment: 1 = Student; 0 = Full-time employed 1st pay quintile (reference)	0.02	4002	231 780
Unpaid Family Worker	Employment: 1 = Unpaid family worker; 0 = Full-time employed 1st pay quintile (reference)	0.00	605	231 780
Underemployed	Employment: 1 = Underemployed; 0 = Full-time employed 1st pay quintile (reference)	0.03	5864	231 780
Part-Time	Employment: 1 = Part-time; 0 = Full-time employed 1st pay quintile (reference)	0.15	34 170	231 780
Full-Time Self-Employed	Employment: 1 = Full-time self-employed; 0 = Full-time employed 1st pay quintile (reference)	0.05	11 954	231 780
	Full-time income: 1 = Full-time 1st pay quintile (reference)	0.06	13 472	231 780
Full-Time 2nd pay quintile	Full-time income: 1 = 2nd pay quintile; 0 = 1st pay quintile (reference)	0.06	13 574	231 780
Full-Time 3rd pay quintile	Full-time income: 1 = 3rd pay quintile; 0 = 1st pay quintile (reference)	0.06	13 514	231 780
Full-Time 4th pay quintile	Full-time income: 1 = 4th pay quintile; 0 = 1st pay quintile (reference)	0.06	13 732	231 780
Full-Time highest pay quintile	Full-time income: 1 = Highest pay quintile; 0 = 1st pay quintile (reference)	0.06	14 453	231 780
Face-to-Face Survey	Survey method: 1 = Face-to-face survey; 0 = Telephone survey (reference)	0.52	125 669	240 808
Airport variable				
MaxDaytime noise	MaxLq16 giving maximum strategic aviation noise map level (L_{Aeq16h}) at a residential dwelling for the Census Output Code (OA): 1 = Presence of maximum daytime noise; 0 = Absence of maximum daytime noise (reference)	0.01	3545	240 680

Table 11.1 (continued)

Variable	Description	Mean	n (= 1)	N
MaxNight time noise	MaxLnight giving 50 dB(A), L_{night} noise contours (11pm to 7am, dB Lnight) for maximum annual strategic aviation noise map levels (L_{night}): 1 = Presence of max. night time noise; 0 = Absence of max. night time noise (reference)	0.01	1777	240 680
Airprox	Airport Proximity is defined as the airport reference point (ARP), the centre point of an airport, located at the geometric centre of all the usable runways: 1 = Within a distance < 5 km from the centre point of an airport; 0 = > 5 km from the centre point of an airport (reference)	0.13	31 584	240 808
Continuous Daytime Noise	Linear continuous maximum daytime noise variable			
Continuous Night time Noise	Linear continuous maximum night time noise variable			

of detail than has been achieved to date, and to compare effects on different types of SWB data, each according with different theoretical concepts of wellbeing (Kahneman et al., 2003).

Living within a daytime aircraft noise contour (at or above 55 dB) is negatively associated with all SWB measures: lower life satisfaction ($\beta = -0.147$), lower sense of worthwhile ($\beta = -0.126$), lower happiness ($\beta = -0.116$), increased anxiety ($\beta = 0.201$), and lower positive affect balance ($\beta = -0.160$). It is well documented that analyses looking at impacts on multiple outcomes lead to increased risk of finding a false positive result just due to chance (Ariely, 2000; Sheskin, 2011). However, the fact that we found consistently negative and significant results across all five SWB variables provides additional confidence concerning these results. It is important to note that the magnitude of these associations were small relative to other common socio-economic drivers of wellbeing (Dolan et al., 2008). The negative effects of unemployment ($\beta = -0.785$), having poor health ($\beta = -0.722$) or being a smoker ($\beta = -0.345$) were at least twice as large as those from aviation noise.

We found no evidence that the presence of night-time aircraft noise (at or above 50 dB) affects people's wellbeing by any of the four SWB measures. These results are not included in this chapter. We note that the sample of residences affected by night-time noise at this level was lower (n = 1777) than those affected by daytime noise (n = 3545), by a proportion of around 50 per cent, which may affect the significance of our results. We also note that average night-time noise levels are restricted to a lower level (as indicated by the lower noise threshold used in this analysis) (European Union Directive 2006/93/EC).

Table 11.2 Presence of daytime aircraft noise (maximum), and SWB (all wellbeing variables measured on a scale of 0–10)

Explanatory variable	Life satisfaction	Sense of worthwhile	Happiness	Anxiety	Positive affect balance
	β (se)	β (se)	β (se)	β (se)	β (se)
MaxDaytime Noise	−0.147***	−0.126**	−0.116*	0.201**	−0.160**
	(0.040)	(0.038)	(0.052)	(0.071)	(0.053)
Airport Proximity (< 5 km)	0.011	0.002	−0.003	0.023	−0.013
	(0.014)	(0.014)	(0.018)	(0.024)	(0.018)
Female	0.163***	0.331***	0.088***	0.205***	−0.059***
	(0.011)	(0.011)	(0.014)	(0.018)	(0.014)
Age	−0.109***	−0.066***	−0.079***	0.081***	−0.080***
	(0.003)	(0.003)	(0.004)	(0.005)	(0.003)
Age Squared	0.001***	0.001***	0.001***	−0.001***	0.001***
	(0.000)	(0.000)	(0.000)	(0.000)	(0.000)
BME	−0.282***	−0.207***	−0.106***	0.187***	−0.147***
	(0.019)	(0.018)	(0.022)	(0.029)	(0.021)
Religion – Yes	0.091***	0.161***	0.124***	0.076***	0.024
	(0.012)	(0.012)	(0.015)	(0.019)	(0.014)
Single	−0.476***	−0.314***	−0.392***	0.148***	−0.270***
	(0.014)	(0.014)	(0.017)	(0.023)	(0.017)
Separated	−0.718***	−0.352***	−0.512***	0.294***	−0.404***
	(0.031)	(0.029)	(0.036)	(0.045)	(0.035)
Divorced	−0.520***	−0.306***	−0.406***	0.209***	−0.308***
	(0.017)	(0.017)	(0.021)	(0.027)	(0.020)
Widowed	−0.788***	−0.417***	−0.614***	0.255***	−0.433***
	(0.032)	(0.030)	(0.038)	(0.047)	(0.037)
Civil partner	0.251***	0.263***	0.201*	0.019	0.094
	(0.060)	(0.064)	(0.089)	(0.150)	(0.105)
One child	0.079***	0.232***	0.092***	−0.065**	0.078***
	(0.015)	(0.015)	(0.019)	(0.025)	(0.018)
Two children	0.156***	0.351***	0.158***	−0.207***	0.182***
	(0.026)	(0.024)	(0.032)	(0.042)	(0.031)
Three children	0.159**	0.421***	0.228***	−0.220**	0.222***
	(0.051)	(0.051)	(0.061)	(0.081)	(0.062)
Four or more children	0.270*	0.425***	0.305*	−0.275	0.277*
	(0.111)	(0.111)	(0.121)	(0.140)	(0.110)
Limiting Health	−0.722***	−0.539***	−0.703***	0.891***	−0.797***
	(0.015)	(0.015)	(0.018)	(0.023)	(0.018)
Smoker – Yes	−0.345***	−0.237***	−0.337***	0.219***	−0.278***
	(0.015)	(0.015)	(0.019)	(0.024)	(0.018)
Smoker – Ex	−0.077***	−0.049***	−0.077***	0.080***	−0.078***
	(0.011)	(0.011)	(0.014)	(0.019)	(0.014)
RentPrivate	−0.128***	−0.048**	−0.058**	0.183***	−0.120***
	(0.015)	(0.015)	(0.019)	(0.025)	(0.019)
RentSocial	−0.258***	−0.120***	−0.243***	0.194***	−0.219***
	(0.019)	(0.018)	(0.022)	(0.028)	(0.021)

Table 11.2 (continued)

Explanatory variable	Life satisfaction	Sense of worthwhile	Happiness	Anxiety	Positive affect balance
	β (se)	β (se)	β (se)	β (se)	β (se)
No rent/squatters	0.218***	0.257***	0.218**	−0.284**	0.250**
	(0.064)	(0.063)	(0.080)	(0.099)	(0.078)
Higher_Ed	0.016	0.010	0.007	−0.163***	0.085***
	(0.017)	(0.017)	(0.022)	(0.030)	(0.022)
Alevel	0.032*	−0.032*	−0.004	−0.174***	0.085***
	(0.014)	(0.014)	(0.018)	(0.024)	(0.018)
GCSE	0.007	−0.055***	0.000	−0.251***	0.125***
	(0.015)	(0.015)	(0.019)	(0.025)	(0.018)
Ed_Other	0.046*	−0.096***	0.026	−0.204***	0.116***
	(0.022)	(0.021)	(0.025)	(0.033)	(0.025)
Ed_None	−0.008	−0.244***	−0.083**	−0.083*	0.000
	(0.023)	(0.022)	(0.027)	(0.034)	(0.026)
Inactive – seeking	−0.426***	−0.237**	−0.303**	0.600***	−0.457***
	(0.080)	(0.075)	(0.095)	(0.113)	(0.086)
Inactive – not seeking but wants to work	−0.649***	−0.479***	−0.479***	0.561***	−0.519***
	(0.036)	(0.036)	(0.043)	(0.053)	(0.041)
Inactive – not seeking not want to work	−0.190***	−0.177***	−0.189***	0.283***	−0.234***
	(0.028)	(0.027)	(0.034)	(0.043)	(0.033)
Inactive – retired	0.376***	0.182***	0.376***	−0.353***	0.363***
	(0.027)	(0.026)	(0.033)	(0.043)	(0.032)
Unemployed	−0.785***	−0.535***	−0.353***	0.426***	−0.390***
	(0.034)	(0.033)	(0.040)	(0.049)	(0.037)
Student	0.073	0.162***	0.009	0.373***	−0.182***
	(0.039)	(0.042)	(0.052)	(0.068)	(0.050)
Unpaid Family Worker	0.089	0.190*	0.229*	0.148	0.043
	(0.086)	(0.079)	(0.103)	(0.147)	(0.109)
Underemployed	−0.391***	−0.192***	−0.196***	0.199***	−0.197***
	(0.037)	(0.036)	(0.046)	(0.057)	(0.042)
Part-Time	0.108***	0.156***	0.077**	0.027	0.025
	(0.023)	(0.023)	(0.029)	(0.038)	(0.028)
Full-Time Self-Employed	0.112***	0.250***	0.096**	0.089*	0.003
	(0.027)	(0.027)	(0.034)	(0.045)	(0.033)
Full-Time 2nd pay quintile	0.052*	0.037	0.006	0.012	−0.003
	(0.026)	(0.026)	(0.034)	(0.043)	(0.032)
Full-Time 3rd pay quintile	0.150***	0.157***	0.036	0.065	−0.014
	(0.026)	(0.025)	(0.033)	(0.043)	(0.032)
Full-Time 4th pay quintile	0.195***	0.231***	0.046	0.063	−0.008
	(0.025)	(0.024)	(0.033)	(0.043)	(0.032)
Full-Time highest pay quintile	0.313***	0.231***	0.100**	0.086*	0.008
	(0.025)	(0.025)	(0.032)	(0.043)	(0.032)
Face-to-Face Survey	−0.130***	−0.110***	−0.085***	−0.014	−0.036**
	(0.011)	(0.011)	(0.014)	(0.018)	(0.013)

Table 11.2 (continued)

Explanatory variable	Life satisfaction	Sense of worthwhile	Happiness	Anxiety	Positive affect balance
	β (se)	β (se)	β (se)	β (se)	β (se)
Data set 1 = APS 2012–13	−0.066	−0.050	−0.218***	0.090	−0.155*
	(0.051)	(0.050)	(0.061)	(0.084)	(0.061)
Constant	10.114***	8.964***	9.347***	1.072***	4.141***
	(0.076)	(0.077)	(0.096)	(0.124)	(0.093)
r2	0.137	0.096	0.068	0.040	0.064
N	189 058	188 491	189 044	188 793	188 684

Notes:
* $p < 0.05$; ** $p < 0.01$; *** $p < 0.001$; standard error in parenthesis.
Variable descriptions in Table 11.1.
Reference groups: (1) for religion variables ref. = no religion; (2) for marital status ref. = married or co-habiting; (3) for children variables ref. = no children; (4) for health variables ref. = good health; (5) for smoker variables ref. = non-smoker; (6) for housing variables ref. = mortgage; (7) for education variables ref. = degree; (8) for employment variables ref. = full-time employed; (9) for income variables ref. = lowest income quintile.
Control variables for days of the week and seasonal change through months of the year are included (not shown).
Sample is restricted to England and those aged 16 and over.

Table 11.3 Daytime continuous aircraft noise and SWB (all SWB variables measured on a scale of 0–10)

Explanatory variable	Life satisfaction	Sense of worthwhile	Happiness	Anxiety	Positive affect balance
	β (se)	β(se)	β(se)	β(se)	β(se)
MaxDaytime Noise	−0.003***	−0.002**	−0.002*	0.003**	−0.003**
	(0.001)	(0.001)	(0.001)	(0.001)	(0.001)
Constant	10.114***	8.964***	9.347***	1.072***	4.141***
	(0.076)	(0.077)	(0.096)	(0.124)	(0.093)
r2	0.137	0.096	0.068	0.04	0.064
N	189058	188491	189044	188793	188684

Notes:
* $p < 0.05$; ** $p < 0.01$; *** $p < 0.001$; standard error in parenthesis.
Variable descriptions in Table 11.1.
Control variables for standard sociodemographic variables, proximity to airport (≤ 5 km), days of the week and seasonal change through months of the year are included (not shown).
Sample is restricted to England and those aged 16 and over.

Evidence of dose–response, marginal association between aviation noise and SWB

There has been limited research to date on the marginal effect of noise on SWB at different ambient noise levels. Case study 1 finds a negative association between marginal changes of +1 dB of daytime aircraft noise (beginning at the 55 dB threshold) for all five SWB measures. The magnitude of the coefficients on SWB was low, ranging from a reduction in life satisfaction of −0.003 points and an increase of anxiety of 0.003 points on a ten-point scale for every additional dB[9] of daytime aircraft noise, to a reduction of reported worthwhile and happiness of −0.002 points on a ten-point scale, all other factors being held constant (Table 11.3). However, it should be remembered that this is a marginal effect estimate on a logarithmic dB scale, and that cumulative effects at multiple dB levels would be more sizeable.

We note that due to the cross-sectional nature of the APS data, causation cannot be directly inferred. Impact estimates may be biased to some degree if there are confounding factors that have not been controlled for in the analysis (Ferrer-i-Carbonell and Frijters, 2004; Fujiwara and Campbell, 2011). This is a risk with any wellbeing analysis using non-experimental data. Notwithstanding, multiple regression analysis (or similar types of analyses based on the same fundamental assumptions, such as matching estimators) have been used extensively in the wellbeing and policy evaluation literature (Clark and Oswald, 2002; Dolan et al., 2011; Ferrer-i-Carbonell and Frijters, 2004). As noted in the health literature (Berry and Flindell, 2009), bias may be introduced to these results when populations living within noisy areas are subject to non-random selection. We tested for possible selection effects by regressing airport proximity on a set of socio-economic variables (equation 11.2).

We found that females, those from ethnic minorities, renters (private and social), those who are inactive from work through retirement or not seeking work, part-time workers and the self-employed have higher odds of living near UK airports. With reference to income variables, those in the highest (3rd, 4th and 5th) income quintiles were successively more likely to live within 5 km of airports. Those with poor health, smokers, and those with education below degree level were less likely to live near an airport. This suggests that, contrary to the expectation that aviation noise would decrease the desirability of living in areas affected by aviation noise, causing those with the economic capability to move out (Nelson, 2008; Wadud, 2009), there is self-selection into airport noise areas by the more economically secure. One possible explanation is self-selection by those who may be resilient to the negative wellbeing effects of aviation noise, and who benefit in some way from living in these areas, through either lower rents or other economic or infrastructure benefits associated with airport proximity. Alternatively, areas around airports may be more rural, and therefore more desirable, providing more green space and larger home or garden space.

11.4.2 Case Study 2: The Impact of Noise on SWB: Panel Data

Case study 2 is based on a large experience sampling method (ESM) iPhone survey app. These results were first published in Fujiwara et al. (2017), and are expanded upon within this chapter. Mappiness is an iPhone application that permits individuals to record their wellbeing scores on a scale of 0–100 via their phone. The data contain more than 1 million observations from tens of thousands of individuals in the UK, collected since August 2010.[10] Individuals who have downloaded the application receive randomly timed signals on their phone to request that they complete a very short survey. The survey asks individuals to rate themselves on three dimensions of momentary wellbeing, stating how happy, and relaxed they feel. Each score is elicited by means of a continuous slider (a form of visual analogue scale; see Couper et al., 2006). The ends of each scale are labelled 'not at all' and 'extremely', and an individual positions themself on the scale by drawing a fingertip across the screen.[11] There is a growing literature which demonstrates the explanatory power of ESM methods in the evaluation of momentary wellbeing, showing that wellbeing in the moment is associated with theoretically consistent drivers (Csikszentmihalyi and Hunter, 2003; Hektner et al., 2007; Kahneman et al., 2004).

We link the Global Positioning System (GPS) signal coded at the time of the response in Mappiness to the locations of airport sites and aircraft noise contours. We can therefore determine whether people are near airports or noise contours when responding to the SWB questions, and for those people inside an airport we can determine what they are doing when responding to the SWB questions. We merged the Mappiness data with the Department for Transport's (DfT) noise contours for London Heathrow (LHR), London Gatwick (LGW) and Stansted (STN).[12] Airport operator strategic noise contour maps from 2012 are matched to GPS locations recorded in Mappiness surveys. A 15 km perimeter was created around the London airports (LHR, LGW, STN). To avoid overlap, if respondents fall within more than one airport perimeter, we choose the nearest one. After the data merge, each Mappiness response is linked with the associated decibel level from the three airports. There are approximately 12000 responses in the 2010–16 Mappiness data from the 57 dB+ noise contours for these three airports (Table 11.4). By including region dummies in all models, we control for differences between London and non-London populations (note: Stansted airport is not classed within the London administrative region, but is considered to be one of the London airports).

The key distinction from case study 1 is that Mappiness captures SWB at multiple points across the year, linked directly to the presence of the individual within/outside aircraft noise contours at the time of the survey. The two case studies also capture different measures of wellbeing: momentary in case study 1, and retrospective in case study 2.

We run fixed effects regressions for a panel data specification of equation (11.1), where SWB_{it} is either happiness or relaxation (in separate specifications) for individual i at time t. SWB variables are measured on a scale of 0–100, where 0 is 'not at all', and 100 is 'completely'. AN_{it} is presence within an airport noise contour at the time of the ESM survey. Separate regressions are run for daytime noise for presence within noise contours of 55 dB and above.

Fixed effects estimation allows us to control for all time-invariant factors specific to

Table 11.4 LHR/LGW/STN standard contours 2012 (dB bands)

dB	N	%
0	2061938	99.50
57	7937	0.38
60	1733	0.08
63	342	0.02
66	182	0.01
69	75	0
72	12	0
Total	2072219	100

the individual. ESM methods do not require the inclusion of sociodemographic controls for time-invariant factors such as education, health or income. The modelling design focuses the analysis on time-variant factors such as respondent activity and location in the moment. We are also able to provide controls for land cover (using the Generalised Land Use Database 2005), distance from the coast, region and day of the week (MacKerron and Mourato, 2013). Standard errors are clustered at the person level to account for non-independent repeat observations, and a robust standard error estimator is deployed to account for heteroscedasticity.

Among the advantages of the ESM is that it allows for more robust levels of causal inference than that involved in the standard OLS regression modelling commonly used for SWB analysis, because it provides people's actual location rather than household postcode. We include only surveys elicited from individuals located within aircraft noise contours at the time of the survey, rather than simply located near to an airport, to increase the causal link between noise and self-reported SWB, allowing us to make stronger inferences around the issue of cause and effect between aircraft noise and wellbeing.

We find a significant negative association between being located within an aircraft noise contour at the 66 dB level at the time of the survey and both happiness and relaxation (Table 11.5). The negative association between aircraft noise at the 66 dB level and happiness ($\beta = -6.344$ on a 0–100 scale) was high compared to the negative effects of an activity such as queuing ($\beta = -3.802$) or caring for adults ($\beta = -4.527$). The negative association between aircraft noise at the 66 dB level and relaxation ($\beta = -5.614$) was greater than the negative effects of travelling or commuting ($\beta = -4.087$). There was also an even higher negative association between happiness and noise at the highest (72 dB) level. However, we disregard this result due to the small sample of respondents within this noise contour ($n = 12$; see Table 11.4).

We note that noise levels of 66 dB and above are particularly high, with less than 1 per cent of flight contours in England reaching this level (95 per cent of aviation noise in the UK sits around the 55–60 dB range).[13] In addition, aircraft noise analysis was restricted to noise contours around three London airports, due to limitations in data available from other English airport operators.

11.4.3 Comparison of Modelling Approaches: Case Studies 1 and 2

Across the two case studies, we have shown that aviation noise is negatively associated with SWB as measured retrospectively and momentarily. The negative effects of aircraft noise are detected on all SWB measures in case study 1, including evaluative (life satisfaction), hedonic (happiness and anxiety) and eudemonic (sense of purpose) measures. In case study 2, we detect the effects of aircraft noise on momentary hedonic SWB (happiness and anxiety).

These results lead us to conclude that noise has an overall negative relationship with people's wellbeing, as experienced in the moment, but also in a cumulative way across their life. This makes sense when we consider the nature of aircraft noise as an environmental complaint. Although flight paths change, and the presence of aviation noise may be intermittent over the short term, long-term exposure to intermittent stressors becomes a regular and unwelcome part of an individual's life, leading to negative effects across the full set of SWB measures, both evaluative and hedonic, retrospective and momentary.

Table 11.5 Fixed effects regressions for Mappiness SWB responses within noise contours for three London airports controlling for background variables (all wellbeing variables measured on a scale of 0–100)

	Happiness		Relaxation	
	β	se	β	se
London Airport (LHR/LGW/STN) standard contours average mode 2012 (dB bands) = 57	1.342	1.206	0.176	1.292
London Airport (LHR/LGW/STN) standard contours average mode 2012 (dB bands) = 60	0.358	0.844	−1.285	1.182
London Airport (LHR/LGW/STN) standard contours average mode 2012 (dB bands) = 63	0.415	1.115	−0.389	1.241
London Airport (LHR/LGW/STN) standard contours average mode 2012 (dB bands) = 66	−6.344**	3.039	−5.614*	3.225
London Airport (LHR/LGW/STN) standard contours average mode 2012 (dB bands) = 69	0.899	2.22	−3.892	2.848
London Airport (LHR/LGW/STN) standard contours average mode 2012 (dB bands) = 72	−10.419*	5.356	−3.015	5.848
Place: Outdoors	3.060***	0.163	2.193***	0.154
Place: Vehicle	−0.007	0.153	−0.261	0.173
Place: Elsewhere	1.573***	0.104	0.308***	0.115
Place: Work	−2.720***	0.167	−4.933***	0.192
Activity: Admin, finances, organizing	−1.214***	0.159	−2.710***	0.167
Activity: Birdwatching, nature watching	4.408***	0.472	5.347***	0.531
Activity: Browsing the Internet	0.718***	0.108	1.496***	0.127
Activity: Care or help for adults	−4.527***	0.658	−5.225***	0.584
Activity: Childcare, playing with children	2.771***	0.179	0.746***	0.193
Activity: Computer games, iPhone games	2.763***	0.134	3.674***	0.141
Activity: Cooking, preparing food	2.187***	0.099	0.666***	0.112
Activity: Drinking alcohol	3.565***	0.127	4.031***	0.138
Activity: Drinking tea/coffee	1.233***	0.087	1.226***	0.099
Activity: Eating, snacking	1.984***	0.068	1.677***	0.071
Activity: Exhibition, museum, library	5.705***	0.377	4.262***	0.504
Activity: Gambling, betting	0.784	0.88	−1.215	0.946
Activity: Gardening, allotment	4.804***	0.364	2.828***	0.409
Activity: Hobbies, arts, crafts	5.196***	0.288	4.433***	0.302
Activity: Housework, chores, DIY	−0.770***	0.103	−3.457***	0.124
Activity: Hunting, fishing	3.066**	1.359	2.105	1.537
Activity: In a meeting, seminar, class	0.204	0.202	−1.307***	0.226
Activity: Intimacy, making love	12.877***	0.359	10.220***	0.354
Activity: Listening to music	3.387***	0.107	3.215***	0.116
Activity: Listening to speech/podcast	2.098***	0.162	2.559***	0.168
Activity: Match, sporting event	2.421***	0.323	−0.382	0.351
Activity: Meditating, religious activities	4.000***	0.544	5.274***	0.598
Activity: Other games, puzzles	2.416***	0.296	2.440***	0.301
Activity: Pet care, playing with pets	3.282***	0.203	2.391***	0.229
Activity: Reading	1.883***	0.115	3.859***	0.134
Activity: Shopping, errands	0.581***	0.121	−1.407***	0.137
Activity: Sick in bed	−19.571***	0.348	−14.363***	0.336
Activity: Singing, performing	5.861***	0.355	2.293***	0.583
Activity: Sleeping, resting, relaxing	0.846***	0.09	5.764***	0.122

Table 11.5 (continued)

	Happiness		Relaxation	
	β	se	β	se
Activity: Smoking	0.531**	0.235	0.06	0.267
Activity: Sports, running, exercise	6.709***	0.212	0.495*	0.3
Activity: Talking, chatting, socialising	4.176***	0.087	3.322***	0.084
Activity: Texting, email, social media	0.941***	0.112	0.785***	0.111
Activity: Theatre, dance, concert	5.684***	0.344	2.391***	0.429
Activity: Travelling, commuting	−1.909***	0.13	−4.087***	0.147
Activity: Waiting, queueing	−3.802***	0.159	−5.394***	0.191
Activity: Walking, hiking	2.687***	0.19	2.283***	0.224
Activity: Washing, dressing, grooming	1.962***	0.105	0.09	0.124
Activity: Watching TV, film	2.211***	0.074	3.915***	0.084
Activity: Working, studying	−1.656***	0.112	−4.229***	0.128
Activity: Something else (original version of Mappiness app)	−1.477***	0.211	−2.646***	0.215
Activity: Something else (version 2 of Mappiness app)	−3.409***	0.188	−4.410***	0.186
People ('who with'): Children	0.460***	0.156	−0.768***	0.164
People: Clients, customers	0.755	0.459	−0.391	0.457
People: Colleagues, classmates	−0.463***	0.173	−1.160***	0.199
People: Friends	4.212***	0.099	3.223***	0.111
People: Other family members	0.618***	0.107	0.175	0.109
People: Other people participant knows	−0.926***	0.229	−1.734***	0.227
People: Spouse, partner, girl/boyfriend	3.726***	0.122	2.408***	0.116
People: Between sunrise and sunset, based on time, date and GPS coords (0/1)	0.464***	0.09	0.354***	0.093
Geography: Proportion domestic gardens coverage	−0.226	0.51	0.781	0.568
Geography: Proportion of green space coverage	0.760**	0.337	1.532***	0.352
Geography: Proportion of water coverage	2.836*	1.483	4.242**	1.714
England Region: East Midlands	0.529	0.328	0.997**	0.388
England Region: East of England	0.955***	0.297	1.256***	0.37
England Region: North East	0.418	0.64	0.28	0.682
England Region: North West	0.652*	0.371	1.359***	0.385
England Region: South East	0.741***	0.229	1.113***	0.265
England Region: South West	1.235***	0.308	1.983***	0.426
England Region: West Midlands	0.843**	0.37	1.103***	0.396
England Region: Yorkshire and The Humber	0.501	0.338	1.244***	0.456
Constant	56.371***	0.808	55.662***	0.927
Observations	1 156 270		1 156 270	
r2	0.124		0.142	

Notes:
* $p < 0.05$; ** $p < 0.01$; *** $p < 0.001$. Fixed effects OLS models.
Reference groups: (1) for location variables ref. = inside; (2) for place ref. = home; (3) for region variables ref. = London. London airports consist of London Heathrow (LHR), London Gatwick (LGW), and Stansted (STN). Control variables for days of the week and national holidays are included (not shown). Sample is restricted to England and those aged 16 and over.

Exploiting the panel nature of the ESM data in case study 2 provides the strongest causal claims to date of the negative association between aviation noise and SWB, by linking actual location within aircraft noise contours to SWB at the time the individual is surveyed, and averaging SWB across multiple observations over time. This is one of the major methodological advantages of the ESM data applied to aircraft noise contours in case study 2, compared to the cross-sectional data in case study 1, which is a retrospective measure taken once a year at the household level.

The ESM method also allows us to control for individual-level fixed effects, which increases the strength of our causal inference. Nonetheless, it is possible that the extent of that impact may have been underestimated if the survey was taken on a day when no flights had occurred on the previous day, or were occurring over the respondent's house on the survey day itself. In such circumstances we would expect overall measures of life satisfaction (as measured in case study 1) to remain significantly affected by the presence of aircraft noise over a prolonged period, but for experiential measures to be lower than expected. In order to more closely examine causal relationships between noise exposure and wellbeing, future research may wish to examine differences in wellbeing immediately before and after change to flight paths or routes, in the form of a quasi-experimental design.

11.5 POLICY IMPLICATIONS AND CONCLUSIONS

The negative association between daytime aviation noise and SWB was significant across two UK case studies, for both retrospective (case study 1) and momentary SWB data (case study 2). However, they were low in magnitude compared to some of the well-known drivers of wellbeing such as unemployment, poor health and family breakdown (Dolan et al., 2008). This suggests that while noise negatively impacts upon an individual's quality of life, other conditions in their life continue to have the greatest effect on their wellbeing.

The results from case study 1 suggest that the marginal effect of aviation noise affects individuals' overall quality of life on a continuous level (Table 11.3). This is the first time that a marginal relationship has been identified between noise and SWB. More research is required on the acute, adaptive and long-term effects on health and wellbeing from exposure to aircraft noise (Morrell et al., 1997). This evidence could enable prediction of the average wellbeing effect associated with each additional decibel of aviation noise for each of the five SWB variables, and has considerable potential for modelling the wellbeing impacts that may arise from changes in aircraft noise, in terms of both its presence and its increase by orders of single decibels. The fact that we found significant marginal results for all five SWB variables increases the reliability of these results.

In terms of policy implications, traditional mitigation for aviation activities entails noise insulation to reduce the negative effect of high levels of aircraft noise (WHO, 2009). The analysis of confounding socio-economic factors in this study provides an important reference for potential mitigation measures. These findings suggest that the negative effects of aviation noise on quality of life and wellbeing can be compensated in other ways, by improving the provision of services that have been known to improve SWB to compensate for the noise. With reference to other significant variables in the Mappiness analysis (case study 2), these would include communication drives to promote a healthier lifestyle, programmes to reduce ambient pollution, and improvements in the quality of health provisioning services. Measures to reduce unemployment and underemployment in the local area should also be an important part of the mitigation plans accompanying airport expansion. Improvements to the local economy are one of the economic factors commonly presented in airport expansion options (Airports Commission, 2014). It is important to ensure that these opportunities are made available to those in the local community who are most likely to be affected by increases in air traffic and aviation noise.

In the future, researchers should seek to exploit more detailed noise contour data that could be made available publicly. There is considerable room to go further in causal analysis of the impacts of noise and SWB with innovation in the Mappiness analysis to exploit the real-time and geolinked nature of the data by inclusion of daily or hourly flight path information that could be temporally linked to the GPS of the Mappiness response. In addition, the Mappiness app may be exploited further to understand in more detail how noise affects people in their daily activities; in particular, whether the effect of noise is heterogenous with the kind of activity undertaken, and conversely, whether the wellbeing associated with different activities is depressed by the presence of noise. Improvements in this area would require the release of more detailed noise contour data by regulatory bodies and the airport operators.

We would like to expand our comparative analysis of confounding factors such as local-level data on green space, community health and social capital, controls for weather (partially captured in month controls), anthropogenic air pollution, and other sources of noise from rail and road, as controls against the negative impacts of aircraft noise. These omissions need to be recognized when using and extrapolating the results.

NOTES

1. Life satisfaction is recommended by the WHO Regional Office for Europe and the Organisation for Economic Co-operation and Development (OECD) as an international measure of SWB.
2. The search for a dose–response relationship also introduces certain assumptions; for instance, the use of fixed marginal values to simplify the difficulties associated with differing impacts due to variations in dispersion of noise. A single dose–response function may inadequately measure noise impacts arising from different sources (for example, modes of transport, industrial) as they disperse noise (and therefore impacts) differently (IGCB(N), 2010).
3. Fujiwara (2013) assessed the reported life satisfaction associated with housing quality variables in the British Household Panel Survey (BHPS), finding that of all the housing problems, neighbour noise has the largest negative association with life satisfaction. The authors suggest that neighbour noise may sit among the number of things that people do not generally adapt to because they are unpredictable negative events (e.g., Diener et al., 1999; Frederick and Loewenstein, 1999; Loewenstein and Ubel, 2008). Noise from neighbours may or may not be unpredictable, but in any case this research would explain why neighbour noise seems to be such a large detriment to wellbeing.
4. High: Major noise problem (≥67.5 dB); Medium: Moderate noise problem (57.5–67.4 dB); Low: No noise problem (≤57.4 dB).
5. http://t1.services.defra.gov.uk/wps/portal/noise/!ut/p/c5. OAs are groups of adjoining postcodes and are the lowest geographic level used in the presentation of census results, typically around 50–80 households.
6. BHX – Birmingham, LBA – Leeds Bradford, MAN – Manchester, BLK – Blackpool, LCY – London City, NCL – Newcastle, BOH – Bournemouth, LGW – London Gatwick, SEN – Southend, BRS – Bristol, LHR – London Heathrow, SOU – Southampton, EMA – East Midlands, LPL – Liverpool, STN – Stansted, ESH – Shoreham, LTN – Luton.
7. The source of this information is the Noise and Track Keeping (NTK) system, which stores radar data supplemented by daily flight plans. Traffic statistics from NTK data are cross-checked with runway logs supplied by National Air Traffic Services.

8. Dropping null and unknown responses and restricting the analysis to England provided an overall sample size of 189058 individuals for waves 2011–12 and 2012–13 of the APS. Thirteen per cent of the sample lived within 5 km of an airport. Among households living within daytime aircraft noise contours (n = 3545), average noise levels (L_{Aeq16h}) were 58.0 dB. Among those living within night-time noise contours (n = 1777), average noise levels (L_{night}) were 53.4 dB. Descriptions of the variables used in the APS can be found in the Appendix (Table 11A.1).
9. Note that the dB scale is logarithmic. Thus, an increase of 1 dB indicates an increase in sound pressure by about 1.26 times, a doubling of sound power corresponds to an increase of 3 dB, and so on.
10. Mappiness responses may be received from one individual on a number of occasions. There is on average approximately a 2:1 ratio of responses to individual respondents.
11. Frijters (2001) shows that the results of OLS (where SWB is assumed to be cardinal) and ordered response models (models where it is assumed that SWB is ordinal) provide very similar results. Tests have found no differences in reliability and concurrent validity between 7-, 11- and 101-point scales (Lewis and Oğuzhan, 2017), and the 101-point scale provides more variation in the outcome data, which not only solves the problems of information loss but also allows for applying advanced robust statistical analyses. This scale issue is pertinent in any kind of SWB measure, where we may ask how consistently a respondent distinguishes between 8 and 9. However, the evidence suggests that SWB questions are responsive theoretical expectations (Dolan and Fujiwara, 2016; Dolan and Peasgood, 2008). The benefit of the Mappiness tool is that it requires the respondent to answer on a sliding scale which is converted into the 0–100 scale. Interactive sliding scales have a long history in psychophysical measurement and have been found to be more accurate than standard Likert scales (Treiblmaier and Filzmoser, 2011).
12. There were some limitations in the noise data that was available from DfT. This meant we had to restrict noise analysis to London airports. By including region dummies in all models, we control for differences between London and non-London populations.
13. Based on Environmental Research and Consultancy Department (ERCD) 2006 L_{DEN} Noise Mapping.

REFERENCES

Airports Commission (2014), 'Airports Commission: appraisal framework', London, UK: Airports Commission.

Ariely, D. (2000), 'Controlling the information flow: effects on consumers' decision making and preferences', *Journal of Consumer Research*, **27** (2), 233–248.

Berry, B.F. and I. Flindell (2009), 'Estimating dose–response relationships between noise exposure and human health impacts in the UK', BEL report 2009-2, London, UK: Department for Transport.

Bjørner, T.B. (2004), 'Combining socio-acoustic and contingent valuation surveys to value noise reduction', *Transportation Research Part D: Transport and Environment*, **9** (5), 341–356.

Black, D.A., Black, J.A., Issarayangyun, T. and S.E. Samuels (2007), 'Aircraft noise exposure and resident's stress and hypertension: a public health perspective for airport environmental management', *Journal of Air Transport Management*, **13** (5), 264–276.

Braubach, M., Tobollik, M., Mudu, P., Hiscock, R., Chapizanis, D., et al. (2015), 'Development of a quantitative methodology to assess the impacts of urban transport interventions and related noise on well-being', *International Journal of Environmental Research and Public Health*, **12** (6), 5792–5814.

Cantril, H. (ed.) (1966), *The Pattern of Human Concerns*, New Brunswick, NJ, USA: Rutgers University Press.

Chapman, L. (2007), 'Transport and climate change: a review', *Journal of Transport Geography*, **15** (5), 354–367.

Clark, A.E. and A.J. Oswald (2002), 'A simple statistical method for measuring how life events affect happiness', *International Journal of Epidemiology*, **31** (6), 1139–1144.

Clark, C. and S.A. Stansfeld (2011), 'The effect of nocturnal aircraft noise on health: a review of recent evidence', London, UK: Report prepared for the London Borough of Hounslow.

Couper, M.P., Tourangeau, R., Conrad, F.G. and E. Singer (2006), 'Evaluating the effectiveness of visual analog scales: a web experiment', *Social Science Computer Review*, **24** (2), 227–245.

Csikszentmihalyi, M. and J. Hunter (2003), 'Happiness in everyday life: the uses of experience sampling', *Journal of Happiness Studies*, **4** (2), 185–199.

Defra (2014), 'Environmental noise: valuing impacts on: sleep disturbance, annoyance, hypertension, productivity and quiet', London, UK: Department for Environment, Food and Rural Affairs.

Diener, E., Suh, E.M., Lucas, R.E. and H.L. Smith (1999), 'Subjective well-being: three decades of progress', *Psychological Bulletin*, **125** (2), 276–302.

Dolan, P. and D. Fujiwara (2016), 'Happiness-based policy analysis', in Matthew D. Adler and Marc Fleurbaey (eds), *The Oxford Handbook of Well-Being and Public Policy*, Oxford, UK: Oxford University Press, pp. 286–317.

Dolan, P. and T. Peasgood (2008), 'Measuring well-being for public policy: preferences or experiences?', *Journal of Legal Studies*, **37** (S2), S5–S31.

Dolan, P., Fujiwara, D. and R. Metcalfe (2011), 'A step towards valuing utility the marginal and cardinal way', CEP Discussion Paper No. 1062.

Dolan, P., Peasgood, T. and M. White (2008), 'Do we really know what makes us happy? A review of the economic literature on the factors associated with subjective well-being', *Journal of Economic Psychology*, **29** (1), 94–122.

EuroControl (2013), 'Challenges of Growth 2013 summary report', Brussels, Belgium: European Organisation for the Safety of Air Navigation.

European Parliament (2002), 'Declaration by the Commission in the Conciliation Committee on the Directive relating to the assessment and management of environmental noise', *Official Journal of the European Communities*, **L189**, 12–26.

Ferrer-i-Carbonell, A. and P. Frijters (2004), 'How important is methodology for the estimates of the determinants of happiness?', *Economic Journal*, **114** (497), 641–659.

Franssen, E.A.M., van Wiechen, C.M.A.G., Nagelkerke, N.J.D. and E. Lebret (2004), 'Aircraft noise around a large international airport and its impact on general health and medication use', *Occupational and Environmental Medicine*, **61** (5), 405–413.

Frederick, S. and G. Loewenstein (1999), 'Hedonic adaptation', in Daniel Kahneman, Ed Diener and Norbert Schwarz (eds), *Well-Being: The Foundations of Hedonic Psychology*, New York, USA: Russell Sage Foundation, pp. 302–329.

Frey, B.S. and A. Stutzer (eds) (2010), *Happiness and Economics: How the Economy and Institutions Affect Human Well-Being*, Princeton, NJ, USA: Princeton University Press.

Frijters, P. (2001), 'Interpretation problems with changes in indices based on categorizations', *Economics Letters*, **72** (3), 375–379.

Fujiwara, D. (2013), 'The social impact of housing providers', London, UK: HACT, Legal & General, Plus Dane Group.

Fujiwara, D. and R. Campbell (2011), 'Valuation techniques for social cost–benefit analysis: stated preference, revealed preference and subjective well-being approaches. A discussion of the current issues', London, UK: HM Treasury and Department for Work and Pensions.

Fujiwara, D., Lawton, R.N. and G. MacKerron (2017), 'Experience sampling in and around airports: momentary subjective wellbeing, airports, and aviation noise in England', *Transportation Research Part D: Transport and Environment*, **56**, 43–54.

Haines, M.M., Stansfeld, S.A., Brentnall, S., Head, J., Berry, B., et al. (2001), 'The west London schools study: the effects of chronic aircraft noise exposure on child health', *Psychological Medicine*, **31** (8), 1385–1396.

Hardoy, M.C., Carta, M.G., Marci, A.R., Carbone, F., Cadeddu, M., et al. (2005), 'Exposure to aircraft noise and risk of psychiatric disorders: the Elmas survey', *Social Psychiatry and Psychiatric Epidemiology*, **40** (1), 24–26.

He, Q., Wollersheim, C., Locke, M. and I. Waitz (2014), 'Estimation of the global impacts of aviation-related noise using an income-based approach', *Transport Policy*, **34**, 85–101.

Hektner, J.M., J.A. Schmidt and M. Csikszentmihalyi (eds) (2007), *Experience Sampling Method: Measuring the Quality of Everyday Life*, Thousand Oaks, CA, USA: SAGE.

Helliwell, J.F., Layard, R. and J. Sachs (2013), 'World Happiness Report', New York, USA: UN Sustainable Development Solutions Network.

Howarth, D. and S. Griggs (eds) (2013), *The Politics of Airport Expansion in the United Kingdom: Hegemony, Policy and the Rhetoric of 'Sustainable Aviation'*, Manchester, UK: Manchester University Press.

IGCB(N) (2010), 'Noise and health – valuing the human health impacts of environmental noise exposure', London, UK: Interdepartmental Group on Costs and Benefits Noise Subject Group.

Kahneman, D. and A. Tversky (1984), 'Choices, values, and frames', *American Psychologist*, **39** (4), 341–350.

Kahneman, D., Diener, E. and N. Schwarz (eds) (2003), *Well-Being: Foundations of Hedonic Psychology*, New York, USA: Russell Sage Foundation.

Kahneman, D., Krueger, A.B., Schkade, D.A., Schwarz, N. and A.A. Stone (2004), 'A survey method for characterizing daily life experience: the day reconstruction method', *Science*, **306** (5702), 1776–1780.

Kroesen, M., Molin, E.J.E., Miedema, H.M.E., Vos, H., Janssen, S.A. and B. van Wee (2010), 'Estimation of the effects of aircraft noise on residential satisfaction', *Transportation Research Part D: Transport and Environment*, **15** (3), 144–153.

Lawton, R.N. and D. Fujiwara (2016), 'Living with aircraft noise: airport proximity, aviation noise and subjective wellbeing in England', *Transportation Research Part D: Transport and Environment*, **42**, 104–118.

Lercher, P. and W.W. Kofler (1996), 'Behavioral and health responses associated with road traffic noise exposure along alpine through-traffic routes', *Science of the Total Environment*, **189–190**, 85–89.

Lewis, J.R. and E. Oğuzhan (2017), 'User experience rating scales with 7, 11, or 101 points: does it matter?', *Journal of Usability Studies*, **12** (2), 73–91.

Loewenstein, G. and P.A. Ubel (2008), 'Hedonic adaptation and the role of decision and experience utility in public policy', *Journal of Public Economics*, **92** (8–9), 1795–1810.
MacKerron, G. and S. Mourato (2013), 'Happiness is greater in natural environments', *Global Environmental Change*, **23** (5), 992–1000.
Morrell, S., Taylor, R. and D. Lyle (1997), 'A review of health effects of aircraft noise', *Australian and New Zealand Journal of Public Health*, **21** (2), 221–236.
Navrud, S. (2002), 'The state-of-the-art on economic valuation of noise (final report to European Commission DG Environment)', Department of Economics and Social Sciences Agricultural University of Norway.
Nelson, J.P. (2008), 'Hedonic property value studies of transportation noise: aircraft and road traffic', in Andrea Baranzini, José Ramirez, Caroline Schaerer and Philippe Thalmann (eds), *Hedonic Methods in Housing Markets*, New York, USA: Springer, pp. 57–82.
O'Donnell, G., Deaton, A., Durand, M., Halpern, D. and R. Layard (2014), 'Wellbeing and policy', London, UK: Legatum Institute.
Organisation for Economic Co-operation and Development (OECD) (2013), *Guidelines on Measuring Subjective Well-Being*, Paris, France: OECD.
Oswald, A.J. and N. Powdthavee (2008), 'Does happiness adapt? A longitudinal study of disability with implications for economists and judges', *Journal of Public Economics*, **92** (5–6), 1061–1077.
Pavot, W. and E. Diener (1993), 'The affective and cognitive context of self-reported measures of subjective well-being', *Social Indicators Research*, **28** (1), 1–20.
Pedersen, E. and K.P. Waye (2007), 'Wind turbine noise, annoyance and self-reported health and well-being in different living environments', *Occupational and Environmental Medicine*, **64** (7), 480–486.
Rehdanz, K. and D. Maddison (2008), 'Local environmental quality and life-satisfaction in Germany', *Ecological Economics*, **64** (4), 787–797.
Riedel, N., Scheiner, J., Müller, G. and H. Köckler (2014), 'Assessing the relationship between objective and subjective indicators of residential exposure to road traffic noise in the context of environmental justice', *Journal of Environmental Planning and Management*, **57** (9), 1398–1421.
Schwarz, N. and G.L. Clore (1983), 'Mood, misattribution, and judgments of well-being: informative and directive functions of affective states', *Journal of Personality and Social Psychology*, **45** (3), 513–523.
Sheskin, D.J. (ed.) (2011), *Handbook of Parametric and Nonparametric Statistical Procedures, Fifth Edition*, Boca Raton, FL: Chapman & Hall/CRC.
Stansfeld, S.A., Sharp, D.S., Gallacher, J. and W. Babisch (1993), 'Road traffic noise, noise sensitivity and psychological disorder', *Psychological Medicine*, **23** (4), 977–985.
Treiblmaier, H. and P. Filzmoser (2011), 'Benefits from using continuous rating scales in online survey research', presented at the ICIS 2011 Proceedings.
Van Praag, B.M.S. and B.E. Baarsma (2005), 'Using happiness surveys to value intangibles: the case of airport noise', *Economic Journal*, **115** (500), 224–246.
Wadud, Z. (2009), 'Depreciation of property prices around airports: meta-regression of hedonic price studies', paper presented at the Transportation Research Board 88th Annual Meeting, Washington, DC.
Welsch, H. (2006), 'Environment and happiness: valuation of air pollution using life satisfaction data', *Ecological Economics*, **58** (4), 801–813.
Wolfe, P.J., Yim, S.H.L., Lee, G., Ashok, A., Barrett, S.R.H. and I.A. Waitz (2014), 'Near-airport distribution of the environmental costs of aviation', *Transport Policy*, **34**, 102–108.
World Health Organization (WHO) (2009), 'Night noise guidelines for Europe', Copenhagen, Denmark: World Health Organization.
World Health Organization (WHO) (2011), 'Burden of disease from environmental noise: quantification of healthy life years lost in Europe', Geneva, Switzerland: World Health Organization.
Yim, S.H.L., Stettler, M.E.J. and S.R.H. Barrett (2013), 'Air quality and public health impacts of UK airports. Part II: Impacts and policy assessment', *Atmospheric Environment*, **67**, 184–192.

APPENDIX 11A.1

Table 11A.1 Variable descriptions

Variable	Description
Gender	1 = female; 0 = male (reference)
Age	Age of respondent as continuous variable
Age Squared	Non-linear function of age
BME	Black or minority ethnic
Religion	Yes 1 = Religious; 0 = no religion (reference)
Single	Marital status: 1 = Single; 0 = Married (reference)
Separated	Marital status: 1 = Separated; 0 = Married (reference)
Divorced	Marital status: 1 = Divorced; 0 = Married (reference)
Widowed	Marital status: 1 = Widowed; 0 = Married (reference)
Civil Partner	Marital status: 1 = Civil partner; 0 = Married (reference)
One child	Number of children: 1 = One child; 0 = No children (reference)
Two children	Number of children: 1 = Two children; 0 = No children (reference)
Three children	Number of children: 1 = Three children; 0 = No children (reference)
Four or more children	Number of children: 1 = Four or more children; 0 = No children (reference)
Limiting Health	1 = Individual reports health to be limiting on their day to day life; 0 = No limiting health conditions (reference)
Smoker – Ex Smoking	1 = Ex-smoker; 0 = No smoking (reference)
Smoker – Yes Smoking	1 = Current smoker; 0 = No smoking (reference)
Own House	Accommodation status: 1 = Owns house; 0 = Mortgage (reference)
Rent Private	Accommodation status: 1 = Private renter; 0 = Mortgage (reference)
Rent Social	Accommodation status: 1 = Social housing; 0 = Mortgage (reference)
No rent/squatters	Accommodation status: 1 = Not paying rent/ squatting; 0 = Mortgage (reference)
Higher Ed	1 = Higher education; 0 = Degree (reference)
A level	1 = A-level; 0 = Degree (reference)
GCSE	1 = GCSE; 0 = Degree (reference)
Ed Other	1 = Other educational training; 0 = Degree (reference)
Ed_None Education	Ed_None Education: 1 = No education; 0 = Degree (reference)
Learn – Yes	1 = Further learning; 0 = Degree (reference)

Table 11A.1 (continued)

Variable	Description
Inactive seeking work	1 = Inactive seeking work; 0 = Full-time employed (reference)
Inactive – not seeking but wants work	1 = Inactive not seeking work but wants work; 0 = Full-time employed (reference)
Inactive – not seeking not want work	1 = Inactive not seeking work doesn't want work; 0 = Full-time employed (reference)
Inactive – retired Employment	1 = Retired; 0 = Full-time employed (reference)
Unemployed	1 = Unemployed; 0 = Full-time employed (reference)
Student	1 = Student; 0 = Full-time employed (reference)
Unpaid FamilyWorker	1 = Unpaid family worker; 0 = Full-time employed (reference)
Underemployed	1 = Underemployed; 0 = Full-time employed (reference)
Part-Time Employment	1 = Part-time; 0 = Full-time employed (reference)
Full Time Self-Employed	1 = Full-Time Self-Employed; 0 = Full-time employed (reference)
Full Time 2nd pay quintile	1 = 2nd pay quintile; 0 = 1st pay quintile (reference)
Full Time 3rd pay quintile	1 = 3rd pay quintile; 0 = 1st pay quintile (reference)
Full Time 4th pay quintile	1 = 4th pay quintile; 0 = 1st pay quintile (reference)
Full Time highest pay quintile	1 = Highest pay quintile; 0 = 1st pay quintile (reference)
Face-to-Face Survey Survey method	1 = Face-to-face survey; 0 = Telephone survey (reference)
MaxDaytime noise MaxLq16 giving maximum strategic aviation noise map level (LAeq16h) at a residential dwelling for the Census Output Code (OA)	1 = Presence of maximum daytime noise; 0 = Absence of maximum daytime noise (reference)
MaxLnight giving 50dB(A), Lnight noise contours (11pm to 7am,dB Lnight) for maximum annual strategic aviation noise map levels (Lnight)	1 = Presence of max night time noise; 0 = Absence of max night time noise (reference)
MeanDaytime noise MeanLq16 giving mean strategic aviation noise map level data (LAeq16h)	1 = Presence of mean daytime noise; 0 = Absence of mean daytime noise (reference)
Mean night time noise MeanLnight giving 50dB(A), Lnight noise contours (11pm to 7am,dB Lnight) for and mean strategic aviation noise map level (Lnight)	1 = Presence of mean night time noise; 0 = Absence of mean night time noise (reference)
Airprox Airport Proximity is defined as the airport reference point (ARP), the centre point of an airport, located at the geometric centre of all the usable runways	1 = Within a distance < 5 km from the centre point of an airport; $0 \geq 5$ km from the centre point of an airport (reference)
Continuous Daytime Noise	Linear continuous maximum daytime noise variable
Continuous Night time Noise	Linear continuous maximum night time noise variable

12. Measuring the wellbeing and health impacts of sewage odour*

Daniel Fujiwara, Iulian Gramatki and Kieran Keohane

12.1 INTRODUCTION

The water industry is required to undertake a number of public maintenance works such as sewage treatment works (STWs), water treatment works, pipe installation and repairs, and drainage works. There is a certain degree of disutility caused by these maintenance works. For example, an STW can emit foul odour, noise, encourage insects or represent a visual disamenity to the neighbouring residents. Disutility from such services is an important input in designing maintenance and incident prevention policies, pricing in the water industry and regulation of water provision. While the cost of these public works is easier to measure, the respective benefits are more difficult to ascertain, as they are non-monetary. In the absence of a market for goods (or bads) such as odour, another way to assess the disutility they generate is through their impact on people's wellbeing.

This chapter gives a brief introduction to the studies on wellbeing and the water industry to date, and complements it with original analysis on the association between subjective wellbeing (SWB) and proximity to STWs. It combines two nationally representative United Kingdom (UK) datasets with data from a large UK water provider using distance calculation algorithms. Life satisfaction is used as the main indicator of subjective wellbeing, because it is an evaluative measure of overall quality of life rather than a momentary experience, and because it has been proven to have a strong degree of retest reliability (Krueger and Schkade, 2008). The findings suggest a negative correlation between proximity to STWs and SWB, which increases in magnitude for STWs with severe odour problems. This supports the recent stated preference research in the UK, which finds that people living close to an STW would be willing to forgo part of their income in exchange for reductions in odour levels. Since the previous literature on odour and STWs has focused on health, we also analyse the health impacts of living within the vicinity of STWs, and confirm that our data supports the general findings in the literature to date.

12.2 LITERATURE REVIEW

Previous academic work assessing the impact of water incidents on wellbeing did not use incident data from water companies and regulatory bodies. Notable work to date includes the assessment of the impacts on life satisfaction of droughts in Australia using the HILDA dataset (Carroll et al., 2009), and of flood disasters in Europe (Luechinger and Raschky, 2009; Sekulova and van den Bergh, 2016). These studies have also introduced an early example of the wellbeing valuation method (also known as the subjective wellbeing regression or the life satisfaction approach), where a monetary value is obtained by comparing the regression coefficients of the negative incident on life satisfaction to the corresponding coefficient on income.

However, no study to date has considered the impact of sewage odour on wellbeing. There is a long history of research in the academic literature on STWs and problems of odour control (Cohn, 1929; Dague, 1972). Whilst there is some literature on the impact of odour emanating from STWs on neighbouring residents, we are unaware of any evidence or research on STWs and local residents' SWB.

There are, however, a number of studies that would indirectly suggest that odour from STWs would be associated with lower levels of wellbeing for local residents. Firstly, within the valuation literature, Batalhone et al. (2002) apply the hedonic pricing method, a revealed preference valuation method, to the issue of strong smells associated with a specific STW in Brasilia and find that apartment prices increase by 1.7–6.5 per cent for a 1 per cent increase in distance to a STW. Secondly, Vantarakis et al. (2016) find a negative association between health (both physical and mental) and proximity to municipal wastewater treatment plants in Greece. Thirdly, in the agricultural science literature, meta-analyses by Nimmermark (2004) and Schiffman (1998) have investigated animal production and the impact of livestock odours on the health and wellbeing of neighbouring communities, finding evidence of impact of odour on mood, stress and perceived health. However, they acknowledge that this evidence is suggestive, with further scientific research being required to assess the causal impact of odours for establishing recommendations for official air quality guidelines (Schiffman, 1998). Von Möllendorff and Welsch (2017) show that living close to biomass plants for power generation is associated with less SWB and argue that this is at least partly related to odour.

There is an established epidemiological literature on the occupational hazards that sewage treatment workers face when working at STWs. Previous studies have highlighted that STW employees have a higher incidence of headache, tiredness and nausea (Melbostad et al., 1994). Inhalation of STW aerosols has also been shown through blood tests to be linked to viral-originated intestinal complications (Melbostad et al., 1994; Thorn et al., 2002). Moreover, a national survey of municipalities in Sweden found an increased risk of disease for sewage workers (Thorn et al., 2002). There is, therefore, a substantial amount of literature on the negative health effects of exposure to odour from STWs for both workers and local residents, and thus, since health is a key driver of wellbeing, we hypothesize there to be a negative impact of odour from STWs on the SWB of local residents as well.

While odour has not been tested explicitly in the SWB field, a number of papers have more generally investigated the link between air quality and wellbeing, and this would suggest that it would be possible to pick up the impacts of odour on SWB through similar methods. For example, Zhang et al. (2015) find that poor air visibility reduces happiness and assign a monetary value to it by using the life satisfaction approach (wellbeing valuation). Zhang et al. (2017) use the same method to value reductions in PM2.5 (particulate matter with a diameter smaller than 2.5 micrometers), a major source of pollution in China. Luechinger (2009) uses life satisfaction data in the wellbeing valuation (WV) approach to value air quality, looking specifically at sulphur dioxide concentration due to power plant emissions, and finds a negative effect of sulphur dioxide pollution on SWB using a difference-in-difference study design. The implicit willingness to pay (WTP) for a reduction in sulphur dioxide concentration was significantly larger than the analogous WTP derived through revealed preferences using house price data. Finally, a recent study by Knight and Howley (2017) using UK data revealed a negative association between life satisfaction and nitrogen dioxide (NO_2) concentration.

This study is a first application of the life satisfaction approach to sewage odour. The method has been previously used to measure other negative externalities of public good provisions, such as airport noise (see, for example, the update of Fujiwara and Lawton, 2016, as presented in Chapter 11 of this *Handbook*). This chapter combines the life satisfaction approach with geolinking analysis partly inspired by the method in Lawton and Fujiwara (2016), who also derive respondents' proximity to the source of disturbance; airport noise in their case. It makes use of three data sources, which include two nationally representative UK general household surveys and a dataset containing the location and capacity of sewage treatment works. The household data and the STWs data are merged together via a distance calculation algorithm which finds the nearest STW for each respondent. We then proceed to investigate the impact on SWB and self-assessed general health of proximity to STWs, as well as the extent to which these impacts vary with the level of odour emissions.

The remainder of this chapter is structured as follows. Section 12.3 presents the data and section 12.4 elaborates on the methodology and the underlying model. Section 12.5 sets out the main findings, with interpretation and concluding comments in section 12.6.

12.3 DATA

We use two nationally representative UK datasets. First, the Annual Population Survey (APS) (four waves, April 2011 to March 2015) is the source of our main results. It is a continuous household survey, covering the UK. The topics include employment, as well as housing, ethnicity, religion, health and education. The pooled four waves of the APS contain about 660 000 observations with subjective wellbeing responses, of which 370 000 have responses to each question used to create the variables included in the baseline regression. We use the secure access version of the APS, which provides the postcode of each respondent.

Second, Understanding Society (USoc) (six waves, 2009–15) is a large longitudinal study of households in the UK. It is a panel dataset that surveys over 70 000 individuals each year on all aspects of their lives. It is representative of England, Scotland, Wales and Northern Ireland. Understanding Society is the largest panel (longitudinal) dataset of households and individuals in the UK. The pooled six waves of USoc contain about 300 000 observations, of which 138 000 can be included in the baseline regression. We use the special licence of the USoc data (usage number 107 826), which provides geographical data at the lower level super output area (LSOA) of its respondents. The LSOA is a statistical subdivision in England and Wales comprising 2000 people on average, whereas a postcode normally contains 100–150 people. Thus the higher precision of the geographical data in the APS than in USoc makes the former more reliable, with the latter serving mainly to check the external validity of the APS findings.

We merge national population-level data provided in the APS and USoc with independently compiled data on the location and operations of STWs collected from several sources (a list of STWs operated by Thames Water, a large UK water company; the 2013–15 pollution inventory; 2005–14 carbon dioxide emissions data and other government environment data). A map of the approximate geographical location of the STWs analysed is provided in Figure 12.1. We calculated the Euclidean distance from each respondent's home postcode or LSOA to the nearest STW (the main treatment variable used in subsequent analysis), based on the geographical information available in the nationally representative surveys: postcodes in the APS and LSOAs in USoc.

12.4 METHODOLOGY

We apply ordinary least squares (OLS) regression based on the following models (for simplicity we drop time notations here, since the APS is cross-sectional):

$$LS_i = \alpha + \gamma_1 STW_i + \boldsymbol{X}_i\boldsymbol{\beta} + \varepsilon_i,\ if\ STW_i < 20km \tag{12.1}$$

$$LS_i = \alpha + \beta_1 STW_i + \beta_2 P_i + \beta_3(P_i \cdot STW_i) + \boldsymbol{X}_i\boldsymbol{\beta} + \varepsilon_i,\ if\ STW_i < 20km \tag{12.2}$$

$$LS_i = \alpha + \delta P_i + \boldsymbol{X}_i\boldsymbol{\beta} + \varepsilon_i,\ if\ STW_i < 1.5km \tag{12.3}$$

where LS_i is the life satisfaction of individual i as obtained from the APS (on a 0–10 scale) or USoc (on a 1–7 scale); STW_i is the Euclidean distance from the respondent's postcode (in the APS) or LSOA (in USoc) to the nearest STW; $\boldsymbol{X}_i$ is a vector of control variables listed further below and enumerated in full in Appendix 12A.1; and P_i is a dummy variable indicating whether the nearest STW has been categorized as a priority STW because of significant odour issues. P_i is based on data on odour frequency, quantity and severity, collected by the water company and transformed into a measure of equivalent odour, comparable across STWs. The top 60 STWs in terms of equivalent odour were designated as priority STWs.

In models (12.1) and (12.2), we remove all those respondents from our analysis that are farther than 20 km away from the nearest STW. This is because those people have a high likelihood of being close to another STW which was not in our data, as we had only a partial register of STWs in England (see Figure 12.1). Furthermore, whilst we control for a wide range of the main determinants of SWB in our models, this approach of narrowing down the sample geographically will provide additional help in ensuring that the people we compare (those who live close to STWs and those who live farther away) are broadly similar, such that we can get a better estimate of the impact of odour on SWB. Finally, there is a limit for STW odour spread, and any wellbeing correlation beyond a certain distance threshold will be spurious.

Model (12.1) captures the overall negative wellbeing correlation of sewage treatment works without discrimination between odour and other sources of disamenity in the coefficient γ_1. For the health analysis, we run a modified version of model (12.1), where we replace the dependent variable with GH_i, the respondent's self-reported general health on a 1–5 scale (very bad, bad, fair, good, very good):

$$GH_i = \alpha + \gamma_2 STW_i + \boldsymbol{X}_i\boldsymbol{\beta} + \varepsilon_i,\ if\ STW_i < 20km \tag{12.4}$$

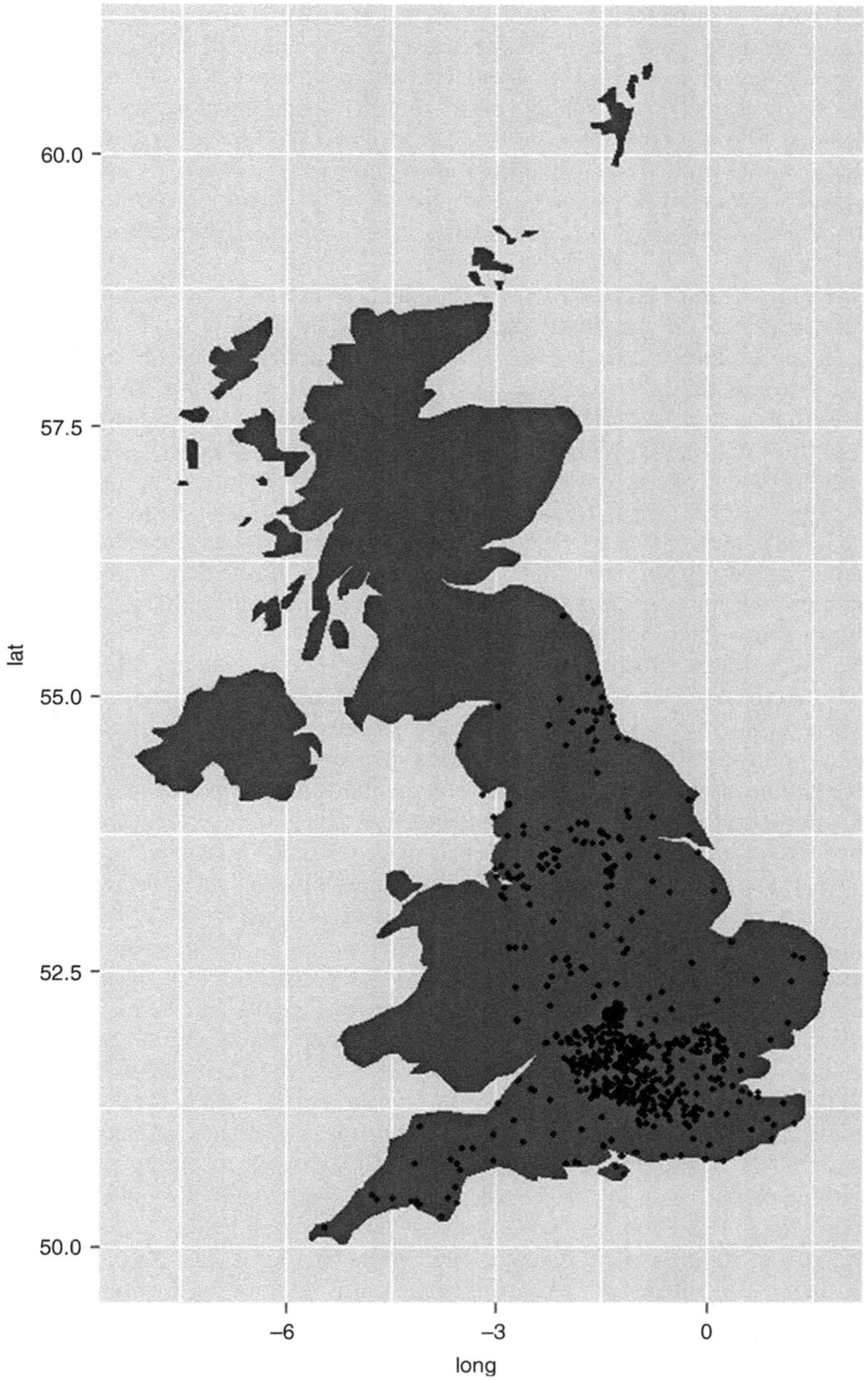

Figure 12.1 *Approximate location of STWs under investigation*

The purpose of model (12.2) is both to assess the overall negative wellbeing correlation of living close to a STW per se (via the coefficient β_1) and to single out the negative correlation associated with STW odour (via the coefficient β_3). The coefficient β_3 of the interactive term $(P_i \cdot STW_i)$ represents the extra correlation between wellbeing and distance that priority STWs have over non-priority STWs. Given that other factors such as noise or visual disamenity are much less likely to vary between high odour and non-high odour STWs, and other main determinants of wellbeing have been controlled for, we attribute this wellbeing association (with caveats in mind) to a detrimental effect of sewage odour.

At the same time, β_2 represents the wellbeing association of moving from a standard STW to a priority STW, provided that the distance to the STW is 0 (the actual association for any given distance will be $\beta_2 + \beta_3 * distance$). To simplify and more clearly capture the contrast between standard and priority STWs in terms of wellbeing, we use model (12.3) as an alternative approach. Restricting the sample to those who are already close to a STW (within 1.5 km), we obtain in the coefficient δ the wellbeing association with having a priority STW nearby as opposed to a non-priority STW, averaged for distances between 0 and 1.5 km. A threshold of 1.5 km from the nearest STW is where bad odour, if present, is much more likely to reach the respondent's perception and thus affect their welfare. This is based on a study by Shafibeik and Lyon (2012) around Cambridge STW, which showed that all areas within a 665 m radius are within a 5 odour unit[1] contour, whereas the 1.5 odour unit contour has a radius above 1 km.

The STW_i variable, which measures proximity of the household to an STW, is calculated as follows. In the APS, we are able to measure the distance from the respondent's postcode to the nearest STW. The postcode is matched to geographical coordinates – easting and northing – via the Office of National Statistics Postcode Directory (ONSPD). Euclidean distance 'as the crow flies' is assumed to be the main factor driving exposure to sewage odour, since it travels by air. The respondents' postcodes were made available via secure access to the Secure Research Service (SRS) of the Office of National Statistics (ONS).

For the USoc data, respondents' locations were only available in terms of the lower level super output area (LSOA), obtained via special licence from the UK Data Service (UKDS). We first calculate the distance to the nearest STW for each postcode in an LSOA, and then estimate the average distance to the nearest STW for all the postcodes in each LSOA. This introduces measurement error, because for some households the discrepancy between the actual distance and LSOA average distance to the nearest STW can be large. In an attempt to reduce measurement error, we also exclude LSOAs in which the standard deviation of the average distance is larger than 500 m when using USoc.

In the vector X_i we control for a wide range of factors which are known to be associated with SWB. These are based on the control variables recommended in Fujiwara and Campbell (2011). They have been obtained from the USoc and APS datasets, which provide information on a wide range of indicators and variables related to survey respondents, including health, demographic characteristics, and socio-economic factors such as income/earnings, age, gender, marital status, ethnicity, education, employment status, religious affiliation, home ownership type and number of children. An alternative specification controls for location in the form of local authority dummies. In USoc we are also able to run a fixed effects model for comparison. Note that controlling for health in the SWB regressions (APS only) implies that the models capture the impact of STWs on wellbeing over and above any health impacts. Health is excluded as a control in the model where it is a dependent variable.

12.4.1 Caveats

We recognize that there are a number of other variables that determine odour dispersion and severity, such as wind and humidity, in addition to proximity to an STW. Strong variation in these other factors may cause external validity problems and make the findings less generalizable. It is possible that the extent of the impact may have been underestimated if the survey was taken on a day when the wind was blowing the sewage odour away from the respondent's house. These environmental variables vary seasonally and by location, and we can partially account for this variation by controlling for location and time of interview. Note that we would expect overall measures of life satisfaction to be less sensitive to such circumstances than experiential measures (happiness and anxiety), but momentary experiences are known to also affect evaluative measures nonetheless.

Secondly, STW odour is not linearly dependent on distance to the STW. In particular, there is a threshold beyond which odour is not perceived at all. This non-linearity can also bias the regression coefficients. We have tried several alternative models to account for this non-linearity:

- a binary proximity variable equal to 1 if the respondent is within 1.5 km of a STW and 0 otherwise;
- a stepwise model of odour dispersion by using a categorical distance variable with thresholds set at various ranges such as < 1 km; 1–2 km; 2–3 km and 3 km+ from the nearest STW;
- a model with a squared distance term.

However, none of the models above yielded statistically significant results, and hence they are not reported here. Finally, measurement error due to the imprecision of the geographical location of respondents can lead to attenuation bias in coefficient estimates for STW proximity, especially since the relative error is higher for lower distances.

12.5 RESULTS

Tables 12.1 and 12.2 show the coefficients of interest for models (12.1), (12.2) and (12.3) in the APS and for model (12.1) in the USoc dataset, respectively (full regression results for selected models are reported in Appendix 12A.2).

From the results of model (12.1) we can see that living farther away from the nearest STW is associated with higher levels of life satisfaction, with an increase of about 0.0029–0.0037 for each extra kilometre of distance. The coefficient is positive since a greater distance to the nearest STW means less exposure to the negative externalities of sewage processing. Although quite small in magnitude, it is statistically significant. The results from the APS are supported by the analysis run on the USoc data as well.

The model in (12.1) may capture many possible externalities associated with living next to an STW, including noise, odour, insect prevalence, visual disamenity and overall

Table 12.1 Coefficients of STW proximity and odour on life satisfaction in a subjective wellbeing OLS regression using the APS dataset

	(1a)	(1b)	(2)	(3)
Distance to STW	0.0037	0.0029	0.0021	
(in km)	(5.49)***	(3.26)**	(1.52)	
High odour STW			−0.0457	−0.0851
			(2.45)**	(2.17)***
Distance (km) *			0.0064	
High odour STW			(2.37)**	
Constant	8.886	8.826	8.737	9.063
	(213.36)***	(84.12)***	(109.94)***	(34.21)***
Controls	YES	YES	YES	YES
Location Controls	NO	YES	NO	NO
N	369 333	369 177	98 661	8186

Notes: * $p < 0.1$, ** $p < 0.05$, *** $p < 0.01$. t-statistics in parentheses.

Table 12.2 Coefficients of STW proximity and odour on life satisfaction in a subjective wellbeing OLS regression using the Understanding Society (USoc) dataset

	(1a)	(1b)	(1c)
Distance to STW	0.0031	0.0035	0.0083
(in km)	(1.97)**	(1.39)	(1.04)
Constant	6.593	6.775	3.427
	(84.12)***	(44.20)***	(5.52)***
Controls	yes	yes	yes
Location controls	no	yes	no
Fixed effects	no	no	yes
R^2	0.098	0.105	0.013
N	143 861	143 861	143 861

Notes: * $p < 0.1$, ** $p < 0.05$, *** $p < 0.01$. t-statistics in parentheses. USoc coefficients have been rescaled from a 1–7 to a 0–10 life satisfaction scale via linear transformation for comparability with the APS results.

neighbourhood quality. However, model (12.2) is used to set aside the wellbeing correlation of odour. Thus, the wellbeing correlation for non-priority STWs (that is, those with lower objective odour levels) is +0.0021 life satisfaction per km and not statistically significant at the 10 per cent level, whereas for those with higher odour levels it is around four times as much, 0.0021 + 0.0064 = +0.0085 life satisfaction per kilometre. Furthermore, those who live very close to a high odour STW have 0.0457 lower life satisfaction on average compared to those who live very close to a regular STW (the actual marginal effect of high odour is −0.0457 + 0.0064 * distance in kilometres). This is around the same magnitude as the marginal effects of being an ex-smoker as opposed to someone who never smoked, having one child as opposed to two, or living in a small town as opposed to a large city.

Table 12.3 Coefficients of STW proximity and odour on general health in an OLS regression

	APS – all STWs	APS – high odour STWs	USoc – all STWs	USoc – high odour STWs	USoc – all STWs	USoc – high odour STWs
Distance to STW (km)	0.0011 (3.49)***	0.0010 (1.87)*	−0.0001 (−0.16)	0.0030 (3.19)***	0.0059 (2.29)**	0.0080 (1.84)*
Constant	5.047 (273.3)***	4.972 (134.4)***	3.504 (98.5)***	3.504 (53.7)***	2.087 (4.91)***	2.471 (3.81)***
Controls	yes	yes	yes	yes	yes	yes
Fixed eff.	no	no	no	no	yes	yes
R^2			0.229	0.219	0.009	0.011
N	369 721	87 000	163 580	47 977	163 580	47 977

Notes: * $p < 0.1$, ** $p < 0.05$, *** $p < 0.01$. t-statistics in parentheses. Dependent variable is self-reported general health on a 1–5 scale in both datasets.

In model (12.3) we find that respondents within 1.5 km of a high odour STW have on average 0.085 units less life satisfaction than those living within 1.5 km of non-high odour STWs. The wellbeing association with high odour STWs as opposed to standard STWs became higher when we reduced the cut-off threshold for our sample from 20 km to the nearest STW to 1.5 km, which is supporting evidence for negative odour effects, because odour is more strongly perceived as one moves closer to its emanating source.

The data also confirms that the negative subjective correlation of proximity to an STW with wellbeing is accompanied by a negative correlation with health (see Table 12.3). Since health is a key driver of wellbeing, the health analysis is a valuable robustness check on our well-being results. Again, the positive coefficients tell us that living farther away from a sewage works is associated with being slightly healthier, everything else held equal. While the coefficients are quite small, they are statistically significant. In the Understanding Society dataset, we can only detect an impact for those STWs that were flagged for high odour emissions, whereas in the APS there does not seem to be a difference between the impact of these particular STWs and that of all STWs in the sample.

12.6 INTERPRETATION AND CONCLUSIONS

This study has demonstrated how wellbeing analysis via the life satisfaction approach can be used to generate insights on water-related issues and problems. It provides a strong case that other water-related problems such as flooding, water supply disruptions, water quality issues, roadworks and maintenance, on-site injuries and accidents, and other health and safety issues at STWs could be assessed and valued using the same approach.

The main results of this study can be summarized in three points. Firstly, based on the consistent correlation between proximity to STWs and SWB across two nationally representative datasets, it is highly likely that there is a negative wellbeing impact of living close to water-related public works, such as sewage treatment works. Secondly, the negative wellbeing impact of STW appears to be driven by foul odour emissions, as STWs with high odour levels have a four times stronger wellbeing correlation than STWs with objectively lower odour levels. Thirdly, given the negative association between proximity to STWs and self-reported general health, after controlling for other health determinants, a negative health impact of STWs on neighbouring respondents is also likely.

These findings, however, are subject to a series of limitations, which we need to be aware of both for adequate interpretation and when probing opportunities for future research. For the impact of distance to STWs, we use multivariate regression analysis. Although we control for all the main determinants of SWB (for example, income, employment and education levels) in our models, in line with best practice academic research in this area, we can never ensure that the exogeneity assumption holds. There may be some factors related to where a person decides to live that we were unable to control for, such as personality traits. To the extent that these are time-invariant, they are accounted for in the fixed effects model using the Understanding Society data. However, time-varying unobservables such as motivation may still cause bias even in a fixed effects setting. In general, it is very difficult to infer causality in non-experimental settings using observational data.

If there is an unobserved selection issue related to STWs – that is, if certain types of people are more likely to live near STWs – then we hypothesize that these types of people will have lower levels of wellbeing to begin with, because they may come from poorer backgrounds or lower socio-economic groups. We therefore believe that the values estimated here should be seen as upper-bound estimates.

Another important concern is adaptation-based selection (Frederick and Loewenstein, 1999). It could be that those who are more resilient to odour are more likely to live near an STW in the long term, because those who are more sensitive to odour will have a higher incentive to move out. In order to more closely examine causal relationships, future research may wish to examine differences in wellbeing immediately before and after changes to public works, in the form of a quasi-experimental design.

As a defence, we note that the problem related to measuring causal effects is pertinent and inherent to most forms of wellbeing research, because very few studies are able to use random assignment. For example, revealed preference studies also require robust causal inference in that we need to ascertain the causal effect of a non-market good on a market price, such as housing prices or wage rates, that also depend on an equilibrium in the target market which is rarely attained due to transaction and information costs. A further advantage of the wellbeing regression approach is that it can analyse actual lived experiences of STWs and odour without asking people their WTP in a hypothetical situation (as in stated preference studies), which has been inherently difficult to research due to people's general lack of knowledge about the impact of STWs.

The wellbeing impacts estimated in this study can provide valuable input for policy evaluation. Recently, new techniques have been developed that can assign monetary values to wellbeing impacts, based on a robust estimate of the income effect on SWB (Fujiwara, 2013). This is known as wellbeing valuation (WV) and can feed into cost–benefit analysis (CBA) in numerous ways. A direct application would be to use the results to assess the impact and value to local residents of reducing odour emissions from priority STWs to the level observed in non-priority STWs.

Overall, the results presented here can be readily used by water and sewage service providers, water industry regulators, government, independent research organizations and academia. The wellbeing impact and the associated social value can be factored into the development and refinement of environmental and social impact strategies, whereas the cost of prevention can feed into future price reviews in the water industry accounting for the benefits to society that odour mitigation would provide, based on the findings here.

In terms of future research areas, there are a number of options. The wellbeing correlation with STW proximity, estimated in this study, represents an average over multiple dimensions: the specific geographic area analysed (parts of England), the levels of odour from STWs, the average environmental conditions experienced during the survey period, and so on. Future research can break these values down for different population groups (for example, young and elderly), different geographic regions or different times of the year, to assess how impact varies across groups. It would also be possible to conduct further analysis on the interaction between the housing market and the impact of odour on wellbeing by combining reliable housing payment data at the postcode level with the APS data. Finally, it may be possible to more accurately define the households impacted upon by STW odour by linking odour contour geographical information systems data, which measure the geographic spread of odour emanating from STWs, to subjective wellbeing responses.

NOTES

* Part of the analysis presented in this report is based on data provided by the Office for National Statistics via its Secure Research Service (SRS) under secure access (project number 1006200). This data remains under Crown Copyright.

1. The odour unit value of a substance is directly proportional to its concentration, that is, diluting a substance in the same amount of water will halve its odour unit value. One odour unit is defined as an odour concentration that half of the panelists can detect in a lab setting.

REFERENCES

Batalhone, S.A., Nogueira, J.M. and B.P.M. Mueller (2002), 'Economics of air pollution: hedonic price model and smell consequences of sewage treatment plants in urban areas', Brasília, Brasil: DF Universidade Brasília.

Carroll, N., Frijters, P. and M. Shields (2009), 'Quantifying the costs of drought: new evidence from life satisfaction data', *Journal of Population Economics*, **22** (2), 445–461.

Cohn, M.M. (1929), 'Sewage works odors and their control', *Sewage Works Journal*, **1** (5), 568–577.

Dague, R.R. (1972), 'Fundamentals of odor control', *Journal (Water Pollution Control Federation)*, **44** (4), 583–594.

Frederick, S. and G. Loewenstein (1999), 'Hedonic adaptation', in Daniel Kahneman, Ed Diener and Norbert Schwartz (eds), *Well-Being, the Foundations of Hedonic Psychology*, New York, USA: Russell Sage Foundation, pp. 302–329.

Fujiwara, D. (2013), 'A general method for valuing non-market goods using wellbeing data: three-stage wellbeing valuation', London School of Economics and Political Sciences, CEP Discussion Paper No. 1233.

Fujiwara, D. and R. Campbell (2011), 'Valuation techniques for social cost–benefit analysis: stated preference, revealed preference and subjective well-being approaches: a discussion of the current issues', London, UK: HM Treasury.

Knight, S.J. and P. Howley (2017), 'Can clean air make you happy? Examining the effect of nitrogen dioxide (NO_2) on life satisfaction', University of York, HEDG Working Paper 17/08.

Krueger, A.B. and D.A. Schkade (2008), 'The reliability of subjective well-being measures', *Journal of Public Economics*, **92** (8–9), 1833–1845.

Lawton, R. and D. Fujiwara (2016), 'Living with aircraft noise: airport proximity, aviation noise and subjective wellbeing in England', *Transportation Research Part D: Transport and Environment*, **42**, 104–118.

Luechinger, S. (2009), 'Valuing air quality using the life satisfaction approach', *Economic Journal*, **119** (536), 482–515.

Luechinger, S. and P.A. Raschky (2009), 'Valuing flood disasters using the life satisfaction approach', *Journal of Public Economics*, **93** (3–4), 620–633.

Melbostad, E., Eduard, W., Skogstad, A., Sandven, P., Lassen, J., et al. (1994), 'Exposure to bacterial aerosols and work-related symptoms in sewage workers', *American Journal of Industrial Medicine*, **25** (1), 59–63.

Nimmermark, S. (2004), 'Odour influence on well-being and health with specific focus on animal production emissions', *Annals of Agricultural and Environmental Medicine*, **11** (2), 163–173.

Parfit, Derek (ed.) (1984), *Reasons and Persons*, Oxford, UK: Oxford University Press.

Schiffman, S.S. (1998), 'Livestock odors: implications for human health and well-being', *Journal of Animal Science*, **76** (5), 1343–1355.

Sekulova, F. and J.C.J.M. van den Bergh (2016), 'Floods and happiness: empirical evidence from Bulgaria', *Ecological Economics*, **126** (C), 51–57.

Shafibeik, O. and R. Lyon (2012), 'Cambridge sewage treatment works: odour dispersion modelling report', August, Peterborough, UK: Anglian Water.

Thorn, J., Beijer, L. and R. Rylander (2002), 'Work related symptoms among sewage workers: a nationwide survey in Sweden', *Occupational and Environmental Medicine*, **59** (8), 562–566.

Vantarakis, A., Paparrodopoulos, S., Kokkinos, P., Vantarakis, G., Fragou, K. and I. Detorakis (2016), 'Impact on the quality of life when living close to a municipal wastewater treatment plant', *Journal of Environmental and Public Health*, **2016**, Article ID 8467023, 1–8.

Von Möllendorff, C. and H. Welsch (2017), 'Measuring renewable energy externalities: evidence from subjective well-being data', *Land Economics*, **93** (1), 109–126.

Zhang, X., Zhang, X. and X. Chen (2015), 'Happiness in the air: how does a dirty sky affect subjective well-being?', Institute for the Study of Labor (IZA) Discussion Paper No. 9312.

Zhang, X., Zhang, X. and X. Chen (2017), 'Valuing air quality using happiness data: the case of China', *Ecological Economics*, **137**, 29–36.

APPENDIX 12A.1

Table 12A.1 Variable description

Name	Description	Type	Mean	Std dev.	Min.	Max.
Priority STW dummy	1 if the nearest STW has been market as priority for being in the top 60 odour-emitting STWs of the water company	Binary	0.125	0.330	0	1
Distance to STW	Distance from the respondent's postcode to the nearest STW in metres	Continuous	6002	3998	64	19984
Distance * priority	The product of the two terms above	Continuous	508	1577	0	12537
male	1 if the respondent is male	Binary	0.460	0.498	0	1
Age	The respondent's age in years	Continuous	45.76	18.33	16	102
Ethnicity	White / Mixed / Asian / Black / Other	Categorical	4.012	8.455	1	97
Religious	1 if the respondent is religious	Binary	0.583	0.492	0	1
Health	Respondent's self-reported general health, 5 levels ranging from very bad to very good	Categorical	3.402	1.130	1	5
Smoking	Current smoker/ex-smoker/never smoked	Categorical	7.902	2.916	0	9
Marital Status	Single/Married/Separated/ Widowed/Divorced/Civil Partner	Categorical	2.218	1.709	1	5
Education	Highest educational level achieved by respondent	Categorical	1.631	1.096	1	5
Tenancy status	Whether respondent owns or rents property	Categorical	2.585	4.512	1	97
Benefits	Whether respondent claims benefits (binary in USoc)	Categorical	0.279	0.448	0	1
Dependent children	Number of dependent children respondent has	Categorical	0.331	0.789	0	10
Employment	Detailed labour force status breakdown (in the APS this also includes earnings quintile for the employed)	Categorical	3.805	7.129	1	97
Income	Natural logarithm of household equivalized income (USoc only)	Continuous	7.150	1.341	−5.298	9.903
Rurality	Whether respondent lives in rural (2) or urban area (1)	Binary	1.080	0.271	1	2
Face-to-face	1 if the respondent was interviewed face-to-face (0 for telephone interviews) (APS only)	Binary				
Interview month	Month of interview	Categorical	6.349	3.465	1	12
Wave	The wave of the APS survey that respondent was part of	Categorical	3.378	1.724	1	6

Note: Statistics provided for the Understanding Society dataset.

APPENDIX 12A.2 EXAMPLE REGRESSION RESULTS

Table 12A.2 APS, model (2)

Variable	Coefficient	Std error	t-statistic	p-value
Priority STW dummy	−0.046	0.019	−2.446	0.014
Distance to nearest STW (m)	2.09E-06	1.37E-06	1.523	0.128
Distance * priority interaction	6.38E-06	2.69E-06	2.372	0.018
Female	0.097	0.012	8.160	0.000
Age	−0.096	0.003	−30.533	0.000
Age squared	0.001	0.000	29.158	0.000
Ethnicity = White (reference group)	0.000			
Ethnicity = Mixed	−0.136	0.047	−2.861	0.004
Ethnicity = Asian	−0.047	0.019	−2.459	0.014
Ethnicity = Black	−0.356	0.027	−13.028	0.000
Ethnicity = Other	−0.065	0.033	−1.996	0.046
Respondent is religious	0.084	0.012	7.177	0.000
Health = Very bad	−1.678	0.090	−18.603	0.000
Health = Bad	−0.772	0.044	−17.700	0.000
Health = Fair (reference)	0.000			
Health = Good	0.613	0.018	33.743	0.000
Health = Very good	1.029	0.018	55.847	0.000
Current cigarette smoker	−0.234	0.017	−14.074	0.000
Ex-smoker	−0.055	0.012	−4.757	0.000
Never smoked (reference)	0.000			
Smoking = Under 18	−0.066	0.063	−1.044	0.297
Smoking = N/A	−0.301	0.280	−1.074	0.283
Single (reference)	0.000			
Married	0.419	0.015	28.333	0.000
Separated	−0.182	0.033	−5.450	0.000
Divorced	0.021	0.023	0.933	0.351
Widowed	−0.254	0.040	−6.324	0.000
Civil Partner	0.544	0.071	7.681	0.000
Education = Degree or equivalent	−0.084	0.026	−3.187	0.001
Higher education	−0.076	0.029	−2.614	0.009
GCE, A-level or equivalent	−0.055	0.027	−2.020	0.043
GCSE grades A*–C or equivalent	−0.018	0.027	−0.648	0.517
Other qualifications	0.036	0.030	1.185	0.236
Education = No qualification (ref.)	0.000			
Housing = Owned outright (ref.)	0.000			
Being bought with mortgage or loan	−0.104	0.015	−6.821	0.000
Part rent	−0.146	0.052	−2.799	0.005
Rented	−0.172	0.019	−8.973	0.000
Rent free	0.029	0.060	0.488	0.625
Squatting	−2.574	0.361	−7.132	0.000
Social renter	−0.186	0.022	−8.400	0.000
Benefits = Doesn't know	−0.362	0.179	−2.024	0.043
Benefits = No (ref.)	0.000			
Benefits = Yes	−0.120	0.015	−8.152	0.000

Table 12A.2 (continued)

Variable	Coefficient	Std error	t-statistic	p-value
No dependent children	0.000			
1 Dependent child	0.035	0.018	1.977	0.048
2 Dependent children	0.079	0.018	4.262	0.000
3 Dependent children	0.153	0.029	5.210	0.000
4+ Dependent children	0.161	0.051	3.173	0.002
Employed full-time, no salary data (ref.)	0.000			
Self-employed full-time	−0.037	0.028	−1.319	0.187
Government training prog.	−0.678	0.134	−5.059	0.000
Unpaid family worker	−0.036	0.091	−0.396	0.692
Unemployed	−0.818	0.037	−21.979	0.000
Student	−0.117	0.041	−2.880	0.004
Looking after family	−0.087	0.032	−2.704	0.007
Temp. sick or injured	−0.642	0.108	−5.965	0.000
Long-term sick or disabled	−0.394	0.049	−8.072	0.000
Unavailable for other reasons	−0.572	0.138	−4.154	0.000
Retired	0.308	0.031	10.001	0.000
Doesn't need a job	0.414	0.049	8.385	0.000
Not looking, believes no job available	−0.443	0.142	−3.115	0.002
Not looking for other reasons	−0.134	0.055	−2.442	0.015
Employed part-time	0.033	0.026	1.255	0.209
Self-employed part-time	0.043	0.034	1.264	0.206
Underemployed	−0.489	0.043	−11.484	0.000
Employed full-time, salary lowest quintile	−0.097	0.033	−2.946	0.003
Employed full-time, salary quintile 2	−0.114	0.031	−3.641	0.000
Employed full-time, salary quintile 3	−0.033	0.027	−1.186	0.236
Employed full-time, salary quintile 4	0.028	0.026	1.069	0.285
Employed full-time, salary highest quntile	0.136	0.024	5.629	0.000
Rurality = City (ref.)	0.000			
Rurality = Town	0.062	0.022	2.798	0.005
Rurality = Village	0.087	0.024	3.654	0.000
Rurality = Hamlet	0.136	0.035	3.880	0.000
Face-to-face interview (ref. = telephone)	0.001	0.011	0.119	0.906
Interview month = January (ref.)	0.000			
Interview month = February	0.034	0.028	1.196	0.232
Interview month = March	0.029	0.027	1.056	0.291
Interview month = April	−0.051	0.027	−1.860	0.063
Interview month = May	−0.005	0.026	−0.195	0.845
Interview month = June	0.011	0.026	0.420	0.675
Interview month = July	0.037	0.026	1.434	0.151
Interview month = August	0.002	0.026	0.059	0.953
Interview month = September	−0.016	0.026	−0.596	0.551
Interview month = October	−0.040	0.026	−1.528	0.127
Interview month = November	−0.006	0.026	−0.220	0.826
Interview month = December	−0.021	0.026	−0.784	0.433

Table 12A.2 (continued)

Variable	Coefficient	Std error	t-statistic	p-value
APS Wave 1 (2011/12)	0.000			
APS Wave 2 (2012/13)	0.034	0.015	2.310	0.021
APS Wave 3 (2013/14)	0.087	0.014	6.068	0.000
APS Wave 4 (2014/15)	0.177	0.016	11.276	0.000
Constant term	8.737	0.079	109.937	0.000
Sample size	98 661			

Table 12A.3 Understanding Society, model (1a)

Variable	Coefficient	Std error	t-statistic	p-value
LSOA-based distance to nearest STW (m)	0.000	0.000	1.970	0.049
Logarithm of eq. household income	0.092	0.006	16.372	0.000
Age	−0.037	0.002	−24.507	0.000
Age squared	0.000	0.000	22.362	0.000
Male	−0.016	0.008	−1.864	0.062
Married	0.286	0.012	23.523	0.000
Divorced	−0.055	0.020	−2.811	0.005
Widowed	0.009	0.023	0.420	0.674
Separated	−0.139	0.032	−4.306	0.000
Single (ref.)	0.000			
No qualification (ref.)	0.000			
A-level or GCSE	−0.016	0.015	−1.107	0.268
Other qualification	−0.039	0.018	−2.211	0.027
Degree or higher	0.093	0.015	6.303	0.000
Self-employed	0.417	0.025	16.998	0.000
Employed	0.432	0.021	21.011	0.000
Unemployed (ref.)	0.000			
Retired	0.601	0.025	23.987	0.000
On maternity leave	0.722	0.047	15.516	0.000
Looking after family	0.334	0.026	12.778	0.000
Student	0.697	0.026	26.776	0.000
Long-term sick or disabled	−0.891	0.031	−28.359	0.000
Govt. training scheme	0.143	0.152	0.945	0.345
Unpaid worker or family business	0.111	0.189	0.587	0.557
Unknown	0.654	0.178	3.682	0.000
Doing something else	0.236	0.060	3.940	0.000
Number of children	0.059	0.007	8.763	0.000
Respondent is religious	0.040	0.008	4.775	0.000
Respondent has carer	−0.249	0.016	−15.907	0.000
House owned outright (ref.)	0.000			
Mortgage	−0.136	0.011	−12.383	0.000
Shared ownership	−0.256	0.051	−5.034	0.000
Rented	−0.272	0.012	−22.083	0.000
Rent-free	−0.070	0.042	−1.688	0.091
Other	−0.187	0.093	−2.014	0.044
White UK (ref.)	0.000			
White Irish	−0.061	0.034	−1.816	0.069
White: gypsy or Irish traveller	−0.087	0.278	−0.315	0.753
White: any other white background	−0.114	0.022	−5.092	0.000
Mixed: white and black Caribbean	−0.250	0.044	−5.650	0.000
Mixed: white and black African	−0.243	0.067	−3.626	0.000
Mixed: white and Asian	−0.079	0.051	−1.554	0.120
Mixed: any other mixed background	−0.115	0.056	−2.061	0.039
Asian/Asian British: Indian	−0.212	0.020	−10.445	0.000
Asian/Asian British: Pakistani	−0.318	0.025	−12.755	0.000

Table 12A.3 (continued)

Variable	Coefficient	Std error	t-statistic	p-value
Asian/Asian British: Bangladeshi	−0.239	0.031	−7.644	0.000
Asian/Asian British: Chinese	−0.233	0.045	−5.200	0.000
Asian/Asian British: any other Asian background	−0.113	0.033	−3.414	0.001
Black: Caribbean	−0.221	0.027	−8.077	0.000
Black: African	−0.135	0.027	−5.047	0.000
Black: any other black background	−0.041	0.079	−0.523	0.601
Other ethnic group: Arab	−0.266	0.058	−4.626	0.000
Other ethnic group: any other ethnic group	−0.185	0.057	−3.219	0.001
Wave 1 (ref.)	0.000			
Wave 2	−0.064	0.012	−5.127	0.000
Wave 3	−0.152	0.013	−11.861	0.000
Wave 4	−0.229	0.013	−18.270	0.000
Wave 5	−0.253	0.013	−19.781	0.000
Wave 6	−0.095	0.014	−6.981	0.000
Interviewed in January (ref.)	0.000			
February	0.010	0.018	0.580	0.562
March	−0.012	0.017	−0.702	0.482
April	−0.017	0.018	−0.934	0.350
May	0.040	0.018	2.221	0.026
June	0.018	0.018	1.039	0.299
July	−0.005	0.018	−0.279	0.781
August	0.043	0.018	2.428	0.015
September	0.017	0.018	0.958	0.338
October	−0.007	0.018	−0.374	0.709
November	−0.012	0.018	−0.696	0.487
December	0.007	0.019	0.393	0.694
Claiming benefits	−0.165	0.011	−15.322	0.000
Smoking	−0.143	0.026	−5.413	0.000
Rural area	0.057	0.013	4.296	0.000
Constant	4.956	0.059	84.118	0.000
R-squared	0.098			
Sample size	98 661			

Table 12A.4 APS health analysis, all STWs

Variable	Coefficient	Std error	t-statistic	p-value
Distance to nearest STW (m)	1.13E-06	3.24E-07	3.491	0.000
Female	0.032	0.003	10.974	0.000
Age	−0.030	0.001	−39.237	0.000
Age squared	0.000	0.000	27.091	0.000
Ethnicity = White (reference group)	0.000			
Ethnicity = Mixed	−0.035	0.014	−2.484	0.013
Ethnicity = Asian	−0.162	0.006	−28.743	0.000
Ethnicity = Black	0.038	0.008	4.814	0.000
Ethnicity = Other	−0.040	0.011	−3.807	0.000
Respondent is religious	−0.005	0.003	−1.638	0.101
Current cigarette smoker	−0.180	0.004	−48.295	0.000
Ex-smoker	−0.070	0.003	−23.683	0.000
Never smoked (reference)	0.000			
Smoking = Under 18	−0.200	0.015	−13.349	0.000
Smoking = N/A	−0.219	0.073	−3.015	0.003
Single (reference)	0.000			
Married	0.028	0.004	7.472	0.000
Separated	−0.013	0.008	−1.768	0.077
Divorced	−0.023	0.005	−4.482	0.000
Widowed	−0.010	0.009	−1.213	0.225
Civil Partner	−0.022	0.025	−0.866	0.386
Education = Degree or equivalent	0.223	0.006	40.014	0.000
Higher education	0.163	0.006	25.983	0.000
GCE, A-level or equivalent	0.121	0.006	21.877	0.000
GCSE grades A*–C or equivalent	0.113	0.005	20.907	0.000
Other qualifications	0.088	0.006	14.173	0.000
Education = No qualification (ref.)	0.000			
Housing = Owned outright (ref.)	0.000			
Being bought with mortgage or loan	−0.060	0.004	−15.529	0.000
Part rent	−0.114	0.017	−6.546	0.000
Rented	−0.088	0.005	−18.165	0.000
Rent free	−0.115	0.016	−7.199	0.000
Squatting	−0.407	0.362	−1.122	0.262
Social Renter	−0.243	0.005	−46.384	0.000
Benefits = Doesn't know	−0.183	0.046	−3.948	0.000
Benefits = No (ref.)	0.000			
Benefits = Yes	−0.114	0.004	−31.440	0.000
No dependent children	0.000			
1 Dependent child	0.080	0.004	18.890	0.000
2 Dependent children	0.140	0.005	30.266	0.000
3 Dependent children	0.149	0.007	21.184	0.000
4+ Dependent children	0.127	0.011	11.343	0.000
Employed full-time, no salary data (ref.)	0.000			
Self-employed full-time	0.029	0.008	3.773	0.000
Government training prog.	−0.334	0.032	−10.587	0.000
Unpaid family worker	−0.069	0.027	−2.550	0.011

Table 12A.4 (continued)

Variable	Coefficient	Std error	t-statistic	p-value
Unemployed	−0.173	0.009	−19.900	0.000
Student	−0.010	0.010	−0.967	0.334
Looking after family	−0.143	0.008	−17.314	0.000
Temp. sick or injured	−1.068	0.022	−48.580	0.000
Long-term sick or disabled	−1.590	0.009	−177.407	0.000
Unavailable for other reasons	−0.165	0.034	−4.925	0.000
Retired	−0.186	0.008	−22.639	0.000
Doesn't need a job	0.014	0.014	0.939	0.348
Not looking, believes no job available	−0.232	0.029	−7.970	0.000
Not looking for other reasons	−0.174	0.014	−12.484	0.000
Employed part-time	−0.021	0.007	−3.030	0.002
Self-employed part-time	−0.027	0.010	−2.787	0.005
Underemployed	−0.075	0.009	−7.884	0.000
Employed full-time, salary lowest quintile	−0.040	0.008	−5.315	0.000
Employed full-time, salary quintile 2	−0.010	0.008	−1.286	0.199
Employed full-time, salary quintile 3	−0.004	0.007	−0.561	0.575
Employed full-time, salary quintile 4	0.032	0.007	4.329	0.000
Employed full-time, salary highest quntile	0.067	0.007	9.285	0.000
Rurality = City (ref.)	0.000			
Rurality = Town	0.019	0.005	3.721	0.000
Rurality = Village	0.071	0.006	12.344	0.000
Rurality = Hamlet	0.054	0.008	6.531	0.000
Face-to-face interview (ref. = telephone)	−0.023	0.003	−8.402	0.000
Interview month = January (ref.)	0.000			
Interview month = February	−0.002	0.007	−0.229	0.819
Interview month = March	−0.008	0.007	−1.160	0.246
Interview month = April	−0.006	0.007	−0.897	0.370
Interview month = May	0.002	0.007	0.365	0.715
Interview month = June	0.000	0.007	0.027	0.978
Interview month = July	0.012	0.006	1.885	0.059
Interview month = August	0.020	0.007	3.087	0.002
Interview month = September	−0.007	0.006	−1.072	0.284
Interview month = October	0.006	0.007	0.912	0.362
Interview month = November	−0.001	0.007	−0.181	0.856
Interview month = December	−0.009	0.006	−1.356	0.175
APS Wave 1 (2011/12)	0.000			
APS Wave 2 (2012/13)	−0.014	0.003	−3.991	0.000
APS Wave 3 (2013/14)	−0.020	0.004	−5.726	0.000
APS Wave 4 (2014/15)	−0.028	0.004	−7.118	0.000
Constant term	5.047	0.018	273.300	0.000
Sample size	369 721			

13. The effect of green areas on life satisfaction: a comparison of subjective and objective measures

Teresa Ruckelshauß

13.1 INTRODUCTION

'In that case, grey' was the title of an article published in the renowned German newspaper *Die Zeit* (Erenz, 2017; own translation). The author argues that in times of serious housing shortage, green space should not be maintained because 'city are [*sic*] buildings, streets, courtyards' (ibid: 60; own translation). Although he admits the necessity of room for nice smaller and larger parks, the overall message of the article is to reduce green space, especially lawns.[1]

The depiction in this article neglects the importance of green space and the positive effect that green areas have on humans through several channels. As shown by many studies, green areas enhance general health, mental health and overall wellbeing (see, among others, Maas et al., 2006; Tzoulas et al., 2007; Triguero-Mas et al., 2015; van den Berg et al., 2015; Coppel and Wüstemann, 2017; Wood et al., 2017). Studies eliciting the pathways through which these effects occur find that the enhancement of physical activity, the provision of psychological relaxation and recreational opportunities, the stimulation of social cohesion and the reduction of air pollution, noise and heat play an important role (see, e.g., Tyrväinen et al., 2005; Gidlöf-Gunnarsson and Öhrström, 2007; Braubach et al., 2017; Markevych et al., 2017).

The European Commission also recognizes that 'green infrastructure' is highly important because of provisioning ecosystem services (see, e.g., European Commission, 2013). This is further emphasized in the European Union Biodiversity Strategy requiring all European Union member states to assess the values of all their ecosystem services by 2020 (European Commission, 2011: 12). The need to assign values to environmental goods and services to make their importance clear to society and policy makers is nowadays widely accepted by scholars and a variety of methodologies are available for this purpose (see, e.g., Freeman III, 2003). The life satisfaction approach is one of the available approaches.

Despite the broad evidence for the positive effect of green areas on health and wellbeing, however, there are still unanswered questions. As Hart et al. (2018: 2) state, there is a lack of studies that investigate 'multiple social and physical environmental factors in the same sample and across different regions in Europe'. Moreover, the authors emphasize that few studies have directly compared objective and subjective measures of environmental aspects. Among the few is an analysis by Weden et al. (2008), who find that perceived and actual neighbourhood characteristics do not have the same correlation with health. Similar results are found regarding physical activity facilities as well as the obesogenic features of neighbourhoods which include recreational areas (Ball et al., 2008; Roda et al., 2016).

Based on this assessment, the research question underlying this chapter is as follows: what is the influence of green areas on life satisfaction using subjective and objective measures comparatively, and what conclusions can be drawn regarding the value of green areas?

In order to answer this question, data from the Third European Quality of Life Survey (EQLS) from 2012 are used and supplemented by other data, mainly from the European Union. The data sources restrict the study area to the member states of the European Union with the exception of Croatia, in the following referred to as the EU27. Individual life satisfaction data will be combined with geographical data mainly provided on the NUTS 2 level.[2]

13.2 LITERATURE REVIEW

This section provides an overview of the application of environmental valuation methods with a focus on green areas. It needs to be emphasized that there is no universally agreed definition of green areas that is used throughout the literature. Instead, the different studies set different foci based on their research question and the available data, meaning that some only look at parks or forests and others apply a broader understanding.

13.2.1 Revealed Preference Methods

The travel cost method is most often applied to large green areas such as forests and national parks that attract not only people living nearby but also visitors from far away. Khan (2006), for example, estimates the recreational benefits of a national park in Pakistan. He finds a considerable annual consumer surplus generated by the recreational opportunities of the park. There are also a few applications of near-urban green areas. Bishop (1992) employs, along with the contingent valuation approach, the travel cost method for eliciting the recreational value of two forests close to urban areas. He concludes that the method is not well suited for green space that is easily accessible on foot or by bike where many visitors come from the immediately surrounding area, maybe viewing the time to travel there as a benefit and not as a cost (ibid.: 68).

Bertram and Larondelle (2017), by contrast, use the travel cost method to value an urban forest site in Berlin. They argue that the application is appropriate due to the fact that travel distances are comparatively large and most visitors use public transport or motorized vehicles. Similarly, Hanauer and Reid (2017) focus on a regional park in California. They justify their use of the travel cost method by the availability of a comparatively accurate measure of the travel distance, thereby avoiding a lack of variation in this variable.

The other revealed preference method, hedonic pricing, explicitly focuses on neighbourhood characteristics including green space to determine differences in property prices. For a city in Spain, Bengochea Morancho (2003) finds an inverse relationship between the house prices and the distance to the nearest green space. Neither the view of, nor the size of, a green space, however, have a significant influence on the property price. Similarly, Anderson and West (2006) find higher house prices to be associated with nearer green space in a metropolitan area in Minnesota in the United States. Similar results are obtained for developing countries. Kong et al. (2007), for example, focus on a city in China and find, among other things, that housing prices are positively affected by the percentage of green space around the property and the accessibility of parks and plaza green areas.

13.2.2 Stated Preference Methods

There are also several applications of stated preference methods to value green space. One example of a choice experiment is a study by Bullock (2006), who surveyed the preferences of inhabitants of Dublin, Ireland, for characteristics of green space. A mix of busy and quiet areas, a moderate level of facilities, and shorter travel time are the preferred attributes. Additionally, the same author finds that the type of green space, in this case small local parks compared with larger municipal parks, influences which characteristics are preferred or have more influence on the choice (Bullock, 2008). For regional parks, for example, travel time emerges as a less relevant aspect. The study by Horne et al. (2005) focuses on the preferences of visitors for forest types. In their choice experiment, they show that most of the respondents value scenic amenities and biodiversity.

Applying the contingent valuation method, Scarpa et al. (2000) focus on forest recreation in 27 forests in Ireland. They find that naturalness is a decisive positive attribute for which visitors are willing to pay. Focusing on the effect of distance, Kim et al. (2015) identify this aspect along with usage of a stream in an urban area in South Korea as important predictors of willingness to pay (WTP) for its restoration.

The valuation of parks is also a common application of the contingent valuation method. Moral norms and attitudes and their influence on visitors' valuation of green space is an aspect that is increasingly the focus of interest and has been found to be significant by many studies, including a recent study by López-Mosquera et al. (2014).

13.2.3 Life Satisfaction Approach

There are several studies that examine the relationship between green space and wellbeing, happiness or life satisfaction. Studies by George MacKerron focus on momentary wellbeing and the effect of direct environmental surrounding using a specially designed application for smartphones (MacKerron, 2012; MacKerron and Mourato, 2013; MacKerron and Mourato, Chapter 14 in this *Handbook*). MacKerron and Mourato (2013) find that people are significantly happier in green and natural environments.

Mitchell et al. (2015) use the World Health Organization (WHO) WHO (Five) Well-Being Index of mental wellbeing and find a positive relationship of this multi-item scale with subjectively reported access to recreational or green areas. Using the less common WHO (Ten) Well-Being Index, Ode Sang et al. (2016) found a positive relationship between perceived naturalness of urban green areas and wellbeing. A similar approach was taken by Larson et al. (2016) who made use of the Gallup–Healthways Wellbeing Index that covers five different aspects of wellbeing, namely physical, community, social, financial and purpose. Park quantity was found to have a positive relationship with wellbeing, while for park quality and accessibility no significant relationship was revealed.

White et al. (2017) investigated four components of subjective wellbeing separately. The life satisfaction item had a positive relationship with natural environments, while other components of subjective wellbeing were found to be influenced to an even greater extent.

A positive relationship between the level of happiness and the amount of green space in the neighbourhood was also found by Hart et al. (2018).

There also exist some studies that apply the life satisfaction approach to green space valuation, as in the present chapter. Kopmann and Rehdanz (2013) use the second wave of the EQLS and combine it with land cover data. They find that different types of natural and artificial land cover are related to life satisfaction. The similarity to this study is limited, however, as green space as such does not constitute a separate category.

Smyth et al. (2008) study the effect of a city's environmental characteristics on life satisfaction. The area of parkland in an urban area is significantly positively related to life satisfaction. Relatedly, using a multi-item measure for life satisfaction Smyth et al. (2011) found access to parkland to be positively associated with life satisfaction in some of their specifications.

White et al. (2013) examined how green space is associated with mental distress and wellbeing. Their conclusions correspond well with the other reported results: a small positive effect of green space on life satisfaction can be observed. Also, Ambrey and Fleming (2014) find a positive effect of public green space in cities on life satisfaction.

Tsurumi and Managi (2015) conduct a more detailed analysis as they consider the amount of green space as well as the distance to it, people's preference for greenery and the quality of the green space respondents usually access. They find an inverted U-shaped relationship between the amount of green space and life satisfaction. Similar results are obtained by Krekel et al. (2016), and Bertram and Rehdanz (2015: 146) who list 'congestion, noise or fear of crime' as possible reasons for this shape. Furthermore, the study by Krekel et al. (2016) found a negative effect of abandoned areas.

13.3 METHOD

Following Frey et al. (2010), the simple life satisfaction function can be stated as follows:

$$LS = f(G, Y, S, M) \tag{13.1}$$

Life satisfaction LS depends on the environmental good G, here green space, household income Y, a set of socio-economic individual attributes denoted S, and a set of macro-level characteristics, summarized in M. In order to infer the value of green space from this relationship, the equation has to be totally differentiated (holding S and M constant) and dLS set to zero. This leads to the marginal willingness to pay (MWTP) that shows the value of a change in green space in terms of a change in income:

$$MWTP = -\frac{dY}{dG} = \frac{\delta f/\delta G}{\delta f/\delta Y} \tag{13.2}$$

In order to estimate the effect of the variables on life satisfaction, an ordinary least squares (OLS) regression is applied. From a theoretical viewpoint, this would require the life satisfaction measure to be cardinal. However, the variable is discrete and ordinal. Thus, a linear regression model would lead to measurement error. Using OLS regression is nonetheless suitable as the expected difference to non-linear approaches has been found to be negligible and OLS regressions are therefore used throughout the literature (see, e.g., Ferrer-i-Carbonell and Frijters, 2004; Brereton et al., 2008; MacKerron and Mourato, 2009; Ferreira and Moro, 2010). For the empirical analysis, the life satisfaction function can be specified as follows:

$$LS_{ijr} = \beta_0 + \beta_g G_{ijr} + \beta_y \ln(Y_i) + \beta_s S_i + \beta_m M_j + \varepsilon_{ijr} \tag{13.3}$$

Here, LS_{ijr} is the self-reported life satisfaction of individual *i* in location *j*. The green space measure is captured by G_{ijr}[3] and household income enters the equation in its natural logarithm $\ln(Y_i)$. With this specification, the decreasing marginal utility of income can be accounted for, meaning that c.p. people with a higher income are willing to give up more income – in absolute terms – for an increase in green space. S_i captures the socio-economic characteristics of individual *i*, while M_j captures all other components of location *j* that are expected to have an influence on individual *i*'s self-reported life satisfaction and ε_{ijr} is an error term.

With this specification, the MWTP turns out to take the following form that will be used for the estimation of the value of green space where the ratio of the estimated coefficients of green space and income is multiplied by the mean income $\overline{Y}$:[4]

$$MWTP = \frac{\widehat{\beta_g}}{\widehat{\beta_y}} \overline{Y} \tag{13.4}$$

13.4 DATA

The analysis is mainly based on the third wave of the EQLS from 2012.[5] This survey includes detailed information on more than 43 000 individuals from 34 European countries, comprising the 27 European Union member states (as of 2012) and seven other countries. This information includes the respondent's region of residence at the NUTS level. Taking advantage of this information we analyse the data on the NUTS 2 level, the finest disaggregation possible, and focus on the EU27 member states.[6]

The measure of subjective wellbeing is based on responses to the question, 'All things considered, how satisfied would you say you are with your life these days?' on a ten-point scale from 1 (very dissatisfied) to 10 (very satisfied). This question format is comparable to other studies where the question was framed similarly.

In line with the literature, a number of control variables are included that have been shown to influence life satisfaction (see Dolan et al., 2008 for a detailed overview). Important individual characteristics include income, gender, employment status, marital status and educational attainment. Information on annual total net household income is available as a categorical variable. Midpoints for each category are used.[7] Age enters in both linear and squared form to account for an inverted U-shaped relationship that has been found in the literature. Furthermore, the number of children and people living in the household, the self-reported health status,[8] and whether one has the citizen status in the country where one is living, are added. With information on the attendance frequency of religious services and the general level of trust further individual traits are captured.

At the macroeconomic level the following variables are captured: population density and the level of urbanization, both at the NUTS 2 level, and whether a country has joined the European Union before 2004 (belonging to the EU15).[9]

Climatic conditions have also gained importance in terms of their impact on subjective wellbeing (Frijters and van Praag, 1998; Rehdanz and Maddison, 2005; Brereton et al., 2008; Maddison and Rehdanz, 2011; Murray et al., 2013; Maddison and Rehdanz, Chapter 6 in this *Handbook*). For the present assessment, climate is especially important as the study area is considerably large, resulting in a sizable variation in climatic conditions. These are captured by three variables, all gathered at the NUTS 2 level, namely the average temperature in summer months (June, July, August), the average temperature in winter months (December, January, February) and average monthly precipitation.[10]

Our analysis aims at comparing the effect of subjective and objective measures of green areas on life satisfaction. Information on a subjective measure of green areas is provided by the EQLS, namely, 'Thinking of physical access, distance, opening hours and the like, how would you describe your access to the following services? Can you access . . . recreational or green areas?' Respondents could answer that they can access these with great or some difficulty, easily or very easily, or that they do not use this service. Objective information on green space, measured as primary land use, was taken from Eurostat's Land Use and Coverage Area Frame Survey (LUCAS) 2012.[11] We use the percentage of the land use category 'Amenities, museums, leisure' (U361) in each NUTS 2 region as green space measure – the highest level of disaggregation available – where parks, botanical and zoological gardens are included.[12] This category choice is based on availability and comparability considerations. We note, however, that this classification does not express the same depiction as the subjective measure of 'recreational or green areas', especially due to the inclusion of museums in the objective measure. The descriptive statistics of all variables are presented in Table 13.1.

13.5 SPECIFICATION AND RESULTS

Due to the fact that data on the individual and the regional level are combined, standard errors are potentially underestimated (Moulton, 1990). To account for this possibility, clustering is applied for all regressions, following, for example, the approach of Brereton et al. (2008) and Kopmann and Rehdanz (2013). The analysis is conducted using the software Stata, version 13.0.

We specify three main models based on equation (13.3) where the green space measure varies. In a first model, we analyse whether there is a difference between using and not using recreational or green areas (Model 1). Model 1 can be viewed as a preliminary investigation, since it compares users and non-users of recreational or green areas. The second model focuses on the users and captures respondents' self-reported access to green space (Model 2). The last model focuses on the objective measure (Model 3).

The results are displayed in Table 13.2. Overall, the models are able to account for about 25 per cent of the variation of the data, which is comparable to other studies of this kind. Across the models, the results for the exogenous variables are similar with regard to the direction of the effect and significance, and correspond well to other findings reported in the literature (see Dolan et al., 2008 for a comprehensive review). In the following we focus on the results of Model 1 as there are only minor differences between the three models.

Table 13.1 Summary statistics and descriptions of the variables used

Variable name	Description	Mean	Std dev.	Min.	Max.
Life satisfaction					
Life satisfaction	Overall life satisfaction, measured on a scale from 1 ('very dissatisfied') to 10 ('very satisfied')	7.045	2.149	1	10
Individual and household characteristics					
Household income	Total net household annual income, in Euros	20 875.74	17 193.13	300	66 000
Gender	Gender dummy, 1 if 'female', 0 if 'male'	0.570	0.495	0	1
Age	Age, measured in years (maximum documented 95 years)	51.18	17.76	18	95
Married	Marital status dummy, 1 if 'married or living with partner', 0 otherwise	0.601	0.490	0	1
Separated	Marital status dummy, 1 if 'separated or divorced and not living with partner', 0 otherwise	0.116	0.320	0	1
Widowed	Marital status dummy, 1 if 'widowed and not living with partner', 0 otherwise	0.130	0.336	0	1
Never married*	Marital status dummy, 1 if 'never married and not living with partner', 0 otherwise	0.153	0.360	0	1
Very good health	Health status dummy, 1 if 'very good health', 0 otherwise	0.197	0.397	0	1
Good health	Health status dummy, 1 if 'good health', 0 otherwise	0.383	0.486	0	1
Fair health	Health status dummy, 1 if 'fair health', 0 otherwise	0.303	0.460	0	1
Bad health	Health status dummy, 1 if 'bad health', 0 otherwise	0.091	0.287	0	1
Very bad health*	Health status dummy, 1 if 'very bad health', 0 otherwise	0.026	0.159	0	1
No education completed*	Education level dummy, 1 if ISCED level 0 (no education completed), 0 otherwise	0.014	0.116	0	1
Primary education	Education level dummy, 1 if ISCED level 1 (primary education), 0 otherwise	0.103	0.304	0	1
Lower secondary education	Education level dummy, 1 if ISCED level 2 (lower secondary education), 0 otherwise	0.209	0.406	0	1
Upper secondary education	Education level dummy, 1 if ISCED level 3 (upper secondary education), 0 otherwise	0.376	0.484	0	1
Post-secondary education	Education level dummy, 1 if ISCED level 4 (post-secondary including pre-vocational or vocational education but not tertiary), 0 otherwise	0.059	0.235	0	1

Table 13.1 (continued)

Variable name	Description	Mean	Std dev.	Min.	Max.
Tertiary education – first level	Education level dummy, 1 if ISCED level 5 (tertiary education – first level), 0 otherwise	0.229	0.420	0	1
Tertiary education – advanced level	Education level dummy, 1 if ISCED level 6 (tertiary education – advanced level), 0 otherwise	0.011	0.105	0	1
Employed	Employment status dummy, 1 if 'employed', 0 otherwise	0.459	0.498	0	1
Unemployed*	Employment status dummy, 1 if 'unemployed', 0 otherwise	0.072	0.259	0	1
Unable	Employment status dummy, 1 if 'unable', 0 otherwise	0.024	0.154	0	1
Retired	Employment status dummy, 1 if 'retired', 0 otherwise	0.327	0.469	0	1
Homemaker	Employment status dummy, 1 if 'homemaker', 0 otherwise	0.066	0.249	0	1
Student	Employment status dummy, 1 if 'student', 0 otherwise	0.038	0.191	0	1
Other	Employment status dummy, 1 if 'other', 0 otherwise	0.013	0.114	0	1
Trust	Level of trust, measured on a scale from 1 ('you can't be too careful') to 10 ('most people can be trusted')	5.103	2.481	1	10
Religious services – (almost) every day	Religious services attendance dummy, 1 if 'every day or almost every day', 0 otherwise	0.018	0.132	0	1
Religious services – at least once a week	Religious services attendance dummy, 1 if 'at least once a week', 0 otherwise	0.150	0.358	0	1
Religious services – 1 to 3 times a month	Religious services attendance dummy, 1 if 'one to three times a month', 0 otherwise	0.102	0.303	0	1
Religious services – less often	Religious services attendance dummy, 1 if 'less often', 0 otherwise	0.320	0.466	0	1
Religious services – never*	Religious services attendance dummy, 1 if 'never', 0 otherwise	0.410	0.492	0	1
Citizen	Citizen dummy, 1 if citizen of the country of residence, 0 otherwise	0.957	0.204	0	1
Children	Number of children of one's own (maximum documented 10 children)	1.614	1.304	0	10
People in household	Number of people living in the household	2.466	1.309	1	10

Macro-level characteristics					
EU15	EU15 country dummy, 1 if country joined the EU before 2004, 0 otherwise	0.612	0.487	0	1
Population density	Population density on NUTS 2 level	327.24	706.27	3.3	7131.1
Open countryside*	Living area dummy, 1 if 'the open countryside', 0 otherwise	0.109	0.312	0	1
Village/small town	Living area dummy, 1 if 'a village/small town', 0 otherwise	0.377	0.485	0	1
Medium to large town	Living area dummy, 1 if 'a medium to large town', 0 otherwise	0.280	0.449	0	1
City/city suburb	Living area dummy, 1 if 'a city or city suburb', 0 otherwise	0.235	0.424	0	1
Average precipitation	Average monthly precipitation in a large city in the NUTS 2 region, measured in mm	57.29	14.38	24	110
Average temperature summer	Average temperature in the months June, July and August in a large city in the NUTS 2 region, measured in °C	18.43	3.336	5.4	27.1
Average temperature winter	Average temperature in the months December, January, February in a large city in the NUTS 2 region, measured in °C	1.795	4.740	−8.7	13
Area variables					
Degree of access green areas	Subjectively perceived access to recreational or green areas, measured on a scale from 1 ('with great difficulty') to 4 ('very easily'); those that do not use this service (see below) excluded	3.267	0.755	1	4
Access green areas – with great difficulty*	Green area access dummy (subjective), 1 if 'with great difficulty', 0 otherwise	0.028	0.165	0	1
Access green areas – with some difficulty	Green area access dummy (subjective), 1 if 'with some difficulty', 0 otherwise	0.088	0.283	0	1
Access green areas – easily	Green area access dummy (subjective), 1 if 'easily', 0 otherwise	0.412	0.492	0	1
Access green areas – very easily	Green area access dummy (subjective), 1 if 'very easily', 0 otherwise	0.389	0.487	0	1
Access green areas – service not used	Green area access dummy (subjective), 1 if 'service not used', 0 otherwise	0.083	0.276	0	1
Green space – objective	Share of green space in the NUTS 2 region, including 'Amenities, museums, leisure'	0.019	0.025	0	0.143

Note: * Reference category; 26 859 observations.

Table 13.2 Results of the OLS regressions

Variable name	Model 1	Model 2[a]	Model 3	Model 4[a]
Individual and household characteristics				
Log household income	0.3251***	0.3113***	0.3296***	0.3117***
	(0.03)	(0.03)	(0.03)	(0.03)
Gender	0.0546**	0.0716***	0.0548**	0.0713***
	(0.02)	(0.02)	(0.02)	(0.02)
Age	−0.0465***	−0.0477***	−0.0455***	−0.0476***
	(0.01)	(0.01)	(0.01)	(0.01)
Age^2	0.0005***	0.0005***	0.0005***	0.0005***
	(0.00)	(0.00)	(0.00)	(0.00)
Married	0.2261***	0.2088***	0.2302***	0.2101***
	(0.04)	(0.05)	(0.04)	(0.05)
Separated	−0.2186***	−0.2075***	−0.2147***	−0.2059***
	(0.05)	(0.05)	(0.05)	(0.05)
Widowed	−0.0850	−0.0591	−0.0862	−0.0581
	(0.06)	(0.06)	(0.06)	(0.06)
Never married	*[Reference category]*			
Very good health	2.4764***	2.2467***	2.5009***	2.2456***
	(0.11)	(0.13)	(0.12)	(0.13)
Good health	2.0706***	1.8725***	2.0941***	1.8722***
	(0.11)	(0.1219)	(0.11)	(0.12)
Fair health	1.6435***	1.4496***	1.6646***	1.4499***
	(0.10)	(0.11)	(0.10)	(0.11)
Bad health	0.8169***	0.6150***	0.8234***	0.6159***
	(0.10)	(0.12)	(0.11)	(0.12)
Very bad health	*[Reference category]*			
No education completed	*[Reference category]*			
Primary education	−0.0795	−0.0856	−0.0882	−0.0832
	(0.12)	(0.13)	(0.12)	(0.13)
Lower secondary education	−0.0708	−0.0705	−0.0624	−0.0681
	(0.12)	(0.13)	(0.12)	(0.13)
Upper secondary education	−0.0062	0.0045	0.0091	0.0066
	(0.12)	(0.13)	(0.12)	(0.13)
Post-secondary education	−0.0083	0.0080	0.0053	0.0102
	(0.14)	(0.16)	(0.14)	(0.16)
Tertiary education – first level	0.0607	0.0660	0.0821	0.0691
	(0.12)	(0.14)	(0.12)	(0.14)
Tertiary education – advanced level	0.2123	0.2374	0.2306	0.2416
	(0.15)	(0.16)	(0.15)	(0.16)
Employed	0.8218***	0.8359***	0.8204***	0.8350***
	(0.06)	(0.06)	(0.06)	(0.06)
Unemployed	*[Reference category]*			
Unable	0.5935***	0.6157***	0.5963***	0.6143***
	(0.11)	(0.12)	(0.11)	(0.12)
Retired	0.9924***	1.0298***	0.9952***	1.0292***
	(0.09)	(0.08)	(0.08)	(0.08)

Table 13.2 (continued)

Variable name	Model 1	Model 2[a]	Model 3	Model 4[a]
Homemaker	0.7573***	0.7625***	0.7559***	0.7622***
	(0.08)	(0.08)	(0.08)	(0.08)
Student	0.9955***	1.0001***	0.9987***	1.0005***
	(0.08)	(0.08)	(0.08)	(0.08)
Other	0.6654***	0.7138***	0.6559***	0.7137***
	(0.12)	(0.12)	(0.12)	(0.12)
Trust	0.1306***	0.1221***	0.1313***	0.1220***
	(0.01)	(0.01)	(0.01)	(0.01)
Religious services – (almost) every day	0.2426**	0.1935*	0.2455**	0.1927*
	(0.11)	(0.11)	(0.11)	(0.11)
Religious services – at least once a week	0.1864***	0.1768***	0.1918***	0.1779***
	(0.05)	(0.05)	(0.05)	(0.05)
Religious services – 1 to 3 times a month	0.0506	0.0483	0.0558	0.0493
	(0.05)	(0.05)	(0.05)	(0.05)
Religious services – less often	0.1014***	0.1013***	0.1050***	0.1029***
	(0.03)	(0.03)	(0.03)	(0.03)
Religious services – never	*[Reference category]*			
Citizen	0.1323*	0.0943	0.1366*	0.0965
	(0.07)	(0.07)	(0.07)	(0.07)
Children	0.0446***	0.0470***	0.0440***	0.0471***
	(0.01)	(0.01)	(0.01)	(0.01)
People in household	−0.0471***	−0.0437***	−0.0474***	−0.0440***
	(0.01)	(0.01)	(0.01)	(0.01)
Macro-level characteristics				
EU15	12.7300***	10.8135**	13.6976***	10.8841**
	(4.43)	(5.26)	(4.77)	(5.31)
Population density	−0.0001*	−0.0001	−0.0000	−0.0001
	(0.00)	(0.00)	(0.00)	(0.00)
Open countryside	*[Reference category]*			
Village/small town	−0.1270**	−0.1275**	−0.1215**	−0.1257**
	(0.05)	(0.05)	(0.05)	(0.05)
Medium to large town	−0.2676***	−0.2660***	−0.2588***	−0.2631***
	(0.06)	(0.06)	(0.06)	(0.06)
City/city suburb	−0.2631***	−0.2462***	−0.2450***	−0.2428***
	(0.06)	(0.06)	(0.06)	(0.06)
Average precipitation	−0.0039*	−0.0028	−0.0035	−0.0027
	(0.00)	(0.00)	(0.00)	(0.00)
Average temperature summer	0.0075	0.0088	0.0092	0.0090
	(0.01)	(0.01)	(0.01)	(0.01)
Average temperature winter	−0.0193	−0.0125	−0.0218*	−0.0123
	(0.01)	(0.01)	(0.01)	(0.01)

Table 13.2 (continued)

Variable name	Model 1	Model 2[a]	Model 3	Model 4[a]
Area variables				
Access green areas – service not used	−0.2758*** (0.05)			
Degree of access green areas		0.2169*** (0.02)		
Green space – objective			−1.8876* (1.11)	
Access green areas – with great difficulty				*[Reference category]*
Access green areas – with some difficulty				0.0261 (0.16)
Access green areas – easily				0.3327** (0.15)
Access green areas – very easily				0.5373*** (0.14)
Number of observations	26859	24623	26859	24623
Adjusted R^2	0.2467	0.2404	0.2457	0.2405

Notes:
* Significant at the 10 per cent level; ** significant at the 5 per cent level; *** significant at the 1 per cent level; standard errors in parentheses. Country dummy variables included but not displayed.
[a] Models 2 and 4 include users, while Models 1 and 3 capture both users and non-users.

Like earlier studies, we find a positive but diminishing marginal effect of income on life satisfaction, and age has an inverted U-shaped relationship with life satisfaction. The effect of better health is also unambiguously positive and substantial. All other respondents have higher levels of life satisfaction than those stating very bad health conditions. Similarly for employment status, respondents who are unemployed report significantly lower levels of life satisfaction compared to all other respondents. The difference is especially large for those who are employed or retired, and for students. Viewed from the reference group of respondents who were never married, those who are married or live with their partner are significantly more satisfied, those who are separated or divorced significantly less so. Additionally, a higher level of trust in other people positively and significantly influences life satisfaction; while wellbeing is lower with more people living in the household.

Female respondents report a higher level of wellbeing compared to male respondents, although the coefficient is only slightly significant. This is in line with Dolan et al. (2008) reporting a tendency towards higher levels of life satisfaction among women. We find no significant effect of education, which is also in line with Dolan et al. A higher number of one's own children also has a small positive and significant effect. Dolan et al., however, find mixed evidence on this aspect and emphasize that the effect of having children varies greatly with other circumstances.

A higher frequency of attending religious services generally has a positive effect, but significant differences are not found for every group. This finding is not completely in line with what was found by Dolan et al., as they report a high consistency of significant effects. Nevertheless, the tendency is comparable with higher attendance levels being associated with higher life satisfaction.

Those who live in the EU15 also report a significantly higher level of life satisfaction. The effect of the living environment is unequivocal.[13] Those living in more urban areas report a significantly lower level of life satisfaction. The difference between the open countryside as reference group and small towns or villages is less clear, as shown by a significance level of only 5 per cent. Being a citizen of the country one is living in, and a country's population density, have no significant effects. The effect of the climate variables is negligible.

Turning to the green space variables, the results of Model 1 reveal that the use of recreational or green areas is associated with higher levels of life satisfaction. Non-users of green space report on average a −0.2758 lower level of life satisfaction compared to users.

Reducing the sample to those who report using green space (Model 2), the number of observations declines from 26 859 to 24 623. The results are as expected: those respondents who have easier access to recreational or green areas obtain higher levels of life satisfaction. The variable is again highly significant, but the effect, as in Model 1, is moderate in size (0.2169).

Turning to Model 3, the effect of a higher share of green area in a NUTS 2 region on life satisfaction is unexpectedly signed. We find a negative coefficient of the objective green space measure; which is, however, only significant at the 10 per cent level.[14]

13.6 DISCUSSION

13.6.1 General Considerations

Focusing on the findings from the models with the subjective measure of green space first, the results fit nicely into earlier research on this topic. What needs to be scrutinized more closely, however, are the monetary values. Taking the results from the former section and equation (13.4), the monetary value of a change in subjectively perceived access to green areas can be estimated. An increase in access of one level is worth €15 083 of annual household income based on average green space availability and average income (€21 648 in this restricted sample).[15] There are substantial differences in the WTP depending on the current level of green space accessibility (see Table 13.2, Model 4 and Table 13.3). To get from the worst level ('with great difficulty') to the second level ('with some difficulty'), the average WTP is €1818 per household per year, mounting from the second to the third ('easily') level is worth €21 318; and to get from the third to the highest ('very easily') level, the average WTP would be €14 231. As there are on average 2.5 people living in a household in this sample (see Table 13.1), the average per capita willingness to pay amounts to €6033 per year.

Although difficult to compare, estimates in other studies are much lower. Bertram

Table 13.3 Average WTP to get from one level of green space accessibility to another

From \ To	Access green areas – with some difficulty	Access green areas – easily	Access green areas – very easily
Access green areas – with great difficulty	€1818	€23 136	€37 367
Access green areas – with some difficulty		€21 318	€35 549
Access green areas – easily			€14 231

Source: Own calculations based on Model 4.

and Rehdanz (2015: 148), for example, derive a marginal rate of substitution of €451 per household per year for an increase of 1 hectare of urban green space in a 1 km radius around households. The results of Krekel et al. (2016: 123) are in a similar range, with an average willingness to pay of €690 per household per hectare per year in the same radius. Even the comparatively higher amounts that were found by Ambrey and Fleming (2014: 1290) lie markedly below the results of this study, with €1737 per household per year for a 1 per cent increase in green space.[16] The discrepancy is striking, but it needs to be mentioned that it is not possible to accurately compare the levels of the present analysis with hectares. Generally, high values seem common for the life satisfaction approach, as is noted by, among others, Dolan and Metcalfe (2008: 3) and MacKerron and Mourato (2009: 1450).

Ferreira and Moro (2010: 270) argue that their high estimate could be due to a relatively low income coefficient. Bertram and Rehdanz (2015: 149) also discuss the reliability of the income coefficient. A downward bias could result from missing information on relative income, as this is seen as having an impact on life satisfaction as well. An upward bias may arise from endogeneity of income, namely that happier people are paid better. Character traits included in the analysis might reduce the endogeneity bias, an aspect that could be considered at least to some extent with the trust variable. With regard to the substantial estimates of the willingness to pay, it is possible that the former aspect – a downward bias on the income variable – might weigh heavier in the present study when comparing to estimates of earlier studies.

Moreover, green space valuation is a broad concept at least in two dimensions. First, as was already mentioned in section 13.2, what is defined as green space greatly varies across studies. Comparisons are thus not always straightforward. Second, there are different approaches to valuing green space. Ode Sang et al. (2016) reflect on this point and emphasize that the amount of green space, its accessibility, use, proximity and naturalness, are all relevant facets. This is also mirrored in the present study, with Model 1 focusing on the use of green space, Model 2 being based on accessibility and Model 3 focusing on the amount of green space available.

The type of green space also seems to play an important role which has an impact on urban planning. As green areas are especially scarce in cities, Saw et al. (2015: 3) argue that optimization is crucial, in the sense that the most useful type of green space is realized; while Byrne et al. (2010: 162) call for 'needs-based' park planning.

Many studies focus on the combination of different facets of green space, such as Liu et al. (2017) who advocate a park system that is both efficient and equally distributed, and Gobster and Westphal (2004) who state that cleanliness, naturalness, aesthetics, safety, access and appropriateness of development together determine people's perception of green areas. Tsurumi and Managi (2015) focus more on individual attributes such as the affection for green space, knowledge about its functions and quality as determinants of willingness to pay. It is also evident from the Schipperijn et al. (2010) study that different components of green areas need to be scrutinized. They find that the nearest park is not the one used most, but that the usage also depends on size, among other things. Many of these aspects could not be included in the present analysis, especially effects resulting from the interaction of different facets.

The unsatisfying results based on the objective measure of green space, which will be further discussed in the next subsection, should nevertheless not necessarily distract from the results based on the subjective measure. A number of studies make the difference between subjective and objective measures the focus of discussion, including Ball et al. (2008), Dadvand et al. (2016) and Dzhambov et al. (2018). Although not focused on life satisfaction, Dadvand et al. (2016) report no effect of objective proximity to green space on perceived general health, whereas subjective proximity indeed emerges as a significant indicator. Moreover, Ode Sang et al. (2016) emphasize that in their study, perceived access to green space is more important than geographical access or proximity for self-reported wellbeing.

13.6.2 Strengths and Weaknesses

Focusing on the first two regressions of the present study, a number of strengths can be identified that result from the database. As Mitchell et al. (2015: 83) remark, the EQLS provides much data on the individual and regional level that allow capturing important influences on life satisfaction. In contrast to surveys conducted solely for one life satisfaction study, the sample is large, comprises many countries, and users and non-users of green space can be identified.

There are, however, still a number of shortcomings mainly stemming from the green space measures applied. The question on green space availability does not give a clear-cut definition but instead asks for 'recreational or green areas'. Depending on the individual background, respondents might also think of sporting facilities or public squares, making it difficult to interpret and compare the results.

Further, despite the wide range of variables there is always unobserved heterogeneity. In the present case, personality traits are not adequately displayed as the so-called 'big five' personality trait controls are not included which might have an influence on the WTP estimates. Their importance is discussed, for example, by Ambrey and Fleming (2014: 1296). This demonstrates that – for some aspects – self-conducted studies have an advantage over large-scale but more general surveys, as there are sometimes variables missing that are crucial for the research purpose. The necessity of including personality measures in large datasets has already been mentioned by Boyce (2010: 13).

Another unobserved variable is privately owned open space. Its importance is debated by, among others, White et al. (2013: 922) and Krekel et al. (2016: 126). Especially, Cameron et al. (2012) elaborate more on this topic and argue that private gardens provide value not only for their owners but also for the general public. Grunewald et al. (2017: 36) go even further and argue that opening private allotments to the public would increase green space provision, especially in areas with deficits. Most life satisfaction studies, however, exclude privately owned green space from their analyses.

As concerns the subjective measure in the present study, the vague formulation of the question on green space may include privately owned gardens, but it is uncertain whether all respondents thought about it in the same way when answering the question. The objective measure does not include private gardens, as these are included in the 'Residential' (U370) class in the LUCAS database (Eurostat, 2013: 76).

Causality is also a topic that needs to be addressed, as it is not always straightforward to infer in which direction a detected relationship between two variables works (see, e.g., Dolan et al., 2008). That this can be also problematic for environmental amenities is shown by Chay and Greenstone (2005), who find some sort of self-selection residence bias for air quality. Nevertheless, Luechinger (2010) shows that this does not totally eliminate the effect of air quality on life satisfaction, by employing instrumental variables. Tsurumi and Managi (2015) also try to account for potential reversed causality by using instrumental variables for income and green space. That causality would be easier to deduce with panel data is shown by, for example, Blanchflower and Oswald (2004).

Beyond these issues, there is one aspect that seems to weaken the present analysis most, namely that the objective green space measure is not robust. The LUCAS data are a rough measure only, as point estimates are being used and there is no complete inventory of the land use for each hectare. Beyond that, the land use categories do not allow a clear-cut extraction of all green space types. The aggregation level on NUTS 2 regions also seems insufficient for a refined analysis. This deficit, however, is not uncommon in this area of study, which is noticed by, among others, MacKerron and Mourato (2009: 1443). For Welsch and Ferreira (2014: 219), the optimal level of aggregation would mirror the area individuals actually perceive as their surrounding.

13.7 CONCLUSION

This chapter aimed to answer the research question, 'What is the influence of green areas on life satisfaction using subjective and objective measures comparatively and what conclusions can be drawn from that for the value of green areas?' Using data for the EU27 from the third wave of the EQLS, the LUCAS dataset and additional sources, no significant influence of the objective measure for green space on life satisfaction was found. Subjectively perceived accessibility of green space, however, has a significant positive influence on life satisfaction in the given sample, even in a regression comprising a wide range of socio-economic and macro-level factors. However, the derived willingness-to-pay value seems inconceivably high. The relatively small income coefficient might give an explanation for this.

Nevertheless, the life satisfaction approach is a promising environmental valuation method, as it has several advantages over other methods. Welsch and Kühling (2009) therefore highlight that this method, due to its dissimilar approach of using life satisfaction data, can serve as a complement to the other environmental valuation methods and as a basis for comparisons. This could be done, for example, to realize the earlier-mentioned ecosystem service assessment requested by the EU Biodiversity Strategy.

What has become apparent in the present analysis, and in reflecting upon other research, is that what facet of green space is considered and what is defined as green space is important. The latter distinction is also made by *Die Zeit* journalist Erenz (2017) with whose work this chapter started. He emphasizes that flat green areas mainly consisting of lawn are not attractive; something that the findings of the literature and of this chapter cannot disprove.

Future research could use the new wave of the EQLS published recently where the question on the accessibility of recreational or green areas is included again (Eurofound, 2018). Beyond that, for a more reliable and profound analysis a better objective measure would be reasonable with a higher spatial resolution and where green space can be defined more precisely, for example the CORINE database (Copernicus Programme, 2018).

Another aspect that was not covered is the importance of interaction effects that is highlighted by, among others, Larson et al. (2016), but is beyond the scope of this study. The different effects of green space on life satisfaction experienced by different groups is investigated by, for example, Ambrey and Fleming (2014) and Bertram and Rehdanz (2015). The heterogeneity, however, emerged to be lower than expected in these studies. Thus, further research in this area would be helpful, as well as to compare the different countries in the analysis.

Additionally, the use of panel data where available could improve the meaningfulness of the analysis, as it would be possible to assess causality. An expansion of the field of study could also lead to interesting results, either with the available EQLS dataset for Europe or even for other climatic regions and less developed countries.

In conclusion, this study shows that there exists a significant relationship between subjectively perceived accessibility of green space and life satisfaction in the 27 member states of the European Union. This finding holds even though we control for a wide range of socio-economic and macro-level factors. The derived monetary value for an increase in green space nevertheless seems large compared to previous results. Objectively measured amounts of green space within the NUTS 2 region have no significant and robust effect on life satisfaction. Further research utilizing more disaggregated data that better reflect the area that people perceive as their surrounding would be welcome.

NOTES

1. In this chapter, the terms 'green space' and 'green areas' are used interchangeably.
2. The Nomenclature of Territorial Units for Statistics (NUTS) classification was introduced by Eurostat in order to have a standardized breakdown of the territory of the European Union for regional statistics and for targeting of policy interventions (European Union, 2015: 4, 6). Where existing, the regions are constituted by already-employed administrative units of the respective countries. The average size of the NUTS 2 regions lies between 800 000 and 3 million inhabitants.
3. Depending on the green space measure applied (subjective or objective), it is either individual-specific (subscript i) or location-specific (subscript j). Detailed information on the different measures can be found below.
4. Using the mean income here is only a convention, but the differences to using different levels of income are expected to be negligible. It would also be possible to show the MWTP for different percentiles of the income distribution.
5. The principal investigator and sponsor of this survey was the European Foundation for the Improvement of Living and Working Conditions; the data were collected by GfK EU3C. They were distributed by the UK Data Archive, University of Essex, January 2014, and can be accessed at https://www.ukdataservice.ac.uk.

6. Since some additional data are only available for the EU27, this chapter concentrates on these countries. For France and the United Kingdom, information is only available at higher levels of aggregation (nine regions for France and ten for the United Kingdom). Note that the EQLS excludes EU27 countries' remote islands (for example, Madeira).
7. Although the EQLS also includes a question on the exact net household income, income categories are used. Otherwise, too many observations would have been excluded due to missing exact income reports. We admit, however, that this might cause a small bias. Converting midpoints to purchasing power parities to account for different price levels in the countries does not change the results.
8. The health channel plays a negligible role in the relationship between green space and life satisfaction, as the results are robust to excluding the self-reported health status.
9. Information on the level of urbanization and the EU15 is provided by the EQLS. Data on population density refer to the year 2011 when the third wave of the EQLS was conducted in the EU (GfK EU3C, n.d.: 4), and were obtained from the online presence of Eurostat: http://ec.europa.eu/eurostat/web/products-datasets/product?code=tgs00024 and http://ec.europa.eu/eurostat/web/products-datasets/product?code=demo_r_d3dens. In the case of Slovenia, data for the year 2014 are taken because earlier statistics at the NUTS 2 level are not available.
10. Data are taken from https://en.climate-data.org/location/17/ for one major city in each NUTS 2 region.
11. http://ec.europa.eu/eurostat/web/lucas/data/primary-data/2012.
12. Detailed information on the exact classification can be found in Eurostat (2013).
13. Although one could expect a relationship with the amount of objective green space, omitting the living area variable does not change the green space coefficient substantially.
14. We tried different specifications of the objective measure in a sensitivity analysis; we add the following categories to the initial one: 'Kitchen garden' (U113), 'Forestry' (U120) and/or 'Seminatural and natural areas not in use' (U420). The coefficients of these specifications are insignificant.
15. Although no formal analysis was conducted, skimming through the mean values of the whole and restricted sample reveals that there are slight differences. Those who use green space not only have higher income on average, but are also more often employed or enrolled as students, more often live in cities and the EU15, and trust more. For the other variables the differences are negligible. A thorough analysis would be necessary to elicit whether these variations are of importance.
16. Given the original value of AU$1172 and an exchange rate of €1.48218/AUD as of 31 December 2014.

REFERENCES

Ambrey, C.L. and C.M. Fleming (2014), 'Public greenspace and life satisfaction in urban Australia', *Urban Studies*, **51** (6), 1290–1321.

Anderson, S.T. and S.E. West (2006), 'Open space, residential property values, and spatial context', *Regional Science and Urban Economics*, **36** (6), 773–789.

Ball, K., Jeffery, R.W., Crawford, D.A., Roberts, R.J., Salmon, J. and A.F. Timperio (2008), 'Mismatch between perceived and objective measures of physical activity environments', *Preventive Medicine*, **47** (3), 294–298.

Bengochea Morancho, A. (2003), 'A hedonic valuation of urban green areas', *Landscape and Urban Planning*, **66** (1), 35–41.

Bertram, C. and N. Larondelle (2017), 'Going to the woods is going home: recreational benefits of a larger urban forest site – a travel cost analysis for Berlin, Germany', *Ecological Economics*, **132**, 255–263.

Bertram, C. and K. Rehdanz (2015), 'The role of urban green space for human well-being', *Ecological Economics*, **120**, 139–152.

Bishop, K. (1992), 'Assessing the benefits of community forests: an evaluation of the recreational use benefits of two urban fringe woodlands', *Journal of Environmental Planning and Management*, **35** (1), 63–76.

Blanchflower, D.G. and A.J. Oswald (2004), 'Well-being over time in Britain and the USA', *Journal of Public Economics*, **88** (7), 1359–1386.

Boyce, C.J. (2010), 'Understanding fixed effects in human well-being', *Journal of Economic Psychology*, **31** (1), 1–16.

Braubach, M., Egorov, A., Mudu, P., Wolf, T., Thompson, C.W. and M. Martuzzi (2017), 'Effects of urban green space on environmental health, equity and resilience', in Nadja Kabisch, Horst Korn, Jutta Stadler and Aletta Bonn (eds), *Nature-Based Solutions to Climate Change Adaptation in Urban Areas, Theory and Practice of Urban Sustainability Transitions*, Cham, Switzerland: Springer, pp. 187–205.

Brereton, F., Clinch, J.P. and S. Ferreira (2008), 'Happiness, geography and the environment', *Ecological Economics*, **65** (2), 386–396.

Bullock, C.H. (2006), 'Using choice experiments to value urban green space', in David Pearce (ed.),

Environmental Valuation in Developed Countries: Case Studies, Cheltenham, UK and Northampton, MA, USA: Edward Elgar Publishing, pp. 240–251.
Bullock, C.H. (2008), 'Valuing urban green space: hypothetical alternatives and the status quo', *Journal of Environmental Planning and Management*, **51** (1), 15–35.
Byrne, J., Sipe, N. and G. Searle (2010), 'Green around the gills? The challenge of density for urban greenspace planning in SEQ', *Australian Planner*, **47** (3), 162–177.
Cameron, R.W.F., Blanuša, T., Taylor, J.E., Salisbury, A., Halstead, A.J., et al. (2012), 'The domestic garden: its contribution to urban green infrastructure', *Urban Forestry and Urban Greening*, **11** (2), 129–137.
Chay, K.Y. and M. Greenstone (2005), 'Does air quality matter? Evidence from the housing market', *Journal of Political Economy*, **113** (2), 376–424.
Copernicus Programme (2018), 'CORINE land cover'. Accessed 1 May 2018 at https://land.copernicus.eu/pan-european/corine-land-cover/view.
Coppel, G. and H. Wüstemann (2017), 'The impact of urban green space on health in Berlin, Germany: empirical findings and implications for urban planning', *Landscape and Urban Planning*, **167**, 410–418.
Dadvand, P., Bartoll, X., Basagaña, X., Dalmau-Bueno, A., Martinez, D., et al. (2016), 'Green spaces and general health: roles of mental health status, social support, and physical activity', *Environment International*, **91**, 161–167.
Dolan, P. and R. Metcalfe (2008), 'Comparing willingness-to-pay and subjective well-being in the context of non-market goods', CEP Discussion Paper No. 890, London School of Economics.
Dolan, P., Peasgood, T. and M. White (2008), 'Do we really know what makes us happy? A review of the economic literature on the factors associated with subjective well-being', *Journal of Economic Psychology*, **29** (1), 94–122.
Dzhambov, A., Hartig, T., Markevych, I., Tilov, B. and D. Dimitrova (2018), 'Urban residential greenspace and mental health in youth: different approaches to testing multiple pathways yield different conclusions', *Environmental Research*, **160**, 47–59.
Erenz, B. (2017), 'Dann lieber grau' (In that case, grey), *Die Zeit*, **40**, 59–60.
Eurofound (2018), '4th European Quality of Life Survey: source questionnaire'. Accessed 1 May 2018 at https://www.eurofound.europa.eu/sites/default/files/ef_survey/field_ef_documents/4th_eqls_final_master_source_questionnaire_12_june_2017_-_updated_07_september_2017.pdf.
European Commission (2011), 'Our Life Insurance, Our Natural Capital: An EU Biodiversity Strategy to 2020. Communication from the European Commission to the European Parliament, the Council, the Economic and Social Committee and the Committee of the Regions'. Accessed 1 February 2018 at https://eur-lex.europa.eu/legal-content/EN/TXT/PDF/?uri=CELEX:52011DC0244&from=EN.
European Commission (2013), *Building a Green Infrastructure for Europe*, Luxembourg: Publications Office of the European Union.
European Union (2015), *Regions in the European Union: Nomenclature of Territorial Units for Statistics NUTS 2013/EU-28*, Luxembourg: Publications Office of the European Union.
Eurostat (2013), 'LUCAS 2012 – Technical Reference Document: C-3 Land Use and Land Cover Classification (Revised) (No. 1/1)'. Accessed 5 May 2018 at http://ec.europa.eu/eurostat/documents/205002/208012/LUCAS2012_C3-Classification_20131004_0.pdf/a71e46b5-a14b-4c9e-83ed-4f973dc139e0.
Ferreira, S. and M. Moro (2010), 'On the use of subjective well-being data for environmental valuation', *Environmental and Resource Economics*, **46** (3), 249–273.
Ferrer-i-Carbonell, A. and P. Frijters (2004), 'How important is methodology for the estimates of the determinants of happiness?', *Economic Journal*, **114** (497), 641–659.
Freeman III, A. Myrick (2003), 'Resource evaluation and public policy', in A. Myrick Freeman III, *The Measurement of Environmental and Resource Values: Theory and Methods*, Washington, DC, USA: Resources for the Future, pp. 1–18.
Frey, B.S., Luechinger, S. and A. Stutzer (2010), 'The life satisfaction approach to environmental valuation', *Annual Review of Resource Economics*, **2** (1), 139–160.
Frijters, P. and B.M.S. van Praag (1998), 'The effects of climate on welfare and well-being in Russia', *Climatic Change*, **39** (1), 61–81.
GfK EU3C (n.d), '3rd European Quality of Life Survey: Technical Report, UK Data Archive Study Number 7316 – European Quality of Life Survey, 2011–2012'. Accessed 29 March 2018 at https://www.eurofound.europa.eu/sites/default/files/ef_files/surveys/eqls/2011/documents/technicalreport.pdf.
Gidlöf-Gunnarsson, A. and E. Öhrström (2007), 'Noise and well-being in urban residential environments: the potential role of perceived availability to nearby green areas', *Landscape and Urban Planning*, **83** (2), 115–126.
Gobster, P.H. and L.M. Westphal (2004), 'The human dimensions of urban greenways: planning for recreation and related experiences', *Landscape and Urban Planning*, **68** (2), 147–165.
Grunewald, K., Richter, B., Meinel, G., Herold, H. and R-U. Syrbe (2017), 'Proposal of indicators regarding the provision and accessibility of green spaces for assessing the ecosystem service "Recreation in the City" in Germany', *International Journal of Biodiversity Science, Ecosystem Services and Management*, **13** (2), 26–39.

Hanauer, M.M. and J. Reid (2017), 'Valuing urban open space using the travel-cost method and the implications of measurement error', *Journal of Environmental Management*, **198**, 50–65.

Hart, E.A.C., Lakerveld, J., McKee, M., Oppert, J.-M., Rutter, H., et al. (2018), 'Contextual correlates of happiness in European adults', *PLOS ONE*, **13** (1), 1–17.

Horne, P., Boxall, P.C. and W.L. Adamowicz (2005), 'Multiple-use management of forest recreation sites: a spatially explicit choice experiment', *Forest Ecology and Management*, **207** (1–2), 189–199.

Khan, H. (2006), 'Willingness to pay for Margalla Hills National Park: evidence from the travel cost method', *Lahore Journal of Economics*, **11** (2), 43–70.

Kim, J.H., Kim, S.-N. and S. Doh (2015), 'The distance decay of willingness to pay and the spatial distribution of benefits and costs for the ecological restoration of an urban branch stream in Ulsan, South Korea', *Annals of Regional Science*, **54** (3), 835–853.

Kong, F., Yin, H. and N. Nakagoshi (2007), 'Using GIS and landscape metrics in the hedonic price modeling of the amenity value of urban green space: a case study in Jinan City, China', *Landscape and Urban Planning*, **79** (3–4), 240–252.

Kopmann, A. and K. Rehdanz (2013), 'A human well-being approach for assessing the value of natural land areas', *Ecological Economics*, **93**, 20–33.

Krekel, C., Kolbe, J. and H. Wüstemann (2016), 'The greener, the happier? The effect of urban land use on residential well-being', *Ecological Economics*, **121**, 117–127.

Larson, L.R., Jennings, V. and S.A. Cloutier (2016), 'Public parks and wellbeing in urban areas of the United States', *PLOS ONE*, **11** (4), e0153211.

Liu, W., Chen, W. and C. Dong (2017), 'Spatial decay of recreational services of urban parks: characteristics and influencing factors', *Urban Forestry and Urban Greening*, **25**, 130–138.

López-Mosquera, N., García, T. and R. Barrena (2014), 'An extension of the Theory of Planned Behavior to predict willingness to pay for the conservation of an urban park', *Journal of Environmental Management*, **135**, 91–99.

Luechinger, S. (2010), 'Life satisfaction and transboundary air pollution', *Economics Letters*, **107** (1), 4–6.

Maas, J., Verheij, R.A., Groenewegen, P.P., de Vries, S. and P. Spreeuwenberg (2006), 'Green space, urbanity, and health: how strong is the relation?', *Journal of Epidemiology and Community Health*, **60** (7), 587–592.

MacKerron, G. (2012), 'Happiness and environmental quality', PhD dissertation, London School of Economics and Political Science.

MacKerron, G. and S. Mourato (2009), 'Life satisfaction and air quality in London', *Ecological Economics*, **68** (5), 1441–1453.

MacKerron, G. and S. Mourato (2013), 'Happiness is greater in natural environments', *Global Environmental Change*, **23** (5), 992–1000.

Maddison, D. and K. Rehdanz (2011), 'The impact of climate on life satisfaction', *Ecological Economics*, **70** (12), 2437–2445.

Markevych, I., Schoierer, J., Hartig, T., Chudnovsky, A., Hystad, P., et al. (2017), 'Exploring pathways linking greenspace to health: theoretical and methodological guidance', *Environmental Research*, **158**, 301–317.

Mitchell, R.J., Richardson, E.A., Shortt, N.K. and J.R. Pearce (2015), 'Neighborhood environments and socioeconomic inequalities in mental well-being', *American Journal of Preventive Medicine*, **49** (1), 80–84.

Moulton, B.R. (1990), 'An illustration of a pitfall in estimating the effects of aggregate variables on micro units', *Review of Economics and Statistics*, **72** (2), 334–338.

Murray, T., Maddison, D. and K. Rehdanz (2013), 'Do geographical variations in climate influence life-satisfaction?', *Climate Change Economics*, **4** (1), 1350004.

Ode Sang, Å., Knez, I., Gunnarsson, B. and M. Hedblom (2016), 'The effects of naturalness, gender, and age on how urban green space is perceived and used', *Urban Forestry and Urban Greening*, **18**, 268–276.

Rehdanz, K. and D. Maddison (2005), 'Climate and happiness', *Ecological Economics*, **52** (1), 111–125.

Roda, C., Charreire, H., Feuillet, T., Mackenbach, J.D., Compernolle, S., et al. (2016), 'Mismatch between perceived and objectively measured environmental obesogenic features in European neighbourhoods', *Obesity Reviews*, **17**, 31–41.

Saw, L.E., Lim, F.K.S. and L.R. Carrasco (2015), 'The relationship between natural park usage and happiness does not hold in a tropical city-state', *PLOS ONE*, **10** (7), e0133781.

Scarpa, R., Hutchinson, W.G., Chilton, S.M. and J. Buongiorno (2000), 'Importance of forest attributes in the willingness to pay for recreation: a contingent valuation study of Irish forests', *Forest Policy and Economics*, **1** (3), 315–329.

Schipperijn, J., Stigsdotter, U.K., Randrup, T.B. and J. Troelsen (2010), 'Influences on the use of urban green space – a case study in Odense, Denmark', *Urban Forestry and Urban Greening*, **9** (1), 25–32.

Smyth, R., Mishra, V. and X. Qian (2008), 'The environment and well-being in urban China', *Ecological Economics*, **68** (1), 547–555.

Smyth, R., Nielsen, I., Zhai, Q., Liu, T., Liu, Y., et al. (2011), 'A study of the impact of environmental surroundings on personal well-being in urban China using a multi-item well-being indicator', *Population and Environment*, **32** (4), 353–375.

Triguero-Mas, M., Dadvand, P., Cirach, M., Martínez, D., Medina, A., et al. (2015), 'Natural outdoor environments and mental and physical health: relationships and mechanisms', *Environment International*, **77**, 35–41.

Tsurumi, T. and S. Managi (2015), 'Environmental value of green spaces in Japan: an application of the life satisfaction approach', *Ecological Economics*, **120**, 1–12.

Tyrväinen, L., Pauleit, S., Seeland K. and S. de Vries (2005), 'Benefits and uses of urban forests and trees', in Cecil C. Konijnendijk, Kjell Nilsson, Thomas B. Randrup and Jasper Schipperijn (eds), *Urban Forests and Trees*, Berlin and Heidelberg, Germany: Springer, pp. 81–114.

Tzoulas, K., Korpela, K., Venn, S., Yli-Pelkonen, V., Kaźmierczak, A., et al. (2007), 'Promoting ecosystem and human health in urban areas using green infrastructure: a literature review', *Landscape and Urban Planning*, **81** (3), 167–178.

van den Berg, M., Wendel-Vos, W., van Poppel, M., Kemper, H., van Mechelen, W. and J. Maas (2015), 'Health benefits of green spaces in the living environment: a systematic review of epidemiological studies', *Urban Forestry and Urban Greening*, **14** (4), 806–816.

Weden, M.M., Carpiano, R.M. and S.A. Robert (2008), 'Subjective and objective neighborhood characteristics and adult health', *Social Science and Medicine*, **66** (6), 1256–1270.

Welsch, H. and S. Ferreira (2014), 'Environment, well-being, and experienced preference', *International Review of Environmental and Resource Economics*, **7** (3–4), 205–239.

Welsch, H. and J. Kühling (2009), 'Using happiness data for environmental valuation: issues and applications', *Journal of Economic Surveys*, **23** (2), 385–406.

White, M.P., Alcock, I., Wheeler, B.W. and M.H. Depledge (2013), 'Would you be happier living in a greener urban area? A fixed-effects analysis of panel data', *Psychological Science*, **24** (6), 920–928.

White, M.P., Pahl, S., Wheeler, B.W., Depledge, M.H. and L.E. Fleming (2017), 'Natural environments and subjective wellbeing: different types of exposure are associated with different aspects of wellbeing', *Health and Place*, **45**, 77–84.

Wood, L., Hooper, P., Foster, S. and F. Bull (2017), 'Public green spaces and positive mental health – investigating the relationship between access, quantity and types of parks and mental wellbeing', *Health and Place*, **48**, 63–71.

14. Mappiness: natural environments and in-the-moment happiness*

George Mackerron and Susana Mourato

14.1 INTRODUCTION

Wellbeing in the United Kingdom (UK) appears to be generally higher in rural than in urban locations (e.g., Berry and Okulicz-Kozaryn, 2009; Gilbert et al., 2016). Several mechanisms may help to explain that finding. Those mechanisms, by which exposure to natural rather than urban environments may be beneficial for subjective wellbeing, include: (1) lower levels of environmental stressors such as air pollution and noise (e.g., Passchier-Vermeer and Passchier, 2000; Day, 2007; Gouveia and Maisonet, 2005; Welsch, 2006); (2) facilitation of behaviours such as exercise and social interaction (e.g., Morris, 2003; Barton and Pretty, 2010a); and (3) biophilia (Wilson, 1993): direct psychological effects presumed to arise from evolutionary history.

In investigating this relationship, there are several ways to conceptualise and measure exposure to natural environments: for example, we can look at neighbourhood proportions of different land cover types, or viewsheds, or the frequency of visits to particular kinds of sites. Similarly, there are several ways to conceptualise and measure subjective wellbeing: for example, a commonly accepted classification recognises evaluative, eudaimonic and experiential (or hedonic) accounts (Dolan and Metcalfe, 2012). This matters, because there is evidence that different types of environmental exposure are associated with different aspects of wellbeing. For example, based on analysis of the Monitoring Engagement with the Natural Environment (MENE) survey data, White et al. (2017: 77) report that 'people who visited nature regularly felt their lives were more worthwhile, and those who visited nature yesterday were happier'.

Evidence comes from both observational and experimental studies. Observational studies have traditionally treated both wellbeing and environment at a relatively high level, assessing wellbeing over periods of months or years in relation to environmental characteristics across wide areas (e.g., Vries et al., 2003; Brereton et al., 2008; Engelbrecht, 2009; Maas et al., 2009; Mitchell and Popham, 2007, 2008; Rehdanz and Maddison, 2008; Vemuri and Costanza, 2006). Experimental studies have more typically looked at shorter time scales and smaller areas, exploring the short-term physiological or psychological effects of immediate exposures to different environments, or representations of them (e.g., Hartig et al., 2003; Barton and Pretty, 2010b; Berto, 2005; Ryan et al., 2010; Valtchanov et al., 2010; White et al., 2010). These approaches each have their own strengths and weaknesses.

In the last decade or so, new approaches have been enabled by new technology. In particular, the rapid uptake of smartphones – offering user-friendly interactivity, always-on connectivity, and Global Positioning System (GPS) and other sensor data – has allowed observational study designs to be applied to the kinds of immediate and highly disaggregated exposure data that were formerly available only in experimental work. Technological advances will of course continue to drive the development of research in this area (Yaden et al., 2018).

Using secondary data, 'sentiment analysis' of geolocated social media activity has been used to infer variation in experiential wellbeing over time and across locations (e.g., Hicks, 2010; Dodds et al., 2011; Frank et al., 2013; Hauthal and Burghardt, 2016; Luhmann, 2017; Mislove et al., 2010; Mitchell et al., 2013; Schwartz et al., 2013), including some limited work on natural environments (e.g., Roberts, 2017; Roberts et al., 2019; Zheng et al., 2019). Key limitations of this approach include the varied motivations of social media participants, the limitations of sentiment analysis (e.g., Maynard and Greenwood, 2014), the lack of contextual control variables (for example, activity), and issues with sampling in terms both of individuals and of the moments and locations of posts. Taken together, the effect of these limitations is that we get a noisy proxy for what people who have already chosen to use a particular social medium choose to say (or imply) about their mood to other people who use that medium, only at the moments and places they choose. Additional methods that, like the use of social media data, do not require active subject participation in research – such as emotion detection using machine learning on facial expressions, tone of voice or even body motion – have to date been of interest primarily to advertisers and the security services (e.g., Janssen et al., 2008; Birch et al., 2016; Chung et al., 2012; Sandulescu et al., 2015; Schwartz, 2019), but could prove valuable in future.

New technology has also enabled new forms of primary data collection, including the collection of experiential wellbeing self-reports, accompanied by relevant contextual variables, potentially at a large scale. This represents an updated form of what psychologists call the experience sampling method or ESM (Hektner et al., 2007) and medical researchers know as ecological momentary assessment or EMA (Shiffman et al., 2008). The addition of sensor data, and especially GPS location used in conjunction with spatial data systems, enables immediate wellbeing measures to be analysed in conjunction with a wealth of objective environmental information. Large-scale smartphone-based ESM/EMA studies include Track Your Happiness (Killingsworth and Gilbert, 2010) and Mappiness (Bryson and MacKerron, 2017; Fujiwara et al., 2017; Geiger and MacKerron, 2016; MacKerron, 2012; MacKerron and Mourato, 2013; Seresinhe et al., 2019). Studies with an environmental focus include Mappiness, Urban Mind (Bakolis et al., 2018), WeSense (Velde et al., 2016) and NatureBuzz (University of Cambridge, 2016). Studies of this kind draw on wider interest in both 'citizen science' (Haklay, 2012) and the 'quantified self' (Swan, 2013), and are discussed in further depth by Beute et al. (2016).

The remainder of this chapter focuses on the authors' own UK-focused ESM/EMA study, Mappiness, which we believe to be by some distance the largest environmentally oriented project of this kind. The chapter builds on our original paper on natural environments (MacKerron and Mourato, 2013) in several respects. Regarding data, we use a longer series from Mappiness: seven years instead of six months. We join response locations with Land Cover Map 2007 categories (Morton et al., 2011), giving more recent and precise land cover information than the 2000 edition used previously. And we use validated Met Office weather data in preference to the crowdsourced data used before. Regarding hypotheses, we investigate the effect of proximity to any coastline, following up on the particularly large positive effect of the 'marine and coastal margin' land cover type in the earlier paper. And we explore whether the positive wellbeing effects of natural environments could be down to simple changes in a respondent's environment, rather than characteristics of the environments themselves, by considering impacts on city-dwellers and non-city-dwellers separately.

14.2 METHODS

14.2.1 Data Collection

App development and participant recruitment

We developed a native app for iPhones using Apple's Software Development Kit (Apple Inc., 2010), back-end server software to receive and store the data, and a public website to reach actual and prospective users (now at http://v1.mappiness.org.uk). The app was distributed free via Apple's App Store, and participants were recruited opportunistically. The app was highlighted in the App Store for two weeks shortly after launch, mentioned in thousands of messages on Facebook and Twitter, and enjoyed quite extensive coverage in broadcast and print media. The app is also somewhat suited to spreading by word of mouth, since its random signals may interrupt social interaction and make it a subject of conversation.

Registration and experience sampling

Participants downloaded the Mappiness app, indicated informed consent to taking part, and provided basic demographic information. They were then signalled (beeped) at random moments, with a frequency and during hours they chose (the defaults were twice a day, between 8 am and 10 pm). When they responded to a signal, they were asked to rate how far they felt 'happy' by sliding an interface control along a continuous scale between endpoints labelled 'not at all' on the far left and 'extremely' on the far right (the control was initially placed centrally). They were also asked whom they were with, where they were, and what they were doing. Example screens are shown in Figure 14.1. If they were outdoors, they were asked to take a photo straight in front of them.[1] During the response process, and subject to further consent, precise location was determined via GPS. All the data were then encrypted and transmitted to our server, or queued for sending if no data connection was available. Participants were given simple feedback, charting their happiness in different contexts, and could opt out of the study whenever they chose.

Key strengths and limitations

To receive a valid response to a signal, the participant had to: have the powered-on iPhone with them; have wireless data reception; be able to hear the signal; be able to respond; and be willing to do so. This rules out a number of activities and locations, including driving, riding on the Underground, and – unfortunately, given our focus on natural environments – some remote rural locations. Regarding the sample of participants, requiring iPhone users to self-select into the study ruled out obtaining a representative or probability sample (we describe some basic characteristics of the sample in section 14.3).

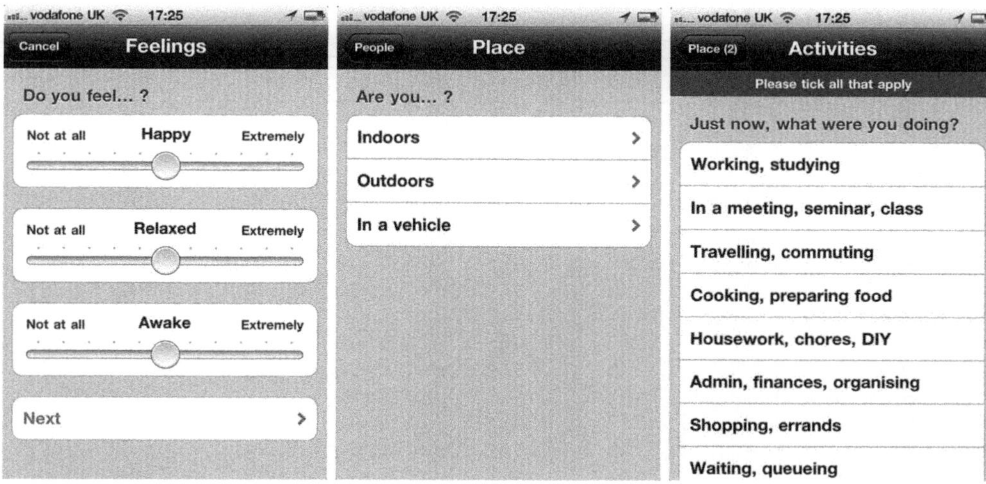

Figure 14.1 *Example ESM questionnaire screens*

Aside from the self-selection issue, iPhone users might differ from non-iPhone users in various ways. In this context it is reassuring to note that personality traits appear to differ little between users of the main smartphone operating systems (Götz et al., 2017).

Using smartphones also has some important advantages over traditional ESM or EMA protocols using paper diaries. They are small and convenient, and likely to be kept charged up, turned on and within easy reach. Responses can be entered only for the current moment.[2] And crucially, the comparatively small burden on respondents, and the low marginal cost to the researchers per respondent, facilitates a sample size enormously greater than previously achievable. The methods outlined here are described in additional detail by MacKerron (2012).

14.2.2 Spatial Analysis

Land cover

We used GPS location to link each signalled response with these spatial and environmental variables: (1) broad habitat or land cover type; (2) weather conditions; and (3) daylight. Our main focus was land cover, including green and blue space. This was evaluated according to the ten 'aggregate classes' of the UK Land Cover Map (LCM) 2007 (Morton et al., 2011: Table 2.2), using the vector format data for maximum precision. These categories are as listed in Table 14.1. Although nearby habitats might also form part of a participant's experience, we consider the land cover type at the exact point location to represent a reasonable proxy for the overall habitat they are currently experiencing.

Coast

We also created a dummy variable indicating proximity to the coast, irrespective of land cover type, using a union of the outlines of England, Wales, Scotland and Northern

Table 14.1 *Descriptive statistics for explanatory variables*

Variable	%	Count
Participant is . . .		
Indoors	83.94	1 705 388
In a vehicle	6.84	138 946
Outdoors	9.22	187 227
LCM 2007 aggregate class, when outdoors		
Broadleaf woodland (1)	0.25	4988
Coniferous woodland (2)	0.05	1016
Arable (3)	0.46	9379
Improved grassland (4)	0.75	15 318
Semi-natural grassland (5)	0.13	2543
Mountain, heath, bog (6)	0.06	1140
Saltwater (7)	0.02	450
Freshwater (8)	0.09	1747
Coastal (9)	0.08	1721
Built-up areas and gardens (10)	7.33	148 925
Coastal proximity, when outdoors		
Less than 50 m inland	0.24	4967
Weather, when outdoors		
Daylight	7.84	159 182
Clear skies (no cloud)	1.63	33 119
Rain (any during 1 hr)	0.61	12 460
Poor visibility (< 100 m)	0.07	1520
Sunshine (any, except whole 1 hr)	3.35	68 055
Full sunshine (whole 1 hr)	1.71	34 795
Wind speed: 0–3 knots	0.97	19 728
Wind speed: 4–8 knots	3.92	79 625
Wind speed: 9–14 knots	3.4	69 135
Wind speed: 15+ knots	0.92	18 739
< 0 °C	0.20	3983
0–4 °C	0.73	14 729
5–9 °C	1.58	32 114
10–14 °C	2.69	54 562
15–19 °C	3.11	63 190
20–24 °C	0.80	16 277
25+ °C	0.12	2372
Selected activities		
Walking, hiking	1.65	33 476
Sports, running, exercise	1.25	25 363
Gardening, allotment	0.34	6930
Bird watching, nature watching	0.17	3492
Hunting, fishing	0.02	479
Participant is with . . .		
Spouse, partner, girl/boyfriend	24.29	493 519
Children	10.82	219 721
Other family members	8.14	165 378
Colleagues, classmates	15.08	306 334
Clients, customers	1.38	28 027
Friends	9.02	183 314
Other people participant knows	1.59	32 336
Nobody (or strangers only)	43.76	888 993
Participant is . . .		
At home	54.15	1 100 165
At work	20.98	426 287
Elsewhere	24.86	505 109

Notes: All variables are 0/1 dummies. All percentages – including where variables are interacted with the variable *Outdoors* – are calculated in relation to the full sample of 2 031 561 responses.

Ireland, clipped to the high water mark (National Records of Scotland, 2001; Northern Ireland Statistics and Research Agency, 2011; Office for National Statistics, 2011). Responses are considered to be at the coast if they are less than 50 m inland of the nearest point on the coastline.

Weather and daylight
Weather conditions represent an important control, since people are more likely to choose to be outside in nature in favourable weather conditions, and those conditions may also affect mood directly (e.g., Klimstra et al., 2011). Using the Met Office Integrated Data Archive System (MIDAS) data (Met Office, 2006a, 2006b), we linked each response with weather conditions reported by the station nearest to the response location at the moment nearest to the response timestamp, and within one hour before or after.[3] Finally, we calculated whether it was daylight at the response date, time and location using the United States National Oceanic and Atmospheric Administration (NOAA) sunrise/sunset calculations of the StreamMetabolism library in *R* (R Development Core Team, 2011; Sefick, 2009).

Home location
For the purpose of identifying which participants live in urban versus natural environments, we use the following heuristic to determine participants' home locations. For each participant, we select UK responses with a GPS accuracy of +/– 250 m or better where they report being at home. If there are no such responses, we drop that participant from this analysis. If there is exactly one, we use the location of that response. If there are several, we check that at least two-thirds of them fall within a 750 m square: if they do not, we drop them from this analysis; otherwise, we use the response closest to the average location of responses within that square.

14.2.3 Response Scope and Validity

Our analysis is based on over 2 million responses from almost 35 000 UK participants. The responses cover a period of over seven years, from the app's launch in mid-August 2010 until early 2018, although many more responses were received in the earlier than the later years. Responses are considered valid as long as they meet three criteria. First, they should be prompted by a signal: we identify those as starting within 60 minutes of a previously unanswered signal, and completed within a further five minutes. Second, they must have a UK GPS location for which, if outdoors, the accuracy reported by the iPhone is +/ 250 m or better. Third, data from a nearby weather station must be available within one hour of the response time. These choices are discussed in more detail by MacKerron and Mourato (2013). Descriptive statistics and econometric analyses are reported for these valid responses and their contributing participants only.

14.2.4 Econometric Model

Fixed effects specification
The Mappiness data represent a very large unbalanced panel, having large N (the count of individuals) and highly variable T (the count of assessments per individual). We use the data to estimate a fixed effects model, explaining the relationship of land cover type, environmental and other control variables to happiness reports. Specifically, we model the reported happiness r of individual i at location l and time t as:

$$r_{ilt} = \alpha_i + \boldsymbol{\beta}_{\mathrm{p}}' \, \mathbf{p}_{ilt} + \boldsymbol{\beta}_{\mathrm{q}}' \, \mathbf{q}_{ilt} + \varepsilon_{ilt}$$

where α is an individual-specific constant or fixed effect, **p** is a vector of situational factors such as activity and companionship, **q** is a vector of local amenities and environmental conditions (both static and time-varying per location), and ε is an error term. The participant-specific intercepts or fixed effects make this equivalent to an ordinary least squares (OLS) regression in which a dummy variable is included for each participant, and they control for all time-invariant individual characteristics, including personality characteristics and demographic variables such as gender (e.g., Wooldridge, 2009).[4]

Variables included

On the left-hand side of the model, happiness self-ratings are scaled from 0 ('not at all') to 100 ('extremely'). On the right-hand side, we include dummies for land cover types when outdoors, which are the main focus of this research. Since experience of different environments may well be associated with other variables that are important to wellbeing, we also include as control variables: indicators of daylight and weather conditions when outdoors; activity; companionship; location type; time of day (separately for weekdays and for weekends and public holidays); and year, public holiday and day-of-week dummy variables. We also include response sequence indicators, capturing the number of previous responses by the same participant, to control for trends in happiness (or response behaviour) over time.

Properties of the model

We cannot include time-invariant individual-level influences on reported happiness, such as gender, since any such influences are soaked up by the individual-level fixed effects. However, the estimator allows for arbitrary correlation between any individual effects, including unobserved effects, and the observed explanatory variables. This property is important, since correlations of this sort could well exist in the data (for example, personality traits might well be associated with the companionship, activity and environment that a person chooses at any given moment in time). Basic fixed effects estimation requires the errors to be homoscedastic and not serially correlated (Wooldridge, 2009). The serial correlation restriction could be problematic here, since unobserved influences on a person's happiness might well persist from one response to the next. Standard errors are therefore calculated using a cluster-robust sandwich estimator (StataCorp, 2009), which is robust in the presence of both heteroscedasticity and serial correlation of the errors (Stock and Watson, 2008).

14.3 RESULTS AND DISCUSSION

14.3.1 Descriptive Statistics

Relying on self-selecting iPhone users means that our sample is not representative of the UK as a whole. Participants are relatively young: at sign-up, 64 per cent are aged under 35, and 93 per cent are under 50, compared to 29 per cent and 56 per cent, respectively, in the UK adult population (Office for National Statistics, 2010). They are also relatively wealthy: median household income is approximately £48 000, which is almost twice the UK median (House of Commons, 2006). Seventy-six per cent of participants are in employment and 15 per cent are in full-time education. These groups are over-represented relative to the UK adult population, in which the proportions are, respectively, 57 per cent and 4 per cent. This is mainly at the expense of retired people, who constitute fewer than 1 per cent of our participants but 22 per cent of the population at large (National Centre for Social Research, 2009). Participants' genders are nearly balanced, however, at 51 per cent male, compared to 49 per cent in the UK adult population (Office for National Statistics, 2010).

We are able to infer home location for 91 per cent of respondents. Of these, 90 per cent live in cities (that is, the 'built-up areas and gardens' aggregate class in the LCM 2007). No direct comparison for this figure is available, but in 2014, 17 per cent of the UK population lived in lower layer super output areas (LSOAs) classified as rural (Defra, 2019).

The number of responses per participant ranges between 1 and 5624, with a mean of 59. Amongst participants who contributed at least one valid response, approximately half of the beeps sent resulted in a valid response.

Responses

All the explanatory variables in our analysis are 0/1 dummies. The land cover type, coastal proximity and weather variables are included only as interactions with being outdoors; although it is possible that these variables are also associated with happiness when participants are indoors or in a vehicle, the same direct link is less clear in such cases. Additionally, when participants are not outdoors their GPS location is usually less precise, making the joined spatial data less reliable.

Response-level variables are summarised in Table 14.1. The happiness report, which is scaled from 0 to 100, has a mean of 66.3 and standard deviation of 21.3. The distribution is negatively skewed, as illustrated in Figure 14.2, which also shows an artefact of the

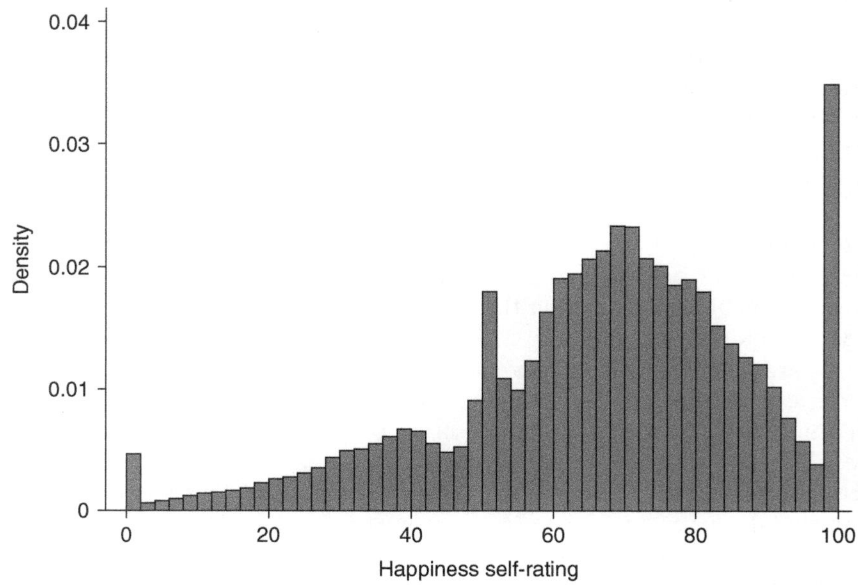

Figure 14.2 Distribution of happiness self-ratings

response process: spikes at the extremes, where the slider is moved to its limit, and small troughs on either side of the middle, where the slider is either left in its initial position or moved some distance left or right. In previous work, we have accounted for the spikes by using a random effects interval regression model, and treating ≤ 0 and ≥ 100 as unbounded upper and lower intervals (e.g., MacKerron and Mourato, 2013). As might be expected, this has always given rise to similar results with somewhat larger coefficients.

The coastal land cover type and the coastal close proximity dummy variables do not overlap excessively (land cover type is seen without proximity in 1037 cases, proximity is seen without land cover type in 6449 cases, and the two coincide in 1433 cases).

14.3.2 Models

Basic model

The basic model is presented in Table 14.2. When participants are outdoors, every land cover type except coniferous woodland is associated with significantly higher happiness levels than the baseline category, built-up areas and gardens.[5] In line with the literature on the benefits of blue space (e.g., White et al., 2010; Ashbullby et al., 2013; Völker and Kistemann, 2011, 2013, 2015; Wheeler et al., 2012), and with our own earlier findings (MacKerron and Mourato, 2013), areas of coastal land cover are the happiest locations. The LCM 2007 coastal aggregate class is linked to happiness responses that are on average approximately 4 points higher on the 0–100 scale than those from built-up areas and gardens. In addition – and, where applicable, the coefficients are indeed additive – being near the coast, irrespective of land cover, is associated with a further 1.4 points in raised happiness. The summed impact of 5.4 points represents 0.26 standard deviations of the dependent variable and is of similar magnitude, for instance, to the impact of attending a museum or exhibition.

All control variables show intuitive relationships with the happiness score, which are (if applicable) in accordance with previous research. For example, participants are happier at home than at work, and also happier in warm, dry, still and sunny weather. Physical exercise, and activities likely to be undertaken in natural environments – including running, gardening and birdwatching – all have substantial positive associations with happiness. Participants are happier outdoors than indoors or in a vehicle.

Land cover contrast

Since 90 per cent of our participants live in the built-up areas and gardens land cover type, it is reasonable to ask whether the positive effects of the natural environment types seen above could be due simply to a change in environment, or to increased distance from the participant's home or average location (see Frank et al., 2013), rather than any intrinsic characteristics of the land cover types themselves. To address this concern, we run a new model, which is estimated using only those responses when participants reported that they were neither at home nor at work, and treats separately (via a set of interaction terms) the 10 per cent of respondents whose home location lies in any natural environment land cover type. Table 14.3 presents this model, which is otherwise identical to the basic model. All the coefficients on land cover are relative to the happiness of participants who live in built-up areas and gardens when they are in built-up areas and gardens (but not at home).

Table 14.2 Estimated parameters of the basic model

Variable	Coeff.	Std err.	Variable	Coeff.	Std err.
Participant is . . .			*Selected activities*		
Indoors (base category)	–		Sports, running, exercise	6.64***	0.16
In a vehicle	0.04	0.12			
Outdoors	1.58***	0.35	Birdwatching, nature watching	4.31***	0.35
LCM 2007 aggregate class, when outdoors			Gardening, allotment	4.75***	0.26
Broadleaf woodland (1)	2.06***	0.29	Hunting, fishing	4.48**	1.69
Coniferous woodland (2)	1.05	0.73	Walking, hiking	2.26***	0.14
Arable (3)	1.64***	0.22	36 further activity dummies	Yes	
Improved grassland (4)	1.27**	0.43			
Semi-natural grassland (5)	3.34***	0.36			
Mountain, heath, bog (6)	3.25***	0.57	*Companionship*		
Saltwater (7)	2.88***	0.80	Spouse, partner, girl/boyfriend	3.66***	0.10
Freshwater (8)	2.09***	0.42			
Coastal (9)	4.01***	0.51	Friends	4.05***	0.08
Built-up areas and gardens (10 – base category)	–		Other family members	0.78***	0.09
			Clients, customers	1.15***	0.29
Coastal proximity, when outdoors			Children	0.42**	0.14
Less than 50 m inland	1.43***	0.37	Colleagues, classmates	−0.29*	0.12
			Other people participant knows	−0.66***	0.16
Weather when participant is outdoors					
Daylight	−0.33*	0.13	*Participant is . . .*		
Clear skies (no cloud)	0.67***	0.13	At home (base category)	–	
Rain (any during 1 hr)	−1.03***	0.17			
Poor visibility (< 100 m)	−0.78+	0.44	At work	−2.00***	0.12
Sunshine (any, except whole 1 hr)	1.08***	0.10	Elsewhere	1.73***	0.08
Full sunshine (whole 1 hr)	1.95***	0.14	Hour-of-weekday/weekend, day-of-week, public holiday, year and sequence dummies	Yes	
Wind speed: 0–3 knots (base category)	–				
Wind speed: 4–8 knots	−0.06	0.13			
Wind speed: 9–14 knots	−0.32*	0.14	Participant-level fixed effects	Yes	
Wind speed: 15+ knots	−0.34+	0.18			
< 0 °C (base category)	–		Constant (mean fixed effect)	57.39***	0.74
0–4 °C	−0.07	0.32			
5–9 °C	0.26	0.32			
10–14 °C	0.59 +	0.33	Observations	2031561	
15–19 °C	1.06**	0.33	Groups (participants)	34542	
20–24 °C	1.06**	0.35			
25+°C	1.63***	0.47	R^2 (within groups)	0.12	

Notes:
+ $p < 0.1$, * $p < 0.05$, ** $p < 0.01$, *** $p < 0.001$.
Dependent variable: reported happiness, scaled 0–100. Model: fixed effects, participants as groups. Standard errors are sandwich estimators clustered at participant level.

Table 14.3 Estimated parameters of the land cover contrast model

Variable	Coeff.	Std err.
Participant is . . .		
Indoors (base category)	–	
In a vehicle	−0.30*	0.12
Outdoors	0.57	0.39
Current LCM 2007 aggregate class, when outdoors, interacted with home location aggregate class (rural = 1 – 9 vs city = 10)		
Rural dweller Broadleaf woodland (1)	0.87	0.69
Rural dweller Coniferous woodland (2)	0.03	1.7
Rural dweller Arable (3)	1.36*	0.53
Rural dweller Improved grassland (4)	1.19*	0.49
Rural dweller Semi-natural grassland (5)	2.60*	1.06
Rural dweller Mountain, heath, bog (6)	2.59+	1.55
Rural dweller Saltwater (7)	0.93	2.14
Rural dweller Freshwater (8)	2.85 *	1.44
Rural dweller Coastal (9)	2.17+	1.29
Rural dweller Built-up areas and gardens (10)	−0.22	0.26
City dweller Broadleaf woodland (1)	2.30***	0.29
City dweller Coniferous woodland (2)	1.67*	0.71
City dweller Arable (3)	2.13***	0.26
City dweller Improved grassland (4)	1.66***	0.19
City dweller Semi-natural grassland (5)	3.48***	0.39
City dweller Mountain, heath, bog (6)	3.71***	0.64
City dweller Saltwater (7)	2.17*	0.96
City dweller Freshwater (8)	2.24***	0.46
City dweller Coastal (9)	4.02***	0.5
City dweller Built-up areas and gardens (10 – base category)	–	
Coastal proximity, when outdoors		
Less than 50 m inland	1.60***	0.31
All other controls from the basic model	Yes	
Participant-level fixed effects	Yes	
Constant (mean fixed effect)	57.39***	0.74
Observations	449 260	
Groups (participants)	26 593	
R^2 (within groups)	0.12	

Notes: Only responses neither at home nor at work. Dependent variable: reported happiness, scaled 0–100. Model: fixed effects, participants as groups. Standard errors are sandwich estimators clustered at participant level.

In this model, coefficients on all the natural land cover types are less strongly positive for those who live in a natural land cover type than for the majority who do not, and a few are no longer statistically significant. Although this may be due in part to reduced sample sizes – for example, we have only 88 responses from rural dwellers from the saltwater land cover type – it would appear to indicate that distance or contrast from the home location does contribute to the positive influence of natural environments reported above, but that there are indeed still intrinsic characteristics of natural land cover types that are associated with higher subjective wellbeing.

14.4 CONCLUSIONS

14.4.1 Key Findings and Limitations

This study builds on a new and very direct line of evidence on the links between subjective wellbeing and natural environments. Amongst participants in the study, immediate experiential happiness is greater in natural environments, even for those who live in a natural environment from day to day and after controlling for a wide range of possible confounders. With a large sample of participants and responses, the relationships we estimate are highly statistically significant, and their magnitudes are substantial. We know that these relationships are not confounded at the participant level (that is, by associations between locations and the kinds of people who spend time there), because our model is estimated exclusively using within-individual variation.

Causation may run in both directions, assuming people choose environments partly according to their mood and that their mood is partly determined by their environment.[6] It seems highly plausible that the latter pathway makes an important contribution to the relationship, but more research on that point would undoubtedly be valuable. It is possible that the use of high-resolution, high-frequency satellite photography, that is able to detect changes in land cover over short time periods, will be helpful here (see, e.g., Duarte et al., 2018 using data from planet.com).

Our sample is not representative of the UK population. Caution is thus required regarding the general applicability of our results, although we know of no clear evidence why the demographic characteristics of our sample – who are relatively young, rich, and likely to be in employment or education – should affect relationships between their happiness and natural environments. Self-selection could also affect the generality of our findings, if there are substantial differentials in individuals' sensitivity to the environmental characteristics we investigate, and if these differentials play a part in an individual's decision to participate in the study. We cannot be sure whether or to what extent that is the case.

14.4.2 Uses

There is value simply in understanding localised patterns in subjective wellbeing, both on the individual level and for policy and planning purposes. At the individual level, Mappiness or similar data can be used, for example, as input to algorithms for optimal route planning that take affective parameters – not just minimum time or distance – into account (Huang et al., 2014). Furthermore, the data collection process can be adapted to offer tailored individual interventions, via a method known as ecological momentary intervention (Runyan et al., 2013; Runyan and Steinke, 2015).[7]

Earlier Mappiness results informed the UK National Ecosystem Assessment (NEA) (Pretty et al., 2011). Tailored ESM/EMA studies could be used to assess the impacts of particular environmental policy interventions – such as improved provision of or public access to green or blue spaces – on subjective wellbeing. They could be used to investigate how persistent such effects are over time, and whether interventions are more beneficial in certain geographical surroundings, or for specific aspects of wellbeing, including not only the experiential or hedonic, but also mental health, evaluative and eudemonic measures.

NOTES

* We thank Josh Hardman for research assistance, and all the Mappiness study participants. The original Mappiness research was funded by the Economic and Social Research Council (grant number PTA-031-2006-00280), UK.

1. Work is now under way to apply deep learning techniques to exploit these photographs more fully.
2. In traditional diary-based studies, a significant proportion of responses are sometimes found to have been fabricated long before or after the signalling time (Stone and Shiffman, 2002).
3. We use only weather stations providing hourly readings and having at least a 90 per cent reporting rate during our data collection period, which limits us to 33 stations for sunshine duration and 125 stations for all other variables. Fewer than 300 responses are lost to missing weather data.
4. Most Mappiness respondents participate for a only a few weeks, and we therefore think it is safe to regard characteristics that vary slowly or infrequently (such as age in years, marital status or employment) as effectively time-invariant, and therefore controlled by the fixed effects.
5. Reasons behind the lack of a significant positive effect of coniferous forest are not immediately apparent. Existing research does not seem to clearly corroborate a lower wellbeing value for these environments. For example, Han (2007) finds coniferous forest to be preferred to grassland (among United States undergraduate students), and Gibbons et al. (2011) find that coniferous forest has one of the larger positive effects on UK land values. However, the absence of an effect here should perhaps not be overinterpreted, given that the number of responses is relatively low, and that the coefficient is positive and would meet a $p < 15$ per cent significance level.
6. In support of the causal hypothesis, assuming that people like to be and try to be happy – approximately, utility maximisation – one would expect visits to natural environments only to be undertaken if the expected happiness change is positive.
7. One of the authors (MacKerron) has integrated breathing, mindfulness and cognitive behavioral therapy (CBT) exercises into a workplace ESM app. These can be offered automatically based on ESM responses, with promising early results in some large organisations.

REFERENCES

Apple Inc. (2010), 'Xcode and iOS Software Development Kit (SDK) 3'. Accessed 22 July 2019 at http://developer.apple.com/ios.

Ashbullby, K.J., Pahl, S., Webley, P. and M.P. White (2013), 'The beach as a setting for families' health promotion: a qualitative study with parents and children living in coastal regions in Southwest England', *Health and Place*, **23**, 138–147. doi:10.1016/j.healthplace.2013.06.005.

Bakolis, I., Hammoud, R., Smythe, M., Gibbons, J., Davidson, N., et al. (2018), 'Urban mind: using smartphone technologies to investigate the impact of nature on mental well-being in real time', *BioScience*, **68** (2), 134–145.

Barton, J. and J. Pretty (2010a), 'Urban ecology and human health and wellbeing', in Kevin J. Gaston (ed.), *Urban Ecology*, Cambridge, UK: Cambridge University Press, pp. 202–229.

Barton, J. and J. Pretty (2010b), 'What is the best dose of nature and green exercise for improving mental health? A multi-study analysis', *Environmental Science and Technology*, **44** (10), 3947–3955. doi:10.1021/es903183r.

Berry, B.J.L. and A. Okulicz-Kozaryn (2009), 'Dissatisfaction with city life: a new look at some old questions', *Cities*, **26** (3), 117–124.

Berto, R. (2005), 'Exposure to restorative environments helps restore attentional capacity', *Journal of Environmental Psychology*, **25** (3), 249–259. doi:10.1016/j.jenvp.2005.07.001.

Beute, F., Kort, Y. de and W. IJsselsteijn (2016), 'Restoration in its natural context: how ecological momentary assessment can advance restoration research', *International Journal of Environmental Research and Public Health*, **13** (4), Article 420.

Birch, I., Birch, T. and D. Bray (2016), 'The identification of emotions from gait', *Science and Justice*, **56** (5), 351–356. doi:10.1016/j.scijus.2016.05.006.

Brereton, F., Clinch, J.P. and S. Ferreira (2008), 'Happiness, geography and the environment', *Ecological Economics*, **65** (2), 386–396. doi:10.1016/j.ecolecon.2007.07.008.

Bryson, A. and G. MacKerron (2017), 'Are you happy while you work?', *Economic Journal*, **127** (599), 106–125. doi:10.1111/ecoj.12269.

Chung, W.J., Patwa, P. and M.M. Markov (2012), 'Targeting advertisements based on emotion', US Patent No. 20120143693A1, assigned to Microsoft Corp.

Day, R. (2007), 'Place and the experience of air quality', *Health and Place*, **13** (1), 249–260.

Defra (2019), 'Official statistics: rural population 2014/15. Revision note', Department for Environment Food and Rural Affairs, UK. https://www.gov.uk/government/publications/rural-population-and-migration/rural-population-201415.

Dodds, P.S., Harris, K.D., Kloumann, I.M., Bliss, C.A. and C.M. Danforth (2011), 'Temporal patterns of happiness and information in a global social network: hedonometrics and Twitter', *PLoS ONE*, **6** (12), e26752. doi:10.1371/journal.pone.0026752.

Dolan, P. and R. Metcalfe (2012), 'Measuring subjective wellbeing: recommendations on measures for use by national governments', *Journal of Social Policy*, **41** (2), 409–427.

Duarte, C.R., de Miranda, F.P., Landau, L., Souto, M.V.S., Sabadia, J.A.B., et al. (2018), 'Short-time analysis of shoreline based on RapidEye satellite images in the terminal area of Pecém Port, Ceará, Brazil', *International Journal of Remote Sensing*, **39** (13), 4376–4389. doi:10.1080/01431161.2018.1457229.

Engelbrecht, H. (2009), 'Natural capital, subjective well-being, and the new welfare economics of sustainability: some evidence from cross-country regressions', *Ecological Economics*, **69** (2), 380–388. doi:10.1016/j.ecolecon.2009.08.011.

Frank, M.R., Mitchell, L., Dodds, P.S. and C.M. Danforth (2013), 'Happiness and the patterns of life: a study of geolocated tweets', *Scientific Reports*, **3**, Article 2625.

Fujiwara, D., Lawton, R.N. and G. MacKerron (2017), 'Experience sampling in and around airports: momentary subjective wellbeing, airports, and aviation noise in England', *Transportation Research Part D: Transport and Environment*, **56**, 43–54. doi:10.1016/j.trd.2017.07.015.

Geiger, B.B. and G. MacKerron (2016), 'Can alcohol make you happy? A subjective wellbeing approach', *Social Science and Medicine*, **156**, 184–191.

Gibbons, S., Mourato, S. and G. Resende (2011), 'The amenity value of English nature: a hedonic price approach', Discussion Paper 74, Spatial Economics Research Centre, London School of Economics.

Gilbert, A., Colley, K. and D. Roberts (2016), 'Are rural residents happier? A quantitative analysis of subjective wellbeing in Scotland', *Journal of Rural Studies*, **44**, 37–45.

Götz, F.M., Stieger, S. and U.-D. Reips (2017), 'Users of the main smartphone operating systems (iOS, Android) differ only little in personality', PLOS ONE, **12** (5), e0176921.

Gouveia, N.C. and M. Maisonet (2005), 'Health effects of air pollution: an overview', in World Health Organization (ed.), *Air Quality Guidelines: Global Update 2005*, Regional Office for Europe, Denmark: World Health Organization, pp. 87–109.

Haklay, Muki (2012), 'Citizen science and volunteered geographic information – overview and typology of participation', in Daniel Sui, Sarah Elwood and Michael Goodchild (eds), *Crowdsourcing Geographic Knowledge: Volunteered Geographic Information (VGI) in Theory and Practice*, Dordrecht, Netherlands: Springer, pp. 105–122.

Han, K. (2007), 'Responses to six major terrestrial biomes in terms of scenic beauty, preference, and restorativeness', *Environment and Behavior*, **39** (4), 529–556.

Hartig, T., Evans, G.W., Jamner, L.D., Davis, D.S. and T. Gärling (2003), 'Tracking restoration in natural and urban field settings', *Journal of Environmental Psychology*, **23** (2), 109–123. doi:10.1016/S0272-4944(02)00109-3.

Hauthal, E. and D. Burghardt (2016), 'Mapping space-related emotions out of user-generated photo metadata considering grammatical issues', *Cartographic Journal*, **53** (1), 78–90. doi:10.1179/1743277414Y.0000000094.

Hektner, J.M., Schmidt, J.A. and M. Csíkszentmihályi (eds) (2007), *Experience Sampling Method: Measuring the Quality of Everyday Life*, London, UK: SAGE.

Hicks, M. (2010), 'A more global view of Gross National Happiness', Facebook data team. Accessed 21 July 2019 at https://www.facebook.com/notes/facebook/a-more-global-view-of-gross-national-happiness/387623222130.

House of Commons (2006), 'Hansard written answers for 18 July 2006', London.

Huang, H., Klettner, S., Schmidt, M., Gartner, G., Leitinger, S., et al. (2014), 'AffectRoute – considering people's affective responses to environments for enhancing route-planning services', *International Journal of Geographical Information Science*, **28** (12), 2456–2473. doi:10.1080/13658816.2014.931585.

Janssen, D., Schöllhorn, W.I., Lubienetzki, J., Fölling, K., Kokenge, H. and K. Davids (2008), 'Recognition of emotions in gait patterns by means of artificial neural nets', *Journal of Nonverbal Behavior*, **32** (2), 79–92. doi:10.1007/s10919-007-0045-3.

Killingsworth, M.A. and D.T. Gilbert (2010), 'A wandering mind is an unhappy mind', *Science*, **330** (6006), 932.

Klimstra, T.A., Frijns, T., Keijsers, L., Denissen, J.J.A., Raaijmakers, Q.A.W., et al. (2011), 'Come rain or come shine: individual differences in how weather affects mood', *Emotion*, **11** (6), 1495–1499. doi:10.1037/a0024649.

Luhmann, M. (2017), 'Using Big Data to study subjective well-being', *Current Opinion in Behavioral Sciences*, **18**, 28–33.

Maas, J., Verheij, R.A., de Vries, S., Spreeuwenberg, P., Schellevis, F.G. and P.P. Groenewegen (2009), 'Morbidity is related to a green living environment', *Journal of Epidemiology and Community Health*, **63** (12), 967–973.

MacKerron, G. (2012), 'Happiness and environmental quality', PhD thesis, London School of Economics; Political Science. Retrieved 22 July 2019 from http://etheses.lse.ac.uk/383/.

MacKerron, G. and S. Mourato (2013), 'Happiness is greater in natural environments', *Global Environmental Change*, **23** (5), 992–1000.

Maynard, D.G. and M.A. Greenwood (2014), 'Who cares about sarcastic tweets? Investigating the impact of sarcasm on sentiment analysis', *LREC 2014 Proceedings*, 4238–4243. http://eprints.whiterose.ac.uk/130763/.

Met Office (2006a), 'MIDAS UK hourly weather observation data', NCAS British Atmospheric Data Centre.

Met Office (2006b), 'MIDAS UK hourly rainfall data', NCAS British Atmospheric Data Centre.

Mislove, A., Lehmann, S., Yong-Yeol Ahn, Onnela, J.-P. and J.N. Rosenquist (2010), 'Pulse of the nation: US mood throughout the day inferred from Twitter'. Retrieved 22 July 2019 from http://www.ccs.neu.edu/home/amislove/twittermood/.

Mitchell, L., Frank, M.R., Harris, K.D., Dodds, P.S. and C.M. Danforth (2013), 'The geography of happiness: connecting Twitter sentiment and expression, demographics, and objective characteristics of place', *PLOS ONE*, **8** (5), e64417.

Mitchell, R. and F. Popham (2007), 'Greenspace, urbanity and health: relationships in England', *Journal of Epidemiology and Community Health*, **61** (8), 681–683. doi:10.1136/jech.2006.053553.

Mitchell, R. and F. Popham (2008), 'Effect of exposure to natural environment on health inequalities: an observational population study', *Lancet*, **372** (9650), 1655–1660.

Morris, N. (2003), 'Health, well-being and open space: literature review', Edinburgh, UK: OPENspace, Edinburgh. http://www.openspace.eca.ed.ac.uk/wp-content/uploads/2015/10/Health-Well-being-and-Open-Space-literature-review.pdf.

Morton, D., Rowland, C., Wood, C., Meek, L., Marston, C., et al. (2011), 'Final report for LCM2007 – the new UK land cover map', Countryside Survey Technical Report No 11/07, NERC/Centre for Ecology and Hydrology. https://www.ceh.ac.uk/sites/default/files/LCM2007%20Final%20Report.pdf.

National Centre for Social Research (2009), 'British Social Attitudes Survey 2009', Economic and Social Data Service.

National Records of Scotland (2001), '2001 Census: boundary data (Scotland), UK Data Service, SN:5819 UKBORDERS: Digitised Boundary Data, 1840–'.

Northern Ireland Statistics and Research Agency (2011), '2011 Census: Boundary data (Northern Ireland), UK Data Service, SN:5819 UKBORDERS: Digitised Boundary Data, 1840–'.

Office for National Statistics (2010), Mid-year population estimates 2009, retrieved 22 July 2019 from http://www.statistics.gov.uk/statbase/product.asp?vlnk=15106.

Office for National Statistics (2011), '2011 Census: Boundary data (England and Wales), [data collection], UK Data Service, SN:5819 UKBORDERS: Digitised Boundary Data, 1840–'.

Passchier-Vermeer, W. and W.F. Passchier (2000), 'Noise exposure and public health', *Environmental Health Perspectives*, **108**, 123–131.

Pretty, J., Barton, J., Colbeck, I., Hine, R., Mourato, S., et al. (2011), 'Health values from ecosystems', in *UK National Ecosystem Assessment: Technical Report*, Cambridge, UK: UNEP-WCMC.

R Development Core Team (2011), *R: A Language and Environment for Statistical Computing*, Vienna, Austria: R Foundation for Statistical Computing.

Rehdanz, K. and D. Maddison (2008), 'Local environmental quality and life-satisfaction in Germany', *Ecological Economics*, **64** (4), 787–797.

Roberts, H.V. (2017), 'Using Twitter data in urban green space research', *Applied Geography*, **81**, 13–20.

Roberts, H., Sadler, J. and L. Chapman (2019), 'The value of Twitter data for determining the emotional responses of people to urban green spaces: a case study and critical evaluation', *Urban Studies*, **56** (4), 818–835.

Runyan, J.D. and E.G. Steinke (2015), 'Virtues, ecological momentary assessment/intervention and smartphone technology', *Frontiers in Psychology*, **6**, Article ID 481. doi:10.3389/fpsyg.2015.00481.

Runyan, J.D., Steenbergh, T.A., Bainbridge, C., Daugherty, D.A., Oke, L. and B.N. Fry (2013), 'A smartphone ecological momentary assessment/intervention "app" for collecting real-time data and promoting self-awareness', *PLOS ONE*, **8** (8), e71325. doi:10.1371/journal.pone.0071325.

Ryan, R.M., Weinstein, N., Bernstein, J., Brown, K.W., Mistretta, L. and M. Gagné (2010), 'Vitalizing effects of being outdoors and in nature', *Journal of Environmental Psychology*, **30** (2), 159–168.

Sandulescu, V., Andrews, S., Ellis, D., Dobrescu, R. and O. Martinez-Mozos (2015), 'Mobile app for stress monitoring using voice features', 2015 E-Health and Bioengineering Conference, IEEE. https://ieeexplore.ieee.org/abstract/document/7391411.

Schwartz, H.A., Eichstaedt, J.C., Kern, M.L., Dziurzynski, L., Lucas, R.E., et al. (2013), 'Characterizing geographic variation in well-being using tweets', Seventh International AAAI Conference on Weblogs and Social Media.

Schwartz, O. (2019), 'Don't look now: why you should be worried about machines reading your emotions', *Guardian*, 6 March 2019. Accessed 24 May 2019 at https://www.theguardian.com/technology/2019/mar/06/facial-recognition-software-emotional-science.

Sefick, S.A., Jr (2009), 'Stream Metabolism: a package for calculating single station metabolism from diurnal oxygen curves', CRAN repository. Accessed 22 July 2019 at http://CRAN.R-project.org/package=StreamMetabolism.

Seresinhe, C.I., Preis, T., MacKerron, G. and H.S. Moat (2019), 'Happiness is greater in more scenic locations', *Scientific Reports*, **9**, Article 4498.

Shiffman, S., Stone, A.A. and M.R. Hufford (2008), 'Ecological momentary assessment', *Clinical Psychology*, **4** (1), 1–32.

StataCorp (2009), *Stata Longitudinal-Data/Panel-Data Reference Manual, Release 11*, Texas: Stata Press.

Stock, J.H. and M.W. Watson (2008), 'Heteroskedasticity-robust standard errors for fixed effects panel data regression', *Econometrica*, **76** (1), 155–174.

Stone, A. and S. Shiffman (2002), 'Capturing momentary, self-report data: a proposal for reporting guidelines', *Annals of Behavioral Medicine*, **24** (3), 236–243. doi:10.1207/S15324796ABM2403_09.

Swan, M. (2013), 'The quantified self: fundamental disruption in Big Data science and biological discovery', *Big Data*, **1** (2), 85–99. doi:10.1089/big.2012.0002.

University of Cambridge (2016), 'Does nature make you happy? Crowdsourcing app looks at relationship between the outdoors and wellbeing', University of Cambridge News, 26 April 2016. Accessed 22 July 2019 at https://www.cam.ac.uk/research/news/does-nature-make-you-happy-crowdsourcing-app-looks-at-relationship-between-the-outdoors-and.

Valtchanov, D., Barton, K.R. and C. Ellard (2010), 'Restorative effects of virtual nature settings', *Cyberpsychology, Behavior, and Social Networking*, **13** (5), 503–512. doi:10.1089/cyber.2009.0308.

van der Velde, J.R., Tisma, A. and R.R. Fransman (2016), 'WeSense: social sensing the quality of urban environments', Poster, KNAW-Symposium Citizen Science. http://resolver.tudelft.nl/uuid:7bb03145-ae47-49fa-a1d7-b8d571c958b3.

Vemuri, A.W. and R. Costanza (2006), 'The role of human, social, built, and natural capital in explaining life satisfaction at the country level: toward a National Well-Being Index (NWI)', *Ecological Economics*, **58** (1), 119–133. doi:10.1016/j.ecolecon.2005.02.008.

Völker, S. and T. Kistemann (2011), 'The impact of blue space on human health and well-being – salutogenetic health effects of inland surface waters: a review', *International Journal of Hygiene and Environmental Health*, **214** (6), 449–460. doi:10.1016/j.ijheh.2011.05.001.

Völker, S. and T. Kistemann (2013), '"I'm always entirely happy when I'm here!" Urban blue enhancing human health and well-being in Cologne and Düsseldorf, Germany', *Social Science and Medicine*, **78** (1), 113–124. doi:10.1016/j.socscimed.2012.09.047.

Völker, S. and T. Kistemann (2015), 'Developing the urban blue: comparative health responses to blue and green urban open spaces in Germany', *Health and Place*, **35**, 196–205. doi:10.1016/j.healthplace.2014.10.015.

Vries, S. de, Verheij, R.A., Groenewegen, P.P. and P. Spreeuwenberg (2003), 'Natural environments – healthy environments? An exploratory analysis of the relationship between greenspace and health', *Environment and Planning A*, **35** (10), 1717–1732.

Welsch, H. (2006), 'Environment and happiness: valuation of air pollution using life satisfaction data', *Ecological Economics*, **58** (4), 801–813.

Wheeler, B.W., White, M., Stahl-Timmins, W. and M.H. Depledge (2012), 'Does living by the coast improve health and wellbeing?', *Health and Place*, **18** (5), 1198–1201.

White, M.P., Pahl, S., Wheeler, B.W., Depledge, M.H. and L.E. Fleming (2017), 'Natural environments and subjective wellbeing: different types of exposure are associated with different aspects of wellbeing', *Health and Place*, **45**, 77–84. doi:10.1016/j.healthplace.2017.03.008.

White, M., Smith, A., Humphryes, K., Pahl, S., Snelling, D. and M.H. Depledge (2010), 'Blue space: the importance of water for preference, affect, and restorativeness ratings of natural and built scenes', *Journal of Environmental Psychology*, **30** (4), 482–493.

Wilson, Edward O. (1993), 'Biophilia and the conservation ethic', in Stephen R. Kellert and Edward O. Wilson (eds), *The Biophilia Hypothesis*, Washington, DC, USA: Island Press, pp. 31–41.

Wooldridge, Jeffrey M. (2009), *Introductory Econometrics: A Modern Approach*, 4th edition, Mason, OH, USA: South-Western Cengage Learning.
Yaden, D.B., Eichstaedt, J.C. and J.D. Medaglia (2018), 'The future of technology in Positive Psychology: methodological advances in the science of well-being', *Frontiers in Psychology*, **9**, Article 962.
Zheng, S., Wang, J., Sun, C., Zhang, X. and M.E. Kahn (2019), 'Air pollution lowers Chinese urbanites' expressed happiness on social media', *Nature Human Behaviour*, **3** (3), 237–243.

15. Legacy effects and individual heterogeneity in the relationship between health and wellbeing*

Peter Howley

15.1 INTRODUCTION

Economists are becoming increasingly interested in basing assessments of welfare on experienced utility (for example, self-reported wellbeing), rather than basing them solely on observed behaviour (see Lowenstein and Ubel, 2008; Dolan and Fujiwara, 2016 for a review of this literature). Proponents of the use of experienced utility as a welfare criterion for public policy consider the factors that affect how happy or otherwise individuals feel, and subsequently use such information to inform economic and social policy (e.g., Donovan and Halpern, 2002; Kahneman and Sugden, 2005; Layard, 2005; Dolan and Metcalfe, 2012). Focusing specifically on health, there is now an extensive literature that has examined the effects of a wide variety of health conditions on subjective indicators of wellbeing using large-scale household surveys (see, e.g., Graham et al., 2011; Powdthavee and van den Berg, 2011; Howley, 2017).

While much progress has been made in relation to understanding the hedonic effects of different health conditions, there is still much to learn. Focusing on cancer or a malignancy as a case study, in this chapter I conduct a preliminary investigation into two aspects of the health and wellbeing relationship that have largely been overlooked in the literature to date. The first of these is potential legacy effects from health conditions. While we know that individual's wellbeing will be negatively affected by health conditions, and moreover these effects can be substantive and long-lasting, we do not yet know what happens to wellbeing once individuals feel that they have fully recovered from their ill-health.

It may be too simplistic to assume that individuals who feel that they have recovered from their ill-health will return to their pre-existing 'baseline' level of wellbeing, that is, the level experienced prior to acquiring the health condition. This is because there could be some negative features of post-illness life that resist adaptation. One could imagine, for example, that many individuals even when fully recovered from cancer may still worry about the health condition returning (or indeed new ones manifesting themselves), or more generally worry about what the future may hold for their health. Additionally, the treatment of certain health conditions can be quite intensive, and so it seems plausible that it could have a lasting impact on individuals' emotional wellbeing.

The second issue I look at is in relation to individual heterogeneity in the health and wellbeing relationship. Focusing on personality differences, the question I explore here is whether individuals with certain personality traits are more likely to feel adversely affected in terms of wellbeing by changes to their health than others. The importance of personality traits is underscored by a nascent, yet rapidly emerging area of research, showing that personality can moderate the extent to which individuals' wellbeing is affected in response to changing life events. Personality moderation analysis shows, for example, that marriage is not beneficial to everyone (Boyce et al., 2016), and that economic losses are easier for some individuals to bear than for others (Boyce et al., 2010). Within this context, it seems reasonable to suggest that personality traits may also affect the extent to which individuals' wellbeing is affected by changes to their health. Previous work generally does not take individual heterogeneity into account when reporting on the relationship between health and wellbeing, and neglecting such heterogeneity may give an incomplete, if not superficial, understanding of the hedonic effects of health. Before moving on to a description of the research design and results, I discuss each of these issues – legacy effects and personality-oriented heterogeneity – in a little more detail in the following sections.

15.2 LEGACY EFFECTS

Much research within economics and psychology has explored whether individuals facing adverse life events such as unemployment, long-term illnesses or disabilities tend to 'adapt' to their new context. This issue has important policy implications, since if people experience full hedonic adaptation to adverse life events such as disability, then one could argue that it would be unnecessary to spend public resources on measures that mitigate these harmful life events, albeit that this would conflict with many people's common intuitions and values (Loewenstein and Ubel, 2008). Perhaps the factor that has attracted the most interest when it comes to the issue of hedonic adaptation and wellbeing is that of health status. The most recent research in this area would suggest that some people may experience partial hedonic adaptation, but at the same time the negative effects of disability are significant and long-lasting (Lucas, 2007; Oswald and Powdthavee, 2008).

While there is compelling evidence to suggest that having a health condition will lead to lasting declines in wellbeing (albeit these negative hedonic effects, at least for certain health conditions, may diminish somewhat over time), we do not yet know whether individuals' wellbeing will revert back to their initial set-point level if they feel that they have fully recovered from such a health condition. This is important, as once an individual reports being fully recovered, they are less likely to seek further assistance, counselling or treatment, and hence such reductions are less likely to be mitigated, leading to long-term loss in quality of life. Moreover, a lack of understanding relating to what happens to wellbeing once individuals feel that they have fully recovered from health conditions makes it impossible to gauge the full hedonic consequences of health conditions, and potentially leads to underestimating the true cost of illnesses.

In order to examine whether individuals' wellbeing returns to the levels experienced before acquiring a health condition, I take advantage of a unique nationally representative dataset which, fortunately for the purposes of this study, not only asked individuals whether they ever had a specified health condition such as cancer or a malignancy, but also asked those same individuals in a follow up question whether they still had that same health condition. Using this information the population can be divided into three subgroups, namely: (1) those with a current diagnosis of cancer or a malignancy; (2) those who report that they have fully recovered from cancer or a malignancy (recoverees); and finally, (3) what serves as a control group for our purposes, those who regard themselves as never having had cancer or a malignancy (never diagnosed). I then compare the wellbeing of all three groups, controlling for observed differences between them.

15.3 INDIVIDUAL HETEROGENEITY: PERSONALITY TRAITS

There has been a growing consensus that there are five basic or primary personality traits, namely neuroticism, extraversion, openness, agreeableness and conscientiousness (McCrae and Costa, 2008). These personality traits have been identified as having considerable public health significance (see Weston et al., 2015 for a review). Specifically, personality traits have been identified as being a significant predictor of the onset of disease. Of the Big Five personality traits, neuroticism in particular has garnered significant attention as an important contributing factor to a wide variety of health conditions. Shipley et al. (2007), for example, in a 21-year prospective study of British adults, found that neuroticism was significantly associated with cardiovascular disease (Shipley et al., 2007). Similarly Wilson et al. (2004, 2005) report that individuals with high neuroticism scores had significantly higher deaths from all causes, compared to those low in neuroticism.

Overall we can see that there is an extensive literature to suggest that apart from directly affecting perceived wellbeing, personality traits can have an indirect effect through influencing the onset of disease. One issue that has been largely overlooked to date, however, is whether personality traits influence the extent to which a health condition will negatively affect an individual's wellbeing. More precisely, apart from predicting the onset of health conditions, personality traits may have a significant role in moderating the extent to which the wellbeing of individuals are negatively affected by a health condition. One pathway through which this moderation may occur is that personality traits may influence how people will respond to a health condition, whether from better adherence to doctor's instructions and overall disease management, to effectively coping with the stress associated with the onset of a health condition. In order to test this idea, I examine whether there are any significant interaction effects between a dummy variable capturing individuals currently suffering with cancer or a malignancy, and each of the Big Five personality traits.

15.4 DATA

The data used in this analysis comes from Understanding Society: the United Kingdom Household Longitudinal Study (UKHLS). This is a comprehensive household survey that started in 2009 with a nationally representative stratified, clustered sample of around 50 000 adults (16+) living in the United Kingdom. The indicator of subjective wellbeing used as the key outcome variable in this analysis is the General Health Questionnaire (GHQ), which consists of a 12-item scale designed to assess somatic symptoms, anxiety and insomnia, social dysfunction and severe depression. It is one of the most common indicators of subjective wellbeing used in the literature to date (Goldberg et al., 1997; Jackson, 2007). Some examples of the items elicited include: 'Have you recently lost much sleep over worry?'; 'Have you recently felt constantly under strain?' and 'Have you recently been able to enjoy your normal day-to-day activities?' Each item is accompanied by four possible responses; two of the answers are positive and two are negative. The GHQ score ranges from 0 (best psychological wellbeing) to 36 (worst psychological wellbeing) for each participant and is computed for each individual by aggregating the item responses;

higher scores indicate a greater likelihood that the respondent is suffering from some form of psychological distress. To simplify interpretation, I reorder this variable so that individuals are scored from 0 (worst) to 36 (best), and label this variable as psychological wellbeing.

15.4.1 Explanatory Variables

The key explanatory variable of interest is derived from participants' response to a question about whether they have been diagnosed with particular health conditions, which was asked in wave 1[1] (2009–11) of the survey. Participants were presented with a card listing 17 health conditions, one of which was 'cancer or a malignancy' and asked, 'Has a doctor or other health professional ever told you that you have any of the conditions listed on this card?'. Participants who reported that they had been diagnosed with one of these conditions were then asked whether they still had that health condition. Using this information, I derive dummy variables indicating: (1) whether a survey participant is currently suffering from cancer or a malignancy; and (2) those who previously had cancer but who now report that they have fully recovered (recoverees). What serves as the reference group are individuals who report that they never had cancer or a malignancy (never diagnosed).[2] One important point to note is that the UKHLS does not capture individuals who have died as a result of the health condition, and hence the estimates in this analysis will act as a lower bound when it comes to the wellbeing losses attributable to having cancer or a malignancy.

15.4.2 Control/Moderating Variables

Personality is typically described as encompassing 'the psychological component of a person that remains from one situation to another' (Wood and Boyce, 2014) and is most typically captured by psychologists using the influential five factor model (McCrae and Costa, 2008). The five factor model consists of five over-arching traits: agreeableness, conscientiousness, extraversion, neuroticism and openness. To obtain these personality traits, participants in wave 3 of the UKHLS (conducted between 2011 and 2013) were asked to what extent they agree/disagree with 15 statements beginning with the quote, 'I see myself as someone who . . .'. Each statement is classed in one of five categories: extraversion, agreeableness, conscientiousness, neuroticism and openness. A composite score for each personality trait is then derived by summing the scores for each of the individual categories. While these personality questions were asked just in wave 3 of the UKHLS, personality is generally regarded as fixed across time (see Borghans et al., 2008) and so we assume these personality measures are an adequate proxy for individuals in subsequent waves of the UKHLS. Given that the same individuals are mostly interviewed from wave to wave we can, therefore, match individuals with their reported health states recorded in wave 1, to their personality traits captured in wave 3.

I include a number of variables to help mitigate the influence of confounding, by controlling for observed differences between groups. These controls include socio-economic variables such as age, equivalent household income, gender, education, relationship status and labour force status. I also add variables reflecting the extent to which individuals talk with their neighbours and participate in religious activities as

Table 15.1 Summary statistics

	Mean	Std dev.	Min.	Max.
Psychological wellbeing – GHQ	24.890	5.512	0	36
Log of equivalent monthly household income	7.416	0.711	−6	11
In a relationship	0.634	0.482	0	1
Age	47	18.605	15	104
Age squared	2538	1854.276	225	10816
Female	0.537	0.499	0	1
Has a degree or higher qualification	0.281	0.450	0	1
Employed	0.478	0.499	0	1
Self-employed	0.073	0.261	0	1
Unemployed	0.049	0.215	0	1
Retired	0.221	0.415	0	1
Family care	0.065	0.246	0	1
Training	0.069	0.254	0	1
Other	0.002	0.043	0	1
Disabled	0.038	0.192	0	1
Regularly attends religious services or meetings	0.149	0.357	0	1
Regularly stops and talks with people in their neighbourhood	0.197	0.398	0	1
Body mass index	26.664	5.207	10	86
Currently has cancer	0.009	0.093	0	1
Recovered from cancer	0.022	0.148	0	1
Neuroticism	3.557	1.439	1	7
Conscientiousness	5.472	1.112	1	7
Agreeableness	5.630	1.038	1	7
Openness	4.535	1.313	1	7
Extraversion	4.592	1.303	1	7

proxy variables for social capital. These variables were supplemented with a full set of regional dummies to help control for any regional differences in access to medical care. To help mitigate any bias due to unmeasured lifestyle or behavioural differences between those with cancer or a malignancy and those fully recovered from this health condition, I also added a measure of body mass index to the model specification (see Table 15.1 for summary statistics).

15.5 ANALYSIS

I first compare the difference in psychological wellbeing (GHQ) scores between respondents that have a current diagnosis for cancer or a malignancy, to those who report that they have recovered from this health condition, and also to those who have never had cancer or a malignancy, using the following model specification:

$$GHQ = a_0 + \beta_1 C_i + \beta_2 RC_i + \beta_3 P_i + \beta_4 X_i + R + \varepsilon_i \tag{15.1}$$

where C_i is a dummy variable representing whether the individual has cancer or a malignancy, and RC_i is a dummy variable representing whether the individual feels that they have recovered from cancer or a malignancy. Each of the five personality measures are captured by (P_i). I also add in a number of control variables (X_i) as outlined earlier to help mitigate the influence of confounding due to observed differences between groups and a set of regional dummies R. ε_i is a random error term. β_1 captures the average difference in psychological wellbeing between individuals who currently have cancer or a malignancy and those who have never had this health condition (never diagnosed). Similarly, β_2 captures the average difference in psychological wellbeing between individuals who feel that they have recovered from cancer or a malignancy (recoverees) and those who have never had cancer or a malignancy (never diagnosed).

To test whether personality traits can moderate the relationship between a health condition such as cancer or a malignancy and wellbeing, I simply interact each of the personality measures (P_i) – namely neuroticism, extraversion, agreeableness, openness and conscientiousness – with the dummy indicator capturing individuals with a current diagnosis of cancer or a malignancy (C_i). Support for the idea that the wellbeing effects from having cancer or a malignancy will be moderated by personality traits can be obtained when the interaction terms between P and C ($P_i * C_i$) are statistically significant.

15.6 RESULTS

15.6.1 Legacy Effects

Specification 1 in Table 15.2 presents the results – pooled ordinary least squares (OLS) – relating to the analysis of psychological wellbeing including the full set of control variables. In specification 2, I match individuals in wave 1 with reported health conditions to their personality traits recorded in wave 3. This reduced the sample size somewhat but has the advantage of allowing us to control for this potentially important source of individual heterogeneity. The key explanatory variables of interest are the dummy variables indicating whether a respondent has a current diagnosis of cancer or a malignancy, and the dummy variable indicating whether individuals have recovered from a cancer or a malignancy (recoverees). The reference group in both cases reflect respondents who report that they have never been diagnosed with cancer or a malignancy.

The coefficient reflecting differences in wellbeing between individuals with a current diagnosis and recoverees is broadly similar across both specifications; that is, accounting for personality differences does not change the main results in any meaningful fashion. In unreported results (available upon request) I also added in controls for other health conditions, and again the results did not change in any meaningful fashion with the addition of these additional controls. Looking at specification 2, we can see that, as expected, individuals with cancer or a malignancy have a significantly lower self-reported level of psychological wellbeing (1.68 unit difference) than individuals never diagnosed with cancer or a malignancy. Given the heterogeneity within cancers, it is worth noting that for some cancers, the average reduction in wellbeing is likely to be much larger than this.

We can test the hypothesis that individuals may not return to pre-disability levels of psychological wellbeing once recovered from a health condition such as cancer by examining

Table 15.2 Psychological wellbeing regression results, pooled OLS

	Specification 1		Specification 2		
	Coef.	Std err.	Coef.	Std err.	
Log of equivalent household income	0.29***	0.04	0.25***	0.05	
In a relationship	0.65***	0.06	0.66***	0.07	
Age	−0.11***	0.01	−0.14***	0.01	
Age squared	0.00***	0.00	0.00***	0.00	
Female	−0.97***	0.06	−0.31***	0.07	
Has a degree	0.16***	0.06	0.08	0.07	
Labour market status – employed is the reference category					
Self-employed	−0.09	0.11	−0.07	0.12	
Unemployed	−2.12***	0.12	−1.88***	0.15	
Retired	0.07	0.12	0.28**	0.13	
Family care	−0.86***	0.11	−0.52***	0.13	
Training	0.17	0.13	0.18	0.17	
Disabled	−6.51***	0.15	−4.82***	0.19	
Other	−0.88	1.01	−0.86	1.11	
Regularly attend religions services	0.45***	0.08	0.30***	0.09	
Regularly talk with neighbours	0.68***	0.07	0.40***	0.08	
Body mass index	−0.04***	0.01	−0.05***	0.01	
Currently has cancer	−2.21***	0.27	−1.68***	0.33	
Recovered from cancer	−0.62***	0.17	−0.62***	0.19	
Regional dummy variables unreported for parsimony					
Neuroticism			−1.15***	0.02	
Conscientiousness			0.26***	0.03	
Agreeableness			−0.01	0.03	
Openness			−0.04	0.03	
Extraversion			0.05**	0.03	
R^2	0.095			0.20	
N = 36 137					
Interaction terms					
Cancer*neuroticism					−0.39*
Cancer*extraversion					−0.41*
Cancer*conscientiousness					−0.66**
Cancer*agreeableness					−0.79***
Cancer*openness					−0.90

Note: * Statistically significant at 10% level, **statistically significant at 5% level, *** statistically significant at 1% level.

the signs and significance of the dummy variable (recoverees) comparing the wellbeing of individuals who have recovered from cancer or a malignancy, to the wellbeing of those who have never had the condition (never diagnosed). The coefficient on this variable is statistically significant and negative, indicating that there is a significant difference in the psychological wellbeing between individuals who feel that they have recovered from cancer or a malignancy, and the group never diagnosed with cancer or malignancy. While this wellbeing gap is much lower than that observed when comparing individuals with a current diagnosis of this health condition and those never diagnosed, it is still substantive (0.62 unit difference).

The results relating to the control variables are all along the expected lines and correspond with the results widely documented in previous literature, and so for parsimony are not discussed in detail here (see Dolan et al., 2008). I do, however, point the reader in the direction of one of our control variables, namely body mass index (BMI). The UKHLS records a measure of individuals' self-reported height and weight which I used to calculate individuals' BMI. BMI has been found to be one of the most important predictors of individuals' general health status (see, e.g., Wang et al., 2011), and this variable was included in the model specification as a means to partially account for any lifestyle or behavioural differences that could explain wellbeing differences between individuals recovered from cancer or a malignancy, and those never diagnosed with this health condition. In keeping with other recent research (see Preiss et al., 2013 and de Wit et al., 2010 for recent systematic reviews), we can observe a negative relationship between BMI and psychological wellbeing.

Taken together, the results outlined in Table 15.2 suggest that having cancer or a malignancy has a substantive and significant adverse relationship with wellbeing, and that when individuals feel that they have recovered, their psychological wellbeing significantly improves, but that part of the negative hedonic effect from having health conditions such as cancer or a malignancy may still linger even after individuals regard themselves as no longer having those same health conditions.

15.6.2 Individual Heterogeneity: Personality Traits

Next, I test whether the Big Five personality traits can moderate the adverse wellbeing effects from having a health condition such as cancer or a malignancy. I do this by interacting the dummy variable capturing individuals who currently have this health condition with each of the measures of personality traits. These interaction effects are illustrated in the figures included here. The absence of moderation would be indicated by parallel lines for both groups; that is, individuals with cancer or a malignancy and those who never had this health condition.

Neurotic individuals are characterised as being more prone to negative emotions such as anxiety and stress (McCrae and Costa, 2003). Much previous research suggests that neuroticism can be an important contributing factor to a wide variety of health conditions (Shipley et al., 2007). Looking at Figure 15.1, we can see that neuroticism is also negatively associated with wellbeing for individuals never diagnosed and those currently diagnosed with cancer or a malignancy. This is in keeping with much prior literature which suggests that neuroticism can be harmful to wellbeing (see Steel et al., 2008 for a review). Of particular interest here is that in addition to having a negative relationship with wellbeing, neuroticism appears to exacerbate, at least to some degree, the adverse wellbeing effects from having cancer or a malignancy. We can see in Figure 15.1, for instance, how the gap in wellbeing between individuals with and without this health condition widens as neuroticism scores also increase. In other words, there is a more substantive difference in wellbeing between individuals with and without this health condition, who have high as opposed to low neuroticism scores.

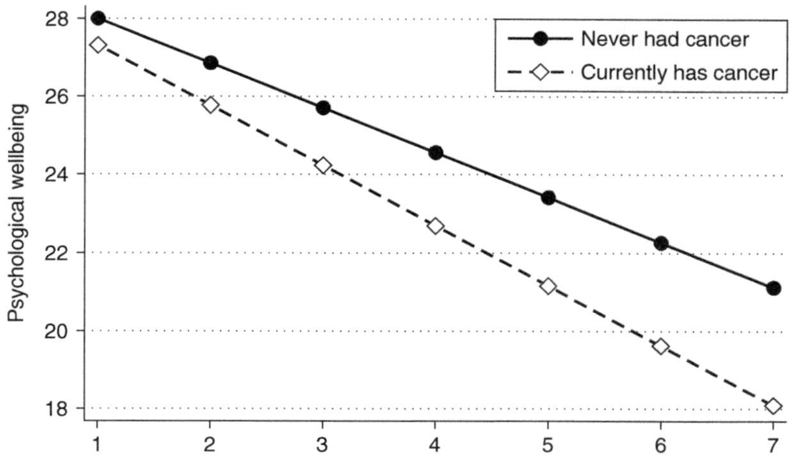

Figure 15.1 *Cancer*neuroticism interaction effect*

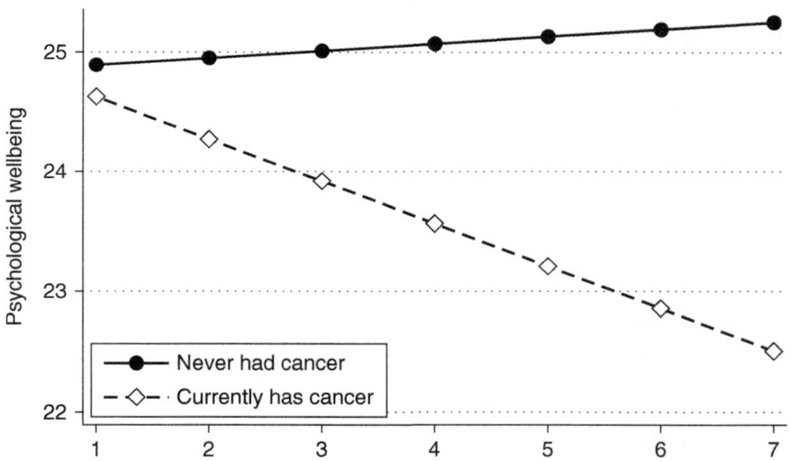

Figure 15.2 *Cancer*extraversion interaction effect*

Individuals who score high on extraversion tend to be outgoing and social, and this personality trait is typically positively related with wellbeing (see Steel et al., 2008). Similar to neuroticism, we observe a significant but even more substantive interaction effect between this personality trait and suffering with cancer or a malignancy (Figure 15.2). Specifically, at low levels of extraversion (introverted individuals) there is a relatively small wellbeing gap between individuals with and without this health condition. This wellbeing gap widens considerably when looking at individuals with relatively high extraversion scores; that is, extraversion, like neuroticism, appears to exacerbate the adverse wellbeing effects from having this health condition.

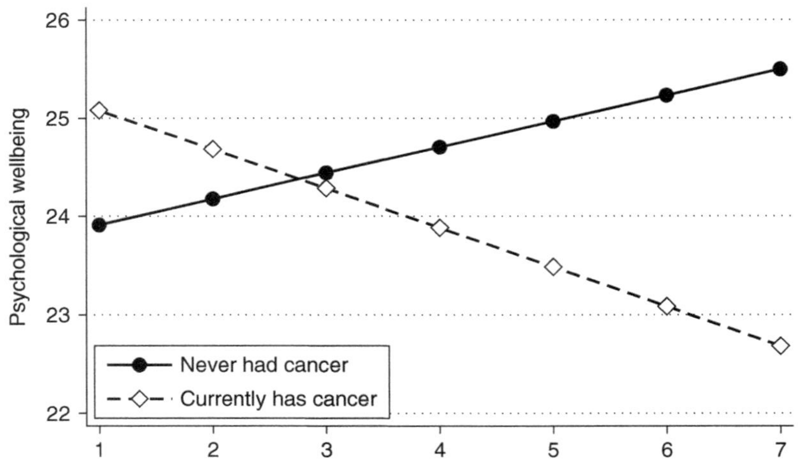

*Figure 15.3 Cancer*conscientiousness interaction effect*

Individuals who score high on conscientiousness tend to be organised and dutiful and to take obligations to others seriously (Bogg and Roberts, 2004). At low levels of conscientiousness, we somewhat strangely observe that individuals with cancer or a malignancy have slightly higher wellbeing scores than individuals without cancer (Figure 15.3). However, these differences are small and I suggest are most likely the result of having a very small comparison group, that is, very small numbers of individuals with cancer or a malignancy who also have very low conscientiousness scores. In keeping with much prior literature which has found that conscientiousness is associated with enhanced wellbeing (see Steel et al., 2008), we see a substantive positive correlation between conscientiousness and wellbeing for those who have never had cancer or a malignancy. On the other hand, we observe a substantive negative correlation between conscientiousness and wellbeing for individuals with this health condition. One possible explanation is that conscientiousness engenders a feeling of obligation to others, and this in turn can lead to greater worry or feelings of being a burden, thus lowering wellbeing.

As illustrated in Figure 15.4, we do not observe any significant association between agreeableness and psychological wellbeing for individuals who do not have cancer or a malignancy. We do, however, observe a substantive negative correlation between agreeableness and the wellbeing of individuals with this health condition (Figure 15.4). This suggests that, similarly to neuroticism, extraversion and conscientiousness, agreeableness appears to exacerbate the wellbeing effects associated with having cancer or a malignancy. Finally, openness does not appear to moderate the wellbeing effects from having cancer or a malignancy (Figure 15.5).

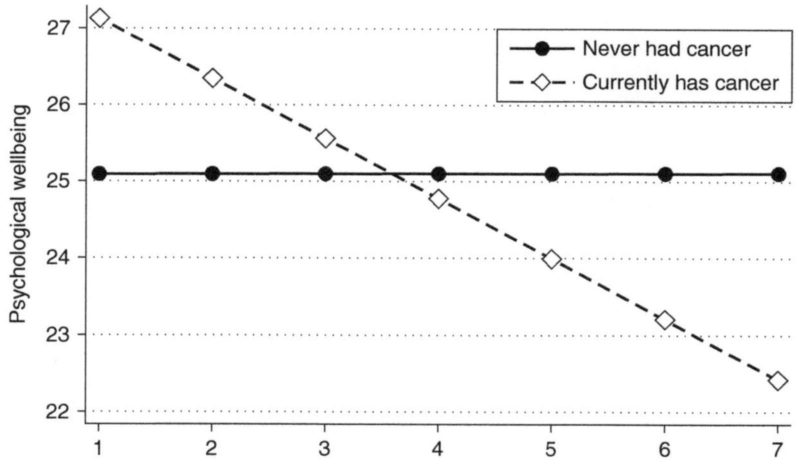

*Figure 15.4 Cancer*agreeableness interaction effect*

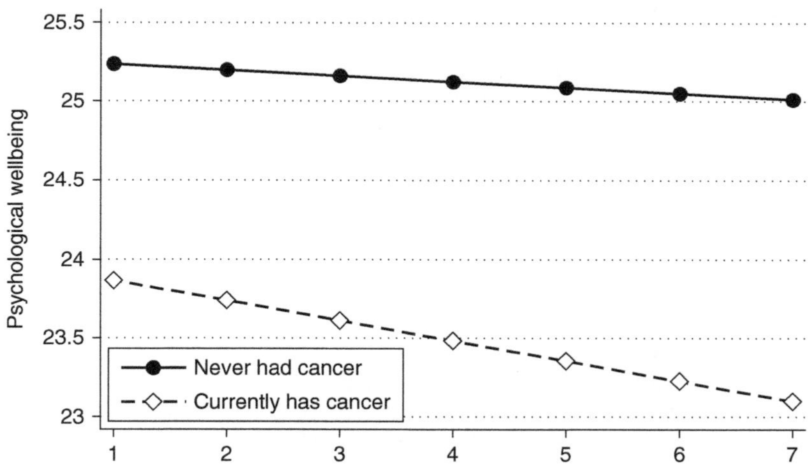

*Figure 15.5 Cancer*openness interaction effect*

15.7 CONCLUSION

One of the most robust findings in the 'economics of happiness' literature is that disability negatively affects psychological wellbeing. However, little is known about the legacy impacts of previous bouts of poor health on current psychological wellbeing. To assess whether individuals fully recover in terms of psychological wellbeing after previously having a health condition, I tested for differences in psychological wellbeing between individuals with a current diagnosis of cancer or a malignancy, those who feel that they have recovered from this health condition, and a control group consisting of individuals with similar characteristics but who have never been diagnosed with this health condition. I found significant differences in psychological wellbeing between all three groups. The differences in psychological wellbeing between individuals with cancer or a malignancy and individuals never diagnosed with this health condition were especially pronounced, and they suggest, in keeping with much recent research, that health conditions such as cancer have a substantive deleterious relationship with psychological wellbeing.

Differences between individuals who feel that they have fully recovered from cancer or a malignancy and those never diagnosed with this health condition were much less pronounced, but still significant and substantial, and therefore suggest that individuals may not fully recover their psychological wellbeing even when they feel that they have recovered from certain health conditions. This means that there may be ongoing ramifications of disability that are not easily adaptable even when individuals have fully recovered in terms of their health status.

It is important to note that, due to the cross-sectional nature of this study, I cannot rule out the possibility that the observed psychological wellbeing differences are the result of unobserved differences between groups. This work is intended as an initial exploration into an issue that has not previously been examined in the health and wellbeing domain (at least to the best of my knowledge), rather than an attempt to establish causal effects. That being said, the detailed set of controls provide some support that the estimates are not significantly biased by confounding factors. My hope is that these findings will stimulate further research into what happens to psychological wellbeing following positive changes in health status, to go along with the emerging and interesting literature concerned with the psychological wellbeing effects (and subsequent adaptation or otherwise) of adverse changes in health. Failure to do so makes it impossible to gauge the full hedonic costs of health. In future work, I hope to extend the analysis of legacy effects to a multitude of health conditions and see whether similar patterns emerge to that described here.

A nascent yet rapidly emerging body of work suggests that personality traits can play a significant role in the probability that one will develop certain health conditions. In this study I find that personality may also play an important role in how an individual copes, in wellbeing terms at least, with health conditions such as cancer or a malignancy. Looking at differences across groups instead of just focusing on main effects helps us in understanding when and to whom health conditions are likely to be particularly important for wellbeing. Neglecting to consider such heterogeneity and focusing on 'average' effects, as is the norm in the literature to date, may lead to an incomplete and perhaps superficial understanding of the hedonic effects of health.

Taking characteristics such as personality traits into account may also improve health assessments as well as decisions on management and service provision. For instance, if patients' personality traits predispose them to being more likely to cope with the onset of disease (for example, both emotional and behavioural aspects), then that patient is likely to experience fewer health complications and lower economic costs in the long term. In future work, I hope to look at other sources of individual heterogeneity as well as examine further health conditions and see whether similar patterns emerge as those described here.

NOTES

* The author is grateful to Stephen on Neill from the Department of Economics at National University of Ireland, Galway, and the editors for helpful comments and suggestions. The usual disclaimer applies.

1. All respondents in wave 1 are asked whether they have been diagnosed with these health conditions. New panel members were subsequently asked this same question in waves 2, 4 and 5. This analysis focused on wave 1 as some of the controls such as BMI are only available in this wave. Furthermore, adding in additional waves does not increase sample size to a significant degree; for example, only six of the new respondents in wave 3 report that they had ever been diagnosed with cancer. Finally, as wave 1 participants are not asked this question again, it is not possible to use fixed effects, albeit it would be unlikely that there would be enough 'transitions' from poor to good health over such a short time period to permit fixed effects analysis in any case.
2. It is of course possible that some of the individuals who report that they have never had cancer, have undiagnosed cancer. If there is a significant number of individuals with cancer in the 'never diagnosed' group, then that will place a downward bias in our estimates relating to the wellbeing gap between those who currently have cancer or those who have recovered from cancer, and those who have never been diagnosed.

REFERENCES

Bogg, T. and B.W. Roberts (2004), 'Conscientiousness and health-related behaviors: a meta-analysis of the leading behavioral contributors to mortality', *Psychological Bulletin*, **130** (6), 887–919.

Borghans, L., Duckworth, A.L., Heckman, J.J. and B. ter Weel (2008), 'The economics and psychology of personality traits', *Journal of Human Resources*, **43** (4), 972–1059.

Boyce, C.J., Wood, A.M. and G.D.A. Brown (2010), 'The dark side of conscientiousness: conscientious people experience greater drops in life satisfaction following unemployment', *Journal of Research in Personality*, **44** (4), 535–539.

Boyce, C.J., Wood, A.M. and E. Ferguson (2016), 'Individual differences in loss aversion: conscientiousness predicts how life satisfaction responds to losses versus gains in income', *Personality and Social Psychology Bulletin*, **42** (4), 471–484.

De Wit, L.M., Luppino, F., Van Straten, A., Penninx, B., Zitman, F. and P. Cuijpers (2010), 'Depression and obesity: a meta-analysis of community-based studies', *Psychiatry Research*, **178** (2), 230–235.

Dolan, P. and D. Fujiwara (2016), 'Happiness-based policy analysis', in Matthew D. Adler and Marc Fleurbaey (eds), *The Oxford Handbook of Well-Being and Public Policy*, Oxford, UK: Oxford University Press, pp. 286–318.

Dolan, P. and R. Metcalfe (2012), 'Measuring subjective wellbeing: recommendations on measures for use by national governments', *Journal of Social Policy*, **41** (2), 409–427.

Dolan, P., Peasgood, T. and M. White (2008), 'Do we really know what makes us happy? A review of the economic literature on the factors associated with subjective well-being', *Journal of Economic Psychology*, **29** (1), 94–122.

Donovan, N. and D. Halpern (2002), 'Life satisfaction: the state of knowledge and implications for government', London, UK: Prime Minister's Strategy Unit.

Goldberg, D.P., Gater, R., Sartorius, N., Ustun, T.B., Piccinelli, M., et al. (1997), 'The validity of two versions of the GHQ in the WHO study of mental illness in general health care', *Psychological Medicine*, **27** (1), 191–197.

Graham, C., Higuera, L. and E. Lora (2011), 'Which health conditions cause the most unhappiness?', *Health Economics*, **20** (12), 1431–1447.

Howley, P. (2017), 'Less money or better health? Evaluating individual's willingness to make trade-offs using life satisfaction data', *Journal of Economic Behavior and Organization*, **135**, 53–65.

Jackson, C. (2007), 'The general health questionnaire', *Occupational Medicine*, **57** (1), 79.

Kahneman, D. and R. Sugden (2005), 'Experienced utility as a standard of policy evaluation', *Environmental and Resource Economics*, **32** (1), 161–181.

Layard, R. (ed.) (2005), *Happiness – Lessons from a New Science*, London, UK: Penguin Books.

Loewenstein, G. and P.A. Ubel (2008), 'Hedonic adaptation and the role of decision and experience utility in public policy', *Journal of Public Economics*, **92** (8–9), 1795–1810.

Lucas, R.E. (2007), 'Long-term disability is associated with lasting changes in subjective well-being: evidence from two nationally representative longitudinal studies', *Personality and Individual Differences*, **92** (4), 717–730.

McCrae, R.R. and P.T. Costa (eds) (2003), *Personality in Adulthood: A Five-Factor Theory Perspective*, New York, USA: Guilford Press.

McCrae, R.R. and P.T. Costa (2008), 'The five-factor theory of personality', in Oliver P. John, Richard W. Robins and Lawrence A. Pervin (eds), *Handbook of Personality: Theory and Research*, New York, USA: Guilford Press, pp. 159–181.

Oswald, A.J. and N. Powdthavee (2008), 'Does happiness adapt? A longitudinal study of disability with implications for economists and judges', *Journal of Public Economics*, **92** (5–6), 1061–1077.

Powdthavee, N. and B. van den Berg (2011), 'Putting different price tags on the same health condition: re-evaluating the well-being valuation approach', *Journal of Health Economics*, **30** (5), 1032–1043.

Preiss, K., Brennan, L. and D. Clarke (2013), 'A systematic review of variables associated with the relationship between obesity and depression', *Obesity Reviews*, **14** (11), 906–918.

Shipley, B.A., Weiss, A., Der, G., Taylor, M.D. and I.J. Deary (2007), 'Neuroticism, extraversion, and mortality in the UK Health and Lifestyle Survey: a 21-year prospective cohort study', *Psychosomatic Medicine*, **69** (9), 923–931.

Steel, P., Schmidt, J. and J. Shultz (2008), 'Refining the relationship between personality and subjective well-being', *Psychological Bulletin*, **134** (1), 138–161.

Wang, Y.C, McPherson, K., Marsh, T., Gortmaker, S.L. and M. Brown (2011), 'Health and economic burden of the projected obesity trends in the USA and the UK', *Lancet*, **378** (9793), 815–825.

Weston, S.J., Hill, P.L. and J.J. Jackson (2015), 'Personality traits predict the onset of disease', *Social Psychological and Personality Science*, **6** (3), 309–317.

Wilson, R.S., Krueger, K.R., Gu, L., Bienas, J.L., Mendes de Leon, C.F. and D.A. Evans (2005), 'Neuroticism, extraversion, and mortality in a defined population of older persons', *Psychosomatic Medicine*, **67** (6), 841–845.

Wilson, R.S., Mendes de Leon, C.F., Bienias, J.L., Evans, D.A. and D.A. Bennett (2004), 'Personality and mortality in old age', *Journal of Gerontology, Series B*, **59** (3), 110–116.

Wood, A.M. and C.J. Boyce (2014), 'Personality, an overview', in Alex C. Michalos (ed.), *Encyclopedia of Quality of Life Research*, Dordrecht, Netherlands: Springer, pp. 4773–4775.

16. Valuing energy infrastructure externalities using wellbeing and hedonic price data: the case of wind turbines*

Christian Krekel

16.1 INTRODUCTION

Renewable energy plants have become a common sight in many countries. In Germany, for example, where the share of renewables in the total electricity mix made up more than 36 per cent in 2017 (BMWi and Arbeitsgruppe Erneuerbare Energien – Statistik, 2018), there were more than 27000 wind turbines operational (OPSD, 2018a), compared to around 120 coal-fired power plant blocks and only nine nuclear plants (OPSD, 2018b).

This, of course, neglects differences in generating capacities between renewable and conventional plants. While Germany is considered a front-runner in the transition towards renewables over the past two decades, other countries are also engaged in phasing in more renewables. In the United Kingdom (UK) and the United States (US), the share of renewables in the total electricity generation mix is 29 per cent (Department for Business, Energy and Industrial Strategy, 2018) and 17 per cent (US EIA, 2018), respectively, not much smaller compared to Germany. These examples illustrate both the growing importance of renewable energy and one of its basic characteristics. Besides coming in (much) larger numbers, plants are, on average, more spatially dispersed and thus, on average, located in closer proximity to places of residence than conventional technologies.[1]

Environmental psychologists argue that this close proximity raises the salience of the energy supply (Pasqualetti, 2000; Wüstenhagen et al., 2007), and gives the landscape an industrialized appearance due to uniform technological structures that run counter to traditional landscape preferences (Kirchhoff, 2014). For wind turbines, beyond noise emissions at close distances (Bakker et al., 2012; McCunney et al., 2014) and adverse effects on wildlife (Pearce-Higgins et al., 2012; Schuster et al., 2015), negative externalities on landscape aesthetics are amongst the chief nuisances reported (Devine-Wright, 2005; Jobert et al., 2007; Wolsink, 2007).[2]

There exists no market-based valuation for intangible, public goods such as landscape aesthetics. Economists, therefore, refer to other methods in order to elicit the willingness to pay for such goods.[3] These include so-called *stated preference approaches* such as contingent valuation, in which respondents are directly asked to attach a monetary value to a public good under various scenarios, or choice experiments; and so-called *revealed preference approaches*, in which the monetary value of a public good is inferred from observed behaviour. The dominant method in the latter category is hedonic pricing, where changes in real estate prices following the provision of a public good are taken as the capitalization of the good in dwelling prices.

All of these valuation methods have their respective advantages and disadvantages.

In stated preference elicitation, respondents may not – consciously or subconsciously – reveal their true willingness-to-pay. For example, they may express their intrinsic attitudes towards a public good, which reflects a rather immediate emotional response, or answer in a strategic or socially desirable way. Further, contingent valuation is prone to the way in which (often quite complex) scenarios are presented, that is, framing effects – and the monetary values attached to them, that is, anchoring effects (Kahneman and Sugden, 2005). When it comes to hedonic pricing, intended behaviour may not always be realized. For example, real estate market frictions such as price rigidity, incomplete information or transaction costs (in particular, direct and indirect moving costs) may prevent a market equilibrium from being realized – a prerequisite for hedonic pricing to yield an unbiased valuation. Individuals may also make prediction errors when making locational decisions, and to the extent that such prediction errors are correlated with the public good (that is, prediction errors are systematic), the valuation obtained from using hedonic pricing may be biased (Krekel and Odermatt, 2019). A practical, often overlooked issue is that, especially in more rural areas, real estate market transactions may be low, rendering hedonic pricing practically infeasible due to a low liquidity of real estate markets.

An alternative valuation method is the so-called *life satisfaction approach* (Welsch, 2007). Here, self-reported subjective wellbeing (typically an ordinal measure of life satisfaction, hence the name) is regressed on the public good and income, alongside other covariates; the effect of the public good on life satisfaction is then traded off against that of income on life satisfaction to yield the *implicit* marginal willingness-to-pay.[4] This particular willingness-to-pay is referred to as implicit because the life satisfaction approach does not reveal the relationship of interest, that is, the relationship between life satisfaction and the public good, to respondents. It thus reduces respondents' propensity to express attitudes and mitigates incentives to answer in a strategic or socially desirable way as they may under contingent valuation. Moreover, it does not rely on the assumption of a real estate market equilibrium as hedonic pricing. Note that, for monetary valuation purposes, it does not matter whether life satisfaction is equal to utility (or at least an approximate measure thereof) or just one component amongst many in a respondent's utility function (Benjamin et al., 2012). One may be tempted to criticize the life satisfaction approach for using a self-reported, subjective outcome. On the other hand, however, one could argue that this is the comparative advantage of the method, because what ultimately matters is the subjective experience of respondents with the public good to be valued (including, for example, anticipation and adaptation effects).

This, of course, is not meant to suggest that the life satisfaction approach is without drawbacks. An often-cited drawback, for example, is that it relies on an unbiased estimation of the income coefficient, which tends to be rather small in typical life satisfaction regressions, and which has led some to argue in favour of wellbeing cost-effectiveness rather than cost–benefit analysis.[5] I discuss such drawbacks in detail below. The method has nevertheless become widely accepted, and has been used in various contexts ranging from air pollution (Levinson, 2012; Ferreira et al., 2013; Ambrey et al., 2014) and noise pollution (van Praag and Baarsma, 2005; Rehdanz and Maddison, 2008) to landscape amenities or disamenities (Ambrey and Fleming, 2011; Kopmann and Rehdanz, 2013) and land use (Bertram and Rehdanz, 2015; Krekel et al., 2016).

We used the life satisfaction approach to value the *total* negative externalities of wind turbines for households in their surroundings (Krekel and Zerrahn, 2017), and discuss complementarity between the life satisfaction approach and hedonic pricing to quantify these externalities (see Heintzelman and Tuttle, 2012; Jensen et al., 2014; Gibbons, 2015; Dröes and Koster, 2016; Sunak and Madlener, 2016 for hedonic pricing studies on the external cost of wind turbines).[6] While both strands of literature have evolved somewhat independently of each other, this chapter argues – in the spirit of Luechinger (2009) – that they should be used, in most cases, complementarily to arrive at an unbiased monetary valuation. In fact, which method is preferable (and whether a combination of methods needs to be used) depends crucially on the degree of real estate market perfection and the extent to which the externality in question is internalized via the price mechanism.

In what follows, I discuss, using the example of our study on wind turbines, the data, methodological and conceptual issues surrounding the use of wellbeing data for valuation purposes. I describe – step by step, summarized in a very simplified way – the data and basic empirical strategy used in our study, and then present its main finding. In doing so, I sacrifice detail for the bigger picture, focusing in every step on the 'why' and 'how' rather than technical details. For the full picture, including technical details, I refer the interested reader to our original study (Krekel and Zerrahn, 2017). Subsequently, I discuss complementarities between using wellbeing and hedonic data. Finally, I give practical recommendations and discuss future developments, including novel opportunities arising from big data and machine learning.

16.2 DATA AND METHODS

The life satisfaction approach has three ingredients, two relating to data and one relating to methods. The first ingredient is household data that, ideally, (1) include some measure of subjective wellbeing as outcome and relevant controls (especially those relating to self-selection of residents into particular geographical areas that are exposed to the public good to a greater or lesser extent, such as income and real estate prices); (2) are longitudinal in nature, that is, have a temporal dimension (ideally including interview dates), to study (within-individual) variation over time; and (3) have a geographical identifier, that is, have a spatial dimension, to study variation across space (the less aggregate this identifier, and hence the more precise, the better).

We used the German Socio-Economic Panel Study (SOEP) for the period 2000 to 2012. The SOEP is a nationally representative household panel, covering almost 30 000 individuals in 11 000 households in its latest wave (Wagner et al., 2007; Wagner et al., 2008). The study has been conducted annually since 1984 and since 2000 records – besides other, more aggregated geographical identifiers such as post or administrative district codes and federal states – the geographical coordinates of households at the street-block level in each interview year.[7] Our primary dependent variable is *life satisfaction*, obtained from a single-item 11-point measure asking respondents: 'How satisfied are you with your life, all things considered?'[8] As a dependent variable for the complementary hedonic analysis, we obtained the annual net rent of the dwelling. Our controls include demographic characteristics, human capital characteristics and economic conditions at the individual level; household characteristics and housing conditions at the household level; and neighbourhood characteristics at the district level.[9]

The second ingredient of the life satisfaction approach are data on the public good (or, in our case, the public bad) to be valued monetarily. To merge them with the household data, and fully exploit both temporal and spatial variation, these data, ideally, mimic the basic features of the household data, that is, they are longitudinal in nature and have geographical identifiers.

We collected data on more than 20000 onshore wind turbines which were constructed between 2000 and 2012 from the environmental authorities in the 16 German federal states, about half of which we used in our analysis.[10] The distinct feature of our data is that they include (1) the exact geographical coordinates of wind turbines, which allowed us to calculate the exact distance between every household and the nearest installation; (2) their construction dates, which allowed us to contrast interview dates of households with construction dates of installations; and (3) some background information on their size or capacity, which allowed us to restrict the analysis to larger, industrial installations that are unlikely to be built by private persons (and that typically, due to their size, are the subject of public nuisance).[11]

Our focus on large turbines, which implies that wind turbine construction is exogenous for a single, private household, brings us to the third, methodological ingredient of the life satisfaction approach. For an unbiased valuation, we must have an identification strategy (for example, a difference-in-differences, regression discontinuity or regression kink design), to estimate the causal effect of the public good (or bad) on life satisfaction. It can be tricky to come up with a credible identification, especially with observational data and when there are no suitable (quasi-)experiments at hand.

The fact that we could calculate the exact distance between every household and the nearest wind turbine, and that we could contrast the interview dates of individuals with the construction dates of wind turbines, made us adopt a difference-in-differences design. In this design, we first allocated an individual to the treatment group if a wind turbine is constructed (present) within a prespecified treatment radius around the household (and to the control group otherwise), and then compared the evolution of life satisfaction between treatment and control group over time. We chose a default treatment radius of 4000 metres, a decision driven mostly by sample size considerations. The construction of a wind turbine in close proximity to households is – even over a long observation period – a rather rare event, and the low sample size is made worse by the tendency of the SOEP to over-sample urban as opposed to rural areas, that is, areas where typically no wind turbines are constructed. The choice was also driven by the fact that there exists no uniform legislation in Germany that could serve as a point of reference. Impact radii for environmental impact assessments vary between federal states and over the observation period, ranging between 1500 and 6000 metres for a wind turbine with a hub height of 100 metres.[12] An interesting application is shown by Currie et al. (2015), who investigated the impact of toxic plant openings and closings on property values and infant health. The authors adopted a design similar to ours but determined the treatment radius empirically by looking at how far toxic plant emissions travel, on average, from a plant to the nearest measurement station. Unfortunately, this approach is not applicable in our case (there exists no objective measurement for landscape intrusion). In addition to the treatment radius, we introduced a ban radius, twice the size of the treatment radius, to arrive at a more clear-cut distinction between treatment and control group. All households outside the treatment but inside the ban radius were excluded from the analysis.

As in every difference-in-differences design, we made two identifying assumptions. The first is (conditional) ignorability, which states that whether an individual is allocated to the treatment or control group is independent of the outcome of that individual (conditional on controls).[13] For example, individuals with a higher income (and hence a higher life satisfaction) may be more capable of resisting the construction of a wind turbine in their surroundings (that is, endogenous construction) or to move away from a newly built installation (that is, endogenous sorting), both of which, in turn, affects their life satisfaction. Endogenous construction is unlikely to be an issue in our case. We focused on large installations (that is, wind turbines with a minimum hub height of 50 metres and a minimum nameplate capacity of 0.5 megawatts) that are typically built by utilities or project developers rather than private persons. Moreover, we excluded farmers from the analysis, as they are more likely to build installations themselves or let land to commercial operators, generating income from renting out or leasing.[14] We worked around the issue of endogenous sorting by focusing – in our baseline specification – on stayers only. In a robustness check, we studied how moving behaviour affects our results, by including all types of movers (that is, movers from treatment to control, from treatment to treatment, from control to treatment, and from control to control group), both jointly and separately; results remain, in most cases, similar to those obtained when focusing on stayers only. This is in line with studies showing that endogenous sorting plays only a minor role when assessing negative environmental externalities (see, Chay and Greenstone, 2003, for example).[15] Assuming that individuals who are more adversely affected by wind turbine construction are more likely to move away, our estimates can be interpreted as lower bounds.

The second identifying assumption is the common trend assumption, which states that treatment and control group would have followed a common trend in the outcome over time had there been no treatment. To ensure a common trend, we applied a spatial matching strategy. We introduced – in addition to our treatment and ban radii – a matching radius. It goes beyond the ban radius, restricting the control group to individuals living between the ban and the matching radius. The idea is to arrive at a control group that lives close to an installation but not close enough to be treated. We chose two matching radii, 10000 metres and 15000 metres. Figure 16.1 illustrates allocation into treatment and control group in our difference-in-differences design.

The common trend assumption is not formally testable (the counterfactual is not observable). However, it can be shown graphically that it is likely to be satisfied. Panels A and B in Figure 16.2 show the evolution of our primary outcome – life satisfaction, covariate-adjusted – over time, respectively, under spatial matching using a 10000 metres and 15000 metres matching radius. As can be seen, treatment group, pre-treatment, and control group exhibit common trend behaviour in mean life satisfaction over time.

Having accounted for the three ingredients of the life satisfaction approach, we estimated a generalized difference-in-differences design in regression form. We refer to this difference-in-differences design as generalized because treatment may occur at different points in time for different individuals. We estimated the following regression equation:

$$y_{it} = \beta_0 + X'_{it}\beta_1 + \delta_1 Wind_{it,r} + \sum_{n=1}^{12} \gamma_n Year_{2000+n} + \mu_i + \varepsilon_{it} \qquad (16.1)$$

where y_{it} is life satisfaction of individual i in year t; X_{it} is a vector of controls at the individual, household and district level; and $Year_{2000+n}$ is a full set of year dummy

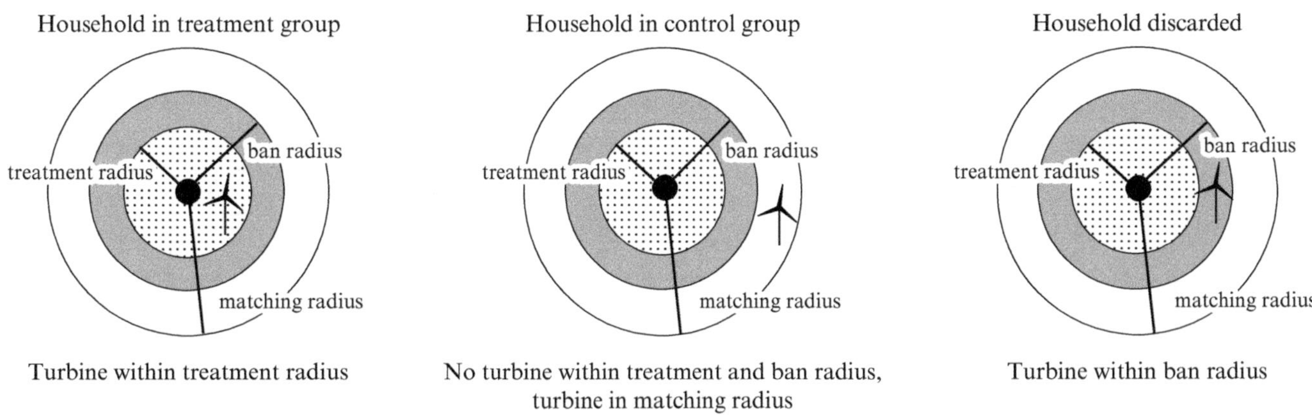

Source: Adapted from Krekel and Zerrahn (2017).

Figure 16.1 Allocation into treatment and control group

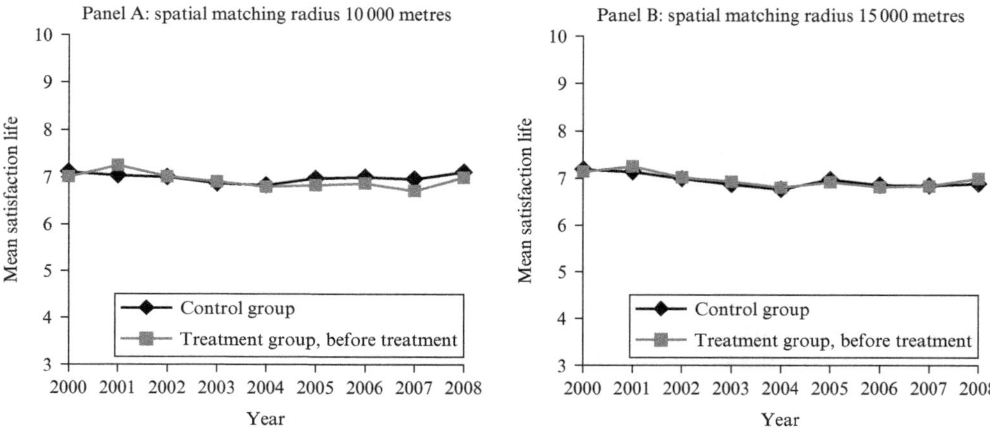

Note: The default treatment radius is 4000 metres, the ban radius 8000 metres (Panels A and B). The outcome is covariate-adjusted.

Source: SOEP v29 (2013), 2000–2012, individuals aged 17 or above, own calculations. Adapted from Krekel and Zerrahn (2017).

Figure 16.2 Common trend behaviour

variables. μ_i denotes time-invariant unobserved heterogeneity at the individual level; ε_{it} the idiosyncratic disturbance. $Wind_{it,r}$ is the regressor of interest. It is equal to one if a wind turbine is constructed (present) within treatment radius r (default of 4000 metres) and zero otherwise. The corresponding average treatment effect on the treated is denoted by δ_1.

The equation was estimated using ordinary least squares after applying a within-transformation to eliminate the individual fixed effect. Note that we apply a linear (rather than discrete) model to life satisfaction as a discrete ordinal variable. Doing so has become common practice, as differences have been found to be minor in panel (Ferrer-i-Carbonell and Frijters, 2004) and (repeated) cross-section data (Brereton et al., 2008; Ferreira and Moro, 2010), although this has been recently contested (see Schröder and Yitzhaki, 2017 for example). Robust standard errors were clustered at the federal state level, the level at which relevant legislation and administrative rules on possible locations and setback distances are enacted. Note that the results remain significant at the 5 per cent level for both matching radii if we cluster at a lower geographical level than federal states, for example, the level of administrative regions (*Regierungsbezirke*), and in case of the 15 000 metres matching radius even if we cluster at the county (*Kreise*) level. They also remain significant at the 5 per cent level when clustering at the individual level. Likewise, applying wild cluster-bootstrapped standard errors (Cameron et al., 2008) with 3999 repetitions to account for the small number of clusters when clustering at the federal state level reduces significance levels slightly; nevertheless, estimates are significant at the 1 per cent level for the 10 000 metres matching radius (originally 1 per cent level) and at the 10 per cent level for the 15 000 metres matching radius (originally 5 per cent level).

16.3 RESULTS

I now turn to our baseline results. Table 16.1 shows the causal effect of wind turbine construction on the life satisfaction of residents in their surroundings for our difference-in-differences design (Equation 16.1), respectively, under spatial matching using a matching radius of 10000 metres (Column 1) and using a matching radius of 15000 metres (Column 2).

As can be seen, wind turbine construction has a statistically significant, negative effect on life satisfaction under both matching specifications, at slightly more than −0.1. Put in standard deviation terms, a newly built installation reduces the life satisfaction of residents in their surroundings by about 8 per cent of a standard deviation, which is about a quarter of the size of the effect of becoming unemployed.[16] This stresses that the identified effect is not only statistically but also economically significant.[17]

The identified effect is also robust. We used placebo tests to check for confounding factors, by including first, second and third leads of the treatment dummy variable ($Wind_{it+3,4000}$ to $Wind_{it+1,4000}$), either separately or jointly with the contemporaneous variable ($Wind_{it,4000}$); we did not find evidence for confounding factors. Treatment appears to be rather ad hoc and unexpected; there seems to be no anticipation. In a different specification, we included up to nine lags of the treatment dummy variable ($Wind_{it-1,4000}$ to $Wind_{it-9,4000}$) to test for adaptation. We find some evidence that residents

Table 16.1 Baseline results

	Life satisfaction	
	Spatial matching (10000 m)	Spatial matching (15000 m)
	(1)	(2)
$Wind_{it,4000}$	−0.1088***	−0.1138**
	(0.0222)	*(0.0366)*
Controls		
Individual level	Yes	Yes
Household level	Yes	Yes
District level	Yes	Yes
Adjusted R^2	0.0678	0.0632
Number of observations	8609	16378
Number of individuals	1317	2586
Individuals in treatment group	506	506
Individuals in control group	811	2080

Notes: * $p < 0.1$, ** $p < 0.05$, *** $p < 0.01$; robust standard errors clustered at the federal state level in parentheses. $Wind_{it,4000}$ is a treatment dummy variable based on the exact interview date that is equal to one if a wind turbine is present within a treatment radius of 4000 metres in interview year *t* and zero else. The dependent variable is *life satisfaction* on a 0/10 scale. All regressions include dummy variables for interview years, individual fixed effects and a constant. All figures are rounded to four decimal places.

Source: SOEP v29 (2013), 2000–2012, individuals aged 17 or above, own calculations. Adapted from Krekel and Zerrahn (2017).

get used to wind turbines in their surroundings. Adaptation appears to be complete after five lags at the latest. However, sample size at higher lags gets lower (the number of treated drops to about half at the sixth lag, from originally 506 to 291 in the spatial matching specification). For illustrative purposes, we focused on permanent as opposed to temporary effects. Note that the construction process of a wind turbine is rather fast. Once the foundations are laid, it is assembled on-site from ready-made components. Identified negative impacts are thus unlikely to be driven (entirely) by the construction process itself.

We also looked at transmission channels, in two ways. First, we interacted our treatment dummy variable ($Wind_{it,4000}$) with different treatment intensity measures (different parametrizations of distances between households and the nearest wind turbine within the treatment radius, as well as the number of wind turbines). Although the coefficients for the different treatment intensity measures have negative signs, they fail to reach statistical significance at conventional levels. Second, we downloaded a digital terrain model for Germany (Federal Agency for Cartography and Geodesy, 2016) and merged it with our combined dataset on households and wind turbines. This allowed us to perform a viewshed analysis by (1) restricting the treatment group to individuals who stand in a direct visual relationship to the nearest wind turbine (that is, defining the new treatment dummy variable $WindVisible_{it,4000}$), and (2) interacting the treatment dummy variable with a measure of the visible height of the nearest installation from the viewpoint of households (that is, interacting $WindVisible_{it,4000}$ with the new treatment intensity measure $HeightVisible_{it,4000}$) as an alternative measure of treatment intensity.[18] To be clear, the digital terrain model only accounts for geographical barriers to visibility such as location-specific elevated terrain (that is, mountains or hills), neglecting natural barriers such as forests or trees, as well as man-made structures such as walls or fences. If such structures are built on purpose to block the view from the household to the nearest installation, our estimates can again be interpreted as lower bounds.

Table 16.2 shows the results of our viewshed analysis, using, for simplicity, the 15000 metres matching radius. We find that, by restricting the treatment group to individuals who stand in a direct visual relationship (Column 1), wind turbine construction still has a statistically significant, negative effect on life satisfaction, of about the same effect size. Moreover, life satisfaction drops significantly for each metre increase in visibility of the nearest installation (Column 2). In fact, the visible height of the nearest installation turns out to be the only statistically significant measure of treatment intensity – perhaps unsurprisingly, as we restricted our analysis to large installations.

An obvious question is whether some individuals are more affected by wind turbine construction than others. To shed light on this question, we conducted a heterogeneity analysis by re-estimating our sample split by several pre-treatment characteristics. Besides looking at heterogeneous effects with respect to worries about environmental protection and climate change (we find that individuals with more pro-environmental attitudes are indeed less affected), most importantly, we looked at heterogeneous effects with respect to home ownership. Table 16.3 shows the causal effect of wind turbine construction on the life satisfaction of residents in their surroundings (using, again, our 15000 metres matching radius), respectively, for owners (Column 1) and for renters (Column 2).

We find that, while owners show statistically significant, negative effects of the order identified previously, effects for renters turn out to be statistically insignificant.[19]

Table 16.2 Robustness check: viewshed analysis

	Life satisfaction	
	Spatial matching (15 000 m)	
	(1)	(2)
$WindVisible_{it,4000}$	−0.1082**	
	(0.0381)	
$WindVisible_{it,4000}$ x $HeightVisible_{it,4000}$		−0.0010**
		(0.0004)
Controls		
Individual level	Yes	Yes
Household level	Yes	Yes
District level	Yes	Yes
Adjusted R^2	0.0615	0.0616
Number of observations	16013	16013
Number of individuals	2538	2538
Individuals in treatment group	458	458
Individuals in control group	2080	2080

Notes: * $p < 0.1$, ** $p < 0.05$, *** $p < 0.01$; robust standard errors clustered at the federal state level in parentheses. $WindVisible_{it,4000}$ is a treatment dummy variable based on the exact interview date that is equal to one if a wind turbine is present within a treatment radius of 4000 metres in interview year t and the household has a direct view on it, and zero else. $HeightVisible_{it,4000}$ is the corresponding visible height of the wind turbine from the viewpoint of the household. The dependent variable is *life satisfaction* on a 0/10 scale. All regressions include dummy variables for interview years, individual fixed effects and a constant. All figures are rounded to four decimal places.

Source: SOEP v29 (2013), 2000–2012, Federal Agency for Cartography and Geodesy (2016), individuals aged 17 or above, own calculations. Adapted from Krekel and Zerrahn (2017).

Aggregate impacts, therefore, appear to be driven by owners as opposed to renters, or put differently, negative external effects on wellbeing appear to be borne predominantly by owners as opposed to renters.

The non-finding for renters is an important observation which can be explained by the notion of a spatial equilibrium. In this equilibrium, we would expect renters to be compensated for a disamenity through a reduction in rental prices. A reduction in rental prices, in turn, would raise disposable income, which would then raise life satisfaction, depending on the degree of rental market perfection, at the most up to a point at which renters are fully compensated and no negative net wellbeing effect may be detectable.

Yet, the interpretation of this compensation mechanism is influenced by transaction costs related to moving, which comprise both direct and indirect moving costs. When we restrict the analysis to stayers, then moving costs could bias the absolute value of the estimated coefficient downward. Some stayers may suffer more from the externality than they are compensated through their rental price but refrain from moving. An analogous argument applies to an analysis that would also include movers. An individual would only decide to relocate, *ceteris paribus*, if the lower rental price at least compensates for

Table 16.3 Heterogenous results

	Life satisfaction	
	Spatial matching (15 000 m)	
	Owns dwelling	Rents dwelling
	(1)	(2)
$Wind_{it,4000}$	−0.1261**	−0.0937
	(0.0488)	*(0.1132)*
Controls		
Individual level	Yes	Yes
Household level	Yes	Yes
District level	Yes	Yes
Adjusted R^2	0.0635	0.0733
Number of observations	12 570	3808
Number of individuals	2047	700
Individuals in treatment group	388	155
Individuals in control group	1659	545

Notes: * $p < 0.1$, ** $p < 0.05$, *** $p < 0.01$; robust standard errors clustered at the federal state level in parentheses. $Wind_{it,4000}$ is a treatment dummy variable based on the exact interview date that is equal to one if a wind turbine is present within a treatment radius of 4000 metres in interview year t and zero else. The dependent variable is *life satisfaction* on a 0/10 scale. All regressions include dummy variables for interview years, individual fixed effects and a constant. All figures are rounded to four decimal places.

Source: SOEP v29 (2013), 2000–2012, individuals aged 17 or above, own calculations. Adapted from Krekel and Zerrahn (2017).

the disamenity plus moving costs. In this case, the coefficient estimate would be biased upwards. For owners, however, this compensation channel does not operate. They may suffer from the disamenity itself and, latently, through the reduction in their house price (see also Welsch, 2016 on electricity externalities and house prices). When they consider moving, they will weigh the disamenity in case of staying against the reduction in their house price.

Internalization through rental markets may, of course, not occur instantaneously, but instead may have a temporal dimension depending on market dynamics. This prediction of a spatial equilibrium is in line with both the stronger impact on owners and the non-finding for renters.

To test this prediction more formally, we conducted an additional hedonic analysis for renters. More specifically, we ran the following (difference-in-differences) hedonic price regression:

$$\ln(R_{dst}) = \beta_0 + X'_{dst}\,\beta_1 + \delta_1 Wind_{dst,r} + \sum_{n=1}^{12} \gamma_n Year_{2000+n} + \eta trend_{st} + \varepsilon_{dst} \quad (16.2)$$

where R_{dst} is the annual net rent of dwelling d in federal state s in year t; X_{dst} is a vector of controls, including dwelling and amenity characteristics (for example, whether the

Table 16.4 Hedonic results for individuals who rent their dwelling

	Log annual net rent
	Spatial matching (15000m)
	(1)
$Wind_{dst,4000}$	−0.0437**
	(0.0186)
Controls	
Dwelling level	Yes
Amenities level	Yes
State-specific linear time trend	Yes
Adjusted R^2	0.1852
Number of observations	3167
Number of individuals	563
Individuals in treatment group	128
Individuals in control group	435

Notes: * $p < 0.1$, ** $p < 0.05$, *** $p < 0.01$; robust standard errors clustered at the district-times-year level in parentheses. $Wind_{dst,4000}$ is a treatment dummy variable based on the exact interview date that is equal to one if a wind turbine is present within a treatment radius of 4000 metres in interview year t and zero else. The dependent variable is *log annual net rent*. Dwelling controls include whether the dwelling is a detached, semi-detached or terraced house; a small or large apartment building; or a high rise (including the number of rooms per individual). Amenity controls include whether the dwelling has a kitchen; an indoor bath or a shower; an indoor toilet; central or under-floor heating; a balcony or terrace; a basement; a garden; or a boiler. All regressions include dummy variables for interview years and a constant. All figures are rounded to four decimal places.

Source: SOEP v29 (2013), 2000–2012, individuals aged 17 or above, own calculations. Adapted from Krekel and Zerrahn (2017).

dwelling is a detached, semi-detached or terraced house; a small or large apartment building; or a high rise; and the number of rooms per individual); $Year_{2000+n}$ is a full set of year dummy variables; $trend_{st}$ is a linear federal state-specific time trend; and ε_{it} is the idiosyncratic disturbance. $Wind_{dst,r}$ is again the regressor of interest. It is equal to one if a wind turbine is constructed (present) within treatment radius r (default of 4000 metres) and zero otherwise. The corresponding average treatment effect on the treated is denoted by δ_1.

Table 16.4 presents the results of estimating the log-level hedonic price regression in Equation (16.2), respectively, using the 15000 metres matching radius. We find that wind turbine construction has a statistically significant, negative effect on rental prices, reducing them by about 4 per cent. At the mean, this amounts to a decrease of about 11 per cent of a standard deviation, roughly comparable to the standard deviation decrease in life satisfaction (about 8 per cent) found earlier. Given that annual net rental prices are about €5000 in our sample, it corresponds to a reduction of about €200.

How does this compare to our wellbeing impacts when monetized? To answer this question, we apply the logic of the life satisfaction approach, trading off the impact of income on life satisfaction with that of wind turbine construction. As monetization using wellbeing data crucially depends on the income coefficient and income coefficients from life satisfaction regressions are rather problematic (see the discussion below), we follow the approach suggested by Fujiwara (2013) and take an established income coefficient estimate from the literature (Sacks et al., 2010): the estimate is about 0.35 for a level-log specification in which life satisfaction as level, standardized, is regressed on annual net household income as log. This estimate becomes about $0.35 \times 1.75 = 0.61$ when translating life satisfaction into natural units (standard deviation of about 1.75). A 1 per cent increase in annual net household income, therefore, raises life satisfaction by about $0.61/100 = 0.0061$ points. The mean annual net household income in our final sample is about €39 000. Wind turbine construction is estimated to reduce life satisfaction by about 0.11 points in our spatial-matching specifications (regardless of matching radius). We thus have:

$$390 \triangleq 0.0061$$
$$X \triangleq -0.11$$

It follows that:

$$X/(-0.11) \triangleq 390/0.0061$$
$$X \triangleq (390 \times (-0.11))/0.0061$$
$$X \triangleq -7033$$

An individual would be willing to forego about €7000 of annual net household income in order to avoid wind turbine construction in a 4000 metres radius around the household.[20]

16.4 DISCUSSION

The life satisfaction approach and hedonic pricing yield a very different willingness-to-pay (valued at, respectively, €7000 and €200 per household per year). In fact, the willingness-to-pay obtained when using the life satisfaction approach is about 35 times larger than that obtained when using hedonic pricing. How does this difference come about?

First, it may be that wellbeing data captures aspects of the externality that rental prices are unable to capture. Another, more technical, reason may be an inherent weakness of the life satisfaction approach: it hinges on the correct estimation of the marginal utility of income (that is, the income coefficient) when translating wellbeing benefits or disbenefits into a monetary equivalent (see the calculation above). It is well known in the literature that life satisfaction regressions yield relatively small income coefficients (Clark et al., 2018). How this comes about is still subject to ongoing research, but the consequences are a relatively large willingness-to-pay as well as a relatively small trade-off ratio between the public good or bad to be valued and individual characteristics such as unemployment. Income is clearly an endogenous regressor (that is, happier people may generate more income, and vice versa), which is why some authors suggest taking the coefficient estimate from other studies (Fujiwara, 2013), and in particular, from studies estimating the causal effect of income on life satisfaction through exogenous lottery wins (see Kuhn et al., 2011; Apouey and Clark, 2015; Lindqvist et al., 2018, for example). The problem is that there are not many of these studies, and most find relatively modest income coefficients as well. There may be, besides endogeneity and measurement issues (that is, happier people may systematically understate or overstate income, and vice versa), more subtle factors at play such as, for example, loss aversion (income losses may produce larger coefficient estimates than equivalent income gains; see Boyce et al., 2013, for example), reverse causality (happier people may be more prone to understating their income than unhappy ones, or may attach less importance to money) or relative income comparisons, either with oneself in the past (Clark et al., 2008a; Clark et al., 2016) or with others (Clark et al., 2008b; Senik, 2009; Clark and Senik, 2010).

When discussing the absence of wellbeing impacts for renters and conducting the complementary hedonic analysis, we implicitly assumed that rental markets are perfect: that is, that the negative external effect of wind turbine construction is completely internalized in the rental price, which in turn raises disposable income and hence life satisfaction, leaving overall life satisfaction unchanged. If, however, rental markets are not perfect (for example, due to market frictions such as information or adjustment costs) and the absence of wellbeing impacts for renters arises as a statistical artefact due to loss of power, then it is conceivable that we would be able to detect a statistically significant negative wellbeing impact for renters as well. The total monetary value of the externality is then comprised of both the monetized wellbeing impact and the rental price impact. In such situations, the life satisfaction approach and hedonic pricing complement each other. In fact, using the life satisfaction approach alone would deliver an unbiased willingness-to-pay only in cases in which rental markets do not internalize the public good via the price mechanism; likewise, using hedonic pricing alone would deliver an unbiased willingness-to-pay only in cases in which rental markets perfectly internalize the public good. Both are extreme cases, and in between is a continuum of cases in which the degree of rental market completion varies. In these cases, the life satisfaction approach and hedonic pricing are complementary, as part of the externality is internalized via the price mechanism and wellbeing impacts are residuals. Which empirical strategy is best, therefore, depends on underlying real estate market characteristics. There is also a temporal dimension. Depending on how long it takes for rental markets to fully internalize the externality (if they do so in the first place), the life satisfaction approach may be more suitable early on when the externality arises for the first time, whereas hedonic pricing may be more suitable later on. Note that, in practice, data availability and sample size often determine the method used. We can test the real estate market channel implicitly by selectively including rental prices into our life satisfaction regressions. Table 16.5 replicates Table 16.1 by including, in addition to our standard set of controls, rental prices.

As can be seen, when including rental prices, the coefficient estimate of wind turbine construction on life satisfaction is greatly reduced and becomes statistically insignificant, suggesting that, indeed, part if not all of the internalization occurs via real estate markets. Should one then routinely include rental prices into life satisfaction regressions? It depends.

If there are no unobservables which are correlated with wind turbine construction and affect both rental prices and life satisfaction at the same time, then including rental prices into life satisfaction regressions allows decomposing the total effect of wind turbine construction on life satisfaction into the part that is internalized via rental markets and the residual that is not. If, however, such unobservables exist – for example, targeted

Table 16.5 Baseline results

	Life satisfaction	
	Spatial matching (10000 m)	Spatial matching (15000 m)
	(1)	(2)
$Wind_{it,4000}$	−0.0424	−0.0708
	(0.0552)	*(0.0792)*
Controls		
Individual level	Yes	Yes
Household level	Yes	Yes
District level	Yes	Yes
Adjusted R^2	0.0657	0.0588
Number of observations	5060	9868
Number of individuals	1198	2345
Individuals in treatment group	457	457
Individuals in control group	741	1888

Notes: * $p < 0.1$, ** $p < 0.05$, *** $p < 0.01$; robust standard errors clustered at the federal state level in parentheses. $Wind_{it,4000}$ is a treatment dummy variable based on the exact interview date that is equal to one if a wind turbine is present within a treatment radius of 4000 metres in interview year t and zero else. The dependent variable is *life satisfaction* on a 0/10 scale. All regressions include dummy variables for interview years, individual fixed effects and a constant. All figures are rounded to four decimal places.

Source: SOEP v29 (2013), 2000–2012, individuals aged 17 or above, own calculations. Adapted from Krekel and Zerrahn (2017).

compensation measures to upgrade the quality of the surroundings which may affect rental prices and life satisfaction at the same time – then we have a problem of 'bad controls' (Angrist and Pischke, 2009). In such situations, one should abstain from including rental prices into life satisfaction regressions.

So far, in this discussion, I have focused on renters, but a similar logic applies to owners as well. For owners, however, there is no compensation for the externality via rental markets. In fact, for them, house prices may decrease, implying that the total monetary value of the externality comprises both the monetized wellbeing impact and the house price impact. Owners, therefore, may suffer twice: from the disamenity itself and, latently, from capital losses as a result of the disamenity, which may raise important distributional questions.[21] This is an interesting avenue for future research which could test, for example, how the life satisfaction of affected owners relates to price changes of statistically similar houses in their surroundings, Unfortunately, the SOEP does not include house prices to test this double impact more formally. House prices from the Federal Statistical Office/Federal Office for Building and Regional Planning are available at the district level, which is, however, a rather crude geographical referencing, as we allocate individuals into treatment and control group based on exact distances between households and nearest installations. It may be possible to scrape online data on house (and rental) prices with more precise geographical referencing (at least street-block level, if not complete addresses), approximate timestamps (date, and hence duration, of advertising), and characteristics of dwellings from online real estate marketplaces, which would allow for a more accurate, high-powered hedonic analysis.

We know that individuals spend large amounts of their (non-sleeping) time outside their homes – that is, commuting, working or travelling for various reasons – yet household panels survey mostly private households, interviewing individuals when they are at home. That said, our analysis neglects externalities close to places where individuals spend large amounts of their time (mostly at work); at the same time, externalities close to their homes cannot be completely accounted for. Needless to say, our analysis also neglects temporary visitors to places, such as tourists, or tourists who would have visited had there been no externality.[22] As a result, the coefficient estimate of the externality may be downward-biased and the calculated willingness-to-pay should be interpreted as a lower bound – a desirable feature in econometrics but a less meaningful one for policy, which is preoccupied with designing efficient and equitable compensation mechanisms or effective measures for nuisance mitigation. High-frequency experience-sampling methods may help to shed light on that blind spot. For example, the *Mappiness* study, originally developed at London School of Economics, uses a smartphone and an app that records, randomly during the day at different points in time, the wellbeing of individuals, including their activities, exact geographical locations and relevant background characteristics (especially income). Such big data sources, which include millions of data points, are already being used, albeit only sparsely.[23] They bring, of course, their own set of problems. For example, users of smartphones and apps may be selected and non-representative of the general population (they may be more technologically competent and environmental-friendly, which has been shown to mediate the size of the externality). Such problems need to be carefully addressed and discussed.

Big data combined with novel methods such as machine learning – algorithms that automatically detect and evaluate externalities and that improve upon themselves – may also help to shed light on the exact nature of externalities, in two ways. First, remember that, in our viewshed analysis, we restricted the treatment group to individuals who stand in a direct visual relationship to the nearest plant, accounting for location-specific elevated terrain such as hills. Although powerful, this analysis neglects natural barriers to visibility such as trees, or man-made structures such as fences (implying again that the coefficient estimate of the externality is downward-biased and the calculated willingness-to-pay a lower-bound estimate). High-frequency experience-sampling methods such as *Mappiness* now ask respondents, when sampling their momentary wellbeing and activities at their current location, to also take a picture of their surroundings using their smartphone camera. Another potential image depository that offers a panoramic, aerial view is Google Street View. Such images may help to identify natural and built barriers to visibility, for example, by employing machine learning algorithms that could be trained to automatically detect them, eliminating respective observations and refining the treatment group. Second, although we have data on basic characteristics of plants such as capacity and size, we know little about the extent to which architectural features matter for the extent of the externality. For example, as a suggested measure for nuisance mitigation, built structures (pertaining not only to wind turbines but also to biomass plants and cooling towers) are sometimes coloured in ways that reduce disharmony with landscape aesthetics. Deep learning algorithms, trained on a small sample of respondents' ratings of images, may help to evaluate the extent to which such architectural features can mitigate externalities, thereby providing a more nuanced picture of the exact nature of the externality itself.[24]

Taken together, novel opportunities arising from big data and machine learning can meaningfully complement our traditional toolkit for impact-evaluating externalities, enriching both the life satisfaction approach and hedonic analysis. Methodological discussions that currently centre around benefits and disbenefits of the respective method should move towards practical guidance on which method (or, rather, combination of methods) is preferable under which circumstances, including how to practically assess these circumstances. This would also be an important step towards developing a common methodology for including monetary valuations of intangibles in systems of national accounts.

NOTES

* I thank David Maddison, Katrin Rehdanz and Heinz Welsch for valuable comments and suggestions on a previous version of this chapter.

1. The average distance between households and the nearest nuclear power plant in Germany is about 104 kilometres (Goebel et al., 2015). Considering only turbines within a 15 kilometres radius around households, the average distance between households and the nearest wind turbine is about 3 kilometres (Krekel and Zerrahn, 2017).
2. Besides local externalities due to wind turbines (see Zerrahn, 2017 for a review), the use of wind power entails a costly redesign of the system of energy supply as a whole; for example, the need to build new transmission lines or backup facilities. Such system-wide effects are beyond the scope of this chapter.
3. There is a conceptual difference between willingness-to-pay and willingness-to-accept: the former is defined as the maximum amount that an individual is willing to pay in order to acquire a public good, the latter as the minimum amount that an individual is willing to accept in order to abandon it (the difference is called 'social surplus'). In this chapter, the concept of willingness-to-pay is employed.
4. In case of a dichotomous public good the term 'marginal' is redundant.
5. The main difference between cost–benefit and cost-effectiveness analysis is that, under cost–benefit analysis, wellbeing benefits are converted, via the income coefficient, into a monetary value, which is then contrasted with the costs of achieving these benefits. Under cost-effectiveness analysis, wellbeing benefits are added up and divided by the costs of achieving these benefits; the resulting coefficient is then contrasted with a prespecified threshold (Clark et al., 2018).
6. A related study to ours (Krekel and Zerrahn, 2017) is von Möllendorff and Welsch (2017): the authors used the same data but a different empirical specification, which yields a lower willingness-to-pay than our study.
7. Geographical coordinates at the street-block level tend to be more accurate in urban than in rural areas.
8. There are different measures of life satisfaction in different datasets. The SOEP includes a single-item 11-point measure, whereas the British Household Panel Survey (BHPS)/Understanding Society includes a single-item seven-point measure. Longer scales (which convey more information) have been shown to outperform shorter ones (Kroh, 2006) and are recommended for policy and programme evaluation (Dolan and Metcalfe, 2012).
9. Demographic characteristics include age, gender, marital status, health and migration background. Human capital characteristics include whether the respondent is currently in education and the highest degree obtained. Economic conditions include the labour force status and employment type. Household characteristics include the household income and number of individuals per household. Housing conditions include the dwelling type and number of rooms per individual. Neighbourhood characteristics include the unemployment rate and average household income.
10. For the other half, relevant information was missing or inaccurate. We still accounted for these installations by excluding households in their surroundings if we were unsure whether and to which extent these installations affected households.
11. Calculations of distances between households and wind turbines need to be performed on-site in the SOEP Research Data Centre at the German Institute for Economic Research (DIW Berlin). See Goebel and Pauer (2014) for a description of data access and protection principles.
12. Apart from the default treatment radius of 4000 metres, we ran sensitivity analyses using other treatment radii (8000 and 10000 metres) and different distance bins (2000 to 3000; 2000 to 4000; 2500 to 4000; and

3000 to 4000 metres) around wind turbines; results point towards a localized, spatially limited negative externality that rapidly declines in size and significance for treatment radii larger than 4000 metres. In this chapter, I focus on the default treatment radius of 4000 metres for illustrative purposes.

13. A related assumption is 'stable unit treatment value', which states that whether an individual is allocated to the treatment or control group is independent of the outcome of another individual. There is little reason to believe that there exist behavioural spillovers in our case.
14. Unfortunately, our data do not include information on ownership structure of installations. They do not include information on planning and construction processes either, and in particular, on community involvement during these processes (Loring, 2007; Pasqualetti, 2011; Graziano and Gillingham, 2015). Such participatory elements have been shown to be an important mediating variable through which negative external effects of new build projects can be mitigated (see Zerrahn, 2017 for a review).
15. Geographical mobility in Germany is low: in the SOEP, only about 6 per cent of individuals move every year.
16. The effect of becoming unemployed is about −0.5 under both matching specifications.
17. A better, more related comparison may be the presence of urban green and abandoned areas in the surroundings of households. Krekel et al. (2016) find that increasing the coverage of urban green areas in a 1 kilometre radius around households by 1 hectare (mean coverage of 23 hectares) raises the life satisfaction of household members by about 0.4 per cent of a standard deviation; increasing the coverage of abandoned areas by 1 hectare (mean coverage of 1 hectare) reduces the life satisfaction of household members by about 2 per cent of a standard deviation.
18. More than 90 per cent of respondents stand in a direct visual relationship to the nearest installation.
19. A caveat of this analysis is that there are more than twice as many owners (388) than renters (155) in our sample. Non-findings for renters may thus arise as a statistical artefact due to loss of power. There is indeed some evidence for loss of power: the standard error in Column 2 is more than twice as large as that in Column 1. Note, however, that the coefficient estimate in Column 2 is also reduced by about a third, compared to the coefficient estimate for all individuals pooled. Hence, both may be at play: a power issue and less negative impacts on renters.
20. Von Möllendorff and Welsch (2017) find that the presence of at least one wind turbine in one's postcode district in Germany is equivalent to a reduction in equivalized yearly income of about €2183.
21. Of course, if owners let dwellings, they may also suffer from a reduction in rental prices.
22. Evidence on effects of wind turbine developments on tourism is both scarce and mixed: Broekel and Alfken (2015) find a negative relationship between turbine construction and tourism demand for Germany; Landry et al. (2012) indicate only a very weak impact on coastal tourism demand.
23. See MacKerron and Mourato (2013) for an application using *Mappiness* to study the wellbeing impact of being exposed to the natural as opposed to the urban environment.
24. Similar techniques have already been used to evaluate the impact of landscape beauty on residential wellbeing and health (Seresinhe et al., 2015, 2017).

REFERENCES

Ambrey, C.L. and C.M. Fleming (2011), 'Valuing scenic amenity using life satisfaction data', *Ecological Economics*, **72**, 106–115.

Ambrey, C.L., Fleming, C.M. and A.Y.-C. Chan (2014), 'Estimating the cost of air pollution in South East Queensland: an application of the life satisfaction non-market valuation approach', *Ecological Economics*, **97**, 172–181.

Angrist, J.D. and J-S. Pischke (eds) (2009), *Mostly Harmless Econometrics: An Empiricist's Companion*, Princeton, NJ, USA: Princeton University Press.

Apouey, B. and A.E. Clark (2015), 'Winning big but feeling no better? The effect of lottery prizes on physical and mental health', *Health Economics*, **24** (5), 516–538.

Bakker, R.H., Pedersen, E., van den Berg, G.P., Stewart, R.E., Lok, W. and J. Bouma (2012), 'Impact of wind turbine sound on annoyance, self-reported sleep disturbance and psychological distress', *Science of the Total Environment*, **425**, 42–51.

Benjamin, D.J., Heffetz, O., Kimball, M.S. and A. Rees-Jones (2012), 'What do you think would make you happier? What do you think you would choose?', *American Economic Review*, **102** (5), 2083–2110.

Bertram, C. and K. Rehdanz (2015), 'The role of urban green space for human well-being', *Ecological Economics*, **120**, 139–152.

Boyce, C., Wood, A., Banks, J. and A.E. Clark (2013), 'Money, well-being, and loss aversion: does an income

loss have a greater effect on well-being than an equivalent income gain?', *Psychological Science*, **24** (12), 2557–2562.
Brereton, F., Clinch, J-P. and S. Ferreira (2008), 'Happiness, geography and the environment', *Ecological Economics*, **65** (2), 386–396.
Broekel, T. and C. Alfken (2015), 'Gone with the wind? The impact of wind turbines on tourism demand', *Energy Policy*, **86**, 506–519.
Cameron, C.A., Gelbach, J.B. and D.L. Miller (2008), 'Bootstrap-based improvements for inference with clustered errors', *Review of Economics and Statistics*, **90** (3), 414–427.
Chay, K.Y. and M. Greenstone (2003), 'The impact of air pollution on infant mortality: evidence from geographic variation in pollution shocks induced by a recession', *Quarterly Journal of Economics*, **118** (3), 1121–1167.
Clark, A.E. and C. Senik (2010), 'Who compares to whom? The anatomy of income comparisons in Europe', *Economic Journal*, **120** (544), 573–594.
Clark, A.E., D'Ambrosio, C. and S. Ghislandi (2016), 'Adaptation to poverty in long-run panel data', *Review of Economics and Statistics*, **98** (3), 591–600.
Clark, A.E., Diener, E., Georgellis, Y. and R.E. Lucas (2008a), 'Lags and leads in life satisfaction: a test of the baseline hypothesis', *Economic Journal*, **118** (529), F222–F243.
Clark, A.E., Flèche, S., Layard, R., Powdthavee, N. and G. Ward (eds) (2018), *The Origins of Happiness: The Science of Well-Being Over the Life Course*, Princeton, NJ, USA: Princeton University Press.
Clark, A.E., Frijters, P. and M. Shields (2008b), 'Relative income, happiness, and utility: an explanation for the Easterlin paradox and other puzzles', *Journal of Economic Literature*, **46** (1), 95–144.
Currie, J., Davis, L., Greenstone, M. and R. Walker (2015), 'Environmental health risks and housing values: evidence from 1,600 toxic plant openings and closings', *American Economic Review*, **105** (2), 678–709.
Department for Business, Energy and Industrial Strategy (2018), *Digest of UK Energy Statistics (DUKES): Renewable Sources of Energy, Chapter 6: Statistics on Energy from Renewable Sources*. Accessed 10 October 2018 at https://assets.publishing.service.gov.uk/government/uploads/system/uploads/attachment_data/file/736153/Ch6.pdf.
Devine-Wright, P. (2005), 'Beyond NIMBYism: towards an integrated framework for understanding public perceptions of wind energy', *Wind Energy*, **8** (2), 125–139.
Dolan, P. and R. Metcalfe (2012), 'Measuring subjective wellbeing: recommendations on measures for use by national governments', *Journal of Social Policy*, **41** (2), 409–427.
Dröes, M.I. and H.R.A. Koster (2016), 'Renewable energy and negative externalities: the effect of wind turbines on house prices', *Journal of Urban Economics*, **96**, 121–141.
Federal Agency for Cartography and Geodesy (Bundesamt für Kartographie und Geodäsie) (2016), *Digitales Geländemodell Gitterweite 200m*.
Federal Ministry for Economic Affairs and Energy (BMWi) and Arbeitsgruppe Erneuerbare Energien – Statistik (2018), *Zeitreihen zur Entwicklung erneuerbarer Energien in Deutschland*. Accessed 10 October 2018 at https://www.erneuerbare-energien.de/EE/Redaktion/DE/Downloads/zeitreihen-zur-entwicklung-der-erneuerbaren-energien-in-deutschland-1990-2017.pdf?__blob=publicationFile&v=15.
Ferreira, S., Akay, A., Brereton, F., Cuñado, J., Martinsson, P., et al. (2013), 'Life satisfaction and air quality in Europe', *Ecological Economics*, **88**, 1–10.
Ferreira, S. and M. Moro (2010), 'On the use of subjective well-being data for environmental valuation', *Environmental and Resource Economics*, **46** (3), 249–273.
Ferrer-i-Carbonell, A. and P. Frijters (2004), 'How important is methodology for the estimates of the determinants of happiness?', *Economic Journal*, **114** (497), 641–659.
Fujiwara, D. (2013), 'A general method for valuing non-market goods using wellbeing data: three-stage wellbeing valuation', CEP Discussion Paper No. 1233.
Gibbons, S. (2015), 'Gone with the wind: valuing the visual impacts of wind turbines through house prices', *Journal of Environmental Economics and Management*, **72**, 177–196.
Goebel, J. and B. Pauer (2014), 'Datenschutzkonzept zur Nutzung von SOEPgeo im Forschungsdatenzentrum SOEP am DIW Berlin', *Zeitschrift für amtliche Statistik Berlin-Brandenburg*, **3**, 42–47.
Goebel, J., Krekel, C., Tiefenbach, T. and N.R. Ziebarth (2015), 'How natural disasters can affect environmental concerns, risk aversion, and even politics: evidence from Fukushima and three European countries', *Journal of Population Economics*, **28** (4), 1137–1180.
Graziano, M. and K. Gillingham (2015), 'Spatial patterns of solar photovoltaic system adoption: the influence of neighbors and the built environment', *Journal of Economic Geography*, **15** (4), 815–839.
Heintzelman, M.D. and C.M. Tuttle (2012), 'Values in the wind: a hedonic analysis of wind power facilities', *Land Economics*, **88** (3), 571–588.
Jensen, C.U., Panduro, T.E. and T.H. Lundhede (2014), 'The vindication of Don Quixote: the impact of noise and visual pollution from wind turbines', *Land Economics*, **90** (4), 668–682.

Jobert, A., Laborgne, P. and S. Mimler (2007), 'Local acceptance of wind energy: factors of success identified in French and German case studies', *Energy Policy*, **35** (5), 2751–2760.

Kahneman, D. and R. Sugden (2005), 'Experienced utility as a standard of policy evaluation', *Environmental and Resource Economics*, **32** (1), 161–181.

Kirchhoff, T. (2014), 'Energiewende und Landschaftsästhetik', *Naturschutz und Landschaftsplanung*, **46** (1), 10–16.

Kopmann, A. and K. Rehdanz (2013), 'A human well-being approach for assessing the value of natural land areas', *Ecological Economics*, **93**, 20–33.

Krekel, C. and R. Odermatt (2019), 'Behavioural spatial economics: utility misprediction in locational choices and spatial sorting', mimeo.

Krekel, C. and A. Zerrahn (2017), 'Does the presence of wind turbines have negative externalities for people in their surroundings? Evidence from well-being data', *Journal of Environmental Economics and Management*, **82**, 221–238.

Krekel, C., Kolbe, J. and H. Wüstemann (2016), 'The greener, the happier? The effect of urban land use on residential well-being', *Ecological Economics*, **121**, 117–127.

Kroh, M. (2006), 'An experimental evaluation of popular well-being measures', DIW Discussion Paper, 546.

Kuhn, B.P., Kooreman, P., Soetevent, A. and A. Kapteyn (2011), 'The effects of lottery prizes on winners and their neighbors: evidence from the Dutch postcode lottery', *American Economic Review*, **101** (5), 2226–2247.

Landry, C.E., Allen, T., Cherry, T. and J.C. Whitehead (2012), 'Wind turbines and coastal recreation demand', *Resource and Energy Economics*, **34** (1), 93–111.

Levinson, A. (2012), 'Valuing public goods using happiness data: the case of air quality', *Journal of Public Economics*, **96** (9–10), 869–880.

Lindqvist, E., Östling, R. and D. Cesarini (2018), 'Long-run effects of lottery wealth on psychological well-being', NBER Working Paper No. 24667.

Loring, J. (2007), 'Wind energy planning in England, Wales and Denmark: factors influencing project success', *Energy Policy*, **35** (4), 2648–2660.

Luechinger, S. (2009), 'Valuing air quality using the life satisfaction approach', *Economic Journal*, **119** (536), 482–515.

MacKerron, G. and S. Mourato (2013), 'Happiness is greater in natural environments', *Global Environmental Change*, **23** (5), 992–1000.

McCunney, R.J., Mundt, K.A., Colby, W.D., Dobie, R., Kaliski, K. and M. Blais (2014), 'Wind turbines and health: a critical review of the scientific literature', *Journal of Occupational and Environmental Medicine*, **56** (11), 108–130.

Open Power System Data (OPSD) (2018a), *Data Package Renewable Power Plants. Version 2018-03-08*. Accessed 10 October 2018 at https://doi.org/10.25832/renewable_power_plants/2018-03-08.

Open Power System Data (OPSD) (2018b), *Data Package Conventional Power Plants. Version 2018-02-27*. Accessed 10 October 2018 at https://doi.org/10.25832/conventional_power_plants/2018-02-27.

Pasqualetti, M.J. (2000), 'Morality, space, and the power of wind-energy landscapes', *Geographical Review*, **90** (3), 381–394.

Pasqualetti, M.J. (2011), 'Opposing wind energy landscapes: a search for common cause', *Annals of the Association of American Geographers*, **101** (4), 907–917.

Pearce-Higgins, J.W., Stephen, L., Douse, A. and R.H.W. Langston (2012), 'Greater impacts of wind farms on bird populations during construction than subsequent operation: results of a multi-site and multi-species analysis', *Journal of Applied Ecology*, **49** (2), 386–394.

Rehdanz, K. and D. Maddison (2008), 'Local environmental quality and life-satisfaction in Germany', *Ecological Economics*, **64** (4), 787–797.

Sacks, D.W., Stevenson, B. and J. Wolfers (2010), 'Subjective well-being, income, economic development, and growth', NBER Working Paper No. 16441.

Schröder, C. and S. Yitzhaki (2017), 'Revisiting the evidence for cardinal treatment of ordinal variables', *European Economic Review*, **92**, 337–358.

Schuster, E., Bulling, L. and J. Köppel (2015), 'Consolidating the state of knowledge: a synoptical review of wind energy's wildlife effects', *Environmental Management*, **56** (2), 300–331.

Senik, C. (2009), 'Direct evidence on income comparisons and their welfare effects', *Journal of Economic Behavior and Organization*, **72** (1), 408–424.

Seresinhe, C.I., Preis, T. and H.S. Moat (2015), 'Quantifying the impact of scenic environments on health', *Nature: Scientific Reports*, **5**, 16899.

Seresinhe, C.I., Preis, T. and H.S. Moat (2017), 'Using deep learning to quantify the beauty of outdoor places', *Royal Society Open Science*, **4**, 170170.

Sunak, Y. and R. Madlener (2016), 'The impact of wind farm visibility on property values: a spatial difference-in-differences analysis', *Energy Economics*, **55**, 79–91.

United States Energy Information Authority (US EIA) (2018), *Electric Power Monthly*, September 2018. Accessed 10 October 2018 at https://www.eia.gov/electricity/monthly/current_month/epm.pdf.
van Praag, B.M.S. and B.E. Baarsma (2005), 'Using happiness surveys to value intangibles: the case of airport noise', *Economic Journal*, **115** (500), 224–246.
von Möllendorff, C. and H. Welsch (2017), 'Measuring renewable energy externalities: evidence from subjective well-being data', *Land Economics*, **93** (1), 109–126.
Wagner, G.G., Frick, J.R. and J. Schupp (2007), 'The German Socio-Economic Panel Study (SOEP): scope, evolution and enhancements', *Schmollers Jahrbuch*, **127** (1), 139–170.
Wagner, G.G., Goebel, J., Krause, P., Pischner, R. and I. Sieber (2008), 'Das Sozio-oekonomische Panel (SOEP): Multidisziplinäres Haushaltspanel und Kohortenstudie für Deutschland – Eine Einführung (für neue Datennutzer) mit einem Ausblick (für erfahrene Anwender)', *AStA Wirtschafts- und Sozialstatistisches Archiv*, **2** (4), 301–328.
Welsch, H. (2007), 'Environmental welfare analysis: a life satisfaction approach', *Ecological Economics*, **62** (3–4), 544–551.
Welsch, H. (2016), 'Electricity externalities, siting, and the energy mix: a survey', *International Review of Environmental and Resource Economics*, **10** (1), 57–94.
Wolsink, M. (2007), 'Wind power implementation: the nature of public attitudes: equity and fairness instead of "backyard motives"', *Renewable and Sustainable Energy Reviews*, **11** (6), 1188–1207.
Wüstenhagen, R., Wolsink, M. and M.J. Bürer (2007), 'Social acceptance of renewable energy innovation: an introduction to the concept', *Energy Policy*, **35** (5), 2683–2691.
Zerrahn, A. (2017), 'Wind power and externalities', *Ecological Economics*, **141**, 245–260.

17. Happiness and energy supply

Heinz Welsch

17.1 INTRODUCTION

While the wellbeing repercussions from pollution and environmental change have been studied for almost two decades, wellbeing effects of energy supply started to be investigated only recently. Given that some forms of environmental change are caused by the use of fossil fuels (coal, oil and gas), a branch of the wellbeing–environment literature has indirectly been concerned with energy. Nevertheless, several aspects of energy supply affect wellbeing independently of environmental concerns and are worthy of special investigation. Examples include nuclear safety, disamenity effects of energy facilities, and energy affordability.

Wellbeing effects of energy supply are a timely issue in the light of efforts around the world to restructure the energy system. Against the background of climate change, many countries have started phasing out fossil-fueled power generation and phasing in renewable energies. Renewable energy facilities, however, can be expected to have wellbeing effects of their own, such as visual or acoustic impairments. Similar to renewable energies, nuclear power avoids emission of air pollutants and greenhouse gases but poses problems of nuclear risk that have the potential to affect wellbeing. In addition, to the extent that restructuring the energy system involves higher costs, the issue of energy affordability has gained in importance.

Responding to the various wellbeing concerns related to energy supply, the recent literature has addressed the following questions. How do actual or perceived nuclear risks affect wellbeing? What are the wellbeing consequences of living close to energy facilities? How do energy-related natural hazards (for example, droughts, floods, hurricanes) affect wellbeing? How does the affordability of energy affect wellbeing? What are citizens' preferences for alternative configurations of the energy system in terms of wellbeing?

The remainder of this chapter is organized according to these questions, discussing the wellbeing consequences of nuclear accidents (section 17.2), perceived nuclear risks (section 17.3), renewable energy facilities (section 17.4), energy resource extraction (section 17.5), energy-related natural hazards (section 17.6), energy affordability (section 17.7) and the electricity mix (section 17.8). Section 17.9 concludes.

17.2 NUCLEAR ACCIDENTS

The nuclear disasters at Chernobyl (Ukraine) in 1986 and Fukushima (Japan) in 2011 are the only "Level 7" nuclear events ever recorded on the seven-point International Nuclear Event Scale. They led to large-scale releases of radiation and ensuing consequences for humans, fauna and flora. In both cases, fatalities and injuries were registered, electricity supply was disrupted, and agricultural and industrial production were stopped in the affected areas. Thousands of people were permanently evacuated from their homes.

While some of the consequences of nuclear accidents occur within a short period of time, others are of a more long-term nature. In particular, radioactive isotopes (iodine-131, caesium-137, strontium-90 and plutonium-239) are linked to increased risk of several kinds of cancer, some of which may materialize only after a considerable time. Accordingly, studying the wellbeing effects of the Fukushima disaster shortly after the event may capture only some of the channels through which the disaster affected wellbeing, whereas the Chernobyl disaster offers the potential to uncover slightly longer-term effects.

The Chernobyl and Fukushima disasters differ not only in terms of the time elapsed since the respective events. In contrast to the Chernobyl case, the Fukushima nuclear meltdown was one facet of a larger disaster comprising an earthquake and tsunami (actually being the causes of the nuclear accident), which led to large-scale destruction of residential and industrial structures.

Like other disasters, the Chernobyl and Fukushima nuclear accidents may have affected subjective wellbeing (SWB) in a variety of ways, some of which involve physical consequences of the disaster whereas others refer to psychological mechanisms. The physical consequences of the disaster may have led to income losses, job losses or health impairments. In addition to physical effects, the disaster may have caused psychological impacts in terms of fear, anxiety or mental distress related to fatalities, injuries or radioactive contamination. Some of those psychological impacts need not be restricted to persons directly affected by the event. Due to media coverage, they may spill over and cause distress in other, more distant places. Notably in the case of a major nuclear accident, people may become worried about nuclear power in general, especially if they live close to nuclear facilities themselves. Depending on the severity of a disaster's consequences, they may imply fundamental changes in how people evaluate not just their current SWB, but happiness with their entire life up to the present.

The wellbeing effects of the Chernobyl nuclear accident were studied by Danzer and Danzer (2016). They combined data on the geographic variation in radioactive fallout with data from a nationally representative survey in Ukraine 20 years after the disaster, accounting for respondents' place of residence at the time of the disaster. By excluding individuals who were exposed to high levels of radiation (about 4 percent of the population), they focused on the remaining majority of Ukrainians who received subclinical radiation doses. They found that those persons exhibit lower subjective wellbeing and higher depression rates than unaffected individuals. Specifically, one additional dose of natural background radiation leads to a reduction in SWB by 20 percent of a standard deviation. The monetized annual wellbeing losses caused by the disaster amount to 2–6 percent of current Ukrainian gross domestic product (GDP). These psychological costs are in addition to the direct costs of about 5–7 percent of GDP for recovery work, disaster relief and monetary compensation of victims.

Rehdanz et al. (2015) used panel data elicited in Japan in the two years before and after the Fukushima disaster to analyze the disaster's effect on people's SWB. Employing a difference-in-differences methodology, they found no wellbeing variation with distance from the Fukushima-Daiichi plant before the disaster, but a significant distance gradient after the disaster. For individuals living within 150 km from the power plant, there was a drop in wellbeing whose monetary compensation amounts to 240 percent of average annual household income. By running several specifications of their wellbeing regressions, they found that effects through induced deteriorations in the health, income or employment situation, if any, seem not to have contributed to the wellbeing effects of the disaster. Effects directly related to the radiation level could not be established, given that the period of analysis ended less than a year after the event and radiation-related impairments are of a more long-term nature (as was found in the case of Chernobyl by Danzer and Danzer, 2016). For Japanese nuclear power plants other than the Fukushima-Daiichi plant, a wellbeing variation with distance was found neither before nor after the disaster. In contrast to current SWB, no effect of the disaster on people's happiness with their entire life was found.

Tiefenbach and Kohlbacher (2015) investigate wellbeing effects of the Great East Japan Earthquake (which coincided with the Fukushima nuclear accident) and find that people living closer to the Fukushima prefecture are less happy after the disaster, whereas no drop in nationwide happiness can be found. Ohtake et al. (2016) use data elicited after the disaster to explore the spatial and temporal SWB pattern post-Fukushima. They find the entire Japanese society to be affected by the media coverage of the disaster, but are unable to analyze the difference in SWB before and after the event.

The effects of the Fukushima disaster on SWB can be compared to the effect on other outcome variables. Yamane et al. (2013) found that property values around the Fukushima-Daiichi plant decreased with increasing levels of local nuclear contamination, but not with proximity to the plant. There thus seems to exist a remarkable difference between wellbeing effects and property price effects of the disaster, suggesting that wellbeing and property prices capture different aspects of the disaster in different ways. While SWB effects refer to actual (experienced) utility consequences of the disaster – whose severity may be distance-dependent – to affected individuals, property values capture the expected utility consequences not only on currently affected individuals, but also on individuals in the future, provided that the effects are persistent. Since (low- and intermediate-level) nuclear contamination has long-term rather than short-term effects, it may be more likely capitalized in house prices than reflected in current wellbeing (Welsch, 2016).

17.3 PERCEIVED NUCLEAR RISK

In addition to actual nuclear events, fear of such events – that is, perceived nuclear risk – may affect SWB. Conceptually, perceived nuclear risk is composed of the perceived (subjective) probability of a nuclear event and the expected severity of damage from an event. From a citizen's perspective, both components of perceived risk (probability and expected severity) have the character of beliefs, and those beliefs may change in response to actual events such as the Chernobyl and Fukushima disasters.

In a cross-national (macro) perspective, the perceived probability of a nuclear event may be assumed to depend on the share of nuclear power in the national electricity mix. Invoking such an assumption, Welsch and Biermann (2014a) used survey data for almost 140000 individuals in 25 European countries, 2002–11, to measure the relationship between people's life satisfaction and the share of nuclear power in their national electricity supply. Using a difference-in-differences design, they found that European citizens' life satisfaction was unrelated to the nuclear share before the Fukushima disaster, but significantly negatively related to the nuclear share after the disaster (12 March to 31 December 2011). This effect applies to both sexes, all age groups, and to both environmentalists and non-environmentalists.

While the relationship between SWB and the nuclear share turned from non-significant to negative after Fukushima, Welsch and Biermann (2014a) found no evidence of a drop in the level of SWB. On the contrary, SWB increased in countries with no nuclear power, while being constant in others. The latter is consistent with Goebel et al. (2015) and Berger (2010), who found no changes in SWB in Germany after the Fukushima and Chernobyl disasters, respectively (though finding an increase in environmental concern).

While a country's nuclear share may be a macro indicator of nuclear risk, a more detailed (micro) analysis is needed to account for spatial aspects. Specifically, an individual's expectation of the severity of damage facing them in the case of an event should depend on their distance from nuclear plants and on topographical and meteorological conditions (such as mountains and wind directions).

An issue to be considered when dealing with spatial aspects in the relationship between SWB and nuclear risk is the possible endogeneity of an individual's location with respect to their personal risk perception. Assuming that people expect damage to increase with proximity to nuclear plants, they *ceteris paribus* prefer to be further away from them. Nuclear risk, however, is not the only factor in people's locational preference function. Important other factors are wages (incomes) and housing costs, and these too may vary with location. Hedonic spatial equilibrium theory suggests that people sort across locations according to location-specific (perceived) nuclear risk, wages and housing costs, and as a consequence of locational choice, wages and housing costs adjust so as to capitalize the externality from nuclear risk and to eliminate any location-dependent differences in utility (Schneider and Zweifel, 2013).

Accounting for such considerations, Welsch and Biermann (2016) conducted an analysis of the relationship between Swiss citizens' SWB and their place of residence relative to nuclear power plants (NPPs). Using several parametric and non-parametric specifications for the distance to the nearest NPP they found a statistically and economically significant SWB–distance gradient at fixed income and housing costs. Its monetary equivalent amounts to CHF291 (US$305 as of 2015) income per kilometre at mean income. The gradient is smaller for those who may feel protected by wind direction and mountains. The SWB–distance relationship remains significant when incomes and housing costs are omitted from the SWB regressions, indicating a violation of the condition for locational equilibrium. In spite of the significant SWB–distance relationship for the overall population, there exists considerable heterogeneity with respect to demographic characteristics. Specifically, the benefit from greater distance to NPPs is statistically significant only for women, not for men, for individuals of younger age, and for individuals that have no tertiary education. This heterogeneity may reflect differences in preferences or, alternatively, differences in the ability or willingness to adjust location according to individual-specific risk perception (Schneider and Zweifel, 2013).

In addition, Welsch and Biermann (2016) found that the SWB–distance relationship in Switzerland changed significantly after the Fukushima disaster. In particular, life satisfaction of individuals whose nearest NPP was at an intermediate distance (40–85 km) dropped, which the authors take to indicate that, due to an information shock provided by the spatial extent of the Fukushima event, individuals at places previously considered safe reassessed distance-dependent expectations of potential damage size. People more proximate, by contrast, did not seem to update their expectations, nor did people farther away. While before the disaster people at intermediate distances felt substantially less exposed to nuclear risk than people more proximate to NPPs, their perceived relative safety dropped by about 84 percent after the disaster.

17.4 RENEWABLE ENERGY FACILITIES

The massive deployment of renewable energy facilities in recent years has spurred an interest in studying their wellbeing consequences. Wind, solar and biomass-based energy facilities may affect SWB through visual and acoustic impairments and odor nuisance. By their nature, these effects are more local in character. Since, in contrast to nuclear plants, many of the existing renewable energy facilities were built within the time frame for which wellbeing data exist, it is possible to investigate whether and to what extent people grow accustomed to the presence of such facilities.

Krekel and Zerrahn (2017) studied the relationship between German citizens' SWB (measured as stated life satisfaction) and the presence of wind turbines in their vicinity and found wellbeing to be significantly lower in individuals who live within 4 km of wind turbines. While this effect applies to the overall population, it does not exist in individuals with a high level of environmental and climate concern. In addition, they found wellbeing effects to be transitory due to hedonic adaptation, vanishing after five years at the latest.

Von Möllendorff and Welsch (2017) also used German data on SWB and combined them with data on several types of renewable energies. With respect to wind turbines, they found statistically and economically significant wellbeing externalities. Quantitatively, the presence of at least one wind turbine in the individual's postcode district is associated with a reduction in 11-point life satisfaction by about 0.0346 points. An increase in installed wind power capacity by 1 MW is associated with a drop in wellbeing by 0.0011 points, whose monetary equivalent amounts to 0.35 percent of equivalized monthly income, or €5.8 per MW per person/month. Considering the average capacity of turbines in the sample, this translates into €6.2 per turbine per person/month. Similar to Krekel and Zerrahn (2017) they find the wellbeing effects of wind turbines to be transitory, becoming insignificant in the second year after installation.

Von Möllendorff and Welsch (2017) also investigated the relationship between German citizens' SWB and the presence of solar and biomass facilities in their neighborhood. With respect to solar power, they found no significant wellbeing effects of solar panels in residents' own postcode districts, but significant negative effects from adjacent districts. The latter amount to €6.8 per MW per person/month. As an explanation for the lack of effect in close vicinity (own postcode district), they refer to possible financial and moral benefits ("warm glow" or status effects) to local owners of solar panels, which may offset negative externalities. Shedding more light on this issue is hampered by a lack of differentiation between owners and non-owners, and between rooftop and free-standing solar facilities. In contrast to solar installations, the presence of biomass plants negatively affects the life satisfaction of individuals in the same postcode district and in adjacent ones. In monetary terms, a 1 MW increase in installed biomass capacity in the own district and the adjacent districts is associated with a drop in life satisfaction corresponding to €20.5 and €6.6 per person/month, respectively. In contrast to wind power, the wellbeing externalities from biomass remain significant over time and do not decrease in magnitude.

17.5 EXTRACTION OF ENERGY RESOURCES

The extraction of energy resources creates both benefits and costs. While the benefits accrue to mineral owners and workers in energy and related industries or to the economy at large, the costs largely accrue to local residents. Maguire and Winters (2017) examined the net effects of oil and gas development on SWB across Texas in the United States (US), by combining time-varying county-level oil and gas drilling data with individual SWB measures for 2005 through 2010, a period of heightened oil and gas development. They differentiated between conventional and horizontally drilled wells because horizontal drilling implies increased environmental concerns, as the hydraulic fracturing process requires massive injections of water and chemicals into wells to free the oil and gas trapped in shale. In addition, it implies a much larger footprint due to the storage of water, and increased surface disturbance due to the construction of access roads. They found statistically significant deleterious effects of horizontal drilling, but no significant effects of conventional drilling. Effects are concentrated in the Dallas–Fort Worth metropolitan area, an area that contains both very high levels of horizontal drilling and a large urban population (amounting to 6 million people). This suggests that for the typical resident, the costs of drilling in the area exceed the benefits and reduce their SWB. The results suggest that a one standard deviation increase in horizontal drilling implies that about 1.7 percent of the sample would be moved to a lower life satisfaction category on the four-point scale.

Li et al. (2017) studied wellbeing impacts of coal mining in the Shanxi province of China, an area that holds 27 percent of China's coal resources, with coal mining typically co-located with coal stockpiling and coal washing. Rather than using general life satisfaction, they focused on satisfaction in 29 life domains. Differentiating their 542 survey respondents into several categories of distance between their place of residence and the nearest coal mines, they found no statistically significant difference in income satisfaction between residents within 10 km and residents farther than 20 km from coal mining. While no difference in satisfaction with health was found either, nearby residents scored significantly lower on satisfaction with air and water quality than did respondents in the more distant category.

17.6 CLIMATE-RELATED ENERGY EXTERNALITIES

While the impairments from nuclear power and renewable energies are of a regional and immediate nature, the bulk of climate-related effects of energy supply are global and expected to happen in the future. Climate-related effects are therefore less likely to affect individuals' wellbeing than the more direct and contemporaneous effects of locally undesired (nuclear and renewable) energy facilities.

In spite of this, however, climate-related wellbeing effects of energy supply can be captured in two ways. One is by studying how wellbeing varies with spatial and temporal variation in climate parameters that are likely to change in the future, such as levels and seasonal patterns of temperature or precipitation. Studies along those lines are the subject of Chapter 6 in this *Handbook*. The other approach is by studying how wellbeing is affected by extreme events whose intensity and frequency are expected to increase due to climate change, such as storms, floods, droughts or wildfires. While those natural disasters' wellbeing effects are discussed in detail in Chapter 7 in this *Handbook*, this section gives a brief account of some of the relevant research.[1]

In one of the first studies linking global self-reports of SWB to natural disasters, Kimball et al. (2006) find that reported happiness of US citizens dipped significantly after the severity of the damage done by Hurricane Katrina along the US Gulf coast became clear. The impulse response of happiness is not limited to, but strongest in the region closest to the devastation of Katrina. In a cross-country setting, Berlemann (2016) finds a negative effect of hurricane risk on life satisfaction in both developing and developed countries. The effect is stronger in poor countries due to people's more limited possibilities for taking protective measures against storms.

Other studies have analyzed the impacts of flood disasters on life satisfaction. In a cross-country study of Europeans, Luechinger and Raschky (2009) estimate a large willingness to pay to avoid a sure flood event, amounting to $6505. Sekulova and Van den Berg (2016) study the relationship between floods and SWB using survey data from 15 municipalities in Bulgaria. They find that the material damages done do not capture floods' entire impact on happiness, and that effects occur even with low-intensity floods.

Von Möllendorff and Hirschfeld (2016) study the effect of both storm and hail events, and flood events, on life satisfaction in Germany. Using representative panel data, they find that both types of event engender statistically and economically significant wellbeing losses, which are lower in regions with higher insurance rates. While the effect of storm and hail events is of a short-term nature, the effect from floods persists for much longer.

Carroll et al. (2009) estimate the effect of droughts on the life satisfaction of Australians. They find a large effect of drought events on SWB, whose monetary equivalent amounts to A$18000 for residents in rural areas to prevent a spring drought. Kountouris and Remoundou (2011) estimate the impact of the frequency and extent of wildfires on the life satisfaction of residents of the European Mediterranean region (Italy, France, Spain and Portugal). As expected, the negative impact of forest incidents is larger for larger-scale fires and more pronounced for rural residents, but even in this case WTP to prevent an additional forest fire incident is estimated at only €0.26. Jones (2017) investigates the effect of wildfire smoke on US citizens' life satisfaction and finds an implicit willingness to pay of $373 to avoid one day of wildfire smoke over their county of residence within a six-month period. Residents of rural areas are willing to pay $130 more than urban residents to avoid one smoke day. Ambrey et al. (2017) investigate the effect of forest fire danger on the life satisfaction of Australians. Using the McArthur Forest Fire Danger Index, which combines rainfall, evaporation, wind speed, temperature and humidity and takes values from 0 to 100, they find an implicit willingness to pay of $10 per year to avoid a one-unit increase of the daily Fire Danger Index over the previous 12 months.

17.7 ENERGY AFFORDABILITY

The affordability of energy has been an important issue in public debates, in particular in the context of the expansion of renewable energies, on the presumption that the phasing-in of renewables leads to higher costs of energy supply. A specific aspect of the energy affordability debate is so-called fuel poverty. Fuel poverty refers to a situation in which prevailing energy prices prevent a household from satisfying a minimum requirement of energy, or if the costs of satisfying the minimum energy requirement exceed a certain threshold, even if those costs stay within the limits of the budget constraint.

Based on the theoretical insight that the effect of energy prices on wellbeing (utility) is greater when the fuel poverty ratio – the ratio of required energy costs to income – is higher, Welsch and Biermann (2017) identify the degree of fuel poverty with the strength of the wellbeing effect of higher energy prices. Using data on the life satisfaction of more than 100 000 individuals in 21 European countries from 2002 to 2011, they study the relationship between SWB and the prices for households of electricity, heating oil and natural gas. They find that energy prices have statistically and economically significant effects on wellbeing. The effect sizes are smaller than but comparable to the effects of important personal factors of wellbeing. Effects above average are found in individuals from the lowest income quartile. In addition, adverse effects follow a seasonal pattern, being particularly strong at times when required energy expenditures can be expected to be high (for instance, at the start of the heating season).

Biermann (2016) studies the wellbeing effects of fuel poverty more directly, using several fuel poverty indicators discussed in the literature. Using panel data on life satisfaction, energy expenditures and income of more than 40 000 individuals in Germany from 1994 to 2013, he computes the relevant indicators and estimates their effect on SWB. For each measure, he considers whether a household is classified as fuel poor (incidence) and, if so, how far from the respective poverty line the household is (intensity). He finds that for the subset of measures that involve energy expenditures relative to income, both the incidence and intensity of fuel poverty are associated with lower wellbeing, and the effects are sizeable. Interestingly, the effects remain significant, though smaller, when controlling for income poverty (which itself affects wellbeing significantly negatively). This suggests that living in fuel poverty inflicts hardship on affected individuals beyond purely budgetary effects.

While the fuel poverty problem and the related literature mainly refer to residential heating, some wellbeing literature has been concerned with gasoline prices. Boyd-Swan and Herbst (2012) used data for about 75 000 US citizens over the period 1985–2005 to estimate the relationship between gasoline prices and self-reported life satisfaction. They found significant wellbeing losses from higher gasoline prices in rural areas with high household vehicle ownership rates. Although rising gasoline prices lead to an immediate deterioration in subjective wellbeing, analyses of lagged prices suggest that wellbeing almost fully rebounds one year later and changes very little each year thereafter. Referring to literature that has found a negative impact of higher gasoline prices on obesity, they find that the SWB effects likely offset some of those physical health benefits. With respect to channels of influence, the authors speculate that in addition to the substitution and income effects associated with increases in gasoline prices, such increases might be perceived as signals of international political unrest or as a threat to social stability at the national level.

17.8 ENERGY MIX

The literature discussed up to this point has largely focused on single technologies or technology categories. The corresponding wellbeing effects are heterogeneous in nature, differing both in their spatial and temporal range and in their quality (environmental and amenity effects, costs, risks). Complementing those studies, overall wellbeing assessments of several technologies have been conducted by correlating individuals' SWB with the shares of the various technologies in their countries' electricity mix. Such exercises capture the wellbeing-relevant attributes of the different technologies in an implicit yet encompassing way.

As mentioned in section 17.3, Welsch and Biermann (2014a) found no significant relationship between European citizens' wellbeing and their countries' nuclear electricity share up to the Fukushima nuclear disaster. This means that, from an experienced-preference perspective, individuals were indifferent between nuclear power and other electricity sources, that is, fossil-fueled and renewable. Welsch and Biermann (2014b) provide a more detailed analysis of the relationship between wellbeing and the electricity mix by differentiating fossil-fueled and renewable energies into several more specific types. Using survey data for almost 140000 individuals in 25 European countries, 2002–11, they measured the relationship between people's life satisfaction and the shares of the following technologies in the national electricity mix: nuclear, coal, oil, gas, hydro power, solar and wind power, and biofuels. Interpreting their results as indicating a preference order over the set of technologies, they find that solar and wind power as well as electricity from gas are preferred to nuclear power. Electricity from biofuels is the least-preferred type of electricity. Individuals are indifferent between gas, solar and wind power, and between nuclear, coal, oil and hydropower. Most remarkable is the sharp difference between the renewable energies solar and wind (being the most-preferred technologies along with gas) and biofuels, being the least-preferred. This result, based on international "macro" indicators, is consistent with the finding that the local wellbeing repercussions from biomass facilities in Germany are far greater than those from solar and wind power (see section 17.4). Focusing on nuclear power alone (vis-à-vis all other technologies), Welsch and Biermann (2014b) found in a similar set-up that European citizens' life satisfaction was unrelated to the nuclear share before the Fukushima disaster, but significantly negatively related to the nuclear share at the time after the disaster (12 March to 31 December 2011). The preference for solar and wind over biofuels derived from national production shares (Welsch and Biermann, 2014a) is consistent with the finding that zonal wellbeing externalities from biomass facilities in Germany are far greater (by a factor of more than three) than those from wind and solar power (von Möllendorff and Welsch, 2017).

17.9 CONCLUSIONS

Happiness research has the potential to shed light on the welfare significance of energy supply beyond energy's value expressed in market prices. Recent research has found that not only actual nuclear accidents but also the latent threat of such accidents affect subjective wellbeing. Alternative sources of electricity based on renewable energies, however, have been found to be associated with wellbeing impairments of their own, particularly at the local scale. Fossil fuel energies, by changing the climate, impact on wellbeing by increasing the frequency and intensity of natural hazards. The mining or drilling of fossil energy resources affects local subjective wellbeing.

In addition to the wellbeing externalities of the energy system, happiness research has studied the welfare significance of energy affordability. It has found that the unavailability of affordable energy leaves affected people suffering considerable wellbeing losses. In particular, so-called fuel poverty has wellbeing repercussions distinct from mere income poverty. Rising gasoline prices may affect wellbeing not only through conventional economic channels but also by signaling the risk of political and social unrest.

Energy policy in many countries has recently taken steps to transform the energy system towards a more sustainable energy supply. Happiness research can inform policy makers on the wellbeing consequences of alternative options. Available evidence suggests that from the point of view of experienced utility (wellbeing), people have a preference for at least some forms of environment-friendly energy supply over more polluting or more risky alternatives. This evidence, however, is preliminary, being mainly based on multi-country studies of the relationship between wellbeing and the electricity mix. A comparative assessment of the spatial wellbeing effects of fossil fuel, nuclear and renewable energy facilities is missing as yet. It would be interesting to know the geographical extent of the respective impacts on wellbeing and, relatedly, the number of affected individuals. Another area for future research is the valuation of energy infrastructure such as high-voltage power lines, as local resistance to such investments has been an important issue in recent energy policy debates.

From the point of view of methodology, two issues deserve further attention. One is identification: can we ascribe a causal effect from energy supply decisions to wellbeing? To address this question, difference-in-differences techniques may be useful, but locational sorting may still create a challenge to reliable inference. Another issue is the extent to which disamenity impacts are reflected in wellbeing rather than property markets. In this regard, a comparison of different valuation techniques would be interesting.

NOTE

1. In addition to climate change, energy supply causes a variety of other environmental problems, notably air pollution. On air pollution, see Chapter 9 in this *Handbook*.

REFERENCES

Ambrey, C.L., Fleming, C.M. and M. Manning (2017), 'Forest fire danger, life satisfaction and feelings of safety: evidence from Australia', *International Journal of Wildland Fire*, **26** (3), 240–248.

Berger, E. (2010), 'The Chernobyl disaster, concern about the environment, and life satisfaction', *Kyklos*, **63** (1), 1–8.

Berlemann, M. (2016), 'Does hurricane risk affect individual well-being? Empirical evidence on the indirect effects of natural disasters', *Ecological Economics*, **124**, 99–113.

Biermann, P. (2016), 'How fuel poverty affects subjective well-being: panel evidence from Germany', Discussion Paper V-395-2016, Department of Economics, University of Oldenburg.

Boyd-Swan, C. and C.M. Herbst (2012), 'Pain at the pump: gasoline prices and subjective well-being', *Journal of Urban Economics*, **72** (2–3), 160–175.

Carroll, N., Frijters, P. and M. Shields (2009), 'Quantifying the costs of drought: new evidence from life satisfaction data', *Journal of Population Economics*, **22** (2), 445–461.

Danzer, A.M. and N. Danzer (2016), 'The long-run consequences of chernobyl: evidence on subjective well-being, mental health and welfare', *Journal of Public Economics*, **135**, 47–60.

Goebel, J., Krekel, C., Tiefenbach, T. and N. Ziebarth (2015), 'How natural disasters can affect environmental concerns, risk aversion, and even politics: evidence from Fukushima and three European countries', *Journal of Population Economics*, **28**, 1137–1180.

Jones, B.A. (2017), 'Are we underestimating the economic costs of wildfire smoke? An investigation using the life satisfaction approach', *Journal of Forest Economics*, **27**, 80–90.

Kimball, M., Levy, H., Othake, F. and Y. Tsutsui (2006), 'Unhappiness after Hurricane Katrina', NBER Working Paper No. 12062.

Kountouris, Y. and K. Remoundou (2011), 'Valuing the welfare cost of forest fires: a life satisfaction approach', *Kyklos*, **64** (4), 556–578.

Krekel, C. and A. Zerrahn (2017), 'Does the presence of wind turbines have negative externalities for people in their surroundings? Evidence from well-being data', *Journal of Environmental Economics and Management*, **82**, 221–238.

Li, Q., Stoeckl, N., King, D. and E. Gyuris (2017), 'Exploring the impact of coal mining on host communities in Shanxi, China – using subjective data', *Resources Policy*, **53**, 125–134.

Luechinger, S. and P.A. Raschky (2009), 'Valuing flood disasters using the life satisfaction approach', *Journal of Public Economics*, **93** (3–4), 620–633.

Maguire, K. and J.V. Winters (2017), 'Energy boom and gloom? Local effects of oil and gas drilling on subjective well-being', *Growth and Change*, **48** (4), 590–610.

Ohtake, F., Yamada, K. and S. Yamane (2016), 'Appraising unhappiness in the wake of the Great East Japan Earthquake', *Japanese Economic Review*, **67** (4), 403–417.

Rehdanz, K., Welsch, H., Narita, D. and T. Okubo (2015), 'Well-being effects of a major natural disaster: the case of Fukushima', *Journal of Economic Behavior and Organization*, **116**, 500–517.

Schneider, Y. and P. Zweifel (2013), 'Spatial effects in willingness to pay for avoiding nuclear risks', *Swiss Journal of Economics and Statistics*, **149** (3), 357–379.

Sekulova, F. and J.C.J.M. van den Bergh (2016), 'Floods and happiness: empirical evidence from Bulgaria', *Ecological Economics*, **126**, 51–57.

Tiefenbach, T. and F. Kohlbacher (2015), 'Happiness in Japan in times of upheaval: empirical evidence from the National Survey on Lifestyle Preferences', *Journal of Happiness Studies*, **16** (2), 333–366.

Von Möllendorff, C. and J. Hirschfeld (2016), 'Measuring impacts of extreme weather events using the life satisfaction approach', *Ecological Economics*, **121**, 108–116.

Von Möllendorff, C. and H. Welsch (2017), 'Measuring renewable energy externalities: evidence from subjective well-being data', *Land Economics*, **93** (1), 109–126.

Welsch, H. (2016), 'Electricity externalities, siting, and the energy mix: a survey', *International Review of Environmental and Resource Economics*, **10** (1), 57–94.

Welsch, H. and P. Biermann (2014a), 'Fukushima and the preference for nuclear power in Europe: evidence from subjective well-being data', *Ecological Economics*, **108**, 171–179.

Welsch, H. and P. Biermann (2014b), 'Electricity supply preferences in Europe: evidence from subjective well-being data', *Resource and Energy Economics*, **38**, 38–60.

Welsch, H. and P. Biermann (2016), 'Measuring nuclear power plant externalities using life satisfaction data: a spatial analysis for Switzerland', *Ecological Economics*, **126**, 98–111.

Welsch, H. and P. Biermann (2017), 'Energy affordability and subjective well-being: evidence from European countries', *Energy Journal*, **38** (3), 159–176.

Yamane, F., Ohgaki, H. and K. Asano (2013), 'The immediate impact of the Fukushima Daiichi accident on local property values', *Risk Analysis*, **33** (11), 2023–2040.

18. Green with satisfaction: the relationship between pro-environmental behaviours and subjective wellbeing*

Kate Laffan

18.1 INTRODUCTION

Pro-environmental behaviour (PEB) on the part of individuals is imperative to the wellbeing of future generations (Dietz et al., 2009; Stern, 2007). How individuals' engagement in PEB relates to people's own wellbeing, however, remains unclear. In particular, although we are increasingly learning more about the positive and negative instigators of PEB (Gosling and Williams, 2010; Mallett, 2012; Mallett et al., 2013; Priolo et al., 2016; Rees et al., 2015; Scannell and Gifford, 2010), our understanding of the wellbeing consequences of PEB is limited. This represents an important gap; understanding the wellbeing effects of PEB will inform both how it is conceptualised and the strategies used to promote it (Kasser, 2009).

Pro-environmental behaviour has long been equated with sacrifice. This view of PEB has its basis in traditional ideas around what welfare constitutes. According to a narrow standard economic framework, utility is based on individuals' consumption (Binder and Blankenberg, 2017). Within such a framework, PEB, which often requires individuals to forgo consumption, is understood to reduce the utility of the individual engaging in it (Brown and Kasser, 2005). Relatedly, much of environmental psychology has characterised PEB as altruistically motivated behaviour (Allen and Ferrand, 1999; Geller, 1995; Schultz, 2001; Schwartz, 1977; Stern, 2000), where altruism is defined as a feeling or action that prioritises the wellbeing of others independent of one's own interests (Jencks, 1990).

Some existing empirical work supports these traditional views of PEB; several research studies document evidence of individuals associating PEB engagement with inconvenience and discomfort, and viewing it as costly in terms of time, money and effort (Lorenzoni et al., 2007; Stoll-Kleemann et al., 2001). Such negative perceptions of the consequences of PEB for the individual are understood to inhibit individuals' engagement in these activities. For example, anticipated feelings of anger and frustration about public transport and recycling have been negatively linked to a desire to engage in those activities (Carrus et al., 2008).

Over past decades utility theory has broadened to incorporate not just what people consume, but also what they do (Juster, 1990). In line with this reconceptualisation, theoretical work in both economics and psychology has questioned the idea that there is a conflict between individual wellbeing and pro-social actions. This work suggests that these behaviours can provide individuals with a 'warm glow' – a positive emotional feeling – and contribute to people's needs for autonomy, relatedness and competence (Andreoni, 1990; Ryan et al., 2013). A number of authors have linked these concepts to PEB and have suggested that intrinsic benefits are underexplored motivators of these actions (De Young, 2000; Kaplan, 2000; Kasser, 2009; Van Der Linden, 2015).

Recently, researchers have turned to subjective wellbeing (SWB) data – individuals' reports of their own wellbeing – to explore these ideas empirically. The resulting literature uses these data to examine how engaging in behaviours which promote the wellbeing of others affects the actor (Dunn et al., 2008; Meier and Stutzer, 2008; Son and Wilson, 2012). Although the focus of most of the research has been pro-social spending and volunteering (Aknin et al., 2012; Aknin et al., 2013; Dunn et al., 2008; Son and Wilson, 2012), a growing number of studies in both environmental economics and psychology explore the relationship between SWB and PEB (see Chapter 18 for a review).

Overall, this literature provides suggestive evidence that PEB promotes individual wellbeing. In particular, a number of studies have documented positive relationships between PEB and individuals' reports of their life satisfaction (Brown and Kasser, 2005; Corral-Verdugo et al., 2011; Jacob et al., 2009; Kaida and Kaida, 2016; Welsch and Kühling, 2010, 2011). Related work has also found that individuals who engage in lifestyles based on voluntary simplicity – freely choosing to live frugally – also report being more satisfied with their lives (Boujbel and d'Astous, 2012; Jackson, 2005). These findings appear to be at odds with the theoretical and empirical work that highlights negative consequences for the individual of engaging in PEB.

One potential explanation for the seemingly conflicting ideas about the wellbeing consequences of PEB engagement may relate to different ideas of what wellbeing is. Within the philosophical work around wellbeing, a distinction is commonly made between hedonic wellbeing and eudemonic wellbeing. Hedonic wellbeing relates to the positive and negative emotions that individuals experience, such as joy and anger; and eudemonic wellbeing reflects people's sentiments of purpose and purposelessness (Son and Wilson, 2012; Stone and Mackie, 2013). The SWB–PEB literature has generally failed to recognise the distinction between these types of wellbeing (Venhoeven et al., 2013). In relying on life satisfaction, a measure which assesses both hedonic and eudemonic wellbeing (Dolan and Kudrna, 2016), as the sole measure of wellbeing, the existing research may be obscuring a more nuanced story about how acting in a pro-environmental way influences how people feel.

There are good reasons to think that the distinction between these different types of wellbeing will matter. First, other activities are differently related to measures of hedonic and eudemonic wellbeing. Research which has included a range of SWB measures capturing these two types of wellbeing has found that activities such as working and spending time with children are more closely related to eudemonic than hedonic wellbeing, while the opposite is true of watching television (White and Dolan, 2009). Second, and specific to PEB, while some actions, such as bike riding, could be construed as being pleasurable, many other PEBs are more readily associated with discomfort and sacrifice (Venhoeven et al., 2017). As pleasure is not an inherent characteristic of PEB, engagement may not be expected to yield consistent hedonic benefits. In contrast, to the extent that an individual feels that all PEB represents doing 'good', it may all feel purposeful and yield eudemonic wellbeing across the board. Accounting for the multidimensional nature of SWB may produce new insights into how PEB engagement might both contribute to and detract from individual wellbeing.

Beyond the need for conceptual clarity around SWB, there is also the question of what constitutes PEB. Existing literature has largely focused on investigating single behaviours or groups of behaviours which have an environmental impact (Binder and Blankenberg, 2016; Corral-Verdugo et al., 2011; Verhofstadt et al., 2016; Xiao and Li, 2011). Within the environmental psychology literature, however, authors have argued that in order to understand an individual's overall impact it is necessary to examine behavioural patterns relating to different types of PEBs (Kaiser and Wilson, 2004; Stern, 2000). This recommendation is made on the basis that: (1) individuals arguably only have substantive positive ecological impacts through PEB when these behaviours are aggregated across many different activities (Markowitz et al., 2012); (2) looking at any one behaviour may also misrepresent their overall levels of PEB engagement as individuals may license themselves to act in environmentally damaging ways as a result of engaging in a given PEB (Thøgersen and Ölander, 2003; Tiefenbeck et al., 2013); and (3) focusing on single behaviours precludes a comparison of the relationships between the SWB measures and clusters of PEBs which may have important shared characteristics (Larson et al., 2015; Lynn, 2014; Stern, 2000).

Additionally, to understand the psychological processes that relate to conscious PEB engagement (Markowitz et al., 2012), it is important to investigate PEBs that the individual is aware are linked to benefits for the environment, not just those actions that people take which have unintended positive impacts. Existing SWB–PEB work has focused largely on behaviours which impact upon the environment by using measures of individuals' ecological footprints (Lenzen and Cummins, 2013; Verhofstadt et al., 2016), or investigating PEBs which positively affect the environment, such as eating seasonal food, regardless of whether or not they are undertaken as a result of pro-environmental motives (Corral-Verdugo et al., 2011). However, research based on intentional PEB is crucial to our understanding and targeting of pro-environmental activities (Stern, 2000; Kaiser and Wilson, 2004). The wellbeing benefits of PEB may be dependent, as existing research suggests is the case for pro-social spending, on individuals' awareness of the behaviour's positive impact (Aknin et al., 2013). Research by Binder and Blakenberg (2017), which demonstrates that green identity partially explains the relationship between green behaviour and life satisfaction, supports this idea.

This chapter seeks to address the issues mentioned above. It uses a range of SWB measures to investigate how wellbeing relates to composite measures of PEBs explicitly linked to environmental goals. The data come from Natural England's Monitor of Engagement with the Natural Environment survey (MENE), which contains both SWB measures and self-reported measures of PEB. The analysis is carried out in two stages. First, multiple correspondence analysis is undertaken to explore relationships between the different types of PEB contained in the survey and as a data reduction technique. Second, ordinary least squares regression analysis is used to investigate the relationship between the variables derived from the correspondence analysis and the SWB measures of interest.

The results show that, on average, the more an individual engages in PEB, the more satisfied they are with their lives and the more worthwhile they consider their activities to be (a eudemonic measure of wellbeing). In contrast, no relationship is documented between the general measure of PEB and the purely hedonic measures of SWB in the analysis: happiness and anxiety yesterday. Additionally, whether different types of PEB are differently related to wellbeing is investigated. The results find that at any level of PEB engagement, undertaking relatively more common PEBs, compared to less common ones, is positively associated with all the measures of wellbeing investigated. Possible explanations for these relationships may relate to the social norms or costs associated with these different types of PEB (Kaiser and Wilson, 2004; Stern, 2000).

Together, these findings represent the first empirical evidence on the wellbeing correlates of PEB engagement to examine a range of SWB measures. The results emphasise the importance of taking into account both the multidimensional nature of wellbeing and the different types of PEB when considering how they relate to one another. The chapter proceeds as follows: Section 18.2 describes the data, Section 18.3 presents the methods and results, and Section 18.4 discusses the findings and concludes.

18.2 DATA

All of the data used in the analysis come from two pooled cross-sections from the 2013–13 wave[1] and 2014–15 wave[2] of the MENE. The MENE survey consists of weekly waves of face-to-face interviews with a representative sample of the English adult population (aged 16 and over) (Natural England, 2016). Four SWB questions were introduced to the MENE survey as a trial in 2012 and ran quarterly for a year starting in June 2012. From May 2014, the questions were formally adopted into the main survey, and the question frequency was increased to weekly. The questions, sometimes referred to as the 'ONS 4', are the standard questions used by the Office for National Statistics in the United Kingdom (UK) to measure citizens' SWB. The questions are currently being used in over 20 surveys across the UK government. The questions capture both hedonic and eudemonic SWB. They are:

- Overall, how satisfied are you with your life nowadays?
- Overall, to what extent do you feel that the things you do in your life are worthwhile?
- Overall, how happy did you feel yesterday?
- Overall, how anxious did you feel yesterday?

The responses are measured on a scale from 0 to 10, where 0 represents 'not at all' and 10 is 'completely'.

The life satisfaction question is the most traditional indicator in the set. It represents an evaluative SWB measure which can be considered a combination measure, incorporating both hedonic and eudemonic dimensions of wellbeing (Dolan and Kudrna, 2016). The 'worthwhile' question is a purely eudemonic measure of SWB which involves both evaluative wellbeing and experiential wellbeing, in that it asks about people's activities overall. The happiness and anxiety-based questions are measures of positive and negative hedonic wellbeing, respectively (Dolan and Metcalfe, 2012). These questions are global 'yesterday' measures which are considered a practical methodology to assess people's experienced SWB in large population surveys (Stone and Mackie, 2013). They are used in this context as a proxy measure for people's hedonic experiential SWB. The analysis is carried out on the sample of 5206 respondents for whom SWB measures, demographic characteristics, PEBs and other individual characteristics such as self-reported work status are available. Descriptive statistics for the SWB measures appear in Appendix 18A.1.

To investigate the relationship between wellbeing and PEB, responses to all environment-related activity questions contained in the MENE for the years 2012–15 were considered.

Table 18.1 Descriptive statistics for individual PEB measures (N = 5206)

Variable	Mean	Min.	Max.
Recycle	0.745	0	1
Buy eco-friendly	0.238	0	1
Encourage others	0.242	0	1
Member	0.068	0	1
Volunteer	0.054	0	1

These questions asked individuals to reflect on the past 12 months and agree or disagree with the following statements:

- I usually recycle items rather than throw them away.
- I usually buy seasonal or locally grown food.
- I choose to walk or cycle instead of using my car when I can.
- I usually buy eco-friendly products and brands.
- I encourage other people to protect the environment.
- I am a member of an environmental or conservation organisation.
- I volunteer to help care for the environment.

Five of the seven were then selected on the basis that they are unambiguously connected to the environment. Responses relating to whether an individual bought seasonal or locally grown food, and whether they chose to walk or cycle, were excluded on the basis that these responses related to activities which individuals may engage in out of health or other concerns without being aware of their environmental impact. The descriptive statistics for the five measures used in the analysis appear in Table 18.1. The prevalence of engagement in the PEBs varies substantially across the different behaviours. For example, 74.5 per cent of the sample report recycling items rather than throwing them away, whereas only 5.4 per cent volunteer to help care for the environment.

18.3 METHODS AND RESULTS

18.3.1 Multiple Correspondence Analysis

Multiple correspondence analysis (MCA) was first carried out on the group of binary PEB variables. MCA is a technique which allows for the identification of underlying patterns of associations between a group of categorical variables (>2). It also identifies individuals with similar response profiles. MCA was chosen as a result of its suitability for the analysis of the binary variables (Greenacre, 2007; Greenacre and Blasius, 2006). It is analogous to principal component analysis for categorical data. Similarly to principal component analysis, MCA gathers the initial information from the original set of variables in a reduced number of dimensions. The number of dimensions retained for interpretation is guided by selection criteria relating to the amount of information carried by each of the dimensions generated by the analysis.

In the current work, the results of the analysis suggested that there were two important dimensions to the group of PEBs examined. The first dimension represented general engagement in PEB; higher scores on this dimension can be interpreted as higher levels of engagement in PEB in general. The second dimension sees certain subsets of the group of PEBs cluster together. More specifically, across this dimension recycling, buying eco-friendly products and encouraging others to engage in PEB – the more prevalent or common PEBs – cluster together; as do being a member of an environmental organisation and volunteering, the less common PEBs. Higher scores on this dimension can be understood to represent engaging in relatively more common, compared to less common PEBs. Please see Appendix 18A.2 for the output and a more technical discussion of the analysis. The predicted individual scores derived from MCA analysis are then used in multivariate regression analysis to investigate the relationship between SWB and PEB.

18.3.2 Regression Analysis

Ordinary least squares regression analysis was then carried out to explore the relationship between the measures of PEB constructed using the MCA analysis and the four measures of SWB (see Table 18.2 and Appendix 18A.3). Model I of the analysis examines how the first and second dimension scores derived from the MCA above relate to each of the four measures of wellbeing. The first dimension represents a general measure of engagement in PEB, with higher scores indicating higher levels of engagement. The second component represents the level of engagement in common relative to uncommon behaviours. Model II incorporates control variables relating gender, ethnicity, age group; whether the person has a long-standing illness, health problem or disability; work and marital status, tenure and socio-economic status (descriptive statistics can be found in Appendix 18A.1).

18.3.3 Results for the First Dimension

The first dimension represents a general measure of PEB engagement. The results relating to this dimension suggest that people gain satisfaction and eudemonic wellbeing from engaging in PEB, without incurring a hedonic cost. Life satisfaction is found to be significantly positively associated with general PEB engagement in both Model I (without controls) and Model II (with controls). There is also a positive link documented between PEB and eudemonic wellbeing; higher levels of engagement in PEB are positively associated with how worthwhile individuals consider their activities to be in both Model I and II. Interestingly, PEB engagement appears to be much more closely related to eudemonic wellbeing than it is to people's evaluations of life overall; the coefficient in the adjusted Model (II) with worthwhile activities as the dependent variable is over twice the size of the coefficient on the life satisfaction model. In contrast, neither happiness nor anxiety – two measures of hedonic wellbeing – were found to be linked to general PEB engagement. The relationship between the first dimension and happiness yesterday appears to be significant in Model I, but is no longer so once individual-level controls are included. PEB engagement is not associated with levels of anxiety yesterday in either Model I or II. Importantly, however, as no negative associations were found, PEB does not appear to come at a hedonic cost. The results of Model II for all four SWB measures and a general measure of PEB engagement are presented in the upper part of the coefficient plot in Figure 18.1.

Table 18.2 Subjective wellbeing and pro-environmental behaviour

Variables	Satisfaction	Satisfaction	Worthwhile	Worthwhile	Happiness	Happiness	Anxiety	Anxiety
	Model I	Model II	Model I	Model II	Model I	Model II	Model I	Model II
MCA Dimension 1 – General PEB	0.115***	0.0668**	0.218***	0.155***	0.106***	0.0542	−0.000861	0.0564
	(0.0308)	(0.0294)	(0.0285)	(0.0283)	(0.0369)	(0.0350)	(0.0403)	(0.0419)
MCA Dimension 2 – Common/ uncommon PEB	0.104***	0.0814***	0.114***	0.0814***	0.0852***	0.0683**	−0.194***	−0.163***
	(0.0297)	(0.0293)	(0.0263)	(0.0265)	(0.0315)	(0.0321)	(0.0373)	(0.0381)
Constant	7.323***	7.725***	7.559***	7.528***	7.414***	7.722***	2.679***	2.796***
	(0.0324)	(0.120)	(0.0339)	(0.115)	(0.0383)	(0.143)	(0.0607)	(0.196)
Controls	No	Yes	No	Yes	No	Yes	No	Yes
N	5206	5206	5206	5206	5206	5206	5206	5206
R-squared	0.006	0.097	0.017	0.077	0.004	0.058	0.005	0.041

Notes: Ordinary least squares regression with standard errors clustered at local authority level in parentheses. *** $p < 0.01$, ** $p < 0.05$, * $p < 0.1$.

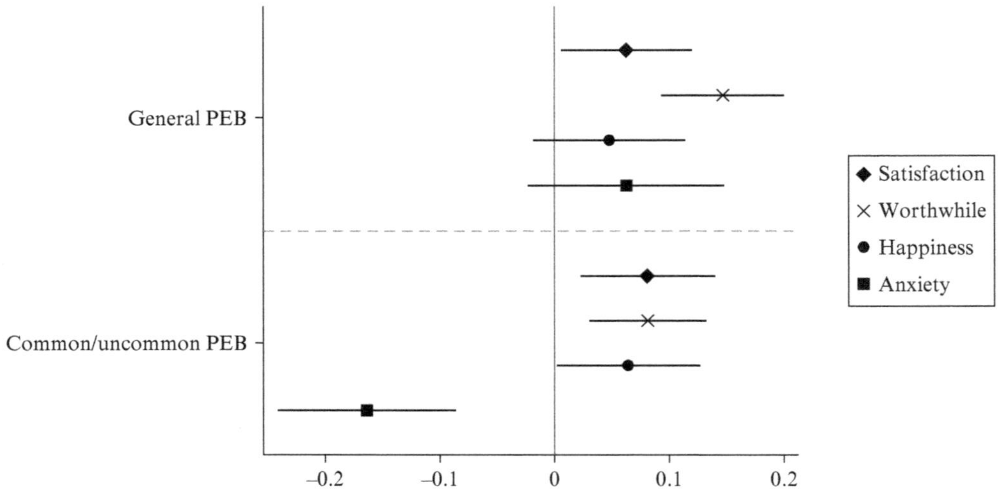

Note: The symbols represent the point estimates from Model II, and the bars indicate the 95% confidence intervals.

Figure 18.1 Pro-environment behaviour measures and the range of SWB measures

18.3.4 Results for the Second Dimension

The second dimension contrasts engagement in relatively more common PEBs (recycling, buying eco-friendly products and encouraging others) and with engaging in the less common activities (being a member of an environmental organisation or volunteering to protect the environment). The coefficients on the SWB regressions relating to the second dimension can be interpreted as the association between SWB and engagement in relatively more common compared to less common PEBs, holding constant overall levels of engagement. This component is similarly related to all four measures of SWB in that it is significantly positively associated with life satisfaction, the worthwhileness of activities and happiness yesterday, and negatively associated with anxiety yesterday at the 5 per cent level in Models I and II. This suggests that at any level of PEB engagement people are more satisfied, consider their activities to be more worthwhile, and have higher levels of happiness and lower levels of anxiety if they demonstrate their pro-environmentalism through behaviours that are commonly engaged in by others, compared to behaviours that a small minority of people carry out. The results of Model II for all four SWB measures and a measure which contrasts engaging in more common compared to less common PEBs are presented in the lower part of the coefficient plot in Figure 18.1.

18.4 DISCUSSION

By going beyond life satisfaction as the sole measure of SWB, focusing on PEBs that have explicit environmental goals, and using multiple correspondence analysis to explore patterns of relationships between these behaviours, this chapter provides new insights into the relationship between individual wellbeing and PEB.

18.4.1 General PEB and Subjective Wellbeing

The results indicate that PEB engagement is significantly associated with life satisfaction and how worthwhile individuals consider their activities to be, but not how happy or anxious they report feeling on the previous day. The positive relationship between life satisfaction and general PEB engagement echoes other literature in both environmental economics and psychology which has documented positive links between a range of PEBs and peoples' evaluations of their own lives (see Chapter 19 in this *Handbook*). This result builds on existing work by documenting a PEB–life satisfaction relationship in a group of behaviours which are explicitly related to environmental goals. This chapter also presents the first evidence of a positive link between PEB and eudemonic wellbeing: higher levels of engagement in PEB are positively associated with how worthwhile individuals consider their activities to be. Relative to the relationship between PEB and life satisfaction, PEB seems to be far more closely related to eudemonic wellbeing.

General levels of PEB engagement are not associated with people's reports of happiness or anxiety yesterday, suggesting that individuals do not derive hedonic benefits from engaging in PEB. Given previous theoretical and empirical work associating PEB with sacrifice, however, it is equally important to note that these findings suggest that PEB does not come at a hedonic cost either. That no relationship is found may be attributable to the temporal mismatch between the happiness and anxiety yesterday measures and the PEB variables that relate to the past 12 months. Future work should explore the relationship between PEB and hedonic wellbeing in more detail, perhaps through the use of experience sampling which captures people's activities alongside their feelings in the moment (Stone and Mackie, 2013).

Despite this limitation, the results suggest that the literature documenting relationships between PEB and life satisfaction, which can be considered a combination measure of eudemonic and hedonic wellbeing (Dolan and Kudrna, 2016), capture a eudemonic, rather than hedonic, link between PEB and SWB that feeds into people's satisfaction with their lives overall. Similar results were documented in relation to volunteer work by Son and Wilson (2012). They find evidence that volunteering enhances eudemonic and social, but not hedonic wellbeing in the National Survey of Middle Age in the United States. Together, the findings suggest that PEB may benefit people by making their activities and lives feel more purposeful.

18.4.2 Common/Uncommon PEBs and Subjective Wellbeing

The four measures of SWB tell different stories about how wellbeing relates to general levels of engagement in PEB. Where the results do cohere across different measures of SWB, however, is in relation to the second dimension. This dimension contrasts engagement in relatively more common compared to less common PEBs. Controlling for their overall level of PEB engagement, individuals who report undertaking relatively more common, compared to less common, behaviours are significantly more satisfied with their lives, consider their activities to be more worthwhile, and report higher levels of happiness and lower levels of anxiety on the previous day. These findings suggest that PEBs which are commonly engaged in by many people are those which yield more wellbeing.

Existing theoretical literature suggests some potential explanations for these findings, highlighting, in particular, a couple of characteristics of these categories of behaviours which may be relevant: namely social norms and costs (Nyborg et al., 2006; Diekmann and Preisendörfer, 2003). The descriptive social norms relating to the PEBs – that is, the extent to which they are perceived as behaviour which people commonly engage in or not – will likely be stronger for the common behaviours than for the relatively uncommon ones. The degree to which an individual perceives engaging in a given behaviour as being the 'done thing' may influence their perception of the 'goodness' of carrying out such behaviour and their moral responsibility to engage in it (Brekke et al., 2010; Thøgersen, 2006). Nyborg et al. (2006: 353), for example, propose a theoretical model in which internal rewards for green consumption behaviours depend on 'the perception that the action in question is governed by an applicable norm that is recognized and observed in the subject's community'. Related empirical work by Welsch and Kühling (2018) looks at the relationship between people having an environmentally friendly self-image and life satisfaction across 35 different countries. They find that the positive association between these variables is stronger in societies where pro-environmental attitudes are widely held, suggesting that the wellbeing benefits of conforming to social norms may help to explain the link between pro-environmental attitudes and actions and wellbeing. The results of the current work are in line with this view.

A second interpretation based on the relative prevalence of these behaviours is also possible. It has been argued elsewhere that the proportion of individuals engaging in an activity can act as a proxy measure of how costly it is (in terms of time, money or effort) (Diekmann and Preisendörfer, 2003; Kaiser and Wilson, 2004). Although recycling, which is engaged in by over 70 per cent of the individuals in the sample, could be more costly for some individuals than volunteering, which is engaged in by only around 5 per cent of the sample, in aggregate it is likely that a PEB engaged in by the majority of the population is less costly than one engaged in by a small minority of people. This argument is supported by research which suggests that the most popular PEBs tend to be those that require minimal effort and personal cost (Dunlap and Scarce, 1991). Based on this line of reasoning, the results may reflect that engaging in relatively less costly PEB, as compared to more costly ones, is positively related to all measures of wellbeing investigated here. Importantly, however, a recent study by Schmitt et al. (2018) on the relationship between PEB and life satisfaction found evidence of a stronger positive link between PEB and wellbeing for those actions which were rated as entailing greater direct costs on the part of the individual. The researchers also find evidence that life satisfaction is more strongly predicted by PEBs that involved social interaction and those that are more easily observed.

While the current work cannot test the merits of these various explanations for why engaging in relatively more common PEBs compared to less common ones is more positively associated with wellbeing – and, importantly, these reasons may vary across the different dimensions of SWB – what is clear from this chapter is that the relationship between PEB and SWB does vary across different types of PEB.

18.4.3 Limitations and Future Research

Further work on the topic of SWB and PEB is imperative, as several important caveats apply to the current work. As the analysis is based on cross-sectional data, it is unclear whether the links documented between SWB and PEB represent causal relationships. Individuals who engage in these PEBs may derive both a sense of purpose and feelings of satisfaction from doing so. It is also possible, however, that those who have higher levels of eudemonic wellbeing and life satisfaction are more likely to engage in PEB (Kasser, 2017). Additionally, the results may suffer from omitted variable bias; nature connectedness, for example, has been found in separate studies to be significantly associated with meaning in life and, separately, PEB (Howell et al., 2011; Pereira and Forster, 2015). Due to data limitations, this variable could not be included in the current analysis. Existing experimental and longitudinal work has found evidence of a bi-directional relationship between SWB and other pro-social behaviours, including volunteering and charitable giving (Aknin et al., 2012; Son and Wilson, 2012). While PEB shares many common characteristics with these behaviours, it is also different in ways that may influence its relationship with well-being; for example, many PEBs typically involve less social interaction than volunteering (Son and Wilson, 2012), and the impact of pro-environmental actions may appear less salient than charitable donations elicited to help identifiable victims, for example (Aknin et al., 2013). As such, future work must establish the extent to which engaging in PEB actually causes SWB.

Beyond issues around causality, only five self-reported measures of PEB were incorporated into this analysis. Though the self-reported behaviour is used widely in environmental psychology, estimates of the validity of these measures vary widely (Steg and Vlek, 2009). Furthermore, these measures do not cover all dimensions of PEB previously found in the existing literature; for example, no measure relates to environmental policy support. This PEB has been recognized as an important PEB from an impact perspective and has been found in previous studies to represent a separate dimension of PEB engagement to consumer behaviours such as buying eco-friendly goods, or environmental citizenship behaviours such as signing petitions (Stern et al., 1999). In addition, there is a temporal mismatch between the hedonic measures of SWB and the PEB measures: they relate to 'yesterday' and 'the past 12 months', respectively. Future work should look to incorporate experimental methods to establish causality and directly measure a more comprehensive range of PEBs and the hedonic wellbeing experienced during the action to better understand whether and how various dimensions of actual PEB engagement affect wellbeing.

Despite these limitations, the results of this chapter present valuable new insights into the nature of the relationship between SWB and PEB which challenge the view of PEB as entailing sacrifice. They suggest that individuals may derive a eudemonic wellbeing gain from engaging in PEBs without paying a hedonic cost and that they may be better off doing their bit by engaging in common PEBs compared to uncommon behaviours. Future research should build on these findings to establish whether the associations presented here reflect causal relationships from PEB to wellbeing. If these relationships are found to be causal, then policy makers should take these findings into account in the pursuit of the important goals of promoting both environmental protection and human wellbeing.

NOTES

* The author would like to thank Professor Paul Dolan for his extensive comments and methodological guidance on the work. Additionally, the author gratefully acknowledges the input and advice provided by Dr Barbara Fasolo, Dr Heather Kappes and the attendees of the LSE's Department of Psychological and Behavioural Science and Department of Social Policy seminar series. The research was supported by a Grantham Research Institute on Climate Change and the Environment LSE studentship.

1. n = 3521.
2. n = 1685.

REFERENCES

Aknin, L., Dunn, E. and M. Norton (2012), 'Happiness runs in a circular motion: evidence for a positive feedback loop between prosocial spending and happiness', *Journal of Happiness Studies*, **13** (2), 347–355.

Aknin, L., Dunn, E., Whillans, A., Grant, A. and M. Norton (2013), 'Making a difference matters: impact unlocks the emotional benefits of prosocial spending', *Journal of Economic Behavior and Organization*, **88**, 90–95.

Allen, J. and J. Ferrand (1999), 'Environmental locus of control, sympathy, and proenvironmental behaviour – a test of Geller's actively caring hypothesis', *Environment and Behavior*, **31** (3), 338–353.

Andreoni, J. (1990), 'Impure altruism and donations to public goods: a theory of warm-glow giving', *Economic Journal*, **100** (401), 464–477.

Binder, M. and A. Blankenberg (2016), 'Environmental concerns, volunteering and subjective well-being: antecedents and outcomes of environmental activism in Germany', *Ecological Economics*, **124**, 1–16.

Binder, M. and A. Blankenberg (2017), 'Green lifestyles and subjective well-being: more about self-image than actual behaviour?', *Journal of Economic Behavior and Organization*, **137**, 304–323.

Boujbel, L. and A. d'Astous (2012), 'Voluntary simplicity and life satisfaction: exploring the mediating role of consumption desires', *Journal of Consumer Behaviour*, **11** (6), 487–494.

Brekke, K., Kipperberg, G. and K. Nyborg (2010), 'Social interaction in responsibility ascription: the case of household recycling', *Land Economics*, **86** (4), 766–784.

Brown, K.W. and T. Kasser (2005), 'Are psychological and ecological well-being compatible? The role of values, mindfulness, and lifestyle', *Social Indicators Research*, **74** (2), 349–368.

Canuel, M., Abdous, B., Bélanger, D. and P. Gosselin (2014), 'Development of composite indices to measure the adoption of pro-environmental behaviours across Canadian provinces', *PloS ONE*, **9** (7), e101569.

Carrus, G., Passafaro, P. and M. Bonnes (2008), 'Emotions, habits and rational choices in ecological behaviours: the case of recycling and use of public transportation', *Journal of Environmental Psychology*, **28** (1), 51–62.

Corral-Verdugo, V., Mireles-Acosta, J., Tapia-Fonlle, C. and B. Fraijo-Sing (2011), 'Happiness as correlate of sustainable behaviour: a study of pro-ecological, frugal, equitable and altruistic actions that promote subjective wellbeing', *Human Ecology Review*, **18** (2), 95–104.

Costa, P., Santos, N., Cunha, P., Cotter, J. and N. Sousa (2013), 'The use of multiple correspondence analysis to explore associations between categories of qualitative variables in healthy ageing', *Journal of Aging Research*, **2013**, Article ID 302163.

Deeming, C. (2013), 'Addressing the social determinants of subjective wellbeing: the latest challenge for social policy', *Journal of Social Policy*, **42** (3), 541–565.

De Young, R. (2000), 'New ways to promote proenvironmental behaviour: expanding and evaluating motives for environmentally responsible behaviour', *Journal of Social Issues*, **56** (3), 509–526.

Diekmann, A. and P. Preisendörfer (2003), 'Green and greenback: the behavioural effects of environmental attitudes in low-cost and high-cost situations', *Rationality and Society*, **15** (4), 441–472.

Dietz, T., Gardner, G., Gilligan, J., Stern, P. and M. Vandenbergh (2009), 'Household actions can provide a behavioural wedge to rapidly reduce US carbon emissions', *PNAS*, **106** (44), 18452–18456.

Dolan, P. and L. Kudrna (2016), 'Sentimental hedonism: pleasure, purpose, and public policy', in Joar Vittersø (ed.), *Handbook of Eudaimonic Well-Being*, Basel, Switzerland: Springer International Publishing, pp. 437–452.

Dolan, P. and K. Laffan (2016), 'Bad air days: the effects of air quality on different measures of subjective well-being', *Journal of Benefit–Cost Analysis*, **7** (1), 147–195.

Dolan, P. and R. Metcalfe (2012), 'Measuring subjective wellbeing: recommendations on measures for use by national governments', *Journal of Social Policy*, **41** (2), 409–427.

Dunlap, R. and R. Scarce (1991), 'Poll trends: environmental problems and protection', *Public Opinion Quarterly*, **55** (4), 651–672.

Dunn, E., Aknin, L. and M. Norton (2008), 'Spending money on others promotes happiness', *Science*, **319** (5870), 1687–1688.
Geller, E. (1995), 'Actively caring for the environment: an integration of behaviourism and humanism', *Environment and Behaviour*, **27** (2), 184–195.
Gosling, E. and K. Williams (2010), 'Connectedness to nature, place attachment and conservation behaviour: testing connectedness theory among farmers', *Journal of Environmental Psychology*, **30** (3), 298–304.
Greenacre, M. (ed.) (2007), *Correspondence Analysis in Practice*, Boca Raton, FL, USA: Chapman & Hall/CRC.
Greenacre, M. and J. Blasius (eds) (2006), *Multiple Correspondence Analysis and Related Methods*, Boca Raton, FL, USA: Chapman & Hall/CRC.
Hair, J., Black, W. and B. Babin (eds) (2009), *Multivariate Data Analysis: A Global Perspective*, Upper Saddle River, NJ, USA: Pearson Education.
Howell, A., Dopko, R., Passmore, H. and K. Buro (2011), 'Nature connectedness: associations with well-being and mindfulness', *Personality and Individual Differences*, **51** (2), 166–171.
Jackson, T. (2005), 'Live better by consuming less? Is there a "double dividend" in sustainable consumption?', *Journal of Industrial Ecology*, **9** (1–2), 19–36.
Jacob, J., Jovic, E. and M. Brinkerhoff (2009), 'Personal and planetary well-being: mindfulness meditation, pro-environmental behaviour and personal quality of life in a survey from the social justice and ecological sustainability movement', *Social Indicators Research*, **93** (2), 275–294.
Jencks, C. (1990), 'Varieties of altruism', in Jane Mansbridge (ed.), *Beyond Self-Interest*, Chicago, IL, USA: University of Chicago Press, pp. 53–67.
Johnson, R. and D. Wichern (eds) (2002), *Applied Multivariate Statistical Analysis*, Upper Saddle River, NJ, USA: Prentice Hall.
Juster, F. (1990), 'Rethinking utility theory', *Journal of Behavioral Economics*, **19** (2), 155–179.
Kaida, N. and K. Kaida (2016), 'Pro-environmental behaviour correlates with present and future subjective well-being', *Environment, Development and Sustainability*, **18** (1), 111–127.
Kaiser, F and M. Wilson (2004), 'Goal-directed conservation behaviour: the specific composition of a general performance', *Personality and Individual Differences*, **36** (7), 1531–1544.
Kaplan, S. (2000), 'New ways to promote proenvironmental behaviour: human nature and environmentally responsible behaviour', *Journal of Social Issues*, **56** (3), 491–508.
Kasser, T. (2009), 'Psychological need satisfaction, personal well-being, and ecological sustainability', *Ecopsychology*, **1** (4), 175–180.
Kasser, T. (2017), 'Living both well and sustainably: a review of the literature, with some reflections on future research, interventions and policy', *Philosophical Transactions of the Royal Society A*, **375** (2095), 20160369.
Larson, L., Stedman, R., Cooper, C. and D. Decker (2015), 'Understanding the multi-dimensional structure of pro-environmental behaviour', *Journal of Environmental Psychology*, **43**, 112–124.
Lenzen, M. and R. Cummins (2013), 'Happiness versus the environment: a case study of Australian lifestyles', *Challenges*, **4** (1), 56–74.
Lorenzoni, I., Nicholson-Cole, S. and L. Whitmarsh (2007), 'Barriers perceived to engaging with climate change among the UK public and their policy implications', *Global Environmental Change*, **17** (3), 445–459.
Lynn, P. (2014), 'Distinguishing dimensions of pro-environmental behaviour', ISER Working Paper Series, 29 April.
Mallett, R. (2012), 'Eco-guilt motivates eco-friendly behaviour', *Ecopsychology*, **4** (3), 223–231.
Mallett, R., Melchiori, K. and T. Strickroth (2013), 'Self-confrontation via a carbon footprint calculator increases guilt and support for a proenvironmental group', *Ecopsychology*, **5** (1), 9–16.
Markowitz, E., Goldberg, L., Ashton, M. and K. Lee (2012), 'Profiling the "pro-environmental individual": a personality perspective', *Journal of Personality*, **80** (1), 81–111.
Meier, S. and A. Stutzer (2008), 'Is volunteering rewarding in itself?', *Economica*, **75** (297), 39–59.
Natural England (2016), 'Monitor of Engagement with the Natural Environment: 2012–2015'. http://publications.naturalengland.org.uk/category/47018.
Nyborg, K., Howarth, R. and K. Brekke (2006), 'Green consumers and public policy: on socially contingent moral motivation', *Resource and Energy Economics*, **28** (4), 351–366.
Pereira, M. and P. Forster (2015), 'The relationship between connectedness to nature, environmental values, and pro-environmental behaviours', *Reinvention: An International Journal of Undergraduate Research*, **8** (2).
Priolo, D., Milhabet, I., Codou, O., Fointiat, V., Lebarbenchona, E. and F. Gabarrot (2016), 'Encouraging ecological behaviour through induced hypocrisy and inconsistency', *Journal of Environmental Psychology*, **47**, 166–180.
Rees, J., Klug, S. and S. Bamberg (2015), 'Guilty conscience: motivating pro-environmental behaviour by inducing negative moral emotions', *Climatic Change*, **130** (3), 439–452.
Ryan, R., Huta, V. and E. Deci (2013), 'Living well: a self-determination theory perspective on eudaimonia', in Antonella Delle Fave (ed.), *The Exploration of Happiness*, Dordrecht, Netherlands: Springer, pp. 117–139.
Scannell, L. and R. Gifford (2010), 'The relations between natural and civic place attachment and pro-environmental behaviour', *Journal of Environmental Psychology*, **30** (3), 289–297.

Schmitt, M.T., Aknin, L.B., Axsen, J. and R.L. Shwom (2018), 'Unpacking the relationships between pro-environmental behavior, life satisfaction, and perceived ecological threat', *Ecological Economics*, **143**, 130–140.

Schultz, P. (2001), 'The structure of environmental concern: concern for self, other people, and the biosphere', *Journal of Environmental Psychology*, **21** (4), 327–339.

Schwartz, S. (1977), 'Normative influences on altruism', *Advances in Experimental Social Psychology*, **10**, 221–279.

Son, J. and J. Wilson (2012), 'Volunteer work and hedonic, eudemonic, and social well-being', *Sociological Forum*, **27** (3), 658–681.

Steg, L. and C. Vlek (2009), 'Encouraging pro-environmental behaviour: an integrative review and research agenda', *Journal of Environmental Psychology*, **29** (3), 309–317.

Stern, N. (ed.) (2007), *The Economics of Climate Change: The Stern Review*, Cambridge, UK: Cambridge University Press.

Stern, P. (2000), 'New environmental theories: toward a coherent theory of environmentally significant behaviour', *Journal of Social Issues*, **56** (3), 407–424.

Stern, P., Dietz, T., Abel, T., Guagnano, G. and L. Kalof (1999), 'A value–belief–norm theory of support for social movements: the case of environmentalism', *Human Ecology Review*, **6** (2), 81–97.

Stoll-Kleemann, S., O'Riordan, T. and C. Jaeger (2001), 'The psychology of denial concerning climate mitigation measures: evidence from Swiss focus groups', *Global Environmental Change*, **11** (2), 107–117.

Stone, A.A. and C.E. Mackie (2013), *Subjective Well-being: Measuring Happiness, Suffering, and Other Dimensions of Experience*, Washington, DC: National Academies Press.

Thøgersen, J. (2006), 'Norms for environmentally responsible behaviour: an extended taxonomy', *Journal of Environmental Psychology*, **26** (4), 247–261.

Thøgersen, J. and F. Ölander (2003), 'Spillover of environment-friendly consumer behaviour', *Journal of Environmental Psychology*, **23** (3), 225–236.

Tiefenbeck, V., Staake, T., Roth, K. and O. Sachs (2013), 'For better or for worse? Empirical evidence of moral licensing in a behavioural energy conservation campaign', *Energy Policy*, **57**, 160–171.

Van Der Linden, S. (2015), 'Intrinsic motivation and pro-environmental behaviour', *Nature Climate Change*, **5** (7), 612–613.

Venhoeven, L., Bolderdijk, J. and L. Steg (2013), 'Explaining the paradox: how pro-environmental behaviour can both thwart and foster well-being', *Sustainability*, **5** (4), 1372–1386.

Venhoeven, L., Steg, L. and J. Bolderdijk (2017), 'Can engagement in environmentally-friendly behaviour increase well-being?', in Ghozlane Fleury-Bahi, Enric Pol and Oscar Navarro (eds), *Handbook of Environmental Psychology and Quality of Life Research*, Basel, Switzerland: Springer International Publishing, pp. 229–237.

Verhofstadt, E., Van Ootegem, L., Defloor, B. and B. Bleys (2016), 'Linking individuals' ecological footprint to their subjective well-being', *Ecological Economics*, **127**, 80–89.

Welsch, H. and J. Kühling (2010), 'Pro-environmental behaviour and rational consumer choice: evidence from surveys of life satisfaction', *Journal of Economic Psychology*, **31** (3), 405–420.

Welsch, H. and J. Kühling (2011), 'Are pro-environmental consumption choices utility-maximizing? Evidence from subjective well-being data', *Ecological Economics*, **72**, 75–87.

Welsch, H. and J. Kühling (2018), 'How green self image is related to subjective well-being: pro-environmental values as a social norm', *Ecological Economics*, **149**, 105–119.

White, M. and P. Dolan (2009), 'Accounting for the richness of daily activities', *Psychological Science*, **20** (8), 1000–1008.

Xiao, J. and H. Li (2011), 'Sustainable consumption and life satisfaction', *Social Indicators Research*, **104** (2), 323–329.

APPENDIX 18A.1

Table 18A.1 Descriptive statistics

	N	Mean	Std dev.	Min.	Max.
Dependent [a]					
Satisfaction	5206	7.323	2.034	0	10
Worthwhile	5206	7.559	1.890	0	10
Happiness	5206	7.414	2.259	0	10
Anxiety	5206	2.679	2.883	0	10
Independent					
MCA dimension 1 – General PEB	5206	−1.51e-09	1.0001	−1.0489	4.1198
MCA dimension 2 – Common/Uncommon PEB	5206	5.92e-09	1.0001	−5.2664	1.4256
Controls					
Gender	5206	1.0			
Male	2418	0.48		0	1
Female	2788	0.52		0	1
Age group (in years)	5206	1.0			
16–24	757	0.15		0	1
25–34	894	0.17		0	1
35–44	744	0.14		0	1
45–54	778	0.15		0	1
55–64	734	0.14		0	1
65+	1299	0.25			
Health condition[b]	5206	1.0			
No	3985	0.77		0	1
Yes	1221	0.23		0	1
Socio-economic group	5206	1.0			
Upper and middle class	945	0.18		0	1
Lower middle class	1357	0.26		0	1
Skilled working class	977	0.19		0	1
Lower working	1927	0.37		0	1
Marital Status	5206	1.0			
Single	1415	0.55		0	1
Separated/divorced/widow	929	0.27		0	1
Married	2862	0.18		0	1
Work status	5206	1.0			
In full-time work	1725	0.33		0	1
In education	661	0.12		0	1
Not working	1482	0.28		0	1
Part-time work	362	0.07		0	1
Retired	976	0.19		0	1
Housing Tenure	5206	1.0			
Mortgage	1236	0.24		0	1
Owned outright	1595	0.19		0	1

Table 18A.1 (continued)

	N	Mean	Std dev.	Min.	Max.
Other tenure (incl. rent)	2375	0.4		0	1
Ethnicity	5206	1.0			
White	4431	0.85		0	1
Non-white	775	0.15		0	1

Notes:
[a] All dependent variables are measured on a scale of 0–10, where 0 is 'not at all' and 10 is 'completely'.
[b] Response to the question, 'Do you have any long-standing illness, health problem or disability that limits your daily activities or the kind of work you can do?'

APPENDIX 18A.2

Prior to carrying out the regression analysis to explore the relationship between SWB and PEB, multiple correspondence analysis (MCA) was carried out as a data reduction technique and to explore patterns of relationship between the original PEB variables. MCA was chosen as a result of its suitability for the analysis of the binary PEB variables (Greenacre, 2007; Greenacre and Blasius, 2006). The predicted individual scores derived from MCA were then used in multivariate regression analysis to investigate the relationship between SWB and PEB.

MCA was carried out on the indicator matrix of the five measures of PEB using the 'mca' command in STATA 14 (see Table 18A.2). The axes were then assessed using a number of common considerations in MCA (Canuel et al., 2014; Costa et al., 2013). First, the principal inertia scores were examined using the criterion of including MCA dimensions with inertia above 0.2 (Hair et al., 2009). The first dimension meets this criterion with a principal inertia value of 0.34; the second component also does with a value of 0.21; all other components do not. Second, the scree-plot, which presents the proportions of variance explained, was examined. As can be seen in Figure 18A.1, the elbow occurs at the second dimension, indicating that the proportion of variance explained drops faster up to two dimensions and less rapidly after that (Johnson and Wichern, 2002). Third, the cumulative variance explained was considered. The first two components together capture notably larger amounts of the variance in the data than the subsequent ones (see Table 18A.2). The first dimension explains 34 per cent of the total variation in the data while the first two in combination explain 55 per cent, and the first three in combination explain over 71 per cent. Lastly, retaining two dimensions allows for the construction of two-dimensional pictures of data which facilitates interpretation (see Figure 18A.2). On the basis of the above considerations, two dimensions were retained for further analysis. It is, however, important to note that these two dimensions collectively explain just under 55 per cent of the variance in the data, which suggests that the original variables are somewhat heterogeneous.

The category coordinates were then plotted, and the resulting graph (Figure 18A.2) was used to interpret the dimensions. The first dimension under MCA explains as much of the variance as possible and appears to group all of the PEBs. The first dimension, therefore, can be interpreted as a general measure of PEB. The second dimension is orthogonal to the first and displays as much of the remaining variance as possible. This dimension

Table 18A.2 Multiple correspondence analysis dimensions

Dimension		Principle inertia	%	Cumulative %
Dimension 1		0.3439	34.39	34.39
Dimension 2		0.2053	20.53	54.92
Dimension 3		0.1654	16.54	71.46
Dimension 4		0.1456	14.56	86.02
Dimension 5		0.1398	13.98	100.00
N	5206			
Number of axes	4			

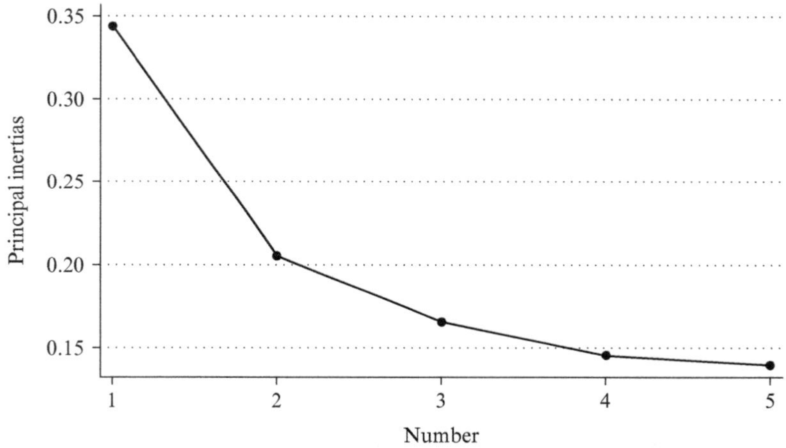

Figure 18A.1 Multiple correspondence analysis scree plot

appears to contrast recycling, encouraging others to protect the environment and buying eco-friendly products with volunteering and being a member of an environmental organisation. In Figure 18A.2 the first dimension is plotted on the horizontal axis and the second dimension is plotted on the vertical axis. Considering the horizontal axis for all five variables, engaging in the PEB in question is shown to be associated with a lower score on dimension 1, than is not engagement. This suggests that this dimension captures engagement in PEB in a general sense.

In contrast, looking at the vertical axis, engagement in the first three PEBs – recycling, buying eco-friendly products and encouraging others – are related to lower scores on the second dimension, whereas engagement in the other two PEBs (being a member and volunteering) are associated with higher scores. Interestingly, when the prevalence of the behaviours which are contrasted in dimension two are compared (see Table 18A.2), it is clear that this dimension contrasts relatively more common behaviour with less common behaviours. Predicted values for both of the dimensions were calculated for each individual. The scores were then reverse coded so higher scores on the first dimension represent a higher level of engagement in PEB, and higher scores on the second dimension represents a greater level of engagement in common relative to uncommon behaviours.

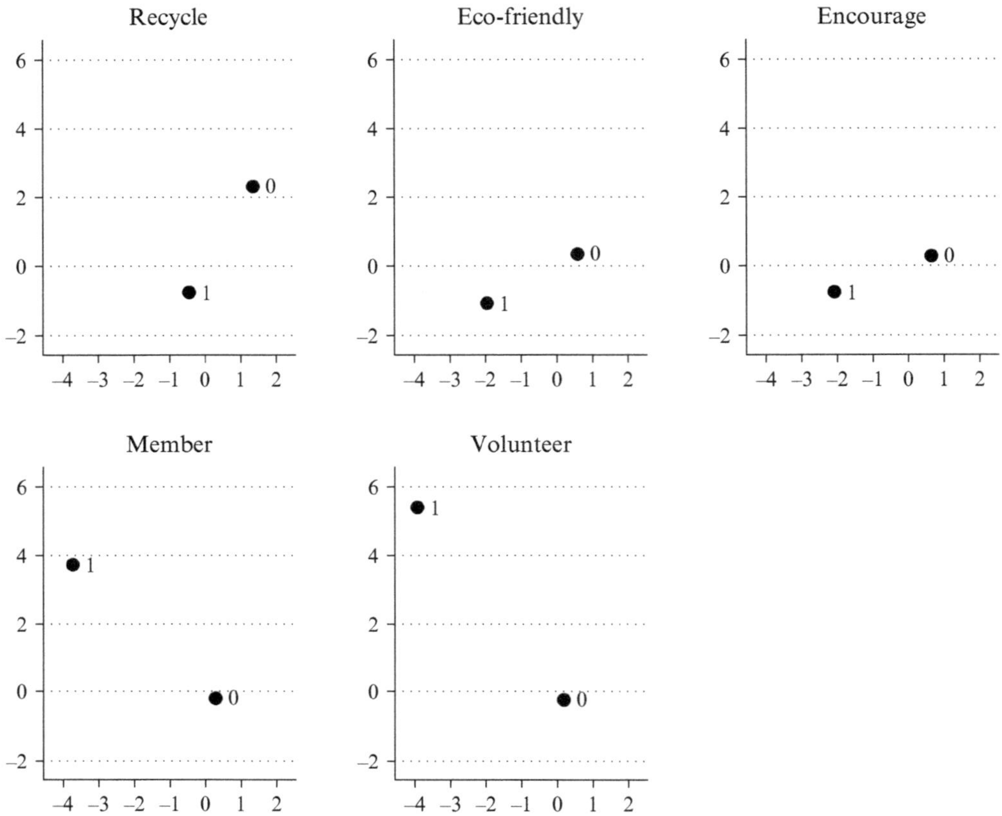

Notes:
Dimension 1 (horizontal) explains 34.4% inertia.
Dimension 2 (vertical) explains 20.5% inertia.

Figure 18A.2 Multiple correspondence analysis coordinate plot

APPENDIX 18A.3

Table 18A.3 details the results for the full specification of Model I (without controls) and Model II (with controls) across the four SWB measures. The results relating to the independent variables of interest are discussed in the results and discussion sections of the main text. The results relating to the controls are similar to those found in other work using these SWB measures (Deeming, 2013; Dolan and Laffan, 2016). For example, married people report higher levels of SWB than their single counterparts across all four SWB measures, and people out of employment report lower levels of SWB across all four measures than those in full-time employment. Other variables such as ethnicity and gender are associated with some measures of SWB but not others.

Table 18A.3 SWB and PEB

Variables	Satisfaction	Satisfaction	Worthwhile	Worthwhile	Happiness	Happiness	Anxiety	Anxiety
	Model I	Model II	Model I	Model II	Model I	Model II	Model I	Model II
MCA dimension 1 – General PEB	0.115***	0.0668**	0.218***	0.155***	0.106***	0.0542	−0.000861	0.0564
	(0.0308)	(0.0294)	(0.0285)	(0.0283)	(0.0369)	(0.0350)	(0.0403)	(0.0419)
MCA dimension 2 – Common/Uncommon PEB	0.104***	0.0814***	0.114***	0.0814***	0.0852***	0.0683**	−0.194***	−0.163***
	(0.0297)	(0.0293)	(0.0263)	(0.0265)	(0.0315)	(0.0321)	(0.0373)	(0.0381)
Gender – Reference group: Male								
Female		0.105*		0.294***		0.0950		0.105
		(0.0555)		(0.0585)		(0.0605)		(0.0774)
Age group – Reference group: 16–24								
25–34		−0.700***		−0.312***		−0.394***		0.228
		(0.113)		(0.110)		(0.131)		(0.153)
35–44		−0.917***		−0.347***		−0.676***		0.547***
		(0.140)		(0.119)		(0.139)		(0.172)
45–54		−1.037***		−0.483***		−0.597***		0.416**
		(0.130)		(0.122)		(0.141)		(0.185)
55–64		−0.804***		−0.340***		−0.456***		0.430**
		(0.129)		(0.122)		(0.150)		(0.207)
65+		−0.485***		−0.0596		−0.0754		0.152
		(0.155)		(0.132)		(0.159)		(0.258)
Health – Reference group: no health condition								
Suffers from a health condition		−0.799***		−0.520***		−0.680***		0.854***
		(0.0860)		(0.0790)		(0.0837)		(0.123)
Socio-economic group – Reference: Upper and middle class								
Lower middle class		−0.0861		−0.159**		−0.0281		0.106
		(0.0765)		(0.0625)		(0.0753)		(0.102)
Skilled working class		−0.104		−0.0933		−0.0900		−0.0755
		(0.0855)		(0.0768)		(0.0949)		(0.109)

Table 18A.3 (continued)

Variables	Satisfaction	Satisfaction	Worthwhile	Worthwhile	Happiness	Happiness	Anxiety	Anxiety
	Model I	Model II	Model I	Model II	Model I	Model II	Model I	Model II
Lower worker class and lower class		−0.179**		−0.235***		−0.235**		0.0971
		(0.0838)		(0.0785)		(0.0932)		(0.127)
Marital status – Reference group: Single								
Separated/divorced/widowed		0.0139		−0.0749		−0.102		−0.162
		(0.111)		(0.0998)		(0.117)		(0.159)
Married		0.587***		0.484***		0.504***		−0.309***
		(0.0725)		(0.0794)		(0.0776)		(0.111)
Work status – In full-time work								
In education		−0.0772		0.0740		−0.0633		0.212
		(0.118)		(0.112)		(0.157)		(0.198)
Not working		−0.554***		−0.460***		−0.433***		0.303**
		(0.102)		(0.0939)		(0.103)		(0.134)
Part-time work		−0.0765		−0.0953		0.1000		−0.150
		(0.0811)		(0.0612)		(0.0980)		(0.127)
Retired		0.174		−0.0272		0.157		−0.275
		(0.119)		(0.107)		(0.132)		(0.191)
Housing tenure – Reference: Other tenure including rental								
Mortgage		0.0747		0.00635		−0.0560		−0.202*
		(0.0800)		(0.0798)		(0.0777)		(0.110)
Owned outright		0.161**		0.130*		0.0559		−0.283**
		(0.0773)		(0.0731)		(0.0861)		(0.123)
Ethnicity – Reference group: Non-white								
White		0.202***		0.244***		0.0169		−0.445***
		(0.0705)		(0.0676)		(0.0826)		(0.0979)
Constant	7.323***	7.725***	7.559***	7.528***	7.414***	7.722***	2.679***	2.796***
	(0.0324)	(0.120)	(0.0339)	(0.115)	(0.0383)	(0.143)	(0.0607)	(0.196)
Observations	5206	5206	5206	5206	5206	5206	5206	5206
R-squared	0.006	0.097	0.017	0.077	0.004	0.058	0.005	0.041

Notes: Ordinary least squares regression with standard errors clustered at local authority level in parentheses. *** $p < 0.01$, ** $p < 0.05$, * $p < 0.1$.

19. Happiness and green lifestyle

Heinz Welsch

19.1 INTRODUCTION

A growing literature within the broader field of happiness research has found green lifestyles to be positively related to subjective wellbeing. This finding has sometimes been taken to suggest that engaging in pro-environmental behavior (PEB) is conducive to greater wellbeing, and that it refutes views which equate PEBs with hardship and sacrifice (Brown and Kasser, 2005; Binder and Blankenberg, 2017).

While such conclusions are striking, their significance seems ambiguous. The first part of the assertion – that PEB is conducive to wellbeing – is unsurprising and seems hard to deny even without referring to research on happiness: from a revealed-preference perspective, the very fact that people voluntarily engage in such behaviors plausibly suggests that they derive some utility (wellbeing) from doing so. By contrast, the second part – that PEB involves no sacrifice – seems to be overselling the evidence. On the contrary, wellbeing research has studied PEBs that are costly (in terms of money, time and effort), and some of this research has found that engaging in more costly PEBs is particularly strongly related to wellbeing.

These observations suggest that our understanding of the relationship between green lifestyle and subjective wellbeing is incomplete in parts. In particular, the roles of wellbeing benefits and wellbeing costs involved in empirical PEB–wellbeing relationships seem to be surrounded by some ambiguity.

This chapter discusses the available evidence with the aim of contributing to a better understanding of how green lifestyle and wellbeing are related. Section 19.2 provides an overview of available evidence on the relationship between pro-environmental behavior and wellbeing. Section 19.3 discusses possible motives underlying pro-environmental behavior and how they fit into explanatory models of the occurrence of PEBs. Section 19.4 is devoted to interpreting the evidence in the light of those models, discussing in particular what the evidence implies with respect to the wellbeing benefits and costs of PEBs. Section 19.5 concludes by discussing the policy implications that may follow from different interpretations of the evidence.

Throughout the chapter, the term "green lifestyle" will be used to include both people's pro-environmental behavior and people's "green" self-image. While the bulk of the literature has been concerned with actual (self-reported) behavior, some recent studies have focused on self-image as a predictor of wellbeing. The term "happiness" will mostly be used in the wider sense, as a synonym for subjective wellbeing. When referring to happiness in the narrow sense, denoting affective as opposed to evaluative subjective wellbeing, it will be stated explicitly.

19.2 SURVEY OF EMPIRICAL STUDIES

Studies on the relationship between subjective wellbeing and pro-environmental behaviors (PEBs) and attitudes have been conducted by psychologists and economists using datasets from Canada, China, Germany, Mexico, Spain, Sweden, the United Kingdom (UK) and the United States (US), as well as multi-country datasets (Table 19.1). While a great variety of PEBs was studied in these works, subjective wellbeing was mostly measured as life satisfaction. This strategy seems to be justified in the light of Chapter 18 in this *Handbook* which demonstrates that an aggregate PEB indicator is significantly related to evaluative measures of subjective wellbeing (life satisfaction, sense of purpose), but not to affective measures (happiness, anxiety). This section describes the designs and findings of the various studies, whereas comparative interpretations of the findings are the subject of subsequent sections.

19.2.1 Environmental Psychology

Brown and Kasser (2005) investigated the relationship between subjective wellbeing (happiness and life satisfaction) and a variety of pro-environmental behaviors in samples of adolescents and adults in the US and found this relationship to be significantly positive. The study identified an intrinsic value orientation (in particular, generosity) and dispositional mindfulness (receptive attention to and awareness of ongoing internal states and behavior) as common explanatory factors for wellbeing and pro-environmental behaviors.

Following up on the role of mindfulness, Jacob et al. (2009) studied the wellbeing–PEB relationship in a sample from Canada and the US. They found an eight-item construct of subjective wellbeing to be significantly positively related to an indicator of "sustainable food practice" (in particular, buying locally grown produce and organic food), but not to indicators of recycling behavior and "sustainable household choices." Sustainable behaviors were found to be positively related to the frequency of "mindful meditation," and the relationship between wellbeing and sustainable food practice was found to be weaker (but significant) when the wellbeing regression controlled for meditation frequency.

Corral-Verdugo et al. (2011) analyzed data from a sample of students at a Mexican university. They found a construct of "sustainable behavior," composed of pro-ecological, frugal, altruistic and equitable conducts, to significantly influence a "happiness" construct within a structural equation modeling (SEM) framework.

Xiao and Li (2011) conducted an analysis of sustainable consumption and life satisfaction using data collected in 14 cities from all regions in China. They found a significantly positive association between life satisfaction and both green purchase intentions (yes/no) and green purchase behavior (never/sometimes/always). No significant association was found between life satisfaction and "green lifestyle intentions," that is, the willingness to forego a "lifestyle of high consumption" to avoid environmental pollution.

Kaida and Kaida (2016) used data elicited in Stockholm county, Sweden, to investigate structural relationships between water and energy saving at home and present as well as expected future satisfaction with life. Path analysis using SEM revealed that water and energy saving enhanced present life satisfaction, which in turn enhanced expected future life satisfaction. While water and energy saving were positively related to values

Table 19.1 Survey of empirical studies

Study	Countries	Dependent variable	Behaviors/attitudes
Brown and Kasser (2005)	USA	Happiness, life satisfaction	12 ecological footprint questions on diet, transportation and housing + 54 positive environmental behaviors (e.g., turning off lights in unoccupied rooms)
Videras and Owen (2006)	27 countries worldwide	Life satisfaction	Buying environment-friendly products; recycling or reuse of goods; water conservation
Jacob et al. (2009)	Canada and USA	8-item SWB construct	Constructs of recycling behavior (3 items), sustainable household practice (3 items) and sustainable food practice (4 items)
Welsch and Kühling (2010)	27 countries worldwide	Life satisfaction	Buying environment-friendly products; recycling or reuse of goods; water conservation
Corral-Verdugo et al. (2011)	Mexico	Happiness	Latent "sustainable behavior" (pro-ecological, frugal, altruistic and equitable)
Welsch and Kühling (2011)	Germany	Life satisfaction	Buying organic food, low-energy light bulbs and household appliances; using solar heating system; subscription to "green" energy
Xiao and Li (2011)	China	Life satisfaction	Green lifestyle intentions, green purchase intentions, green purchase behavior
Kühling (2014)	Germany	Life satisfaction	Use of solar energy for lighting, cooking, water and space heating
Kaida and Kaida (2016)	Sweden	Life satisfaction	Water and energy saving at home
Suarez-Varela et al. (2016)	Spain	Life satisfaction	Water-saving behaviors (using washing machine/dishwasher, tap, shower); water-saving devices (toilet, tap); voluntary work in environmental organization
Binder and Blankenberg (2017)	UK	Life satisfaction	Environmental behaviors relating to TV, lights, water, heating, packaging, recycled paper, shopping bags, public transport, short journeys, car sharing, fewer flights; environmental attitudes (intentions, lifestyle, willingness to pay)
Schmitt et al. (2018)	Canada and USA	Life satisfaction	Participate in local environmental activities; buy food at farmer's market; talk to children about environmental issues; buy locally produced foods; buy energy-efficient appliances; make your own products instead of purchasing; talk to children about how food is grown; attend pro-environmental meetings; buy environmentally friendly soaps or cleaners; buy organic food; eat a diet based on organic, local or free-range food; trade or share products with others rather than buy; buy products made from recycled materials; avoid excess packaging in purchases;

Table 19.1 (continued)

Study	Countries	Dependent variable	Behaviors/attitudes
			compost garden or kitchen waste; grow your own food; walk or cycle; support pro-environmental candidates in elections; buy an efficient vehicle; buy high-efficiency light bulbs; use reusable bag when shopping; turn off tap when soaping up; turn off tap when brushing teeth; eat a vegetarian diet; minimize number of baths or showers; reduce hot water temperature; shut off electrical appliances when not in use; minimize water use in yard or garden; reduce home air-conditioning use; fix something rather than buy new; turn off tap when washing dishes; reuse paper or glass; hang clothes to dry instead of using dryer; buy used products instead of new ones; minimize use of home heating; turn off lights when not in use; use recycling bins for paper, cardboard, cans, glass; use public transit or carpool; run washer/dryer only when full
Welsch and Kühling (2018)	35 European countries	Life satisfaction	Pro-environmental attitude/self-image

of "universalism" (social justice, equality, unity with nature, a world of peace) and to measures of "intrinsic satisfaction," water and energy saving were negatively related to higher expectations of future life satisfaction. The authors interpreted the latter finding as suggesting that expectations of a less happy life in the future may reflect pessimism as to future environmental conditions, which may drive people's engagement in pro-environmental actions in the present. While "universalism" was found to indirectly influence subjective wellbeing through its effect on PEB, it was not tested whether a direct influence of universalism on wellbeing existed, and what allowing for such an influence implied for the PEB–wellbeing relationship.

19.2.2 Environmental Economics

Videras and Owen (2006) studied the relationships between life satisfaction and three pro-environmental behaviors (buying green products, recycling/reuse, water conservation) in a multi-country database, the World Values Surveys, and found those relationships to be significantly positive. They interpreted their findings as evidence of the "warm glow of giving" (Andreoni, 1990), meaning that altruistic behaviors per se yield utility independent of their real-world consequences (see section 19.3).

Using the same database, Welsch and Kühling (2010) confirmed those findings and offered a choice-theoretic background for their analysis, addressing in particular the issue of the rationality of pro-environmental behaviors in a benefit–cost framework (to be discussed in section 19.4).

Welsch and Kühling (2011) used data from Germany to study the issue of rational choice and the possibility of "decision errors" (see section 19.4) more thoroughly. In addition to people's intensity of several pro-environmental behaviors their data include information on how long people have been engaging in those behaviors and whether their peers (neighbors, friends and relatives) behave in similar ways. Controlling for pro-environmental attitudes, they found significantly positive associations between individuals' PEBs and their life satisfaction (except for organic food), the strength of the association being weaker when people had engaged in those behaviors for a longer period of time and when their peers displayed similar behaviors.

While the studies discussed to this point used cross-section data or pooled cross-sections, Kühling (2014) employed a panel dataset, the German Socio-Economic Panel (SOEP). Using fixed-effects regressions allowed him to control for characteristics of the individuals that may confound evidence based on cross-section data. He focused on different types of energy used in households, of which the use of solar energy was considered to constitute an environment friendly behavior. He found individuals in whose households solar energy was used (yes/no), or was used for more purposes (space heating, heating of water, cooking, lighting), to have significantly higher levels of life satisfaction. Breaking down the overall sample by home owners and renters, he found that the positive association between solar energy and wellbeing remained significant only for home owners. Similarly, differentiating between the decider within the household and other household members, the positive solar–wellbeing association remained significant only for the decider. Both results are consistent with the view that the psychological benefits from environmental friendliness stem from an action per se (yielding a "warm glow"), not from its consequences for the environment (see section 19.3). If this is the case, those benefits are likely to accrue only to those actually taking the action.

Suarez-Varela et al. (2016) analyzed data from Granada, Spain, on water-saving behaviors, water-saving devices, and volunteering in environmental organizations, motivating the focus on water saving by the prevalence of water scarcity in the study region. The study finds life satisfaction to be significantly positively related to volunteering and to the availability of water-saving devices in the household, but not to water-saving behaviors (relating to usage of washing machine/dishwasher, tap and shower). The authors argue that the non-significance of water-saving behaviors may be explained in a cost–benefit framework where the perceived benefits and costs (in terms of inconvenience and discomfort) of these behaviors just balance.

19.2.3 Further Studies

A number of recent studies (Schmitt et al., 2018; Binder and Blankenberg, 2017; Welsch and Kühling, 2018) aimed at shedding more light on the mechanisms behind the relationship between subjective wellbeing and pro-environmental behaviors and attitudes. These studies will be discussed in the following sections which aim at interpreting and understanding the empirical evidence.

19.3 WHY PEOPLE ENGAGE IN PRO-ENVIRONMENTAL BEHAVIOR

While PEB studies by environmental psychologists have emphasized the role of mentalities and value orientations for the emergence of PEBs, environmental economists conceive of such behaviors as choices taken subject to cost–benefit considerations. This section discusses the emergence of PEBs in such frameworks, starting with the standard economic model and proceeding with more elaborated models that take into account insights from psychology.

19.3.1 The Standard Economic Model

From an economics perspective, pro-environmental behaviors can be conceptualized as the private provision of a public (environmental) good. Private public-good provision has long puzzled economists because the extent to which individuals contribute to public goods (for example, through charitable giving) often far exceeds what is economically rational in the traditional sense (see below). This observation has spurred developing behavioral models that extend the standard microeconomic model of consumer choice. A characteristic of those extensions is that they transcend the consequentialist setting of the standard economic model, that is, the assumption that actions or choices are evaluated on the basis of their consequences alone, without regard to the possibility that actions may have value per se, independently of or in addition to their consequentialist value.

The standard public good model involves a strictly increasing and concave utility function defined over quantities of a private (consumption) good, c, and a public (environmental) good, Q:

$$u_i = \widetilde{H}(c_i, Q). \tag{19.1}$$

In this formulation, individual i may value the public good out of pure self-interest (egoism) or, in addition, out of concern for the good's benefit to others (altruism).

Assuming that the quantity of the public good is the sum of individual contributions q_i, available at unit cost p (consumption foregone), and denoting exogenous income by y_i, the model is completed by the following public good provision function and budget constraint:

$$Q = \sum_j q_j \text{ and } c_i = y_i - pq_i.^1 \tag{19.2}$$

By inserting (19.2) into (19.1), one gets a semi-reduced utility function of the following form:

$$u_i = \widetilde{H}(y_i - pq_i, \sum_j q_j) =: H(p, y_i, q_i)$$

Given the strict concavity of $\widetilde{H}(c_i, Q)$, the semi-reduced form is hump-shaped in q_i. An interior utility maximum is then characterized by the following first-order condition:

$$\frac{dH}{dq_i} = \frac{\partial \widetilde{H}}{\partial c_i}(-p) + \frac{\partial \widetilde{H}}{\partial Q} = 0, \tag{19.3}$$

which tells us that at the utility maximum the marginal utility from the public good equals the marginal disutility from consumption foregone.

It is easy to demonstrate that in large populations there are negligible incentives to contribute to the public good. To illustrate, consider the following specification:

$$\widetilde{H} = \alpha \log c_i + \beta \log Q. \tag{19.4}$$

Again inserting (19.2), the condition (19.3) takes the following form:

$$\frac{dH}{dq_i} = \frac{\alpha}{c_i}(-p) + \frac{\beta}{Q} = 0$$

Assuming (for simplicity) a symmetrical solution (which presumes equal income of all individuals) and denoting the population size by n, we can write $Q = n\, q_i$ and restate this condition as:

$$\frac{q_i}{c_i} = \frac{\beta/\alpha}{n \cdot p}. \tag{19.5}$$

This illustrates the property of the consequentialist model (demonstrated more generally by Andreoni, 1988) that in large economies (with large n) virtually no one gives to the public good, even if preferences are altruistic. The intuitive reason is that one individual's contribution has a negligible influence on the overall quantity of the public good. Similarly, in the case of pro-environmental behavior, an individual's behavior has a negligible influence on environmental quality.

In spite of this logic, significant donations to public goods such as charity are widely observed. Similarly, the data used in wellbeing–PEB studies show that large portions of people engage in pro-environmental behaviors in spite of significant costs in terms of money, time, effort or inconvenience. The standard model is inadequate in explaining such observations.

19.3.2 The Deontological Model

The inadequacy of the standard consequentialist model in explaining pro-social or pro-environmental behavior has led researchers to incorporate deontological motives in choice-theoretical models; that is, to assume that people attach value to certain actions per se, not just to their consequences. The benefits that people derive from such actions can be intrinsic (internal) or extrinsic (external). Intrinsic benefits arise from the individual's own knowledge of their action, either through the "warm glow of giving" (Andreoni, 1989, 1990) that derives from acting in a generous or altruistic way, or through conformity to a social norm (Farrow et al., 2017). Extrinsic benefits, involving prestige or reputation, may arise when other people know about the action (Harbaugh, 1998).

Deontological factors are easily incorporated into the utility function by including q_i as a separate argument:

$$u_i = \widetilde{H}(c_i, Q, q_i).$$

If we extend the specification (19.4) accordingly:

$$\widetilde{H} = \alpha \log c_i + \beta \log Q + \gamma \log q_i$$

and insert the equations (19.2), we obtain the following analog to equation (19.5):

$$\frac{q_i}{c_i} = \frac{\beta/\alpha}{n \cdot p} + \frac{\gamma/\alpha}{p}.$$

This shows that non-negligible individual contributions to the public good can arise even in large populations, depending on the utility weight γ that is placed on the action itself.

With respect to the latter, it is interesting to note that the wellbeing benefit from acting pro-socially has been found to be greater when the costs involved (p) are larger (Aknin et al., 2012). Reasons for this might be that contributing one's own resources enhances one's self-image as being a generous person (Aknin et al., 2013; Batson and Weeks, 1996). In terms of the presumed utility function, such an effect would manifest itself in a greater parameter γ when costs are higher, that is, $\gamma = \gamma(p)$, and would imply greater contributions.

A further factor that might contribute to a greater utility weight on pro-social or pro-environmental behavior derives from the fact that some such behaviors may provide opportunities for social connection. It is well known that people report the highest levels of wellbeing when socializing or connecting with other people (Kahneman et al., 2004). Similar to costs, considerations of socialness, as a co-benefit, would also be captured through the parameter γ.

19.3.3 Evidence

To date, the most encompassing study aiming at unpacking the relationship between pro-environmental behavior and subjective wellbeing is Schmitt et al. (2018). This study used samples from Canada and the United States to examine how performing a variety of pro-environmental behaviors predicts life satisfaction of more than 2000 individuals in the two nations. Specifically, they studied 39 pro-environmental behaviors, each of which was rated by two of the authors and five undergraduate research assistants in terms of the extent to which they were observable by others, involved direct costs (or cost savings), and provided opportunities for social interaction and building of relationships. This way, the authors were able to study how those factors influence the behavior–satisfaction relationship.

Overall, Schmitt et al. (2018) found that 37 behaviors were significantly correlated with greater life satisfaction and two non-significantly so. This finding suggests that a positive behavior–satisfaction relationship is detectable across a wide range of behaviors and thus not limited to any particular type(s) of behavior. The size of the relationship displayed a considerable range, the strongest relationship ("participate in local environmental activities") being seven times as large as the weakest ("run washer/dryer only when full"). Using the ratings of the behaviors in terms of observability, costs and socialness, it was found that all three factors were significantly correlated with a stronger behavior–satisfaction gradient, the correlations with observability, costs and socialness amounting to $r = 0.37$, $r = 0.74$ and $r = 0.50$, respectively.

The correlation of the behavior–satisfaction gradient with observability suggests that considerations of prestige and reputation play a role in the behavior–satisfaction relationship (Harbaugh, 1998). The correlation with costs may reflect that costly behaviors are more prestigious, or that individuals perceive them as more efficacious in helping the environment, or it may indicate that contributing one's own resources enhances one's self-image as being a generous person (Aknin et al., 2013; Batson and Weeks, 1996; Binder and Blankenberg, 2017). The correlation with socialness is consistent with findings mentioned earlier that people report the highest levels of wellbeing when socializing or connecting with other people (Kahneman et al., 2004). Overall, the findings of Schmitt et al. (2018) suggest that concerns of prestige and self-image as well as co-benefits through socializing with others are factors that motivate people to engage in PEBs. In addition to observability, costs and socialness, Laffan (Chapter 18 in this *Handbook*) found PEBs that are more common to be more strongly related to wellbeing, which suggests that conformity to a social norm may be a factor that furthers pro-environmental behavior.

19.4 UNDERSTANDING THE BEHAVIOR–WELLBEING RELATIONSHIP

19.4.1 The Issue

The preceding sections have discussed empirical studies of the relationship between pro-environmental behaviors and subjective wellbeing, and the channels that may explain why such a relationship exists. These channels involve self-regarding (egoistic) and other-regarding (altruistic) preferences with respect to the environment (consequentialist motives) as well as considerations of self-image with respect to a moral norm (generosity), conformity to a social norm and prestige (deontological motives). While these factors may rationalize the existence of a positive relationship between pro-environmental behavior and subjective wellbeing, the pertinent empirical studies nevertheless pose a conceptual puzzle, as will be demonstrated now.

As with other forms of economic behavior, the default explanatory model for pro-environmental behaviors is rational choice; that is, people choose the level or intensity of PEBs such as to attain an optimal trade-off between benefits and costs. As discussed in the preceding section, rational choice of environment-friendly behavior involves the maximization of a utility function that can be restated as follows:

$$u_i = \widetilde{H}(c_i, Q, q_i) = \widetilde{H}(y_i - pq_i, \sum_j q_j, q_i) =: H(p, y_i, q_i).$$

In this formulation, there is a trade-off between the utility from behaving in an environment-friendly way and the disutility in terms of consumption foregone. It should be noted that alternative formulations of trade-offs involved in environment-friendly behavior are conceivable. For instance, a PEB may be time-consuming, reducing the amount of leisure time, or it may require additional effort and imply inconvenience and discomfort in comparison to alternative behaviors. All such trade-offs manifest themselves in the semi-reduced function $H(p, y_i, q_i)$, or versions thereof, being hill-shaped in q_i. An interior maximum of $H(p, y_i, q_i)$ with respect to q_i thus implies that its derivative – that is, the net marginal utility of pro-environmental behavior – be zero.

The studies of the behavior–wellbeing relationship discussed earlier typically estimate a specification of the form:

$$H_i = a + b^*q_i + c^*y_i + d^*controls_i + e_i,$$

where $controls_i$ is a vector of the usual correlates of happiness and e_i is an error term. The constant a captures factors common to all individuals (in particular the cost parameter p). The typical estimating equation thus represents a linearized version of the semi-reduced function $H(p, y_i, q_i)$. The crucial parameter is b. This parameter measures the net marginal utility of pro-environmental behavior; that is, the derivative of $H(p, y_i, q_i)$ with respect to q_i. While the parameter should be zero according to the rational choice (utility maximization) assumption, it has been found to be significantly positive for a large set of behaviors. This means that the existing evidence is consistent with a positive marginal utility of pro-environmental behavior, on the basis of the factors discussed earlier, but inconsistent with the rational choice model of the preceding section. In terms of the theoretical model, the evidence suggests that people end up on the left-hand, rising branch of the hill-shaped behavior–utility schedule, rather than on the top of the utility hill. As a consequence, they could increase their utility by behaving in a more environment-friendly way. The remainder of this section discusses possible reasons for this inconsistency.

19.4.2 Boundary Solutions

The theoretical analysis presented above refers to an interior utility maximum, characterized by the first-order condition:

$$\frac{dH}{dq_i} = \frac{\partial \widetilde{H}}{\partial c_i}(-p) + \frac{\partial \widetilde{H}}{\partial Q} + \frac{\partial \widetilde{H}}{\partial q_i} = 0.$$

For an interior solution to exist, it is necessary that $p > 0$. In the case of costless pro-environmental behaviors or those that save costs, the expression between the two equality signs is necessarily positive. Then, the behaviors observed can only be boundary solutions, where people would rather choose higher levels of the behavior but cannot do so due to non-economic constraints.

This reasoning would predict that the behavior–wellbeing gradient is large for behaviors that are constrained by non-economic factors rather than by high costs (boundary solution), while being small or non-significant for costly but otherwise unconstrained behaviors (interior solution). Referring to her finding that more common PEBs yield greater wellbeing, Laffan (Chapter 18 in this *Handbook*) argues that more common PEBs coincide with those that are less costly, which suggests that less costly behaviors yield more wellbeing. Contrary to such reasoning, however, Schmitt et al. (2018) found behavior–satisfaction gradients to be non-significant for behaviors with negative costs, and larger for more costly behaviors. In addition, there is no indication of stricter non-economic bounds to behaviors strongly associated with greater wellbeing than to those less strongly associated with wellbeing. On the contrary, some behaviors with small gradients (for example, "use public transit or carpool") seem to face stronger non-economic restrictions (availability or quality of public transport) than behaviors with large gradients (for example "buy energy-efficient appliances," "buy organic food"). It is thus unclear whether the occurrence of positive net marginal utility from environment-friendly behavior can be explained as a boundary solution in the presence of non-economic restrictions.

19.4.3 Decision Errors

Another possible reason why empirical studies have found a positive net marginal utility of pro-environmental behavior is decision error. The notion of decision error relies on the distinction between decision utility and experienced utility introduced by Kahneman et al. (1997). Experienced utility – measured by subjective wellbeing – is the *ex post* hedonic quality (satisfaction) associated with an act of choice; whereas decision utility is the *ex ante* expectation of experienced utility.

Given the conceptual distinction between the two notions of utility, an important issue is whether or not the decision utility function and the experienced utility function coincide, or in other words, whether people know and correctly apply their experienced utility function when making economic choices, or whether they make systematic errors. As will be seen immediately, available evidence suggests that there may be systematic decision errors to the disadvantage of non-material choices, such as pro-environmental consumption.

A major reason for decision errors to occur is that people adapt to consumption levels attained, but fail to correctly anticipate this adaptation when taking consumption decisions, due to a failure in affective forecasting (Wilson and Gilbert, 2003; Loewenstein et al., 2003). While adaptation is well established with respect to consumption (Clark et al., 2008), such adaptation does not seem to apply to all sorts of activities and outcomes alike. Especially, people do not seem to adapt their utility evaluation in the case of outcomes which relate to intrinsic motivations, as opposed to extrinsic motivations. In the case of intrinsic motivation, utility derives from an internal reward as a direct result of a particular activity or choice, for example the "warm glow." In the case of extrinsic motivation, choice is instrumental to some external goal such as acquisition and possession.

Since failures of affective forecasting results from failures to anticipate hedonic adaptation, and since hedonic adaptation is more important for some categories of outcomes than for others, it follows that some sorts of outcomes are more likely to involve inaccurate utility forecasting than others. This asymmetry in the accuracy of utility forecasting is an origin of distorted, non-utility-maximizing choice. Especially, it implies that choice is distorted towards extrinsically motivated choices, such as consumption, relative to activities which serve less material goals.

This reasoning suggests that, when facing a consumption–PEB trade-off, people choose levels of pro-environmental behavior that are less than optimal *ex post*; that is, people could achieve an increase in net experienced utility by behaving in a more environment-friendly way (Welsch and Kühling, 2010, 2011). In this sense, decision error due to asymmetric unforeseen hedonic adaptation provides a possible explanation for the evidence of a positive net marginal utility from pro-environmental behaviors.

The idea that a positive net marginal utility of pro-environmental behavior may be due to decision errors is supported by evidence that the behavior–wellbeing gradient is smaller in better-educated people and in people with less materialistic values, on the presumption that more materialistic, extrinsically motivated individuals are more likely to overrate *ex ante* the wellbeing benefits from consumption (Welsch and Kühling, 2010). Further evidence supporting the decision error hypothesis is that the PEB–wellbeing gradient is smaller in people who have engaged in these behaviors for a longer time, as this may have helped them to learn their experienced utility function and bring their decision utility function more in line with it (Welsch and Kühling, 2011). In addition, Welsch and Kühling (2011) found no statistically significant association between wellbeing and buying organic food (in contrast to low-energy light bulbs and appliances), and explained this by the likely dominance of non-intrinsic or non-deontological motives (relating to perceived healthiness and taste) in the purchase of organic food.

19.4.4 Simultaneity Bias

A further possible reason for a biased estimate of the behavior–wellbeing gradient is simultaneity bias. Specifically, it is possible that happier people engage more in pro-environmental behaviors, rather than or in addition to pro-environmental behavior boosting happiness.

While the issue of simultaneity does not seem to have been studied with representative survey data, experimental studies of causality (Richins, 1997; Rucker and Petty, 2004) found evidence that although happier people consume less, the other causal direction also exists: more sustainable consumption leads to greater happiness. In a similar vein, experimental studies confirm that pro-social behavior has a causal effect on wellbeing: people randomly assigned to spend a given amount of money on others were significantly happier afterwards than people assigned to spend this amount on themselves (Dunn et al., 2008). Similarly, people randomly assigned to commit kind deeds for others or "the world" were found to be happier than people randomly assigned to commit those deeds to themselves (Nelson et al., 2016).

This evidence suggests that positive behavior–wellbeing gradients likely are not – or at least not entirely – the result of reverse causation. Nevertheless, a rigorous study of simultaneity using survey data on wellbeing and involving instrumental variables techniques has yet to be conducted.

19.4.5 Self-Image Concerns

One challenge to the usual finding of a positive association between pro-environmental behavior and subjective wellbeing comes from studies that involve a pro-environmental (green) self-image in addition to green behaviors. While Welsch and Kühling (2010) found positive PEB–wellbeing relationships to be robust to controlling for conservation-related preferences in multi-country data, Binder and Blankenberg (2017) failed to find such robustness with respect to indicators of "green" self-image using representative longitudinal data from the UK. In pooled estimates (that is, disregarding the longitudinal character of the data) they found the intensity of the behaviors to be significantly positively correlated with life satisfaction when the indicators of green attitudes (self-image) were omitted. When the latter were included, the behavior index turned out to be non-significant, whereas green self-image attracted significantly positive coefficients. In fixed-effects estimations, the behavior index was found to be non-significant, no matter whether self-image was included or not, whereas a more environment-friendly self-image continued to be significantly correlated with greater satisfaction.

The relationship between green self-image and subjective wellbeing was further explored by Welsch and Kühling (2018); disregarding, however, green behaviors. They used data from a series of cross-sections from 35 European countries and found life satisfaction to be significantly positively correlated with an indicator of green self-image in the pool of all countries as well as in 23 individual countries, and non-significantly so in the rest of countries. They further investigated what might explain differences in the relationship between self-image and wellbeing, invoking the hypothesis that this relationship might be stronger in societies in which being "green" is a shared social norm. Conceptualizing the validity of the presumed social norm by either the mean societal level of the attitudinal (self-image) variable or measures of diversity of the green attitude, they found the attitude–wellbeing relationship to be stronger in societies that are less polarized on green issues, whereas the mean level of the green attitude did not affect the attitude–wellbeing relationship.

In interpreting their results, Welsch and Kühling (2018) argued in favor of a causal understanding of the attitude–wellbeing relationship. According to their argument, it makes sense that being green is psychologically more beneficial in societies where greenness is a relatively uncontested social norm, yielding satisfaction through conformity. A reverse interpretation of the attitude–wellbeing relationship, mediated by the greenness norm, would imply that happier (more satisfied) people are greener in green societies, whereas less happy people are less green in green societies; an effect which the authors find difficult to explain.

19.4.6 Wellbeing–Utility Discrepancy

A further possibility to explain why people may come up with choices that imply positive net marginal wellbeing (life satisfaction) relies on the idea that, rather than committing decision errors, people do not even strive to maximize subjective wellbeing. Instead, they maximize a utility function U that includes wellbeing as an argument that trades off against other non-wellbeing factors, X (Benjamin et al., 2012).

Assuming that X is negatively related to q_i, an assumption to be discussed below, as well as a utility trade-off between wellbeing and X, we can extend our choice-theoretic model as follows:

$$u_i = U(H(p, y_i, q_i), X(q_i)).$$

Assuming the utility function to be increasing and strictly concave in both arguments, the first-order condition for utility maximization then reads:

$$\frac{dU}{dq_i} = \frac{\partial U \partial H}{\partial H \partial q_i} + \frac{\partial U \partial X}{\partial X \partial q_i} = 0$$

Thus, when H (wellbeing) and X optimally trade off against each other and, as assumed, $\frac{\partial X}{\partial q_i} < 0$, the above condition implies that the net marginal wellbeing from pro-environmental behavior, $\frac{\partial H}{\partial q_i}$, is positive.[2]

The idea that people trade off subjective wellbeing against other goals and make choices that they expect to lead to less than maximum wellbeing was tested empirically in choice experiments by Benjamin et al. (2012). Using a variety of choice scenarios and both happiness and life satisfaction as indicators of subjective wellbeing, they found that in 17 percent of cases individuals chose options that they themselves had rated as yielding less wellbeing than the respective alternative options. Differentiating wellbeing into life satisfaction (evaluative wellbeing) and happiness (affective wellbeing), the latter measure was found to be a weaker predictor of choice than the former. Nevertheless, the paper found people's "own happiness" to be the single most important factor in explaining observed choices. Specifically, considering all choice scenarios, the explanatory power in predicting choices increased by just under 8 percent (from 0.38 to 0.41) when a set of 11 other factors were added to own happiness as explanatory variables. The factors that turned out to be the most important were sense of purpose, control over one's life, family happiness and social status.

In evaluating the potential relevance of this study for the relationship between pro-environmental behavior and wellbeing, it is worthwhile considering the choice scenarios in more detail. None of those scenarios involved pro-environmental or pro-social behavior. Among the choices studied, the one that may appear most relevant to the question at hand is that between "money" and "time," as the evaluation of these two options may involve a trade-off between extrinsic and intrinsic motives, similar to environment-related choices. With respect to this choice, adding other explanatory factors to "own happiness" led to an increase in explanatory power by 5 percent (from 0.40 to 0.42). The only other factor found to be significant (at the 5 percent level) was "family happiness."

While those tests involved own happiness and family happiness, it stands to reason that both factors are contributors to a person's life satisfaction. With respect to own happiness, the mediator model of life satisfaction (Suh et al., 1998) and related evidence (Schimmak et al., 2002; Welsch and Kühling, 2016) suggest that people in part directly rely on their affective wellbeing (happiness) when judging life satisfaction. With respect to family happiness, it is difficult to imagine an individual enjoying a high level of life satisfaction while their family is unhappy. Thus, one might conjecture that life satisfaction would perform rather well as the sole predictor of the "money versus time" choice; that is, "family happiness" may have no independent influence on the "time versus money" choice over and above life satisfaction (a proposition not tested).

Returning to the relationship between wellbeing and pro-environmental behavior, it should be recalled that any wellbeing–utility discrepancy may provide an explanation for positive net marginal wellbeing from acting in an environment-friendly way only when other (non-wellbeing) goals are negatively related to environment-friendly behavior. Considering the alternative goals studied by Benjamin et al. (2012) – notably sense of purpose, control over one's life, family happiness and social status – it is difficult to see why such a negative relationship should exist. On the contrary, in light of the typical motives for pro-environmental behaviors, it is likely that those behaviors positively affect sense of purpose (through altruism) or social status (through prestige). Indeed, Laffan (Chapter 18 in this *Handbook*) found sense of purpose to be positively affected by pro-environmental behavior.

Overall, it seems unlikely that goals that: (1) are valid factors for utility, in addition to life satisfaction; and (2) are negatively affected by pro-environmental activities provide an explanation for positive net marginal satisfaction from acting in an environment-friendly way.

19.5 DISCUSSION AND CONCLUSIONS

Research in both environmental psychology and environmental economics has accumulated impressive evidence that engaging in pro-environmental behaviors is associated with greater life satisfaction. While the standard economic model of private public-good provision, which considers only real-world consequences of actions, is unable to explain the occurrence of such behaviors in large populations, accounting for direct psychological benefits of those behaviors provides plausible explanations for their occurrence. Channels through which PEBs may yield such benefits are self-image concerns (yielding a "warm glow" of acting in accordance with a moral norm) as well as prestige, conformity to a social norm, and the satisfaction from interacting with others who engage in similar activities.

Available evidence suggests that all of those channels may play a role in the PEB–wellbeing relationship. In particular, the PEB–wellbeing gradient was found to be larger for PEBs that are more observable, which suggests that prestige may be a relevant factor. In addition, the gradient was found to be larger for more costly behaviors. In combination with observability, this also points to the relevance of prestige motives. However, since not all PEBs that were found to be associated with greater wellbeing are observable, "warm glow" benefits also seem to be involved in the PEB–wellbeing relationship. Finally, evidence that the relationship is stronger for behaviors that are more common and those that involve more social interaction suggest that conformity to a social norm and co-benefits from socialness, respectively, contribute to the wellbeing from engaging in PEBs.

While a positive PEB–wellbeing relationship is theoretically plausible in the light of those psychological channels, it is not immediately clear how the evidence can be squared with rational choice. As with other economic behaviors, rational choice is the default explanatory model for PEBs. As it was argued, the evidence suggests that not just the gross marginal wellbeing from PEBs, but the marginal wellbeing net of marginal costs is positive. This means that people could attain higher levels of wellbeing by behaving in a more environment-friendly way than they do; a result that provides a puzzle from the point of view of rational choice.

Possible explanations for this puzzle are of a methodological nature (involving reverse causation and omitted variables) or a substantive nature (involving boundary solutions, wellbeing–utility discrepancies and decision errors). Regarding methodological explanations, related evidence suggests that omitted variables may be a more relevant concern than reverse causation. Specifically, while one study found a positive PEB–wellbeing relationship to be robust to controlling for conservation-related preferences, another found the PEB–wellbeing relationship to become non-significant when controlling for pro-environmental self-image. Similarly, a potentially confounding variable could be "universalism," as this construct was found to indirectly influence subjective wellbeing through its effect on PEB, whereas it was not tested whether a direct influence of universalism on wellbeing existed and whether the PEB–wellbeing relationship was robust to allowing for such a direct influence.

Regarding substantive explanations of positive net marginal wellbeing from engaging in PEBs, it was argued that explanations in terms of boundary solutions and wellbeing–utility discrepancies are not likely to resolve the puzzle, whereas decision error may well do so. This explanation entails that individuals' choices between standard behaviors and their environment-friendly alternatives are distorted to the disadvantage of the latter due to a systematic bias in forecasting choices' wellbeing consequences. Due to such errors, individuals may end up on the upward-sloping branch of the hill-shaped PEB–wellbeing schedule rather than at its maximum. Consistent with such reasoning, findings of better-educated individuals and those with more experience with PEBs displaying smaller PEB–wellbeing gradients can be interpreted as indicating that those individuals are closer to the wellbeing maximum where PEBs' benefits just balance the associated costs.

It is evident that resolving the "PEB–wellbeing puzzle" has important policy implications. If a positive net marginal wellbeing from PEBs is the result of decision error to the disadvantage of PEBs, it is important to educate people about the wellbeing benefits of behaving in a more environment-friendly way. If it is an artifact of omitted variables (or reverse causation), there may be little potential for such a strategy. This implies that resolving the puzzle is an important direction for future research.

From a policy point of view, another finding from PEB–wellbeing research is worth considering, namely the evidence from one study that more costly PEBs yield greater wellbeing. If this finding can be generalized, it suggests that incentive-based policies that aim at reducing the costs of PEBs may be counterproductive as they may crowd out intrinsic motivations for engaging in PEBs. The robustness and magnitude of the positive cost effect is a further direction for future research.

NOTES

1. The budget constraint captures the financial trade-off between the individual's consumption and their contribution to the public good. In the case of pro-environmental behaviors, one can conceive of a "standard" consumption good and an environment-friendly alternative, available at different costs (Welsch and Kühling, 2011).
2. Similar reasoning has been invoked as one reason for spatial variation in wellbeing (see Chapter 3 in this *Handbook*).

REFERENCES

Aknin, L.B., Hamlin, J.K. and E.W. Dunn (2012), 'Giving leads to happiness in young children', *PLoS One*, **7** (6), e39211.

Aknin, L.B., Dunn, E.W., Whillans, A.V., Grant, A.M. and M.I. Norton (2013), 'Making a difference matters: impact unlocks the emotional benefits of prosocial spending', *Journal of Economic Behavior and Organization*, **88**, 90–95.

Andreoni, J. (1988), 'Privately provided public goods in a large economy: the limits of altruism', *Journal of Public Economics*, **35** (1), 57–73.
Andreoni, J. (1989), 'Giving with impure altruism: applications to charity and Ricardian equivalence', *Journal of Political Economy*, **97** (6), 1447–1458.
Andreoni, J. (1990), 'Impure altruism and donations to public goods: a theory of warm-glow giving', *Economic Journal*, **100** (401), 464–477.
Batson, C.D. and J.L. Weeks (1996), 'Mood effects of unsuccessful helping: another test of the empathy–altruism hypothesis', *Personality and Social Psychology Bulletin*, **22** (2), 148–157.
Benjamin, D.J., Heffetz, O., Kimball, M.S. and A. Rees Jones (2012), 'What do you think would make you happy? What do you think you would choose?', *American Economic Review*, **102** (5), 2083–2110.
Binder, M. and A.-K. Blankenberg (2017), 'Green lifestyles and subjective well-being: more about self-image than actual behavior?', *Journal of Economic Behavior and Organization*, **137**, 304–323.
Brown, K. and T. Kasser (2005), 'Are psychological and ecological well-being compatible? The role of values, mindfulness, and lifestyle', *Social Indicators Research*, **74**, 349–368.
Clark, A.E., Frijters, P. and M.A. Shields (2008), 'Relative income, happiness and utility: an explanation for the easterlin paradox and other puzzles', *Journal of Economic Literature*, **46** (1), 95–144.
Corral-Verdugo, V., Mireles-Acosta, J., Tapia-Fonllem, C. and B. Fraijo-Sing (2011), 'Happiness as correlate of sustainable behavior: a study of pro-ecological, frugal, equitable and altruistic actions that promote subjective well-being', *Human Ecology Review*, **18** (2), 95–104.
Dunn, E.W., Aknin, L.B. and M.I. Norton (2008), 'Spending money on others promotes happiness', *Science*, **319** (5870), 1687–1688.
Farrow, K., Grolleau, G. and L. Ibanez (2017), 'Social norms and pro-environmental behavior: a review of the evidence', *Ecological Economics*, **140**, 1–13.
Harbaugh, W.T. (1998), 'What do donations buy? A model of philanthropy based on prestige and warm glow', *Journal of Public Economics*, **67** (2), 269–284.
Jacob, J., Jovic, E. and M. Brinkerhoff (2009), 'Personal and planetary well-being: mindfulness meditation, pro-environmental behavior and personal quality of life in a survey from the social justice and ecological sustainability movement', *Social Indicators Research*, **93** (2), 275–294.
Kahneman, D., Wakker, P.P. and R. Sarin (1997), 'Back to Bentham? Explorations of experienced utility', *Quarterly Journal of Economics*, **112** (2), 375–406.
Kahneman, D., Krueger, A.B., Schkade, D.A., Schwarz, N. and A.A. Stone (2004), 'A survey method for characterizing daily life experience: the day reconstruction method', *Science*, **306** (5702), 1776–1780.
Kaida, N. and K. Kaida (2016), 'Pro-environmental behavior correlates with present and future subjective well-being', *Environment, Development and Sustainability*, **18** (1), 111–127.
Kühling, Jan (2014), *Nachhaltiger Konsum und individuelle Konsumwahl: Eine Analyse umweltfreundlichen Konsumverhaltens*, Marburg, Germany: Metropolis-Verlag.
Loewenstein, G., O'Donohue, T. and M. Rabin (2003), 'Projection bias in predicting future utility', *Quarterly Journal of Economics*, **118** (4), 1209–1248.
Nelson, S.K., Layous, K., Cole, S.W. and S. Lyubomirsky (2016), 'Do unto others or treat yourself? The effects of prosocial and self-focused behavior on psychological flourishing', *Emotion*, **16** (6), 850–861.
Richins, M.L. (1997), 'Measuring emotions in the consumption experience', *Journal of Consumer Research*, **24** (2), 127–146.
Rucker, D.D. and R.E. Petty (2004), 'Emotion specificity and consumer behavior: anger, sadness, and preference for activity', *Motivation and Emotion*, **28** (1), 3–21.
Schimmak, U., Diener, E. and S. Oishi (2002), 'Life satisfaction is a momentary judgement and a stable personality characteristic: the use of chronically accessible and stable sources', *Journal of Personality*, **70** (3), 345–384.
Schmitt, M.T., Aknin, L.B., Axsen, J. and R.L. Shwom (2018), 'Unpacking the relationships between pro-environmental behavior, life satisfaction, and perceived ecological threat', *Ecological Economics*, **143**, 130–140.
Suárez-Varela, M., Guardiola, J. and F. González-Gómez (2016), 'Do pro-environmental behaviors and awareness contribute to improve subjective well-being?', *Applied Research in Quality of Life*, **11** (2), 429–444.
Suh, E., Diener, E., Oishi, S. and H.C. Triandis (1998), 'The shifting basis of life satisfaction judgements across cultures: emotions versus norms', *Journal of Personality and Social Psychology*, **74** (2), 482–493.
Videras, J.R. and A.L. Owen (2006), 'Public goods provision and well-being: empirical evidence consistent with the warm glow theory', *B.E. Journal of Economic Analysis and Policy*, **5** (1), 1–40.
Welsch, H. and J. Kühling (2010), 'Pro-environmental behavior and rational consumer choice: evidence from surveys of life satisfaction', *Journal of Economic Psychology*, **31** (3), 405–420.
Welsch, H. and J. Kühling (2011), 'Are pro-environmental consumption choices utility maximizing? Evidence from subjective well-being data', *Ecological Economics*, **72**, 75–87.
Welsch, H. and J. Kühling (2016), 'Affective states and the notion of happiness', *Journal of Happiness and Well-Being*, **4**, 101–114.

Welsch, H. and J. Kühling (2018), 'How green self image is related to subjective well-being: green values as a social norm', *Ecological Economics*, **149**, 105–119.
Wilson, Timothy D. and Daniel T. Gilbert (2003), 'Affective forecasting', in Mark P. Zanna (ed.), *Advances in Experimental Social Psychology Vol. 35*, New York, USA: Elsevier, pp. 345–411.
Xiao, J. and H. Li (2011), 'Sustainable consumption and life satisfaction', *Social Indicators Research*, **104** (2), 323–329.

20. How environmental ethics affect the consumption–wellbeing relationship: evidence from Japan*

Tetsuya Tsurumi, Kazuki Kagohashi and Shunsuke Managi

20.1 INTRODUCTION

If developing countries were able to emulate the prevailing consumption patterns of developed countries, the entire world would be on an equal footing in terms of consumer behavior, thereby exacerbating the fears of increasing environmental burdens. Moreover, if consumption in developed countries is maintained at, or continues to rise beyond current levels, the problems will only increase. In order to engender the sustainable consumption advocated in the ongoing discourse on ecological footprints, planetary boundaries and the Sustainable Development Goals (SDGs), current consumption levels in developed countries need to be re-examined. If there is an acknowledgment that an increase in consumption is not related to an increase in the subjective wellbeing at least by people with high environmental ethics, rampant consumption can be mitigated.

Neoclassical economic theory eliminates systematic errors in consumption choice and basically assumes that individuals are able to choose activities and goods whose utility can be maximized (Stutzer and Frey, 2006). Recent research in behavioral economics, however, has shown that specific consumption decisions taken by particular individuals do not maximize their utility, according to the individuals' own evaluation (e.g., Loewenstein and Adler, 1995; Loewenstein and Schkade, 1999; Loewenstein et al., 2003; Wilson and Gilbert, 2003). Stutzer and Frey (2006) mention that, "based on proxy measures for experienced utility, it is, in principle, possible to directly address whether some observed behavior is sub-optimal and is therefore reducing a person's well-being," and suggest that some observed behaviors, such as smoking and eating habits, TV viewing and commuting choice, can be suboptimal and therefore reduce a person's wellbeing.[1] In light of environmental issues, Welsch and Kühling (2010) suggest a positive and statistically significant association between life satisfaction and pro-environmental behavior, which is consistent with environment-friendly consumption being lower than the individual optimal. The above-mentioned literature implies that the consumption–wellbeing relationship may differ according to the difference in people's attitude toward the environment (that is, environmental ethics). Previous empirical literature has not considered the role of environmental ethics on the consumption–wellbeing relationship. This chapter thus investigates how environmental ethics affect the consumption–wellbeing relationship.

Kahneman and Deaton (2010) show that "high income improves evaluation of life but not emotional well-being" using United States (US) data. If there is the same tendency for the consumption–wellbeing relationship, people may endlessly accelerate their consumption to improve their wellbeing (in terms of evaluation of life). Research on happiness economics has focused mainly on the effects of income; relatively little interest has been shown about the effects on happiness of how earnings are spent (Stanca and

Veenhoven, 2015). Indeed, a small number of empirical studies have considered the relationship between consumption and subjective wellbeing (e.g., DeLeire and Kalil, 2010; Dumludag, 2015; Gokdemir, 2015; Headey et al., 2008; Noll and Weick, 2015; Wang et al., 2019; Zhang and Xiong, 2015). Utilizing Chinese data, Wang et al. (2019) find that the total amount of consumption expenditure tends to be positively correlated to life satisfaction; while, utilizing British and Hungarian data, Headey et al. (2008) clarify the positive correlation between life satisfaction and both income and consumption. Using the satisfaction-with-life scale, which is a five-component measure, DeLeire and Kalil (2010) analyze US data for nine consumption categories and measure the influence of these on subjective wellbeing. Among all the measured consumption categories, only one, leisure, shows a positive correlation with subjective wellbeing. Dumludag (2015) analyzes countries at different stages of development in Europe and shows that the relationship between life satisfaction and each consumption category varies in accordance with the development stage. Noll and Weick (2015) investigate the relationship between life satisfaction and amounts of German consumption expenditures in various categories. The results show that life satisfaction rises in some categories but declines in others. Zhang and Xiong (2015) utilize 77 consumption categories and 13 subjective wellbeing indicators to examine the relationship between consumption and subjective wellbeing in Japan. One notable finding in their study is the particularly strong correlation between relational consumption and subjective wellbeing. Gokdemir (2015) reports that, in Turkey, only the consumption of durable goods has a correlation with life satisfaction. Moreover, this result varies depending on personal attributes (for example, gender and age).

In short, the literature on the consumption–wellbeing relationship shows that the consumption–wellbeing relationship may vary according to the type of consumption, personal attributes, the country's stage of development and the country itself. Among the literature on the consumption–wellbeing relationship, our chapter's original aspects are twofold. First, we focus on the role of environmental ethics on the consumption–wellbeing relationship. To the best of our knowledge, this is the first empirical study that investigates the consumption–wellbeing relationship in light of environmental ethics. Second, we hypothesize the non-linearity of the consumption–wellbeing relationship to consider a more flexible functional form than previous literature, which was not considered sufficiently in that literature, by using the generalized additive models.

The rest of this chapter proceeds as follows. Section 20.2 describes the estimation methodology, while section 20.3 presents the results. Section 20.4 shows the extended estimation results using subsamples. Finally, section 20.5 offers the study's conclusions and discusses them.

20.2 ESTIMATION STRATEGY

This study explores the relationship between consumption and life satisfaction.[2] The estimations are calculated by an employing equation (20.1) as follows:

$$SWB_i = c + f(consumption_i) + \sum_j \alpha_j X_{ij} + \varepsilon \tag{20.1}$$

where i represents the individual and SWB_i represents life satisfaction. Further, c is a constant term, consumption is the amount of monthly household expenditure ($), and X_{ij} is a control variable that consists of principal determinants derived from prior literature on subjective wellbeing (that is, age, gender, level of subjective health, education, marriage, presence of children, presence of grandchildren, and personality indicator).[3] Further, since consumption expenditure amounts are reported per household, the control variable includes the number of people in the household. Finally, α_j is the coefficient, while ε is the error term.

This study aims to clearly define the functional forms of consumption; thus, we utilize non-parametric functions for consumption. Regarding the other explanatory variables, we consider parametric functions and thus apply semiparametric regression. In this study, we use generalized additive models (see Hastie and Tibshirani, 1990). We use a cubic spline smoothing[4] iteratively to minimize the partial residuals, which are the residuals after removing the influence of the other variables in the model. In this model, a Bayesian approach is used to derive standard errors and confidence intervals.[5]

With respect to the aforementioned variables, this study relies on data from 9635 subjects who submitted valid responses from a total of 13 690 respondents to our questionnaire survey conducted in March 2017 across Japan.[6] The main variables used in our analysis are summarized in Table 20.1, while Table 20.2 shows the control variables.

In addition to full sample estimation, to consider how environmental ethics affect the consumption–wellbeing relationship, this study addresses subsample estimation. We consider the following six factors that can influence the relationship. They are listed in Table 20.3.

To reveal individual attributes or beliefs that determine each respondent's perception towards the level of the criticality of natural environment, this study adopts the questions related to the viewpoints of environmental ethics (see Table 20.3). Following the previous literature of critical natural capital (e.g., Ekins et al., 2003), we pick up four main perspectives: (1) "irreversibility," which is a physical property of natural capital that cannot be recovered once it is destroyed; (2) "immoderate damage," which denotes the attitude towards the loss of natural capital in the future; (3) "non-substitutability," which denotes the importance of natural capital stock in the physical term by stressing the inability to substitute natural capital with other capital assets such as produced capital and human capital; and (4) "intergenerational equity," which focuses on the equity between current and future generations.

The first three perspectives are deeply related to the concept of "critical natural capital" (CNC), which was firstly proposed by Pearce et al. (1993) as the ecological assets that are essential for human wellbeing and survival (Pearce et al., 1993: 16). This concept obviously focuses on the non-substitutability of natural capital; that is, natural capital cannot be substituted or replaced by other forms of capital stocks. This position is called "strong sustainability" in the literature of sustainable economic development, which claims that Hartwick's rule – the assumption of which is to regards natural capital as substitutable with produced capital assets – is not appropriate especially when it is applied to the natural environment that provides not only the provisioning services but also other essential services such as regulating, cultural or supporting services (e.g., Daly, 1974; Georgescu-Roegen, 1971; Pearce and Atkinson, 1993: 103; Victor, 1991: 210; Neumayer, 2003).

Table 20.1 Survey questions for life satisfaction and consumption

	Survey question	Notes
Life satisfaction	Overall, how satisfied are you with your life? Responses are given on an integer scale from 1 (not at all satisfied) to 5 (completely satisfied).	5 = completely satisfied, 1 = not at all satisfied; five-point scale (standardized: 0 to 1)
Monthly household consumption expenditure: unit ($)*	Overall, approximately how much does your household spend monthly on consumption? Please see the consumption categories under "Reference" and include all expenses before answering this question. * Reference. Consumption categories in the Public Opinion Survey on the Life of the People conducted by the Cabinet Office in Japan: Clothing apparel (clothes and shoes) Food expenses (foodstuffs and dining costs) Housing expenses (loans, rent, land fees, equipment repairs/maintenance expenses, construction, other housing-related services, and utility fees) Durable consumer goods (electrical appliances, furniture, bedding, automobiles/motorcycles/bicycles, etc.) Miscellaneous expenses (sundries, consumables, and hairdressing) Medical expenses Transportation expenses Social expenses Insurance Communications expenses (postage, mobile phone, and Internet) Educational expenses Entertainment expenses	

Note: * In our survey questionnaire, we use Japanese yen as a currency unit. We use the exchange rate $1=111.31 yen (averaged exchange rate during survey periods) to transform yen into dollars.

The framework to identify CNC was elaborated by Ekins et al. (2003), in which the distinctive features of CNC are recognized as the non-substitutability of natural capital and the services and functions therefrom, the irreversibility of the loss of natural capital, and the immoderate damage occurred by the loss of natural capital. Ekins et al. set "important environmental functions" that cannot be replaced or substituted by other services from produced or human capital, and/or the loss of which is irreversible, and/or the damage from the loss of natural capital is immoderate (that is, the social cost from that is unacceptably high). These are the conditions of criticality of natural capital defined under the service flow from natural capital. In addition to these conditions, the classical

Table 20.2 Definition of control variables

Variables	Survey question	Notes
Age	Please tell us your age.	Unit: years old.
Gender	Please tell us your gender.	Male dummy (1: man, 0: woman).
Subjective health	All in all, how would you describe your state of health?	4: very good, 3: good, 2: poor, 1: very poor; four-point scale.
Education	Please tell us your highest academic qualification (if a student, please tell us which school you graduated from most recently).	College graduate and above dummy (college graduate and above: 1, others: 0).
Marriage	Are you married?	Marriage dummy (1: married, 0: others).
Children	Do you have children?	"Presence of children" dummy (1: yes, 0: no).
Grandchildren	Do you have grandchildren?	"Presence of grandchildren" dummy (1: yes, 0: no).
Big five personality domains	Big five personality traits taken from the Ten-Item Personality Inventory (TIPI) proposed by Gosling et al. (2003).	Five types of indicators: extroversion, agreeableness, neuroticism, conscientiousness, and openness to experience.

definition of the non-substitutability of natural capital – both within the category of natural capital and between natural capital and other forms of capital stocks – is also set in Ekins et al. (2003). These conditions of CNC are refrained in Ekins (2014) as well as Ekins et al. (2003).

The questions on the perspectives of irreversibility and immoderate damage, which can be categorized by "threat" (de Groot et al., 2003) arising from the loss of natural capital, are to ask each respondent's perception on the possibility of restoration of natural capital after it is destroyed and on the degree how the damage from the loss of natural environment is immoderate (that is, unacceptably high). These criteria can determine each respondent's attitude toward the future. If a repondent regards the loss of natural capital as "reversible" and the damage from that as "not immoderate," then they may no longer express their willingness to conserve natural capital for the future generations. We elaborated the questions to reveal each respondent's perception on irreversibility (whether one agrees with the notion that "Once destroyed, the natural environment can never be restored to its prior state") and immoderate damage ("If things go on this way, there will be enormous environmental destruction and disasters in the future").

By "non-substitutability," we ask for each respondent's perception on the importance of the environmental functions and services. If a respondent agrees with the question (that is, we can overcome the negative effect even if the natural environment has been destroyed), they should not perceive the environmental functions and services as important, and vice versa. If a respondent reveals that natural capital is non-substitutable, and the loss of it is irreversible and immoderate, they regard the natural capital as critical (that is, CNC).

The criteria of non-substitutability of natural capital and intergenerational equity are intertwined. On the topic of intergenerational equity, there have been extensive economic

Table 20.3 Definition of environmental ethics

	Definition	Notes
Irreversibility	Please tell us whether you agree with the following: "Once destroyed, the natural environment can never be restored to its prior state." (Sample selecting "Agree": N = 3027)	Observations: Agree = 3027, Somewhat agree = 4467, Somewhat disagree = 1775, Disagree = 366
Immoderate damage	Please tell us whether you agree with the following: "If things go on this way, there will be enormous environmental destruction and disasters in the future." (Sample selecting "Agree": N = 3438)	Observations: Agree = 3438, Somewhat agree = 4747, Somewhat disagree = 1271, Disagree = 179
Non-substitutability	Please tell us whether you agree with the following: "Even if the natural environment is destroyed, technology and human ingenuity will overcome any resulting problems." (Sample selecting "Disagree": N = 2486)	Observations: Agree = 333, Somewhat agree = 2146, Somewhat disagree = 4670, Disagree = 2486
Intergenerational equity	Please tell us whether you agree with the following: "We must pass on to future generations the natural and cultural legacy we have received from prior generations." (Sample selecting "Agree": N = 2967)	Observations: Agree = 2967, Somewhat agree = 5530, Somewhat disagree =1015, Disagree =123
Intergenerational equity (with the cost of sacrifices)	Please tell us whether you agree with the following: "Even at the cost of sacrifices from our generation, we must leave behind a natural environment in good shape for future generations." (Sample selecting "Agree": N = 1836)	Observations: Agree = 1836, Somewhat agree = 5930, Somewhat disagree = 1607, Disagree = 262
Intergenerational equity (temporal discounting rate)	"Please tell us if you would prefer to receive ¥10 000 today or a certain amount two weeks later. Please select A or B from each pair of choices provided." ("Discounting rate = 0"; Sample: N = 1732)	Discounting rate = 0, 1, 2, 5, 10, 40, 70 or 100

analyses from the 1970s in the literature of sustainable economic development (e.g., Dasgupta and Heal, 1974; Hartwick, 1977, 1978a, 1978b; Solow, 1986, 1974; Stiglitz, 1974). These researches are focusing on the possibility of long-term economic growth concordant with the condition of intergenerational equity. Solow (1986) showed that the Hartwick's rule – investing the rents from natural capital into the accumulation of produced capital to maintain the production output – can be theoretically interpreted as holding the total capital stock intact to pass on it for the sake of future generations (Hartwick, 1994; Pearce et al., 1994; Solow, 1986). This theory underpins the paradigm of "weak sustainability" in which natural capital is regarded as substitutable to other forms of capital (cf. strong sustainability).

To investigate in depth each respondent's attitude on intergenerational equity, we set

Table 20.4 Basic statistics

Variable	Number of observations	Mean	Standard deviation	Minimum	Maximum
Life satisfaction (standardized: 0 to 1)	9635	0.571	0.263	0	1
Total monthly household expenditure (unit: $)	9635	1715	997	224	4938
Male dummy	9635	0.583	0.493	0	1
Age	9635	49.5	11.2	18	75
Subjective health	9635	2.79	0.778	1	4
Marriage dummy	9635	0.698	0.459	0	1
Children dummy	9635	0.603	0.489	0	1
Number of persons in household	9635	2.70	1.26	1	10
Grandchildren dummy	9635	0.141	0.348	0	1
College graduate or above dummy	9635	0.502	0.500	0	1
Extroversion	9635	1.86	0.635	1	3
Agreeableness	9635	2.39	0.508	1	3
Neuroticism	9635	2.15	0.574	1	3
Conscientiousness	9635	1.96	0.588	1	3
Openness to experience	9635	2.00	0.547	1	3

three questions on it. First, we ask each respondent's valuation of the cultural services from natural capital by the question "We must pass on to future generations the natural and cultural legacy we have received from prior generations" (the fifth row in Table 20.3). The cultural services from natural capital such as the historical and natural landscape are deemed as critical in the literature of CNC, in that the criticality of natural capital should include the importance of cultural services (Chiesura and de Groot, 2003; Ekins et al., 2003; Turner et al., 1994). Second, by the question "Even at the cost of sacrifices from our generation, we must leave behind a natural environment in good shape for future generations" (which is labeled as "Intergenerational equity (with the cost of sacrifices)" in Table 20.3), we ask whether each respondent agrees with the paradigm of "strong sustainability" which requires maintaining natural capital stocks for the sake of future generations. This question is also related to environmental justice, which appears in the literature of environmental ethics (e.g., Dobson, 1998). Third, the question on the temporal discounting rate (labeled as "Intergenerational equity (temporal discounting rate)" in Table 20.3) is also included to investigate each respondent's intertemporal time preference from the economic point of view. The basic statistical values for the full sample are shown in Table 20.4.

20.3 ESTIMATION RESULTS

The estimation results of functional form of consumption for the full sample are shown in Figure 20.1.[7] Total monthly household consumption expenditure (unit: $) is on the

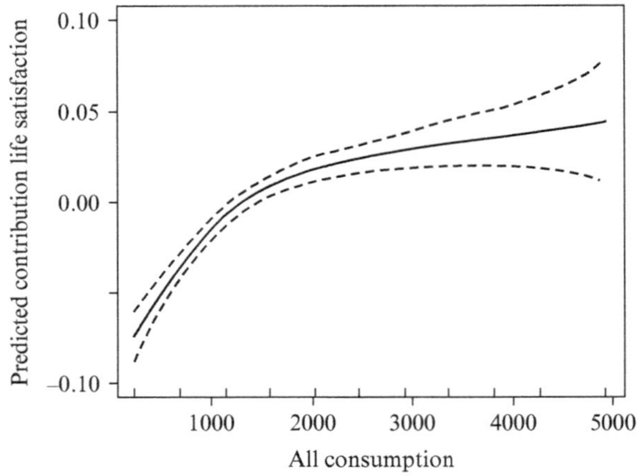

Note: The vertical axis represents the predicted contribution to life satisfaction, while the horizontal axis represents the monthly household consumption expenditure (unit: $). The solid lines constitute the non-parametric function curves, while the dotted lines denote the 95% confidence interval.

Figure 20.1 Relationship between consumption and life satisfaction in the full sample

Table 20.5 Predicted contribution to life satisfaction at moderately high and high consumption levels and model fit statistics (full sample)

	Predicted contribution to life satisfaction (Moderately high: $3000)	Predicted contribution to life satisfaction (High: $5000)	Approximate significance of smooth term of equation (1): F statistics	R squared
Full sample	0.0291	0.0441	30.06***	0.285

Note: *, ** and *** indicate "significant" at the 10% level, the 5% level and the 1% level, respectively.

horizontal axis, while the subjective wellbeing indicator, life satisfaction, is on the vertical axis. The solid line is the estimated consumption function curve, while the dotted lines represent the 95 percent confidence intervals. The "0" on the vertical axis denotes the sample's average subjective wellbeing. Table 20.5 shows predicted contribution to life satisfaction at moderately high and high consumption levels and model fit statistics. We find the smooth term ($f(consumption)$) of equation (20.1) to be statistically significant. We also find that predicted contribution to life satisfaction continues to increase as consumption levels increase, which suggests that there is no satiation point for consumption even at a moderately high consumption level ($3000) and a high consumption level ($5000).

As mentioned in the introduction, if there is an acknowledgment that an increase in consumption is not related with an increase in subjective wellbeing, rampant consumption can be mitigated. However, our result implies that people are not satisfied with the current level of consumption even at moderately high or high levels of consumption expenditure, which may accelerate future consumption in Japan.

Next, Figure 20.2 shows the estimated functional forms of consumption for each subsample, while Table 20.6 shows each sample's predicted contribution to life satisfaction at moderately high ($3000) and high ($5000) consumption levels and model fit statistics. We omit parameter estimates of control variables because they are almost the same as that of the full sample. It is notable that the result implies that there are satiation points in the cases of irreversibility, intergenerational equity, intergenerational equity (with the cost of sacrifices), and intergenerational equity (temporal discounting rate), which is not observed for the full sample. We show the satiation points' consumption expenditures ($) for these samples in Table 20.6.

20.4 EXTENSION

Our estimation results imply that environmental ethics related with future generation or irreversibility can have a crucial role in the existence of saturation points. In this section, we extend the concept of environmental ethics to broader concepts. Specifically, we investigate how the following four factors affect the consumption–wellbeing relationship:

1. Generational cohort.
2. "The best possible life for you"; leading a simple life with minimal material possessions.
3. Belief in the Confucian precept that "a contented mind is a perpetual feast."
4. Maslow's hierarchy of needs.

The first factor, generational cohort, is included to determine whether a change of attitude can be detected in a group that has experienced material abundance.[8] The second and third factors are also related to material abundance. The fourth factor focuses on Maslow's hierarchy of needs: once material needs are sufficiently satisfied, people may change their attitudes to consumption. The list of the above five factors is shown in Table 20.7.

Figure 20.3 and Table 20.8 show the results of the predicted consumption–wellbeing relationship. First, when classified by generational cohort, only the group aged in their forties, who experienced Japan's high economic growth in their childhoods (the 1970s and 1980s) and then the collapse of the bubble economy (in the early 1990s), shows satiation points ($2326). For those of the younger generation (in their thirties and younger), who have less experience of superfluous consumption, and the subsamples in their fifties or older, who presumably have abundant consumption experience, an increase in consumption tends to be linked to greater predicted contributions to life satisfaction. The results imply that all those who have experienced mass consumption do not necessarily feel that material abundance is meaningless.

Results show that there exists a satiation point in the subsample in which the respondents answered that the best possible life is "leading a simple life with minimal material possessions" and the subsample who supported the Confucian precepts which advocate a way of life that is content with less consumption without expanding one's desires. Those who expressed satisfaction in each step of Maslow's hierarchy of needs also show satiation

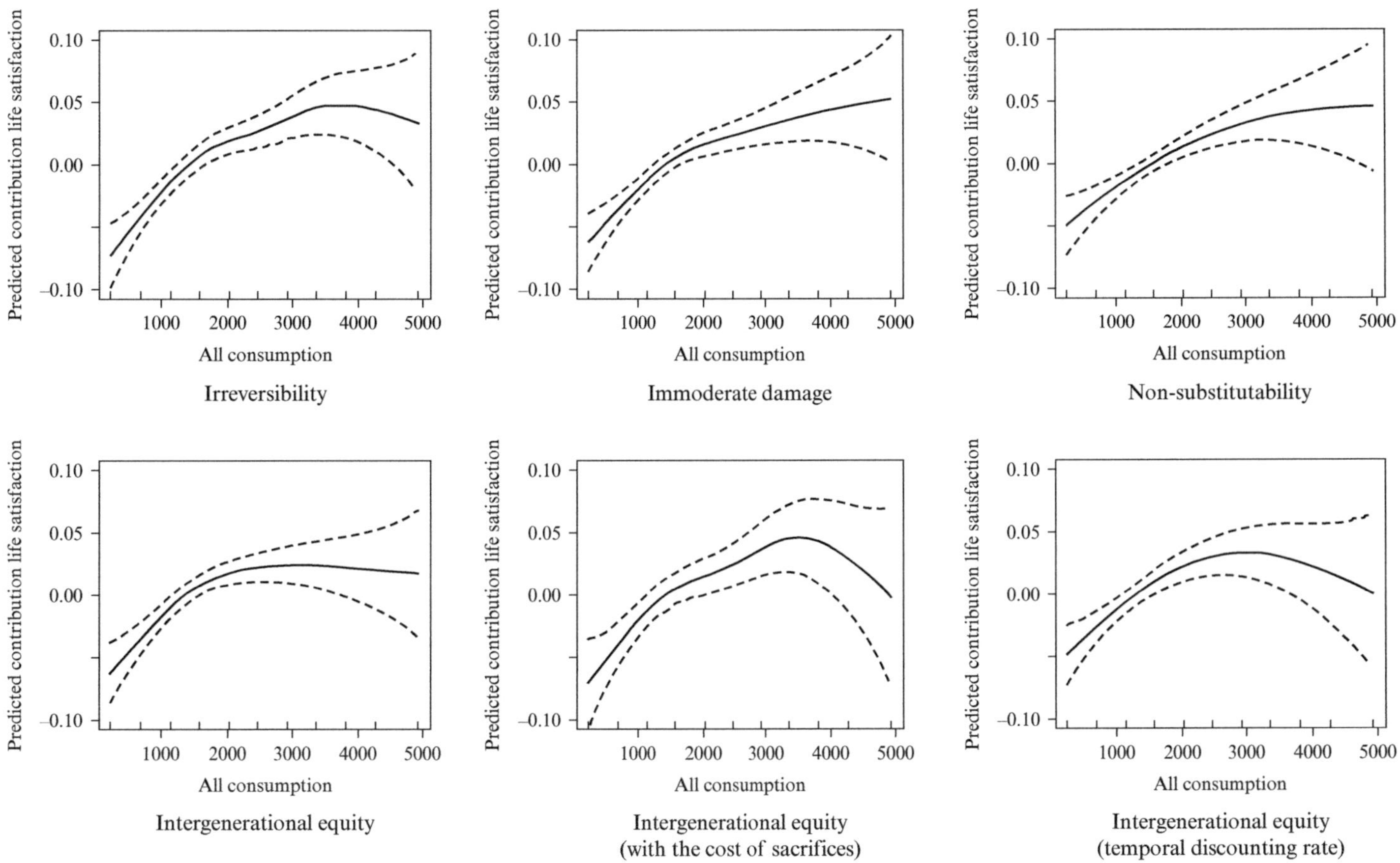

Note: See Figure 20.1.

Figure 20.2 Relationship between consumption and life satisfaction in the sub-sample

Table 20.6 Predicted contribution to life satisfaction at moderately high and high consumption level, satiation point, and model fit statistics (subsample)

Subsample with regard to environmental ethics	Predicted contribution to life satisfaction (Moderately high: \$3000)	Predicted contribution to life satisfaction (High: \$5000)	Satiation point for monthly consumption expenditure (\$)	Approximate significance of smooth term of equation (1): F statistics	R squared
Irreversibility	0.0433	0.0368	3721	12.12***	0.287
Immoderate damage	0.0359	0.0578	–	12.08***	0.287
Non-substitutability	0.0343	0.0482	–	9.898***	0.291
Intergenerational equity	0.0269	0.0188	3205	9.148***	0.288
Intergenerational equity (with the cost of sacrifices)	0.0433	−0.00045	3488	6.423***	0.254
Intergenerational equity (Temporal discounting rate)	0.0335	−0.0000059	3006	7.101***	0.268

Note: *, ** and *** indicate "significant" at the 10% level, the 5% level and the 1% level, respectively.

points. In particular, the graph of those who professed fulfillment of their need for love (belonging) demonstrates a notable negative slope after the satiation point (\$3604). We note we also find negative slopes in the case of "Intergenerational equity (with the cost of sacrifices)" in Figure 20.2. The reason why we find a negative slope in the case of those who professed fulfillment of their need for love (belonging) could be that people who are satisfied with love (belonging) tend to place a relatively high value on future generations or intergenerational equity.

20.5 CONCLUSIONS

Our estimation results show that, although there are no satiation points concerning the consumption–wellbeing relationship for people in Japan on average, there are satiation points for people who have the perspectives on environmental ethics concerning irreversibility or intergenerational equity. It is also notable that there is no satiation point for people who have environmental ethics concerning immoderate damage or non-substitutability. We thus need to acknowledge that, even if we merely recognize the seriousness of environmental problems (that is, immoderate damage), it is difficult to change our consumption–wellbeing relationship. We also need to acknowledge the difference between irreversibility and non-substitutability. The former is related to the loss of the very existence of natural capital, while the latter is related to the loss of the function of natural capital. We also note that our estimation results suggest that holding a perspective

Table 20.7 Definition of factors related with environmental ethics

	Definition	Notes
Generational cohort	Age: 30s and younger, 40s, 50s, 60s and older	Observations: 30s and younger = 1987; 40s = 2866; 50s = 2582; 60s and older = 2200
"The best possible life for you"; leading a simple life with minimal material possessions	Which of the following statements best describes your "ideal life"? Please choose all of those (as many as you wish) that describe your ideal life (sample selecting "Living a simple life with minimal material possessions": N = 2752).	
Belief in the Confucian teaching that "a contented mind is a perpetual feast"	Belief in Confucian Precepts Question: "A contented mind is a perpetual feast" is a Confucian teaching. In other words, "Human desires are endless, but a person who is satisfied living within one's means and does not crave for more is happy and rich. A person who is pleased with today and has no complaints about the present is blessed with a life of contentment." Do you believe in this teaching? (sample selecting "I believe in it": N = 3541)	Observations: I believe in it = 3541; I more or less believe in it = 5106; I more or less do not believe in it = 780; I do not believe in it = 208
Maslow's hierarchy of needs (basic needs, safety, love, esteem, self-actualization)	How satisfied are your needs at the following stage? Stage 1 (basic needs); sample selecting "Satisfied": N = 3323 Stage 2 (safety); sample selecting "Satisfied": N = 2515 Stage 3 (love); sample selecting "Satisfied": N = 1393 Stage 4 (esteem); sample selecting "Satisfied": N = 881 Stage 5 (self-actualization); sample selecting "Satisfied": N = 744	Stage 1, physiological needs: satisfied = 3323; more or less satisfied = 4955; more or less dissatisfied = 1060; dissatisfied = 297 Stage 2, safety (a secure and healthy life): satisfied = 2515; more or less satisfied = 5284; more or less dissatisfied = 1438; dissatisfied = 398 Stage 3, love (belonging): satisfied = 1393; more or less satisfied = 5178; more or less dissatisfied = 2446; dissatisfied = 618 Stage 4, esteem (respect from others): satisfied = 881; more or less satisfied = 5080; more or less dissatisfied = 2941; dissatisfied = 733 Stage 5, self-actualization (drawing on one's capabilities to engage in creative activities): satisfied = 744; more or less satisfied = 4422; more or less dissatisfied = 3414; dissatisfied = 1055

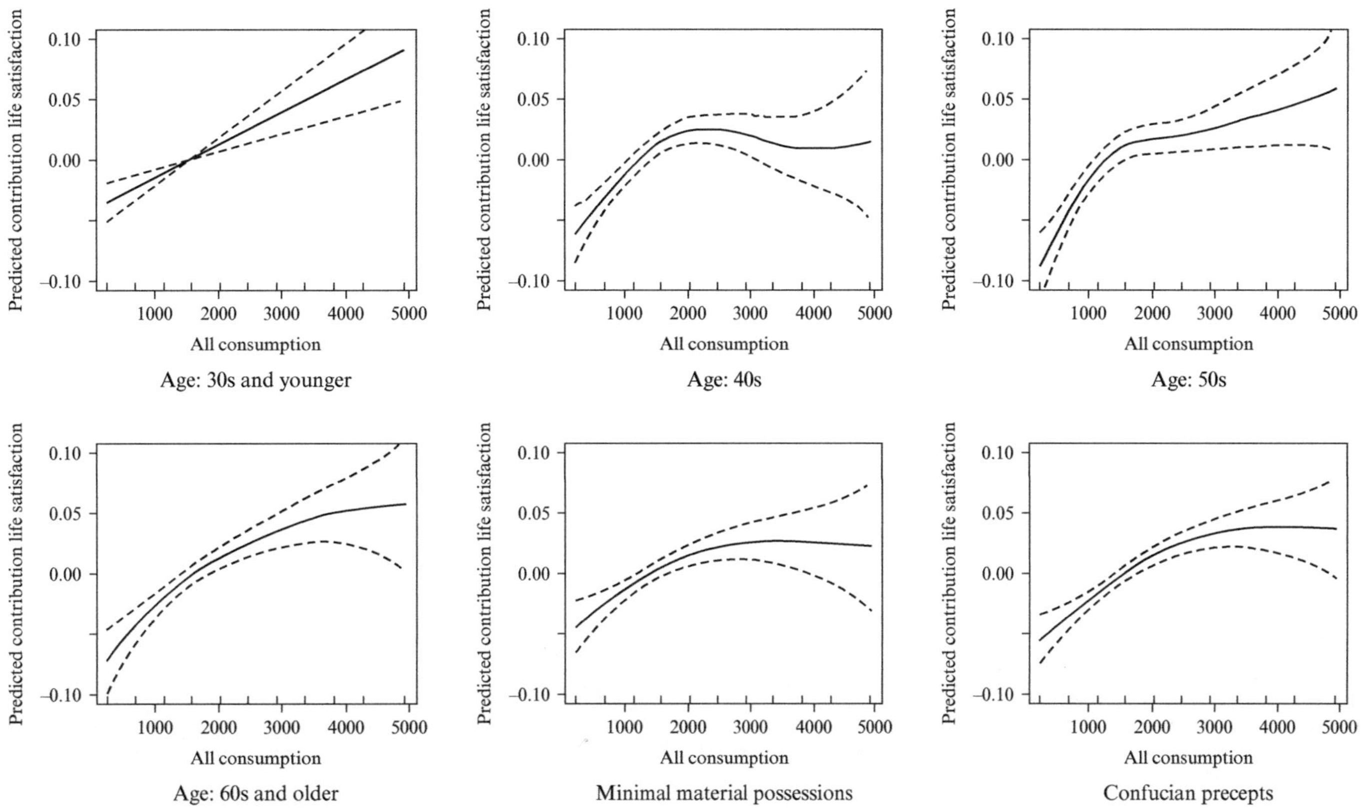

Note: See Figure 20.1.

Figure 20.3 Relationship between consumption and life satisfaction in the extended subsample

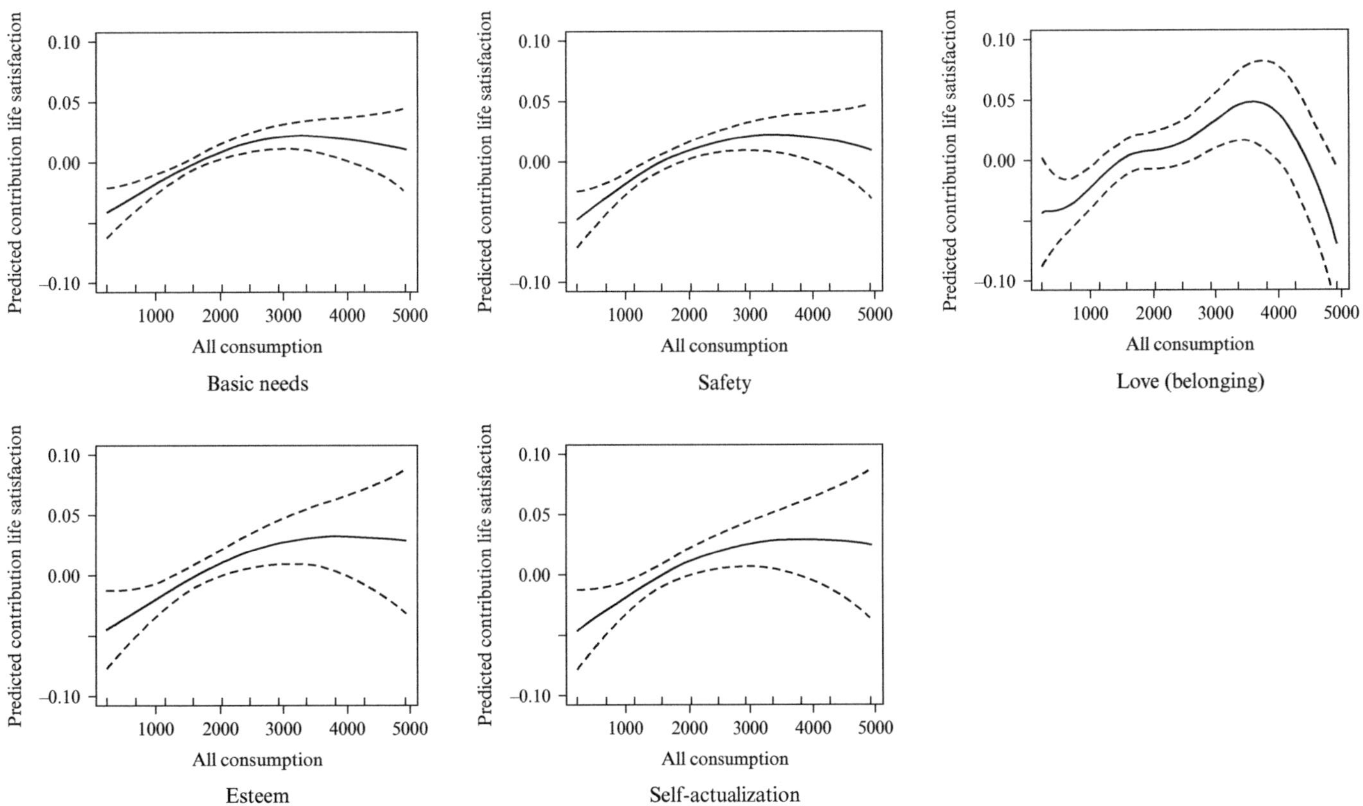

Figure 20.3 (continued)

Table 20.8 Predicted contribution to life satisfaction at moderately high and high consumption level, satiation point, and model fit statistics (extended subsample)

Subsample	Predicted contribution to life satisfaction (Moderately high: $3000)	Predicted contribution to life satisfaction (High: $5000)	Satiation point for monthly consumption expenditure ($)	Approximate significance of smooth term of equation (1): F statistics	R squared
Age: 30s and younger	0.0401	0.0935	–	19.63***	0.294
Age: 40s	0.0158	0.0110	2326	9.305***	0.288
Age: 50s	0.0242	0.0572	–	11.24***	0.287
Age: 60s and older	0.0406	0.0614	–	13.5***	0.247
Minimal material possessions	0.0298	0.0254	3363	7.7***	0.255
Confucian precepts	0.0348	0.0390	4111	15.66***	0.250
Basic needs	0.0250	0.0134	3308	8.836***	0.207
Safety	0.0297	0.0169	3401	7.955***	0.166
Love (belonging)	0.0403	−0.0719	3604	5.692***	0.224
Esteem	0.0320	0.0321	3882	4.326**	0.298
Self-actualization	0.0282	0.0278	3847	4.159*	0.281

Note: *, ** and *** indicate "significant" at the 10% level, the 5% level and the 1% level, respectively.

of intergenerational equity robustly affects one's consumption–wellbeing relationship, because all three kinds of subsamples concerning intergenerational equity show satiation points. We further note, as we have already shown in the previous section, that people who professed fulfillment of their need for love (belonging) demonstrate notable satiation points. There would be some overlaps among the respondents who are satisfied with love (belonging) and who put stress on the interests of future generations, since the idea of love (belonging) is one form of altruism which can be applied not only to the current generation, but also to future generations.

To sum up, our results imply that from the point of view of environmental ethics it is necessary for us to promote the concepts of intergenerational equity and irreversibility, rather than the concepts of non-substitutability or immoderate damage, to mitigate rampant consumption.

NOTES

* This research was supported by the Environment Research and Technology Development Fund (S-16) of the Ministry of the Environment, Japan.

1. For a comprehensive review of subjective well-being, see Tsurumi and Managi (2015, 2017) and Tsurumi et al. (2018).
2. For our robustness check, we use not only life satisfaction but also Cantril ladder and eudaimonia as indicators of life evaluation, which is in accordance with Kahneman and Deaton (2010). The estimation results are almost the same as life satisfaction.
3. In the panel data, it is possible to consider the fixed effects from individuals in order to discount personality and temperament. However, because this study utilizes cross-sectional data, it is not possible to consider the fixed effects of individual attributes. When questions regarding life satisfaction are answered, the statistical dispersion from the choice of either positive or negative responses may cause a response bias. In order to account for this dispersion, the indicators reflecting personality are subsumed in the explanatory variables.
4. When we used the loess function instead of the cubic spline function, the results were almost the same.
5. Our estimation technique follows Wood (2004, 2008).
6. There were a total of 13690 respondents. After eliminating samples responding "I don't know/I don't want to answer this question" to questions regarding consumption, and samples deemed incompatible based on criteria established to weed out invalid responses, 9635 eligible subjects remained.
7. We show parameter estimated of control variables in Table 20A.1, Appendix 20A.1. The results are consistent with the literature.
8. With regard to the first factor, the Opinion Survey on the Quality of Life of the People conducted every year by the Cabinet Office in Japan serves as a reference. After World War II, Japan experienced a period of high economic growth at annual rates exceeding 10 percent. Eventually, Japan casts off its post-war status as a developing country to join the ranks of the world's developed countries. Until the first half of the 1970s, which are considered the peak years of Japan's high economic growth, most people valued material over spiritual wealth. However, from the latter half of the 1970s, a growing trend in the opposite direction has been observed (Government of Japan, 2016). It can be said that, after experiencing mass consumption, a certain segment of the population had begun to feel emptiness in the midst of material abundance.

REFERENCES

Chiesura, A. and R. De Groot (2003), 'Critical natural capital: a socio-cultural perspective', *Ecological Economics*, **44** (2–3), 219–231.

Daly, H.E. (1974), 'The economics of the steady state', *American Economic Review*, **64** (2), 15–21.

Dasgupta, P. and G. Heal (1974), 'The optimal depletion of exhaustible resources', *Review of Economic Studies*, **41**, 3–28.

De Groot, R., Van der Perk, J., Chiesura, A. and A. Van Vliet (2003), 'Importance and threat as determining factors for criticality of natural capital', *Ecological Economics*, **44** (2–3), 187–204.

DeLeire, T. and A. Kalil (2010), 'Does consumption buy happiness? Evidence from the United States', *International Review of Economics*, **57** (2), 163–176.

Dobson, Andrew (ed.) (1998), *Justice and the Environment: Conceptions of Environmental Sustainability and Theories of Distributive Justice*, Oxford, UK: Oxford University Press.

Dumludag, D. (2015), 'Consumption and life satisfaction at different levels of economic development', *International Review of Economics*, **62** (2), 163–182.

Ekins, P. (2014), 'Strong sustainability and critical natural capital', in Giles Atkinson, Simon Dietz, Eric Neumayer and Matthew Agarwala (eds), *Handbook of Sustainable Development*, 2nd edn, Cheltenham, UK and Northampton, MA, USA: Edward Elgar Publishing, pp. 55–71.

Ekins, P., Simon, S., Deutsch, L., Folke, C. and R. De Groot (2003), 'A framework for the practical application of the concepts of critical natural capital and strong sustainability', *Ecological Economics*, **44** (2–3), 165–185.

Georgescu-Roegen, N. (ed.) (1971), *The Entropy Law and the Economic Process*, Cambridge, MA, USA: Harvard University Press.

Gokdemir, O. (2015), 'Consumption, savings and life satisfaction: the Turkish case', *International Review of Economics*, **62** (2), 183–196.

Government of Japan (2016), 'Overview of the Public Opinion Survey on the Life of the People'. Accessed April 4, 2019 at https://www.gov-online.go.jp/eng/pdf/summaryk16.pdf.

Hartwick, J.M. (1977), 'Intergenerational equity and the investing of rents from exhaustible resources', *American Economic Review*, **67** (5), 972–974.

Hartwick, J.M. (1978a), 'Investing returns from depleting renewable resource stocks and intergenerational equity', *Economics Letters*, **1** (1), 85–88.
Hartwick, J.M. (1978b), 'Substitution among exhaustible resources and intergenerational equity', *Review of Economic Studies*, **45** (2), 347–354.
Hartwick, J.M. (1994), 'National wealth and net national product', *Scandinavian Journal of Economics*, **96** (2), 253–256.
Hastie, T.J. and R.J. Tibshirani (eds) (1990), *Generalized Additive Models*, New York, USA: Chapman & Hall.
Headey, B., Muffels, R. and M. Wooden (2008), 'Money does not buy happiness: or does it? A reassessment based on the combined effects of wealth, income and consumption', *Social Indicators Research*, **87** (1), 65–82.
Kahneman, D. and A. Deaton (2010), 'High income improves evaluation of life but not emotional well-being', *PNAS*, **107** (38), 16489–16493.
Loewenstein, G. and D. Adler (1995), 'A bias in the prediction of tastes', *Economic Journal*, **105** (431), 929–937.
Loewenstein, G. and D.A. Schkade (1999), 'Wouldn't it be nice? Predicting future feelings', in Daniel Kahneman, Ed Diener and Norbert Schwarz (eds), *Well-Being: The Foundation of Hedonic Psychology*, New York, NY, USA: Russell Sage Foundation, pp. 85–105.
Loewenstein, G., O'Donoghue, T. and M. Rabin (2003), 'Projection bias in predicting future utility', *Quarterly Journal of Economics*, **118** (4), 1209–1248.
Neumayer, E. (ed.) (2003), *Weak versus Strong Sustainability: Exploring the Limits of Two Opposing Paradigms*, Cheltenham, UK and Northampton, MA, USA: Edward Elgar Publishing.
Noll, H.H. and S. Weick (2015), 'Consumption expenditures and subjective well-being: empirical evidence from Germany', *International Review of Economics*, **62** (2), 101–119.
Pearce, D.W. and G.D. Atkinson (1993), 'Capital theory and the measurement of sustainable development: an indicator of "weak" sustainability', *Ecological Economics*, **8** (2), 103–108.
Pearce, D.W., Atkinson, G.D. and W.R. Dubourg (1994), 'The economics of sustainable development', *Annual Review of Energy and the Environment*, **19** (1), 457–474.
Pearce, D., Turner, R.K., O'Riordan, T., Adger, N., Atkinson, G., Brisson, I., et al. (eds) (1993), *Blueprint 3: Measuring Sustainable Development*, London, UK: Earthscan.
Solow, R.M. (1974), 'Intergenerational equity and exhaustible resources', *Review of Economic Studies*, **41**, 29–45.
Solow, R.M. (1986), 'On the intergenerational allocation of natural resources', *Scandinavian Journal of Economics*, **88** (1), 141–149.
Stanca, L. and R. Veenhoven (2015), 'Consumption and happiness: an introduction', *International Review of Economics*, **62** (2), 91–99.
Stiglitz, J. (1974), 'Growth with exhaustible natural resources: efficient and optimal growth', *Review of Economic Studies*, **41**, 123–137.
Stutzer, A. and B.S. Frey (2006), 'What happiness research can tell us about self-control problems and utility misprediction', IZA Discussion Paper No. 1952.
Tsurumi, T. and S. Managi (2015), 'Environmental value of green spaces in Japan: an application of the life satisfaction approach', *Ecological Economics*, **120**, 1–12.
Tsurumi, T. and S. Managi (2017), 'Monetary valuations of life conditions in a consistent framework: the life satisfaction approach', *Journal of Happiness Studies*, **18** (5), 1275–1303.
Tsurumi, T., Imauji, A. and S. Managi (2018), 'Greenery and well-being: assessing the monetary value of greenery by type', *Ecological Economics*, **148**, 152–169.
Turner, R.K., Pearce, D.W. and I.J. Bateman (eds) (1994), *Environmental Economics: An Elementary Introduction*, New York: Harvester Wheatsheaf.
Victor, P.A. (1991), 'Indicators of sustainable development: some lessons from capital theory', *Ecological Economics*, **4** (3), 191–213.
Wang, H., Cheng, Z. and R. Smyth (2019), 'Consumption and happiness', *Journal of Development Studies*, **55** (1), 120–136.
Welsch, H. and J. Kühling (2010), 'Pro-environmental behavior and rational consumer choice: evidence from surveys of life satisfaction', *Journal of Economic Psychology*, **31** (3), 405–420.
Wilson, T.D. and D.T. Gilbert (2003), 'Affective forecasting', *Advances in Experimental Social Psychology*, **35** (35), 345–411.
Wood, S.N. (2004), 'Stable and efficient multiple smoothing parameter estimation for generalized additive models', *Journal of the American Statistical Association*, **99** (467), 673–686.
Wood, S.N. (2008), 'Fast stable direct fitting and smoothness selection for generalized additive models', *Journal of the Royal Statistical Society: Series B (Statistical Methodology)*, **70** (3), 495–518.
Zhang, J. and Y. Xiong (2015), 'Effects of multifaceted consumption on happiness in life: a case study in Japan based on an integrated approach', *International Review of Economics*, **62** (2), 143–162.

APPENDIX 20A.1

Table 20A.1 Parameter estimates of control variables for full sample

Variables	Parameter estimates
Male dummy	−0.029***
	(0.005)
Age	−0.0005
	(0.0003)
Subjective health	0.128***
	(0.003)
Marriage dummy	0.086***
	(0.007)
Children dummy	0.004
	(0.007)
Number of persons in household	−0.004
	(0.002)
Grandchildren dummy	0.024**
	(0.008)
College graduate or above dummy	0.039***
	(0.005)
Extraversion	0.023***
	(0.004)
Agreeableness	0.016***
	(0.005)
Conscientiousness	0.013**
	(0.004)
Neuroticism	−0.029***
	(0.004)
Openness to experience	0.003
	(0.004)
Constant term	0.117***
	(0.026)
Obs.	9635

Note: *, **, and *** indicate "significant" at the 10% level, the 5% level and the 1% level, respectively. Standard errors are in parenthesis.

21. An empirical assessment of the indigenous *Sumak Kawsay* (living well): the importance of nature and relationships*

Carmen Amelia Coral-Guerrero, Jorge Guardiola and Fernando García-Quero

21.1 INTRODUCTION

The indigenous philosophy and way of life *Sumak Kawsay* ("living well" in Kichwa) is related to several principles of life such as reciprocity, solidarity, respect, complementarity, dignity, collective participation and social justice, set within an overall sense of harmony with Mother Nature and with the community (CELADE, 2014). Although there are similar philosophies in the Andes, *Sumak Kawsay* is mainly found in Ecuador. Due to the importance of this philosophy for indigenous people, it played an important role not only in the Constitution of Ecuador, but also in the country's development plans from 2008 onwards.

The environment and relationships are key in *Sumak Kawsay*, a philosophy that offers a holistic vision of life in which everything is interconnected (Maldonado, 2010b; Medina, 2001). Therefore, it offers a particular idea of what happiness is. In this chapter we explore this idea by addressing the importance of *Sumak Kawsay* in people's subjective wellbeing (SWB) using a representative sample of Ecuador for 2017 comprising 7478 households. To do so, we estimate a standard happiness model, including satisfaction with life and satisfaction with the environment as measures of SWB.

In order to proxy the complexity of *Sumak Kawsay*, we propose several variables that are related to this way of life. Even if it is impossible to capture this complexity via a set of variables, the empirical exercise we present offers some clues on how certain important features of *Sumak Kawsay* relate to people's SWB. In order to proxy *Sumak Kawsay,* we include the following variables: living in a rural area, participation in *mingas* (collective work in which the entire community participates, contributing to tasks such as cleaning neighborhood roads, building a house or planting potatoes), participation in community activities other than *mingas*, having a *chakra* (a small piece of land that constitutes an ecological, symbolic and social space in which the economy is developed as well as the spirit, and which provides food such as yucca, corn, cacao, pineapples, vanilla, avocados, coffee, oranges and plantain, among other ornamental and medicinal plants), and the self-perception of oneself as being indigenous.[1]

This study has a political dimension. Even though *Sumak Kawsay* enjoyed great importance in political terms at the beginning of the century, recent development plans have turned against the very essence of it (Acosta, 2011; Gudynas, 2016). Resource extraction plans in Ecuador have left indigenous people disappointed in the state, and an internal debate has opened up in the country. On February 4, 2018, a Referendum and Popular

Consultation was held in Ecuador to gauge opinion in favor of and against fundamental aspects of *Sumak Kawsay*, such as the rights of nature defined in terms of restrictions on metal mining, and the reduction of the area of oil exploitation in the Yasuní National Park.[2]

Considering its importance, relatively few efforts have been made to study indigenous people's SWB in Ecuador. Exceptions are García-Quero and Guardiola (2017), Guardiola and García-Quero (2014) and Ramírez (2011). The novelty of our research with respect to these studies is the use of a recent national representative sample, along with the incorporation of additional variables related to SWB, and the environment domain as an additional dependent variable.[3]

The results are in line with previous research, as they indicate that most of the *Sumak Kawsay* variables are positively related to the two measures of SWB. However, considering oneself to be indigenous is related to lower levels of life satisfaction. We argue that this might be because the Ecuadorian development process over the last decade has rejected the concept of *Sumak Kawsay*, and does not benefit indigenous people's lives.

The remainder of this chapter is structured as follows: in section 21.2, we present the theoretical framework, explaining in further detail the significance of *Sumak Kawsay* as well as the relationship between *Sumak Kawsay* and SWB. In section 21.3, we outline the data, the variables, the method and the hypotheses. In section 21.4, we report the results, and finally in section 21.5 we conclude, discussing the results and proposing a new political direction following the results.

21.2 LITERATURE REVIEW

21.2.1 Definition of *Sumak Kawsay*

Sumak Kawsay is an indigenous term, linked to the worldview of the Andes–Amazonian region, and is related to the following principles of life: reciprocity, solidarity, respect, complementarity, dignity, collective participation and social justice, all within a sense of harmony with Mother Nature and with the community (CELADE, 2014). This Kichwa term is translated into English as "living well" and into Spanish as *buen vivir*. Similar concepts in the region are known as *Suma Qamaña* ("good living" in Aymara), *Ñandereco* ("harmonious life" in Guaraní), *Qhapaj Ñan* ("road" or "noble life" in Quechua) (Huanacuni-Mamani, 2010a). For some indigenous people, the correct term to define living well is *Alli Kawsay*, which means "full life" (Macas, 2010b; Maldonado, 2010b).

In this chapter, we work with the indigenous concept of *Sumak Kawsay*, which is a two-word phrase: *Kawsay* means "life," and *Sumak* means "good, full, precious, beautiful or abundant" (Ministerio de Educación Ecuador, 2009). *Sumak Kawsay* thus indicates a state of fullness of the whole vital community involved in the interaction between human and natural existence (Macas, 2010a). Similar to this concept, for the Aymara, *Suma Qamaña* is defined as "to live in fullness," while *Suma Qamasiña* is "(co)living well," not better than others and not at the expense of others (Albó, 2009; Macas, 2010b; Medina, 2001).

The processes of reform and constituent assembly led to the promulgation of the new Constitutions of Ecuador in 2008 and Bolivia in 2009, both of which clearly reflect the concept of *Sumak Kawsay*. The preamble of the Political Constitution of Ecuador (PCE) points out that the decision has been taken to build "a new form of citizen coexistence, in diversity and harmony with nature, to achieve *Sumak Kawsay*" (Asamblea Nacional Ecuador, 2008). The PCE emphasizes that economic development focuses on *Sumak Kawsay*. Article 275 of the PCE states that "the development structure is the organized, sustainable and dynamic set of economic, political, socio-cultural and environmental systems that guarantee the achievement of good living, of *Sumak Kawsay*" (Asamblea Nacional Ecuador, 2008).

21.2.2 Important Aspects of *Sumak Kawsay* Concerning Nature, Relationships and the Economic System

In *Sumak Kawsay*, nature and good relations with people and nature play an important role. For the indigenous peoples of the Abya Yala (as they call Latin America), the conception of the environment includes all the beings that inhabit it: "our mother earth is a living being, we not only know that there is life on earth, we know with certainty that the earth is a living being bodily and spiritually" (Torres, 2011). According to Kowii (2009), nature is a living being that has a spirit and is sacred; within this dimension, development actions were restricted under the mandate to take from nature only what is needed and not to abuse it. For the people in the Amazon jungle, "nature not only provides a home for all of its inhabitants, it also emotionally, psychologically, physically, and spiritually revitalizes them. In this way it regenerates the indigenous peoples who live in community with these sylvan selves. That is, the living forest nourishes and augments life" (Sarayaku, 2015).

The connection that indigenous people have with their land is fundamental to understanding what nature means to them. In agrarian communities, *kamari* (offerings) are made, that is, indigenous people request Mother Earth's intervention, using the lunar cycle to assure a good harvest (Kowii, 2009). Offerings to the earth are standard in indigenous cultures, in order to show gratitude in their relationship with the *allpa-mama* or Mother Earth. This is a reciprocal relationship that involves sharing the commitment to continue generating life (Huanacuni-Mamani, 2010b). In the indigenous worldview, a relationship of mutual respect is established: the land is part of the human being and vice versa. Therefore:

> when a *wawa* (baby) is born, the umbilical cord and the placenta are planted under the ground next to a tree, which will then flower, bear fruit and provide shelter or shade. Likewise, when death occurs, which is another way of living, we return to the earth again, to our *allpa-mama* and we are once again part of it. (Pacari, 2013a)

The space where relations with nature take place is called the *chakra*: it is a space where the communities of the Andes constitute a micro-territory, an ecological, symbolic and social space in which life is developed materially and spiritually. It provides food such as yucca, corn, potatoes, vegetables and fruits, as well as aromatic, medicinal, ornamental and artisanal plants. Each family unit usually has one of these little pieces of land (at least in rural or wild environments), and *chakras* thus play an important role as a pillar of the indigenous economy and community participation (Lehmann and Rodríguez, 2013; Medina, 2001). The *chakras* form the central dimension of the family and community relations and the economy, constituting the basis of food security and family welfare.

They therefore help to create self-sufficiency, enjoyment and autonomy, which are historically fundamental values in indigenous societies (Viteri, 2003).

For indigenous peoples, relations with the community are fundamental to their worldview. In Aymara, the *ayllú* – a term which means "community" – is a system of life organization. It differs from the Western idea of community, which is understood as "unity and social structure"; specifically, the components of community are exclusively human in the Western idea. For the worldview of indigenous peoples, community is understood as the unity and structure of life, and:

> [the] human being is only a part of this unit; animals, insects, plants, mountains, air, water, sun, even what is not seen, our ancestors and other beings, are part of the community. Everything lives and everything is important for the balance and harmony of life; the disappearance or deterioration of species is the deterioration of life. (Huanacuni-Mamani, 2010a)

The community, understood as people's relationships with their peers, their environment and everything that surrounds it, is fundamental to the understanding of *Sumak Kawsay*. The way communities organize in order to work together is known as the *minga*: this term comes from the Kichwa word *minka* and means "community work." The *mingas* are agreed by the members of a community, who identify the existing needs, and then plan and prioritize the activities to be carried out; for example: cleaning neighborhood roads, constructing the communal house or dwellings, carrying out maintenance of the territorial limits, planting yucca, and so on. Members actively and consciously participate in the *minga* to improve life in the community (Universidad de Cuenca and UNICEF, 2012). The *minga* endures in many communities as a form of ritual and ceremonial assembly that encourages cohesion between people. Their collective participation allows them to maintain the interests of the community while engaging in a full expression of solidarity and internal redistribution, with goods and services produced and consumed within the community (De la Torre et al., 2004).

The economy of the *Sumak Kawsay* promotes a diverse, healthy, sufficient production, with no surpluses or shortages, intended for sharing, trading and self-consumption. With respect to trading, it involves a fair price that does not harm or affect the producer or those who acquire the product (Chuji, 2010). Carlos Viteri has called this economy self-sufficient, communitarian, supportive, equitable and sustainable, based on the principles of self-sufficiency and solidarity; that is, to obtain from nature what is needed for subsistence and to share surplus production with the community. The basis of self-sufficiency, or food sovereignty in the most current expression, is the family unit (Viteri, 2003).

21.2.3 Different Visions of *Sumak Kawsay*

Sumak Kawsay is an indigenous concept. However, it should be borne in mind that other agents have perceived this idea in different ways. *Sumak Kawsay* debates are complex and undergo constant review. Some papers have managed to classify or categorize this concept from different perspectives, as well as analyzing the term.[4] Two lines of work can be identified that support the present study: the indigenous approach, and the 21st century socialist approach.

From the indigenous perspective, *Sumak Kawsay* involves an element of resistance against development projects that entail the destruction of nature, and has influenced the processes of drafting the Constitution and the development plans of both Ecuador and Bolivia. The following elements are fundamental to an understanding of this line of thought: defense of the rights of nature and feeling part of nature (Chancosa, 2010; Chuji, 2010; Pacari, 2013b; Quirola, 2009), the *runa* or self-sufficient economy in tune with nature (Taxo, 1999; Viteri, 2003), holistic thinking (Maldonado, 2010b; Medina, 2001; Oviedo, 2014a), and alternatives to the development and resistance to neoliberalism (Macas, 2010a; Simbaña, 2011; Viteri, 2002).

Twenty-first century socialism is mainly identified with the governments of Rafael Correa in Ecuador (from 2007 to 2017) and Evo Morales in Bolivia (from 2006 to 2019). This line of thought is also defined as the socialism of the citizen revolution or the "bio-socialism" of the 21st century (Steffan, 2008; Garcia-Linera, 2010; Ramírez, 2012). *Sumak Kawsay* from a political perspective, in search of social equity, is included in programs such as the Citizen Revolution (SENPLADES, 2009, 2013). A model for a popular, solidarity economy has been defined, and agencies have been created for its implementation and execution (Asamblea Nacional Ecuador, 2008; Coraggio, 2007; Patiño, 2010).

These categories allow us to analyze the current processes of the *Sumak Kawsay* from two opposing positions, as the recent Ecuadorian Referendum and Popular Consultation has shown. On the one hand, there is the indigenous standpoint, which seeks to defend nature, understood as a living being with constitutional rights, in a relationship of reciprocity between human beings and nature with a long-term vision that allows food sovereignty and self-sufficiency within the community. On the other hand, there is the vision of 21st century socialism, which has characterized the public policies executed by the governments of Ecuador and Bolivia, using the *Sumak Kawsay* to justify resource extraction in all its forms with the aim of eliminating poverty and social exclusion (Correa, 2012, 2013).

21.2.4 Happiness and *Sumak Kawsay*

Happiness studies have traditionally focused on different aspects of life. Results indicate that having better relations with others (family and friends), not being unemployed, being a woman and being married all have a positive effect on SWB (Frey and Stutzer, 2002; Layard, 2011). Meanwhile, poor health, separation and lack of social contact are all strongly negatively associated with SWB (Dolan et al., 2008).

To the authors' knowledge, there are three SWB studies that empirically build on the *Sumak Kawsay* ethos. The first comes from Ramírez (2011), who concludes, using data from 2006 and 2007, that social and family aspects are the most important life domains in relation to SWB. A negative relationship between SWB and being indigenous was found in his study, using regression analysis; however, the study did not distinguish between rural but in the community, and urban but separated from the community. Secondly, the research paper by Guardiola and García-Quero (2014), based on rural areas in Ecuador, uses SWB and *Sumak Kawsay* to frame the political discussion on the conflict between resource extraction and conservation of natural resources. Their research finds that variables associated with *Sumak Kawsay* philosophy, such as participation in the community and self-production, increase people's life satisfaction, while concern for environmental issues decreases it. Thirdly, and in a similar vein, García-Quero and Guardiola (2017) conclude that the approach based on using income as a proxy for wellbeing, and lack of income as a proxy for lack of wellbeing, may fail to account for the many ways that exist to satisfy human needs in rural Ecuador.

Even though little SWB research has focused on *Sumak Kawsay*, some studies have nonetheless centered on other cultures that involve key aspects of *Sumak Kawsay*. Regarding the natural environment, evidence suggests that people's contact with nature is related to a sense of biophilia: as Wilson (1984 [2003]) concluded, "to the degree that we come to understand other organisms, we will place a greater value on them, and on ourselves." In this vein, Albrecht et al. (2007) use the term "solastagia" for understanding the psychological impact of the increasing incidence of environmental change worldwide and the detrimental impact of environmental degradation. Empirical studies considering the relationship between SWB and nature have referred to issues such as: action and volunteering in organizations that foster environmental awareness and sustain behaviors (Suárez-Varela et al., 2016), environmental concern and attitudes (Ferrer-i-Carbonell and Gowdy, 2007), and environmental degradation (Di Tella et al., 2003). Generally, however, these studies are related to cities and urban scenarios in developed countries, and therefore differ from our research, which is based on indigenous communities in rural populations in a developing country.

Research on the environment and conservation attitudes have found that direct and continuous contact with nature generates a very positive effect on the wellbeing of the individual, and that green behavior and sustainable consumption are positively related to life satisfaction (Binder and Blankenberg, 2017; MacKerron and Mourato, 2013), in line with the concept of biophilia. Respectful and responsible attitudes and actions towards nature, such as water saving, recycling, participating in voluntary organizations or buying organic products, also have a positive relationship with happiness (Binder and Blankenberg, 2016).

Relations with the community is another important dimension of *Sumak Kawsay*. This is something which has also been analyzed empirically with respect to SWB, albeit generally in very different contexts to the indigenous worldview of *Sumak Kawsay*. Several studies have focused on the participation of people in the community. Helliwell (2002) conducted a study in 49 countries, finding that people who belong to or have some involvement with a community organization are more satisfied than those who do not (Helliwell, 2002). Bruni and Stanca (2008) obtain similar results with a longer dataset of 80 countries at different times, including correlations between relational goods and individual wellbeing: time spent with parents and friends, volunteering, charity, church and art-related activities impact positively on life satisfaction. The studies of Helliwell (2001, 2006) found that healthy relations with other people are found to reduce mortality and that social capital characteristics, such as trust, are found to be positively related to SWB. In addition, spending money on others rather than spending on oneself is also found to positively influence SWB (Aknin et al., 2013; Dunn et al., 2008). In Latin America, the study of Mariano Rojas, with a sample of 1560 questionnaires in Central Mexico, found that that achievement in several life domains such as leisure time and family ties may explain some people's high life satisfaction in spite of living in poverty (Rojas, 2008).

21.3 DATA, VARIABLES, METHOD AND HYPOTHESES

In this study we utilize a nationally representative sample in Ecuador: the National Survey on Employment, Unemployment and Underemployment or Encuesta de Empleo, Desempleo y Subempleo (ENEMDU), produced by the Instituto Nacional de Estadísticas y Censos (INEC). This is a representative survey at the national level that has been used by the government and researchers to monitor public policies. We use the dataset[5] from June 2017. Excluding observations with missing variables, we have a sample size of 7 478 households.

There is an ample set of variables in the dataset, and we have chosen those that are most useful for our study. For our dependent variable, we take life satisfaction as indicated by the response to the question: "How do you feel about your overall satisfaction with your life, that is, taking into account all aspects of your life?" As an alternative dependent variable, the life domain is taken from the response to "How do you feel about the environment?". The possible responses to both of these questions range from 0 (very unhappy) to 10 (very happy). We refer to these variables as *satvida* and *satenvironment* respectively.

For the *Sumak Kawsay* variables, we include a dummy that indicates whether the household lives in a rural or urban area. This variable is interpreted as a *Sumak Kawsay* variable, as *Sumak Kawsay* communities are found in rural areas, as explained in the previous section. The variable *indigenous* indicates whether the respondents consider themselves to be indigenous rather than other options such as white, black, mestizo, mulatto or montubio. Participation in *Sumak Kawsay* is captured by two different variables. The first one is called *mingas*, which is a variable that indicates the number of hours per week the respondent participates in *mingas*. The other variable, community *participation*, indicates the number of hours per week committed to meetings in the community. Finally, the binary variable *chakra* equals 1 if the respondent's household has a *chakra*.

As for the socio-economic variables, the EDEMDU includes a large section detailing income from every person in the household and from all sources. We consider the household income per capita, that is, we divide the household income by the number of members in the household, and then take logs. We consider marital status, and include *married* and *free union* as dummies in our model to indicate people living with a partner as compared to those living without. The gender and age of the respondent are also taken into account. As a proxy for the educational capabilities of the respondent, we choose a dummy variable that indicates whether or not the respondent can read and write.

Given the fact that our two dependent variables, life and environmental satisfaction, range from 0 to 10, we estimate using ordinary least squares with robust standard errors.[6] We build alternative models to account for the influence of *Sumak Kawsay* on SWB.

21.4 RESULTS AND PRELIMINARY DISCUSSION

The descriptive statistics of the sample are included in Table 21.1. Satisfaction with life is higher than satisfaction with the environment. Almost 50 percent of the sample live in rural areas and 15 percent are indigenous.

In Tables 21.2 and 21.3, we present several models with life satisfaction and environmental satisfaction, respectively, as the dependent variable. The goodness of fit of every

Table 21.1 Descriptive statistics (N = 7478)

Variable	Mean	Std dev.	Min.	Max.
satlife	7.333	1.745	0	10
satenvironment	6.923	1.889	0	10
income (per cap in logs)	4.825	0.868	0	8.933
married	42.9%		0	1
free union	21.5%		0	1
female	29.0%		0	1
age (years)	55.0	16.5	12	96
rural	49.9%		0	1
no read and write	14.4%		0	1
indigenous	15.2%		0	1
mingas (hours per week)	0.311	1.362	0	16
participation (hours per week)	0.133	0.763	0	12
chakra	35.9%		0	1

model indicates that they are adequate for inference, as the F test is significant at 1 percent in every case. That is, in all cases the null hypothesis of zero slope can be rejected at the 1 percent level of significance using an F-test. In every table, we estimate a model with the socio-economic factors, and then add the *Sumak Kawsay* variables.

The socio-economic variables are similar to what would be expected from previous models of life satisfaction (Dolan et al., 2008), with the only exception being gender.[7] For the environmental satisfaction model (Table 21.3), it is interesting to observe that income is significant and positive, but being unable to read and write is not significant. It seems that earning more allows individuals to appreciate the environment more, instead of devoting their attention to worrying about how to meet their subsistence needs (that is, getting food and clean water). This reflects the need satisfaction theories which imply that there is an order or hierarchy of needs to be satisfied (Maslow, 1943), and that subsistence needs take priority over affective needs such as enjoying others and the environment. That is, people who have a low income may not be satisfying their subsistence needs, and as a result they may not be able to appreciate the environment.[8]

According to the results, indigenous people are more dissatisfied with life, but no significant differences are found concerning environmental satisfaction. People living in rural areas are more satisfied with the environment, but this variable was not significantly related to satisfaction with life. In the last model estimated for every dependent variable (models 3 and 6), we add an interaction of indigenous and rural to check whether indigenous people living in rural areas are in fact more satisfied than other indigenous people, but this interaction is not significant in every case.

Concerning the rest of the *Sumak Kawsay* variables, participation in the community shows a positive and significant relationship with both satisfaction variables (models 2, 3, 5 and 6). The *mingas* are significant and positive for life satisfaction, but not for environmental satisfaction. Having a *chakra* is positively associated with both SWB measures.

Table 21.2 Life satisfaction estimations

	(1)	(2)	(3)
income	0.247***	0.270***	0.270***
	(0.024)	(0.026)	(0.026)
married	0.194***	0.189***	0.189***
	(0.061)	(0.061)	(0.061)
free union	0.170**	0.163**	0.163**
	(0.069)	(0.070)	(0.070)
female	−0.0499	−0.0235	−0.0236
	(0.060)	(0.061)	(0.060)
age	−0.006***	−0.007***	−0.007***
	(0.001)	(0.001)	(0.001)
no read and write	−0.193***	−0.180***	−0.180***
	(0.063)	(0.064)	(0.064)
indigenous		−0.256***	−0.278**
		(0.062)	(0.137)
rural		0.044	0.0419
		(0.050)	(0.051)
mingas		0.0328**	0.0326**
		(0.016)	(0.016)
participation		0.0558**	0.0555**
		(0.024)	(0.024)
chakra		0.171***	0.171***
		(0.052)	(0.052)
indigrural			0.0267
			(0.150)
constant	6.664***	6.491***	6.493***
	(0.192)	(0.205)	(0.205)
Observations	7478	7478	7478
R-squared	0.023	0.028	0.028

Notes: Robust standard errors in parentheses. *** $p < 0.01$, ** $p < 0.05$, * $p < 0.1$.

21.5 CONCLUSIONS, DISCUSSION AND POLICY IMPLICATIONS

In this chapter, we examine the indigenous *Sumak Kawsay* philosophy and way of life, which places an important emphasis on harmony with Mother Nature, the interconnectedness of all life forms, and a holistic vision of reality. We estimate how *Sumak Kawsay*-related variables influence two SWB measures: life satisfaction and environmental satisfaction. The results indicate that most *Sumak Kawsay* features are positively related to the two measures of SWB. The variables positively related to life satisfaction are involvement in *mingas*, community participation and having a *chakra*. For environmental satisfaction, the relevant variables are living in a rural area, participation and having a *chakra*. The relationship between being indigenous and SWB is negatively related to life satisfaction and not significant for environmental satisfaction.

Table 21.3 Environmental satisfaction estimations

	(4)	(5)	(6)
income	0.140***	0.238***	0.238***
	(0.026)	(0.028)	(0.028)
married	0.110*	0.0857	0.0869
	(0.065)	(0.065)	(0.065)
free union	−0.0565	−0.0193	−0.0184
	(0.076)	(0.076)	(0.076)
female	−0.147**	−0.0673	−0.0664
	(0.064)	(0.064)	(0.064)
age	−0.005***	−0.005***	−0.005***
	(0.001)	(0.001)	(0.002)
no read and write	0.0181	−0.0624	−0.0627
	(0.066)	(0.067)	(0.067)
indigenous		0.0208	0.154
		(0.069)	(0.140)
rural		0.326***	0.338***
		(0.054)	(0.056)
mingas		0.00379	0.00507
		(0.018)	(0.018)
participation		0.0584**	0.0599**
		(0.030)	(0.030)
chakra		0.202***	0.203***
		(0.057)	(0.057)
indigrural			−0.167
			(0.156)
constant	6.711***	5.970***	5.962***
	(0.201)	(0.215)	(0.215)
Observations	7478	7478	7478
R-squared	0.008	0.022	0.022

Notes: Robust standard errors in parentheses. *** $p < 0.01$, ** $p < 0.05$, * $p < 0.1$.

The results closely reflect the *Sumak Kawsay* worldview concerning Mother Earth, and the sense of belonging to the community. Therefore, spaces that permit participation make it easier for people to develop spiritually. The fact that being indigenous is not significant for environmental satisfaction and was negatively related to life satisfaction is in line with previous empirical results in the Ecuadorian context (Ramírez, 2011).[9] Nevertheless, this evidence requires further explanation.

With the empirical evidence we provide, it is difficult to fully explain why indigenous people are less satisfied with life. The most we can do is to offer our interpretation, taking into account the Ecuadorian context. There may be many reasons for indigenous people's perceived unhappiness. The first explanation we propose concerns the long tradition of resistance in the indigenous movement, from the process of colonization until the present day. In the words of Atawallpa Oviedo, "this sadness is not something contemporary or natural of the peoples of the Andean highlands but it is post-Columbian" (Oviedo,

2014b). Indigenous people have historically been very aggrieved by governments and liberal concepts of individual rights and the creation of private property (Ranta, 2016). The passing of the Ecuadorian Constitution in 2008, supported by a broad majority of indigenous movements and parties, allowed the possibility that this situation could change. However, the growing conflict between the ideas of the government – 21st-century socialism – and indigenous positions has deepened the disputes on topics that are considered vital according to the indigenous worldview.

This confrontation leads us to a second explanation of why indigenous people may be more dissatisfied: the clash between the government's development ideas and *Sumak Kawsay*. From the indigenous viewpoint, poverty is not only associated with loneliness, isolation and disengagement from the community, *wakcha* (orphan) (Maldonado, 2010a), but also refers to a "circumstantial poverty," *mutsui*, generated by external agents such as development, which destroys the ecosystem, deteriorates the sources that provide food security and contributes to the absence of a long-term vision (Viteri, 2002). In this regard, despite the political importance that has been granted to *Sumak Kawsay* in Ecuador, government development plans go against the very essence of it (Acosta, 2011; Gudynas, 2016). This could be the reason for the negative association with life satisfaction (models 2 and 3) and the non-significant association for environmental satisfaction (models 5 and 6) observed in indigenous people.

If those explanations hold true, then indigenous people's subjective wellbeing would benefit if their culture were given more consideration in the political arena. In fact, as we presented in section 21.2, there is an open conflict between indigenous people and the government over the preservation of indigenous people's culture. The results in this chapter focus attention on features related to the *Sumak Kawsay* way of life, which seems to be important for satisfaction. In light of these results, it is reasonable to argue that public policies should seek to preserve and respect those features.

NOTES

* This research has been partially supported by the Ministry of Economy, Industry and Competitiveness, the State Research Agency (SRA) and European Regional Development Fund (ERDF) (project reference ECO2017-86822-R). We are also grateful for the comments made by the editors, which helped to improve the quality of this chapter. The usual disclaimers apply.

1. The Declaration on the Rights of Indigenous Peoples underlines the importance of self-identification: that indigenous peoples themselves define their own identity as indigenous in accordance with their customs and traditions (United Nations, 2008).
2. The Ecuador Referendum and Popular Consultation consisted of seven questions for voters to approve or reject. It had a participation rate of 80.7 percent of the population, and three of the questions were set in the context of *Sumak Kawsay*. These were: "Do you agree with amending the Constitution of the Republic of Ecuador so that metal mining in all its stages, in protected areas, untouchable zones and urban centers, is prohibited without exception, in accordance with the provisions of Annex 5?"; "Do you agree with the repeal of the Organic Law to Prevent Speculation on the Value of Land and Speculation of Taxes, known as the Capital Gains Law, according to Annex I?"; "Do you agree with increasing the untouchable zone by at least 50 000 hectares and reducing the area of oil exploitation authorized by the National Assembly in the Yasuní National Park from 1030 hectares to 300 hectares?" The three questions were approved with 68.62 percent, 63.10 percent and 67.31 percent of the votes, respectively (CNE, 2018).
3. In this chapter, we use a representative sample of the whole country, whereas the Guardiola and García-Quero (2014) analysis is based on a representative sample from two cantons in southern Ecuador. Regarding our database, Ramírez (2011) uses the same database as we use in this study, but from years 2006 and 2007 and with fewer variables related to *Sumak Kawsay*.

4. According to Hidalgo-Capitán and Cubillo-Guevara (2014), there are six open debates that could be informed by three theoretical approaches: the indigenous and *pachamamista*, the socialist and the ecologist.
5. The dataset can be freely accessed at http://www.ecuadorencifras.gob.ec/enemdu-2017/.
6. Similar results are obtained using an ordered logit technique. We prefer to show the results from ordinary least squares (OLS) as they are easier to depict and interpret.
7. Models including the square of age were also estimated, but this variable was found to be non-significant in every model. As such, we decided to eliminate this quadratic term from all estimations.
8. In order to further test this claim, we regressed environmental satisfaction with a measure of perceived poverty (equals 1 if the person perceives themself to be poor, and 0 otherwise). The two are negatively related with a significance level of 1 percent.
9. Using the ENEMDU representative national survey – the same that we use, but from years 2006 and 2007 – Ramírez (2011) finds that indigenous people are more dissatisfied than non-indigenous. By way of justification, he argues that Latin American countries such as Peru, Ecuador and Bolivia have the lowest happiness levels in the region, while at the same time having the highest indigenous populations.

REFERENCES

Acosta, A. (2011), 'Extractivismo y neoextractivismo: Dos caras de la misma maldición', in Miriam Lang and Dunia Mokrani (eds), *Mas allá del desarrollo*, Mexico City, Mexico: Abya-Yala – Rosa Luxemburgo, pp. 83–121.

Aknin, L.B., Dunn, E.W., Helliwell, J., Biswas-Diener, R., Nyende, P., et al. (2013), 'Prosocial spending and well-being: cross-cultural evidence for a psychological universal', *Journal of Personality and Social Psychology*, **104** (4), 635–652.

Albó, X. (2009), 'Suma qamaña = convivir bien. ¿Cómo medirlo?', *OBETS. Revista de Ciencias Sociales*, **4**, 25–40.

Albrecht, G., Sartore, G.M., Connor, L., Higginbotham, N., Freeman, S., et al. (2007), 'Solastalgia: the distress caused by environmental change', *Australasian Psychiatry*, **15** (1), 95–98.

Asamblea Nacional Ecuador (2008), *Constitución de la República del Ecuador*, Ecuador.

Binder, M. and A.K. Blankenberg (2016), 'Environmental concerns, volunteering and subjective well-being: antecedents and outcomes of environmental activism in Germany', *Ecological Economics*, **124**, 1–16.

Binder, M. and A.K. Blankenberg (2017), 'Green lifestyles and subjective well-being: more about self-image than actual behavior?', *Journal of Economic Behavior and Organization*, **137**, 304–323.

Bruni, L. and L. Stanca (2008), 'Watching alone: relational goods, television and happiness', *Journal of Economic Behavior and Organization*, **65** (3–4), 506–528.

CELADE (2014), *Los pueblos indígenas en América Latina: Avances en el último decenio y retos pendientes para la garantía de sus derechos*, Santiago de Chile, Centro Latinoamericano y Caribeño de Demografía – CEPAL, Naciones Unidas.

Chancosa, B. (2010), 'El Sumak Kawsay desde la visión de la mujer', in Antonio Luis Hidalgo-Capitán, Alejandro Guillén García and Nancy Deleg Guazha (eds), *Sumak Kawsay Yuyay – Antología del Pensamiento Indigenista Ecuatoriano sobre Sumak Kawsay*, Huelva y Cuenca: Universidad de Huelva, pp. 161–170.

Chuji, M. (2010), 'Altermundos. El sumak kawsay: una opción de vida'. Accessed August 31, 2016 at http://miradoriu.org/spip.php?article168.

Consejo Nacional Electoral Ecuador (CNE) (2018), 'Resultados Referéndum y Consulta Popular 2018'. Accessed February 10, 2018 at https://resultados2018.cne.gob.ec/.

Coraggio, J. (2007), 'La economía social y la busqueda de un programa socialista para el siglo XXI', paper presented at El Encuentro de los Socialismos del Siglo XXI, Quito, August 21–22.

Correa, R. (2012), 'Rafael Correa: "No podemos ser mendigos sentados en un saco de oro"', *Andes Agencia Pública de Noticias de Ecuador y Suramérica*, July 2012, Quito (Ecuador). Accessed May 25, 2017 at https://www.andes.info.ec/es/noticias/actualidad/1/9675.

Correa, R. (2013), 'Correa pone fin a iniciativa Yasuní-ITT porque "el mundo nos ha fallado"', *El Confindencial*, Quito (Ecuador). Accessed May 25, 2017 at https://www.elconfidencial.com/ultima-hora-en-vivo/2013-08-16/correa-pone-fin-a-iniciativa-yasuni-itt-porque-el-mundo-nos-ha-fallado_18605/.

De la Torre, Luz M. and Carlos S. Peralta (eds) (2004), *La reciprocidad en el mundo Andino: el caso del pueblo de Otavalo*, Quito, Ecuador: Abya-Yala.

Di Tella, R., MacCulloch, R. and A.J. Oswald (2003), 'The macroeconomics of happiness', *Review of Economics and Statistics*, **85** (4), 809–827.

Dolan, P., Peasgood, T. and M. White (2008), 'Do we really know what makes us happy? A review of the economic literature on the factors associated with subjective well-being', *Journal of Economic Psychology*, **29** (1), 94–122.

Dunn, E.W., Aknin, L.B. and M.I. Norton (2008), 'Spending money on others promotes happiness', *Science*, **319** (5870), 1687–1688.
Ferrer-i-Carbonell, A. and J.M. Gowdy (2007), 'Environmental degradation and happiness', *Ecological Economics*, **60** (3), 509–516.
Frey, B.S. and A. Stutzer (2002), 'What can economists learn from happiness research?', *Journal of Economic Literature*, **40** (2), 402–435.
Garcia-Linera, A. (2010), 'El socialismo comunitario. Un aporte de Bolivia al mundo', *Revista de Análisis. Reflexiones Sobre La Coyuntura*, **3** (5), 7–18.
García-Quero, F. and J. Guardiola (2017), 'Economic poverty and happiness in rural Ecuador: the importance of Buen Vivir (living well)', *Applied Research in Quality of Life*, **13** (4), 909–926.
Guardiola, J. and F. García-Quero (2014), 'Buen Vivir (living well) in Ecuador: community and environmental satisfaction without household material prosperity?', *Ecological Economics*, **107**, 177–184.
Gudynas, E. (2016), 'Beyond varieties of development: disputes and alternatives', *Third World Quarterly*, **37** (4), 721–732.
Helliwell, J. (2001), 'Social capital, the economy and well-being', *Review of Economic Performance and Social Progress*, **1**, 43–60.
Helliwell, J. (2002), 'How's life? Combining individual and national variables to explain subjective well-being', *Economic Modelling*, **20** (2), 331–360.
Helliwell, J. (2006), 'Well-being, social capital and public policy: what's new?', *Economic Journal*, **116** (510), C34–C45.
Hidalgo-Capitán, A. and A.P. Cubillo-Guevara (2014), 'Six open debates on Sumak Kawsay', *Íconos. Revista de Ciencias Sociales*, **48** (Enero), 25–40.
Huanacuni-Mamani, F. (2010a), 'Buen Vivir / Vivir Bien: Filosofía, políticas, estrategias regionales andinas', Lima, Peru: Coordinadora Andina de Organizaciones Indígenas-CAOI, M.P. Quishpe.
Huanacuni-Mamani, F. (2010b), 'Paradigma Occidental y Paradigma Indígena Originario', *América Latina En Movimiento*, **452**, 17–22.
Kowii, A. (2009), 'El Sumak Kawsay', in Antonio Luis Hidalgo-Capitán, Alejandro Guillén García and Nancy Deleg Guazha (eds), *Sumak Kawsay Yuyay – Antología del Pensamiento Indigenista Ecuatoriano sobre Sumak Kawsay*, Huelva y Cuenca: Universidad de Huelva, pp. 161–170.
Layard, R. (ed.) (2011), *Happiness: Lessons from a New Science*, London, UK: Penguin Books.
Lehmann, S. and J. Rodríguez (2013), 'La Chakra Kichwa: Criterios para la conservación y fomento de un sistema de producción sostenible en la Asociación Kallari y sus organizaciones socias', Quito, Ecuador: GIZ.
Macas, L. (2010a), 'El Sumak Kawsay', *Yachaykuna*, **13**, 13–39.
Macas, L. (2010b), 'Sumak Kawsay: La vida en Plenitud', *América Látina En Movimiento*, **452**, 14–16.
MacKerron, G. and S. Mourato (2013), 'Happiness is greater in natural environments', *Global Environmental Change*, **23** (5), 992–1000.
Maldonado, L. (2010a), 'El Sumak kawsay/ Buen Vivir/ Vivir Bien', in Antonio Luis Hidalgo-Capitán, Alejandro Guillén García and Nancy Deleg Guazha (eds), *Sumak Kawsay Yuyay – Antología del Pensamiento Indigenista Ecuatoriano sobre Sumak Kawsay*, Huelva y Cuenca: Universidad de Huelva, pp. 195–211.
Maldonado, L. (2010b), 'Interculturalidad y políticas públicas en el marco del buen vivir', in Gerardo Fernandez-Juárez (ed.), *Salud, Interculturalidad y Derechos – Claves para la Reconstrucción del Sumak Kawsay-Buen Vivir*, Quito, Ecuador: Ministerio de Salud Pública, pp. 81–90.
Maslow, A. (1943), 'A theory of human motivation', *Psychological Review*, **50** (4), 370–396.
Medina, J. (2001), 'La Buena Vida occidental y la Vida Dulce amerindia', in Javier Medina (ed.), *Suma Qamaña: La Comprensión Indígena de la Vida Buena*, La Paz, Bolivia: PADEP/GTZ, pp. 31–36.
Ministerio de Educación Ecuador (2009), *KICHWA: Yachakukkunapa Shimiyuk Kamu*. Accessed May 28, 2017 at http://www.illa-a.org/cd/diccionarios/diccionarioKichwaEcuador.pdf.
Oviedo, A. (ed.) (2014a), *Bifurcaciones del Buen Vivir y el Sumak Kawsay*, Quito, Ecuador: Ediciones Sumak.
Oviedo, A. (2014b), 'La Felicidad de la Revolución Ciudadana'. Accessed September 14, 2016 at https://lalineadefuego.info/2014/11/25/la-felicidad-de-la-revolucion-ciudadana-por-atawallpa-oviedo-wakakue/.
Pacari, N. (2013a), 'Naturaleza y territorio desde la mirada de los pueblos indígenas', in Antonio Luis Hidalgo-Capitán, Alejandro Guillén García and Nancy Deleg Guazha (eds), *Sumak Kawsay Yuyay – Antología del Pensamiento Indigenista Ecuatoriano sobre Sumak Kawsay*, Huelva y Cuenca: Universidad de Huelva, pp. 129–132.
Pacari, N. (2013b), 'Sumak Kawsay para que tengamos vida', in Antonio Luis Hidalgo-Capitán, Alejandro Guillén García and Nancy Deleg Guazha (eds), *Sumak Kawsay Yuyay – Antología del Pensamiento Indigenista Ecuatoriano sobre Sumak Kawsay*, Huelva y Cuenca: Universidad de Huelva, pp. 345–355.
Patiño, R. (2010), 'Diferencias entre el socialismo del Siglo XX y el socialismo del siglo XXI. La democracia participativa y el nuevo sujeto revolucionario', in Secretaría Nacional de Planificación y Desarrollo, SENPLADES (ed.), *Los nuevos retos de América Latina: Socialismo y Sumak Kawsay*, Quito, Ecuador: Secretaría Nacional de Planificación y Desarrollo (SENPLADES), pp. 133–140.

Quirola, D. (2009), 'Sumak Kawsay. Hacia un nuevo pacto social en armonía con la naturaleza', in Alberto Acosta and Esperanza Martínez (eds), *El Buen Vivir: Una vía para el desarrollo*, Quito, Ecuador: Abya Yala, pp. 103–114.
Ramírez, R. (2011), *La felicidad como medida del buen vivir en Ecuador*, Quito, Ecuador: Secretaría Nacional de Planificación y Desarrollo (SENPLADES).
Ramírez, R. (2012), *La Vida (Buena) como riqueza de los Pueblos Hacia Una Socioecología Política del Tiempo* (1st edn), Quito, Ecuador: Instituto de Altos Estudios Nacionales IAEN.
Ranta, E.M. (2016), 'Toward a decolonial alternative to development? The emergence and shortcomings of Vivir Bien as state policy in Bolivia in the era of globalization', *Globalizations*, **13** (4), 425–439.
Rojas, M. (2008), 'Experienced poverty and income poverty in Mexico: a subjective well-being approach', *World Development*, **36** (6), 1078–1093.
Sarayaku (2015), 'Kawsak Sacha – the living forest: an indigenous proposal for confronting climate change', paper presented by the Amazonian Kichwa people of Sarayaku at COP 21, Paris, pp. 1–3.
SENPLADES (2009), 'Plan Nacional para el Buen Vivir 2009–2013: Construyendo un estado Plurinacional e Intercultural', Quito, Ecuador.
SENPLADES (2013), 'Plan Nacional para el Buen vivir 2013–2017', Quito, Ecuador.
Simbaña, F. (2011), 'El Sumak Kawsay como proyecto político', in Miriam Lang and Dunia Mokrani (eds), *Más Allá del Desarrollo. Grupo permanente de trabajo sobre alternativas al desarrollo*, Mexico City, Mexico: Abya-Yala – Rosa Luxemburgo, pp. 219–226.
Steffan, H.D. (2008), 'El socialismo del siglo XXI', México, Fondo de Cultura Económica.
Suárez-Varela, M., Guardiola, J. and F. González-Gómez (2016), 'Do pro-environmental behaviors and awareness contribute to improve subjective well-being?', *Applied Research Quality Life*, **11** (2), 429–444.
Taxo, A. (1999), 'La concepción runa de la economía', in Vladimir Serrano (ed.), *Economía de solidaridad y cosmovisión indígena*, Quito, Ecuador: Abya Yala, pp. 155–166.
Torres, W. (2011), 'Medicina De La Tierra : El Sendero de la Madre Ancestral', *Cultura y Droga -Universidad de Caldas*, **16** (18), 137–148.
United Nations (2008), 'Declaration on the rights of indigenous peoples', United Nations. Accessed July 10, 2017 at http://www.un.org/esa/socdev/unpfii/documents/DRIPS_en.pdf.
Universidad de Cuenca and UNICEF (2012), 'Sabiduría de la cultura Kichwa de la Amazonía Ecuatoriana', in Universidad de Cuenca (ed.), *Sabiduría de la cultura Kiwcha de la amazonía Ecuatoriana*, Cuenca, Ecuador: Universidad de Cuencia, pp. 341–400.
Viteri, C. (2002), 'Visión Indígena del desarrollo en la Amazonía', *Polis*, **3**, 2–6.
Viteri, C. (2003), 'Súmak Kaúsai. Una respuesta viable al desarrollo', dissertation presented at Universidad Politécnica Salesiana.
Wilson, E. (ed.) (1984 [2003]), *Biophilia,* 12th printing, 2003, Cambridge, MA, USA: Harvard University Press.

22. Mother Earth and household welfare functions of First Nations peoples of Canada

Shashi Kant, Ilan Vertinsky and Bin Zheng

22.1 INTRODUCTION

More than 1.6 million people identified themselves as Aboriginals during the 2016 Census of Canada. This count included 977235 First Nations, 587545 Metis and 65025 Inuit people, which are about 58 percent, 35 percent and 4 percent, respectively, of those with Aboriginal identity (Statistics Canada, 2017). Wellbeing of Aboriginal peoples is substantially different compared to the wellbeing of non-Aboriginal peoples of Canada and is closer to the wellbeing of peoples living in developing countries (Salée et al., 2006). In other words, a developing country of Aboriginal peoples exists within "developed Canada."

The evaluation of Aboriginal peoples' wellbeing is, generally, based on the material aspects of their lives such as income, personal consumption and unemployment (Michalski, 2001; Zagon, 2001) or composite measures such as the Community Wellbeing Index, a composite index of income, education and housing conditions. However, the use of such measures has a problem because the constructs used to measure wellbeing of people in industrialized cultures may not be appropriate to measure wellbeing of people in a non-industrialized culture (Kleinman, 1977). These measures ignore the most common and predominant First Nations cultural notion of a person's connections to "Mother Earth and nature" (Kirmayer, 2007; Tanner, 2004) and other cultural and social perspectives of Aboriginal peoples on their own experiences and characteristics of their wellbeing.

Aboriginal peoples' traditional wisdom about Mother Earth and nature – which is based on respecting and living in harmony with Mother Earth and nature and seeing all things as interconnected (Mussell et al., 2004) – are integral parts of their wellbeing. Mother Earth to Aboriginal people encompasses the holism of the Aboriginal worldview. Mother Earth is the lifeline that sustains Aboriginal peoples' way of living (CFS, 2012), practiced through traditional land use activities such as fishing, gathering, hunting and trapping that are still an important source of livelihood for Aboriginal people, specifically First Nations people who live on reserves. These activities are not only a source of material goods such as the traditional food items and income but are also the primary source of their knowledge, beliefs and cultural practices (Smith, 1995; Kinsella, 1999; Garvin et al., 2001). In addition, traditional food gathered through fishing, hunting and gathering is a source of good health for Aboriginal people, and locally collected medicinal plants (for example, sweet flag, bearberry, pipsissewa) are widely used in traditional treatments (Perley, 1999). Hence, Aboriginal people, through their lifestyle, establish a unique relationship with the land, and land-based social, cultural and other traditional activities, values and beliefs are critical inputs to their wellbeing (Adelson, 2000; Parsons and Prest, 2003).

An assessment of Aboriginal wellbeing based on only material aspects, therefore, is inappropriate and incomplete. An understanding and incorporation of Aboriginal worldview is essential to understand and analyze Aboriginal peoples' wellbeing. The Canadian Council on Learning (CCL) (2007) proposed three holistic life-long learning models, one each for First Nations, Metis and Inuit people; all three models are based on a holistic approach to lifelong learning and its relations to wellbeing. All three models include emotional, mental, physical and spiritual dimensions of the self, and wellbeing is rooted in relations with other people and nature. As per these models, the measures of Aboriginal peoples' wellbeing should incorporate multiple dimensions of the self, and their relations with nature and other people; and this is possible only through comprehensive measures of wellbeing and not by measures focused on materialistic aspects only.

In recent years, some scholars have analyzed single-domain subjective wellbeing of Aboriginal peoples of Canada. For example, Fernando (2002), using the data from 1997 National Survey of Giving, Volunteering and Participating, found that the average life satisfaction of Aboriginal people (3.15, on the increasing scale of life satisfaction ranging from 1 to 5), was slightly lower than the life satisfaction of the whole sample (3.35); but this study was limited to only those Aboriginal people who were living within non-Aboriginal populations. Barrington-Leigh and Sloman (2016) analyzed overall life satisfaction among Aboriginal peoples in the Canadian prairies; the authors found mean values of satisfied-with-life scores to be similar for Aboriginal and non-Aboriginal samples, and a positive relationship between household income and satisfied-with-life scores for the general population, but a negative relationship for Aboriginal peoples. This opposite relationship between income (monetary income only) and satisfied-with-life scores may be a reflection of fundamental differences between Aboriginal and Non-Aboriginal (European) worldviews with respect to the weights placed on different domains of life and the role of monetary income in their wellbeing.

Subjective wellbeing may be assessed using a holistic concept of satisfaction with life (Helliwell and Putnam, 2004; Deaton, 2008; Kapteyn et al., 2010) or by satisfaction with different domains of life (Cummins, 1996; Van Praag and Ferrer-i-Carbonell, 2008). The holistic life-long learning models (CCL, 2007) that articulate the Canadian Aboriginals' worldviews are based on multiple domains of wellbeing and the basic tenet of subjective wellbeing being internal construct. These characteristics make the use of the concept of satisfaction with multiple domains of life the most suitable framework for assessing wellbeing of Aboriginal peoples of Canada. In addition, participation of community members in the process of identification, selection and definitions of domains, the factors that contribute to the satisfaction of each domain, and the interrelationships between satisfactions of various domains, is essential to ensure that they reflect the perceptions, beliefs and judgments of the peoples of the community being assessed. Kant et al. (2014) and Kant et al. (2016) have used the concept of multiple domains satisfaction to assess wellbeing of on-reserve First Nations (ORFN)[1] people of Canada. The results of these two papers confirmed the ORFN peoples' view that the social, cultural and land use (SCLU) domain is the most important determinant of overall wellbeing of First Nations peoples and SCLU factors also contribute to other domains' satisfactions. The results also confirm that Aboriginal peoples' wellbeing cannot be measured by focusing only on materialistic aspects.

This chapter is a part of a major project of the authors on the subjective wellbeing of First Nations peoples of Canada. Kant et al. (2013) analyzed the social and cultural determinants of First Nations peoples' health, while Kant et al. (2014) analyzed the multi-domain subjective wellbeing of First Nations peoples using path analysis.[2] Kant et al. (2016) used the model of multi-domain subjective wellbeing to value social, cultural, land use and other factors that contribute to their wellbeing. In these three papers, the authors used overall life satisfaction and domain satisfaction questions to analyze different aspects of multi-domain subjective wellbeing. Kant et al. (2019) reviewed the current state of research on the subjective wellbeing of Aboriginal peoples of Canada, and suggested future research directions. In this chapter, we extend the analysis by using the concept of individual welfare functions (IWF) to analyze the First Nations peoples' wellbeing.

The concept of IWF of income and the methodology of data collection to estimate it – the income evaluation question (IEQ) – were proposed by Van Praag (1968). IWF, a forerunner to the life satisfaction question (LSQ),[3] is a cardinal utility function, with values ranging from 0 to 1, that differs among individuals (Kapteyn and Wansweek, 1985). IWF being different among individuals means that the same level of change in the income will lead to different levels of changes in welfare of different people (Van Praag, 1968). This has important implications for designing welfare policies. The IEQ has two key differences compared to the LSQ: it does not refer to own income of respondents; instead, it presents verbal labels of income such as bad, insufficient, sufficient and good, and asks respondents to assign monetary values to each verbal label (Van Praag, 1968). The advantage of the IEQ compared to the LSQ is that a respondent is forced to think more deeply about the exact positioning of each verbal label of income, and therefore probably the answers are more exact (Kapteyn and Wansweek, 1985). In addition, the IEQ provides more data points per respondent which allows for different types of statistical analyses.

Many scholars, including Van Praag (1971), Van Praag and Kapteyn (1973), and Van Herwaarden et al. (1977), have estimated the IWF of income, using IEQ data, and examined the influence of some demographic and economic factors such as family size, education, employment category and spousal employment on the two parameters, "want" and "welfare sensitivity," of IWF. The concepts of IWF and the IEQ with some modifications have been used to analyze welfare policy issues such as the definition of a poverty line (Danziger et al., 1984; Van Praag et al., 1982; Hagenaars and Van Praag, 1985), optimal income redistribution (Van Praag, 1977), and municipal welfare (Van Praag and Linthorst, 1976). Kijazi and Kant (2011) estimated the IWF of forest biomass fuels of residents of Mount Kilimanjaro, Tanzania, and included environmental factors, in addition to demographic and economic factors, to explain the variation in the two parameters of IWF.

Our previous analyses of subjective wellbeing of ORFN peoples have already demonstrated the important role of many social, cultural and land use factors in their wellbeing. In this chapter, we extend our analysis by evaluating ORFN people's household welfare functions (HWF)[4] of income as well as of two key SCLU contributors to wellbeing: traditional diet and trapping income. In our analysis of the two parameters of HWF, we also use SCLU factors that were found to influence various domains' satisfaction in our subjective wellbeing analysis.

The chapter is organized in five sections. A summary of the multi-domain subjective wellbeing results, published in Kant et al. (2014) and Kant et al. (2016), is presented in section 22.2. A brief introduction to the IWF and estimation methods are presented in section 22.3, followed by results in section 22.4. Conclusions are provided in section 22.5.

22.2 SUBJECTIVE WELLBEING OF ORFN PEOPLES OF CANADA

The subjective wellbeing project focuses on one Oji-Cree First Nation in Ontario (ON) with about 850 people living on the reserve, and one Secwepemc First Nation in British Columbia (BC) with about 750 people living on the reserve. The Community Wellbeing Index of the ON First Nation is equal to the average value, while the index for the BC First Nation is higher than the average value of the index for all First Nations. Both First Nations are within 25 km of non-Aboriginal townships, have road access and are active participants in economic development projects.

22.2.1 Data Collections Methods

The data for the whole project was collected through a three-step participatory approach rooted in First Nations culture. People from both First Nations were active participants in all three steps. First, to develop a basic understanding of cultural perspectives and wellbeing of First Nations peoples, researchers conducted open-ended discussions with elders and members of band (local government) offices of the two First Nations. The researchers started the discussion with the introduction of the project's research objectives and the purpose of open-ended discussions. After introductory remarks, the researchers acted as silent listeners and recorders. Second, domains of First Nations peoples' wellbeing, contributing factors and their measurement units were identified through semi-structured interviews with elders and focus groups. Third, a preliminary questionnaire was designed using the information collected in the first two steps. The questionnaire included questions on: (1) life satisfaction questions (LSQ) for each domain and overall life satisfaction; (2) the state of the factors that contribute to the satisfaction with each domain; (3) income evaluation question that was modified to capture household income instead of individual income, and similar questions to evaluate household traditional diet and household trapping income; and (4) cultural, demographic, economic, land use and social variables. The questionnaire was finalized by incorporating the results of pre-testing and suggestions of the participants in the first two steps.

First Nations participants felt very strongly about the unit of survey and analysis, and they believed that an individual cannot evaluate their wellbeing in isolation from their household. Hence, the unit of the survey, and therefore of the analysis, was the household and not an individual. As a result, life and domain satisfaction questions were about household satisfaction and a seven-point Likert scale (1: worst possible satisfaction, and 7: best possible satisfaction) was used for all LSQs. The question for overall household satisfaction with life was:

> After evaluation of your satisfaction with different domains of life, where on the ladder below do you rate your household's satisfaction with life as a whole for a period of one year preceding this survey?

Domain satisfaction questions were similar to the overall life satisfaction question. Seven domains – income, employment, education, health, housing, land use, and social and cultural activities – were included and there was one question for each domain. Similarly, the income as well as traditional diet and trapping income evaluation questions were about the household's income, traditional diet and trapping income, respectively. In all three questions, six labels (very low, low, insufficient, sufficient, good and very good) were used. The income was measured in Canadian dollars, while traditional diet and trapping income were measured as a percentage of the total diet, and the total income, respectively. For details of the income evaluation methodology, please refer to section 22.3. The IEQ was:

> Whether you feel an income is good or not so good depends on your household's circumstances and expectations:
> In your case, you would call your household's gross income from all sources

A very low income if it equaled	CAN $	________
A low income if it equaled	CAN $	________
An insufficient income if it equaled	CAN $	________
A sufficient income if it equaled	CAN $	________
A good income if it equaled	CAN $	________
A very good income if it equaled	CAN $	________

The states of factors contributing to domain's satisfaction were measured during the same one-year period as of the domain's satisfaction, and four types of measurement scales were used: (1) standard measurement units such as dollars, hours and years; (2) binary units (BU), yes/no response; (3) percentage; and (4) Likert scale. Details of all factors and their measurement units are given in Table 22.1.

A postdoctoral fellow (PDF), in person, delivered the questionnaire to 355 households (out of about 400 households) where an adult person was available, and collected back completed questionnaires after one week. The response rate was 90 percent; 315 questionnaires, 167 completed by males and 148 by females, had complete information. Both males and females responded to questions designed to measure the household's satisfaction or evaluation and not their own satisfaction or evaluation.

The data has two important distinguishing features not included in the previous literature. First, the First Nations peoples participating in the development of the conceptual measurement model underlying our study included the land use domain and a richer more complex social and cultural domain that has not received enough attention in the previous literature. Other domains included were: education, income, employment, health and housing. Second, the First Nations peoples included various land use, social and cultural contributing factors. Some examples of these factors are factors related to cultural ceremonies, cultural sites, gathering, spiritual activities, traditional diets, trapping, and the unique nature of factors related to health such as frequent and occasional occurrence of problems related to internal organs, external organs and mental health. These two distinguishing features confirm the distinctive nature of First Nations' worldviews and cultures.

In this chapter, as stated earlier, we extend ORFN people's subjective wellbeing analysis by presenting the results of household welfare functions of income, traditional diet and trapping income. We also examine the role of social, cultural and land use factors, that

Table 22.1 Explanation and measurement of factors influencing overall and different domain's satisfaction

	Details of factor	Measurement Units
AcceCultu	Access to First Nation's cultural sites	LS1[a]
Age	Age of the head of household	Year
BreWorkdays	Breadwinner's work days per week	Hours
Ceremony	Frequency of household participation in cultural ceremonies	LS2[b]
Children	Number of children younger than 16 years in household	#
ChildEdu	Perception of transmission of traditional knowledge in children's education	LS1
ChildEsteem	Effectiveness of children's education in imparting self-esteem	LS1
Edu	Number of years of formal education of head of household	#
Fsize	Family size – number of people including children in household	#
Gatherhrs	Average hours per day spent on gathering	Hours
GatherQualit	Quality of time spent on gathering	LS1
Gathers	Numbers of people in household that gather wild produce	#
ExtOrgFreq	Frequent occurrence of external organ illnesses in household	BU
HealServ	Satisfaction with government health services	LS1
HousTitle	Ownership of house	BU
HousSpac	Satisfaction with space in house	LS1
HousLoc	Satisfaction with the location of house	LS1
HousMaint	Satisfaction with house maintenance	LS1
IntOrgFreq	Frequent occurrence of internal organ illnesses in household	BU
LawLanduse	Satisfaction with the government laws that influence household's land use activities	LS1
LawCultu	Satisfaction with the government laws that influence household's cultural and social life	LS1
LogInc	Log of income	
MaritalStatus	Respondent's marital status	BU
MentalFreq	Frequent occurrence of mental and psychological problems in household	BU
MentalOc	Occasional occurrence of mental and psychological problems in the household	BU
SocTies	Sense of belonging to local community and social ties	LS1
SpouUnemFull	Spouse of breadwinner is full-time unemployed	BU
SpouEdu	Educational level of spouse	LS1
Spiritual	Household freedom to participate in spiritual activities	LS1
StatCSAreas	State of areas of cultural significance	LS1
TradDiets	Percentage of typical household meal that comes from traditional foods (diets obtained from land use activities such as hunting, fishing, gathering, etc.)	%
TrapInc	The percentage of income attributable to trapping	%

Table 22.1 (continued)

	Details of factor	Measurement Units
TradMed	State of traditional medicinal and healing practices	LS1
Trappers	Number of trappers in household	#
HuntFish	Members of household that hunt and fish	#
Traphrs	Average number of hours per day spent on trapping	Hours
Unemplfull	Breadwinner is full time unemployed	BU

Notes:
[a] LS1: Likert scale 1 (4 points scale, 1 = very low, 4 = very high).
[b] LS2: Likert scale 2 (3 points scale (0 = never, 1 = occasionally, 2 = often).

Source: Kant et al. (2014).

were found to influence various domains' satisfaction in our subjective wellbeing analysis, in the two parameters of household welfare functions. Hence, to put this chapter in the perspective of the continuation of our previous published work, first we present a brief summary of the results published in Kant et al. (2014) and Kant et al. (2016).

22.2.2 Summary of Kant et al. (2014): Multi-Domain Subjective Wellbeing of Two Canadian First Nations Communities

In both First Nations, every household used traditional food items and participated in some activity related to the collection of food items such as fishing, gathering, hunting and trapping, but no household participated in all the activities. In the BC First Nation (BCFN), the average contribution of traditional food items to the total diet was 23 percent, while in the ON First Nation (ONFN) it was 18 percent. In terms of activities, the lowest participation was in trapping. The values for some other important demographic, social and economic factors are given in Table 22.2.

In the preliminary analysis of the data, a very high (0.80) and significant (at 1 percent level) correlation was found between the satisfaction scores of the social and cultural activities domain and land use activities domain. Hence, these two domains were combined in one domain of social, cultural and land use (SCLU) activities, and the average of the satisfaction scores of the social and cultural domain and land use domain was used as the score of the SCLU domain.

The average values of each domain's satisfaction and overall satisfaction for all respondents, male respondents and female respondents are given in Table 22.3. The average overall wellbeing (greater than 5) for both First Nations is in the upper half of the satisfaction range (5 means "satisfied" and 7 means "extremely satisfied"). The average satisfaction for the health domain was higher than 5 for all groups, while average satisfaction levels for all other domains were between 4 and 5. Hence, the overall, as well as all domains' satisfaction levels, were quite far from the (maximum) "extremely satisfied" level (7). The ONFN households, as compared to BCFN households, were more satisfied in all domains. As per two-group t-tests, the differences between the average values of satisfaction of ONFN and BCFN people were statistically significant at 1 percent for overall wellbeing and the

Table 22.2 A comparative view of demographic, social and economic factors of households

Demographic, social, economic factors	Ontario First Nation	BC First Nation
Average size of household	4 (2 adults and 2 children)	4 (2 adults and 2 children)
Average annual income of household	\$25911	\$27223
Average age of head of household (HOH)	45 years	49 years
Average years of formal education of HOH	11	12
Percentage of HOH attended residential schools only and non-residential schools only	24 and 60	29 and 51
Percentage of HOH who have college diploma and higher degree	16	47
Percentage of fully employed and fully unemployed HOH	31 and 4	56 and 7

Table 22.3 Average levels and standard deviations of overall wellbeing and domains' satisfaction

	Average for all households N = 315	Average for ON people N = 203	Average for BC people N = 112	Average for all female responses N = 148	Average for all male responses N = 167
Overall wellbeing	5.12 (0.86)	5.30*** (0.94)	5.02*** (0.81)	5.21 (0.97)	5.11 (0.82)
SCLU domain	4.50 (1.22)	4.62 (1.30)	4.44 (1.17)	4.24*** (1.32)	4.54*** (1.25)
Income domain	4.57 (1.16)	4.70 (1.38)	4.49 (1.02)	4.50 (1.34)	4.68 (1.25)
Employment domain	4.72 (1.49)	4.79 (1.82)	4.67 (1.29)	4.30* (1.88)	4.78* (1.53)
Education domain	4.52 (1.32)	4.71* (1.67)	4.42* (1.06)	4.59 (1.64)	4.42 (1.00)
Housing domain	4.61 (1.53)	5.18*** (1.66)	4.31*** (1.36)	4.61 (1.74)	4.65 (1.34)
Health domain	5.18 (1.11)	5.32* (1.18)	5.10* (1.07)	5.28** (1.16)	5.10** (1.13)

Notes:
A two-group t-test was conducted between the ON and BC groups, and female and male groups. Respective null hypotheses were: (1) average level of satisfaction for ON and BC groups are the same; and (2) average level of satisfactions for female and male respondents are the same.
Numbers in brackets – standard deviation.
* Indicates statistical significance at the 10% significance level; ** indicates statistical significance at the 5% significance level; *** indicates statistical significance at the 1% significance level.
The same symbols are used for 10%, 5% and 1% significance levels in all tables in this chapter.

Source: Kant et al. (2014).

housing domain, and at 10 percent for the health and the education domains. The satisfaction levels of female respondents with their household's health domain were higher than those of male respondents (5 percent significance), but were lower than those of male respondents for satisfaction with the SCLU (1 percent significance) and employment (10 percent significance) domains.

Using the data from open-ended discussions and semi-structured interviews with First Nations peoples, the authors conceptualized a multi-domain life satisfaction model of First Nations peoples. The model included six domains – social, cultural and land use (SCLU), income, education, employment, health and housing. The models of overall wellbeing and six domains of wellbeing were estimated using a path analysis technique with IBM SPSS Amos 19.0 software (Byrne, 2001).

The path coefficients of the overall wellbeing model are given in Figure 22.1. The estimated model indicated that the SCLU domain contributed directly as well as indirectly through the health domain to the overall wellbeing. Similarly, the education and employment domains contributed directly and indirectly through the income domain to the overall wellbeing. In the case of female head of household, the ranking of different domains in terms of the total contributions (measured by unstandardized path coefficients) to the overall wellbeing was: (1) SCLU; (2) education; (3) income; (4) health; (5) housing; and (6) employment. In the case of male head of household, the ranking of domains was: (1) SCLU and income; (3) health; (4) housing; (5) employment; and (6) education. Hence, the SCLU ranked top for all households irrespective of the gender of the HOH, while the ranking of other domains varied depending upon the gender of the HOH. The total contributions of the employment, health, housing and income domains to overall wellbeing were not significantly different, but the total contributions of the SCLU and the education domains were significantly different for the male and female models.

In brief, the SCLU domain was the most important domain. The unstandardized path coefficients indicated that an increase of 1 unit in the SCLU domain increased the overall satisfaction by 0.228 units for the females' model, and by 0.136 units for the males' model. The contributions of the unstandardized path coefficients from the education domain to overall wellbeing were 0.026 and 0.138 for males' and females' models, respectively, indicating the big difference in the contributions of the education domain for households headed by males and females. The health domain was as important as the income domain for households headed by both males and females.

These results provided empirical evidence of the First Nations peoples' view about Mother Earth and nature in their wellbeing. The SCLU domain, which captures the holistic relationship between First Nations peoples and Mother Earth, was found to be the most important determinant of overall wellbeing. The SCLU factors contributed to the overall wellbeing through the SCLU domain as well as all other domains.

The SCLU factor, on the basis of their contributions to a number of domains, can be classified in four groups. The groups and the SCLU factor belonging to the groups are: (1) factors that contributed to overall wellbeing through five domains: the freedom to participate in spiritual activities; (2) factors that contributed through four domains: the satisfaction with the government laws that impact land use activities, and the satisfaction with the access to cultural sites; (3) factors that contributed through two domains: gathering hours, number of gatherers, trapping income, state of areas of cultural significance, and satisfaction with the government laws that impact social and cultural activities; and (4)

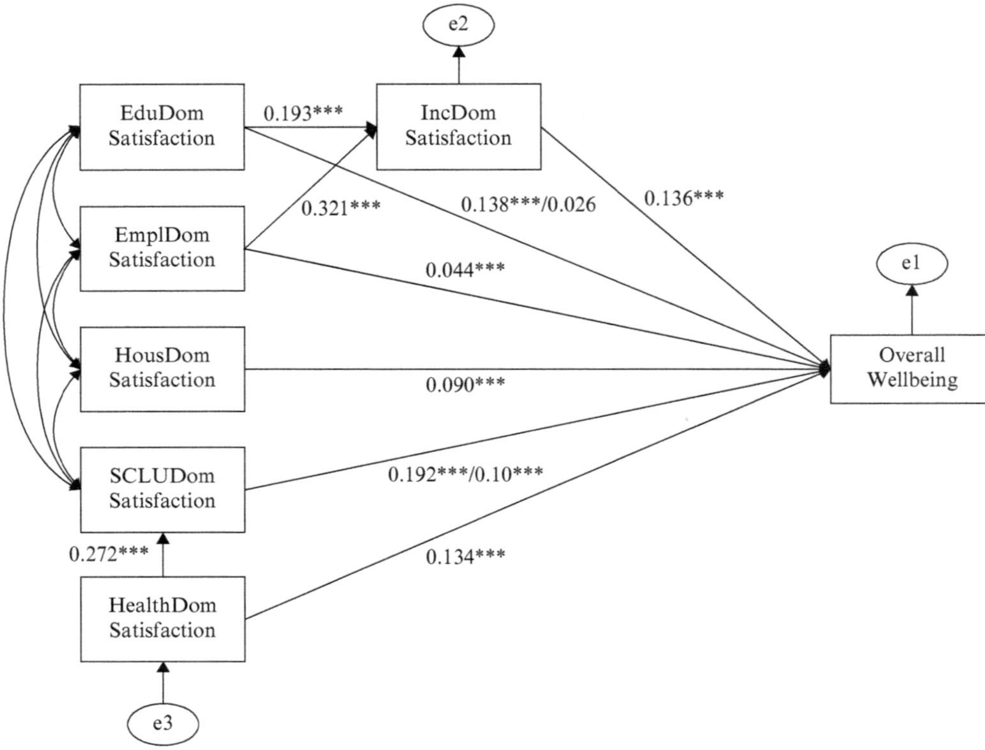

Notes:
One-way arrow shows the contribution of determining variables; and two-headed arrow with curved line indicates unanalyzed correlations between variables.
In the case of the same coefficient for males and females, a single path coefficient is given; in the case of two numbers, the first number is for females and the second number for males.
Error terms are represented by e.
*, ** and *** indicate statistical significance at the 10%, 5% and 1% significance levels, respectively.

Source: Kant et al. (2014).

Figure 22.1 Path coefficients of overall wellbeing of First Nations people (female versus male)

factors that contributed through one domain: number of trappers, social ties, gathering quality, trapping hours and participation in cultural ceremonies. These results provide further empirical evidence of a holistic relationship between First Nations peoples and Mother Earth.

22.2.3 Summary of Kant et al. (2016): Valuation of Social Cultural and Land Use Activities

As per the Aboriginal worldview, a dollar value should not and indeed cannot be assigned to their social, cultural and land use activities. Even activities that produce outputs that are traded in markets cannot be assessed through the income they generate through the market, because engagement in the activities, rather than the output, may be a dominant source of satisfaction with life. For example, fish is traded in the market, but not the Aboriginal fishing activity that includes many family and community activities such as transfer of traditional knowledge to children. Hence, Kant et al. (2016) argued that the standard market-oriented valuation methods are not suitable to value SCLU activities due to non-substitution of these activities with market-traded commodities (refer to Adamowicz et al., 1998 for a detailed discussion). Instead, the authors proposed a multi-domain life satisfaction model consisting of a general satisfaction (GS) equation and one equation for each domain's satisfaction (DS). In their final model, they included four domains – SCLU, income, health and housing – and estimated the model, a system of five equations, using 3SLS.[5]

On the basis of estimated coefficients of the GS equation, the authors found that a one-unit change in the SCLU domain, the health domain and the housing domain satisfaction resulted in 2.29, 2.28 and 2.05 times the changes in GS, respectively, as compared to changes in GS resulting from a unit change in the financial domain satisfaction. The authors compared values of different domains as well as values of different SCLU activities by using the unit-free measure of elasticity. The mean values of elasticities of different domains and SCLU activities are given in Table 22.4.

The GS was inelastic with respect to domain satisfaction. The GS has the highest elasticity (0.23) with respect to the health domain and the lowest elasticity (0.09) with respect to the financial domain, while elasticities with respect to the housing and the SCLU domains were 0.19 and 0.20, respectively. Hence, for the same change in GS, the financial domain satisfaction has to be increased by more than the double of the percentage change in the SCLU, health or housing domain satisfaction.

The GS was also inelastic with respect to all the SCLU activities. GS elasticities with respect to SCLU activities, except gathering days, were quite a bit higher than the GS elasticity with respect to income. The GS elasticity with respect to gathering quality was highest, and with respect to gathering days was lowest.

The ratios of mean GSEF (GS elasticity with respect to a factor) and mean GSEIF (GS elasticity with respect to income) indicated that for the same incremental change in GS, income has to be increased by 31.32 percent, 7.97 percent and 5.41 percent for a 1 percent increase in gathering quality, social ties and the traditional diets, respectively. The GS was also inelastic with respect to all housing factors and health services. Among these factors, the GS elasticity was highest with respect to housing utilities and lowest with respect to housing maintenance. The ratios of mean GSEF and mean GSEIF indicated that to achieve the same incremental change in GS, income has to be increased by 10.58 percent, 5.68 percent, 9.64 percent and 15.11 percent for a 1 percent increase in the satisfaction with health services, housing maintenance, housing space and housing utilities, respectively.

The coefficient of different domains in the GS equation reconfirmed the importance of SCLU, health and housing domains in First Nations peoples' subjective wellbeing. The relatively higher elasticities of GS with respect to SCLU factors as compared to with respect to income demonstrate the higher sensitivity of subjective wellbeing with respect to SCLU factors.

Table 22.4 General satisfaction elasticity with respect to different domains and factors

General satisfaction elasticities with respect to domain

	Financial domain	SCLU domain	Health domain	Housing domain
Mean GSED	0.09	0.20	0.23	0.19
Mean GSED/ mean GSEFD	1.00	2.22	2.55	2.11

General satisfaction elasticities with respect to SCLU factors

	Breadwinner's income	Traditional diet	Social ties	Law land use	Gathering quality	Gathering days
Mean GSEF	0.0034	0.0184	0.0271	0.0318	0.1065	0.0028
Mean GSEF/ mean GSEIF	1.00	5.41	7.97	9.35	31.32	0.82

General satisfaction elasticities with respect to health and housing factors

	Breadwinner's income	Housing space	Housing utility	Housing maintenance	Health services
Mean GSEF	0.0034	0.0328	0.0514	0.0193	0.0360
Mean GSEF/ mean GSEIF	1.00	9.64	15.11	5.68	10.58

Source: Kant et al. (2016).

22.3 CONCEPTUAL FOUNDATIONS OF INDIVIDUAL WELFARE FUNCTION

Van Praag (1968) introduced the concept of the individual welfare function (IWF) of income, which is similar to the cardinal utility function of income. The basic philosophy behind IWF of income is that an individual evaluates their annual income level (y) on some scale in terms of the degree of bad and good. Or, in other words, an individual evaluates their income by comparing the income with the worst income level (can be assumed as zero) and the best income level (can be assumed to be infinite). If the evaluation of income level y is denoted by $U(y)$, it will be natural to denote $U(0) = 0$ and $U(\infty) = 1$. However, the interval scale need not to be [0 1] and it can be any finite interval, say [a b]; the only essential aspect is that it is bounded. In this interval, "a" represents the position of complete dissatisfaction and "b" represents the position of complete satisfaction. In this interval, the evaluation can be done by verbal qualifications (such as good or bad) used in daily language to express satisfaction or dissatisfaction, corresponding with different levels of wellbeing, which are then translated into numbers in the [0, 1] scale. $U(y)$ is called the individual welfare function of income and it is monotonically non-decreasing. It is important to understand that IWF of income represents only the relative welfare as perceived by the individual and not any objectively measurable property of income (Van Praag, 1971).

It is well established in the literature that the best function specification of IWF is a log-normal distribution (Van Herwaarden and Kapteyn, 1981) which means $U(z;\mu,\sigma) = \Lambda(z;\mu,\sigma)$ where $\Lambda(z;\mu,\sigma) = N(\ln(z);\mu,\sigma)$. The function $\Lambda(.)$ stands for the log-normal distribution function, and μ and σ are the parameters of the welfare function which have psychological as well as economic interpretations (Van Praag and Kapteyn, 1973).

Parameter μ is known as the "want parameter" and sometimes μ and its exponential (e^{μ}) has been referred to as the "natural unit"; which means the income level corresponding with the median value of welfare evaluation. In other words, the value of μ for an IWF of income indicates the level of income that an individual needs to attain the median welfare evaluation of 0.5. Parameter σ is known as the "welfare sensitivity parameter"; a large value of σ means that the welfare is less sensitive to a unit change in income, while a low value ofσ indicates high sensitivity of welfare due to a unit change in income.

22.3.1 Estimation Methods of Parameters of Individual Welfare Function

On the basis of the formulation of the IEQ, an individual divides the income range into a number of intervals proposed in the IEQ. In our IEQ, we offered six intervals, and therefore the individual gave us a division of their income range into six intervals: $[0, Z_2]$, $(Z_2\ Z_3]$,. . ., (Z_6, ∞). The corresponding utility values $U(Z_2)$, $U(Z_3)$. . ., $U(Z_6)$ can be calculated by $y_i = U(Z_i) = (i-1)/n$, ($n = 6$ in this case), or, in words, the brackets are chosen in such a way that each bracket contains the same welfare mass 1/n which is called the equal-quantile assumption (see Van Praag, 1991).

The parameters μ and σ for each IWF (welfare function for each individual) are calculated as following:

$$\hat{\mu}_n = \frac{1}{6}\sum_{i=1}^{6}\ln(z_{in}) \text{ and } \hat{\sigma}_n^2 = \frac{1}{5}\sum_{i=1}^{6}\ln(z_{in} - \hat{\mu}_n)^2. \tag{22.1}$$

The contributions of various explanatory variables to the variation of the estimated parameters μ and σ are calculated using the following two regression equations:

$$\hat{\mu}_n = \alpha \ln(y_n) + \beta x_{in} + \gamma \tag{22.2}$$

$$\hat{\sigma}_n = \alpha \ln(y_n) + \beta x_{in} + \gamma \tag{22.3}$$

where y_n is the actual income of individual n, and x_{in} is the ith explanatory factor.

In our data, the questions related to income evaluation and traditional diet evaluation were answered by all respondents, while the question of trapping income evaluation was answered by 43 respondents only. Hence, 272 out of 315 people choose not to answer this question, or they just did not have trapping income, which means the use of simple regression model will have selection or non-response bias. To address the selection bias issue, a two-step sample selection model (Heckman, 1976, 1979) has been widely used (Fink and Rork, 2003; Bushway et al., 2007). We also use Heckman's estimator to estimate the welfare function of trapping income. The two-step model includes a probit model, and a regression model that is observed only for the part of the sample which is "selected," that is, the respondents. The model can be formulated as follows.

In the first step, a probit model used to estimate the probability that households responded:

$$T_i^* = \beta_i' X_i + \varepsilon_i \tag{22.4}$$

where, $Ti^* = 1$ if an individual responds to the trapping income evaluation question, and $Ti^* = 0$ for those who did not answer the question, and X_i are explanatory factors for participation in trapping income activities which are SCLU factors.

In the second step, an OLS regression model is applied to the sample of individuals where $Ti^* = 1$:

$$\hat{\mu}_n^{trap} = \alpha \ln(y_n) + \beta x_{in} + v \tag{22.5}$$

$$\hat{\sigma}_n^{trap} = \alpha \ln(y_n) + \beta x_{in} + v \tag{22.6}$$

These equations are the same as equations (22.2) and (22.3), respectively. The assumption is that the error system follows a bivariate normal distribution; correlation between ε in equation (22.4) and υ in equations (22.5) and (22.6) lead to biased estimation if equations (22.5) and (22.6) are estimated alone.

22.4 ESTIMATED PARAMETERS OF HOUSEHOLD WELFARE FUNCTIONS AND THEIR ANALYSIS

As we stated in section 22.1, our unit of analysis is the household and not an individual, and therefore we are using a household welfare function (HWF), and not an IWF, in this section. We discuss the results of HWF of income and traditional diet together because their estimation methods are the same. The results of HWF of trapping income are discussed separately.

22.4.1 Results of HWF of Income and Traditional Diet

In the case of HWF of income, the estimated mean value of μ is 10.22 and the mean value of **σ** is 0.51. The corresponding HWF for the estimated mean values is sketched in Figure 22.2. Hence, for average annual income of $26 377, that is $ln(y) = 10.18$, the corresponding HWF value is 0.47, which means the head of household with average income feels halfway to total satisfaction. However, most household heads (over 60 percent of our sample) have very low income of 0–$17 500 (in log form this is equal to 9.58); for these heads of households, the corresponding evaluation level is only 0.15 which means that most heads of households evaluate their income as "very low" or "low." Only heads of households with higher income ($17 500–$37 500) were quite satisfied with their financial situation, with $\mathbf{\Lambda} = 0.73$.

In the case of an HWF with a traditional diet, the estimated mean value of μ is 2.59, which is slightly lower than the mean traditional diet of 2.98. Hence, a household head with a mean value of the want parameter evaluates its welfare position slightly above the

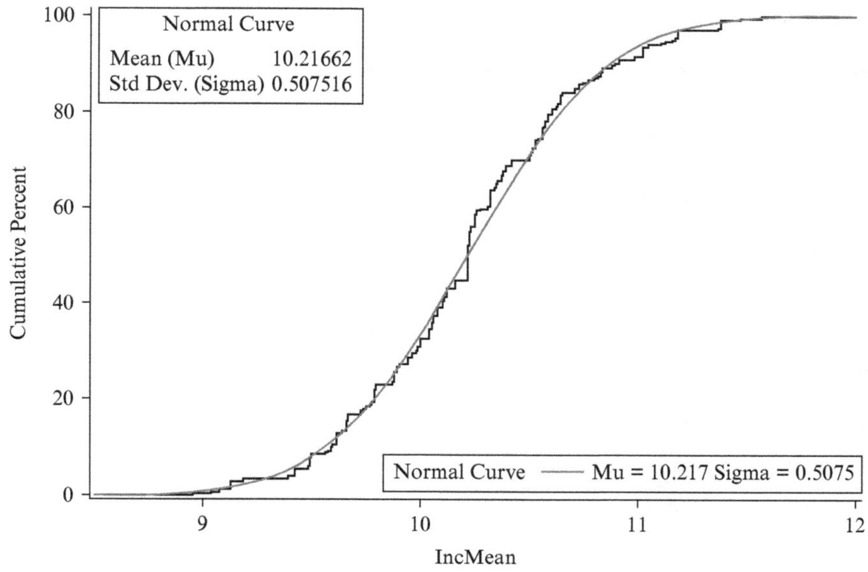

Figure 22.2 Household welfare function of income for the estimated mean values

midpoint of the evaluation scale. The estimated mean value of σ is 0.53, which means the sensitivity parameter of income and traditional diet are similar.

The regression results for want and sensitivity parameters of HWF of income and traditional diet are given in Table 22.5. F-values for want and sensitivity models of income and traditional diet are significant. The R^2 for the want parameter models of income and traditional diet are 0.64 and 0.60, respectively; while the R^2 for sensitivity parameter models are 0.28 and 0.12, respectively. Hence, our estimated models capture a very good proportion of variance in want parameters, but the explanatory power of sensitivity parameter models is not that good. However, there are many significant coefficients in the sensitivity models of income as well as traditional diet, and we discuss the contributions of different explanatory factors next.

In the case of HWF of income, the coefficients of income and family size are positive and significant at the 1 percent level, and these results are similar to results reported in the previous literature including Van Pragg (1971) and Van Praag and Kapteyn (1973). A positive income coefficient indicates that as the head of household's income increases, the head of household needs more money to attain an average level of want parameter; this is called the "preference drift" (Van Pragg, 1971; Van Praag and Kapteyn, 1973). This phenomenon is similar to the notions of adaptation and the endowment effect in psychology (Nettle, 2005). The coefficient of income is referred to as the preference drift rate, the rate at which preference shifts with income.

In the case of the HWF of income, other results are specific to our First Nations context. For example, the coefficient of *Female* is positive and significant at the 1 percent level, which indicates that households headed by females need more income, as compared to households headed by males, for the average value of want (satisfaction). The coefficients

Table 22.5 Regression results of two parameters of HWF of income and traditional diet

	μ-income	σ-income	μ-traditional diet	σ-traditional diet
Intercept	5.14***	1.27***	1.09***	1.28***
LogInc	0.51***	−0.07***	0.06*	−0.03
LogFsize	0.22***	0.06***	0.06	0.05*
Female	0.13***	−0.05***	−0.01	−0.02
LogTradDiets	0.01	−0.02*	0.44***	−0.09***
Ontario	−0.02	−0.06***	−0.11**	−0.04
MentalFreq	0.13*	−0.20***	0.19**	−0.07
ExtOrgFreq	0.03	0.04*	0.10**	−0.06*
TradMed	0.01	−0.00	0.04***	0.002
Unemplfull	−0.22***	0.11***	−0.01	0.01
HousLoc	−0.11***	0.06***	−0.09***	0.03
LogEdu	−0.12***	0.06**	0.04	0.0005
Trappers	0.02	−0.01	0.08***	−0.002
GatherQualit	−0.05***	−0.003	−0.002	−0.02
SocTies	−0.03*	−0.02**	−0.04**	0.02
LawCultu	0.01	−0.02**	−0.07***	0.02
N	314	314	314	314
R-square	0.64	0.28	0.60	0.12
F-value	35.81***	7.86***	30.41***	2.62***

of house location, gathering quality and social ties are negative and significant. The coefficient of house location means that households that are more satisfied with their house location need less money for their satisfaction. Similarly, households that enjoy higher levels of gathering quality need less income for an average level of satisfaction. The negative relationship between social ties and the want parameter means that stronger social ties reduce the amount of income needed for average satisfaction. These results indicate that the household's income evaluation of the welfare function is also influenced by social and cultural factors. The financial aspiration depends not only on current level of income and employment but also on social and cultural factors that contribute to their level of satisfaction from the financial domain.

The R^2 of the sensitivity parameter model is low but most of the coefficients are significant, which means there are some additional explanatory variables but the variables included are also important. The coefficient of income is significant and negative, which implies that increase in income leads to decrease in σ and therefore increase in welfare sensitivity, and vice versa. The positive and significant coefficients of family size, education, house location and unemployment suggest that a bigger family size, better education, good house location and unemployment can enhance the efficient use of money and therefore reduce sensitivity. The negative and significant coefficient of *Female* indicates that income sensitivity of households headed by females is higher than that of households headed by males. Similarly, negative coefficients of severe mental problem, social ties and traditional diet indicate that the increase in the values of these variables increases the sensitivity of the welfare function.

In the case of HWF of traditional diet, similar to HWF of income, the want parameter is significantly positive related to individual's actual level of traditional diet, which means that the phenomenon of preference drift is also true for the traditional diet. As the diet percentage increases, the individual needs more traditional food for an average level of the want parameter. Also, family income contributes positively to the traditional food want parameter.

Other interesting results are the positive and significant coefficients of health-related variables (*Mentalsev*, *ExtOrgsev*, *TradMed*), and number of trappers (*Trappers*), suggesting that the want parameter for First Nations people with severe mental and physical problems is higher, and the want parameter also increases with the satisfaction with traditional medicines and number of trappers in the household.

Consistent with the finding made in the income welfare function, the satisfaction of house location and social ties have negative and significant coefficients. Aboriginals who are more satisfied with where they live and who have stronger social ties can be more easily satisfied with a relatively lower traditional diet percentage. It was found that *LawCultu* also has a significant negative effect on the want parameter, which means the better evaluation of the impact of government law on household aboriginal cultural and social life can reduce the amount of traditional diet needed for an average satisfaction.

In the sensitivity parameter model of traditional diet, the coefficient of traditional diet percentage is significant and negative, which implies that an increase in the traditional food percentage leads to reduced σ and increased welfare sensitivity. The coefficient of family size is positive and significant. So the effect of traditional diet and family size of the sensitivity of HWF of traditional diet are similar to the effect of income and family size of the sensitivity of HWF of income. The only other significant negative coefficient is of frequent external organ problems, which means that sensitivity of HWF of traditional diet increases with severe external organ problems. This result may indicate that households with frequent external organ problems may be hampered in their ability to collect traditional food items, and as a result they may adjust their expectations to a narrow range (higher sensitivity) of the collection of traditional food items.

22.4.2 Results of Individual Welfare Functions of Trapping Income

In the case of HWF of trapping, the estimated mean value of μ is 2.69 which is slightly lower than the mean trapping income of 3.00. Hence, a household with mean value of want parameter evaluates its welfare position above the midpoint of the evaluation scale ($\lambda = 0.64$). The estimated mean value of σ is 0.84, which means the sensitivity parameter of trapping income is quite high (sensitivity is quite low) as compared to income and traditional diet.

The regression results of selection model are given in Table 22.6. The model indicates that income, severe external organ problems, satisfaction with health services, education and house title reduced the probability of having trapping income, while the frequency of participation in traditional ceremonies and satisfaction with the government laws that influence their social and cultural life increase the probability of having trapping income. The regression results for the want parameter and sensitivity parameter of trapping income are given in Table 22.7. The want parameter model explains about 79 percent of variation, while the sensitivity model explains 46 percent variation which is quite high compared to the R^2 of the sensitivity parameter models of HWF of income and traditional diet. The coefficient of actual trapping income is positive and significant which

Table 22.6 Heckman two-step selection correction estimation: the probit regression result (Trap = 1)

Variables	Trap (1/0) N = 315
Intercept	2.08
LogInc	−0.197
ON	−0.57***
ExtOrgsev	−0.89***
HealServ	−0.30***
HousTitle	−0.33*
LogEdu	−0.63***
Ceremony	0.45***
LawCultu	0.15**
−2 Log L	210.825
Likelihood ratio	40.2761***
RHO (ρ)	−0.1670***

Table 22.7 Regression results of two parameters of HWF of trapping income

Variables	μ-Trapping income	σ-Trapping income
Intercept	5.79***	−0.46
LogInc	−0.14	−0.002
TrapInc	0.02***	−0.001
LogAge	−0.31*	0.23**
Married	0.49***	−0.14
TradMed	0.13***	−0.05**
WorkEnv	−0.32***	0.10***
TradDiets	−0.02***	0.01**
LawLanUs	−0.09*	0.06**
N	43	43
R-square	0.79	0.46
F-value	14.41***	3.07***

means that the phenomenon of preference drift is true for trapping income also. As the actual trapping income increases, the individual needs more trapping income to achieve average satisfaction with trapping income, or the trapping income aspiration shifts with the actual trapping income.

The coefficient of age is significant and negative while the coefficient of marriage is significant and positive. These coefficients mean that trapping income required for the mean value of want parameter is higher for households headed by a young person as compared to households headed by an old person, and it is higher for households having a married person as head as compared to households having a non-married person as head. The positive and significant coefficient of *TradMed* indicates that households that experience a more positive state of these practices need higher trapping income for their satisfaction. In the case of the sensitivity parameter model, the coefficients of *LogAge*, *TradMed*, *WorkEnv*, *TradDiets* and *LawLanUs* are significant but signs are opposite to the signs in the want parameter model, which means that the impact on sensitivity is in the same direction as on want (higher σ means low sensitivity).

22.5 SUMMARY AND CONCLUSIONS

In this chapter, we investigate the subjective wellbeing of two First Nations peoples of Canada living on reserves, using multi-domain models of subjective wellbeing and household welfare functions. We discuss the results of the three HWFs of income, traditional diet and trapping income. We used primary data collected through participatory methods. In our open-ended and focus group discussions, the First Nations participants emphasized that their wellbeing analysis should be done at the household level and not the individual level, because they cannot imagine themselves in isolation from their household, therefore our unit of analysis in this chapter has been a household and not an individual.

Our analysis of multi-domain subjective wellbeing, which has been published earlier and summarized in this chapter, has provided empirical evidence in the support of First Nations peoples' view that the social, cultural and land use (SCLU) domain is the most important determinant of overall wellbeing of First Nations peoples. Moreover, SCLU factors also contribute to satisfaction with other domains. We therefore focused our analysis on the impact of SCLU factors on want and sensitivity parameters of HWF of income, and two key First Nations-specific contributors to satisfaction with life: traditional diet and trapping income.

The results of our analyses indicated that the HWF of traditional diet and trapping income also have the key characteristic of preference drift that has been reported for HWF of income. Preference drift means that the higher the current level of traditional diet and trapping income, the higher amounts of these contributors will be required to feel satisfied with these traditional ways of life.

Our results indicate that the want and sensitivity parameters of HWF of income not only depend on conventional economic and demographic factors, such as income, family size, employment and education, but also that First Nations SCLU, health and housing factors affect these parameters. Some of the SCLU factors affecting these parameters are gathering quality, social ties and number of trappers. Similarly, First Nations SCLU, health, housing and laws related to First Nations lifestyle affect the want and sensitivity parameters of HWF of traditional diet and trapping income.

It is quite interesting to note that an improvement of gathering quality or a stronger tie to the community can reduce the amount of income for average income satisfaction. That is to say, even when income is low, Aboriginal people can still improve their wellbeing by having a better experience with land use activities and social life. It also appears that raising incomes in an Aboriginal community would not necessarily lead to decreases in the aspiration for traditional ways of life (especially with respect to the need for traditional food). It is also interesting to note that a higher level of satisfaction with government laws related to Aboriginal cultural and social life, and laws related to Aboriginal land use activities, can significantly reduce the amount required for average satisfaction from traditional diet and trapping income, respectively. This indicates the importance of having a government that shows sensitivity and understanding of Aboriginal perspectives on life and wellbeing and therefore is trusted. Non-timber forest products are the main sources of traditional medicine and traditional diet. Thus, more efficient management of forest land should be promoted to adapt the increasing aspiration of First Nations peoples' wellbeing.

Our results are based on data from two First Nations which may not be a true representation of all First Nations in Canada, specifically First Nations from other provinces and First Nations that are not participating in economic development at the same level as these two First Nations. Hence, the results cannot be treated as representatives of all ORFN peoples in Canada. More studies are required to get the holistic picture of subjective wellbeing of all First Nations peoples of Canada.

NOTES

1. Nearly one-half of First Nations people live on Indian reserves: tracts of land set apart by the Canadian government for the use and benefit of a particular First Nations people (Statistics Canada, 2013).
2. Path analysis, similar to regression analysis, is a statistical method to examine whether or not a multivariate set of non-experimental data fits well with an a priori causal model. A path analysis model, unlike a regression model, includes all causal mechanisms through which independent variables produce direct as well as indirect effects on a dependent variable. Path analysis is also considered to be a better option in the case of two or more dependent variables, because path analysis decomposes the sources of the correlations among the dependent variables. Readers interested in more details of path analysis may like to refer Li (1975) and Olobatuyi (2006), or Google the term "path analysis."
3. Van Praag introduced IEQ prior to the LSQ but the concepts of life satisfaction and happiness have been discussed by psychologists, philosophers, and other social scientists much before Van Praag. Some examples of earlier work are the life satisfaction index by Neugarten et al. (1961) and the scale of happiness by Havighurst and Albrecht (1953). Given the interest of multiple streams of social scientists, including economists, social psychologists, sociologists and philosophers, the LSQ has become more popular.
4. The First Nations people consulted, as discussed in the next section, suggested to use a household (and not an individual) as the unit of wellbeing analysis, and therefore our whole analysis in previous papers as well as in this chapter is based on the household.
5. First, the system of five equations was estimated using 2SLS, but DWH test confirmed the presence of endogeneity. Hence, the 3SLS was used to estimate the model, and Durbin–Wu–Hausman (DWH) test confirmed the absence of endogeneity in these results.

REFERENCES

Adelson, N. (ed.) (2000), *'Being Alive Well': Health and the Politics of Cree Wellbeing*, Toronto, Canada: University of Toronto Press.

Barrington-Leigh, C.P. and S. Sloman (2016), 'Life satisfaction among Aboriginal peoples in the Canadian prairies: evidence from the equality, security and community survey', *International Indigenous Policy Journal*, **7** (2), Article 2.

Bushway, S., Johnson, B.D. and L.A. Slocum (2007), 'Is the magic still there? The use of the Heckman two-step correction for selection bias in criminology', *Journal of Quantitative Criminology*, **23** (2), 151–178.

Byrne, B.M. (2001), *Structural Equation Modeling with AMOS: Basic Concepts, Applications and Programming*, Hove, UK: Psychology Press.

Canadian Council on Learning (CCL) (2007), 'Redefining how success is measured in First Nations, Inuit and Métis learning, Report on Learning in Canada 2007', Ottawa, Canada.

Canadian Forest Service (CFS) (2012), 'The state of Canada's forests 2011–2012', Ottawa, Canada: Natural Resources Canada.

Cummins, R.A. (1996), 'The domains of life satisfaction: an attempt to order chaos', *Social Indicators Research*, **38**, 303–332.
Danziger, S., van der Gaag, J., Smolensky, E. and M. Taussig (1984), 'The direct measurement of welfare level: how much does it cost to make ends meet?', *Review of Economics and Statistics*, **66** (3), 500–505.
Deaton, A. (2008), 'Income, aging, health and wellbeing around the world: evidence from the Gallup World Poll', *Journal of Economic Perspectives*, **22** (2), 53–72.
Fernando, M. (2002), 'A look at life satisfaction and ethnicity in Canada', *Canadian Ethnic Studies*, **34** (1), 51–64.
Fink, S. and J. Rork (2003), 'The importance of self−selection in casino cannibalization of state lotteries', *Economics Bulletin*, **8** (10), 1−8.
Garvin, T., Nelson, S., Ellehoj, E. and B. Redmond (2001), 'A guide to conducting a traditional knowledge and land use study', Edmonton, Canada: Natural Resources Canada, Canadian Forest Service.
Hagenaars, A.J.M. and B.M.S. van Praag (1985), 'A synthesis of poverty line definition', *Review of Income and Wealth*, **31**, 139–153.
Havighurst, R.J. and R. Albrecht (eds) (1953), *Older People*, Harlow, UK: Longmans, Green & Company.
Heckman, J.J. (1976), 'The common structure of statistical models of truncation, sample selection, and limited dependent variables and a simple estimator for such models', *Annals of Economic and Social Measurement*, **5**, 475–492.
Heckman, J.J. (1979), 'Sample selection bias as a specification error', *Econometrica*, **47**, 153–161.
Helliwell, J.F. and R.D. Putnam (2004), 'The social context of wellbeing', *Philosophical Transactions of the Royal Society B*, **359**, 1435–1446.
Kant, S., Vertinsky, I. and B. Zheng (2016), 'Valuation of ecosystem services using the life satisfaction approach: the case of land use activities of the First Nations peoples of Canada', *Forest Policy and Economics*, **72**, 46–55.
Kant, S., Vertinsky, I. and B. Zhang (2019), 'Subjective wellbeing of Aboriginal peoples of Canada', in M. Manning and C. Fleming (eds), *Routledge Handbook of Indigenous Wellbeing*, Abingdon, UK: Routledge, pp. 283–301.
Kant, S., Vertinsky, I., Zheng, B. and P. Smith (2013), 'Social, cultural, and land use determinants of the health and well-being of Aboriginal peoples of Canada: a path analysis', *Journal of Public Health Policy*, **34** (3), 462–476.
Kapteyn, A. and T. Wansweek (1985), 'The individual welfare function: a review', *Journal of Economic Psychology*, **6** (4), 333–363.
Kapteyn, A., Smith, J.P. and A. van Soest (2010), 'Life satisfaction', in Ed Diener, John F. Helliwell and Daniel Kahneman (eds), *International Differences in Wellbeing*, New York, USA: Oxford University Press, pp. 70–104.
Kijazi, M.H. and S. Kant (2011), 'Evaluation of welfare functions of environmental amenities: a case of forest biomass fuels in Mount Kilimanjaro, Tanzania', *Ecological Economics*, **72**, 129–139.
Kinsella, E. (1999), 'Traditional ecological knowledge within the Government of Canada's First Nation Forestry Program: a case study', Ottawa, Canada: Natural Resources Canada, Canadian Forest Service.
Kirmayer, L.J. (2007), 'Psychotherapy and the cultural concept of the person', *Transcultural Psychiatry*, **44** (2), 232–257.
Kleinman, A.M. (1977), 'Depression somatization and the "new cross-cultural psychiatry"', *Social Science and Medicine*, **11** (1), 3–10.
Li, C.C. (ed.) (1975), *Path Analysis – A Primer*, Pacific Grove, CA, USA: Boxwood Press.
Michalski, J.H. (2001), 'Asking citizens what matters for quality of life in Canada. Results of CPRN'S Public Dialogue Process', Ottawa, Canada: Canadian Policy Research Network.
Mussell, B., Cardiff, K. and J. White (2004), 'The mental health and wellbeing of Aboriginal children and youth: guidance for new approaches and services', Vancouver, Canada: Sal'I'Shan Institute and University of British Columbia.
Nettle, D. (ed.) (2005), *Happiness: The Science behind Your Smile*, Oxford, UK: Oxford University Press.
Neugarten, B.L., Havighurst, R.J. and S.S. Tobin (1961), 'The measurement of life satisfaction', *Journal of Gerontology*, **16** (2), 134–143.
Olobatuyi, M.E. (ed.) (2006), *A User's Guide to Path Analysis*, Lanham, MD, USA: University Press of America.
Parsons, R. and G. Prest (2003), 'Aboriginal forestry in Canada', *Forestry Chronicle*, **79** (4), 779–784.
Perley, D. (1999), 'Overview of the medicinal plants of Eel Ground First Nation', Sussex, New Brunswick, Canada: Fundy Model Forest.
Salée, D., Newhouse, D. and C. Levesque (2006), 'Quality of life of Aboriginal people in Canada: an analysis of current research', *IRPP Choices*, **12** (6), 1–38.
Smith, P. (1995), 'Aboriginal participation in forest management: not just another "stakeholder"', Ottawa, Canada: National Aboriginal Forestry Association.
Statistics Canada (2013), 'Aboriginal peoples in Canada: First Nations people, Metis and Inuit: National Household Survey, 2011', Catalogue No. 99, 011-X2011001.

Statistics Canada (2017), 'Highlight tables: Aboriginal peoples highlight tables', 2016 Census, Catalogue No. 98-402-X2016009.

Tanner, A. (2004), 'The cosmology of nature, cultural divergence, and the metaphysics of community healing', in John Clammer, Sylvie Poirier and Eric Schwimmer (eds), *Figured Worlds: Ontological Obstacles in Intercultural Relations*, Toronto, Canada: University of Toronto Press, pp. 189–222.

Van Herwaarden, F.G. and A. Kapteyn (1981), 'Empirical comparison of the shape of welfare functions', *European Economic Review*, **15** (3), 261–286.

Van Herwaarden, F.G., Kapteyn, A. and B.M.S. Van Praag (1977), 'Twelve thousand individual welfare functions: a comparison of six samples in Belgium and the Netherlands', *European Economic Review*, **9** (3), 283–300.

Van Praag, B.M.S. (ed.) (1968), *Individual Welfare Functions and Consumer Behavior*, Amsterdam, Netherlands: North Holland Publishing.

Van Praag, B.M.S. (1971), 'The welfare function of income in Belgium: an empirical investigation', *European Economic Review*, **2** (3), 337–369.

Van Praag, B.M.S. (1977), 'The perception of welfare inequality', *European Economic Review*, **10** (2), 189–207.

Van Praag, B.M.S. (1991), 'Ordinal and cardinal utility: an integration of the two dimensions of the welfare concept', *Journal of Econometrics*, **50** (1–2), 69–89.

Van Praag, B.M.S. and Ada Ferrer-i-Carbonell (eds) (2008), *Happiness Quantified: A Satisfaction Calculus Approach*, New York, USA: Oxford University Press.

Van Praag, B.M.S. and A. Kapteyn (1973), 'Further evidence on the individual welfare function of income: an empirical investigation in The Netherlands', *European Economic Review*, **4** (1), 33–62.

Van Praag, B.M.S. and J. Linthorst (1976), 'Municipal welfare functions', *Regional Science and Urban Economics*, **6** (1), 51–79.

Van Praag, B.M.S., Hagenaars, A.J.M. and H. Van Weeren (1982), 'Poverty in Europe', *Review of Income and Wealth*, **28** (3), 345–359.

Zagon, S. (2001), 'Indicators of quality of life in Canada: a citizen's prototype', Ottawa, Canada, Canadian Research Network.

PART III

CONCLUSION

23. Happiness in retrospect and prospect

Bruno S. Frey

23.1 RETROSPECT

Research on subjective wellbeing – in short, 'happiness' – has produced remarkable results over the last few years.[1] As documented in this *Handbook*, there are many important contributions showing the relationship between the natural environment and happiness.

23.1.1 Determinants of Happiness

The identification of the determinants of happiness has received most attention in research on subjective wellbeing. Among the most important findings are the following (always *ceteris paribus*; that is, holding all other determinants constant).

Individuals and households with higher income state that they are happier – that is, their subjective life satisfaction is higher – than those with lower income. There is a diminishing marginal effect of income on happiness. People rather quickly adapt to higher income, and they tend to compare themselves with people of higher income; this reduces their level of wellbeing because they consider themselves to be relatively less well off.

One of the most important factors for individual wellbeing are satisfactory personal relationships. Persons having a good family life, friends and acquaintances are more satisfied with their lives than are isolated persons.

Good physical and psychological health are among the most significant contributors to happiness.

To live in a democracy makes people happy; individuals value the possibility to participate politically in a meaningful and effective way. If citizens can directly participate via popular initiatives and referenda – that is, if there are elements of direct democracy – then they are even more satisfied with their lives. People are also happier if as many political decisions as possible are taken on a decentralized level.

These results are in line with economic thinking. However, they do not necessarily correspond to what laypersons think and believe. Many people, for example, think that persons in poor developing nations are happier than those living in countries with higher average income, presumably because they lead a less stressful life or are closer to nature. The empirical research on happiness has demonstrated in a great number of studies that this idea is mistaken. It greatly contributes to happiness if one lives in a rich country. Research on wellbeing has also produced results not in line with standard economic theory. But the theory is flexible enough to provide *ex post* explanations. Here are three examples.

First, the unemployed are dramatically less happy than persons having a job. This result holds even when income is kept constant. Unemployed persons are much less happy not (only) due to reduced income. This result appears surprising to conventional economics where work is considered a burden or a cost. People work solely because of the income they receive. The analyses on the wellbeing effects of unemployment focus on the pure effect of losing one's job; income is therefore kept constant. As according to conventional economics work is a cost, not having to work (and receiving the same income) should raise wellbeing. But the empirical results suggest the opposite: people without work are much less happy.

This result can easily be explained by putting *ex post* additional arguments into the utility function. When social relationships, reputation, recognition and self-esteem are relevant factors in individual utility functions, the unemployed are in an unfortunate position. They quickly lose social contacts because they have to leave their work environment, and they may even be ridiculed and disregarded by other persons. Above all, their self-esteem is hampered. These negative factors overshadow the possible advantages of getting income without having to work.

Second, the self-employed work more hours and on average have a lower income and higher risk than employees of a firm or other organization. Nevertheless, careful happiness studies reveal that the self-employed (*ceteris paribus*) are happier than those working as employees.

To explain this result one can introduce that people are risk-loving. Those persons seeking independent work probably have a strong desire to take risks, and are therefore happy with working hard and long hours. People can also be assumed to overestimate the probability of being successful in what they engage in. One can observe many self-employed persons being happy with their situation, but who nevertheless fail at a later stage. To introduce autonomy as an element in the utility function is another way of providing an *ex post* explanation for the happy self-employed. Such workers enjoy their autonomy and are therefore more satisfied with their lives than those working in a hierarchical setting.

Third, making donations, or engaging in voluntary work, raises happiness. In contrast, standard economic theory assumes that more money and leisure always contribute to utility. Empirical studies on wellbeing suggest that the opposite – namely, giving money, and engaging in work for others – also holds.

This result can be explained by a desire to induce reciprocity by the persons receiving a gift. If such reciprocity is strong enough, it is rational to give. Givers may also raise their reputation in society. They thereby demonstrate that they are rich enough to afford to be generous. Such action may help them to raise their status in society.

Such explanations made after having observed an empirical outcome need to be clearly distinguished from predictions made before the empirical result has been reached. The explanations offered make sense and can well be introduced into economic theory. However, in each case additional assumptions are required to reach reasonable explanations. This procedure is in order as long as the additional explanations are not introduced ad hoc. If instead the extensions are introduced to explain observed phenomena *ex post*, it is impossible to empirically test theoretical hypotheses. This undermines one of the major strengths of economics.

23.1.2 Consequences of Happiness

Persons considering themselves to be happy act differently in many life circumstances. Happier persons are more successful in their jobs. The more satisfied people are with their lives, the more willing they are to work hard. Such people work more intensively, are more engaged and more creative, which leads to a higher per-capita income for individuals and the country as a whole.

Happy persons find it easier to get married. Happier people have the opportunity to attract a larger number of suitable partners. Due to their companionship they are less affected by happiness-reducing loneliness.

Happier persons are more cooperative and more inclined to help others by engaging in informal neighbourhood help or in formal voluntary work. In contrast, unhappy people tend to isolate themselves from their social environment.

Happier persons are in better psychological and physical health and are also less likely to commit suicide. Positive effects of happiness on health are thus no fairy tale.

Happy persons enjoy a longer life. Their lives are almost 15 per cent longer than those of persons considering themselves to be unhappy. In industrial countries this means that happy persons can expect to live around ten years longer than unhappy ones.

23.1.3 Causality

Observing a correlation between some variable and happiness does not inform us in what direction the influence works. Often it is difficult to establish what is cause and what is effect. For instance, it is not obvious whether married people get happier, or happy people find it easier to get married. The same applies to work: are employed persons happier, or is it easier for happy persons to find a job because they are more active, creative and open? The same factors can be both determinants or consequences of subjective wellbeing.

The causality issue has received great attention in happiness research, as well as in economic research generally. It may even be argued that the causality issue has been overrated because, after all, in society everything depends on everything. There is rarely, if ever, a totally exogenous event. While in the past natural disasters such as hurricanes, floods or landslides could be considered as such, today they tend to be attributed to human intervention causing climate change.

For future empirical research on happiness a pragmatic approach is commendable. This means that less attention should be placed on trying to identify exactly which variables are endogenous, and which are exogenous. Viewed in a larger perspective, all variables that may theoretically be influenced by human action are endogenous to the system. In that sense, everything depends on everything. However, some events are exogenous from the point of view of a particular person. An example is winning a public lottery. The buyer of a lottery ticket cannot influence its outcome. The change in subjective life satisfaction for the winner can therefore be considered a consequence. Lottery winners indeed state that they are happier. This allows us to conclude that higher income and wealth raise happiness, though only for a short time period. After some time has passed, lottery winners are not much happier than they were before winning. The reason is that they get used to having more money, and that they compare themselves to well-endowed persons.

23.1.4 Integration into Standard Economics?

Happiness research has received great attention outside economics. The results of happiness research have been discussed in thousands of books and newspaper articles. Within economics, the reception has been less enthusiastic because economics is a rather traditional science with a well-determined core which graduate students have to fully master. Many economists still believe that it is impossible to measure utility (because Robbins and Hicks wrote so in the 1930s), and even reject the notion that the various measures of subjective wellbeing are useful empirical approximations to the purely theoretical concept of utility. Many economists still rely on the concept of revealed preference to capture individual utility, though this has been heavily criticized for a long time (especially by Sen, 1977).

Happiness research has been treated lightly even in so-called 'behavioural economics' (which is a misnomer because economics has always been behavioural), though happiness research is one of the few truly interdisciplinary areas; in this case, between psychology and economics.

However, subjective wellbeing has been taken up by a large number of young economists who consider it to be a lively area in which relevant results and insights are achieved. This confirms the often-made statement that in well-established academic fields progress is achieved only when the old scholars who framed the established theory are no longer active.

23.1.5 Policy Consequences

Some happiness scholars have been eager to integrate happiness into orthodox economics.[2] They see it as a way to at last achieve an old dream of the economic theory of policy *à la* Tinbergen (1956) and Theil (1968), namely to be able to maximize an empirically determined social welfare function. This is taken to be the task of government.

This approach assumes that government politicians are purely benevolent, and do not have any incentive to also pursue their own material and ideological interests. Looking at real life, this assumption is far away from what governments do. Research in the fields of political economy and public choice (see Mueller, 2003) has for a long time theoretically and empirically established how naïve such an assumption is. To presume that governments pursue aggregate social welfare is mistaken for several reasons.

First, even benevolent government politicians in democracies would not know what goals they should pursue to maximize social welfare. Indeed, it has been shown long ago that it is not possible to determine aggregate social welfare based on individual preferences (Arrow, 1951; Sen, 1982).

Second, many goals that may be important to individuals are vague and difficult to isolate. This applies in particular to environmental issues affecting not only the present but also the future generations. The politicians in charge have no way of knowing what the preferences of the individuals living in the future will be.

Third, in many cases the politicians in power have little or no incentive to closely follow the wishes of the population as long as they can build on a majority of votes in parliament. This allows them to pursue their own ideological or material interests. Only if they fear losing votes in a forthcoming election, and being thrown out of their present position, do they have an incentive to take the wishes of the population into account (see the literature on political business cycles; for example, Frey and Schneider, 1978a, 1978b; Frey, 1997).

Finally, governments are subject to many restrictions; that is, they are not free to pursue their preferred policies. Most importantly, the members of the public administration guard their own interests. As a rule, they strongly oppose any changes in policy proposed by government because this would endanger their position and influence. Experience and scientific research (Niskanen, 1971, 1994; Dunleavy, 2013) clearly show that the position of bureaucracy is strong relative to the government, not least because in general its members occupy their positions for a far longer time than do politicians.

The insights gained in happiness research should be used in a quite different way (Frey and Stutzer, 2012). They should be communicated to the voters in order to provide them with valuable information to be debated in the democratic political process. The researchers should in no circumstances try to tell voters what is an 'optimal' policy; this can only be determined in a democracy by a well-informed political discourse.

23.2 PROSPECTS

23.2.1 Some Areas which Happiness Research has only Partly Explored

Happiness research has established that the general unemployment level in the economy strongly reduces the level of happiness of the unemployed as well as for the rest of society. A government should therefore put much emphasis on combating unemployment. Most importantly, joblessness among young workers should be fought against, because they are scarred by this for their whole lives. Economic growth, in contrast, should be emphasized less, as the adaptation processes in many cases do not raise the happiness level in a sustainable way. These relationships should be further explored.

The inequality of incomes is another area deserving future research on happiness. The existing results suggest that in most countries large income differences between individuals reduce the overall happiness level of the population. For this reason, it has often been suggested to impose high tax rates on high-income recipients in order to achieve a more equal income distribution. However, highly taxing upper-income recipients tends to produce negative incentive effects. Some of the most productive members of society have less incentive to work hard and may shift their activity into the hidden economy. Such change negatively affects the whole population and reduces overall welfare. It may therefore well be the case that the people living in such societies feel less satisfied than before.

How the inequality of income affects happiness also depends on the opportunity of people to move upwards. An individual earning a low income but who sees a chance to gain a higher income in the future is less unhappy than persons who feel trapped in their income position. People confident that they will be able to leave a low-income position may even welcome a large spread in income; they want to have the opportunity to gain very large incomes in the future.

Existing happiness research does not come to an unequivocal result. There is some evidence that some United States Americans believe that they will move up the income ladder in the future, and therefore they are not unhappy about large differences in income (Alesina et al., 2004). However, recent developments in the United States strongly suggest that this feeling is no longer shared by a significant number of persons. Many of them consider themselves to be left alone by the rest of society. These aspects should be analyzed more deeply by future happiness research.

Doing good deeds for others raises one's own happiness; this is an important and a rather surprising result from the point of view of orthodox economic theory, which assumes human beings to be egotistic. An important area is the natural environment. Happiness research should analyze whether people acting in an environmentally sound and responsible way indeed feel happier. This is likely to be the case but it should be enquired more deeply under which conditions this proposition holds. It may be that this feeling only applies to actions having a visible and obvious effect on the natural environment. In contrast, when the positive effects on the environment lie far in the future, are uncertain or are controversial, it may well be that people are not prepared to act in an environmentally sustainable way. On the other hand, it cannot be excluded that persons wish to exhibit their moral commitment, or an 'expressive' action, to safeguarding the natural environment, irrespective of whether the effects can be identified or not.

In addition, happiness research should deal more deeply with already visible important problems due to future societal changes. This means that challenges coming from the real world – rather than problems formulated inside a more or less closed research community – should be at the centre of future scholarly inquiries.

For example, first, is an ageing population. A strong change in age distribution in economically advanced countries is well under way. Aged persons will have a stronger weight in the overall population. What individuals consider to be important for their wellbeing is likely to shift. Physical and psychological health will have more weight in the econometrically estimated happiness functions. This also includes considerations of what a desirable length of life is. A serene self-administered termination of life – for example, by rejection of food and drink – differs basically from many suicides at a younger age. Clearly, these are fundamental issues going beyond narrowly conceived happiness research, but they are important to take into account rather than to disregard.

Second is changing preferences. Per capita income in many countries has strongly increased over the last decades; China just being one case. Non-material aspects such as personal self-fulfilment, but also new companionships going beyond the family, will – at least in the long run – gain more weight compared to the material determinants of happiness.

A third example is digitization. Many persons spend a large number of hours on the Internet. There are divergent effects on subjective wellbeing. Some studies find that Internet contacts are helpful for individuals' social interactions, but trust in other people seems to be reduced. Other studies find other negative effects on happiness. Social network users are more likely to compare their income to that of those with whom they interact. They therefore are less satisfied with their own income. Persons who concentrate on whether they are 'liked' on Facebook are also less satisfied with the life they lead. They also feel lonelier, which hampers their subjective wellbeing. The overall consequences of digital developments on happiness are largely open (see, e.g., Sabatini and Sarracino, 2017), making it worthwhile to further explore them.

23.2.2 Possible Decreasing Returns

Over the last few years there has been almost an explosion of contributions to happiness research, mainly by the younger generation of economists. More and more refined measures of subjective wellbeing, of the determinants and consequences, and more advanced estimation techniques, have been employed, and ever more detailed and particular aspects have been studied. This is, of course, welcome but it should be noted that it comes at a cost. The main messages of happiness research as spelled out in this chapter may be lost as they are swamped by increasingly sophisticated approaches applying to very specific situations. In the end, outsiders may lose orientation, and therefore tend to disregard the highly valuable insights of happiness research, especially compared to traditional approaches or pure guesses.[3] This would certainly be a loss to be considered.

23.2.3 Particularly Fruitful Future Research Areas

In my view there are two general topics in happiness research to which most attention should be devoted. The first are the constitutional and institutional conditions enabling, and helping, individuals to achieve happiness according to their own liking. A crucially important negative impact on subjective wellbeing is civil wars and violent political conflicts, as well as outright conventional war. People having to live under these conditions are much less happy than those living under peaceful conditions. On those issues there has only been restricted research.

The second general area in which subjective wellbeing research should engage are the sociological conditions correlated with happiness, such as norms and traditions. In both cases this also means that future happiness research should go beyond the rather dominant emphasis on psychological aspects. It should, in particular, put more attention on the heterogeneity of happiness functions both within and between societies.

23.3 CONCLUSION

Happiness research is one of the most interesting and lively areas in social science research. Provided it does not turn to mainly issues of interest to the academic community – such as those related to econometric estimation and causality – it is likely to add important new insights, allowing us to improve the lives of human beings.

NOTES

1. In order not to overload this contribution, only a few citations to specific issues are provided. For general surveys over happiness research see, for example, Kahneman et al. (1999), Frey and Stutzer (2002a, 2002b), Layard (2005), Gilbert (2005), Diener and Biswas-Diener (2008), Frey (2008), Dolan et al. (2008), David et al. (2013), Clark et al. (2017) and Frey (2018).
2. In particular Helliwell, Layard and Sachs, for example in their publication in 2019.
3. Ambiguous results of extensive econometric research can also be observed in other areas of economics. An example is the economics of crime, which has generated an entire literature. In their survey of 228 papers from the last 20 years, Chalfin and McCrary (2017: 5) find 'little conclusive evidence' that 'crime responds to the severity of criminal sanctions'. See also Kirchgässner (2011) for the effect of death sentences on crime. Another example refers to school vouchers, where Epple et al. (2017) on the basis of 166 papers conclude that, 'the evidence to date is not sufficient to warrant recommending vouchers to be adopted on a widespread basis' (ibid.: 485).

REFERENCES

Alesina, A., Di Tella, R. and R. MacCulloch (2004), 'Inequality and happiness: are Europeans and Americans different?', *Journal of Public Economics*, **88** (9–10), 2009–2042.

Arrow, K.J. (ed.) (1951), *Social Choice and Individual Values*, New York, USA: John Wiley & Sons.
Chalfin, A. and J. McCrary (2017), 'Criminal deterrence: a review of the literature', *Journal of Economic Literature*, **55** (1), 5–48.
Clark, A.E., Flèche, S., Layard, R., Powdthavee, N. and G. Ward (eds) (2017), *The Origins of Happiness: The Science of Well-Being over the Life Course*, Princeton, NJ, USA: Princeton University Press.
David, S.A., Boniwell, I. and A. Conley Ayers (eds) (2013), *The Oxford Handbook of Happiness*, Oxford, UK: Oxford University Press.
Diener, E. and R. Biswas-Diener (eds) (2008), *Happiness: Unlocking the Mysteries of Psychological Wealth*, Malden, MA, USA: Blackwell Publishing.
Dolan, P., Peasgood, T. and M. White (2008), 'Do we really know what makes us happy? A review of the economic literature on the factors associated with subjective well-being', *Journal of Economic Psychology*, **29** (1), 94–122.
Dunleavy, P. (ed.) (2013), *Democracy, Bureaucracy and Public Choice: Economic Approaches to Political Science*, New York, USA and London, UK: Routledge.
Epple, D., Romano, R.E. and M. Urquiola (2017), 'School vouchers: a survey of the economics literature', *Journal of Economic Literature*, **55** (2), 441–492.
Frey, B.S. (ed.) (1997), *Political Business Cycles*, Cheltenham, UK and Lyme, NH, USA: Edward Elgar Publishing.
Frey, B.S. (ed.) (2008), *Happiness – A Revolution in Economics*, Cambridge, MA, USA: MIT Press.
Frey, B.S. (ed.) (2018), *Economics of Happiness*, Cham, Switzerland: Springer International Publishing.
Frey, B.S. and F. Schneider (1978a), 'An empirical study of politico-economic interaction in the United States', *Review of Economics and Statistics*, **60** (2), 174–183.
Frey, B.S. and F. Schneider (1978b), 'A politico-economic model of the United Kingdom', *Economic Journal*, **88** (350), 243–253.
Frey, B.S. and A. Stutzer (2002a), 'What can economists learn from happiness research?', *Journal of Economic Literature*, **40** (2), 402–435.
Frey, B.S. and A. Stutzer (eds) (2002b), *Happiness and Economics: How the Economy and Institutions Affect Human Well-Being*, Princeton, NJ, USA: Princeton University Press.
Frey, B.S. and A. Stutzer (2012), 'The use of happiness research for public policy', *Social Choice and Welfare*, **38** (4), 659–674.
Gilbert, D. (ed.) (2005), *Stumbling on Happiness*, New York, USA: Knopf.
Helliwell, J., Layard, R. and J. Sachs (2019), 'World Happiness Report 2019', New York, USA: Sustainable Development Solutions Network.
Kahneman, D., Diener, E. and N. Schwarz (eds) (1999), *Well-Being: The Foundations of Hedonic Psychology*, New York, USA: Russell Sage Foundation.
Kirchgässner, G. (2011), 'Econometric estimates of deterrence of the death penalty: facts or ideology?', *Kyklos*, **64** (3), 448–478.
Layard, R. (ed.) (2005), *Happiness: Lessons from a New Science*, London, UK: Penguin.
Mueller, D.C. (ed.) (2003), *Public Choice III*, Cambridge, UK: Cambridge University Press.
Niskanen, W.A. (ed.) (1971), *Bureaucracy and Representative Government*, Chicago, IL and New York, USA: Aldine-Atherton.
Niskanen, W.A. (ed.) (1994), *Bureaucracy and Public Economics*, Aldershot, UK and Brookfield, VT, USA: Edward Elgar Publishing.
Sabatini, F. and F. Sarracino (2017), 'Online networks and subjective well-being', *Kyklos*, **70** (3), 456–480.
Sen, A.K. (1977), 'Rational fools: a critique of the behavioral foundations of economic theory', *Philosophy and Public Affairs*, **6** (4), 317–344.
Sen, A.K. (ed.) (1982), *Choice, Welfare and Measurement*, Oxford, UK: Blackwell.
Theil, H. (ed.) (1968), *Optimal Decision Rules for Government and Industry*, Amsterdam, Netherlands: North Holland.
Tinbergen, J. (ed.) (1956), *Economic Policy: Principles and Design*, Amsterdam, Netherlands: North Holland.

Index